Risk Ratios
Short-Term Liquidity Risk

$$\text{Current Ratio} = \frac{\text{Current Assets}}{\text{Current Liabilities}}$$

$$\text{Quick Ratio} = \frac{\text{Quick Assets}}{\text{Current Liabilities}}$$

$$\text{Operating Cash Flow to Current Liabilities Ratio} = \frac{\text{Cash Flow from Operations}}{\text{Average Current Liabilities}}$$

$$\text{Accounts Receivable Turnover} = \frac{\text{Sales}}{\text{Average Accounts Receivable}}$$

$$\text{Days Receivable Outstanding} = \frac{365}{\text{Accounts Receivable Turnover}}$$

$$\text{Inventory Turnover} = \frac{\text{Cost of Goods Sold}}{\text{Average Inventories}}$$

$$\text{Days Inventory Outstanding} = \frac{365}{\text{Inventory Turnover}}$$

$$\text{Accounts Payable Turnover} = \frac{\text{Purchases}}{\text{Average Accounts Payable}}$$

$$\text{Days Payable Outstanding} = \frac{365}{\text{Accounts Payable Turnover}}$$

$$\text{Operating Cash Flow to Cash Interest Costs Ratio} = \frac{(\text{Cash Flow from Operations} + \text{Cash Outflow for Interest} + \text{Cash Outflow for Income Taxes})}{\text{Cash Outflow for Interest}}$$

Long-Term Solvency Risk

$$\text{Long-Term Debt Ratio} = \frac{\text{Long-Term Debt}}{\text{Long-Term Debt} + \text{Shareholders' Equity}}$$

$$\text{Debt-Equity Ratio} = \frac{\text{Long-Term Debt}}{\text{Shareholders' Equity}}$$

$$\text{Long-Term Debt to Assets Ratio} = \frac{\text{Long-Term Debt}}{\text{Total Assets (Equities)}}$$

$$\text{Interest Coverage Ratio} = \frac{(\text{Income from Continuing Operations} + \text{Interest Expense} + \text{Income Tax Expense})}{\text{Interest Expense}}$$

$$\text{Operating Cash Flow to Total Liabilities Ratio} = \frac{\text{Cash Flow from Operations}}{\text{Average Total Liabilities}}$$

$$\text{Operating Cash Flow to Capital Expenditures Ratio} = \frac{\text{Cash Flow from Operations}}{\text{Capital Expenditures}}$$

FINANCIAL REPORTING AND STATEMENT ANALYSIS

A Strategic Perspective

THIRD EDITION

FINANCIAL REPORTING AND STATEMENT ANALYSIS

A Strategic Perspective

THIRD EDITION

CLYDE P. STICKNEY

The Signal Companies Professor of Management
Amos Tuck School of Business Administration
Dartmouth College

THE DRYDEN PRESS
Harcourt Brace College Publishers

Fort Worth   Philadelphia   San Diego   New York   Orlando   Austin   San Antonio
Toronto   Montreal   London   Sydney   Tokyo

Acquisitions Editor   Mike Reynolds
Developmental Editor   Yvette Rubio
Project Editor   Sandy Walton
Production Manager   Carlyn Hauser
Art Director   Brian Salisbury
Art & Literary Rights Editor   Susan Stutzman
Product Manager   Craig Johnson

Copy Editor   JaNoel Lowe
Proofreader   Jody St. John
Indexer   Lois Oster
Compositor   Beacon Graphics
Text Type   10/12 Fairfield light

Cover Image   Photo: Eduardo Garcia/FPG. Prudential Plaza, Chicago. Architect Loebl, Schlossman & Hackl, reprinted by permission of Premisys Real Estate Services, Inc.

Address for Editorial Correspondence
The Dryden Press, 301 Commerce Street, Suite 3700, Fort Worth, TX   76102

Address for Orders
The Dryden Press, 6277 Sea Harbor Drive, Orlando, FL   32887
1-800-782-4479, or 1-800-433-0001 (in Florida)

ISBN: 0-03-011698-8

Library of Congress Catalog Card Number: 95-67391

Printed in the United States of America

5 6 7 8 9 0 1 2 3 4   090   9 8 7 6 5 4 3 2 1

The Dryden Press
Harcourt Brace College Publishers

To my students,
with thanks for permitting me to take
the journey with you

THE DRYDEN PRESS SERIES IN ACCOUNTING

Introductory

Bischoff
Introduction to College Accounting
Third Edition

Principles

Hanson, Hamre, and Walgenbach
Principles of Accounting
Sixth Edition

Computerized

Bischoff and Wanlass
The Computer Connection: General Ledger and Practice Sets to accompany Introductory Accounting
Second Edition

Wanlass
Computer Resource Guide: Principles of Accounting
Fourth Edition

Financial

Hanson and Hamre
Financial Accounting
Eighth Edition

Porter and Norton
Financial Accounting: The Impact on Decision Makers

Stickney and Weil
Financial Accounting: An Introduction to Concepts, Methods, and Uses
Seventh Edition

Managerial

Maher, Stickney, and Weil
Managerial Accounting: An Introduction to Concepts, Methods, and Uses
Fifth Edition

Intermediate

Williams, Stanga, and Holder
Intermediate Accounting
Fifth Edition

Advanced

Pahler and Mori
Advanced Accounting
Fifth Edition

Financial Statement Analysis

Stickney
Financial Reporting and Statement Analysis: A Strategic Perspective
Third Edition

Auditing

Guy, Alderman, and Winters
Auditing
Fourth Edition

Rittenberg and Schwieger
Auditing: Concepts for a Changing Environment

Theory

Belkaoui
Accounting Theory
Third Edition

Bloom and Elgers
Foundations of Accounting Theory and Policy: A Reader

Bloom and Elgers
Issues in Accounting Policy: A Reader

Taxation

Everett, Raabe, and Fortin
1995 Income Tax Fundamentals

Reference

Miller and Bailey
Miller Comprehensive GAAS Guide
College Edition

Williams and Miller
Miller Comprehensive GAAP Guide
College Edition

Miller
Electronic GAAP Guide
College Edition

Governmental and Not-For-Profit

Douglas
Governmental and Nonprofit Accounting: Theory and Practice
Second Edition

PREFACE

The effective analysis of a set of financial statements requires an understanding of (1) the economic characteristics and current conditions of a firm's businesses; (2) the particular strategies the firm selects to compete in each of these businesses; and (3) the accounting principles and procedures underlying the firm's financial statements. Equipped with these three essential building blocks, the analyst can assess the success of the strategies as measured by profitability, relative to the level of risk involved. The analyst can then use this information to project the firm's future earnings and cash flows as a basis for valuation. This three-fold approach to financial statement analysis elevates it from one involving the mechanical calculation of a long list of financial statement ratios to one where the analyst has an opportunity to integrate concepts from economics, business strategy, accounting, and other business disciplines. This synthesizing experience rewards the student both intellectually and practically.

The premise of this textbook is that students learn financial statement analysis most effectively by performing the analysis on actual companies. The text portion of this book sets forth the important concepts and analytical tools and then demonstrates their application using the financial statements of Coca-Cola and Pepsi. Each chapter contains a set of problems, and some chapters contain cases, both based for the most part on financial data of actual companies. A financial statement analysis package (FSAP), running on either IBM-compatible PCs or Apple Macintosh computers with Excel, is available to aid in the analytical tasks.

OVERVIEW OF TEXT

Following is a brief description of the contents of each chapter, indicating the major changes from the previous edition.

Chapter 1 describes the various settings in which an analyst might perform a financial statement analysis (for example, equity investment, credit extension, antitrust investigation), emphasizing the need to specify the purpose of the analysis before selecting the analytical tools. This chapter presents a framework for assessing a firm's industry economics and business strategies. It also reviews the purpose and content of each of the three principal financial statements, including those of non-U.S. companies appearing in a different format.

Chapter 2 reviews the statement of cash flows and presents a model for relating the cash flows from operating, investing, and financing activities to a firm's position in its product life cycle. This chapter also demonstrates procedures for preparing the statement of cash flows when a firm either provides no cash flow information or presents such information in a sources and uses format.

Chapter 3 introduces analytical tools for assessing profitability and risk. This material was presented in Chapters 7, 8, and 9 of the previous edition, but my experience in using the previous edition, as well as that of other adopters with whom I have had discussions regarding its usage, indicate that profitability and risk analysis serves as a useful framework for studying the effects of alternative accounting principles discussed in Chapters 4 through 7. Thus, Chapter 3 introduces the analytical tools. Chapters 8 and 9 explore in greater depth the economic and strategic factors affecting the interpretation of the financial statement ratios. Chapter 3 contains entirely new problem material using high-profile companies such as Hasbro, Lands' End, Microsoft, NIKE, Sony, and Wal-Mart that are of high interest to students. Case 3.1 examines the profitability and risk of two specialty retailers, The GAP and The Limited. This edition places the industry analysis cases in the chapter to which they most appropriately relate instead of at the end of the book as in the previous edition.

Chapter 4 discusses data issues that the analyst should address before embarking on a financial statement analysis. These issues include the effects of nonrecurring income items (for example, the effects of restructuring charges, discontinued operations, extraordinary items, and changes in accounting principles), the use of originally reported versus restated data (for example, relating to acquisitions and divestitures), the effect of alternative accounting principles, and the impact of different reporting periods. This chapter includes substantial new material regarding the nature and analytical treatment of nonrecurring income items because of their increasing prevalence in corporate annual reports. This material now precedes the discussion of alternative accounting principles in Chapters 5 through 7, instead of following it as in the previous edition. Chapter 4 contains four new problems and a case study of International Paper Company relating to nonrecurring income items. This chapter also summarizes alternative accounting principles in major industrialized countries and contains problems and cases involving firms in the United Kingdom, Italy, and Japan.

Chapter 5 discusses alternative accounting principles that primarily affect the analysis of profitability, including income recognition, inventory cost-flow assumption, and accounting for depreciable and intangible assets. New to this edition is Appendix 5.1, a discussion of accounting for the effects of changing prices. This topic is of increasing importance as developing countries play an increasing role in international markets. New problem and case materials involve income recognition (Deere), inventory cost-flow and depreciation method (USX), research and development arrangements (Chiron), and changing prices (Corporacion Industrial Sanluis). The Arizona Land Development Case (Case 5.1) is included in this edition because it continues to be a rich illustration of the effect of alternative income recognition methods.

Chapter 6 examines topics that primarily affect the assessment of risk, including off-balance sheet financing arrangements, derivative financial instruments, leases, pension and other retirement benefits, income taxes, and reserves. This chapter incorporates new reporting standards on derivative securities and other financial instruments, health care and other retirement benefits, and income taxes. The problem material, taken from annual reports of publicly-held companies, emphasizes the interpretation of disclosures related to the above reporting issues. Case 6.1 analyzes the effect of operating leases and underfunded pension and health-care obligations on the risk assessments of American Airlines and United Airlines. Case 6.2 interprets the income tax position of Sun Microsystems. Case 6.3 illustrates the use of reserves by the Mexican company CIFRA to shift earnings between accounting periods.

Chapter 7 explores accounting principles that affect many accounts on the financial statements, including corporate acquisitions, investments in securities, foreign currency translation, and segment reporting. This chapter incorporates the new reporting standard on investments in securities. New problem materials involve the AT&T merger with NCR, Time Warner's minority investment in Seagram, the accounting by Mylan Laboratories for a substantial investment in a joint venture, the effect of different functional currencies on assessments of the profitability of Hewlett-Packard and Sun Microsystems and of Bristol Myers-Squibb and Merck. Case 7.1 uses Fisher Corporation to illustrate the effects of accounting, tax, and financing decisions on the structure of a corporate acquisition and the related financial statement impact. Case 7.2 uses Clark Equipment Company to analyze the effect on the financial statements of alternative ways of accounting for a joint venture. Loucks Corporation is used in Case 7.3 to illustrate the choice of a functional currency and the financial statement impact of alternative methods of foreign currency translation.

Chapter 8 discusses economic factors (for example, degree of capital intensity, regulation, and other barriers to entry, stage in the product life cycle, and the commodity nature of products) and strategic factors (for example, product differentiation versus low-cost leadership) that affect the interpretation of the rate of return on assets and the rate of return on common shareholders' equity. This chapter incorporates recent research on the time-series behavior of the rate of return on common shareholders' equity. Case 8.1 asks students to suggest economic and strategic reasons for differences in the rates of return of various segments of eight different industries. Cases 8.2, 8.3, and 8.4 involve the analysis of the profitability and risk of competitors in three different industries. For example, Case 8.2 analyzes Hewlett-Packard and Sun Microsystems, competitors in the engineering workstation computer market, Case 8.3 studies Bristol-Myers Squibb, Merck, and Mylan Laboratories, pharmaceutical companies pursuing different strategies, and Case 8.4 examines Adia Services and Kelly Services, leading firms in the temporary, personnel-supply business. These cases covering the material in the first eight chapters, serve as excellent synthesizing experiences for students. The cases contain the necessary information for students to adjust the financial statements for nonrecurring income items, operating leases, and similar factors. The *Instructor's Manual/Solutions Manual* contains the financial statements and notes for the companies analyzed. Instructors may wish to photocopy these financial statements for use with these cases. The financial statement analysis package (FSAP) available with the text contains data files for these companies, as well.

Chapter 9 explores risk analysis in greater depth than the introduction in Chapter 3. The emphasis is on the prediction of financial distress. This chapter incorporates research on bankruptcy prediction and presents both discriminant and logit prediction models. Case 9.1 uses Fly-By-Night International Group to study bankruptcy prediction and to raise ethical questions about dealings between a firm and its chief executive officer, who is also its majority shareholder. Case 9.2 involves a credit lending decision in an industry experiencing downsizing to Massachusetts Stove Company, a small, privately held wood stove company. Case 9.3 uses Kroger to illustrate the effects of a special dividend to fight a hostile takeover on the firm's risk.

Chapter 10 describes and illustrates the procedures for preparing pro forma financial statements, which later play an important role in the valuation of companies discussed in Chapters 11 and 12. Case 10.1 illustrates the preparation of pro forma financial statements for Wal-Mart, a firm that has shifted its product mix toward warehouse clubs and food products. Case 10.2 illustrates the preparation of pro forma financial statements for McDonald's under two scenarios: one involving greater use of franchising and one involving decreased use of franchising. These two cases specify the pro forma assumptions students are to use to illustrate the preparation procedure. The cases in Chapters 11 and 12 require students make their own pro forma assumptions.

Chapters 11 and 12 include an expanded discussion of valuation. Chapter 11 explores cash-based approaches to valuation with emphasis on the present value of future cash flows. This chapter considers various issues in applying this valuation model, including the appropriate measure of cash flows, the measurement of the terminal value, and the nature of the discount rate. Case 11.1 uses Holmes Company, as an excellent introduction to valuation. This case includes additional information in this edition to permit valuation using both cash-based approaches (Chapter 11) and earnings-based approaches (Chapter 12). Case 11.2 looks at Massachusetts Stove Company three years after the loan decision (Case 9.2) and values it using both cash-based approaches and valuation of individual assets and liabilities.

Chapter 12 discusses the use of the price-earnings ratio and the market value to book value of shareholders' equity ratio to value companies. This chapter explores recent research that attempts to link earnings and book values with stock prices. The research underlying the material in this chapter is still evolving. Case 12.1 involves the valuation of Rodriguez Home Center, a small family-owned business. Case 12.2 uses Revco to illustrate valuation in a fraudulent conveyance case. Case 12.3 relates to pricing an initial public offering of Kleen Cleaners, a rapidly-growing company.

Appendixes A and B include the financial statements and notes for Coca-Cola and Pepsi, respectively. The text makes frequent references to these financial statements. Appendix C includes printouts of the financial statement analysis package for Coke and Pepsi.

SIGNIFICANT CHANGES IN THIS EDITION

The preceding section discussed the major changes in this edition. These changes are summarized below.

1. Chapter 3 introduces financial statement analysis tools for assessing profitability and risk. Chapters 4 through 7 use these analytical tools as a framework for studying the effects of alternative accounting principles on the financial statements. Chapters 8 and 9 explore more fully the economic and strategic factors that help explain differences in profitability and risk. These chapters also incorporate recent research on the behavior and predictive power of financial statement ratios.

2. Chapter 4 on data issues includes an expanded discussion of nonrecurring income items (for example, restructuring charges, discontinued operations, extraordinary items, and changes in accounting principles).

3. Chapters 5 through 7 incorporate new financial reporting standards on derivative securities and other financial instruments, health care and other retirement benefits, income taxes, and investments in securities.

4. Chapter 5 includes an appendix on the accounting for changing prices, a topic of increasing interest with the emergence of developing countries in international markets.

5. Chapters 11 and 12 include an expanded discussion of cash-based and earnings-based approaches to valuation, incorporating recent research linking accounting data and stock prices.

6. All the chapters contain substantially new assignment material, with fifty new problems and sixteen new cases. These problems and cases use more companies of high interest to students, including Lands' End, Microsoft, NIKE, McDonald's, Wal-Mart, and others.

OVERVIEW OF THE SUPPLEMENT PACKAGE

A financial statement analysis package (FSAP) is available as a free master disk to all adopters of the textbook. The package performs various analytical tasks (for example, common size and trend statements and ratio computations) and displays the results both numerically and graphically. By altering data files for the companies in the cases—also included on the software disk—students can study the impact of the capitalization of operating leases, the conversion from LIFO to FIFO, the elimination of nonrecurring income items, and similar adjustments of reported data. Using FSAP to perform the tedious number crunching frees time and energy that the analyst may devote to the more important interpretive task. The master disk contains a user manual for FSAP.

An *Instructor's Manual/Solutions Manual* is also available to adopters. It contains suggestions for using the textbook, solutions to problems, teaching notes to cases, and the financial statements and notes for companies included in the industry analysis cases in Chapter 8.

The Dryden Press will provide complimentary supplements or supplement packages to those adopters qualified under our adoption policy. Please contact your sales representative to learn how you may qualify. If as an adopter or potential user you receive supplements you do not need, please return them to your sales representative or send them to:

Attn: Returns Department
Troy Warehouse
465 South Lincoln Drive
Troy, MO   63379

ACKNOWLEDGMENTS

Many individuals provided invaluable assistance in the preparation of this textbook and I wish to acknowledge their help in a formal manner here. The following professional colleagues have assisted in the development of this textbook by reviewing or providing helpful comments on the previous edition:

Richard Baker, Fordham University
Joseph Bylinski, University of North Carolina
Grace M. Conway, Adelphi University
Benny Copeland, North Texas State University
Jim W. Deitrick, University of Texas at Austin
Marc J. Epstein, Stanford University
Joseph G. Fisher, Indiana University
Peter R. Grierson, Slippery Rock University
J. Larry Hagler, East Carolina University
James A. Largay, Lehigh University
Belinda Mucklow, University of Wisconsin-Madison
Paul A. Pacter, University of Connecticut-Stamford
James Patton, University of Pittsburgh
Larry Prober, Rider College
Stephen G. Ryan, New York University
David Smith, Claremont-McKenna College
Walter Teets, Gonzaga University
Harold Wyman, Florida International University

The following individuals at The Dryden Press contributed to the development, production, and marketing of this edition: Carlyn Hauser, Craig Johnson, Michael Reynolds, Yvette Rubio, Brian Salisbury, Susan Stutzman, Sandy Walton, and Kelly Whidbee.

A number of former students and colleagues have worked on the financial statement analysis package, helping to keep it up to date with changing technology. I wish in particular to thank Mark Boughter and John Ehlers. Thanks also to Kristen Loucks and Tucker Scott, who checked the solutions to all of the problems and cases.

My own thinking about accounting and financial statement analysis has been influenced over the years by five colleagues, coauthors, and friends: Paul R. Brown, New York University; Sidney Davidson, University of Chicago; Tom Selling, American Graduate School of International Management; Virginia Soybel, Babson College; and Roman Weil, University of Chicago.

I owe a particular debt of gratitude to my secretary, Tammy Stebbins, whose organizational skills, perseverance, and patience have kept me going. Thanks, Tammy.

Finally, I wish to acknowledge the role played by former students in my financial accounting and financial statement analysis courses at The Amos Tuck School of Business Administration, Dartmouth College. Learning is a mutual endeavor, and you have certainly been challenging and encouraging partners. This book is dedicated to each of you, with thanks.

Clyde P. Stickney

Brief Contents

CONTENTS

CHAPTER 5   Generally Accepted Accounting Principles:
Income Recognition and Asset Valuation   225

CHAPTER 6   Generally Accepted Accounting Principles:
Liability Recognition and Related
Expenses   291

**CHAPTER 7   Generally Accepted Accounting Principles:
Intercorporate Entities   369**

CHAPTER 1

OVERVIEW OF FINANCIAL REPORTING AND FINANCIAL STATEMENT ANALYSIS

Learning Objectives

1. Understand the role of financial statement analysis in an efficient capital market.
2. Review the purpose, underlying concepts, and format of the balance sheet, income statement, and statement of cash flows.
3. Learn the sources of financial information about publicly held firms beyond that provided in the financial statements.

Financial statements attempt to portray the operating performance and financial health of a business firm during a recent period of time. Financial analysts study these financial statements both to evaluate a firm's success in the past in conducting its activities and to project its likely future performance.

Common settings for performing financial statement analysis include the following:

1. Making an investment in a firm's common or preferred stock.
2. Extending credit, either for a short-term period (for example, a bank loan used to finance accounts receivable or inventories) or for a longer-term period (for example, a bank loan or public bond issue used to finance the acquisition of property, plant, or equipment).
3. Assessing the operating performance and financial health of a supplier, customer, or competitor.
4. Valuing another firm being considered as an acquisition candidate.
5. Forming a judgment about damages sustained in a lawsuit.

1

6. Assessing the extent of audit tests needed by an auditor to form an opinion on a client's financial statements.
7. Assessing the extent to which certain firms in an industry might generate unreasonable (monopoly) returns and require antitrust action by government regulators.

Analyzing a set of financial statements involves using ratios of key financial statement items and other analytical tools to gain insight into the *profitability* (operating performance) and *risk* (financial health) of a firm. Later chapters make clear that the purpose of the analysis drives the particular analytical tools used. This book discusses the underlying rationale for important financial statement ratios and illustrates their usefulness in analyzing financial statements, using as examples the financial statements of The Coca-Cola Company (Coke) and PepsiCo, Inc. (Pepsi). Appendix A and Appendix B at the end of the book include the financial statements and notes for Coke and Pepsi, respectively.

The easiest job facing the analyst is calculating the financial ratios. In fact, the availability of computerized databases and financial analysis packages permits the analyst to do much of the *analytical* work "on line." The real challenge is *interpreting* the resulting analyses. Effective interpretation requires the analyst to (1) identify the economics and current conditions facing the business, (2) identify the strategies that the firm selects to compete in the business, and (3) understand the important concepts and principles underlying the financial statements used in computing the financial ratios. Economics, business strategy, and financial accounting serve as the three key building blocks for effective interpretation of financial statement analyses.

ROLE OF FINANCIAL STATEMENT ANALYSIS IN AN EFFICIENT CAPITAL MARKET

There are differing views as to the benefits of analyzing a set of financial statements. One view is that the stock market is efficient in reacting to published information about a firm. That is, market participants react intelligently and quickly to information they receive, so that market prices continually reflect underlying economic values. One implication of an efficient capital market is that financial statement users cannot routinely analyze financial statements to find "undervalued" or "overvalued" securities. The market quickly impounds new information in security prices. Appendix 1.1 describes the research methodology employed in studies of market efficiency. Later chapters discuss many of the research studies linking financial statement data and market prices.

Opponents of the view that capital markets are efficient points to the market crash in October 1987 and the sharp increases in the market prices of potential merger buyout candidates as evidence that the stock market does not always price securities efficiently. Opponents also point out that empirical research on capital market efficiency focuses on average aggregate market reactions to information, which does not preclude the possibility that the market might misprice shares of individual firms. As a consequence, the analyst can study the financial statements and other information of firms to identify misvalued securities. In addition, opponents note that various empirical studies on capital market efficiency often generate conflicting results. It is seldom clear whether the conflicting results emanate from flaws in the research design, data problems, or market inefficiencies.

Even if one accepts the notion of capital market efficiency, financial statement analysis still has a role to play. Someone, presumably a sophisticated financial analyst, must perform the analysis if the market is to react appropriately to new information. Analysts perform the analysis, however, soon after firms release the information and market prices respond accordingly. Also, financial statement analysis serves a role in settings other than capital markets. The previous section described a number of such situations. In most of them, a particular firm or other entity, such as a commercial bank (credit analysis) or accounting firm (auditor's opinion), performs the analysis rather than the many buyers and sellers involved in capital market settings.

The strength of the research findings on capital market efficiency during the 1970s and 1980s led many academics to downplay the benefits of financial statement analysis. Several research studies, for example, found that current market prices were better predictors of future earnings than were current earnings predictors of future stock prices. The implication of this research is that analysts learn very little of value in analyzing financial statements that the market has not already reflected in security prices. This situation placed academics at odds with securities analysts, who make their living identifying undervalued or overvalued securities and making buy/sell recommendations to customers. Recent academic research has demonstrated anew the benefits of performing "fundamental analysis" using information from the financial statements. Two studies by Ou and Penman showed that financial statements contain useful information for distinguishing permanent and transitory components of past earnings.[1] This information enhances predictions of future earnings and stock price changes. These two widely acclaimed research studies have led to a new stream of research linking financial statement information and stock prices. Chapter 12 discusses this research more fully.

Before embarking on a study of the tools of financial statement analysis, we will review the purpose and content of the three principal financial statements included in corporate reports and relate them to the principal business activities of a firm. Chapters 1 and 2 provide such a review.

OVERVIEW OF BUSINESS ACTIVITIES

Financial statements serve as "score sheets" of a firm's business activities. That is, accounting is a system for measuring the results of a firm's business transactions and summarizing them in a form that interested parties can understand. Enhanced understanding results from relating these financial statements to the business activities

---

[1]Jane A. Ou and Stephen H. Penman, "Financial Statement Analysis and the Prediction of Stock Returns," *Journal of Accounting and Economics,* November 1989, pp. 295–329; and "Accounting Measurement, Price-Earnings Ratio, and the Information Content of Security Prices," *Journal of Accounting Research—Supplement 1989,* 1989, pp. 111–144.

they attempt to portray. Figure 1.1 summarizes the business activities discussed in this section.

ENVIRONMENTAL FACTORS

The economic characteristics and current conditions in the industries in which a firm participates are critical factors to consider when interpreting the results of financial statement analysis. Some of the questions an analyst is likely to address are:

1. What is the competitive market (output) profile of the industry? Are there few competitors with well-differentiated products or many competitors with similar, commodity-like products? Is foreign competition a factor of concern?
2. What is the production (input) profile of the industry? Is it labor intensive or capital intensive? Is it unionized or not? Are there constraints on the availability of raw materials or labor?
3. How important is technological change? Are products mature with few technological innovations, or do new products continually emerge to shorten the life cycle of existing products?
4. What are the growth characteristics of the industry? Is the industry growing rapidly, stable, or declining?
5. What is the regulatory status of the industry? Are there barriers to entry, such as licenses or patents? Is the antitrust environment encouraging or discouraging to mergers in the industry?
6. How sensitive is the industry to demographic changes or trends (aging of the population, two-wage earner families)?

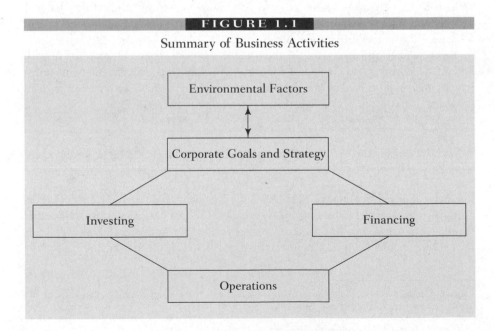

FIGURE 1.1
Summary of Business Activities

7. How sensitive is the industry to macroeconomic forces such as inflation or deflation, changes in interest rates, unemployment, and business cycles?

Coke derives over 87 percent of its revenues from soft drinks, with the remainder coming from consumer food products. Pepsi is more diversified, with approximately equal portions of sales derived from soft drinks, consumer foods, and restaurants. Exhibit 1.1 summarizes the more important economic characteristics and current conditions in these industries.

CORPORATE GOALS AND STRATEGY

The *goals* of a firm are the targets, or end results, toward which it directs its energies. A firm's managers serve as agents for owners in striving to increase its value, a principal goal of all businesses. Other important corporate goals may include maintaining a contented work force, supporting community activities, or promoting government policy objectives.

The *strategies* of a firm are the means for achieving its goals. Firms adopt company-level strategies and specific product strategies. At a company level, firms must decide whether to operate primarily in one industry (for example, soft drinks) or to pursue a diversified strategy. Coke operates almost exclusively in soft drinks, whereas Pepsi conducts operations in soft drinks, consumer foods, and restaurants. Firms must also decide whether they intend to operate primarily in the domestic market or they plan to have foreign operations make up a significant part of their activities. The business segment data for Coke and Pepsi indicate the following for Year 8:

	Sales Mix		Income Mix		Asset Mix	
	U.S.	Non-U.S.	U.S.	Non-U.S.	U.S.	Non-U.S.
Coke	34%	66%	21%	79%	32%	68%
Pepsi	73%	27%	82%	18%	66%	34%

Coke's foreign operations dominate its activities, whereas Pepsi has a smaller foreign involvement.

The business strategy literature uses several methods for classifying product-level strategies. One such method classifies products along a continuum from product differentiation to low-cost leadership. In a product differentiation strategy, a firm attempts to identify a specific market need and to develop a unique product (good or service) to meet that need. For example, a firm might base its product differentiation on technological or other inherent product advantages, a reputation for consistent quality, broad product selection, timely delivery, or similar characteristics. The aim is to build customer loyalty and generate attractive profit margins. The low-cost

EXHIBIT 1.1

Summary of Economic Characteristics and Current Conditions in the Soft Drink,
Consumer Foods, and Restaurant Industries

	Soft Drinks	Consumer Foods	Restaurants
Competitive Profile	Small number of direct competitors but large number of competitors with substitute products. Established brand names create customer loyalty.	Many competitors with similar products but customer loyalty created by established brand names.	Intensive competition in a highly saturated market with similar product offerings; some opportunities for brand recognition.
Production Profile	Production process of moderate capital intensity. Quality control is important.	Production process of moderate capital intensity. Quality control is critical.	Capital-intensive restaurant facilities combined with labor-intensive rendering of services. Quality control is critical.
Technological Change	Not significant.	Not significant, although some recent advances in packaging.	Not significant, although some recent advances in information accumulation and dissemination.
Growth Profile	Mature market in the United States but growth opportunities abroad.	Mature market in the United States but significant growth opportunities abroad.	Mature market in the United States but growth opportunities abroad.
Regulatory Attitude	Not an issue despite Coke's and Pepsi's dominance in the industry.	Increased pressure on accurate labeling and advertising of products.	Not an issue.
Sensitivity to Demographic Changes	Could have negative impact on demand in future years due to aging of population.	The need for speed and convenience in meal preparation increased by two-wage earner families. Price is somewhat less important.	The demand for restaurant foods increased by two-wage earner families.
Sensitivity to Macroeconomic Trends	Not particularly sensitive due to low relative price of product.	Not particularly sensitive because everyone has to eat.	Somewhat sensitive to recessionary conditions.

leadership strategy aims more to compete on the basis of low prices, low profit margins, and high inventory turnover. The objective is to keep costs to a minimum (through quantity purchases, lean administrative organizations, attainment of economies of scale, and so on) and to position products to underprice the competition.

Few firms actually pursue one of these strategies to the exclusion of the other. Most firms, for example, attempt to develop customer loyalty for their products and at the same time maintain control over their costs. It is helpful when comparing firms to understand the relative emphasis that each firm places on product differentiation, low-cost leadership, or other strategies.

Later chapters use this overview of the strategies of Coke and Pepsi and the environmental assessment of their principal businesses to aid in interpreting the financial statement analysis.

The narrative portion of a firm's annual report often describes, at least in general terms, the strategies it pursues. Firms typically structure this narrative around their principal business segments, describing the products, current conditions, and financial performance of each segment.

FINANCING

A firm obtains financing for its business activities from creditors and owners. Short-term creditors, such as banks, suppliers, employees, and governmental units, provide financing for receivables, inventories, and operating expenses. Long-term creditors, purchasers of a firm's bonds and lessors, usually provide financing for property, plant, and equipment. Owners provide financing directly through capital contributions and indirectly by permitting firms to retain earnings rather than distribute dividends. The nature of a firm's assets usually dictates the amount of its short-term versus long-term financing. Retailers, with heavy investments in receivables and inventories, tend to rely on short-term financing. Electric utilities use a preponderance of long-term financing for their large investments in plant assets. Firms base their decision on the mix of long-term financing obtained from creditors versus owners on such factors as the firm's attitude toward risk (debt is more risky than equity because of the fixed interest and principal payments), its tax position (interest payments are tax deductible; dividend payments are not), and its ability to benefit from financial leverage. Chapter 3 describes and illustrates financial leverage.

INVESTING

A firm must invest the funds obtained from financing. It can use the funds to finance receivables or to acquire inventories; property, plant, and equipment; securities of other firms; patents, licenses, or other contractual rights; or simply leave it as cash. The nature of a firm's businesses usually determines the particular investments made.

OPERATIONS

A firm obtains financing and invests in various resources to generate a profit. That is, it strives to sell its goods and services for a higher price than the cost of the investments made in those goods and services, including the cost of any financing. Through operations, a firm accomplishes the primary goal of business activities: increasing its value and thereby the wealth of its owners.

PRINCIPAL FINANCIAL STATEMENTS

Businesses typically prepare three principal financial statements:

1. Balance sheet.
2. Income statement.
3. Statement of cash flows.

These financial statements report the results of financing, investing, and operating activities and serve as a basis for assessing the success of corporate strategies. This section presents a brief overview of the purpose and content of each of these three financial statements.

Generally accepted accounting principles, or GAAP, determine the valuation and measurement methods underlying financial statements. Official rule-making bodies set these principles. The Securities and Exchange Commission (SEC), an agency of the federal government, has the legal authority to specify acceptable accounting principles in the United States. The SEC has, for the most part, delegated the responsibility for setting GAAP to private-sector bodies within the accounting profession. Since 1973, that rule-making body has been the Financial Accounting Standards Board (FASB). The FASB specifies acceptable accounting principles only after receiving extensive comments from various preparers and users of financial statements.

The process followed in countries outside the United States in setting accounting principles varies widely. In some countries, the amounts reported for financial and tax reporting closely conform. In these cases, legislative arms of the government play a major role in setting acceptable accounting principles. Other countries employ a model similar to the one in the United States, where financial and tax-reporting methods differ and the accounting profession plays a major role in establishing GAAP.

The International Accounting Standards Committee, or IASC, strives to reduce diversity in accounting principles across countries and to encourage greater standardization. The IASC, established in 1973, comprises members from approximately 70 countries. Its pronouncements have no enforceability of their own. Rather, the representatives to the IASC pledge their best efforts in establishing the pronouncements of the IASC as GAAP within their countries.

Most references to GAAP in this book are to accounting standards in the United States, although we point out instances in which practices abroad differ from those in the United States.

BALANCE SHEET — MEASURING FINANCIAL POSITION

The balance sheet, or statement of financial position, presents a snapshot of the resources of a firm (assets) and the claims on those resources (liabilities and shareholders' equity) as of a specific time. The assets portion of the balance sheet reports the effects of a firm's past investment decisions. The liabilities and shareholders' equity portion of the balance sheet reports the effects of a firm's past financing decisions.

The balance sheet derives its name from the fact that it shows the following balance or equality:

$$\text{Assets} = \text{Liabilities} + \text{Shareholders' Equity}$$

That is, a firm's assets or resources are in balance with, or equal to, the claims on those assets by creditors and owners. The balance sheet views resources from two perspectives: a list of the specific forms in which a firm holds the resources (for example, cash, inventory, equipment) and a list of the persons or entities that provided the funds to obtain the assets and therefore have claims on them (for example, suppliers, employees, governments, shareholders). Thus, the balance sheet portrays the equality of investing (assets) and financing (liabilities plus shareholders' equity) activities.

The format of the balance sheet in some countries differs from that in the United States. In Germany and France, for example, property, plant, and equipment and other noncurrent assets appear first, followed by current assets. On the financing side, shareholders' equity appears first, followed by noncurrent liabilities and current liabilities. This format maintains the balance between investing and financing but presents accounts in the opposite sequence to that common in the United States.

In the United Kingdom, the balance sheet equation takes the following form:

$$\frac{\text{Noncurrent}}{\text{Assets}} + \left(\frac{\text{Current}}{\text{Assets}} - \frac{\text{Current}}{\text{Liabilities}}\right) - \frac{\text{Noncurrent}}{\text{Liabilities}} = \frac{\text{Shareholders'}}{\text{Equity}}$$

This format takes the perspective of shareholders by reporting the assets available for shareholders after subtracting claims by creditors. Financial analysts can rearrange the components of published balance sheets to whatever format they consider most informative.

Assets—Recognition, Valuation, and Classification.   Which of its resources does a firm recognize as assets? At what amount does the firm report these assets? How does it classify them within the assets portion of the balance sheet? GAAP determines responses to these questions.

Assets are resources that have the potential for providing a firm with future economic benefits: the ability to generate future cash inflows or to reduce future cash outflows. A firm recognizes as assets those resources (1) for which it has acquired rights to their future use as a result of a past transaction or exchange and (2) for which the firm can measure, or quantify, the future benefits with a reasonable degree of precision.[2] Resources that firms do not normally recognize as assets because they fail to meet one or both of the criteria include purchase orders received from customers, employment contracts with corporate officers, and a quality reputation with employees, customers, or citizens of the community.

---

[2]Financial Accounting Standards Board, *Statement of Financial Accounting Concepts No. 6*, "Elements of Financial Statements," 1985, para. 25.

Assets on the balance sheet are either *monetary* or *nonmonetary*. Monetary assets include cash and claims to a fixed amount of cash receivable in the future, including accounts and notes receivable and investments in bonds that a firm intends to hold to maturity. The balance sheet reports monetary assets at the amount of cash the firm expects to receive in the future. If the date or dates of receipt extend beyond one year, the firm reports the monetary asset at the present value of the future cash flows (using a discount rate that reflects the underlying uncertainty of collecting the cash at the time the claim initially arose). Nonmonetary assets include inventories, plant, equipment, and other assets that do not represent a claim to a fixed amount of cash. A firm could report nonmonetary assets at the amount initially paid to acquire them (historical cost), the amount required currently to acquire them (current replacement cost), the amount for which the firm could currently sell them (current realizable value), or the present value of the amounts the firm expects to receive in the future from selling or using the assets (present value of future cash flows). GAAP generally requires the reporting of nonmonetary assets on the balance sheet at their historical cost amounts because this valuation is usually more objective and verifiable than other possible valuation bases. GAAP in some countries, such as the United Kingdom and the Netherlands, permits periodic revaluations of property, plant, and equipment to current values. Chapter 5 discusses alternative valuation methods and their implications for measuring earnings.

The classification of assets within the balance sheet varies widely in published annual reports. The principal asset categories are as follows:

Current Assets.   Current assets include cash and other assets that a firm expects to sell or consume during the normal operating cycle for its business, usually within one year. Cash, accounts receivable, inventories, and prepayments are the most common current assets.

Investments.   This category includes long-term investments in the debt or equity securities of other entities. If a firm makes such investments for short-term purposes, it classifies them under current assets.

Property, Plant, and Equipment.   This category includes the tangible, long-lived assets that a firm uses in operations over a period of years. Property, plant, and equipment includes land, buildings, machinery, automobiles, furniture, fixtures, computers, and other equipment.

Intangibles.   Intangibles include the rights established by law or contract to the future use of property. Patents, trademarks, and franchises are intangible assets. The most troublesome asset recognition questions revolve around which rights satisfy the criteria for an asset. For example, should firms recognize the value of brand names as intangible assets? Intangibles also include goodwill, which arises when one firm acquires another firm and pays an amount that exceeds the market value of the identifiable net assets. GAAP defines the excess as goodwill.

Liabilities—Recognition, Valuation, and Classification.   A liability represents a firm's obligation to make payments of cash, goods, or services in a reasonably definite amount at a reasonably definite future time for benefits or services received in the past.[3] Liabilities include obligations to financial institutions, suppliers, employees, and governments. Most troublesome questions regarding liability recognition relate to unexecuted contracts. GAAP does not recognize labor union agreements, purchase order commitments, and some lease agreements as liabilities because firms will receive the benefits from these items in the future instead of having received them in the past. Notes to the financial statements disclose material, unexecuted contracts, and other contingent claims.

Most liabilities are monetary, requiring payments of fixed amounts of cash. GAAP reports those due within one year at the amount of cash the firm expects to pay to discharge the obligation. If the payment dates extend beyond one year, then GAAP states the liability at the present value of the required future cash flows (discounted at an interest rate that reflects the underlying uncertainty of paying the cash at the time the obligation initially arose). Some liabilities, such as warranties, require the delivery of goods or services instead of the payment of cash. The balance sheet states these liabilities at the expected future cost of these goods or services.

Published balance sheets classify liabilities in various ways. Virtually all firms use a current liabilities category, which includes obligations expected to be settled within one year. Balance sheets report the remaining liabilities in a section labeled *noncurrent liabilities* or *long-term debt*.

Shareholders' Equity Valuation and Disclosure. The shareholders' equity in a firm is a residual interest or claim. That is, the owners have a claim on all assets not required to meet the claims of creditors. The valuation of assets and liabilities in the balance sheet therefore determines the valuation of total shareholders' equity.[4]

Balance sheets separate the total shareholders' equity into amounts initially contributed by shareholders for an interest in a firm (that is, preferred stock, common stock) and the amount of net income a firm subsequently realizes in excess of dividends declared (that is, retained earnings).

Common Size Balance Sheets. One useful analytical tool for gaining insight about the structure of a firm's assets, liabilities, and shareholders' equity is a common size balance sheet. Exhibit 1.2 presents a common size balance sheet for Coke and Pepsi for December 31, Year 7 and Year 8. Note that the common size balance sheet expresses each amount as a percentage of total assets or total liabilities plus shareholders' equity. Observe the following:

1. Receivables and inventories represent a smaller proportion of Pepsi's total assets than Coke's, reflecting Pepsi's greater involvement in restaurants (where sales are for cash and inventory turnover is higher than for soft drinks and consumer foods).

---

[3]Ibid., para 35.

[4]The issuance of bonds with equity characteristics, such as convertible bonds, and the issuance of preferred stock with debt characteristics, such as redeemable preferred stock, cloud the distinction between liabilities and shareholders' equity.

EXHIBIT 1.2

Common Size Balance Sheets for Coke and Pepsi

	Coke		Pepsi	
	Year 7	Year 8	Year 7	Year 8
Assets				
Cash and Marketable Securities	9%	9%	10%	8%
Accounts Receivable	10	10	7	8
Inventories	9	9	4	4
Other Current Assets	10	9	2	2
Total Current Assets	38%	37%	23%	22%
Investments	26	27	8	7
Property, Plant, and Equipment	32	31	36	37
Intangible and Other Assets.	4	5	33	34
Total Assets	100%	100%	100%	100%
Liabilities and Shareholders' Equity				
Accounts Payable.	20%	18%	5%	6%
Short-Term Borrowing	19	14	3	9
Other Current Liabilities	9	11	12	13
Total Current Liabilities	48%	43%	20%	28%
Long-Term Debt	10	12	38	31
Other Noncurrent Liabilities	7	7	16	14
Total Liabilities	65%	62%	74%	73%
Common Stock	11	12	3	4
Retained Earnings.	74	79	26	28
Cumulative Translation Adjustment	(3)	(4)	—	(1)
Treasury Stock.	(47)	(49)	(3)	(4)
Total Shareholders' Equity	35%	38%	26%	27%
Total Liabilities and Shareholders' Equity . . .	100%	100%	100%	100%

---

2. Investments represent a higher proportion of total assets for Coke than for Pepsi. Coke maintains a minority ownership position in its bottling operations whereas Pepsi owns most of its bottling operations.

3. Property, plant, and equipment make up a higher proportion of total assets for Pepsi than for Coke, reflecting the greater capital intensity of Pepsi's restaurant operations.

4. Intangible assets, principally goodwill, represent a significantly higher percentage of total assets for Pepsi than for Coke, reflecting Pepsi's greater emphasis on growth through acquisitions (Pizza Hut, Taco Bell, Kentucky Fried Chicken).

5. The long-term debt percentages for Pepsi significantly exceed those for Coke, reflecting Pepsi's need to finance capital-intensive restaurant operations and corporate acquisitions.

6. The retained earnings percentages of Coke exceed those of Pepsi, due in part to Coke's higher profitability (analyzed more fully in later chapters).

7. The treasury stock percentages for Coke exceed those of Pepsi because Coke has followed a strategy of reacquiring its common shares on the market in recent years.

Analysts should interpret common size financial statements carefully because the percentages for individual accounts are not independent of the percentages for other accounts. For example, Pepsi's goodwill arising for acquisitions represents a larger proportion of its total assets, leaving a smaller proportion for other assets. The fact that Pepsi's percentages for current assets are smaller than those for Coke does not *necessarily* mean that Pepsi needs fewer receivables or inventories for its operations.

Percentage Change Balance Sheets.   A useful analytical tool for gaining insights about changes in the amount and structure of a firm's assets, liabilities, and shareholders' equity is a percentage change balance sheet. Exhibit 1.3 presents a percentage change balance sheet for Coke and Pepsi for December 31, Year 7 and

EXHIBIT 1.3

Percentage Change Balance Sheet for Coke and Pepsi

	Coke			Pepsi		
	Year 7	Year 8	Five-Year Compound Annual Growth Rate	Year 7	Year 8	Five-Year Compound Annual Growth Rate
Assets						
Cash and Marketable Securities ..	(4.8%)	1.4%	(2.6%)	1.1%	(9.9%)	2.8%
Accounts Receivable	12.0%	14.5%	9.7%	7.2%	18.6%	14.0%
Inventories	3.1%	2.9%	6.1%	16.3%	20.3%	15.9%
Current Assets.................	2.5%	4.4%	6.4%	6.0%	6.7%	9.6%
Investments	0.3%	14.3%	6.7%	1.5%	2.9%	16.3%
Property, Plant, and Equipment ..	18.0%	6.7%	14.0%	15.2%	17.8%	16.4%
Accumulated Depreciation	10.4%	8.7%	10.2%	19.1%	15.9%	19.7%
Intangibles and Other Assets.....	26.0%	43.3%	57.3%	17.3%	13.9%	25.2%
Total Assets	8.1%	8.8%	10.0%	11.6%	13.1%	16.3%
Liabilities						
Accounts Payable...............	17.7%	(1.6%)	15.4%	(2.7%)	19.3%	9.5%
Short-Term Borrowing	73.7%	(20.2%)	3.9%	210.1%	209.9%	8.6%
Current Liabilities..............	28.8%	(2.5%)	12.5%	16.2%	52.1%	11.2%
Long-Term Debt	13.7%	27.5%	13.4%	2.0%	(6.6%)	22.9%
Total Liabilities	23.6%	3.8%	12.6%	17.9%	11.4%	16.8%
Shareholders' Equity						
Common Stock	26.2%	19.4%	13.8%	38.9%	30.9%	23.0%
Retained Earnings..............	10.0%	15.8%	16.6%	(0.5%)	20.3%	14.5%
Treasury Stock.................	31.9%	13.1%	23.2%	(10.6%)	36.9%	12.4%
Total Shareholders' Equity	(12.2%)	17.9%	6.5%	(3.4%)	18.3%	14.9%

Year 8. It also shows the compound annual growth rate in various balance sheet accounts for the five years ending December 31, Year 8. Observe the following:

1. Pepsi's total assets grew more rapidly than Coke's during each of the last two years as well as over the last five years. The higher growth is evident in most of Pepsi's individual assets. Pepsi's largest growth item during the period is goodwill (included in other assets) arising from acquisitions.
2. Pepsi financed this growth with both debt and shareholders' equity.
3. Coke's retained earnings increased at a faster rate during the last five years than Pepsi's, but Coke's total shareholders' equity increased more slowly due to its more aggressive repurchases of its common stock.

As with the common size balance sheet, the analyst should interpret percentage change balance sheets cautiously. A large percentage change in one year for a particular item (for example, other assets for Coke in Year 7 and Year 8) may simply reflect a relatively small amount from the previous year that serves as a base. Also, a large percentage change for a particular item may not be significant if that item represents a small proportion of total assets or total liabilities plus shareholders' equity. Note, for example, that intangible and other assets for Coke represent only 4 percent of total assets in Year 7 (refer to Exhibit 1.2). Thus, the large percentage change for other assets in Year 8 and over the last five years plays only a minor role in explaining the changes in its total assets.

INCOME STATEMENT — MEASURING OPERATING PERFORMANCE

The total assets of a firm change over time because of investing and financing activities. For example, a firm may issue common stock for cash, acquire a building by assuming a mortgage for part of the purchase price, or issue common stock in exchange for convertible bonds. These investing and financing activities affect the amount and structure of a firm's assets and equities.

The total assets of a firm also change over time because of operating activities. A firm sells goods or services to customers for a larger amount than the cost to the firm to acquire or produce the goods and services. Creditors and owners provide capital to a firm with the expectation that the firm will use it to generate a profit and provide an adequate return to the suppliers of capital. The second principal financial statement, the income statement, provides information about the operating performance of a firm for some particular time period.

Net income equals revenues and gains minus expenses and losses. Revenues measure the inflows of net assets (that is, assets less liabilities) from selling goods and providing services. Expenses measure the outflows of net assets that a firm uses, or consumes, in the process of generating revenues. As a measure of operating performance, revenues reflect the services rendered by a firm, and expenses indicate the efforts required or expended. Gains and losses arise from sales of assets or settlements of liabilities that relate only peripherally to a firm's primary operating activities (for example, the sale of a building, the early extinguishment of long-term debt). These gains and losses arise when a firm receives or pays a different amount than the amount at which the accounting records state the asset or liability.

Accrual Basis of Accounting. Figure 1.2 depicts the operating, or earnings, process for a manufacturing firm. Net income from this series of activities equals the amount of cash received from customers minus the amount of cash paid for raw materials, labor, and the services of production facilities. If the entire operating process occurred within one accounting period, few difficulties would arise in measuring operating performance. Net income would equal cash inflows minus cash outflows. However, a firm acquires raw materials in one accounting period and uses them in several future accounting periods. It acquires plant and equipment in one accounting period and uses them during many accounting periods. A firm often sells goods or services in an earlier period than the one in which it receives cash from customers.

Under a cash basis of accounting, a firm recognizes revenue when it receives cash from customers and recognizes expenses when it pays cash to suppliers, employees, and other providers of goods and services. Because a firm's operating process usually extends over several accounting periods, the cash basis of accounting provides a poor matching of revenues and expenses and, therefore, a poor measure of operating performance for specific periods of time. To overcome this deficiency of the cash basis, GAAP requires that firms use the accrual basis of accounting in measuring operating performance.

Under the accrual basis of accounting, a firm recognizes revenue when it performs all, or a substantial portion, of the services it expects to perform and receives either cash or a receivable whose cash-equivalent amount the firm can measure objectively. Most firms recognize revenue at the time they sell goods or render services. They match expenses with the associated revenues. Consider the accrual basis of accounting applied to a manufacturing firm. The cost of manufacturing a product remains on the balance sheet as an asset until the time of sale. At the time of sale, the firm recognizes revenue in the amount of the cash it expects to collect. It recognizes the cost of manufacturing the product as a matching expense. When a firm cannot easily link costs with a particular revenue (for example, the corporate president's salary), it recognizes an expense in the period when it consumes services in operations. The accrual basis of accounting focuses on the acquisition and use of economic resources in operations, not on their associated cash flows. The accrual basis provides a better measure of operating performance than the cash basis because it matches more accurately inputs with outputs.

Classification and Format within the Income Statement. The future earnings stream of an asset or collection of assets is often the basis for placing

---

FIGURE 1.2

Operating Process for a Manufacturing Firm

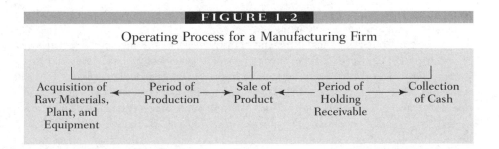

Acquisition of Raw Materials, Plant, and Equipment ← Period of Production → Sale of Product ← Period of Holding Receivable → Collection of Cash

a value on the asset(s). Analysts form predictions of the future earnings, or net income, of a firm by studying its past trend of earnings. Inaccurate projections from past data can occur if net income includes unusual or nonrecurring amounts. To provide more useful information for prediction, GAAP requires that the income statement include some or all of the following sections or categories, depending on the nature of the firm's income for the period:

1. Income from continuing operations.
2. Income, gains, and losses from discontinued operations.
3. Extraordinary gains and losses.
4. Adjustments for changes in accounting principles.

The first section, Income from Continuing Operations, reports the revenues and expenses of activities in which a firm anticipates an ongoing involvement. A firm that intends to remain in a line of business (for example, soft drinks for Coke and Pepsi) but decides to sell or close down some portion of that line of business (for example, a particular bottling operation) would report any income, gain, or loss from such an action under continuing operations. On the other hand, if a firm decides to terminate its involvement in a line of business (for example, restaurants for Pepsi), it would report the income, gain, or loss in the second section of the income statement labeled Income, Gains and Losses from Discontinued Operations.

"Extraordinary gains and losses" arise from events that are (1) unusual, given the nature of a firm's activities, (2) nonrecurring, and (3) material in amount. Corporate annual reports rarely disclose such items (except for gains or losses on early debt retirements, which GAAP requires firms to report as an extraordinary item). Many firms in recent years have reported restructuring charges in their income statements. Such charges reflect the cost of inventories, fixed assets, intangibles, or other assets that the firm does not expect to recover from future revenues. These charges also reflect expected future cash outflows to settle obligations that the firm had not previously recognized as a liability. Because restructuring charges do not usually satisfy the criteria for discontinued operations or for extraordinary gains and losses, firms report these charges in the continuing operations section of the income statement. Such charges usually appear, however, on a separate line to distinguish them clearly from recurring income items.

When firms change their methods of accounting, GAAP generally requires them to report the cumulative difference between the income reported under the old and new methods in a separate section of the income statement. Note in Appendix A and Appendix B that both Coke and Pepsi report adjustments for changes in accounting principles in their income statements.

Each of the four categories of income items appears in the income statement net of any income tax effects. The majority of income statements include only the first section. Firms add the other sections as appropriate for a particular year.

The continuing operations section of the income statement commonly appears in one of two formats. A *single step* format lists and sums all revenues, lists and sums all expenses, and then derives net income in a single mathematical calculation. A *multiple step* format groups similar kinds of revenues and expenses and computes several subtotals before deriving net income. The income statements of Coke and Pepsi in Appendix A and Appendix B appear in a multiple step format, with subtotals for operating profit, income from continuing operations before income taxes and adjustments for changes in accounting principles, income from continuing operations before adjustments for changes in accounting principles, and net income.

Firms also report their expenses in various ways. Most firms in the United States report expenses by their function: cost of goods sold for manufacturing, selling expenses for marketing, administrative expenses for administrative management, interest expense for financing. Other firms report expenses by their nature: raw materials, compensation, advertising, research and development.

The income statements of firms in countries outside the United States typically contain sections for continuing operations and extraordinary items (if any). These income statements commonly report expenses by their nature rather than by their function.

Common Size Income Statements. These statements provide useful insights about the profitability of firms. Most common size income statements express expenses and net income as a percentage of sales. Exhibit 1.4 presents common size income statements for Coke and Pepsi. Note the following:

1. Coke is more profitable than Pepsi in all three years.
2. Coke's higher other revenues percentages reflect its share of the earnings of its minority-owned bottling operations (appears as "equity income" on Coke's income statement.

EXHIBIT 1.4

Common Size Income Statements for Coke and Pepsi

	Coke			Pepsi		
	Year 6	Year 7	Year 8	Year 6	Year 7	Year 8
Sales	100%	100%	100%	100%	100%	100%
Other Revenues	2	1	2	1	1	—[a]
Cost of Goods Sold...................	(40)	(39)	(37)	(48)	(48)	(48)
Selling and Administrative Expenses	(40)	(40)	(41)	(41)	(41)	(41)
Interest Expense	(2)	(1)	(1)	(3)	(3)	(2)
Income Before Income Taxes...........	20%	21%	23%	9%	9%	9%
Income Tax Expense..................	(6)	(7)	(7)	(3)	(3)	(3)
Income from Continuing Operations	14%	14%	16%	6%	6%	6%
Adjustments for Changes in Accounting Principles...............	—	(1)	—[a]	—	(4)	—
Net Income	14%	13%	16%	6%	2%	6%

[a]Amount rounds to zero.

3. Coke's lower cost of goods sold percentages reflect either more efficient manufacturing operations, a greater ability to obtain premium prices for its products relative to Pepsi, or a different product mix. The difference in the cost of goods sold percentages for the two firms accounts for most of Coke's superior profitability.

4. Coke's higher income tax expense to sales percentages occur because of Coke's higher percentage for income before taxes to sales. Both firms have average tax rates between 30 and 35 percent of net income before income taxes.

Percentage Change Income Statements. A percentage change income statement, such as that shown in Exhibit 1.5 for Coke and Pepsi, provides insights about the rate of growth of operations. Consistent with the picture portrayed in the percentage change balance sheet, Pepsi's sales grew more rapidly than Coke's over the last five years. Both Coke's and Pepsi's income growth occurred because cost of goods sold increased less rapidly than sales, suggesting either increased efficiencies in manufacturing, reduced material or labor costs, or increased ability to raise selling prices. Selling and administrative expenses increased more rapidly than sales during this five-year period, suggesting either expansion into new markets abroad or increased competition. Income from continuing operations for Pepsi grew more rapidly than for Coke during the last two years, largely because Pepsi's earnings for Year 6 were somewhat depressed.

STATEMENT OF CASH FLOWS

The third principal financial statement is the statement of cash flows. This statement reports for a period of time the net cash flow (inflows minus outflows) from three of the principal business activities depicted in Figure 1.1: operating, investing, and financing.

EXHIBIT 1.5

Percentage Change Income Statements for Coke and Pepsi

	Coke			Pepsi		
	Year 7	Year 8	Four-Year Compound Annual Growth Rate	Year 7	Year 8	Four-Year Compound Annual Growth Rate
Sales	13.0%	6.8%	11.7%	12.0%	13.9%	13.2%
Cost of Goods Sold.............	8.7%	2.1%	7.3%	11.7%	13.8%	12.6%
Selling and Administrative Expenses....................	14.0%	8.5%	14.2%	12.6%	11.7%	13.9%
Interest Expense	(11.4%)	(1.8%)	(14.1%)	(4.9%)	(2.2%)	(1.6%)
Income Tax Expense...........	12.8%	15.5%	14.9%	3.0%	39.8%	16.0%
Income from Continuing Operations	16.4%	16.1%	16.4%	20.6%	22.0%	15.2%

Rationale for the Statement of Cash Flows.   Profitable firms, especially those growing rapidly, sometimes find themselves strapped for cash and unable to pay suppliers, employees, and other creditors. This occurs for two principal reasons:

1. The timing of cash receipts from customers does not necessarily coincide with the recognition of revenue, and the timing of cash expenditures to suppliers, employees, and other creditors does not necessarily coincide with the recognition of expenses under the accrual basis of accounting. In the usual case, cash expenditures precede the recognition of expenses and cash receipts occur after the recognition of revenue. Thus, a firm might have positive net income for a period but the cash outflow for operations exceeds the cash inflow.
2. The firm may retire outstanding debt or acquire new plant and equipment at a time when there is insufficient cash available.

In many cases, a profitable firm finding itself short of cash can obtain the needed funds from either short- or long-term creditors or from owners. The firm must repay with interest the funds borrowed from creditors. Owners may require that the firm pay periodic dividends as an inducement to invest in the firm. Eventually, the firm must generate cash internally from operations if it is to survive. Cash flows are the connecting link between investing, financing, and operating activities. They permit each of these three principal business activities to continue functioning smoothly and effectively.

Classification of Cash Flows.   The statement of cash flows reports the net amount of cash flow from a firm's operating, investing, and financing activities. It also shows the principal inflows and outflows of cash from each of these three activities. Figure 1.3 presents the major types of cash flows, which the following sections describe.

   Operating.   Selling goods and providing services are among the most important ways to generate cash for a financially healthy company. When assessed over several years, cash flow from operations indicates the extent to which operating activities have generated more cash than they have used. The firm can use excess cash from operations to pay dividends, acquire buildings and equipment, repay long-term debt, and support other investing and financing activities.

   Investing.   The acquisition of noncurrent assets, particularly property, plant, and equipment, usually represents a major ongoing use of cash. Firms must replace such assets as they wear out and acquire additional noncurrent assets if they are to grow. Firms obtain a portion of the cash needed to acquire noncurrent assets from sales of existing noncurrent assets. However, such cash inflows are seldom sufficient to cover the cost of new acquisitions.

   Financing.   A firm obtains cash from short- and long-term borrowing and from issuing capital stock. It uses cash to pay dividends to shareholders, to repay short- or long-term borrowing, and to reacquire shares of outstanding capital stock. The amount of cash flow from these financing activities is the third major component reported in the statement of cash flows.

FIGURE 1.3

Components of the Statement of Cash Flows

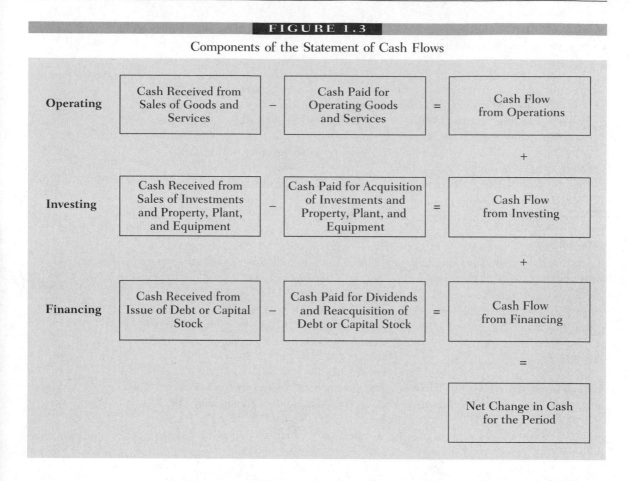

Firms sometimes engage in investing and financing transactions that do not directly involve cash. For example, a firm may acquire a building by assuming a mortgage obligation. It might exchange a tract of land for equipment. The firm might issue common stock upon conversion of long-term debt. Firms disclose these transactions in a supplementary schedule or note to the statement of cash flows in a way that clearly indicates that they are investing and financing transactions that do not affect cash. See the lower portion of Pepsi's statement of cash flows in Appendix B for an example of these disclosures.

The statement of cash flows is not a required financial statement in many countries around the world. Common practice in Europe is to present a statement of sources and uses of funds in which firms define *funds* as current assets minus current liabilities, or working capital. Chapter 2 describes and illustrates analytical procedures for preparing a statement of cash flows. It also demonstrates the conversion of a statement of sources and uses of funds into a statement of cash flows.

Figure 1.4 summarizes the principal business activities and principal financial statements. The five business activities might be viewed as interconnected cogwheels. Cash flows reported in the statement of cash flows tie these activities together and keep them running smoothly.

FIGURE 1.4

Summary of Principal Business Activities and Financial Statements

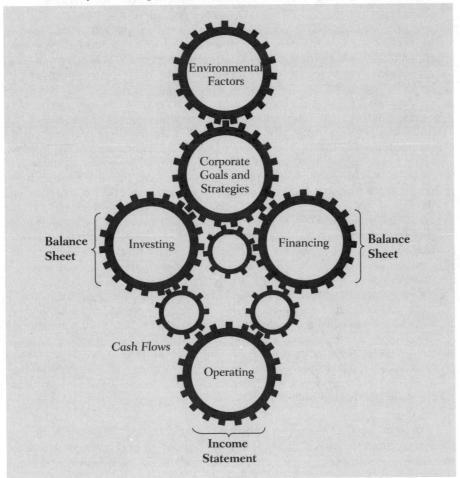

It might be helpful at this point to study the financial statements and notes for Coke and Pepsi presented in Appendix A and Appendix B. We make frequent reference to these financial statements throughout the book.

SOURCES OF FINANCIAL STATEMENT INFORMATION

Firms in the United States whose bonds or capital stock trade in public capital markets typically make available the following financial information:

1. Annual report to shareholders—The "glossy" annual report includes balance sheets for the most recent two years and income statements and statements of

cash flows for the most recent three years, along with various notes and supporting schedules. The notes describe the accounting principles that a firm uses in preparing its financial statements (see Note 1 to Coke's and Pepsi's financial statements). The notes also include more detailed information about inventories; property, plant, and equipment; debt; leases; pensions; postretirement benefits; income taxes; and other items than the principal financial statements provide. Supporting schedules usually include a reconciliation of the change in individual shareholders' equity accounts (this schedule follows the statement of cash flows for Coke and Pepsi).

The annual report includes a letter from the firm's chairman of the board or chief executive officer summarizing the activities of the most recent year. It also includes a discussion and analysis by management of the firm's operating performance, financial position, and liquidity. Firms vary with respect to the information provided in this Management Discussion and Analysis section of the annual report. Some firms simply describe in narrative form information already reported in the principal financial statements. Other firms offer insights regarding the reasons for changes in operating performance or financial health.

2. Form 10K annual report—The Form 10K annual report filed with the SEC includes the same financial statements and notes as the corporate annual report plus additional supporting schedules required by the SEC. For example, the 10K annual report includes more detailed information than the annual report to shareholders provides on changes in the components of property, plant, and equipment and the subsidiaries included in consolidated financial statements.

3. Form 10Q quarterly report—The Form 10Q quarterly report filed with the SEC includes condensed balance sheet and income statement information for the most recent three months, as well as comparative data for earlier quarters.

4. Prospectus or registration statement—Firms intending to issue new bonds or capital stock file a prospectus that describes the offering (amount, intended uses of proceeds). The prospectus includes much of the financial statement information found in the 10K annual report.

Most firms send single copies of these financial reports to anyone requesting them. The corporate annual report usually lists the person or department within the firm to whom to communicate such requests. Documents filed with the SEC are available at SEC offices, generally requiring a photocopying charge. For a fee, Disclosure, Inc., provides copies of each of these documents. Most business libraries subscribe to the services of Disclosure, Inc. Depending on the particular subscription arrangement, libraries may receive these documents on microfiche, optical disk, or photocopy.

Several information services firms offer databases or summaries of information extracted from corporate annual reports. Compustat, owned by Standard & Poors, offers on-line databases of detailed financial statement items. Lotus One Source, a comprehensive on-line information source about firms (products, divisions, officers, analyst reports) contains summary financial statements. Standard & Poor's *Corporation Records,* Moody's *Industrial Manual,* and other industry manuals provide summary financial statement information. Most of these sources do not provide the full text of notes to the financial statements that the original documents contain.

SUMMARY

When performing financial statement analysis, there is a tendency to want to "get cranking;" that is, to start calculating a long list of financial statement ratios. This chapter discussed several important preliminary steps that the analyst should take:

1. Identify the purpose or objective of the analysis. This step better focuses the particular analyses performed and analytical tools used.
2. Gain an understanding of the economics and current conditions of the industries in which a firm operates and the firm's particular strategies for competing in these industries. This step aids in the interpretive process.

A third preliminary step is to study the financial statements to gain an understanding of the accounting methods used, account classification scheme followed, and other data issues that might affect the comparability of the financial statement amounts over time or across firms. Chapters 4 through 7 describe several of the more important data issues that a financial analysis is likely to confront.

Perhaps the least challenging aspect of financial statement analysis is the calculation of financial statement ratios. An analysis package referred to as *Financial Statement Analysis Package,* or *FSAP,* is available to adopters of this textbook from the publisher. *FSAP* runs on either an IBM or Macintosh platforms. Appendix C includes a user manual for FSAP. It also presents the output of *FSAP* for Coke and Pepsi.

OVERVIEW OF RESEARCH METHODOLOGY EXAMINING STOCK MARKET EFFICIENCY

Empirical research examining the effect of new information on security returns generally uses a statistical regression model that filters out the effect of economywide, or marketwide, phenomena. The researcher begins by regressing a particular firm's security returns (the sum of dividends plus changes in the market price of common shares divided by the market price at the beginning of the period) on an index of returns for all shares in the market. The researcher uses either a daily, weekly, or monthly return series for some period that excludes the period of release of the new information being studied. A regression equation of the following form results:

$$\text{Firm Specific Rate of Return} = \alpha + \beta \left(\text{Market Wide Rate of Return} \right) + \text{Residual}$$

The β, or beta coefficient, measures the covariability of a firm's returns with that of the market. As Chapter 9 discusses more fully, analysts use beta as a measure of systematic, or market, risk. The α, or alpha, coefficient and the residual measure firm-specific elements of return. The regression that generates the alpha and beta coefficients has positive and negative residuals for individual firms but a zero residual using ordinary least squares regression techniques for all firms combined (that is, positive and negative residuals net to zero). The coefficients from this regression serve as a basis for generating expected firm-specific rates of return in future periods. The underlying assumption is that the return-generating process is constant (that is, the alpha and beta coefficients do not change). The release of new (unexpected) information about a firm to the market should cause the actual rate of return to deviate from the expected rate of return. The differential return gets captured in the residual. Thus, the researcher can study the behavior of the residual around the time of release of new information to ascertain whether the market reacts quickly and intelligently to the information.

A significant portion of the research on efficient capital markets uses recently released financial statement data as the new item of information. Most of these studies use earnings for this purpose. Because a firm's return-generating process, as captured in the alpha and beta coefficients in the regression, implicitly incorporates an expectation about the level of earnings (as well as other factors), the researcher examines the correlation between *unexpected* earnings and firm-specific return residuals. High correlations for a particular item of information when studied across a large number of firms suggest that the market reacts to that information. The direction and speed of that reaction indicates the degree of market efficiency with respect to the information.

PROBLEMS

1.1 EFFECT OF INDUSTRY CHARACTERISTICS ON FINANCIAL STATEMENT RELATION-SHIPS. Effective financial statement analysis requires an understanding of a firm's economic characteristics. The relations between various financial statement items provide evidence of many of these economic characteristics. Exhibit 1.6 presents common size condensed financial statement information for 13 firms in different industries. These common size balance sheets and income statements express various items as a percentage of total revenues (that is, the statement divides all amounts by total revenues for the year). Exhibit 1.6 also shows the cash flow from operations to capital expenditures ratio. The 13 companies and a brief description of their activities appear below.

1. Biogen: Engages in biotechnology research. Biogen licenses other firms to manufacture and sell products and technologies developed in its research laboratories and receives a royalty fee. Biogen also conducts research for other firms and receives a fee for its services.
2. Burlington Northern: Provides railroad freight transportation services.
3. Circus Circus Enterprises: Offers casino gaming services for adults and theme park entertainment for youths around a circus theme. Circus Circus has recently expanded its existing facilities and added new sites.
4. Ford Motor Company: Manufactures and markets automobiles and provides financing for its customers' purchases.
5. Hershey Foods Corporation: Manufactures and markets candies. Hershey has recently acquired other candy companies in an effort to diversify its product line.
6. J. P. Morgan: Provides commercial banking and financial consulting services, primarily to business firms.
7. Kelly Services: Provides temporary office services to business and other firms.
8. Lands' End: Sells apparel through catalogs.
9. McDonald's: Offers restaurant services.
10. Microsoft: Develops and sells computer software.

11. Tele-Communications: Offers cable television services. The firm must pay a franchise fee to obtain access to local television markets.
12. Toys "R" Us: Sells entertainment products through a network of retail stores.
13. Walt Disney: Generates revenues from theme parks and resorts, motion film production, and consumer products.

REQUIRED

Use whatever clues you can to match the companies in Exhibit 1.6 with the firms listed above.

1.2 EFFECT OF INDUSTRY CHARACTERISTICS ON FINANCIAL STATEMENTS. Effective financial statement analysis requires an understanding of a firm's economic characteristics. The relations between various financial statement items provide evidence of many of these economic characteristics. Exhibit 1.7 presents common size condensed financial statement information for firms in 13 different industries. These common size balance sheets and income statements express various items as a percentage of total revenues (that is, the statements divide all amounts by total revenues for the year). The 13 companies shown (all corporations except the professional basketball franchise) represent the following industries:

1. Advertising agency.
2. Aerospace manufacturer (significant government contracts).
3. Beer brewery.
4. Computer manufacturer.
5. Department store chain.
6. Distiller of hard liquor.
7. Electric utility.
8. Finance company (also involved in leasing).
9. Grocery store chain.
10. Life insurance company.
11. Pharmaceutical company.
12. Professional basketball franchise (a partnership).
13. Steel manufacturer.

REQUIRED

Use whatever clues you can to match the companies in Exhibit 1.7 with the industries listed above.

1.3 USING COMMON SIZE AND TREND FINANCIAL STATEMENTS. Wal-Mart Stores are the largest retailing firm in the world. Its sales mix during three recent years is as follows.

	Year 6	Year 7	Year 8
Discount Stores	78.8%	72.8%	72.6%
Warehouse Clubs.	20.2	21.5	22.2
Food Distribution	1.0	5.7	5.2
Total	100.0%	100.0	100.0%

Exhibit 1.8 presents a common size balance sheet and Exhibit 1.9 presents a common size income statement for Wal-Mart Stores for Year 6, Year 7, and Year 8. Exhibit 1.10 presents trend information and Exhibit 1.11 presents a statement of cash flows for these same years.

EXHIBIT 1.6

Common Size Financial Statement Data for Firms in 13 Industries
(Problem 1.1)

	Company Numbers				
	(1)	(2)	(3)	(4)	(5)
Balance Sheet at End of Year					
Cash and Marketable Securities	9.3%	2.5%	10.0%	0.5%	61.0%
Accounts and Notes Receivable	12.7	0.4	1.2	8.5	9.0
Inventories	—	17.2	22.4	13.0	3.4
Property, Plant, and Equipment (net)	3.5	9.1	40.1	41.9	23.1
Other Assets.	2.2	2.3	3.7	17.9	4.9
Total Assets	27.7%	31.5%	77.4%	81.8%	101.4%
Current Liabilities.	8.0%	10.5%	26.1%	23.3%	15.0%
Long-Term Debt	—	—	9.1	4.8	—
Other Noncurrent Liabilities	—	0.6	2.6	13.3	—
Shareholders' Equity	19.7	20.4	39.6	40.4	86.4
Total Equities.	27.7%	31.5%	77.4%	81.8%	101.4%
Income Statement for Year					
Sales Revenue	—	100.0%	100.0%	100.0%	97.8%
Service and Other Revenues	100.0%	—	—	—	2.2
Total Revenues.	100.0%	100.0%	100.0%	100.0%	100.0%
Cost of Goods Sold.	—	58.9%	69.2%	57.2%	16.9%
Operating Expenses	96.4%	33.0	20.2	29.7	33.3
Research and Development	—	—	—	—	12.5
Interest	—	—	0.9	0.8	—
Income Taxes.	1.3	3.2	3.6	5.3	11.9
Total Expenses.	97.7%	95.1%	93.9%	93.0%	74.6%
Net Income	2.3%	4.9%	6.1%	7.0%	25.4%
Cash Flow from Operations/Capital Expenditures	2.5	1.3	1.2	1.8	4.6

EXHIBIT 1.6

continued

			Company Numbers				
(6)	**(7)**	**(8)**	**(9)**	**(10)**	**(11)**	**(12)**	**(13)**
25.8%	4.1%	0.4%	2.5%	18.8%	181.1%	—	528.6%
15.9	0.9	12.5	4.2	111.7	21.2	5.6%	520.0
22.6	2.1	1.9	0.6	5.1	—	—	—
60.0	123.9	125.8	136.1	21.1	25.8	118.8	15.5
10.5	4.9	9.3	19.1	25.6	11.0	273.4	57.1
134.8%	135.9%	149.9%	162.5%	182.3%	239.1%	397.8%	1,121.2%
32.4%	9.6%	32.5%	14.9%	135.5%	21.3%	101.3%	984.5%
27.4	59.4	32.5	47.1	6.5	—	238.4	44.2
17.3	8.2	44.1	15.8	24.8	—	—	10.0
57.7	58.7	40.8	84.7	15.5	217.8	58.1	82.5
134.8%	135.9%	149.9%	162.5%	182.3%	239.1%	397.8%	1,121.2%
16.2%	—	—	100.0%	83.9%	—	—	—
83.8	100.0%	100.0%	—	16.1	100.0%	100.0%	100.0%
100.0%	100.0%	100.0%	100.0%	100.0%	100.0%	100.0%	100.0%
12.2%	—	—	61.4%	78.1%	—	—	—
67.8	78.9	85.9	11.8	11.7	23.7%	77.9%	30.0%
—	—	—	—	—	53.1	—	—
1.8	1.9	3.0	4.2	6.7	—	17.6	47.5
6.7	7.0	4.8	8.0	1.2	1.5	1.5	8.1
88.5	87.8%	93.7%	85.4%	97.7%	78.3%	97.0	85.6%
11.5%	12.2%	6.3%	14.6%	2.3%	21.7%	3.0%	14.4%
1.9	0.5	0.9	1.3	2.1	4.4	1.3	—

EXHIBIT 1.7

Common Size Financial Statement Data for Firms in 13 Industries
(Problem 1.2)

| | Company Numbers | | | | |
	(1)	(2)	(3)	(4)	(5)
Balance Sheet at End of Year					
Cash and Marketable Securities	0.7%	19.1%	9.0%	0.9%	11.9%
Current Receivables....................	0.2	4.5	16.3	4.9	15.2
Inventories	7.5	—	11.9	5.6	13.2
Property, Plant, and Equipment Cost......	17.0	0.8	42.9	79.4	54.0
Accumulated Depreciation	(5.5)	(0.7)	(21.0)	(21.7)	(26.9)
Net	11.5	0.1	21.9	57.7	27.1
Other Assets..........................	1.4	23.2	12.5	6.9	8.7
Total Assets	21.3%	46.9%	71.6%	76.0%	76.1%
Current Liabilities......................	7.8%	21.0%	32.7%	13.2%	22.3%
Long-Term Debt	3.6	—	6.3	14.7	8.7
Other Noncurrent Liabilities	1.4	15.6	5.5	14.2	4.9
Owners' Equity	8.5	10.3	27.1	33.9	40.2
Total Equities......................	21.3%	46.9%	71.6%	76.0%	76.1%
Income Statement for Year					
Sales	100.0%	100.0%	100.0%	100.0%	100.0%
Cost of Goods Sold (excluding depreciation) or Operating Expenses[a]....	76.9	61.8	74.8	62.0	71.1
Depreciation	1.4	0.1	4.1	3.6	6.8
Interest	0.4	1.9	0.7	0.8	0.5
Advertising...........................	3.6	0.5	—	8.0	—
Research and Development	—	—	3.5	—	7.7
Income Taxes..........................	1.1	—	4.5	5.5	2.8
All Other Items (net)...................	15.5	(0.7)	7.2	13.4	6.5
Total Expenses......................	98.9%	63.6%	94.8%	93.3%	95.4%
Net Income	1.1%	36.4%	5.2%	6.7%	4.6%
Cash Flow from Operations/Capital Expenditures	1.22	—	2.95	1.17	1.09

[a]Represents operating expenses for the following companies: advertising agency, finance company, life insurance company, professional basketball franchise.

EXHIBIT 1.7

continued

			Company Numbers				
(6)	(7)	(8)	(9)	(10)	(11)	(12)	(13)
1.6%	4.4%	22.7%	5.1%	14.4%	245.6%	1.0%	25.2%
36.2	13.5	21.3	13.2	70.6	11.9	7.8	562.5
14.4	21.7	13.0	10.5	7.5	—	11.4	—
37.5	25.3	65.9	162.5	18.4	3.6	398.4	70.8
(12.0)	(11.8)	(27.4)	(80.5)	(9.3)	(1.8)	(109.6)	(21.4)
25.5	13.5	38.5	82.0	9.1	1.8	288.8	49.4
2.2	31.8	16.7	4.0	22.1	51.9	8.7	57.5
79.9%	84.9%	112.2%	114.8%	123.7%	311.2%	317.7%	694.6%
35.1%	15.3%	43.6%	12.5%	87.1%	203.9%	30.4%	437.5%
11.6	17.4	3.3	18.0	4.3	21.4	126.0	196.1
6.8	10.8	12.9	5.0	7.8	8.4	23.1	12.2
26.4	41.4	52.4	79.3	24.5	77.5	138.2	48.8
79.9%	84.9%	112.2%	114.8%	123.7%	311.2%	317.7%	694.6%
100.0%	100.0%	100.0%	100.0%	100.0%	100.0%	100.0%	100.0%
72.1	46.5	26.6	86.1	89.6	86.6	57.8	21.8
2.6	2.0	4.2	6.6	2.6	0.9	10.2	14.8
1.3	2.0	1.1	1.8	1.2	3.4	10.1	47.3
3.3	11.2	4.0	—	—	—	—	—
—	—	11.2	—	—	—	—	—
2.9	6.6	9.9	(4.1)	3.9	2.5	8.2	7.0
13.5	23.5	25.1	6.4	(1.3)	(1.2)	(5.5)	—
95.7%	91.8%	82.1%	96.8%	96.0%	92.2%	80.8%	90.9%
4.3%	8.2%	17.9%	3.2%	4.0%	7.8%	19.2%	9.1%
1.09	5.20	5.20	1.36	3.06	44.80	0.95	0.80

EXHIBIT 1.8

Common Size Balance Sheet for Wal-Mart Stores
(Problem 1.3)

	January 31			
	Year 5	Year 6	Year 7	Year 8
Assets				
Cash	0.2%	0.1%	0.2%	0.1%
Accounts Receivable	1.9	2.7	2.7	2.6
Inventories	54.0	51.0	47.8	45.1
Prepayments........................	1.4	2.5	4.8	1.8
Total Current Assets	57.5%	56.3%	55.5%	49.6%
Property, Plant, and Equipment (net)....	41.8	41.4	41.7	47.6
Other Assets........................	0.7	2.3	2.8	2.8
Total Assets	100.0%	100.0%	100.0%	100.0%
Liabilities and Shareholders' Equity				
Accounts Payable.....................	22.3%	23.3%	22.4%	18.8%
Short-Term Borrowing	2.5	3.7	3.2	8.0
Other Current Liabilities	9.9	8.0	6.8	6.0
Total Current Liabilities	34.7%	35.0%	32.4%	32.8%
Long-Term Debt	15.5	16.7	21.2	23.6
Deferred Tax Liability.................	1.4	1.2	1.1	1.0
Total Liabilities	51.6%	52.9%	54.7%	57.4%
Common Stock	2.9%	4.6%	4.7%	3.7%
Retained Earnings....................	45.5	42.5	40.6	38.9
Total Shareholders' Equity	48.4%	47.1%	45.3%	42.6%
Total Liabilities and Shareholders' Equity.........................	100.0%	100.0%	100.0%	100.0%

EXHIBIT 1.9

Common Size Income Statement for Wal-Mart Stores
(Problem 1.3)

	January 31		
	Year 6	Year 7	Year 8
Sales	100.0%	100.0%	100.0%
Other Revenues	0.8	0.9	0.9
Cost of Goods Sold..............	(78.2)	(79.2)	(79.6)
Selling and Administrative........	(15.8)	(15.2)	(15.0)
Interest	(0.5)	(0.6)	(0.6)
Income Taxes...................	(2.3)	(2.2)	(2.1)
Net Income	4.0%	3.7%	3.6%

EXHIBIT 1.10

Trend Information for Wal-Mart Stores
Year 5 = 100
(Problem 1.3)

	January 31		
	Year 6	Year 7	Year 8
Sales	126.3	170.0	214.9
Net Income	120.0	149.5	185.6
Inventories	131.2	166.8	209.3
Property, Plant, and Equipment	137.3	187.6	285.5
Total Assets	138.9	188.3	250.9
Long-Term Debt	149.2	257.5	380.6
Shareholders' Equity.................	135.3	176.2	220.7

REQUIRED

a. The common size percentage for inventories continually decreased during the three-year period, but the statement of cash flows shows that inventories increased each year. Explain this apparent paradox.

b. What is the likely reason for the decrease in the common size percentage for accounts payable in Exhibit 1.8?

c. What is the likely reason for the increase in the common size percentage for long-term debt in Exhibit 1.8?

d. The common size percentage for retained earnings continually decreased, yet the statement of cash flows shows that net income exceeded dividends by a substantial amount each year. Explain this apparent paradox.

e. What is the likely explanation for the increase in the cost of goods sold percentage in Exhibit 1.9?

f. What is the likely explanation for the decrease in the selling and administrative expense percentage in Exhibit 1.9?

g. Does the decreasing common size percentage for income taxes in Exhibit 1.9 indicate that the income tax rate decreased during the three-year period?

h. The trend information in Exhibit 1.10 indicates that inventories increased at approximately the same rate as sales but that property, plant, and equipment increased at a faster rate than sales. What are the likely explanations for these trend results?

i. The decreasing net income to sales percentages in Exhibit 1.9 suggest that Wal-Mart's strategy of shifting from discount stores to warehouse clubs and food distribution is not working successfully. Do you agree? Why or why not?

j. Exhibit 1.11 indicates that cash flow from operations is significantly less than net income in Year 7 and Year 8. Why should the analyst expect such a relation for a firm like Wal-Mart?

k. Exhibit 1.11 indicates that the cash outflow for investing exceeds the cash inflow from operations each year in an increasing dollar amount. How should the analyst interpret this result?

l. Why might Wal-Mart pay a dividend to shareholders when it appears to need the cash to finance its growth?

1.4 **INTERPRETING COMMON SIZE FINANCIAL STATEMENTS.** R.V. Suppliers manufactures Kaps, a relatively low-cost camping unit attached to a pickup truck. Most units consist

EXHIBIT 1.11

Statement of Cash Flows for Wal-Mart Stores
(amounts in millions)
(Problem 1.3)

	January 31		
	Year 6	Year 7	Year 8
Operations			
Net Income	$ 1,291	$ 1,608	$ 1,995
Depreciation and Amortization	347	475	649
Other Addbacks (Subtractions)	3	(8)	13
Increase in Accounts Receivable...........	(58)	(114)	(106)
Increase in Inventories	(1,088)	(1,460)	(1,884)
(Increase) Decrease in Prepayments	12	(11)	(20)
Increase in Accounts Payable..............	689	710	420
Increase in Other Current Liabilities	99	157	211
Cash Flow from Operations.............	$ 1,295	$ 1,357	$ 1,278
Investing			
Sale of Property, Plant, and Equipment.....	$ 91	$ 369	$ 416
Acquisition of Property, Plant, and Equipment	(1,624)	(2,511)	(3,782)
Other Investing Transactions..............	7	(8)	(140)
Cash Flow from Investing	$(1,526)	$(2,150)	$(3,506)
Financing			
Increase in Short-Term Borrowing.........	$ 30	$ 58	$ 1,135
Increase in Long-Term Borrowing	500	1,010	1,367
Increase in Common Stock	5	13	16
Decrease in Long-Term Borrowing.........	(134)	(75)	(67)
Dividends Paid.........................	(159)	(195)	(241)
Other Financing Transactions	(11)	—	—
Cash Flow from Financing	$ 231	$ 811	$ 2,210
Increase (Decrease) in Cash	—	$ 18	$ (18)
Cash—Beginning of Year.................	13	13	31
Cash—End of Year.....................	$ 13	$ 31	$ 13

of an aluminum frame and a fiberglass skin. The firm experienced a 59 percent increase in sales between Year 4 and Year 5 as a result of heightened interest in camping and other outdoor activities. However, fears of conflict in the Middle East beginning early in Year 6 led potential buyers to shun pickup trucks in preference for more energy-efficient small domestic and foreign automobiles, resulting in a sales decrease between Year 5 and Year 6. Exhibit 1.12 presents common size balance sheets as of December 31, Year 4, 5, and 6. Exhibit 1.13 presents common size income statements for Years 4, 5, and 6. Exhibit 1.14 presents a comparative statement of cash flows in dollars for Years 5 and 6.

REQUIRED

a. What is the likely explanation for the increased common size percentage for property, plant, and equipment between December 31, Year 4, and December 31, Year 5?

EXHIBIT 1.12

R.V. Suppliers
Common Size Balance Sheets
(Problem 1.4)

December 31	Year 4	Year 5	Year 6
Assets			
Cash	10.6%	5.1%	2.7%
Accounts Receivable	21.9	23.8	12.5
Inventories	41.0	36.6	41.9
Prepayments	3.6	3.1	5.5
Total Current Assets	77.1%	68.6%	62.6%
Property, Plant, and Equipment (net)	22.9	31.4	37.4
Total Assets	100.0%	100.0%	100.0%
Liabilities and Shareholders' Equity			
Notes Payable	7.6%	6.5%	15.7%
Accounts Payable	24.0	22.8	9.0
Other Current Liabilities	7.6	5.9	2.3
Total Current Liabilities	39.2%	35.2%	27.0%
Long-Term Debt	11.5	22.2	28.4
Total Liabilities	50.7%	57.4%	55.4%
Common Stock	22.3%	12.6%	15.2%
Retained Earnings	27.0	30.0	29.4
Total Shareholders' Equity	49.3%	42.6%	44.6%
Total Liabilities and Shareholders' Equity	100.0%	100.0%	100.0%

EXHIBIT 1.13

R.V. Suppliers
Common Size Income Statements
(Problem 1.4)

For the Year Ended December 31	Year 4	Year 5	Year 6
Sales	100.0%	100.0%	100.0%
Cost of Goods Sold	(71.9)	(74.2)	(85.1)
Selling and Administrative Expense	(12.4)	(12.7)	(18.3)
Interest Expense	(0.9)	(1.1)	(4.0)
Income Tax Expense	(4.6)	(3.8)	2.0
Net Income	10.2%	8.2%	(5.4%)

EXHIBIT 1.14

R.V. Suppliers
Comparative Statement of Cash Flows
(amounts in millions)
(Problem 1.4)

For the Year Ended December 31	Year 5	Year 6
Operations		
Net Income (Loss)	$ 34.6	$(13.4)
Plus Depreciation Expense	4.8	7.6
(Increase) Decrease in Accounts Receivable	(26.8)	31.4
(Increase) Decrease in Inventories	(31.6)	4.6
(Increase) Decrease in Prepayments	(2.6)	(3.2)
Increase (Decrease) in Accounts Payable	21.8	(36.0)
Increase (Decrease) in Other Current Liabilities	3.8	(9.4)
Cash Flow from Operations	$ 4.0	$(18.4)
Investing		
Acquisition of Property, Plant, and Equipment	$(48.0)	$ (6.4)
Financing		
Increase in Notes Payable	$ 5.3	$ 15.0
Increase in Long-Term Debt	36.7	3.0
Cash Flow from Financing	$ 42.0	$ 18.0
Change in Cash	$ (2.0)	$ (6.8)

b. The statement of cash flows indicates that inventories increased $31.6 million between December 31, Year 4, and December 31, Year 5. Why then did the common size percentage for inventories decline from 41.0 percent to 36.6 percent?

c. What is the likely explanation for the shift in the common size percentages for long-term debt and common stock between December 31, Year 4, and December 31, Year 5?

d. What is the likely explanation for the increased common size percentage for property, plant, and equipment between December 31, Year 5, and December 31, Year 6?

e. What is the likely explanation for the increased common size percentage for notes payable between December 31, Year 5, and December 31, Year 6?

f. What is the likely explanation for the decreased common size percentage for net income between Year 4 and Year 5?

g. What is the likely explanation for the decreased common size percentage for net income between Year 5 and Year 6?

1.5   RECASTING THE FINANCIAL STATEMENTS OF A U.K. COMPANY INTO U.S. FORMATS, TERMINOLOGY, AND ACCOUNTING PRINCIPLES. WPP Group, headquartered in the United Kingdom, is one of the largest marketing services firms in the world. It offers advertising, market research, public relations, and other marketing services through a worldwide network of offices. The financial statements of WPP Group for Year 2 and Year 3 appear in Exhibit 1.15 (balance sheet), Exhibit 1.16 (profit and loss account), and Exhibit 1.17 (cash flow statement). These financial statements reflect reporting formats, terminology, and accounting principles employed in the United Kingdom.

REQUIRED

Recast the financial statements of WPP Group using reporting formats, terminology, and accounting principles customarily used in the United States. Include a separate analysis of the changes in retained earnings.

EXHIBIT 1.15

WPP Group
Consolidated Balance Sheet
(amounts in millions of pounds)
(Problem 1.5)

	December 31	
	Year 2	Year 3
Fixed Assets		
Intangible Assets (Note 1)	£ 350	£ 350
Tangible Assets	147	132
Investments	20	22
Total Fixed Assets	£ 517	£ 504
Current Assets		
Stocks..	£ 66	£ 77
Debtors (Note 2)	715	680
Investments	39	31
Cash at Bank and In Hand	251	288
	£ 1,071	£ 1,076
Creditors: Amounts Falling Due within One Year (Note 3)	(1,132)	(1,225)
Net Current Liabilities	£ (61)	£ (149)
Total Assets Less Current Liabilities	£ 456	£ 355
Creditors: Amounts Falling Due after One Year	(580)	(412)
Provisions for Liabilities and Charges (Note 4)........	(118)	(104)
Net Liabilities...................................	£ (242)	£ (161)
Capital and Reserves		
Called-Up Share Capital (Note 5)...................	£ 36	£ 62
Share Premium Account	323	393
Goodwill Write-Off Reserve (Note 6)	(856)	(829)
Other Reserves (Note 7)...........................	48	1
Profit and Loss	196	211
Share Owners' Funds.............................	£ (253)	£ (162)
Minority Interest	11	1
Total Capital Employed........................	£ (242)	£ (161)

NOTES TO EXHIBIT 1.15

Note 1: Intangible assets represent the portion of the purchase price of marketing services agencies acquired that WPP allocated to the brand names of these agencies.

Note 2: Debtors include the following:

	December 31	
	Year 2	**Year 3**
Trade Debtors.............	£ 583	£ 539
Other Debtors	89	98
Prepayments..............	43	43
Total	£ 715	£ 680

Note 3: Creditors falling due within one year include the following:

	December 31	
	Year 2	**Year 3**
Bank Loans	£ 38	£ 79
Trade Creditors	715	757
Taxation	55	65
Other Creditors and Accruals	324	324
Total	£ 1,132	£ 1,225

Note 4: Provisions include the following:

	December 31	
	Year 2	**Year 3**
Deferred Taxation	£ 36	£ 21
Pensions	51	62
Other.....................	31	21
Total	£ 118	£ 104

Note 5: Called-up share capital includes the following:

	December 31	
	Year 2	**Year 3**
Preference Shares	£ 13	£ 10
Ordinary Shares	23	52
Total	£ 36	£ 62

Note 6: GAAP in the United Kingdom allows firms to write off goodwill in the year of an acquisition against share owners' equity.

Note 7: Other reserves includes the amounts on the top of page 38.

EXHIBIT 1.16

WPP Group
Consolidated Profit and Loss Account
(amounts in millions of pounds)
(Problem 1.5)

	Year 2	Year 3
Turnover..	£ 1,273	£ 1,431
Gross Profit	£ 1,070	£ 1,209
Other Operating Expenses.........................	(982)	(1,100)
Operating Profit.................................	£ 88	£ 109
Nonoperating Exceptional Items		
Loss on Sale or Closure of Advertising Agencies	£ (15)	£ (11)
Restructuring Costs	(31)	(14)
Profit on Ordinary Activities before Interest	£ 42	£ 84
Interest Receivable...............................	11	11
Interest Payable	(15)	(41)
Profit on Ordinary Activities before Taxation	£ 8	£ 54
Tax on Profit on Ordinary Activities	(17)	(29)
Profit/(Loss) on Ordinary Activities after Taxation......	£ (9)	£ 25
Minority Interest	(3)	(2)
Profit/(Loss) for the Financial Year..................	£ (12)	£ 23
Preference Dividend	—	(3)
Profit Attributable to Ordinary Share Owners	£ (12)	£ 20
Ordinary Dividends	—	(5)
Retained Profit/(Loss) for the Year	£ (12)	£ 15

	December 31	
	Year 2	Year 3
Cumulative Translation Adjustment.......	£ (35)	£ (76)
Revaluation of Tangible Fixed Assets......	83	77
Total................................	£ 48	£ 1

EXHIBIT 1.17

WPP Group—Consolidated Cash Flow Statement
(amounts in millions of pounds)
(Problem 1.5)

	December 31	
	Year 2	Year 3
Operating Activities		
Operating Profit..................................	£ 88	£ 109
Depreciation Charge..............................	23	26
(Increase) Decrease in Stocks	6	(16)
(Increase) Decrease in Debtors	23	(6)
Increase (Decrease) in Trade Creditors...............	(9)	99
Decrease in Provisions	(6)	(5)
Other Adjustments	(21)	(22)
Net Cash Flow from Operating Activities	£ 104	£ 185
Returns on Investments and Servicing of Finance		
Interest and Dividends Received	£ 11	£ 13
Interest Paid......................................	(54)	(41)
Dividend Paid	(1)	(8)
Net Cash Flow from Investments and Servicing of Finance..	£ (44)	£ (36)
Taxation	£ (17)	£ (26)
Investing Activities		
Purchase of Tangible Fixed Assets	£ (21)	£ (24)
Proceeds from Sale of Tangible Fixed Assets	2	1
Other Investing Activities..........................	(13)	(6)
Net Cash Outflow from Investing Activities	£ (32)	£ (29)
Financing Activities		
Proceeds from Issue of Share Capital	—	£ 85
Increase (Decrease) in Bank Loans	£ 30	£ (139)
Net Cash Flow from Financing Activities	£ 30	£ (54)
Effect of Exchange Rate Changes on Cash and Cash Equivalents................................	£ 38	£ (3)
Cash and Cash Equivalents—Beginning of Year	£ 172	£ 251
Cash and Cash Equivalents—End of Year.............	£ 251	£ 288

1.6 RECASTING THE FINANCIAL STATEMENTS OF A GERMAN COMPANY INTO U.S. FORMATS AND TERMINOLOGY. Bayerische Motoren Werke (BMW) manufacturers and markets automobiles and provides financing for its customers' purchases. Exhibit 1.18 presents an income statement and Exhibit 1.19 presents a balance sheet for BMW for Year 5 and Year 6.

REQUIRED
a. Prepare an income statement for BMW for Year 5 and Year 6 using terminology commonly encountered in the United States. Separate operating revenues and expenses from nonoperating revenues and expenses. Note that BMW's disclosures do not permit the calculation of cost of goods sold or selling and administrative expenses.
b. Prepare a balance sheet for BMW on December 31, Year 5, and Year 6 using reporting formats and terminology commonly encountered in the United States.

EXHIBIT 1.18

BMW AG
Statement of Income
for the Year Ended December 31
(Problem 1.6)

	Year 5 DM million	Year 6 DM million
Net Sales	31,241	29,016
Increase in Product Inventories and Other Company-Produced Additions to Tangible Fixed Assets	1,430	1,916
Total Value of Production....................	32,671	30,932
Other Operating Income	1,269	1,252
Expenditure on Materials....................	18,542	17,368
Expenditure on Personnel	6,387	6,245
Depreciation on Intangible Assets and on Fixed Assets	1,827	1,836
Other Operating Expenditures	5,787	5,921
Income from Investment in Subsidiaries and Associated Companies	4	13
Interest Income	382	407
Interest Expenditure	306	402
Income from Normal Business	1,477	832
Taxes on Income and Profits.................	608	192
Other Taxes	143	124
Net Income	726	516
Allocation of Net Income		
Minority Interest Share of Profits.............	8	2
Minority Interest Share of Losses.............	2	10
Transfer to Profit Reserve	494	298
Net Income Available for Distribution	226	226
	726	516

EXHIBIT 1.19

BMW AG
Balance Sheet
(Problem 1.6)

	December 31, Year 5 DM million	December 31, Year 6 DM million
Assets		
Intangible Assets	196	229
Tangible Fixed Assets	6,469	6,728
Financial Assets	169	194
Fixed Assets	6,834	7,151
Inventories	3,140	3,020
Trade Receivables	11,596	13,440
Other Receivables	988	1,541
Marketable Securities	2,408	2,218
Liquid Funds	2,187	2,554
Current Assets	20,319	22,773
Prepaid Expenses	351	371
Total Assets	27,504	30,295
Shareholders' Equity and Liabilities		
Subscribed Capital	899	902
Capital Reserve	817	834
Profit Reserves	4,685	4,953
Net Income Available for Distribution	226	226
Minority Interest	91	110
Shareholders' Equity	6,718	7,025
Registered Dividend Right Certificates	101	89
Pension Fund Provisions	1,599	1,675
Other Provisions	5,671	6,059
Provisions	7,270	7,734
Bonds	1,670	1,943
Due to Banks	7,230	9,044
Trade Payables	1,579	1,523
Other Liabilities	2,936	2,937
Liabilities	13,415	15,447
Total Liabilities and Shareholders' Equity	27,504	30,295

1.7 UNDERSTANDING EFFICIENT CAPITAL MARKETS RESEARCH METHODOLOGY. Jim Seward, chief financial officer of Victoria Corporation, recently attended an alumni seminar at the business school where he received his MBA. A finance professor teaching at the seminar described the results of recent research on the efficiency of capital markets. Jim was impressed by the obvious rigor of the research and the fervor with which the finance professor expounded on the wisdom of the marketplace in pricing a firm's securities. Jim believed that he remembered enough from the statistical regression course that he took as part of the MBA program to try out some of the efficient market ideas using data for Victoria Corporation.

Victoria Corporation, a publicly held firm traded on the over-the-counter market, manufactures optical scanning disks. For many years, Victoria Corporation used a first-in, first-out cost-flow assumption for inventories and cost of goods sold. It recently switched to a last-in, first-out cost-flow assumption. Jim is interested in how the market reacted to this change in accounting method.

To study this question, Jim obtained weekly closing prices for Victoria Corporation's common stock for the three-year period ending three months prior to the announcement of the accounting method change. This announcement was part of the firm's first-quarter earnings report. He then computed the weekly market rate of return for Victoria Corporation's common stock by dividing the change in market price (Friday closing price of the week minus Friday closing price of the preceding week) plus any dividends for which the record date occurred during the week by the market price at the end of the preceding week. This step resulted in a series of 156 weekly rates of return for Victoria Corporation. He also computed similar weekly rates of return using the Standard & Poor 500 stock price index to measure marketwide price changes. Jim then regressed Victoria Corporation's rates of returns on the market-indexed rates of return. He obtained the following results:

$$\frac{\text{Victoria Corporation's}}{\text{Market Rate of Return}} = 0.02 + 1.2 \left(\frac{\text{Market Index}}{\text{Rate of Return}} \right)$$

Statistical tests of significance revealed that both coefficients were significantly different from zero.

Jim was ready to study the market's reaction to the announced change in cost-flow assumption for inventories. He computed an *expected* market rate of return for Victoria Corporation for each week during the three months preceding the announcement and each week during the three months after the announcement. He based the calculation of this expected rate of return on weekly changes in the Standard & Poor's 500 stock price index and the alpha and beta coefficients in the regression shown above. He then compared those rates of return to the *actual* rates of return for Victoria Corporation for these same weekly periods. Jim interpreted the difference between expected and actual rates of return to reflect the effect of new information about Victoria Corporation coming to the market.

REQUIRED

    a. Assume that actual rates of return closely parallel expected rates of return for the three months preceding and the three months succeeding the announcement of a change in accounting method for inventories. Would it be appropriate to conclude that the market reacted irrationally to this accounting change (that is, it accepted the reported earnings numbers as reported with no apparent consideration given to the different cost-flow assumption)? Elaborate.

    b. Assume that actual rates of return equaled expected rates of return for the 13 weeks prior to the announcement but that actual rates of return exceeded those expected for the 13 weeks after the announcement (most of the excess return occurred in the first few weeks after the announcement). Would it be appropriate to conclude that the market reacted rationally to the accounting change? Elaborate.

CHAPTER 2

INCOME FLOWS VERSUS CASH FLOWS: KEY RELATIONSHIPS IN UNDERSTANDING THE DYNAMICS OF A BUSINESS

Learning Objectives

1. Understand the relation between net income and cash flow from operations for firms in various stages of their life cycles.
2. Understand the relation between cash flows from operating, investing, and financing activities for firms in various stages of their life cycles.
3. Prepare a statement of cash flows from balance sheet and income statement data.
4. Convert a statement of changes in financial position (funds defined as working capital) to a statement of cash flows.

The income statement reports a firm's revenues and expenses during a period of time. Accountants measure revenues and expenses using the accrual basis of accounting. The objective in preparing an income statement is to obtain a measure of operating performance that matches a firm's outputs (revenues) with associated inputs (expenses). Chapter 1 points out that a firm's cash flows do not precisely track, or mirror, its income flows because (1) cash receipts from customers do not necessarily occur in the same period that a firm recognizes revenues, (2) cash expenditures to employees, suppliers, and governments do not necessarily occur in the same period that a firm recognizes expenses, and (3) cash inflows and outflows occur relating to investing and financing activities that do not flow directly through the income statement.[1] Thus, although the accrual basis of accounting properly measures operating performance each period, its use does not result in reporting the critical variable for remaining in business: cash flows. The statement of cash flows reports the relation between income flows and cash flows from operations. It also reports the cash flow effects of investing and financing activities. An understanding of the relation between income flows and cash flows is an important ingredient in analyzing both the profitability and financial health of a business.

This chapter explores the statement of cash flows in greater depth than did the overview presented in Chapter 1. We look at the relation between income flows and cash flow from operations for various types of businesses and at the relation between the cash flows from operating, investing, and financing activities for firms in various stages of their life cycles. We also describe and illustrate procedures for preparing the statement of cash flows using information from the balance sheet and income statement, as well as procedures for converting a statement of sources and uses of funds, commonly found in countries outside the United States, into a statement of cash flows.[2]

INCOME FLOWS, CASH FLOWS, AND LIFE-CYCLE RELATIONS

Interpreting the statement of cash flows requires an understanding of two relations:

1. The relation between net income and cash flow from operations.
2. The relation among the net cash flows from operating, investing, and financing activities.

NET INCOME AND CASH FLOW FROM OPERATIONS

The first section of the statement of cash flows reconciles net income with cash flow from operations. This reconciliation involves two types of adjustments. First, certain revenues and expenses relate to changes in noncurrent asset or noncurrent liability accounts and have cash flow effects that differ from their income effect. For example, depreciation expense reduces net property, plant, and equipment and net income. The addback of depreciation expense to net income offsets the effect of depreciation since it does not use cash flow for operations. Firms that sell an item of property, plant, or equipment report the full cash proceeds as an investing activity. Because net income includes the gain or loss on the sale (that is, sales proceeds minus the book value of the item sold), the operating section of the statement of cash

---

[1]This chapter uses *income flows* to mean net income, not revenues.

[2]The Financial Accounting Standards Board's *Statement No. 95* defines cash flows in terms of their effect on cash and cash equivalents. Cash equivalents include highly liquid investments that are both readily convertible into cash and so near to maturity that changes in interest rates present an insignificant risk to their market value. Cash equivalents usually include Treasury bills, commercial paper, and money market funds. Throughout this book, we use the term *cash* to mean cash and cash equivalents.

flows shows an addback for a loss and a subtraction for a gain to offset their inclusion in net income. Chapter 7 points out that a firm holding an investment of 20 percent to 50 percent in another entity uses the equity method to account for the investment (a noncurrent asset). The investor recognizes its share of the investee's earnings each period, increasing the investment account and net income. It reduces the investment account for dividends received. Thus, net income reflects the investor's share of earnings, not the cash received. The statement of cash flows usually shows a subtraction from net income for the excess of the investor's share of the investee's earnings in excess of dividends received. Other examples of revenues and expenses that relate to changes in noncurrent asset or noncurrent liability accounts include amortization of intangible assets, the deferred portion income tax expense, minority interest in the earnings of consolidated subsidiaries, and some restructuring charges and adjustments for changes in accounting principles. Later chapters discuss each of these items more fully. Published statements of cash flows sometimes report a subtotal after adjusting net income for the above items and label the subtotal Working Capital Provided by Operations.

The second type of adjustment to reconcile net income to cash flow from operations involves changes in operating current asset and current liability accounts. For example, an increase in accounts receivable indicates that the firm did not collect as much cash from customers as the amount of sales revenue for the period. A subtraction from net income for the increase in accounts receivable converts accrual basis revenues to cash receipts from customers. Similar adjustments for changes in inventories, prepayments, accounts payable, and other operating current liabilities convert accrual basis income amounts to their associated cash flow amounts.

A study of the relation between net income and various measures of operating cash flows revealed (1) a high correlation between net income and working capital from operations and (2) a low correlation between net income and cash flow from operations and between working capital from operations and cash flow from operations.[3] The primary difference between net income and working capital from operations for most firms is the addback for depreciation expense. If a firm's income growth tracks its additions to property, plant, and equipment, one would expect a high correlation between net income and working capital from operations. The low correlation between these two measures and cash flow from operations suggests that changes in operating working capital accounts do not track changes in net income. The next section uses the product life-cycle concept to enhance understanding of the behavior of working capital accounts as a firm grows, matures, and declines.

RELATION BETWEEN CASH FLOWS FROM OPERATING, INVESTING, AND FINANCING ACTIVITIES

A helpful framework for understanding more fully the relation between income flows and cash flows is the product life-cycle concept from marketing and microeconomics. Individual products (goods or services) move through four more or less

[3]Robert M. Bowen, David Burgstahler, and Lane A. Daley, "Evidence on the Relationship between Earnings and Various Measures of Cash Flow," *Accounting Review,* October 1986, pp. 713–725.

identifiable phases: introduction, growth, maturity, and decline, as the top panel of Figure 2.1 depicts. The length of these phases and the steepness of the revenue curve vary by the type of product. Although it is generally difficult to pinpoint the precise location of a product on its life-cycle curve at any particular time, it is usually possible to identify its phase and whether it is in the early or later portion of that phase.

The middle panel of Figure 2.1 shows the trend of net income over the product life cycle. Net losses usually occur in the introduction and early growth phases be-

FIGURE 2.1

Relation of Income Flows and Cash Flows from Operations, Investing, and Financing at Various Stages of Product Life Cycle

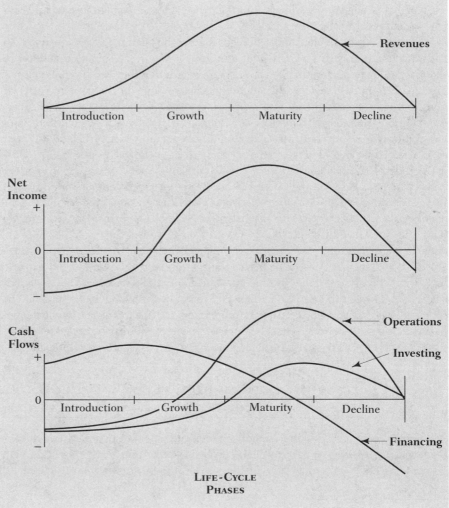

cause revenues do not cover the cost of designing and launching new products. Net income peaks during the maturity phase and then begins its decline.

The lower panel of Figure 2.1 shows the cash flow from operating, investing, and financing activities during the four life-cycle phases. During the introduction and early growth phases, negative cash flow from operations results from the cash outflows needed to launch the product. Negative cash flow from investing activities also occurs during these early phases to build productive capacity. The relative size of this negative cash flow for investing activities depends on the degree of capital intensity of the business. Firms must obtain the cash needed for operating and investing activities during these early phases from external sources (debt and shareholders' equity).

As the growth phase accelerates, operations become profitable and begin to generate cash. However, firms must use the cash generated to finance accounts receivable and to build inventories for expected higher sales levels in the future. Thus, net income usually turns positive earlier than cash flow from operations. The extent of the negative cash flow from investing activities depends on the rate of growth and the degree of capital intensity. As in the introduction phase, firms obtain most of the cash needed during the growth phase from external sources (a multiproduct firm can use cash generated from products in the maturity phase of their life cycles to finance products in the introduction and growth phases and therefore does not need as much external financing).

As products move through the maturity phase, the cash-flow pattern changes dramatically. Operations become a net provider of cash, both because the market accepts the product and working capital needs level off. Also, with revenues leveling off, firms invest to maintain rather than increase productive capacity. During the later stages of the maturity phase, net cash flows from investing activities may even turn positive as cash inflows from sales of unneeded plant assets exceed new investments. Firms can use the excess cash flow from operations and to a lesser extent the sale of investments to repay debt incurred during the introduction and growth phases and to pay dividends.

During the decline phase, cash flows from operating and investing activities tail off as sales decrease. Firms repay their remaining debt.

The product life-cycle model provides helpful insights about the relation between sales, net income, and cash flows from operating, investing, and financing activities for a single product. Few business firms, however, rely on a single product; most have a range of products at different stages of their life cycles. Furthermore, the statement of cash flows reports amounts for a firm as a whole, not for each product. If the life-cycle concept is to assist in interpreting published statements of cash flows, the analyst needs a multiproduct view.

The analyst obtains such a multiproduct view by aggregating the positioning of each of a firm's products in their respective life cycles into a reading on the average life-cycle positioning of the firm. For example, the average positioning of a firm in technology-driven industries, such as biotechnology, is probably in the growth phase. Although such firms will have some products fresh off the drawing board and other products in their decline phase because of the emergence of new technologies, most of these firms' products are in their high-growth phase. Most consumer foods companies have an average life-cycle positioning in the maturity phase. Branded consumer foods products can remain in their maturity phase for many years with proper product quality control and promotion (consider, for example, Coke and Pepsi). Such companies continually bring new products to the market and eliminate products that do not meet consumer acceptance, but their average positioning is probably in the maturity phase. Certain industries in the United States, such as textiles and steel, are probably in the early decline phase because of foreign competition and outdated technology. Some companies in these industries have built technologically advanced production facilities to compete more effectively on a worldwide basis and essentially have reentered the maturity phase. Other firms have diversified into more growth-oriented industries.

Refer to the statements of cash flows for Coke and Pepsi in Appendix A and Appendix B, respectively. Both firms tend to experience an excess of cash inflows from operations over cash outflows for investing, typical of mature firms. These firms have used the excess cash flow to repurchase their common stock in recent years. Note that the excess of cash inflow from operations over cash outflow for investing is less for Pepsi than for Coke, consistent with Pepsi's higher growth rate and the greater capital intensity of its restaurant business.

Exhibits 2.1 through 2.5 present statements of cash flows for firms in five different industries to illustrate the point that a firm's phase in its aggregate product life cycle affects the interpretation of its statement of cash flows.

Exhibit 2.1 shows a statement of cash flows for Callaway Golf Company, a designer and manufacturer of golf clubs. Callaway Golf Company is in the growth phase of its life cycle. Note that net income increased rapidly over the five years. Its cash flow from operations was either negative or less than net income each year. The rapid growth required Callaway Golf Company to carry accounts receivable and invest in inventories. Although suppliers provided some of the needed cash to finance these current assets, such financing was not sufficient. The rapid increase in capital expenditures to acquire fixed assets reported among the investing activities indicates the building of manufacturing capacity to support the increasing levels of sales. To finance its growth, Callaway Golf Company obtained cash primarily by issuing capital stock.

Exhibit 2.2 presents a statement of cash flows for Wal-Mart, a rapidly growing discount store and warehouse club chain. Wal-Mart's net income increased rapidly during the five-year period, but so did its cash flow from operations. Wal-Mart sells either for cash or uses bank credit cards, so it does not need to carry heavy investments in receivables. It used suppliers to finance part of its increasing investments in inventories. The remaining cash needed for inventories came from operating cash flows. Thus, cash flow from operations was less than net income in most years. Wal-Mart's positive cash flow from operations, however, was not sufficient to fully finance the rapid expansion of stores and buildup of fixed assets. It relied primarily on long-term borrowing to make up the difference.

Exhibit 2.3 shows the statement of cash flows for Merck, a pharmaceutical company. Merck, like Callaway Golf Company and Wal-Mart, experienced rapid growth in net income. Its cash flow from operations also increased rapidly. Merck has used its suppliers and other creditors to finance its working capital needs so that cash flow from operations approximately equals net income plus depreciation. Merck's cash

EXHIBIT 2.1

Callaway Golf Company
Statement of Cash Flows
(amounts in thousands)

	Year 4	Year 5	Year 6	Year 7	Year 8
Operations					
Net Income	$ 329	$ 1,842	$ 6,416	$ 19,280	$ 42,862
Depreciation.............................	136	258	618	1,372	3,016
Other Addbacks...........................	451	123	1,090	1,501	5,486
Other Subtractions	—	—	—	—	—
Working Capital Provided by Operations	$ 916	$ 2,223	$ 8,124	$ 22,153	$ 51,364
(Increase) Decrease in Receivables	(1,068)	(643)	(3,989)	(5,205)	(6,271)
(Increase) Decrease in Inventories	(1,177)	(6,020)	(2,660)	(4,097)	(13,771)
(Increase) Decrease in Other Current Assets	(159)	(519)	(2,701)	(5,975)	(8,563)
Increase (Decrease) in Accounts Payable	810	1,292	3,326	1,189	5,055
Increase (Decrease) in Other Current Liabilities ..	176	38	2,908	5,485	5,178
Cash Flow from Operations..................	$ (502)	$(3,629)	$ 5,008	$ 13,550	$ 32,992
Investing					
Fixed Assets Acquired......................	$ (411)	$(1,329)	$(1,540)	$(11,370)	$(20,939)
Other Investing Transactions..................	—	12	4	3	17
Cash Flow from Investing	$ (411)	$(1,317)	$(1,536)	$(11,367)	$(20,922)
Financing					
Increase in Short-Term Borrowing..............	—	$ 1,000	—	—	—
Increase in Long-Term Borrowing	—	2,084	$ 1,416	—	—
Issue of Capital Stock......................	—	4,620	—	$ 17,658	$ 18,864
Decrease in Short-Term Borrowing	—	—	(1,000)	—	—
Decrease in Long-Term Borrowing..............	—	—	—	—	—
Acquisition of Capital Stock..................	$ (1)	(4,263)	(32)	(5,000)	(336)
Dividends	—	—	—	—	(1,591)
Other Financing Transactions	—	—	—	—	(30)
Cash Flow from Financing	$ (1)	$ 3,441	$ 384	$ 12,658	$ 16,907
Change in Cash...........................	$ (914)	$(1,505)	$ 3,856	$ 14,841	$ 28,977
Cash—Beginning of Year....................	3,741	2,827	1,322	5,178	20,019
Cash—End of Year........................	$ 2,827	$ 1,322	$ 5,178	$ 20,019	$ 48,996

flow from operations was more than sufficient to finance capital expenditures on fixed assets. It used the excess cash flow from operations and from additional short- and long-term borrowing to pay dividends, reacquire capital stock, and acquire marketable securities. The reacquisition of common stock had the effect of increasing the proportion of debt in its capital structure and provided additional benefits of financial leverage, a topic discussed in Chapter 3. Such actions also increased the price of Merck's stock and made it a less attractive candidate for an unfriendly takeover by another firm.

EXHIBIT 2.2

Wal-Mart
Statement of Cash Flows
(amounts in millions)

	Year 5	Year 6	Year 7	Year 8	Year 9
Operations					
Net Income	$ 1,076	$ 1,291	$ 1,608	$ 1,995	$ 2,333
Depreciation	269	347	475	649	849
Other Addbacks	5	3	0	13	0
Other Subtractions	0	0	(8)	0	(75)
Working Capital Provided by Operations	$ 1,350	$ 1,641	$ 2,075	$ 2,657	$ 3,107
(Increase) Decrease in Receivables	(29)	(58)	(114)	(106)	(165)
(Increase) Decrease in Inventories	(1,077)	(1,088)	(1,460)	(1,884)	(1,324)
(Increase) Decrease in Other Current Assets	(11)	12	(10)	(20)	(1)
Increase (Decrease) in Accounts Payable	437	689	710	420	230
Increase (Decrease) in Other Current Liabilities	197	100	156	211	349
Cash Flow from Operations	$ 867	$ 1,296	$ 1,357	$ 1,278	$ 2,196
Investing					
Fixed Assets Acquired	$(1,086)	$(1,533)	$(2,142)	$(3,366)	$(3,644)
Other Investing Transactions	7	7	(8)	72	(446)
Cash Flow from Investing	$(1,079)	$(1,526)	$(2,150)	$(3,294)	$(4,486)
Financing					
Increase in Short-Term Borrowing	$ 166	$ 30	$ 58	$ 1,135	0
Increase in Long-Term Borrowing	189	500	1,010	1,367	$ 3,108
Issue of Capital Stock	6	5	13	16	10
Decrease in Short-Term Borrowing	0	0	0	0	(14)
Decrease in Long-Term Borrowing	(25)	(134)	(75)	(67)	(456)
Acquisition of Capital Stock	0	(26)	0	0	0
Dividends	(124)	(159)	(195)	(241)	(299)
Other Financing Transactions	0	14	0	0	(51)
Cash Flow from Financing	$ 212	$ 230	$ 811	$ 2,210	$ 2,298
Change in Cash	0	0	$ 18	$ (18)	$ 8
Cash—Beginning of Year	$ 12	$ 12	12	30	12
Cash—End of Year	$ 12	$ 12	$ 30	$ 12	$ 20

Exhibit 2.4 presents a statement of cash flows for American Airlines. Cash flow from operations significantly exceeds net income or net loss in each year because of the addback of depreciation expense. Depreciation is an expense that does not use cash. The cash outflow occurred when American acquired its fixed assets. The relation between net income and cash flow from operations for American is typical of capital-intensive firms. Although American experienced a positive cash flow from operations each year, this cash flow was not sufficient to finance capital expenditures. It used long-term debt to finance these acquisitions. Airlines tend to use debt rather than equity financing for their fixed asset acquisitions. Debt is usually a less

EXHIBIT 2.3

Merck & Co.
Statement of Cash Flows
(amounts in millions)

	Year 4	Year 5	Year 6	Year 7	Year 8
Operations					
Net Income	$1,495	$1,781	$ 2,122	$ 2,446	$ 2,941
Depreciation and Amortization	222	254	264	321	386
Other Addbacks................................	4	0	0	0	0
Other Subtractions	(66)	(208)	(12)	(92)	(230)
Working Capital Provided by Operations..........	$1,655	$1,827	$ 2,374	$ 2,675	$ 3,097
(Increase) Decrease in Receivables	(304)	(52)	(195)	(298)	(263)
(Increase) Decrease in Inventories	(122)	(113)	(99)	(177)	(47)
Increase (Decrease) in Accounts Payable	104	201	226	101	(123)
Increase (Decrease) in Other Current Liabilities ...	48	193	128	203	384
Cash Flow from Operations....................	$1,381	$2,056	$ 2,434	$ 2,504	$ 3,048
Investing					
Fixed Assets Acquired..........................	$ (433)	$ (671)	$(1,042)	$(1,067)	$(1,013)
Change in Marketable Securities	(189)	(336)	(282)	(273)	342
Other Investing Transactions....................	27	26	23	(12)	(1,917)
Cash Flow from Investing	$ (595)	$ (981)	$(1,301)	$(1,352)	$(2,588)
Financing					
Increase in Short-Term Borrowing..............	$ 123	$ 472	0	$ 480	$ 911
Increase in Long-Term Borrowing	52	17	$ 560	141	354
Issue of Capital Stock..........................	36	38	48	52	83
Decrease in Short-Term Borrowing	0	0	(591)	0	0
Decrease in Long-Term Borrowing..............	(329)	(14)	(94)	(121)	(39)
Acquisition of Capital Stock.....................	(208)	(745)	(184)	(863)	(371)
Dividends	(650)	(750)	(893)	(1,064)	(1,174)
Other Financing Transactions	21	28	12	0	30
Cash Flow from Financing	$ (955)	$ (954)	$(1,142)	$(1,375)	$ (206)
Change in Cash................................	$ (169)	$ 121	$ (9)	$ (223)	$ 254
Cash—Beginning of Year.......................	855	686	807	798	575
Cash—End of Year.............................	$ 686	$ 807	$ 798	$ 575	$ 829

costly source of capital than equity. The assets acquired serve as collateral for the borrowing. Also, some of this financing comes in the form of capital leases (discussed in Chapter 6) in which the lessor, not American, takes advantage of income tax deductions for depreciation. Airlines usually operate at a net loss for income tax purposes because of the low profit margins in this highly competitive industry and the use of accelerated depreciation methods. Airlines lease certain equipment rather than purchasing it, allowing the lessor to claim the tax benefits, and, it is hoped, passing some of these benefits to the airlines by way of lower lease payments.

Finally, Exhibit 2.5 presents a statement of cash flows for Interpublic Group, an advertising agency. Depreciation represents a less significant addback for Interpublic,

EXHIBIT 2.4

American Airlines
Statement of Cash Flows
(amounts in millions)

	Year 4	Year 5	Year 6	Year 7	Year 8
Operations					
Net Income	$ 455	$ (40)	$ (240)	$ (475)	$ (110)
Depreciation and Amortization	613	723	883	1,041	1,223
Other Addbacks	135	32	77	165	196
Other Subtractions	(88)	(152)	(110)	(101)	(30)
Working Capital Provided by Operations	$ 1,115	$ 563	$ 610	$ 630	$ 1,279
(Increase) Decrease in Receivables	(47)	(77)	148	(144)	37
(Increase) Decrease in Inventories	(90)	(102)	(55)	(85)	(27)
(Increase) Decrease in Other Current Assets	6	(35)	15	244	(128)
Increase (Decrease) in Accounts Payable	219	37	35	(53)	(27)
Increase (Decrease) in Other Current Liabilities	122	300	(9)	251	243
Cash Flow from Operations	$ 1,325	$ 686	$ 744	$ 843	$ 1,377
Investing					
Fixed Assets Sold	$ 32	0	0	0	0
Fixed Assets Acquired	(2,395)	$(2,901)	$(3,536)	$(3,299)	$(2,080)
Investments Acquired	0	(355)	(319)	0	0
Other Investing Transactions	647	(482)	(716)	345	326
Cash Flow from Investing	$(1,716)	$(3,738)	$(4,571)	$(2,954)	$(1,754)
Financing					
Increase in Short-Term Borrowing	$ 59	$ 1,175	$ 425	$ 122	0
Increase in Long-Term Borrowing	672	2,265	4,379	2,397	$ 1,811
Issue of Capital Stock	5	0	300	454	0
Decrease in Short-Term Borrowing	0	(129)	(246)	(153)	(380)
Decrease in Long-Term Borrowing	(133)	(266)	(1,096)	(779)	(1,069)
Acquisition of Capital Stock	(150)	0	0	0	0
Dividends	(12)	0	0	0	(49)
Other Financing Transactions	15	0	45	21	82
Cash Flow from Financing	$ 456	$ 3,045	$ 3,807	$ 2,062	$ 395
Change in Cash	$ 65	$ (7)	$ (20)	$ (49)	$ 18
Cash—Beginning of Year	56	121	114	94	45
Cash—End of Year	$ 121	$ 114	$ 94	$ 45	$ 63

a service firm, than for American. The primary source of variation between net income and cash flow from operations is management of working capital, particularly accounts receivable and accounts payable. An advertising agency serves as a conduit between clients wishing to place advertisements (giving rise to an accounts receivable for the agency) and the various media in which they place advertisements (giving rise to an accounts payable). Interpublic manages its position so that the

EXHIBIT 2.5

Interpublic Group
Statement of Cash Flows
(amounts in millions)

	Year 4	Year 5	Year 6	Year 7	Year 8
Operations					
Net Income	$ 70	$ 80	$ 95	$ 112	$ 126
Depreciation and Amortization	30	38	54	40	43
Other Addbacks...................................	21	20	21	45	49
Other Subtractions	(24)	(27)	(16)	(11)	(9)
Working Capital Provided by Operations...........	$ 97	$ 111	$ 154	$ 186	$ 209
(Increase) Decrease in Receivables	(190)	(167)	(69)	24	(66)
(Increase) Decrease in Inventories	0	0	0	0	0
(Increase) Decrease in Other Current Assets	(1)	(12)	(7)	(17)	(13)
Increase (Decrease) in Accounts Payable...........	92	440	7	(16)	59
Increase (Decrease) in Other Current Liabilities	78	(184)	8	11	14
Cash Flow from Operations....................	$ 76	$ 188	$ 93	$ 188	$ 203
Investing					
Fixed Assets Sold................................	$ 5	$ 6	$ 5	$ 3	$ 1
Fixed Assets Acquired............................	(46)	(37)	(47)	(37)	(79)
Investments Acquired	(11)	(2)	0	(2)	0
Other Investing Transactions.....................	(23)	(81)	(22)	(20)	(83)
Cash Flow from Investing	$ (75)	$(114)	$ (64)	$ (56)	$(161)
Financing					
Increase in Short-Term Borrowing................	$ 6	0	$ 36	0	$ 35
Increase in Long-Term Borrowing	1	$ 78	166	$ 113	42
Issue of Capital Stock............................	5	5	7	11	19
Decrease in Short-Term Borrowing	0	(7)	0	(70)	0
Decrease in Long-Term Borrowing................	(6)	(4)	(132)	(69)	(15)
Acquisition of Capital Stock.....................	(36)	(32)	(17)	(52)	(37)
Dividends..	(22)	(24)	(29)	(32)	(36)
Other Financing Transactions	0	0	0	(17)	(14)
Cash Flow from Financing	$ (52)	$ 16	$ 31	$(116)	$ (6)
Change in Cash..................................	$ (51)	$ 90	$ 60	$ 16	$ 36
Cash—Beginning of Year........................	141	90	180	240	256
Cash—End of Year..............................	$ 90	$ 180	$ 240	$ 256	$ 292

receivables and payables do not closely offset each year, resulting in a varying relationship between net income and cash flow from operations. Because of the low level of capital intensity of an advertising agency, cash flow from operations is more than sufficient to finance capital expenditures. Cash flow from operations was also sufficient to finance acquisitions of other advertising agencies (included in the Other Investing Transactions line). Interpublic uses the excess cash to pay dividends and repurchase its common stock.

These five statements of cash flows present typical patterns for firms in different types of industries and in different stages of their product life cycles. They also illustrate some of the interpretations that an analyst can make about the economic characteristics and performance of an entity by studying its statement of cash flows.

PREPARING THE STATEMENT OF CASH FLOWS

Publicly held firms in the United States must include a statement of cash flows in their published financial statements each period. Smaller privately held firms often prepare just a balance sheet and an income statement. Firms outside the United States also usually include a statement of cash flows in their published statements. Some non-U.S. firms include a "funds flow" statement, which discloses funds in a sources and uses format (instead of classifying items as related to operating, investing, and financing activities) and define "funds" differently than cash. This section illustrates a procedure for preparing a statement of cash flows using information from the balance sheet and income statement. It also illustrates the conversion of a statement of sources and uses of funds into a statement of cash flows. The resulting statement merely approximates the amounts that the statement of cash flows would report if the analyst had full access to a firm's accounting records. However, the estimated amounts should approximate the actual amounts closely enough for the analyst to make meaningful interpretations.

ALGEBRAIC FORMULATION

We know from the accounting equation that:

$$\text{Assets} = \text{Liabilities} + \text{Shareholders' Equity}$$

This equality holds for balance sheets at the beginning and end of each period. If we subtract the amounts from the balance sheet at the beginning of the period from the corresponding amounts from the balance sheet at the end of the period, we obtain the following equality for changes (Δ) in balance sheet amounts:

$$\Delta \text{ Assets} = \Delta \text{ Liabilities} + \Delta \text{ Shareholders' Equity}$$

We can now expand the change in assets as follows:

$$\Delta \text{ Cash} + \Delta \text{ Noncash Assets} = \Delta \text{ Liabilities} + \Delta \text{ Shareholders' Equity}$$

Rearranging terms:

$$\Delta \text{ Cash} = \Delta \text{ Liabilities} + \Delta \text{ Shareholders' Equity} - \Delta \text{ Noncash Assets}$$

The statement of cash flows explains the reasons for the change in cash during a period. We can see that the change in cash equals the change in all other (noncash) balance sheet amounts.

Refer to Exhibit 2.6, which shows the comparative balance sheet of Logue Shoe Store for the years ending December 31, Year 5, Year 6, and Year 7. The balance sheets at the end of Year 5 and Year 6 report the following equalities:

	Cash	+	Noncash Assets	=	Liabilities	+	Shareholders' Equity
Year 5	$13,698	+	$132,136	=	$105,394	+	$40,440
Year 6	$12,595	+	$129,511	=	$ 85,032	+	$57,074

EXHIBIT 2.6

Logue Shoe Store
Balance Sheet

	December 31, Year 5	December 31, Year 6	December 31, Year 7
Assets			
Cash	$ 13,698	$ 12,595	$ 5,815
Accounts Receivable	1,876	1,978	1,816
Inventories	98,824	106,022	123,636
Other Current Assets	3,591	—	1,560
Total Current Assets......................	$117,989	$120,595	$132,827
Property, Plant, and Equipment (cost)	$ 63,634	$ 65,285	$ 64,455
Less Accumulated Depreciation................	(37,973)	(45,958)	(54,617)
Net Property, Plant, and Equipment............	$ 25,661	$ 19,327	$ 9,838
Other Assets.....................................	2,184	2,184	2,184
Total Assets	$145,834	$142,106	$144,849
Liabilities and Shareholders' Equity			
Accounts Payable............................	$ 21,768	$ 15,642	$ 13,954
Notes Payable.................................	—	—	10,814
Current Portion of Long-Term Debt............	18,256	10,997	7,288
Other Current Liabilities	4,353	6,912	5,489
Total Current Liabilities....................	$ 44,377	$ 33,551	$ 37,545
Long-Term Debt	61,017	51,481	43,788
Total Liabilities	$105,394	$ 85,032	$ 81,333
Common Stock	$ 1,000	$ 1,000	$ 1,000
Additional Paid-in Capital	124,000	124,000	124,000
Retained Earnings.............................	(84,560)	(67,926)	(61,484)
Total Shareholders' Equity..................	$ 40,440	$ 57,074	$ 63,516
Total Liabilities and Shareholders' Equity	$145,834	$142,106	$144,849

Subtracting the amounts at the end of Year 5 from the amounts at the end of Year 6, we obtain:

$$\Delta \text{ Cash } + \Delta \text{ Noncash Assets } = \Delta \text{ Liabilities } + \Delta \text{ Shareholders' Equity}$$

$$-\$1,103 + \quad (-\$2,625) \quad = -\$20,362 + \quad \quad \$16,634$$

Rearranging terms:

$$\Delta \text{ Cash } = \Delta \text{ Liabilities } + \Delta \text{ Shareholders' Equity } - \Delta \text{ Noncash Assets}$$

$$-\$1,103 = -\$20,362 + \quad \quad \$16,634 \quad \quad - \quad (-\$2,625)$$

CLASSIFYING CHANGES IN NONCASH BALANCE SHEET ACCOUNTS

The statement of cash flows classifies the reasons for the change in cash as being either an operating, investing, or financing activity. The remaining task then is to classify the change in each noncash balance sheet account (right-hand side of the equation above) into one of these three categories. The analyst injects approximations into the preparation of the statement of cash flows at this step. Some of the changes in balance sheet accounts unambiguously fit into one of the three categories (for example, the change in common stock is a financing transaction). However, some balance sheet changes (for example, retained earnings) result from the netting of several changes, some of which relate to operations (net income) and some of which relate to investing or financing (dividends) activities. The analyst should use whatever information that the financial statements and notes provide about changes in balance sheet accounts to classify the net change each period.[4]

Exhibit 2.7 classifies the changes in the noncash balance sheet accounts. The next section discusses the classification of each account.

1. *Accounts Receivable.* Cash collections from customers during a period equal sales for the period plus accounts receivable at the beginning of the period minus accounts receivable at the end of the period. Thus, the change in accounts receivable clearly relates to operations. Line (17) of Exhibit 2.7 shows net income as a source of cash flow from operations. Net income includes sales revenue. The amount for sales revenue included in the amount on line (17) plus or minus the change in accounts receivable on line (1) results in the amount of cash received from customers.

2. *Marketable Securities.* Firms typically acquire marketable securities when they temporarily have excess cash and sell these securities when they need cash. The holding of marketable securities for a relatively short period might

---

[4]The change in balance sheet accounts does not always equal the amount reported on the statement of cash flows related to these accounts. The usual explanation is that the firm acquired or disposed of a business during the period and classified the change in the balance sheet account partially as an operating activity (for example, cash collections from customers exceeded or fell short of sales) and partially as an investing activity (for example, accounts receivable of an acquired or disposed business).

EXHIBIT 2.7

Worksheet for Preparation of Statement of Cash Flows

	Balance Sheet Changes	Operations	Investing	Financing
(Increase) Decrease in Assets				
(1) Accounts Receivable		x		
(2) Marketable Securities			x	
(3) Inventories..........................		x		
(4) Other Current Assets.................		x		
(5) Investments in Securities			x	
(6) Property, Plant, and Equipment Cost ...			x	
(7) Accumulated Depreciation		x		
(8) Other Assets			x	
Increase (Decrease) in Equities				
(9) Accounts Payable		x		
(10) Notes Payable				x
(11) Current Portion of Long-Term Debt				x
(12) Other Current Liabilities..............		x		
(13) Long-Term Debt.....................				x
(14) Deferred Income Taxes		x		
(15) Other Noncurrent Liabilities				x
(16) Common Stock......................				x
(17) Additional Paid-in Capital.............				x
(18) Retained Earnings		x (net income)		x (dividends)
(19) Treasury Stock				x
(20) Cash...............................				

make purchases and sales appear as operating activities. However, the temporarily excess cash could result from selling fixed assets, from issuing bonds or common stock, or from operating activities. Likewise, firms might use the cash inflow from the sale of marketable securities to purchase fixed assets, retire debt, repurchase common or preferred stock, or finance operating activities. GAAP in the United States ignores the reason for the excess cash (purchase of marketable securities) and the use of the cash proceeds (sale of marketable securities) and classifies the cash flows associated with purchases and sales of marketable securities as investing activities. Because net income includes gains or losses on sales of marketable securities, the analyst must subtract gains and add back losses to net income in deriving cash flow from operations. Failure to offset the gain or loss in earnings results in reporting too much (sales of marketable securities at a gain) or too little (sales of marketable securities at a loss) cash flow from operations. Cash flow from operations should include none of the cash flows associated with sales of marketable securities; such transactions are investing activities.

3. *Inventories.* Purchases of inventory during a period equal cost of goods sold for the period plus inventories at the end of the period minus inventories at the

beginning of the period. Line (17) includes cost of goods sold as an expense in measuring net income. The change in inventories on line (3) coupled with cost of goods sold included in the amount on line (17) results in the amount of purchases for the period. The presumption at this point is that the firm made a cash outflow equal to the amount of purchases. If the firm does not pay cash for all of these purchases, then accounts payable changes. We adjust for the change in accounts payable on line (9), discussed later.

4. *Other Current Assets.* This balance sheet account typically includes prepayments for various operating costs. Unless the financial statements and notes present information to the contrary, the presumption is that the change in line (4) relates to operations.

5. *Investments in Securities.* The Investments in Securities account can change for the following possible reasons:

Source of Change	Classification in Statement of Cash Flows
Acquisition of New Investments	Investing (outflow)
Recognition of Income Using Equity Method	Operations (subtraction)
Receipt of Dividend from Investee	Operations (inflow)
Sale of Investments	Investing (inflow)

If the balance sheet and income statement provide information that permits the disaggregation of the net change in Investments in Securities into these components, then the analyst can make appropriate classifications of the components. Absent such information, we classify the change in the account as an investing activity.

6. *Property, Plant, and Equipment.* We classify the cash flows related to purchases and sales of fixed assets as investing activities. Because net income includes any gains or losses from sales of fixed assets, we offset their effect on earnings by adding back losses and subtracting gains from net income when computing cash flow from operations.

7. *Accumulated Depreciation.* The amount of depreciation recognized each period reduces net income but does not use cash. Thus, we classify depreciation as an operating item with a positive sign on line (7). When we add the amount for depreciation included under operations on line (7) to depreciation expense included as a negative element in net income on line (17), we eliminate the effect of depreciation from the Operations column. This treatment is appropriate since depreciation is not a cash flow (ignoring income tax consequences).

8. *Other Assets.* Other Assets on the balance sheet include patents, copyrights, goodwill, and similar assets. Unless the financial statements and notes provide contrary information, the presumption is that the changes in these accounts are investing activities.

9. *Accounts Payable.* The cash outflow for purchases equals purchases during the period plus accounts payable at the beginning of the period minus accounts payable at the end of the period. We derived the amount for purchases

of the period as part of the calculations in line (3) for inventories. The adjustment on line (9) for the change in accounts payable converts purchases to cash payments on purchases and, like inventories, is an operating transaction.

10. *Notes Payable.* Notes payable is the account generally used when a firm engages in short-term borrowing from a bank or other financial institution. GAAP in the United States classifies such borrowing as a financing activity on the statement of cash flows, even though the firm might use the proceeds to finance accounts receivable, inventories, or other working capital needs. The presumption underlying the classification of bank borrowing as a financing activity is that firms derive operating cash inflows from their customers, but not by borrowing from banks.

11. *Current Portion of Long-Term Debt.* The change in the current portion of long-term debt during a period equals (a) the reclassification of long-term debt from a noncurrent liability to a current liability (that is, debt that the firm expects to repay within one year as of the end-of-the-period balance sheet) minus (b) the long-term debt actually repaid during the period. The latter amount represents the cash outflow from this financing transaction. We consider the amount arising from the reclassification in connection with line (13) below.

12. *Other Current Liabilities.* Firms generally use this account for obligations related to goods and services used in operations other than purchases of inventories. Thus, changes in Other Current Liabilities appear as operating activities.

13. *Long-Term Debt.* This account changes for the following reasons:

> Issuance of new long-term debt.
>
> Reclassification of long-term debt from a noncurrent to a current liability.
>
> Early retirement of long-term debt.
>
> Conversion of long-term debt to preferred or common stock.

These items are clearly financing transactions, but they do not all affect cash. The issuance of new debt and early retirement of old debt do affect cash flows. The reclassification of long-term debt included in the amount on line (13) offsets the corresponding amount included in the change on line (11), and they effectively cancel each other. This is appropriate because the reclassification does not affect cash flow. Likewise, any portion of the change in long-term debt on line (13) due to a conversion of debt into capital stock offsets a similar change on line (16). The analyst enters reclassifications and conversions of debt, such as those described above, on the *worksheet* for the preparation of a statement of cash flows since such transactions help explain changes in balance sheet accounts. However, these transactions do not appear on the formal statement of cash flows because they do not involve actual cash flows.

14. *Deferred Income Taxes.* Income taxes currently payable equal income tax expense (included on line (17) as a negative element of net income) plus or minus the change in deferred taxes during the period. Thus, changes in Deferred Income Taxes appear as an operating activity.

15. *Other Noncurrent Liabilities.* This account includes unfunded pension or retirement benefit obligations, long-term deposits received, and other

miscellaneous long-term liabilities. Changes in pension and retirement benefit obligations are operating activities. Absent information to the contrary, we classify the change in other noncurrent liability accounts as financing activities.

16. *Common Stock and Additional Paid-in Capital.* These accounts change when a firm issues new stock or repurchases and retires outstanding stock and appear as financing activities.

17. *Retained Earnings.* Retained earnings increase by the amount of net income and decrease for dividends each period. Net income is an operating activity and dividends are a financing activity.

18. *Treasury Stock.* Repurchases of a firm's outstanding capital stock are a financing activity.

ILLUSTRATION OF PREPARATION PROCEDURE

We illustrate the procedure for preparing the statement of cash flows using the data for Logue Shoe Stores in Exhibit 2.6. Assume that net income was $16,634 for Year 6 and $6,442 for Year 7.

Exhibit 2.8 presents the worksheet for Year 6. The first column shows the change in each noncash balance sheet account that nets to the $1,103 decrease in cash for

EXHIBIT 2.8

Logue Shoe Stores
Worksheet for Statement of Cash Flows
Year 6

	Balance Sheet Changes	Operations	Investing	Financing
(Increase) Decrease in Assets				
Accounts Receivable	$ (102)	$ (102)		
Inventories	(7,198)	(7,198)		
Other Current Assets	3,591	3,591		
Property, Plant, and Equipment	(1,651)		$(1,651)	
Accumulated Depreciation	7,985	7,985		
Other Assets.	—			
Increase (Decrease) in Equities				
Accounts Payable.	$ (6,126)	$ (6,126)		
Notes Payable.	—			
Current Portion of Long-Term Debt.	(7,259)			$ (7,259)
Other Current Liabilities	2,559	2,559		
Long-Term Debt	(9,536)			(9,536)
Common Stock	—			
Additional Paid-in Capital	—			
Retained Earnings.	16,634	16,634		
Cash	$ (1,103)	$17,343	$(1,651)	$(16,795)

the period. One should observe particular caution with the direction of the change. Recall from the earlier equation:

$$\Delta \text{ Cash} = \Delta \text{ Liabilities} + \Delta \text{ Shareholders' Equity} - \Delta \text{ Noncash Assets}$$

Increase =	Increase		
Decrease =	Decrease		
Increase =		Increase	
Decrease =		Decrease	
Decrease =			Increase
Increase =			Decrease

Thus, changes in liabilities and shareholders' equity have the same directional effect on cash, whereas changes in noncash assets have just the opposite directional effect.

We classify the change in each account as an operating, investing, or financing activity. Observe the following for Year 6:

1. Operating activities were a net source of cash for the period. The firm used the cash derived from operations to repay long-term debt.
2. Inventories increased substantially during the period while accounts payable decreased. The two events reduced operating cash flows. Most firms report increases in accounts payable in amounts approximately equal to the increase inventories.
3. Compared to the level of depreciation during the year, capital expenditures on new property, plant, and equipment were small.

Exhibit 2.9 presents a worksheet for Year 7. The preparation procedure is identical to that in Exhibit 2.8. Note in this case that operations were a net user of cash. This is due primarily to a substantial increase in inventories that was not matched with an increase in accounts payable. Long-term debt was again redeemed in Year 7, but it appears that the firm used short-term bank borrowing to finance the redemption. The negative cash flow from operations coupled with the use of short-term debt to redeem long-term debt suggests an increase in short-term liquidity risk.

Exhibit 2.10 presents the statement of cash flows for Logue Shoe Stores for Year 6 and Year 7 using the amounts taken from the worksheets in Exhibits 2.8 and 2.9.

CONVERTING A FUNDS FLOWS STATEMENT INTO A STATEMENT OF CASH FLOWS

The International Accounting Standards Committee (IASC) issued IASC *Standard No. 7* on the statement of cash flows in 1992. This standard recommends that the accounting standards board within each of its member countries require the presentation of a statement of cash flows that classifies cash flows into operating, investing, and financing activities beginning with the 1994 annual reports. Most firms whose common shares trade in international markets adopted this reporting standard earlier than 1994. Thus, statements of cash flows in the format discussed in this chapter are readily available. Some firms have delayed adoption, awaiting a requirement

EXHIBIT 2.9

Logue Shoe Stores
Worksheet for Statement of Cash Flows
Year 7

	Balance Sheet Changes	Operations	Investing	Financing
(Increase) Decrease in Assets				
Accounts Receivable	$ 162	$ 162		
Inventories	(17,614)	(17,614)		
Other Current Assets	(1,560)	(1,560)		
Property, Plant, and Equipment	830		$830	
Accumulated Depreciation	8,659	8,659		
Other Assets.	—			
Increase (Decrease) in Equities				
Accounts Payable.	$ (1,688)	$ (1,688)		
Notes Payable.	10,814			$10,814
Current Portion of Long-Term Debt. . . .	(3,709)			(3,709)
Other Current Liabilities	(1,423)	(1,423)		
Long-Term Debt	(7,693)			(7,693)
Common Stock	—			
Additional Paid-in Capital	—			
Retained Earnings.	6,442	6,442		
Cash	$ (6,780)	$ (7,022)	$830	$ (588)

EXHIBIT 2.10

Logue Shoe Stores
Statement of Cash Flows

	Year 6	Year 7
Operations		
Net Income	$ 16,634	$ 6,442
Depreciation.	7,985	8,659
(Increase) Decrease in Accounts Receivable	(102)	162
(Increase) Decrease in Inventories	(7,198)	(17,614)
(Increase) Decrease in Other Current Assets	3,591	(1,560)
Increase (Decrease) in Accounts Payable	(6,126)	(1,688)
Increase (Decrease) in Other Current Liabilities	2,559	(1,423)
Cash Flow from Operations.	$ 17,343	$ (7,022)
Investing		
Sale (Acquisition) of Property, Plant, and Equipment	$ (1,651)	$ 830
Financing		
Increase in Notes Payable.	—	$ 10,814
Repayment of Long-Term Debt.	$(16,795)	$(11,402)
Cash Flow from Financing	$(16,795)	$ (588)
Net Change in Cash.	$ (1,103)	$ (6,780)

from their national standard body. Such firms often present a statement of sources and uses of funds, with funds defined as working capital. This section illustrates the procedure for converting a statement of sources and uses of funds into a statement of cash flows.

The conversion involves the following steps:

1. Converting the definition of *funds* that a firm used in the sources and uses of funds statement into a cash and cash equivalents definition.
2. Reclassifying the sources and uses into an operating, investing, and financing format.

Exhibit 2.11 presents a sources and uses of funds statement (called here a *statement of changes in financial position*) for Mazda Motor Corporation, a Japanese automobile manufacturer. Mazda defines funds as working capital (that is, current assets minus current liabilities). The top portion of Exhibit 2.11 shows the sources and uses of working capital that net to ¥7,945 million increase for Year 6. The lower portion of Exhibit 2.11 shows the changes in individual current asset and current liability accounts that net to the ¥7,945 million increase in working capital explained in the top portion.

The statement of cash flows defines funds as cash. Thus, we wish to account for the ¥69,334 decrease in cash. To do this, we classify the change in all noncash balance sheet accounts as either an operating, investing, or financing activity. Exhibit 2.12 presents a statement of cash flows for Mazda. Most items are easy to classify into one of these three categories. The following discussion elaborates on a few items.

Provision for Employee Retirements, Net. Japanese GAAP requires firms to provide annually, as a charge against net income, a portion of the estimated cost of employee retirement benefits that the firms will pay later to employees. Japanese firms rarely set aside funds equal to the expense each period. Rather, such firms pay the benefits out of their Cash account when employees retire. Thus, the actual cash outflow during the year to retired employees seldom equals the provision for employee retirements. Mazda shows an addition to net income for this item, suggesting that the provision for Year 5 and Year 6 exceeded the cash outflow.

Increase in Trade Receivables, Inventories, and Other Current Assets. Increases in operating current asset accounts use cash and require a subtraction from net income in computing cash flow from operations. The subtraction for the increase in accounts receivable indicates that cash flow from operations did not increase by the full amount of sales revenue included in net income. The subtraction for the increase in inventories indicates that Mazda used more cash to acquire inventory than the amount of cost of goods sold subtracted in computing net income.

Changes in Operating Current Liability Accounts. Some current liability accounts (for example, Accrued Income Taxes, Accrued Expenses) relate to operating activities; other accounts (Short-Term Bank Loans, Long-Term Debt Due

EXHIBIT 2.11

Mazda Motor Corporation
Consolidated Statement of Changes in Financial Position

	Millions of Yen	
	Year Ended March 31, Year 6	**Year Ended March 31, Year 5**
Source		
Net Income	¥ 23,438	¥ 17,064
Charges to Income Not Requiring Current Outlay of Working Capital:		
Depreciation.	73,070	30,445
Provision for Employees' Retirement Benefits (net). . . .	1,916	503
Working Capital Provided from Operations.	98,424	48,012
Increase in Long-Term Debt	31,075	110,775
Common Stock Issued Upon Conversion of Convertible Bonds and Notes.	29,600	9,452
Disposal of Property, Plant, and Equipment	6,813	1,997
Other, Net	10,045	1,801
	175,957	172,037
Application		
Additions to Property, Plant, and Equipment	71,626	49,089
Increase in Investments and Other Assets	46,503	11,394
Decrease in Long-Term Debt	24,542	30,248
Cash Dividends Paid.	6,921	4,016
Conversion of Convertible Bonds and Notes	18,420	6,331
	168,012	101,078
Increase in Working Capital	¥ 7,945	¥ 70,959
Changes in Components of Working Capital:		
Increase (Decrease) in Current Assets:		
Cash	¥(69,334)	¥ 59,002
Marketable Securities	6,718	2,388
Trade Notes and Accounts Receivable	73,399	11,926
Inventories	14,873	19,033
Other Current Assets	7,203	4,048
	32,859	96,397
Increase (Decrease) in Current Liabilities:		
Short-Term Bank Loans.	3,744	13,653
Long-Term Debt Due within One Year	(46,097)	16,476
Trade Notes and Accounts Payable	42,233	(2,717)
Accrued Income Taxes	(908)	(2,019)
Accrued Expenses.	16,774	(3,329)
Other Current Liabilities	9,168	3,374
	24,914	25,438
Increase in Working Capital	¥ 7,945	¥ 70,959

EXHIBIT 2.12

Mazda Motor Corporation
Statement of Cash Flows
(in millions of Yen)

	Year Ended March 31, Year 6	Year Ended March 31, Year 5
Operating		
Net Income	¥ 23,438	¥ 17,064
Depreciation...	73,070	30,445
Provision for Employees' Retirements, Net.......................	1,916	503
Loss on Conversion of Bonds and Notes	11,180	3,121
(Increase) Decrease in Trade Note and Accounts Receivable	(73,399)	(11,926)
(Increase) Decrease in Inventories	(14,873)	(19,033)
(Increase) Decrease in Other Current Assets	(7,203)	(4,048)
Increase (Decrease) in Trade Notes and Accounts Payable	42,233	(2,717)
Increase (Decrease) in Accrued Income Taxes	(908)	(2,019)
Increase (Decrease) in Accrued Expenses	16,774	(3,329)
Increase (Decrease) in Other Current Liabilities	9,168	3,374
Cash Flow from Operations....................................	¥ 81,396	¥ 11,435
Investing		
Disposal of Property, Plant, and Equipment	¥ 6,813	¥ 1,997
Additions to Property, Plant, and Equipment	(71,626)	(49,089)
Increase in Investments and Other Assets........................	(46,503)	(11,394)
(Increase) Decrease in Marketable Securities	(6,718)	(2,388)
Cash Flow from Investing	¥(118,034)	¥(60,874)
Financing		
Increase (Decrease) in Short-Term Bank Loans....................	¥ 3,744	¥ 13,653
Increase in Long-Term Debt	31,075	110,775
Decrease in Long-Term Debt	(24,542)	(30,248)
Increase (Decrease) in Long-Term Debt Due within One Year	(46,097)	16,476
Dividends	(6,921)	(4,016)
Other, Net	10,045	1,801
Cash Flow from Financing	¥ (32,696)	¥108,441
Change in Cash..	¥ (69,334)	¥ 59,002

within One Year) relate to financing activities. Unless the notes provide information to the contrary, we classify changes in Other Current Liabilities (as well as Other Current Assets) as operating activities.

The analyst should use particular caution when entering changes in current liability accounts on a statement of cash flows worksheet. Firms follow different practices with respect to their use of parentheses in their published statements. Mazda shows the effect of change in individual current liability accounts on *total current liabilities*. Thus, trade notes and accounts payable increased current liabilities by

¥42,233 during Year 6. Mazda's statement of changes in financial position reports this increase as a positive amount. Because increases in current liabilities increase cash (that is, delay the time when the firm must pay cash), they appear as a positive amount as well in the statement of cash flows in Exhibit 2.12.

Other firms report changes in current liabilities in terms of their effect on working capital. Because increases in current liabilities reduce working capital, the published statement reports these items with parentheses, indicating a negative change. The proper treatment still adds increases in operating current liability accounts to net income in computing cash flow from operations. In this case, therefore, the analyst changes the directional sign from that reported in the published statement of sources and uses of funds. When doubt exists as to the direction of the change, the analyst should examine the comparative balance sheet.

Changes in Marketable Securities.   Firms with temporary excess cash not needed in operations invest in government or other marketable securities to generate a return. These firms sell the securities when they need cash. GAAP in the United States classifies purchases and sales of marketable securities as investing activities.

Changes in Short-Term Bank Loans.   Firms temporarily needing cash for operations often obtain bank loans. They usually repay the loans soon thereafter with cash generated from operations. Bank loans are also sometimes a substitute for supplier financing. Classifying changes in bank loans as an operating activity may therefore seem appropriate. GAAP in the United States, however, classifies changes in short-term bank loans as a financing activity. Accounting standard-setters in the United States apparently desired to keep cash flow from operations as a measure of cash flows directly relating to dealings with customers, suppliers, employees, and others.

Change in Long-Term Debt.   The analyst should aggregate the lines "decrease in long-term debt" and "increase (decrease) in long-term debt due within one year" to obtain the cash outflow for debt retirement during the year. During Year 6, Mazda transferred ¥24,542 from long-term debt to the current liability account, Long-Term Debt Due within One Year. The latter account decreased by ¥46,097 net during the year. Thus, Mazda repaid debt totaling ¥70,639 as shown in the first column below:

Analysis of Changes in the Account, Long-Term Debt Due within One Year	Year Ended March 31, Year 6	Year Ended March 31, Year 5
Increases in Account: Transfer from Long-Term Debt Account.............................	¥ 24,542	¥ 30,248
Decreases in Account: Long-Term Debt Repaid	(70,639)	(13,722)
Increase (Decrease) in Account during the Year....	¥(46,097)	¥ 16,526)

During Year 5, Mazda transferred ¥30,248 from long-term debt to the current liability account. Because the latter account increased by ¥16,476 net, Mazda repaid long-term debt totaling ¥13,772 during the year (see second column on previous page).

Debt Conversion Transactions.   When a firm's creditors convert convertible bonds into common stock, GAAP in the United States accounts for the transaction by transferring an amount equal to the book value of the bonds from long-term debt to common shareholders' equity accounts. The firm recognizes no gain or loss on the conversion. Because no cash inflow or outflow occurs, the entity should report the conversion on the statement of cash flows. Mazda reports bond conversions on its statement of changes in financial position on two lines: common stock issued upon conversion of bonds and notes (a source) and bonds and notes converted (a use). The firm reports a larger amount for the common stock issued than for the bonds converted, suggesting that it recognized a loss upon conversion. The loss reduced net income in the operations section of the statement of cash flows. The following summarizes Mazda's reporting for Year 6:

	Year Ended March 31, Year 6
Operating	
Net Income: Loss on Conversion of Bonds	¥(11,180)
Cash Flow from Operations................................	¥(11,180)
Financing	
Common Stock Issued upon Conversion of Bonds and Notes....	29,600
Conversion of Bonds and Notes.............................	(18,420)
Cash Flow from Financing	¥ 11,180
Net Effect on Cash Flow..................................	¥ 0

Consistency with reporting practices in the United States requires an addback to net income in the amount of the loss and elimination of the two lines for the conversion of bonds and notes into common stock. This restatement results in reporting the transaction as having no effect on either net cash flow or on any of the three component activities of the statement of cash flows.

Other, Net.   Firms usually aggregate funds flow items that are immaterial in amount into an Other, Net line. The analyst usually cannot determine the portion of this single-line item that relates to operating, investing, and financing activities. The analyst should select a classification rule for such items and follow it consistently across firms and across years. We treat such items as financing activities in Exhibit 2.12.

SUMMARY

Compared to the balance sheet and income statement, the statement of cash flows is a relatively new statement. The Financial Accounting Standards Board issued its most recent comprehensive standard on the statement of cash flows in 1987, although GAAP in the United States has required some form of "funds flow" statement since the late 1960s. When firms outside the United States issue funds flow statements, they sometimes define *funds* more broadly than cash (usually either as cash plus marketable securities net of short-term borrowing or as net working capital).

The statement of cash flows will likely increase in usefulness during the next several years for the following reasons:

1. Analysts will understand better the types of information that this statement presents and the kinds of interpretations that are appropriate.
2. Analysts will increasingly recognize that cash flows do not necessarily track income flows. A firm with a healthy income statement is not necessarily financially healthy. Cash requirements to service debt may outstrip the ability of operations to generate cash.
3. Differences in accounting principles have less of an impact on the statement of cash flows than on the balance sheet and income statement. Such differences in accounting principles between countries are a major issue as capital markets become more integrated across countries.

PROBLEMS

2.1 INTERPRETING THE STATEMENT OF CASH FLOWS. H. J. Heinz Company (Heinz) manufactures a wide range of consumer foods products in the United States and abroad. Exhibit 2.13 presents a statement of cash flows for Heinz for Year 7 to Year 11.

REQUIRED
Discuss the relationship between net income and cash flow from operations and the pattern of cash flows from operating, investing, and financing activities for the firm over the five-year period.

2.2 INTERPRETING THE STATEMENT OF CASH FLOWS. Inland Steel Industries manufactures steel used in the automotive, construction, heavy equipment, appliance, and similar industries. Exhibit 2.14 presents a statement of cash flows for Inland Steel Industries for Year 7 to Year 11.

REQUIRED
Discuss the relationship between net income and cash flow from operations and the pattern of cash flows from operating, investing, and financing activities for this firm over the five-year period.

2.3 INTERPRETING THE STATEMENT OF CASH FLOWS. Exhibit 2.15 presents a statement of cash flows for Biogen, Inc., a biotechnology company.

REQUIRED
Discuss the relationship between net income and cash flow from operations and the pattern of cash flows from operating, investing, and financing activities over the five-year period.

EXHIBIT 2.13

H. J. Heinz Company
Statement of Cash Flows
(amounts in millions)
(Problem 2.1)

	Year 7	Year 8	Year 9	Year 10	Year 11
Operating					
Net Income	$ 504	$ 568	$ 417	$ 530	$ 603
Depreciation.....................................	169	196	212	235	260
Other Addbacks..................................	38	38	51	179	107
Other Subtractions	(32)	(53)	(127)	(126)	(194)
Working Capital from Operations...............	$ 679	$ 749	$ 553	$ 818	$ 776
(Increase) Decrease in Accounts Receivable	(105)	(36)	(132)	(138)	135
(Increase) Decrease in Inventories	(87)	38	(25)	(114)	10
(Increase) Decrease in Prepayments...............	18	(1)	26	(47)	15
Increase (Decrease) in Accounts Payable...........	47	34	(11)	15	68
Increase (Decrease) In Other Current Liabilities	(24)	(10)	66	(122)	(73)
Cash Flow from Operations....................	$ 528	$ 774	$ 477	$ 412	$ 931
Investing					
Fixed Assets Acquired...........................	$(355)	$(345)	$(331)	$(431)	$(275)
Change in Marketable Securities	20	(48)	(14)	13	82
Other Investing Transactions.....................	(33)	(94)	(259)	(412)	166
Cash Flow from Investing	$(368)	$(487)	$(604)	$(830)	$ (27)
Financing					
Increase in Short-Term Borrowing................	$ 88	$ 42	$ 757	$ 12	0
Increase in Long-Term Borrowing	231	5	1	969	$ 1
Issue of Capital Stock...........................	60	101	64	72	23
Decrease in Short-Term Borrowing	0	0	0	0	(398)
Decrease in Long-Term Borrowing.................	(28)	(95)	(134)	(240)	(18)
Acquisition of Capital Stock......................	(280)	(68)	(398)	(149)	(223)
Dividends	(208)	(239)	(271)	(297)	(326)
Other..	0	(8)	50	27	67
Cash Flow from Financing	$(137)	$(262)	$ 69	$ 394	$(874)
Change in Cash..................................	$ 23	$ 25	$ (58)	$ (24)	$ 30
Cash—Beginning of Year........................	102	125	150	92	68
Cash—End of Year..............................	$ 125	$ 150	$ 92	$ 68	$ 98

2.4 INTERPRETING THE STATEMENT OF CASH FLOWS. Exhibit 2.16 presents a statement of cash flows for Mitsubishi Corporation, a diversified industrial firm engaged in steel, petroleum, chemical, textiles, food, and information system industry segments.

REQUIRED
Discuss the relationship between net income and cash flow from operations and the pattern of cash flows from operating, investing, and financing activities for this firm over a five-year period.

EXHIBIT 2.14

Inland Steel Industries
Statement of Cash Flows
(amounts in millions)
(Problem 2.2)

	Year 7	Year 8	Year 9	Year 10	Year 11
Operating					
Net Income	$ 119.7	$ (20.6)	$ (62.7)	$ (159.4)	$ (37.6)
Depreciation and Amortization	131.2	119.7	118.2	129.6	131.8
Other Addbacks	56.3	16.6	14.0	423.9	76.1
Other Subtractions	(31.0)	(33.6)	(108.0)	(478.2)	(36.8)
Working Capital Provided by Operations	$ 276.2	$ 82.1	$ (38.5)	$ (84.1)	$ 133.5
(Increase) Decrease in Receivables	10.3	47.6	53.8	(27.1)	(46.4)
(Increase) Decrease in Inventories	2.9	39.9	72.1	5.6	(4.2)
(Increase) Decrease in Other Current Assets	(16.3)	(1.2)	14.3	33.2	(11.4)
Increase (Decrease) in Accounts Payable—Trade	(3.4)	60.2	(74.0)	22.8	34.0
Increase (Decrease) in Other Current Liabilities	(29.5)	(39.4)	(2.7)	28.2	6.5
Cash Flow from Operations	$ 240.2	$ 189.2	$ 25.0	$ (21.4)	$ 112.0
Investing					
Fixed Assets Sold	$ 7.7	$ 19.5	$ 13.9	$ 28.1	$ 6.5
Fixed Assets Acquired	(196.5)	(261.1)	(140.2)	(64.4)	(105.6)
Investments in Joint Steel-Making Ventures	(58.3)	(49.8)	(24.9)	(6.3)	(1.9)
Cash Flow from Investing	$(247.1)	$(291.4)	$(151.2)	$ (42.6)	$(101.0)
Financing					
Increase in Long-Term Borrowing	$ 3.1	$ 146.9	$ 121.4	$ 145.4	$ 46.8
Issue of Capital Stock	185.0	—	72.8	97.9	178.7
Decrease in Short-Term Borrowing	(13.3)	—	—	—	—
Decrease in Long-Term Borrowing	(32.8)	(25.6)	(39.3)	(49.4)	(78.5)
Acquisition of Capital Stock	(144.1)	(126.5)	(2.3)	(3.5)	(9.5)
Dividends	(58.9)	(71.7)	(37.6)	(35.8)	(35.7)
Cash Flow from Financing	$ (61.0)	$ (76.9)	$ 115.0	$ 154.6	$ 101.8
Net Change in Cash	$ (67.9)	$(179.1)	$ (11.2)	$ 90.6	$ 112.8
Cash—Beginning of Year	305.3	237.4	58.3	47.1	137.7
Cash—End of Year	$ 237.4	$ 58.3	$ 47.1	$ 137.7	$ 250.5

2.5 PREPARING A STATEMENT OF CASH FLOWS FROM BALANCE SHEETS AND INCOME STATEMENTS. GTI, Inc., manufactures parts, components, and processing equipment for electronics and semiconductor applications for the communication, computer, automotive, and appliance industries. Its sales tend to be cyclical since the sales of most of its customers are cyclical. Exhibit 2.17 presents balance sheets for GTI as of December 31, Year 7 through Year 9 and Exhibit 2.18 presents income statements for Year 8 and Year 9.

| | | **EXHIBIT 2.15** | | | |

Biogen, Inc.
Statement of Cash Flows
(amounts in thousands)
(Problem 2.3)

	Year 7	Year 8	Year 9	Year 10	Year 11
Operating					
Net Income	$ (2,616)	$ 7,720	$ 7,186	$ 38,311	$ 32,417
Depreciation.............................	3,326	3,786	5,064	7,141	6,657
Other Addbacks.........................	—	967	—	5,424	1,803
Other Subtractions	(849)	—	(1,155)	—	(330)
Working Capital Provided by Operations	$ (139)	$ 12,473	$ 11,095	$ 50,876	$ 40,547
(Increase) Decrease in Receivables	(4,190)	(7,448)	(5,174)	(15,026)	1,720
(Increase) Decrease in Other Current Assets	(1,185)	(1,062)	(1,372)	(2,359)	(234)
(Increase) Decrease in Accounts Payable and Other Current Liabilities	(2,001)	6,737	1,335	9,561	5,537
Cash Flow from Operations..............	$ (7,515)	$ 10,700	$ 5,884	$ 43,052	$ 47,570
Investing					
Fixed Assets Acquired.....................	$ (3,138)	$(11,066)	$(37,274)	$(11,557)	$(53,228)
Change in Marketable Securities	(51,976)	(15,318)	(8,426)	(9,379)	(10,770)
Other Investing Transactions	4,174	(3,158)	(2,634)	(2,933)	(2,697)
Cash Flow from Investing	$(50,940)	$(29,542)	$(48,334)	$(23,869)	$(66,695)
Financing					
Increase in Short-Term Borrowing	—	—	—	—	—
Increase in Long-Term Borrowing	—	—	—	—	—
Issue of Capital Stock	$ 71,426	$ 4,068	$ 89,455	$ 10,033	$ 7,808
Decrease in Short-Term Borrowing	—	—	—	—	—
Decrease in Long-Term Borrowing..........	(4,173)	—	—	—	—
Dividends	(2,736)	(5,865)	(2,932)	—	—
Other Financing Transactions	(167)	12	—	—	—
Cash Flow from Financing	$ 64,350	$ (1,785)	$ 86,523	$ 10,033	$ 7,808
Change in Cash.........................	$ 5,895	$(20,627)	$ 44,073	$ 29,216	$(11,317)
Cash—Beginning of Year..................	27,306	33,201	12,574	56,647	85,863
Cash—End of Year.......................	$ 33,201	$ 12,574	$ 56,647	$ 85,863	$ 74,546

REQUIRED

a. Prepare a worksheet for the preparation of a statement of cash flows for GTI, Inc., for Year 8 and Year 9. Follow the format in Exhibit 2.7 in the text. Footnotes to the firm's financial statements reveal the following (amounts in thousands):

   (1) Depreciation expense was $641 in Year 8 and $625 in Year 9.

   (2) Other assets represent patents. Patent amortization was $25 in Year 8 and $40 in Year 9.

EXHIBIT 2.16

Mitsubishi Corporation
Statement of Cash Flows
(amounts in millions)
(Problem 2.4)

	Year 7	Year 8	Year 9	Year 10	Year 11
Operating					
Net Income	¥ 46,131	¥ 60,356	¥ 65,290	¥ 52,717	¥ 28,658
Depreciation.....................	32,640	45,613	58,417	59,527	68,437
Other Addbacks..................	14,520	35,788	53,286	46,383	54,637
Other Subtractions	(20,184)	(7,931)	(60,075)	(24,691)	(22,923)
Working Capital Provided by Operations	¥ 73,107	¥ 133,826	¥116,918	¥ 133,936	¥128,809
(Increase) Decrease in Receivables ..	(398,834)	(497,901)	(139,385)	569,254	83,751
(Increase) Decrease in Inventories ..	(25,063)	(78,126)	(26,734)	(99,402)	8,961
(Increase) Decrease in Other Current Assets.................	(30,591)	(23,004)	(44,220)	(171,470)	(15,176)
Increase (Decrease) in Accounts Payable	162,914	318,755	423,587	(407,188)	(193,740)
Increase (Decrease) in Other Current Liabilities	32,482	27,781	34,136	(15,613)	(11,167)
Cash Flow from Operations......	¥ (185,985)	¥ (118,669)	¥ 364,302	¥ 9,517	¥ 1,438
Investing					
Fixed Assets Acquired.............	¥ (56,207)	¥ (87,651)	¥(131,697)	¥ (120,289)	¥(129,353)
Change in Marketable Securities ...	(1,326,736)	(306,520)	2,753	1,233,508	294,172
Other Investing Transactions.......	(131,336)	(692,087)	(30,239)	1,784	233,355
Cash Flow from Investing	¥(1,514,279)	¥(1,086,258)	¥(159,183)	¥ 1,115,003	¥ 398,174
Financing					
Increase in Short-Term Borrowing..	¥ 1,047,107	¥ 26,507	—	—	—
Increase in Long-Term Borrowing ..	697,418	1,437,979	¥ 943,803	¥ 853,704	¥ 910,289
Issue of Capital Stock.............	9,120	26,912	272	580	816
Decrease in Short-Term Borrowing .	—	—	(702,771)	(570,648)	(816,656)
Decrease in Long-Term Borrowing..	(95,891)	(272,049)	(433,022)	(1,393,125)	(473,955)
Dividends	(10,742)	(12,362)	(13,276)	(12,508)	(12,515)
Other Financing Transactions	142	2,539	(1,480)	(1,565)	(1,128)
Cash Flow from Financing	¥ 1,647,154	¥ 1,209,526	¥(206,474)	¥(1,123,562)	¥(393,149)
Change in Cash..................	¥ (53,110)	¥ 4,599	¥ (1,355)	¥ 958	¥ 6,463
Cash—Beginning of Year..........	107,226	54,116	58,715	57,360	58,318
Cash—End of Year...............	¥ 54,116	¥ 58,715	¥ 57,360	¥ 58,318	¥ 64,781

(3) Changes in deferred income taxes are operating transactions.

b. Discuss the relation between net income and cash flow from operations and the pattern of cash flows from operating, investing, and financing activities for Year 8 and Year 9.

2.6 PREPARING A STATEMENT OF CASH FLOWS FROM BALANCE SHEETS AND INCOME STATEMENTS. New Oji Paper Company is the largest forest products company in Japan.

EXHIBIT 2.17

GTI, Inc.
Balance Sheets
(amounts in thousands)
(Problem 2.5)

	December 31		
	Year 7	Year 8	Year 9
Assets			
Cash	$ 430	$ 475	$ 367
Accounts Receivable	3,768	3,936	2,545
Inventories	2,334	2,966	2,094
Prepayments	116	270	122
Total Current Assets	$ 6,648	$ 7,647	$ 5,128
Property, Plant, and Equipment (net)	3,806	4,598	4,027
Other Assets	193	559	456
Total Assets	$10,647	$12,804	$ 9,611
Liabilities and Shareholders' Equity			
Accounts Payable	$ 1,578	$ 809	$ 796
Notes Payable to Banks	11	231	2,413
Other Current Liabilities	1,076	777	695
Total Current Liabilities	$ 2,665	$ 1,817	$ 3,904
Long-Term Debt	2,353	4,692	2,084
Deferred Income Taxes	126	89	113
Total Liabilities	$ 5,144	$ 6,598	$ 6,101
Preferred Stock	$ —	$ 289	$ 289
Common Stock	83	85	85
Additional Paid-in Capital	4,385	4,392	4,395
Retained Earnings	1,035	1,440	(1,259)
Total Shareholders' Equity	$ 5,503	$ 6,206	$ 3,510
Total Liabilities and Shareholders' Equity	$10,647	$12,804	$ 9,611

Exhibit 2.19 presents the firm's balance sheets for the years ending March 31, Year 8 to Year 11, and Exhibit 2.20 presents the firm's income statements for the years ending March 31, Year 9 to Year 11.

REQUIRED

a. Prepare a worksheet for the preparation of a statement of cash flows for Oji Paper Company for each of the years ending March 31, Year 9 to Year 11. Follow the format of Exhibit 2.7 in the text. Notes to the firm's financial statements indicate the following:

(1) The changes in the Investments account relate to additional investments in affiliated companies.

(2) The changes in the Employee Retirement Benefits account relate to provisions made for retirement benefits net of payments made to retired employees, both of which the statement of cash flows classifies as operating activities.

EXHIBIT 2.18

GTI, Inc.—Income Statements
(amounts in millions)
(Problem 2.5)

	Year 8	Year 9
Sales	$ 22,833	$ 11,960
Cost of Goods Sold.......................	(16,518)	(11,031)
Selling and Administrative Expenses	(4,849)	(3,496)
Interest Expense	(459)	(452)
Income Tax Expense.......................	(590)	328
Net Income	$ 417	$ (2,691)
Dividends on Preferred Stock	(12)	(8)
Net Income Available to Common	$ 405	$ (2,699)

EXHIBIT 2.19

New Oji Paper Company—Balance Sheets
(amounts in millions of yen)
(Problem 2.6)

	March 31			
	Year 8	Year 9	Year 10	Year 11
Assets				
Cash	¥ 71,655	¥ 55,179	¥ 23,892	¥ 22,499
Accounts and Notes Receivable—Trade........	138,244	123,437	119,480	145,481
Inventories	55,986	56,926	52,352	63,683
Prepayments...............................	1,985	10,709	3,821	11,967
Total Current Assets......................	¥ 267,870	¥ 246,251	¥ 199,545	¥ 243,630
Investments	103,242	129,139	133,831	199,455
Property, Plant, and Equipment	735,993	766,932	792,747	910,421
Less Accumulated Depreciation..............	(383,703)	(425,583)	(465,765)	(517,005)
Total Assets	¥ 723,402	¥ 716,739	¥ 660,358	¥ 836,501
Liabilities and Shareholders' Equity				
Accounts and Notes Payable—Trade	¥ 84,366	¥ 59,693	¥ 52,930	¥ 73,722
Notes Payable to Banks	152,531	144,448	140,363	187,779
Current Portion of Long-Term Debt..........	—	27,362	—	—
Other Current Liabilities	54,474	40,179	36,630	46,681
Total Current Liabilities..................	¥ 291,371	¥ 271,682	¥ 229,923	¥ 308,182
Long-Term Debt	164,611	175,619	155,021	156,803
Employee Retirement Benefits................	29,666	26,441	29,838	38,125
Total Liabilities	¥ 485,648	¥ 473,742	¥ 414,782	¥ 503,110
Common Stock	¥ 46,075	¥ 46,113	¥ 46,143	¥ 83,936
Additional Paid-in Capital	58,146	59,098	59,198	107,346
Retained Earnings..........................	133,533	137,786	140,235	142,109
Total Shareholders' Equity................	¥ 237,754	¥ 242,997	¥ 245,576	¥ 333,391
Total Liabilities and Shareholders' Equity	¥ 723,402	¥ 716,739	¥ 660,358	¥ 836,501

EXHIBIT 2.20

New Oji Paper Company
Income Statements
(amounts in millions of yen)
(Problem 2.6)

	Year Ended March 31		
	Year 9	Year 10	Year 11
Sales	¥ 475,887	¥ 449,976	¥ 486,861
Other Revenues	9,775	8,789	8,432
Total Revenues....................	¥ 485,662	¥ 458,765	¥ 495,293
Cost of Goods Sold.................	(353,874)	(337,530)	(371,363)
Selling and Administrative Expenses ...	(99,688)	(95,594)	(101,648)
Interest Expense	(18,506)	(14,730)	(12,852)
Income Tax Expense................	(3,100)	(3,100)	(2,800)
Net Income	¥ 10,494	¥ 7,811	¥ 6,630

b. Discuss the pattern of cash flows from operating, investing, and financing activities for Year 9, Year 10, and Year 11, indicating the stage in the firm's life cycle suggested by the pattern.

2.7 CONVERTING A STATEMENT OF CHANGES IN FINANCIAL POSITION INTO A STATEMENT OF CASH FLOWS. Mazda Motor Corporation (Mazda) manufactures automobiles. Exhibit 2.21 presents Mazda's statement of changes in financial position for the years ended March 31, Year 7, Year 8, and Year 9.

REQUIRED

a. Prepare a statement of cash flows for Mazda for the years ended March 31, Year 7, Year 8, and Year 9. Classify cash flows into operating, investing, and financing activities.
b. Discuss the relation between net income and cash flow from operations and the pattern of cash flows from operating, investing, and financing activities for Mazda for each year.

2.8 PREPARING A STATEMENT OF CASH FLOWS FROM BALANCE SHEETS AND INCOME STATEMENTS. BASF Group is a diversified German chemical company. Exhibit 2.22 presents the firm's balance sheets for the years ending December 31, Year 7 to Year 10. Exhibit 2.23 presents the firm's income statements for the years ended December 31, Year 8 to Year 10.

REQUIRED

a. Prepare a worksheet for the preparation of a statement of cash flows for BASF Group for each of the years ended December 31, Year 8 to Year 10. Follow the format of Exhibit 2.7 in the text. Notes to the firm's financial statements indicate the following:
(1) Marketable securities include short-term, interest-bearing financial instruments. Because their book value approximates their market value, these securities are generally sold at no gain or loss.

EXHIBIT 2.21

Mazda Motor Corporation
Consolidated Statement of Changes in Financial Position
(amounts in millions of Japanese yen)
(Problem 2.8)

	Year Ended March 31		
	Year 7	Year 8	Year 9
Source			
Net Income	¥ 24,972	¥ 9,314	¥ 90,350
Charges to Income Not Requiring Current Outlay of Working Capital:			
Depreciation..	75,536	84,109	88,181
Provision for Employees' Retirement Benefits, Net.............	2,249	2,060	2,101
Working Capital Provided from Operations...................	¥102,757	¥ 95,483	¥ 180,632
Increase in Long-Term Debt	153,319	71,849	143,252
Common Stock Issued upon Conversion of Convertible Bonds and Notes..	2,531	222	—
Disposal of Property, Plant, and Equipment	4,775	4,659	4,348
Other, Net	8,004	10,208	(1,734)
Total Sources...	¥271,386	¥ 182,421	¥ 326,498
Application			
Additions to Property, Plant, and Equipment	¥166,030	¥ 202,691	¥ 121,288
Increase in Investments and Other Assets......................	7,339	7,012	629
Decrease in Long-Term Debt	27,272	69,161	51,165
Cash Dividends Paid......................................	8,042	8,068	7,532
Conversion of Convertible Bonds and Notes	2,531	222	—
Total Uses..	¥211,214	¥ 287,154	¥ 180,614
Increase in Working Capital	¥ 60,172	¥(104,733)	¥ 145,884
Changes in Components of Working Capital			
Increase (Decrease) in Current Assets			
Cash	¥ 47,499	¥ (66,636)	¥ 25,439
Marketable Securities	16,575	5,396	6,804
Trade Notes and Accounts Receivable	(16,203)	12,028	23,398
Inventories	15,018	288	(13,321)
Other Current Assets	5,310	3,142	3,081
	¥ 68,199	¥ (45,782)	¥ 45,401
Increase (Decrease) in Current Liabilities			
Short-Term Bank Loans.................................	¥(31,921)	¥ 39,366	¥ (31,925)
Long-Term Debt Due within One Year	5,391	36,823	(14,680)
Trade Notes and Accounts Payable	26,870	3,952	(9,881)
Accrued Income Taxes	5,196	(12,248)	(1,411)
Accrued Expenses.....................................	(601)	(731)	(37,927)
Other Current Liabilities	3,092	(8,211)	(4,659)
	¥ 8,027	¥ 58,951	¥(100,483)
Increase in Working Capital	¥ 60,172	¥(104,733)	¥ 145,884

EXHIBIT 2.22

BASF Group
Balance Sheets
(amounts in millions of German mark)
(Problem 2.7)

| | December 31 | | | |
	Year 7	Year 8	Year 9	Year 10
Assets				
Cash	DM 1,538	DM 1,337	DM 1,652	DM 2,318
Marketable Securities	4,425	3,820	2,905	2,921
Accounts Receivable	5,793	5,655	5,446	5,748
Inventories	6,407	6,456	6,748	6,317
Prepayments..............................	2,914	3,233	3,370	2,765
Total Current Assets.....................	DM21,077	DM20,501	DM20,121	DM20,069
Investments in Securities	1,692	1,692	2,955	1,929
Property, Plant, and Equipment (net)..........	13,252	14,629	15,213	17,722
Intangible Assets (net)......................	734	650	684	638
	DM36,755	DM37,472	DM38,973	DM40,358
Liabilities and Shareholders' Equity				
Accounts Payable..........................	DM 3,385	DM 3,224	DM 2,892	DM 2,801
Bank Loans	1,819	1,860	1,755	1,902
Other Current Liabilities	2,137	2,168	2,761	3,242
	DM 7,341	DM 7,252	DM 7,408	DM 7,945
Long-Term Debt	1,550	2,066	3,206	3,463
Other Noncurrent Liabilities	13,634	13,606	13,862	14,166
Total Liabilities	DM22,525	DM22,924	DM24,476	DM25,574
Common Stock	DM 2,850	DM 2,850	DM 2,852	DM 2,922
Additional Paid-in Capital	4,326	4,326	4,330	4,464
Retained Earnings..........................	7,054	7,372	7,315	7,398
Total Shareholders' Equity................	DM14,230	DM14,548	DM14,497	DM14,784
Total Liabilities and Shareholders' Equity	DM36,755	DM37,472	DM38,973	DM40,358

(2) Investments in securities include long-term investments in the common stock of affiliates. Assume that the change in this account each year represents purchases or sales at zero gain or loss.

(3) Depreciation expense was DM 3,176 in Year 8, DM 3,338 in Year 9 and DM 3,174 in Year 10. Amortization of intangibles was DM 267 in Year 8, DM 186 in Year 9, and DM 159 in Year 10.

(4) Other noncurrent liabilities include pension obligations and deferred income taxes.

b. Discuss the relation between net income and cash flow from operations and the pattern of cash flows from operating, investing, and financing activities for Year 8, Year 9, and Year 10.

EXHIBIT 2.23

BASF Group
Income Statements
(amounts in millions of German mark)
(Problem 2.7)

	Year Ended March 31		
	Year 8	**Year 9**	**Year 10**
Sales	DM 46,626	DM 41,933	DM 40,568
Cost of Goods Sold.	(31,839)	(28,237)	(27,647)
Selling Expense.	(7,902)	(7,869)	(7,591)
Administrative Expense	(1,177)	(1,077)	(1,052)
Research and Development Expense . .	(2,063)	(2,048)	(1,934)
Other Operating Expense.	(1,465)	(1,391)	(1,312)
Operating Income	DM 2,180	DM 1,311	DM 1,032
Interest Income	408	409	441
Interest Expense	(478)	(481)	(416)
Income before Income Taxes	DM 2,110	DM 1,239	DM 1,057
Income Tax Expense.	(1,054)	(626)	(296)
Net Income	DM 1,056	DM 613	DM 761

CASE 2.1

W.T. GRANT CO.: A CASE STUDY OF BANKRUPTCY

At the time that it filed for bankruptcy in October 1975, W.T. Grant (Grant) was the 17th largest retailer in the United States, with almost 1,200 stores, more than 82,000 employees, and sales of $1.7 billion. It had paid dividends consistently since 1906. The collapse of Grant came largely as a surprise to the capital markets, particularly to the banks that provided short-term working capital loans. Grant had altered its business strategy in the mid 1960s to transform itself from an urban discount store chain to a suburban housegoods store chain. Its failure serves as a classic study of the poor implementation of what seemed to be a sound business strategy. What happened to Grant, and why, are questions that, with some analysis, can be answered. On the other hand, why the symptoms of Grant's prolonged illness were not diagnosed and treated earlier is difficult to understand.

THE STRATEGIC SHIFT

Prior to the mid 1960s, Grant built its reputation on sales of low-priced softgoods (clothing, linens, sewing fabrics). It placed its stores in large urban locations and appealed primarily to lower income consumers.

SOURCE: This case was coauthored with Professor James A. Largay.

The mid 1960s marked the beginning, however, of urban unrest and a movement to the suburbs. To service the needs of these new homeowners, suburban shopping centers experienced rapid growth. Sears led the way in this movement, establishing itself as the anchor store in many of the more upscale locations. Montgomery Ward and JCPenney followed suit. At this time, Sears held a dominant market share in the middle-income consumer market. It saw an opportunity, however, to move its product line more upscale to compete with the established department stores (Macy's, Marshall Field), which had not yet begun their movement to the suburbs. To implement this new strategy, Sears introduced its Sears Best line of products.

The outward population movement to the suburbs and increased competition from growing discount chains such as KMart caused Grant to alter its strategy as well. One aspect of this strategic shift was the rapid expansion of new stores into suburban shopping centers. Between 1963 and 1973, Grant opened 612 new stores and expanded 91 others. It concentrated most of that expansion in the 1969 to 1973 period when it opened 369 new stores, 15 on one particularly busy day. Because Grant's reputation had been built on sales to lower income consumers, it was often unable to locate its new stores in the choicest shopping centers. Louis C. Lustenberger, president of Grant from 1959 to 1968, started the expansion program, although later, as a director, he became concerned over dimensions of the growth and the problems it generated. After Mr. Lustenberger stepped down, the pace of expansion accelerated under the leadership of Chairman Edward Staley and President Richard W. Mayer.

A second aspect of Grant's strategy involved a change in its product line. Grant perceived a vacuum in the middle-income consumer market when Sears moved more upscale. Grant introduced a higher quality, medium-priced line of products into its new shopping center stores to fill this vacuum. In addition, it added furniture and private-brand appliances to its product line and implemented a credit card system. With much of the movement to the suburbs representing middle-income consumers, Grant attempted to position itself as a primary supplier to outfit the new homes being constructed.

To implement this new strategy, Grant chose a decentralized organizational structure. Each store manager controlled credit extension and credit terms. At most stores, Grant permitted customers 36 months to pay for their purchases; the minimum monthly payment was $1, regardless of their total purchases. Bad debt expenses averaged 1.2 percent of sales each year until fiscal 1975, when a provision of $155.7 million was made. Local store managers also made inventory and pricing decisions. Merchandise was acquired from either regional Grant warehouses or directly from the manufacturer. At this time, Grant did not have an information system in place that permitted one store to check the availability of a needed product from another store. Compensation of employees was considered among the most generous in the industry, with most employees owning shares of Grant's common stock acquired under employee stock option plans. Compensation of store managers included salary plus stated percentages of the stores sales and profits.

To finance the expansion of receivables and inventory, Grant used commercial paper, bank loans, and trade credit. To finance the expansion of store space, Grant entered into leasing arrangements. Because Grant was liquidated before the Financial Accounting Standards Board issued *Statement of Financial Accounting Standards No. 13* requiring the capitalization of capital leases on the balance sheet and the disclosure of information on operating leases in the notes to financial statements, it did not disclose its long-term leasing arrangements. Property, plant, and equipment reported on its balance sheet consisted mostly of store fixtures. Grant's long-term debt included debentures totaling $200 million issued in 1971 and 1973. Based on per square foot rental rates at the time, Grant's disclosures of total square footage of space, and an 8 percent discount rate, the estimated present values of Grant's leases are as follows (in 000s):

January 31	Present Value of Lease Commitments	January 31	Present Value of Lease Commitments
1966	$394,291	1971	$496,041
1967	$400,090	1972	$626,052
1968	$393,566	1973	$708,666
1969	$457,111	1974	$805,785
1970	$486,837	1975	$821,565

ADVANCE AND RETREAT — THE ATTEMPT TO SAVE GRANT

By 1974, it became clear that Grant's problems were not of a short-term operating nature. In the spring of 1974, both Moody's and Standard & Poor's eliminated their credit rating for Grant's commercial paper. Banks entered the picture in a big way in the summer of 1974. To provide financing, a group of 143 banks agreed to offer lines of credit totaling $525 million. Grant obtained a short-term loan of $600 million in September 1974, with three New York money center banks absorbing approximately $230 million of the total. These three banks also loaned $50 million of a total of $100 million provided to Grant's finance subsidiary.

Support by the banks during the summer of 1974 was accompanied by a top management change. Messrs. Staley and Mayer stepped down in the spring and were replaced in August 1974 by James G. Kendrick, brought in from Zeller's Ltd., Grant's Canadian subsidiary. As chief executive officer, Mr. Kendrick moved to cut Grant's losses. He slashed payroll significantly, closed 126 unprofitable stores, and phased out the big-ticket furniture and appliance lines. New store space brought on line in 1975 was 75 percent less than in 1974.

The positive effects of these moves could not overcome the disastrous events of early 1975. In January, Grant defaulted on about $75 million in interest payments; in February, results of operations for the year ended January 31, 1975, were released. Grant reported a loss of $177 million, with substantial losses from credit operations accounting for 60 percent of the total.

The banks now assumed a more active role in what was becoming a struggle to save Grant. Robert H. Anderson, a vice president of Sears, was offered a lucrative $2.5 million contract, decided to accept the challenge to turn the company around, and joined Grant as its new president in April 1975. Mr. Kendrick remained as chairman of the board. The banks holding 90 percent of Grant's debt extended their loans from June 2, 1975 to March 31, 1976. The balance of about $56 million was repaid on June 2. A major problem confronting Mr. Anderson was to maintain the continued flow of merchandise into Grant stores. Suppliers became skeptical of Grant's ability to pay for merchandise and, in August 1975, the banks agreed to subordinate $300 million of debt to the suppliers' claims for merchandise shipped. With the approach of the Christmas shopping season, the need for merchandise became critical. Despite the banks' subordination of their claims to those of suppliers and the intensive cultivation of suppliers by Mr. Anderson, Grant did not receive sufficient quantities of merchandise in the stores.

During this period, Grant reported a $111.3 million net loss for the six months ended on July 31, 1975. Sales had declined 15 percent from the comparable period in 1974. Mr. Kendrick observed that a return to profitability before the fourth quarter was unlikely.

On October 2, 1975, Grant filed a Chapter XI bankruptcy petition. The rehabilitation effort was formally underway and the protection provided by Chapter XI permitted a continuation of the reorganization and rehabilitation activities for the next four months. On February 6, 1976, after store closings and liquidations of inventories had generated $320 million in cash, the creditors committee overseeing the bankruptcy voted for liquidation, and W.T. Grant ceased to exist.

FINANCIAL STATEMENTS FOR GRANT

Two changes in accounting principles affect Grant's financial statements. Prior to fiscal 1970, Grant accounted for the investment in its wholly owned finance subsidiary using the equity method. Beginning with the year ending January 31, 1970, Grant consolidated the finance subsidiary. Prior to fiscal 1975, Grant recorded the total finance charges on credit sales as income in the year of the sale. Accounts receivable therefore included the full amount to be received from customers, not the present value of such amount. Beginning with the fiscal year ending January 31, 1975, Grant recognized finance charges on credit sales over the life of the installment contract.

Exhibit 1 presents comparative balance sheets and Exhibit 2 presents statements of income and retained earnings for Grant based on the amounts as originally reported for each year. Exhibits 3, 4, and 5 present balance sheets, income statements, and statement of cash flow, respectively, based on revised amounts reflecting retroactive restatement for the two changes in accounting principles discussed above. These latter statements consolidate the finance subsidiary for all years. Grant provided the necessary data to restate for the change in income recognition of finance charges for the 1971 to 1975 fiscal years only. Exhibit 6 presents selected other data for Grant, the variety chain store industry, and the aggregate economy.

REQUIRED

Using the narrative information and the financial data provided in Exhibits 1 through 6, your mission is to apply tools of financing analysis to determine the major causes of Grant's financial problems. If you had been performing this analysis contemporaneously with the release of publicly reported information, when would you have become skeptical of Grant's ability to continue as a viable going concern? To assist in this analysis, Exhibits 7, 8, and 9 present selected ratio and growth rate information based on the following assumptions:

Exhibit 7   Based on the amounts as originally reported for each year (Exhibits 1 and 2).

Exhibit 8   Based on the amounts as retroactively restated for changes in accounting principles (Exhibits 3, 4, and 5).

Exhibit 9   Same as Exhibit 8, except assets and liabilities reflect the capitalization of leases using the amounts presented in the case.

EXHIBIT 1

W.T. Grant Company
Comparative Balance Sheets
(as originally reported)
(Case 2.1)

January 31	1966	1967	1968	1969
Assets				
Cash and Marketable Securities	$ 22,559	$ 37,507	$ 25,047	$ 28,460
Accounts Receivable[c]	110,943	110,305	133,406	154,829
Inventories	151,365	174,631	183,722	208,623
Other Current Assets	—	—	—	—
Total Current Assets...............	$284,867	$322,443	$342,175	$391,912
Investments	38,419	40,800	56,609	62,854
Property, Plant, and Equipment (net)...	40,367	48,071	47,572	49,213
Other Assets........................	1,222	1,664	1,980	2,157
Total Assets.....................	$364,875	$412,978	$448,336	$506,136
Equities				
Short-Term Debt	$ —	$ —	$ 300	$ 180
Accounts Payable—Trade.............	58,252	75,885	79,673	102,080
Current Deferred Taxes	37,590	47,248	57,518	64,113
Total Current Liabilities............	$ 95,842	$123,133	$137,491	$166,373
Long-Term Debt	70,000	70,000	62,622	43,251
Noncurrent Deferred Taxes	6,269	7,034	7,551	7,941
Other Long-Term Liabilities	4,784	4,949	4,858	5,519
Total Liabilities	$176,895	$205,116	$212,522	$223,084
Preferred Stock	$ 15,000	$ 15,000	$ 14,750	$ 13,250
Common Stock	15,375	15,636	16,191	17,318
Additional Paid-in Capital	25,543	27,977	37,428	59,945
Retained Earnings...................	132,062	149,249	167,445	192,539
Total	$187,980	$207,862	$235,814	$283,052
Less Cost of Treasury Stock	—	—	—	—
Total Stockholders' Equity	$187,980	$207,862	$235,814	$283,052
Total Equities....................	$364,875	$412,978	$448,336	$506,136

[a]In the year ending January 31, 1970, W.T. Grant changed its consolidation policy and commenced consolidating its wholly owned finance subsidiary.

[b]In the year ending January 31, 1975, W.T. Grant changed its method of recognizing finance income on installment sales. In prior years, Grant recognized all finance income in the year of the sale. Beginning in the 1975 fiscal period, it recognized finance income over the time the installment receivable was outstanding.

[c]Accounts receivable comprises the following:

	1966	1967	1968	1969
Customer Installment Receivables	$114,470	$114,928	$140,507	$162,219
Less Allowances for Uncollectible Accounts..	(7,065)	(9,383)	(11,307)	(13,074)
Unearned Credit Insurance...............	—	—	—	—
Unearned Finance Income	—	—	—	—
Net	$107,405	$105,545	$129,200	$149,145
Other Receivables	3,538	4,760	4,206	5,684
Total Receivables......................	$110,943	$110,305	$133,406	$154,829

EXHIBIT 1

continued

1970[a]	1971	1972	1973	1974	1975[b]
$ 32,977	$ 34,009	$ 49,851	$ 30,943	$ 45,951	$ 79,642
368,267	419,731	477,324	542,751	598,799	431,201
222,128	260,492	298,676	399,533	450,637	407,357
5,037	5,246	5,378	6,649	7,299	6,581
$628,409	$719,478	$831,229	$ 979,876	$1,102,686	$ 924,781
20,694	23,936	32,367	35,581	44,251	49,764
55,311	61,832	77,173	91,420	100,984	101,932
2,381	2,678	3,901	3,821	5,063	5,790
$706,795	$807,924	$944,670	$1,110,698	$1,252,984	$1,082,267
$182,132	$246,420	$237,741	$ 390,034	$ 453,097	$ 600,695
104,144	118,091	124,990	112,896	104,883	147,211
80,443	94,785	112,846	130,137	132,085	2,000
$366,719	$459,296	$475,577	$ 633,067	$ 690,065	$ 749,906
35,402	32,301	128,432	126,672	220,336	216,341
8,286	8,518	9,664	11,926	14,649	—
5,700	5,773	5,252	4,694	4,196	2,183
$416,107	$505,888	$618,925	$ 776,359	$ 929,246	$ 968,430
$ 11,450	$ 9,600	$ 9,053	$ 8,600	$ 7,465	$ 7,465
17,883	18,180	18,529	18,588	18,599	18,599
71,555	78,116	85,195	86,146	85,909	83,914
211,679	230,435	244,508	261,154	248,461	37,674
$312,567	$336,331	$357,285	$ 374,488	$ 360,434	$ 147,652
(21,879)	(34,295)	(31,540)	(40,149)	(36,696)	(33,815)
$290,688	$302,036	$325,745	$ 334,339	$ 323,738	$ 113,837
$706,795	$807,924	$944,670	$1,110,698	$1,252,984	$1,082,267

1970	1971	1972	1973	1974	1975
$381,757	$433,730	$493,859	$556,091	$602,305	$518,387
(15,270)	(15,527)	(15,750)	(15,770)	(18,067)	(79,510)
(5,774)	(9,553)	(12,413)	(8,768)	(4,923)	(1,386)
—	—	—	—	—	(37,523)
$360,713	$408,650	$465,696	$531,553	$579,315	$399,968
7,554	11,081	11,628	11,198	19,484	31,233
$368,267	$419,731	$477,324	$542,751	$598,799	$431,201

EXHIBIT 2

W. T. Grant Company
Statements of Income and Retained Earnings
(as originally reported)
(Case 2.1)

Year Ended January 31	1967	1968	1969
Sales	$920,797	$979,458	$1,096,152
Concessions	2,249	2,786	3,425
Equity in Earnings	2,072	2,987	3,537
Finance Charges	—	—	—
Other Income.....................................	1,049	2,010	2,205
Total Revenues................................	$926,167	$987,241	$1,105,319
Cost of Goods Sold...............................	$631,585	$669,560	$ 741,181
Selling, General & Administration	233,134	253,561	287,883
Interest	4,970	4,907	4,360
Taxes: Current	13,541	17,530	25,600
Deferred	11,659	9,120	8,400
Total Expenses................................	$894,889	$954,678	$1,067,424
Net Income	$ 31,278	$ 32,563	$ 37,895
Dividends	$ (14,091)	$ (14,367)	$ (17,686)
Change in Accounting Principles:			
Consolidation of Finance Subsidiary	—	—	4,885
Recognition of Financing Charges	$ —	$ —	$ —
Change in Retained Earnings	$ 17,187	$ 18,196	$ 25,094
Retained Earnings—Beginning of Period	132,062	149,249	167,445
Retained Earnings—End of Period	$149,249	$167,445	$ 192,539

EXHIBIT 2

continued

1970	1971	1972	1973	1974	1975
$1,210,918	$1,254,131	$1,374,811	$1,644,747	$1,849,802	$1,761,952
3,478	4,986	3,439	3,753	3,971	4,238
2,084	2,777	2,383	5,116	4,651	3,086
—	—	—	—	—	91,141
2,864	2,874	3,102	1,188	3,063	3,376
$1,219,344	$1,264,768	$1,383,735	$1,654,804	$1,861,487	$1,863,793
$ 817,671	$ 843,192	$ 931,237	$1,125,261	$1,282,945	$1,303,267
307,215	330,325	374,334	444,879	491,287	769,253
14,919	18,874	16,452	21,127	78,040	86,079
24,900	21,140	13,487	9,588	(6,021)	(19,439)
13,100	11,660	13,013	16,162	6,807	(98,027)
$1,177,805	$1,225,191	$1,348,523	$1,617,017	$1,853,058	$2,041,133
$ 41,539	$ 39,577	$ 35,212	$ 37,787	$ 8,429	$ (177,340)
$ (19,737)	$ (20,821)	$ (21,139)	$ (21,141)	$ (21,122)	$ (4,457)
(2,932)	—	—	—	—	—
$ —	$ —	$ —	$ —	$ —	$ (28,990)
$ 18,870	$ 18,756	$ 14,073	$ 16,646	$ (12,693)	$ (210,787)
192,539	211,679	230,435	244,508	261,154	248,461
$ 211,409	$ 230,435	$ 244,508	$ 261,154	$ 248,461	$ 37,674

EXHIBIT 3

W. T. Grant Company
Comparative Balance Sheets
(as retroactively reported for changes in accounting principles)
(Case 2.1)

January 31	1966	1967	1968	1969
Assets				
Cash and Marketable Securities	$ 22,638	$ 39,040	$ 25,141	$ 25,639
Accounts Receivable[c]	172,706	230,427	272,450	312,776
Inventories	151,365	174,631	183,722	208,623
Other Current Assets	3,630	4,079	3,982	4,402
Total Current Assets	$350,339	$448,177	$485,295	$551,440
Investments	13,405	14,791	16,754	18,581
Property, Plant, and Equipment (net)...	40,372	48,076	47,578	49,931
Other Assets........................	1,222	1,664	1,980	2,157
Total Assets......................	$405,338	$512,708	$551,607	$622,109
Equities				
Short-Term Debt.....................	$ 37,314	$ 97,647	$ 99,230	$118,125
Accounts Payable....................	58,252	75,885	79,673	102,080
Current Deferred Taxes	36,574	44,667	56,545	65,073
Total Current Liabilities...........	$132,140	$218,199	$235,448	$285,278
Long-Term Debt	70,000	70,000	62,622	43,251
Noncurrent Deferred Taxes	6,269	7,034	7,551	7,941
Other Long-Term Liabilities	4,785	5,159	5,288	5,519
Total Liabilities	$213,194	$300,392	$310,909	$341,989
Preferred Stock	$ 15,000	$ 15,000	$ 14,750	$ 13,250
Common Stock	15,375	15,636	16,191	17,318
Additional Paid-in Capital	25,543	27,977	37,428	59,945
Retained Earnings...................	136,226	153,703	172,329	189,607
Total	$192,144	$212,316	$240,698	$280,120
Less Cost of Treasury Stock	—	—	—	—
Total Stockholders' Equity	$192,144	$212,316	$240,698	$280,120
Total Equities.....................	$405,338	$512,708	$551,607	$622,109

[a]See Note a to Exhibit 1.

[b]See Note b to Exhibit 1.

[c]Accounts receivable comprises the following:

	1966	1967	1968	1969
Customer Installment Receivables	NOT DISCLOSED ON A FULLY			
Less Allowances for Uncollectible Accounts..				
Unearned Credit Insurance..............	CONSOLIDATED BASIS			
Unearned Finance Income				
Net	WITH FINANCE SUBSIDIARY			
Other Receivables				
Total Receivables.....................	$172,706	$230,427	$272,450	$312,776

EXHIBIT 3

continued

1970[a]	1971	1972	1973	1974	1975[b]
$ 32,977	$ 34,009	$ 49,851	$ 30,943	$ 45,951	$ 79,642
368,267	358,428	408,301	468,582	540,802	431,201
222,128	260,492	298,676	399,533	450,637	407,357
5,037	5,246	5,378	6,649	7,299	6,581
$628,409	$658,175	$762,206	$ 905,707	$1,044,689	$ 924,781
20,694	23,936	32,367	35,581	44,251	49,764
55,311	61,832	77,173	91,420	100,984	101,932
2,381	2,678	3,901	3,821	5,063	5,790
$706,795	$746,621	$875,647	$1,036,529	$1,194,987	$1,082,267
$182,132	$246,420	$237,741	$ 390,034	$ 453,097	$ 600,695
104,144	118,091	124,990	112,896	104,883	147,211
80,443	58,536	72,464	87,431	103,078	2,000
$366,719	$423,047	$435,195	$ 590,361	$ 661,058	$ 749,906
35,402	32,301	128,432	126,672	220,336	216,341
8,286	8,518	9,664	11,926	14,649	—
5,700	5,773	5,252	4,694	4,196	2,183
$416,107	$469,639	$578,543	$ 733,653	$ 900,239	$ 968,430
$ 11,450	$ 9,600	$ 9,053	$ 8,600	$ 7,465	$ 7,465
17,883	18,180	18,529	18,588	18,599	18,599
71,555	78,116	85,195	86,146	85,909	83,914
211,679	205,381	215,867	229,691	219,471	37,674
$312,567	$311,277	$328,644	$ 343,025	$ 331,444	$ 147,652
(21,879)	(34,295)	(31,540)	(40,149)	(36,696)	(33,815)
$290,688	$276,982	$297,104	$ 302,876	$ 294,748	$ 113,837
$706,795	$746,621	$875,647	$1,036,529	$1,194,987	$1,082,267

1970	1971	1972	1973	1974	1975
$381,757	$433,730	$493,859	$556,091	$602,305	$518,387
(15,270)	(15,527)	(15,750)	(15,770)	(18,067)	(79,510)
(5,774)	(9,553)	(12,413)	(8,768)	(4,923)	(1,386)
—	(61,303)	(69,023)	(74,169)	(57,997)	(37,523)
$360,713	$347,347	$396,073	$457,384	$521,318	$399,968
7,554	11,081	11,628	11,198	19,484	31,233
$368,267	$358,428	$408,301	$468,582	$540,802	$431,201

EXHIBIT 4

W.T. Grant Company
Statements of Income and Retained Earnings
(as retroactively revised for changes in accounting principles)
(Case 2.1)

	1967	1968	1969
Year Ended January 31			
Sales	$920,797	$979,458	$1,096,152
Concessions	2,249	2,786	3,425
Equity in Earnings	1,073	1,503	1,761
Finance Charges	—	—	—
Other Income.................................	1,315	2,038	2,525
Total Revenues...........................	$925,434	$985,785	$1,103,863
Cost of Goods Sold...........................	$631,585	$669,560	$ 741,181
Selling, General & Administration	229,130	247,093	278,031
Interest	7,319	8,549	9,636
Taxes: Current................................	14,463	18,470	27,880
Deferred.................................	11,369	9,120	8,400
Total Expenses...........................	$893,866	$952,792	$1,065,128
Net Income	$ 31,568	$ 32,993	$ 38,735
Dividends.....................................	$(14,091)	$(14,367)	$ (17,686)
Change in Accounting Principles:			
Consolidation of Finance Subsidiary	—	—	(3,219)
Recognition of Financing Charges	—	—	$ —
Change in Retained Earnings	$ 17,477	$ 18,626	$ 17,830
Retained Earnings—Beginning of Period	136,226	153,703	172,329
Retained Earnings—End of Period	$153,703	$172,329	$ 190,159

EXHIBIT 4

continued

1970	1971	1972	1973	1974	1975
$1,210,918	$1,254,131	$1,374,812	$1,644,747	$1,849,802	$1,761,952
3,478	4,986	3,439	3,753	3,971	4,238
2,084	2,777	2,383	5,116	4,651	3,086
—	63,194	66,567	84,817	114,920	91,141
2,864	2,874	3,102	1,188	3,063	3,376
$1,219,344	$1,327,962	$1,450,303	$1,739,621	$1,976,407	$1,863,793
$ 817,671	$ 843,192	$ 931,237	$1,125,261	$1,282,945	$1,303,267
307,215	396,877	445,244	532,604	601,231	769,253
14,919	18,874	16,452	21,127	78,040	86,079
24,900	22,866	13,579	11,256	(6,021)	(19,439)
13,100	9,738	12,166	14,408	9,310	(98,027)
$1,177,805	$1,291,547	$1,418,678	$1,704,656	$1,965,505	$2,041,133
$ 41,539	$ 36,415	$ 31,625	$ 34,965	$ 10,902	$ (177,340)
$ (19,737)	$ (20,821)	$ (21,139)	$ (21,141)	$ (21,122)	$ (4,457)
—	—	—	—	—	—
—	(21,892)	—	—	—	—
$ 21,802	$ (6,298)	$ 10,486	$ 13,824	$ (10,220)	$ (181,797)
189,607	211,679	205,381	215,867	229,691	219,471
$ 211,409	$ 205,381	$ 215,867	$ 229,691	$ 219,471	$ 37,674

EXHIBIT 5

W.T. Grant Company
Statement of Cash Flows
(as retroactively revised for changes in accounting principles)
(Case 2.1)

	1967	1968	1969
Operations			
Net Income	$ 31,568	$ 32,993	$ 38,183
Depreciation	7,524	8,203	8,388
Other	66	(856)	(1,140)
(Increase) Decrease in Receivables	(57,721)	(42,023)	(40,326)
(Increase) Decrease in Inventories	(23,266)	(9,091)	(24,901)
(Increase) Decrease in Prepayments	(449)	97	(420)
Increase (Decrease) in Accounts Payable	17,633	3,788	22,407
Increase (Decrease) in Other Current Liabilities	8,093	11,878	8,528
Cash Flow from Operations	$(16,552)	$ 4,989	$ 10,719
Investing			
Acquisition of Property, Plant, and Equipment	$(15,257)	$ (7,763)	$(10,626)
Acquisition of Investments	(269)	(418)	(35)
Cash Flow from Investing	$(15,526)	$ (8,181)	$(10,661)
Financing			
Increase (Decrease) in Short-Term Borrowing	$ 60,333	$ 1,583	$ 18,895
Increase (Decrease) in Long-Term Borrowing	—	(1,500)	(1,500)
Increase (Decrease) in Capital Stock	2,695	3,958	844
Dividends	(14,091)	(14,367)	(17,686)
Cash Flow from Financing	$ 48,937	$(10,326)	$ 553
Other	$ (457)	$ (381)	$ (113)
Change in Cash	$ 16,402	$(13,899)	$ 498

EXHIBIT 5

continued

1970	1971	1972	1973	1974	1975
$ 41,809	$ 36,415	$ 31,625	$ 34,965	$ 10,902	$(177,340)
8,972	9,619	10,577	12,004	13,579	14,587
(1,559)	(2,470)	(1,758)	(1,699)	(1,345)	(16,993)
(55,491)	(11,981)	(49,873)	(60,281)	(72,220)	109,601
(13,505)	(38,364)	(38,184)	(100,857)	(51,104)	43,280
(635)	(209)	(132)	(1,271)	(650)	718
2,064	13,947	6,899	(12,094)	(8,013)	42,328
15,370	(21,907)	13,928	14,967	15,647	(101,078)
$ (2,975)	$(14,950)	$(26,918)	$(114,266)	$ (93,204)	$ (84,897)
$(14,352)	$(16,141)	$(25,918)	$ (26,251)	$ (23,143)	$ (15,535)
—	(436)	(5,951)	(2,216)	(5,700)	(5,282)
$(14,352)	$(16,577)	$(31,869)	$ (28,467)	$ (28,843)	$ (20,817)
$ 64,007	$ 64,288	$ (8,679)	$ 152,293	$ 63,063	$ 147,598
(1,687)	(1,538)	98,385	(1,584)	93,926	(3,995)
(17,860)	(8,954)	7,407	(8,227)	1,833	886
(19,737)	(20,821)	(21,139)	(21,141)	(21,122)	(4,457)
$ 24,723	$ 32,975	$ 75,974	$ 121,341	$137,700)	$ 140,032
$ (58)	$ (416)	$ (1,345)	$ 2,484	$ (645)	$ (627)
$ 7,338	$ 1,032	$ 15,842	$ (18,908)	$ 15,008	$ 33,691

EXHIBIT 6

W.T. Grant Company
Other Data
(Case 2.1)

December 31	1965	1966	1967	1968
W.T. Grant Co.				
Sales (millions of dollars)[a]	$ 839.7	$ 920.8	$ 975.5	$1,096.1
Number of Stores	1,088	1,104	1,086	1,092
Store Area (thousands of square feet)[a]		DATA NOT AVAILABLE		
Dividends per Share[a]	$ 0.80	$ 1.10	$ 1.10	$ 1.30
Stock Price—High	$ 31-1/8	$ 35-1/8	$ 37-3/8	$ 45-1/8
—Low	$ 18	$ 20-1/2	$ 20-3/4	$ 30
—Close (12/31)	$ 31-1/8	$ 20-3/4	$ 34-3/8	$ 42-5/8
Variety Chain Store Industry				
Sales (millions of dollars)	$5,320.0	$5,727.0	$6,078.0	$6,152.0
Standard & Poor's Variety Chain Stock				
Price Index—High	31.0	31.2	38.4	53.6
—Low	24.3	22.4	22.3	34.7
—Close (12/31)	31.0	22.4	37.8	50.5
Aggregate Economy				
Gross National Product (billions of dollars)	$ 684.9	$ 747.6	$ 789.7	$ 865.7
Average Bank Short-Term Lending Rate	4.99%	5.69%	5.99%	6.68%
Standard & Poor's 500 Stock				
Price Index—High	92.6	94.1	97.6	108.4
—Low	81.6	73.2	80.4	87.7
—Close (12/31)	92.4	80.3	96.5	103.9

[a]These amounts are for the fiscal year ending January 31 of year after the year indicated in the column. For example, sales for W.T. Grant of $839.7 in the 1965 column are for the fiscal year ending January 31, 1966.

EXHIBIT 6

continued

1969	1970	1971	1972	1973	1974
$1,210.9	$ 1,254.1	$ 1,374.8	$ 1,644.7	$ 1,849.8	$ 1,762.0
1,095	1,116	1,168	1,208	1,189	1,152
—	38,157	44,718	50,619	53,719	54,770
$ 1.40	$ 1.40	$ 1.50	$ 1.50	$ 1.50	$ 0.30
$ 59	$ 52	$ 70-5/8	$ 48-3/4	$ 44-3/8	$ 12
$ 39-1/4	$ 26-7/8	$ 41-7/8	$ 38-3/4	$ 9-7/8	$ 1-1/2
$ 47	$ 47-1/8	$ 47-3/4	$ 43-7/8	$ 10-7/8	$ 1-7/8
$6,426.0	$6,959.0	$6,972.0	$7,498.0	$8,212.0	$8,714.0
66.1	61.4	92.2	107.4	107.3	73.7
48.8	40.9	60.2	82.1	60.0	39.0
59.6	60.4	88.0	106.8	66.2	41.9
$ 932.1	$1,075.3	$1,107.5	$1,171.1	$1,233.4	$1,210.0
8.21%	8.48%	6.32%	5.82%	8.30%	11.28%
106.2	93.5	104.8	119.1	120.2	99.8
89.2	69.3	90.2	101.7	92.2	62.3
92.1	92.2	102.1	118.1	97.6	68.6

EXHIBIT 7

W.T. Grant Company
Financial Ratios and Growth Rates Based on Amounts as Originally Reported
(Case 2.1)

Financial Ratios	1967	1968	1969
Profitability Analysis			
Profit Margin..................................	3.7%	3.6%	3.7%
Assets Turnover................................	2.4	2.3	2.3
Return on Assets...............................	8.7%	8.2%	8.4%
Return on Common Shareholders' Equity............	16.8%	15.5%	15.2%
Operating Performance			
Cost of Goods Sold/Sales..........................	68.6%	68.4%	67.6%
Sell. & Admin. Exp./Sales..........................	25.3%	25.9%	26.3%
Asset Turnovers			
Accounts Receivable..............................	8.3	8.0	7.6
Inventory	3.9	3.7	3.8
Fixed Asset.....................................	20.8	20.5	22.7
Short-Term Liquidity Risk			
Current Ratio...................................	2.62	2.49	2.36
Quick Ratio	1.20	1.15	1.10
Days Receivables	44	45	48
Days Inventory..................................	94	98	97
Days Payables...................................	37	42	43
Operating Cash Flow/Current Liabilities	(15.1%)	3.8%	7.1%
Long-Term Solvency Risk			
Liabilities/Assets	49.7%	47.4%	44.1%
Long-Term Debt/Assets	17.0%	14.0%	8.5%
Operating Cash Flow/Liabilities	(8.7%)	2.4%	4.9%
Interest Coverage................................	12.4	13.1	17.5

Growth Rates		1968	1969
Accounts Receivable		20.9%	16.1%
Inventories		5.2%	13.6%
Fixed Assets		(1.0%)	3.4%
Total Assets		8.6%	12.9%
Accounts Payable................................		5.0%	28.1%
Bank Loans		—	(40.0%)
Long-Term Debt		(10.5%)	(30.9%)
Shareholders' Equity..............................		13.4%	20.0%
Sales		6.4%	11.9%
Cost of Goods Sold...............................		6.0%	10.7%
Sell. & Admin. Expense............................		8.8%	13.5%
Net Income		4.1%	16.4%

EXHIBIT 7

continued

1970	1971	1972	1973	1974	1975
4.1%	3.9%	3.2%	3.0%	2.6%	(7.5%)
2.0	1.7	1.6	1.6	1.6	1.5
8.2%	6.5%	5.0%	4.7%	4.1%	(11.4%)
15.1%	13.7%	11.4%	11.7%	2.5%	(84.1%)
67.5%	67.2%	67.7%	68.4%	69.4%	74.0%
25.4%	26.3%	27.2%	27.0%	26.6%	43.7%
4.6	3.2	3.1	3.2	3.2	3.4
3.8	3.5	3.3	3.2	3.0	3.0
23.2	21.4	19.8	19.5	19.2	17.4
1.71	1.57	1.75	1.55	1.60	1.23
1.09	.99	1.11	.91	.93	.68
79	115	119	113	113	107
96	104	110	113	121	120
45	46	46	35	30	37
(1.1%)	(3.6%)	(5.8%)	(20.6%)	(14.1%)	(11.8%)
58.9%	62.6%	65.5%	69.9%	74.2%	85.9%
5.0%	4.0%	13.6%	11.4%	17.6%	20.0%
(0.9%)	(3.2%)	(4.8%)	(16.4%)	(10.9%)	(9.0%)
6.4	4.8	4.8	4.0	1.1	(2.4)

1970	1971	1972	1973	1974	1975
137.9%	14.0%	13.7%	13.7%	10.3%	(28.0%)
6.5%	17.3%	14.7%	33.8%	12.8%	(9.6%)
12.4%	11.8%	24.8%	18.5%	10.5%	0.9%
39.6%	14.3%	17.0%	17.6%	12.8%	(13.6%)
2.0%	13.4%	5.8%	(9.7%)	(7.1%)	40.4%
N/A	35.3%	(3.5%)	64.1%	16.2%	32.6%
(18.1%)	(8.8%)	297.6%	(1.4%)	73.9%	(1.8%)
2.7%	3.9%	7.8%	2.6%	(3.2%)	(64.8%)
10.5%	3.6%	9.6%	19.6%	12.5%	(4.7%)
10.3%	3.1%	10.4%	20.8%	14.0%	1.6%
6.7%	7.5%	13.3%	18.8%	10.4%	56.6%
10.3%	(5.3%)	(11.0%)	7.3%	(77.7%)	(2203.9%)

EXHIBIT 8

W.T. Grant Company
Financial Ratios and Growth Rates Based on Amounts Retroactively Restated
for Changes in Accounting Principles (leases not capitalized)
(Case 2.1)

Financial Ratios	1967	1968	1969
Profitability Analysis			
Profit Margin.....................................	3.8%	3.8%	3.9%
Assets Turnover.................................	2.0	1.8	1.9
Return on Assets................................	7.7%	7.0%	7.4%
Return on Common Shareholders' Equity............	16.6%	15.3%	15.3%
Operating Performance			
Cost of Goods Sold/Sales........................	68.6%	68.4%	67.6%
Sell. & Admin. Exp./Sales	24.9%	25.2%	25.4%
Asset Turnovers			
Accounts Receivable	4.6	3.9	3.7
Inventory	3.9	3.7	3.8
Fixed Asset.....................................	20.8	20.5	22.5
Short-Term Liquidity Risk			
Current Ratio...................................	2.05	2.06	1.93
Quick Ratio	1.23	1.26	1.19
Days Receivables	80	94	97
Days Inventory..................................	94	98	97
Days Payables...................................	37	42	43
Operating Cash Flow/Current Liabilities	(9.4%)	2.2%	4.1%
Long-Term Solvency Risk			
Liabilities/Assets	58.6%	56.4%	55.0%
Long-Term Debt/Assets	13.7%	11.4%	7.0%
Operating Cash Flow/Liabilities	(6.4%)	1.6%	3.3%
Interest Coverage...............................	8.8	8.1	8.7

Growth Rates		1968	1969
Accounts Receivable		18.2%	14.8%
Inventories		5.2%	13.6%
Fixed Assets		(1.0%)	4.9%
Total Assets		7.6%	12.8%
Accounts Payable................................		5.0%	28.1%
Bank Loans		1.6%	19.0%
Long-Term Debt		(10.5%)	(30.9%)
Shareholders' Equity............................		13.4%	16.4%
Sales		6.4%	11.9%
Cost of Goods Sold..............................		6.0%	10.7%
Sell. & Admin. Expense..........................		7.8%	12.5%
Net Income		4.5%	15.7%

EXHIBIT 8

continued

1970	1971	1972	1973	1974	1975
4.1%	3.7%	2.9%	2.8%	2.8%	(7.5%)
1.8	1.7	1.7	1.7	1.7	1.5
7.5%	6.4%	5.0%	4.8%	4.6%	(11.6%)
15.1%	13.2%	11.3%	11.9%	3.6%	(90.2%)
67.5%	67.2%	67.7%	68.4%	69.4%	74.0%
25.4%	31.6%	32.4%	32.4%	32.5%	43.7%
3.6	3.5	3.6	3.8	3.7	3.6
3.8	3.5	3.3	3.2	3.0	3.0
23.0	21.4	19.8	19.5	19.2	17.4
1.71	1.56	1.75	1.53	1.58	1.23
1.09	0.93	1.05	0.85	0.89	0.68
103	106	102	97	100	101
96	104	110	113	121	120
45	46	46	35	30	37
(0.9%)	(3.8%)	(6.3%)	(22.3%)	(14.9%)	(12.0%)
58.9%	62.9%	66.1%	70.8%	75.3%	89.5%
5.0%	4.3%	14.7%	12.2%	18.4%	20.0%
(0.8%)	(3.4%)	(5.1%)	(17.4%)	(11.4%)	(9.1%)
6.4	4.7	4.5	3.9	1.2	(2.4)

1970	1971	1972	1973	1974	1975
17.7%	(2.7%)	13.9%	14.8%	15.4%	(20.3%)
6.5%	17.3%	14.7%	33.8%	12.8%	(9.6%)
10.8%	11.8%	24.8%	18.5%	10.5%	0.9%
13.6%	5.6%	17.3%	18.4%	15.3%	(9.4%)
2.0%	13.4%	5.8%	(9.7%)	(7.1%)	40.4%
54.2%	35.3%	(3.5%)	64.1%	16.2%	32.6%
(18.1%)	(8.8%)	297.6%	(1.4%)	73.9%	(1.8%)
3.8%	(4.7%)	7.3%	1.9%	(2.7%)	(61.4%)
10.5%	3.6%	9.6%	19.6%	12.5%	(4.7%)
10.3%	3.1%	10.4%	20.8%	14.0%	1.6%
10.5%	29.2%	12.2%	19.6%	12.9%	27.9%
9.5%	(12.9%)	(13.2%)	10.6%	(68.8%)	(1726.7%)

EXHIBIT 9

W.T. Grant Company
Financial Ratios and Growth Rates Based on Amounts Retroactively Restated
for Changes in Accounting Principles (leases capitalized)
(Case 2.1)

Financial Ratios	1967	1968	1969
Profitability Analysis			
Profit Margin....................................	3.8%	3.8%	3.9%
Assets Turnover.................................	1.1	1.1	1.1
Return on Assets................................	4.1%	4.0%	4.3%
Return on Common Shareholders' Equity............	16.6%	15.3%	15.3%
Operating Performance			
Cost of Goods Sold/Sales........................	68.6%	68.4%	67.6%
Sell. & Admin. Exp./Sales	24.9%	25.2%	25.4%
Asset Turnovers			
Accounts Receivable	4.6	3.9	3.7
Inventory	3.9	3.7	3.8
Fixed Asset.....................................	2.1	2.2	2.3
Short-Term Liquidity Risk			
Current Ratio...................................	2.05	2.06	1.93
Quick Ratio	1.23	1.26	1.19
Days Receivables	80	94	97
Days Inventory..................................	94	98	97
Days Payables...................................	37	42	43
Operating Cash Flow/Current Liabilities	(9.4%)	2.2%	4.1%
Long-Term Solvency Risk			
Liabilities/Assets	76.7%	74.5%	74.0%
Long-Term Debt/Assets	51.5%	48.3%	46.4%
Operating Cash Flow/Liabilities	(2.5%)	0.7%	1.4%
Interest Coverage...............................	8.8	8.1	8.7

Growth Rates	1968	1969
Accounts Receivable	18.2%	14.8%
Inventories	5.2%	13.6%
Fixed Assets	1.6%	14.9%
Total Assets	3.5%	14.2%
Accounts Payable................................	5.0%	28.1%
Bank Loans	1.6%	19.0%
Long-Term Debt	(3.0%)	9.7%
Shareholders' Equity............................	13.4%	16.4%
Sales	6.4%	11.9%
Cost of Goods Sold..............................	6.0%	10.7%
Sell. & Admin. Expense..........................	7.8%	12.5%
Net Income	4.5%	15.7%

EXHIBIT 9

continued

1970	1971	1972	1973	1974	1975
4.1%	3.7%	2.9%	2.8%	2.8%	(7.5%)
1.1	1.0	1.0	1.0	1.0	0.9
4.4%	3.8%	2.9%	2.8%	2.7%	(6.8%)
15.1%	13.2%	11.3%	11.9%	3.6%	(90.2%)
67.5%	67.2%	67.7%	68.4%	69.4%	74.0%
25.4%	31.6%	32.4%	32.4%	32.5%	43.7%
3.6	3.5	3.6	3.8	3.7	3.6
3.8	3.5	3.3	3.2	3.0	3.0
2.3	2.3	2.2	2.2	2.2	1.9
1.71	1.56	1.75	1.53	1.58	1.23
1.09	0.93	1.05	0.85	0.89	0.68
103	106	102	97	100	101
96	104	110	113	121	120
45	46	46	35	30	37
(0.9%)	(3.8%)	(6.3%)	(22.3%)	(14.9%)	(12.0%)
75.6%	77.7%	80.2%	82.6%	85.3%	94.0%
43.8%	42.5%	50.2%	47.9%	51.3%	54.5%
(0.3%)	(1.6%)	(2.5%)	(8.6%)	(5.9%)	(4.9%)
6.4	4.7	4.5	3.9	1.2	(2.4)

1970	1971	1972	1973	1974	1975
17.7%	(2.7%)	13.9%	14.8%	15.4%	(20.3%)
6.5%	17.3%	14.7%	33.8%	12.8%	(9.6%)
6.9%	2.9%	26.1%	13.8%	13.3%	1.8%
10.6%	4.1%	20.8%	16.2%	14.6%	(4.8%)
2.0%	13.4%	5.8%	(9.7%)	(7.1%)	40.4%
54.2%	35.3%	(3.5%)	64.1%	16.2%	32.6%
4.4%	1.2%	42.8%	10.7%	22.8%	1.1%
3.8%	(4.7%)	7.3%	1.9%	(2.7%)	(61.4%)
10.5%	3.6%	9.6%	19.6%	12.5%	(4.7%)
10.3%	3.1%	10.4%	20.8%	14.0%	1.6%
10.5%	29.2%	12.2%	19.6%	12.9%	27.9%
9.5%	(12.9%)	(13.2%)	10.6%	(68.8%)	(1726.7%)

OVERVIEW OF FINANCIAL STATEMENT ANALYSIS

Learning Objectives

1. Analyze and interpret changes in the operating profitability of a firm using the rate of return on assets and its components, profit margin and total assets turnover.
2. Analyze and interpret the rate of return on common shareholders' equity, including the conditions when a firm uses financial leverage successfully to enhance its rate of return on assets to increase the return to the common shareholders.
3. Understand the importance of effective working capital management and apply analytical tools for assessing short-term liquidity risk.
4. Understand the benefits and risks of financial leverage and apply analytical tools for assessing long-term solvency risk.
5. Calculate earnings per common share and understand the strengths and weaknesses of this financial ratio as a measure of return to common shareholders.

Most financial statement analysis examines some aspect of a firm's *profitability* or a firm's *risk*. Assessments of profitability permit the analyst to study a firm's past operating performance and to project expected returns in the future. Assessments of risk permit the analyst to judge a firm's success in coping with various dimensions of risk in the past and to continue operating as a going concern. This chapter describes several commonly used financial statement ratios for assessing profitability and risk and illustrates their application to the financial statements of Coke and Pepsi. We introduce these financial statement ratios now to provide an analytical framework for the discussion of alternative accounting principles and other data issues in Chapters 4 through 7. Chapters 8 and 9 explore the rationale and usefulness of each of these financial statement ratios in greater depth. Although we will make some preliminary interpretations of the analytical results for Coke and Pepsi in this chapter, a deeper understanding requires consideration of data issues relating to these firms' financial statements and to the effect of economic and strategic factors on the behavior of the financial statement ratios.

PROFITABILITY ANALYSIS

This section discusses and relates two measures of profitability: (1) the rate of return on assets (ROA) and (2) the rate of return on common shareholders' equity (ROCE).

RATE OF RETURN ON ASSETS

The rate of return on assets measures a firm's success in using assets to generate earnings independent of the financing of those assets. Refer to Figure 3.1. ROA takes the particular set of environmental factors and strategic choices that a firm makes as given and focuses on the profitability of its operations relative to the investments (assets) in place. ROA ignores, however, the means of financing these investments. This measure therefore separates financing activities from operating and investing activities. The analyst calculates ROA as follows:

$$\text{ROA} = \frac{\text{Net income} + (1 - \text{Tax Rate})(\text{Interest Expense}) + \text{Minority Interest in Earnings}}{\text{Average Total Assets}}$$

FIGURE 3.1

Summary of Business Activities (shaded area shows the focus of ROA)

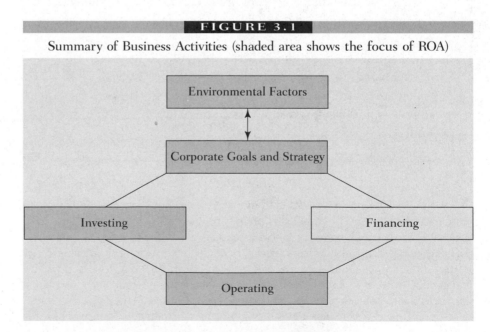

The numerator measures operating income after income taxes, excluding any financing costs. Calculating the numerator is usually easiest if the analyst starts with net income and then adjusts that number for financing costs.[1] Because accountants subtract interest expense in computing net income, the analyst must add it back. However, the firm can deduct interest expense in measuring taxable income. The *incremental* effect of interest expense on net income therefore equals 1 minus the marginal (not average) tax rate times interest expense.[2] That is, the analyst adds back the full amount of interest expense to net income and then subtracts (that is, eliminates) the tax savings from that interest expense. Because accountants do not subtract dividends on preferred and common stocks in measuring net income, calculating the numerator of ROA requires no adjustment for dividends.[3]

The rationale for adding back the minority interest in earnings is as follows: The denominator of ROA includes all assets of the consolidated entity, not just the parent's share. Net income in the numerator, however, represents the parent's earnings plus the parent's share of the earnings of consolidated subsidiaries. The accountant subtracts the minority interest's claim on the earnings of a consolidated subsidiary in measuring net income. Consistency with the inclusion of all of the assets of the consolidated entity in the denominator of ROA requires that the numerator include all of the earnings of the consolidated entity. The analyst accomplishes that objective by adding back the minority interest in earnings. Most publicly held corporations do not disclose the minority interest in earnings because its amount is usually immaterial. Thus, the analyst makes this adjustment only for significant minority interests.

Because operating income in the numerator of ROA reports the results *for a period of time,* the denominator uses a measure of average assets in use during that same period. For a nonseasonal business, an average of assets at the beginning and end of the year is usually satisfactory. For a seasonal business, the analyst should use an average of assets at the end of each quarter.

Refer to the financial statements for Coke and Pepsi in Appendix A and Appendix B, respectively, for the following illustration. The calculation of ROA for Year 8 is as follows:

$$\text{Coke} \quad \frac{\$2,176 + (1 - .35)(\$168) + \$0}{.5(\$11,052 + \$12,021)} = \frac{\$2,285.2}{\$11,536.5} = 19.8\%$$

$$\text{Pepsi} \quad \frac{\$1,587.9 + (1 - .35)(\$572.7) + \$0}{.5(\$20,951.2 + \$23,705.8)} = \frac{\$1,960.2}{\$22,328.5} = 8.8\%$$

---

[1] The analyst should use income from continuing operations instead of net income if the objective is to assess a firm's profitability as a going concern. Chapter 4 discusses this issue more fully.

[2] The marginal tax rate is the statutory tax rate appropriate to a particular type of income or expense. The income tax note discloses the statutory, or marginal, tax rate each year. The income tax note also shows a reconciliation between the statutory tax rate and the effective, or average, tax rate. The latter rate equals income tax expense divided by book income before taxes (see the discussion in Chapter 6). Revenues and expenses that are included in the calculation of book income but do not impact income tax expense (for example, interest on state and municipal securities, goodwill amortization) cause the effective tax rate to differ from the statutory tax rate.

[3] One could argue that the analyst should exclude returns from short-term investments of excess cash (that is, interest revenue) from the numerator of ROA under the view that such investments are really negative financings. We make no such adjustment in this book.

Coke's net income for Year 8 includes an adjustment for changes in accounting principles of $12 million (net of income taxes) relating to postemployment benefits. This nonrecurring charge should not influence the analyst's evaluation of Coke's ongoing profitability. The recomputed ROA for Year 8 excluding this charge is therefore:

$$\text{ROA} \quad \frac{\$2,176 + \$12 + (1 - .35)(\$168) + \$0}{.5(\$11,052 + \$12,021)} = \frac{\$2,297.2}{\$11,536.5} = 19.9\%$$

A comparison of the ROAs of Coke and Pepsi over the last three years after eliminating adjustments for changes in accounting principles from net income[4] is as follows:

	Coke	Pepsi
Year 6	17.9%	8.3%
Year 7	18.8%	8.5%
Year 8	19.9%	8.8%

Thus, Coke has consistently experienced a higher ROA than Pepsi. Both firms experienced an increased ROA during the three-year period.

DISAGGREGATING ROA

The analyst obtains further insight into the behavior of ROA by disaggregating it into profit margin and total assets turnover (hereafter referred to as *assets turnover*) components as follows:

ROA	**=**	**Profit Margin**	**×**	**Assets Turnover**

$$\frac{\begin{array}{c}\text{Net Income} + \\ \text{Interest Expense} \\ \text{(net of taxes)} + \\ \text{Minority Interest in Earnings}\end{array}}{\text{Average Total Assets}} = \frac{\begin{array}{c}\text{Net Income} + \\ \text{Interest Expense} \\ \text{(net of taxes)} + \\ \text{Minority Interest in Earnings}\end{array}}{\text{Sales}} \times \frac{\text{Sales}}{\text{Average Total Assets}}$$

The profit margin indicates a firm's ability to generate operating income from a particular level of sales.[5] The assets turnover indicates the ability to manage the level of investment in assets for a particular level of sales or, to put it another way, the ability to generate sales from a particular investment in assets.

---

[4]Chapter 4 discusses possible balance sheet adjustments for these changes in accounting principles.

[5]One might argue that the analyst should use total revenues, not just sales, in the denominator because assets generate returns in forms other than sales (for example, interest revenue, equity in earnings of affiliates). However, interpretations of various expense ratios (discussed later in this chapter) are usually easier when we use sales in the denominator.

The disaggregation of ROA for Coke and Pepsi for Year 8 is as follows:

$$\textbf{ROA} \quad = \textbf{Profit Margin} \times \textbf{Assets Turnover}$$

Coke $\quad \dfrac{\$2,297.2}{\$11,536.5} \quad = \quad \dfrac{\$2,297.2}{\$13,957} \quad \times \quad \dfrac{\$13,957}{\$11,536.5}$

$$19.9\% = \qquad 16.5\% \quad \times \qquad 1.2$$

Pepsi $\quad \dfrac{\$1,960.2}{\$22,328.5} \quad = \quad \dfrac{\$1,960.2}{\$25,020.7} \quad \times \quad \dfrac{\$25,020.7}{\$22,328.5}$

$$8.8\% = \qquad 7.8\% \quad \times \qquad 1.1$$

Exhibit 3.1 summarizes ROA, profit margin, and assets turnover for the two companies for Year 6, Year 7, and Year 8. Coke's higher ROA than Pepsi's in each of the last three years results from a higher profit margin; these firms realized similar assets turnovers. The next section examines these differences in profitability in greater depth.

FURTHER ANALYSIS OF ROA

Analyzing the Profit Margin. The analyst can identify the reasons for differences in the profit margin percentage by studying the relation between individual expenses and sales. Exhibit 3.2 presents these expense percentages for Coke and Pepsi. Coke's higher profit margin results from two principal factors:

1. Coke has a higher percentage for "other revenues," which primarily represents Coke's share of the earnings of its bottlers. Recall from Chapter 1 that Coke maintains a minority ownership (that is, less than 50 percent) in these bottlers and therefore does not consolidate them. Coke uses the equity method for its investments in these bottlers.

EXHIBIT 3.1

ROAs, Profit Margins, and Assets Turnovers for
Coke and Pepsi—Year 6 to Year 8

	Year 6	Year 7	Year 8
Coke			
ROA	17.9%	18.8%	19.9%
Profit Margin	15.1%	15.3%	16.5%
Assets Turnover	1.2	1.2	1.2
Pepsi			
ROA	8.3%	8.5%	8.8%
Profit Margin	7.7%	7.7%	7.8%
Assets Turnover	1.1	1.1	1.1

	EXHIBIT 3.2					

Analysis of the Profit Margins for Coke and Pepsi—Year 6 to Year 8

	Coke			Pepsi		
	Year 6	Year 7	Year 8	Year 6	Year 7	Year 8
Sales	100.0%	100.0%	100.0%	100.0%	100.0%	100.0%
Other Revenues	2.2	1.1	1.8	0.8	0.5	0.3
Cost of Goods Sold . .	(40.2)	(38.7)	(37.0)	(48.5)	(47.8)	(47.8)
Selling and Admin. .	(39.8)	(40.1)	(40.8)	(40.5)	(41.4)	(40.6)
Income Taxes	(7.1)	(7.0)	(7.5)	(4.1)	(3.6)	(4.1)
Profit Margin	15.1%	15.3%	16.5%	7.7%	7.7%	7.8%

2. Coke has a lower cost of goods sold percentage than Pepsi. Coke's advantage might result from its heavier emphasis on soft drinks relative to Pepsi's more competitive snack foods and restaurants. We explore this possibility more fully later in this chapter.

Note that Coke's higher income tax percentage does not necessarily imply that it has a higher income tax burden. Governmental entities impose taxes on income (that is, revenues minus expenses), not on sales. A more appropriate measure of the income tax burden, referred to as the *effective tax rate,* relates income tax expense to net income before income taxes. By this measure, Coke has a slightly lower effective tax rate, as Exhibit 3.3 shows.

Analyzing Assets Turnover. We can also gain greater insight into the total assets turnover by calculating turnover ratios for particular assets. Analysts frequently calculate three turnover ratios: accounts receivable turnover, inventory turnover, and fixed asset turnover.

Accounts Receivable Turnover. The rate at which accounts receivable turn over gives an indication of how soon they will be converted into cash. The analyst calculates the accounts receivable turnover by dividing net sales on account by average accounts receivable. The calculation of the accounts receivable turnover for Year 8 for Coke and Pepsi, assuming that both companies make all sales on account, is as follows:

$$\frac{\text{Accounts Receivable}}{\text{Turnover}} = \frac{\text{Net Sales on Account}}{\text{Average Accounts Receivable}}$$

$$\text{Coke} \quad 12.0 = \frac{\$13,957}{.5(\$1,055 + \$31 + \$1,210 + \$33)}$$

$$\text{Pepsi} \quad 14.4 = \frac{\$25,020.7}{.5(\$1,588.5 + \$1,883.4)}$$

EXHIBIT 3.3

Calculation of Effective Tax Rate on Operating Income
(amounts taken from Exhibit 3.2)

	Coke			Pepsi		
	Year 6	Year 7	Year 8	Year 6	Year 7	Year 8
Numerator						
(1) Income Taxes.............................	7.1%	7.0%	7.5%	4.1%	3.6%	4.1%
Denominator						
(2) Profit Margin............................	15.1%	15.3%	16.5%	7.7%	7.7%	7.8%
(3) Income Taxes.............................	7.1	7.0	7.5	4.1	3.6	4.1
(4) Profit Margin before Income Taxes	22.2%	22.3%	24.0%	11.8%	11.3%	11.9%
(5) Effective Tax Rate on Operations (1) ÷ (4)...	32.0%	31.4%	31.3%	34.7%	31.9%	34.5%

Coke's accounts receivable turnover was 12.0 in Year 6 and 12.7 in Year 7, while Pepsi's was 13.3 in Year 6 and 14.3 in Year 7. Pepsi's higher accounts receivable turnover probably results from its greater involvements in restaurants where most sales are for cash.

The analyst often expresses the accounts receivable turnover in terms of the average number of days that receivables are outstanding before their conversion into cash. The calculation divides the accounts receivable turnover into 365 days. The average number of days that accounts receivable are outstanding for Coke for Year 8 is 30.4 days (= 365/12.0) and for Pepsi is 25.3 days (= 365/14.4).

The interpretation of the average collection period depends on the terms of sale. If customers must pay within 30 days, then it appears that most customers of both firms pay within the required period. If the terms of sales are, say, 15 days, then neither company collects on average within the required period.

Inventory Turnover.   The rate at which inventories turn over gives an indication of how soon they will be sold. The analyst calculates the inventory turnover by dividing cost of goods sold by the average inventory during the period. The calculation of inventory turnover for Coke and Pepsi for Year 8 is as follows:

$$\frac{\text{Inventory}}{\text{Turnover}} = \frac{\text{Cost of Goods Sold}}{\text{Average Inventories}}$$

$$\text{Coke} \quad 5.0 \;=\; \frac{\$5,160}{.5(\$1,019 + \$1,049)}$$

$$\text{Pepsi} \quad 14.1 \;=\; \frac{\$11,946.1}{.5(\$768.8 + \$924.7)}$$

Thus, Coke's inventory is typically on hand for 73.0 days (= 365/5.0), whereas Pepsi's inventory is on hand an average of 25.9 days (= 365/14.1). Coke's inventory turnover was 4.7 in Year 6 and 5.0 in Year 7, while Pepsi's was 15.0 in Year 6 and 14.7 in Year 7. Pepsi's consistently higher inventory turnover and lower number of days of inventory on hand probably result from its heavier involvement in restaurant activities, which require relatively few inventories.

The interpretation of the inventory turnover figure involves two opposing considerations. A firm would like to sell as many goods as possible with a minimum of capital tied up in inventories. An increase in the rate of inventory turnover between periods seems to indicate more profitable use of the investment in inventory. On the other hand, a firm does not want to have so little inventory on hand that shortages result and the firm must turn away customers. An increase in the rate of inventory turnover in this case may mean a loss of customers and thereby offset any advantage gained by a decreased investment in inventory. Firms must make trade-offs in deciding the optimum level of inventory and thus the desirable rate of inventory turnover.

Some analysts calculate the inventory turnover ratio by dividing sales, rather than cost of goods sold, by the average inventory. As long as there is a reasonably constant relation between selling prices and cost of goods sold, the analyst can identify changes in the *trend* of the inventory turnover with either measure. It is inappropriate to use sales in the numerator if the analyst desires to use the inventory turnover ratio to calculate the average number of days that inventory is on hand until sale.

Fixed Asset Turnover.   The fixed asset turnover ratio is a measure of the relation between sales and the investment in property, plant, and equipment. The analyst calculates the fixed asset turnover by dividing sales by average fixed assets during the year. The fixed assets turnover ratios for Coke and Pepsi for Year 8 are as follows:

$$\frac{\text{Fixed Asset}}{\text{Turnover}} = \frac{\text{Sales}}{\text{Average Fixed Assets}}$$

$$\text{Coke} \quad 3.8 \quad = \frac{\$13,957}{.5(\$3,526 + \$3,729)}$$

$$\text{Pepsi} \quad 3.1 \quad = \frac{\$25,020.7}{.5(\$7,442.0 + \$8,855.6)}$$

The fixed asset turnover for Coke was 4.4 in Year 6 and 4.1 in Year 7, while Pepsi's was 3.1 in Year 6 and 3.1 in Year 7. Pepsi's slower fixed asset turnover probably results from its heavier involvement in the more capital-intensive restaurant activities.

The analyst must interpret changes in the fixed asset turnover ratio carefully. Firms make investments in fixed assets in anticipation of higher sales in future periods. Thus, a low or decreasing rate of fixed asset turnover may indicate an expanding firm preparing for future growth. On the other hand, a firm may cut back its capital expenditures if the near-term outlook for its product is poor. Such an action could lead to an increase in the fixed asset turnover ratio.

Summarizing, the similar total asset turnovers of Coke and Pepsi result from the offsetting effects of higher accounts receivable and inventory turnovers for Pepsi and higher fixed asset turnovers for Coke.

Summary of ROA Analysis.   Our analysis of operating profitability thus far involves three levels of depth:

Level 1:   ROA for the firm as a whole.

Level 2:   Disaggregation of ROA into profit margin and assets turnover for the firm as a whole.

Level 3a: Disaggregation of profit margin into expense ratios for various cost items.

3b: Disaggregation of assets turnover into turnovers for individual assets.

Exhibit 3.4 summarizes this analysis. Coke's higher ROA results from a higher profit margin, which in turn results from higher other revenues and lower cost of goods sold percentages.

Analysis of Segment Data.   Most firms in the United States provide profitability data for product and geographical segments. These disclosures permit the analyst to examine ROA, profit margin, and assets turnover at an additional level (Level 4) of depth. Chapter 7 discusses the accounting issues in preparing segment profitability data.

Exhibit 3.5 presents ROAs, profit margins, and assets turnovers for each of Coke's and Pepsi's product segments. Exhibit 3.6 presents similar data for these firms' geographical segments. Firms report segment income amounts on a pretax basis, so the segment ROAs and profit margins in Exhibits 3.5 and 3.6 exceed those presented in Exhibit 3.4 for Coke and Pepsi.

Coke generated a higher ROA than Pepsi in soft drinks, the result of both a higher profit margin and a higher assets turnover. Pepsi generated a higher ROA than Coke in consumer foods, the result of a higher profit margin. Coke's overall higher ROA and profit margin occur because Coke derives approximately 87 percent of its sales from soft drinks, whereas Pepsi derives only 28 percent of its sales from consumer foods.

The geographical segment data indicate that Coke realizes significantly higher ROAs and profit margins, both inside and outside the United States. Approximately 67 percent of Coke's sales come from other countries, whereas the foreign sales percentage for Pepsi is only 27 percent.

Thus, Coke's higher overall ROA results from more involvement in soft drinks and a proportionally heavier international involvement. Coke expanded internationally earlier than Pepsi and has established itself in many countries as the market share leader in soft drinks. Segment disclosures do not permit analysis of individual expense to sales percentages or individual asset turnovers for product or geographical segments.

RATE OF RETURN ON COMMON SHAREHOLDERS' EQUITY

The rate of return on common shareholders' equity (ROCE) measures the return to common shareholders after subtracting from revenues not only operating expenses

EXHIBIT 3.4

Profitability Analysis for Coke and Pepsi Levels 1, 2, and 3

Level 1

ROA

	Year 6	Year 7	Year 8
Coke	17.9%	18.8%	19.9%
Pepsi	8.3%	8.5%	8.8%

Level 2

Profit Margin

	Year 6	Year 7	Year 8
Coke	15.1%	15.3%	16.5%
Pepsi	7.7%	7.7%	7.8%

Assets Turnover

	Year 6	Year 7	Year 8
Coke	1.2	1.2	1.2
Pepsi	1.1	1.1	1.1

Level 3

	Year 6		Year 7		Year 8	
	Coke	Pepsi	Coke	Pepsi	Coke	Pepsi
Sales	100.0%	100.0%	100.0%	100.0%	100.0%	100.0%
Other Revenues	2.3	0.8	1.2	0.5	1.9	0.3
Cost of Goods Sold	(40.2)	(48.5)	(38.7)	(47.8)	(37.0)	(47.8)
Sell. & Admin.	(39.8)	(40.5)	(40.2)	(41.4)	(40.8)	(40.6)
Inc. Taxes	(7.2)	(4.1)	(7.0)	(3.6)	(7.6)	(4.1)
Oper. Inc.	15.1%	7.7%	15.3%	7.7%	16.5%	7.8%

	Year 6		Year 7		Year 8	
	Coke	Pepsi	Coke	Pepsi	Coke	Pepsi
Receivable Turnover	12.0	13.3	12.7	14.3	12.0	14.4
Inventory Turnover	4.7	15.0	5.0	14.7	5.0	14.1
Fixed Asset Turnover	4.4	3.1	4.1	3.1	3.8	3.1

EXHIBIT 3.5

Profitability Analysis for Coke and Pepsi
Level 4

ROA

	Year 6		Year 7		Year 8	
	Coke	Pepsi	Coke	Pepsi	Coke	Pepsi
Soft Drinks	42.2%	12.6%	42.9%	14.1%	43.4%	12.2%
Consumer Foods	13.8%	18.4%	14.2%	25.7%	16.7%	23.8%
Restaurants	—	13.5%	—	15.3%	—	12.1%

Profit Margin

	Year 6		Year 7		Year 8	
	Coke	Pepsi	Coke	Pepsi	Coke	Pepsi
Soft Drinks	26.4%	12.5%	26.7%	14.6%	27.9%	12.8%
Consumer Foods	6.4%	14.4%	6.7%	19.4%	7.2%	16.9%
Restaurants	—	8.1%	—	9.5%	—	8.3%

Assets Turnover

	Year 6		Year 7		Year 8	
	Coke	Pepsi	Coke	Pepsi	Coke	Pepsi
Soft Drinks	1.6	1.0	1.6	1.0	1.6	0.9
Consumer Foods	2.2	1.3	2.1	1.3	2.3	1.4
Restaurants	—	1.7	—	1.6	—	1.5

EXHIBIT 3.6

Profitability Analysis for Coke and Pepsi
Level 4

ROA

	Year 6		Year 7		Year 8	
	Coke	Pepsi	Coke	Pepsi	Coke	Pepsi
United States	25.9%	17.1%	23.7%	17.2%	27.2%	18.6%
Europe	30.0%	1.3%	34.4%	2.7%	31.4%	1.8%
Other	62.3%	15.7%	60.9%	10.6%	61.8%	11.9%

Profit Margin

	Year 6		Year 7		Year 8	
	Coke	Pepsi	Coke	Pepsi	Coke	Pepsi
United States	13.6%	12.1%	14.0%	12.4%	15.9%	13.8%
Europe	23.0%	2.6%	22.3%	3.9%	22.7%	2.6%
Other	34.1%	10.9%	34.9%	9.6%	34.4%	10.4%

Assets Turnover

	Year 6		Year 7		Year 8	
	Coke	Pepsi	Coke	Pepsi	Coke	Pepsi
United States	1.9	1.4	1.7	1.4	1.7	1.3
Europe	1.3	0.5	1.5	0.7	1.4	0.7
Other	1.8	1.4	1.7	1.1	1.8	1.1

(for example, cost of goods sold, selling and administration expenses, income taxes) but also the costs of financing debt and equity securities that are senior to the common stock. The latter includes interest expense on debt and dividends on preferred stock (if any). Thus, ROCE incorporates the results of a firm's operating, investing, and financing decisions.

The analyst calculates ROCE as follows:

$$\text{ROCE} = \frac{\text{Net Income} - \text{Preferred Stock Dividends}}{\text{Average Common Shareholders' Equity}}$$

The numerator measures the amount of income for the period allocable to the common shareholders after subtracting all amounts allocable to senior claimants. The accountant subtracts interest expense on debt in measuring net income, so the calculation of the numerator of ROCE requires no adjustment for creditors' claims on earnings. The analyst must subtract dividends paid or payable on preferred stock from net income to obtain income attributable to the common shareholders. The denominator of ROCE measures the average amount of common shareholders' equity in use during the period. Common shareholders' equity equals total shareholders' equity minus the par value of preferred stock. Firms seldom issue preferred stock significantly above par value, so the analyst can assume that the amount in the Additional Paid-in Capital account relates to common stock. Because net income to common shareholders in the numerator reflects a subtraction for the minority interest in earnings of consolidated subsidiaries, the denominator should exclude the minority interest in net assets (if any).

The ROCEs of Coke and Pepsi for Year 8 appear below. As was the case with ROA, we base our calculations on income from continuing operations (that is, excluding adjustments for changes in accounting principles).

$$\text{Coke} \quad \frac{\$2,188 - \$0}{.5(\$3,888 + \$4,584)} = 51.7\%$$

$$\text{Pepsi} \quad \frac{\$1,587.9 - \$0}{.5(\$5,355.7 + \$6,338.7)} = 27.2\%$$

Coke's ROCEs were 39.4 percent in Year 6 and 45.3 percent in Year 7, reflecting an increase over the three-year period. Pepsi's ROCEs were 20.7 percent in Year 6 and 23.9 percent in Year 7, also reflecting an increase over the three years. Coke's ROCE consistently exceeds that of Pepsi.

Relating ROA to ROCE.   ROA measures operating performance independent of financing; ROCE explicitly considers the amount and cost of debt and preferred stock financing. The relation between ROA and ROCE is as follows:

Return on Assets		**Return to Creditors**		**Return to Preferred Shareholders**		**Return to Common Shareholders**
$\dfrac{\text{Net Income} + \text{Interest Expense Net of Taxes}}{\text{Average Total Assets}}$	$\rightarrow$	$\dfrac{\text{Interest Expense Net of Taxes}}{\text{Average Total Liabilities}}$	$+$	$\dfrac{\text{Preferred Dividends}}{\text{Average Preferred Shareholders' Equity}}$	$+$	$\dfrac{\text{Net Income to Common}}{\text{Average Common Shareholders' Equity}}$

The accountant allocates each dollar of return generated from using assets to the various providers of capital. Creditors receive their return in the form of interest. The cost of this capital is interest expense net of the income tax benefit derived from deducting interest in calculating taxable income. Many liabilities, such as accounts payable and salaries payable, carry no explicit cost. The preferred stock carries a cost equal to the preferred dividend rate. Firms cannot deduct preferred dividends in calculating taxable income. The income from operations (that is, the numerator of ROA) that is not allocable to creditors or preferred shareholders belongs to the common shareholders as the residual claimants. Likewise, the portion of a firm's assets not financed with capital provided by creditors or preferred shareholders represents the capital provided by the common shareholders.[6]

Consider now the relation between ROA and ROCE. Under what circumstances does ROCE exceed ROA? Under what circumstances is ROCE less than ROA?

ROCE exceeds ROA whenever ROA exceeds the cost of capital provided by creditors and preferred shareholders. If a firm can generate a higher return on capital provided by creditors and preferred shareholders than the cost of that capital, the excess return belongs to the common shareholders.

To illustrate, recall that Coke generated an ROA of 19.9 percent during Year 8. The after-tax cost of capital provided by creditors during Year 8 was 1.5 percent $[= (1 - .35)(168)/.5(7,164 + 7,437)]$. The difference between the 1.5 percent cost of creditor capital and the 19.9 percent ROA generated from using this capital belongs to the common shareholders. The common shareholders also have a full claim on the 19.9 percent ROA generated on the capital that they provided. Thus, Coke's ROCE for Year 8 comprises the following:

Excess Return on Capital Provided by Creditors:
$[.199 - .015][.5(\$7,164 + \$7,437)]$ $1,344.3
Return on Capital Provided by Common Shareholders:
$[.199][.5(\$3,888 + \$4,584)]$ 843.7

Total Return to Common Shareholders $2,188.0

ROCE: $2,188.0/.5(\$3,888 + \$4,584)$ 51.7%

Common business terminology refers to the practice of using lower-cost creditor and preferred stock capital to increase the return to common shareholders as *financial leverage*. Financial leverage worked to the advantage of Coke's and Pepsi's shareholders in Year 6, Year 7, and Year 8.

Disaggregating ROCE.   We can disaggregate ROCE into several components to aid in its interpretation, much as we did earlier with ROA. The disaggregated components of ROCE are ROA, common earnings leverage, and capital structure leverage.

---

[6]If a firm does not own 100 percent of the common stock of a consolidated subsidiary, the accountant must allocate a portion of the ROA to the minority shareholders. Thus, a fourth term appears on the right-hand side of the arrow: minority interest in earnings/average minority interest in net assets.

ROCE	=	ROA	×	Common Earnings Leverage	×	Capital Structure Leverage
$\dfrac{\text{Net Income to Common}}{\text{Average Common Shareholders' Equity}}$	=	$\dfrac{\text{Net Income + Interest Expense (net of taxes)}}{\text{Average Total Assets}}$	×	$\dfrac{\text{Net Income to Common}}{\text{Net Income + Interest Expense (net of taxes)}}$	×	$\dfrac{\text{Average Total Assets}}{\text{Average Common Shareholders' Equity}}$

ROA indicates the return from operations independent of financing. The common earnings leverage (CEL) ratio indicates the proportion of operating income (that is, net income before financing costs and related tax effects) allocable to the common shareholders. The capital structure leverage (CSL) ratio measures the degree to which a firm uses common shareholders' funds to finance assets. CEL and CSL indicate the multiplier effect on ROA of using debt and preferred stock financing to increase the return to common shareholders. Chapter 8 discusses these two components of leverage ratios more fully.

The disaggregation of ROCE for Coke and Pepsi for Year 8 appears as follows:

		ROCE	=	ROA	×	Common Earnings Leverage	×	Capital Structure Leverage
Coke		$\dfrac{\$2,188 - \$0}{.5(\$3,888 + \$4,584)}$	=	$\dfrac{\$2,176 + \$12 + (1 - .35)(\$168)}{.5(\$11,052 + \$12,021)}$	×	$\dfrac{\$2,188 - \$0}{\$2,176 + \$12 + (1 - .35)(\$168)}$	×	$\dfrac{.5(\$11,052 + \$12,021)}{.5(\$3,888 + \$4,584)}$
		51.7%	=	19.9%	×	.96	×	2.7
Pepsi		$\dfrac{\$1,587.9 - \$0}{.5(\$5,355.7 + \$6,338.7)}$	=	$\dfrac{\$1,587.9 + (1 - .35)(\$572.7)}{.5(\$20,951.2 + \$23,705.8)}$	×	$\dfrac{\$1,587.9 - \$0}{\$1,587.9 + (1 - .35)(\$572.7)}$	×	$\dfrac{.5(\$20,951.2 + \$23,705.8)}{.5(\$5,355.7 + \$6,338.7)}$
		27.2%	=	8.8%	×	.81	×	3.8

Coke's higher ROCE results from a higher ROA. Pepsi carries more debt in its capital structure, resulting in a higher capital structure leverage ratio. Pepsi's common earnings leverage ratio is lower than Coke's, because of both a lower ROA and a higher capital structure leverage ratio.

Exhibit 3.7 presents the disaggregation of ROCE of Coke and Pepsi for Year 6 to Year 8. The increasing ROCEs of Coke and Pepsi result from an increasing ROA, CEL, and CSL. The latter results primarily from repurchases of common stock.

EXHIBIT 3.7

Disaggregation of ROCE of Coke and Pepsi Year 6 to Year 8

	ROCE	=	ROA	×	Common Earnings Leverage	×	Capital Structure Leverage
Coke							
Year 6	39.4%	=	17.9%	×	.93	×	2.4
Year 7	45.3%	=	18.8%	×	.94	×	2.6
Year 8	51.7%	=	19.9%	×	.95	×	2.7
Pepsi							
Year 6	20.7%	=	8.3%	×	.73	×	3.4
Year 7	23.9%	=	8.5%	×	.77	×	3.6
Year 8	27.2%	=	8.8%	×	.81	×	3.8

RISK ANALYSIS

The sources and types of risk that a firm faces are numerous and often interrelated. They include:

Source	Type or Nature
International	Host government regulations or attitudes
	Political unrest
	Exchange rate changes
Domestic	Recession
	Inflation or deflation
	Interest rate changes
	Demographic changes
	Political changes
Industry	Technology
	Competition
	Regulation
	Availability of raw materials
	Unionization
Firm Specific	Management competence
	Strategic direction
	Lawsuits

Although a firm should continually monitor each of these types of risk, we focus our attention on the financial consequences of these elements of risk using data from the financial statements. Each of these types of risk ultimately affects net income and cash flows. A firm usually enters bankruptcy because it is unable either to generate sufficient cash internally or to obtain needed cash from external sources to sustain operating, investing, and financing activities. The statement of cash flows, which reports the net amount of cash generated or used by (1) operating, (2) investing, and (3) financing activities, is an important source of information for studying risk.

Exhibit 3.8 relates the factors affecting a firm's ability to generate cash with its need to use cash. Most risk analysis focuses on a comparison of the supply of cash and demand for cash. Risk analysis using financial statement data typically examines (1) the near-term ability to generate cash to service working capital needs and debt service requirements and (2) the longer-term ability to generate cash internally or from external sources to satisfy plant capacity and debt repayment needs. We therefore structure our discussion of the analytical tools for assessing risk around short-term liquidity risk and long-term solvency risk.

SHORT-TERM LIQUIDITY RISK

The analysis of short-term liquidity risk requires an understanding of a firm's *operating cycle*. Consider a typical manufacturing firm. It acquires raw materials on account, promising to pay suppliers within 30 to 60 days. The firm then combines

EXHIBIT 3.8

Structure for Financial Statement Analysis of Risk

Activity	Ability to Generate Cash	Need to Use Cash	Financial Statement Analysis Performed
Operations	Profitability of goods and services sold	Working capital requirements	Short-term liquidity risk
Investing	Sales of existing plant assets or investments	Plant capacity requirements	Long-term liquidity (solvency) risk
Financing	Borrowing capacity	Debt service requirements	

the raw material, labor services, and other factor inputs to produce a product. It pays for some of these costs at the time of incurrence and delays payment of other costs. At some point, the firm sells the product to a customer either for cash or on account. It then collects the customer's account and pays suppliers and others for purchases on account.

If a firm (1) can delay all cash outflows to suppliers, employees, and others until it receives cash from customers and (2) receives more cash than it must disburse, then the firm will not likely encounter short-term liquidity problems. Most firms, however, cannot time their cash inflows and outflows precisely. Employees may require weekly or semimonthly payments, whereas customer may delay payments for 30 days or more. Firms may experience rapid growth and need to produce more units of product during a period than they sell. Even if perfectly timed, the cash outflows to support the higher level of production can exceed cash inflows from customers from the lower level of sales. Firms that operate at a net loss for a period often find that the completion of the operating cycle results in a net cash outflow instead of a net cash inflow.

Short-term liquidity problems also arise from longer-term solvency difficulties. For example, a firm may assume a relatively high percentage of debt in its capital structure as many firms did in the leveraged buyout movement in the late 1980s. This level of debt usually requires periodic interest payments and may require repayments of principal as well. Interest expense is the largest single cost for some firms. The operating cycle must not only generate sufficient cash to supply operating working capital needs but also must throw off sufficient cash to service debt.

Financially healthy firms frequently close any cash-flow gap in their operating cycles with short-term borrowing. Such firms may issue commercial paper on the market or obtain three- to six-month bank loans. Most such firms maintain a line of credit with their banks so they can obtain cash for working capital needs quickly. The notes to the financial statements usually disclose the amount of the line of credit and the level of borrowing utilized on that line during the year.

We discuss seven financial statement ratios for assessing short-term liquidity risk in this section. Three ratios relate the level of resources available to meet short-term commitments with the level of those commitments: (1) current ratio, (2) quick ratio, and (3) operating cash flow to current liabilities ratio. Three ratios relate the amount of working capital required for the level of sales generated: (4) accounts receivable turnover, (5) inventory turnover, and (6) accounts payable turnover. One ratio considers the demands of debt service costs on operating cash flows: (7) operating cash flows to cash interest costs.

Current Ratio.   The current ratio equals current assets divided by current liabilities. It indicates the amount of cash available at the balance sheet date plus the amount of current assets that the firm expects to turn into cash within one year of the balance sheet date (from collection of receivables and sale of inventory) relative to obligations coming due during that period. The current ratios for Coke and Pepsi for Year 8 are:

$$\text{Current Ratio} = \frac{\text{Current Assets}}{\text{Current Liabilities}}$$

$$\text{Coke}\quad .86 = \$4{,}434/\$5{,}171$$

$$\text{Pepsi}\quad .79 = \$5{,}164.1/\$6{,}574.9$$

The current ratio for Coke was 1.01 in Year 6 and .80 in Year 7 and for Pepsi was 1.23 in Year 6 and 1.06 in Year 7. Thus, both Coke and Pepsi experienced a decrease in their current ratios during the last three years, although Coke's current ratio recovered somewhat in Year 8.

Historically, analysts considered a current ratio of 2.0 or 1.5 adequate or satisfactory. As interest rates increased in the early 1980s, firms attempted to stretch their accounts payable and permit suppliers to finance a larger portion of their working capital needs (that is, receivables, inventories). As a consequence, current ratios began moving in the direction of 1.0. Current ratios hovering around this level are now not uncommon. Although this directional movement suggests an increase in short-term liquidity risk, the level of risk is not necessarily intolerable. Recall that accountants report inventories, a major component of current assets for many firms, at acquisition cost. Thus, the amount of cash that the firm expects to generate from inventories is larger than the amount used in calculating the current ratio.

The current ratios of Coke and Pepsi are less than 1.0. Although this level of current ratio is low from an historical perspective, note that 24 percent of current assets for Coke and 36 percent of current assets for Pepsi represent cash and readily marketable securities. Recall also from the discussion earlier in this chapter that these companies realize gross margins (that is, sales minus cost of goods sold) of 50 percent to 60 percent. Thus, inventories have selling prices of 2 to 2.5 times the amount appearing on the balance sheet. Also, Coke reports in Note 6 that it has a $1.4 billion unused line of credit at the end of Year 8, while Pepsi reports in Note 8 that it has a $3.5 billion unused line of credit at the end of Year 8. Thus, a current ratio less than 1.0 is not a major concern for these companies.

Several additional interpretive problems arise with the current ratio:

1. An increase of equal amount in both current assets and current liabilities (for example, purchasing inventory on account) results in a decrease in the current ratio when the ratio is more than 1.0 before the transaction but an increase in the current ratio if it is less than 1.0 before the transaction. Similar interpretive

difficulties arise when current assets and current liabilities decrease by an equal amount. With current ratios for many firms now in the neighborhood of 1.0, this concern with the current ratio gains greater significance.

2. A very high current ratio may accompany unsatisfactory business conditions, whereas a falling ratio may accompany profitable operations. In a recessionary period, businesses contract, firms pay current liabilities, and, even though current assets reach a low point, the current ratio can increase to very high levels. In a boom period, just the reverse can occur.

3. The current ratio is susceptible to "window dressing"; that is, management can take deliberate steps at the balance sheet date to produce a better current ratio than is the normal or average ratio for the period. For instance, toward the end of the period, a firm may accelerate normal purchases on account (current ratio is less than 1.0) or delay such purchases (current ratio is more than 1.0) in an effort to improve the current ratio. Alternatively, a firm may collect loans to officers, classified as noncurrent assets, and use the proceeds to reduce current liabilities.

Given these interpretive problems with the current ratio, the analyst may find its widespread use as a measure of short-term liquidity risk surprising. The explanation lies partially in its ease of calculation. In addition, empirical studies of bond default, bankruptcy, and other conditions of financial distress have found the current ratio to have strong predictive power. Chapter 9 discusses this empirical research more fully.

Quick Ratio.   A variation of the current ratio is the quick ratio or acid test ratio. The analyst computes the quick ratio by including in the numerator only those current assets that the firm could convert quickly into cash. The numerator customarily includes cash, marketable securities, and receivables. However, the analyst should study the facts in each case before deciding whether to include receivables and to exclude inventories. Some businesses can convert their inventory of merchandise into cash more quickly (for example, a retail chain such as Wal-Mart) than other businesses can collect their receivables (for example, an automobile manufacturer such as Ford that provides financing for its customers' purchases).

Assuming that we include accounts receivable but exclude inventories, the quick ratios of Coke and Pepsi for Year 8 are:

$$\text{Quick Ratio} = \frac{\text{Cash} + \text{Marketable Securities} + \text{Receivables}}{\text{Current Liabilities}}$$

$$\text{Coke} \quad .45 = \frac{\$998 + \$80 + \$1,210 + \$33}{\$5,171}$$

$$\text{Pepsi} \quad .57 = \frac{\$226.9 + \$1,629.3 + \$1,883.4}{\$6,574.9}$$

The quick ratio of Coke was .51 in Year 6 and .41 in Year 7, while Pepsi's was .95 in Year 6 and .80 in Year 7. In general, the trends in the quick ratio and the current ratio correlate highly. That is, the analyst obtains the same information about improving or deteriorating short-term liquidity by examining either ratio. Note that the current and quick ratios for each firm follow similar trends. With current ratios recently trending toward 1.0, quick ratios have trended toward 0.5.

Operating Cash Flow to Current Liabilities Ratio.   The analyst can overcome the deficiencies discussed above in using current assets as an indicator of a firm's ability to generate cash in the near term by using cash flow from operations instead. Cash flow from operations, reported on the statement of cash flows, indicates the excess amount of cash that the firm derived from operations after funding working capital needs and making required payments on current liabilities. Because the numerator of this ratio uses amounts for a period of time, the denominator uses an average of current liabilities for the period. This ratio for Coke and Pepsi for Year 8 is:

$$\text{Operating Cash Flow to} \atop \text{Current Liabilities Ratio} = \frac{\text{Cash Flow from Continuing Operations}}{\text{Average Current Liabilities}}$$

$$\text{Coke}\quad .48 = \frac{\$2,508}{.5(\$5,303 + \$5,171)}$$

$$\text{Pepsi}\quad .56 = \frac{\$3,134.4}{.5(\$4,557.6 + \$6,574.9)}$$

The ratio for Coke was .50 in Year 6 and .47 in Year 7 and for Pepsi was .57 in Year 6 and .66 in Year 7. An empirical study utilizing the operating cash flow to current liabilities ratio found that a ratio of .40 or more was common for a healthy manufacturing or retailing firm.[7] Both Coke and Pepsi consistently have an operating cash flow to current liabilities ratio in excess of 40 percent. Thus, even though their current and quick ratios are declining, neither firm appears to have much short-term liquidity risk.

Working Capital Activity Ratios.   The analyst uses three measures of the rate of activity in working capital accounts to study the cash-generating ability of operations and the short-term liquidity risk of a firm:

$$\text{Accounts Receivable Turnover} = \frac{\text{Sales}}{\text{Average Accounts Receivable}}$$

$$\text{Inventory Turnover} = \frac{\text{Cost of Goods Sold}}{\text{Average Inventories}}$$

$$\text{Accounts Payable Turnover} = \frac{\text{Purchases}}{\text{Average Accounts Payable}}$$

An earlier section of this chapter discussed the accounts receivable and inventory turnovers, components of the total assets turnover. We use these ratios here as measures of the speed with which firms turn accounts receivable into cash or sell inventories. The accounts payable turnover indicates the speed at which a firm pays for purchases on account. Purchases is not an amount that the financial statements typically disclose. The analyst can approximate purchases as follows:

$$\text{Purchases} = \text{Cost of Goods Sold} + \text{Ending Inventory} - \text{Beginning Inventory}$$

---

[7]Cornelius Casey and Norman Bartzcak, "Cash Flow—It's Not the Bottom Line," *Harvard Business Review,* July–August 1984, pp. 61–66.

The analyst often expresses these three ratios in terms of the number of days that each balance sheet item (that is, receivables, inventories, accounts payable) is outstanding. To do so, divide 365 days by the three turnover amounts.

Exhibit 3.9 presents the calculation of these three turnover ratios for Coke and Pepsi for Year 8. Pepsi's accounts receivable and inventory turn over more rapidly than Coke's. The faster receivable and inventory turnovers for Pepsi result primarily from its involvement with restaurants. Pepsi's accounts payable turnover substantially exceeds Coke's. The principal explanation for this difference relates to differences in disclosure. Note from Coke's balance sheet in Appendix A that it combines accounts payable and accrued expenses, whereas Pepsi separates accounts payable from other current liabilities. The accounts payable turnovers of these two firms are therefore not comparable. The desirable procedure is to eliminate the liability for accrued expenses from Coke's calculations. Lacking the necessary information to make such an elimination, instead we add other current liabilities to accounts payable for Pepsi to assess the effect of the reporting differences on the accounts payable turnover. The restated amounts for Pepsi are:

$$\text{Restated Accounts Payable Turnover for Pepsi for Year 8} = \frac{\$11,946.1 + \$924.7 - \$768.8}{.5(\$1,164.8 + \$2,064.9 + \$1,390.0 + \$2,170.0)}$$

$$= 3.6$$

EXHIBIT 3.9

Working Capital Activity Ratios for Coke and Pepsi for Year 8

	Accounts Receivable Turnover			**Days Receivables Outstanding**		
Coke	$\dfrac{\$13,957}{.5(\$1,055 + \$31 + \$1,210 + \$33)}$	$=$	12.0 times per year	$\dfrac{365}{12.0}$	$=$	30 days
Pepsi	$\dfrac{\$25,020.7}{.5(\$1,588.5 + \$1,883.4)}$	$=$	14.4 times per year	$\dfrac{365}{14.4}$	$=$	25 days

	Inventory Turnover			**Days Inventory Held**		
Coke	$\dfrac{\$5,160}{.5(\$1,019 + \$1,049)}$	$=$	5.0 times per year	$\dfrac{365}{5.0}$	$=$	73 days
Pepsi	$\dfrac{\$11,946.1}{.5(\$768.8 + \$924.7)}$	$=$	14.1 times per year	$\dfrac{365}{14.1}$	$=$	26 days

	Accounts Payable Turnover			**Days Accounts Payable Outstanding**		
Coke	$\dfrac{(\$5,160 + \$1,049 - \$1,019)}{.5(\$2,253 + \$2,217)}$	$=$	2.3 times per year	$\dfrac{365}{2.3}$	$=$	157 days
Pepsi	$\dfrac{\$11,946.1 + \$924.7 - \$768.8}{.5(\$1,164.8 + \$1,390.0)}$	$=$	9.5 times per year	$\dfrac{365}{9.5}$	$=$	39 days

Pepsi's restated accounts payable turnover still exceeds that of Coke, but the differences are significantly reduced.

Operating Cash Flow to Cash Interest Costs Ratio.   A firm burdened with heavy commitments to service debt can experience short-term liquidity problems just as much as a firm with working capital management problems. A ratio that assesses a firm's ability to service its debt from operating cash flows is the operating cash flow to cash interest costs ratio.

The numerator of this ratio is cash flow from operations before the payment of interest and income taxes. We calculate the numerator by adding the cash outflow for interest and income taxes to cash flow from operations in the statement of cash flows. The denominator is the cash outflow for interest. Coke discloses the cash outflow for interest in Note 8 ($158 million in Year 8) and for income taxes in Note 15 ($650 million in Year 8). Pepsi discloses the amounts for these items at the bottom of its statement of cash flows ($549.5 million and $675.6 million, respectively, for Year 8). The calculation of the operating cash flow to cash interest costs ratio for Year 8 is as follows:

$$\frac{\text{Operating Cash Flow to}}{\text{Cash Interest Costs Ratio}} = \frac{\begin{array}{ccc}\text{Cash Flow from} & \text{Cash Outflow for} & \text{Cash Outflow for} \\ \text{Operations} + & \text{Interest} + & \text{Income Taxes}\end{array}}{\text{Cash Outflow for Interest}}$$

Coke   21.0 = ($2,508 + $158 + $650)/$158

Pepsi   7.9 = ($3,134.4 + $549.5 + $675.6)/$549.5

Each of the companies generated more than sufficient cash flow from operations to meet both working capital needs and interest service requirements on debt. As the next section discusses more fully, Pepsi carries heavier long-term debt financing than Coke and therefore has a lower operating cash flow to cash interest costs ratio.

Analysts often approximate this ratio using amounts from the income statement instead of the statement of cash flows. Referred to as the *interest coverage ratio,* the computation is as follows:

$$\text{Interest Coverage Ratio} = \frac{\begin{array}{c}\text{Income from} \\ \text{Continuing Operations} + \text{Interest Expense} + \end{array}\begin{array}{c}\text{Income Tax} \\ \text{Expense}\end{array}}{\text{Interest Expense}}$$

Coke   20.0 = ($2,188 + $168 + $997)/$168

Pepsi   5.2 = ($1,587.9 + $572.7 + $834.6)/$572.7

Note that the interest coverage ratio provides the same insights about the ability of operations to service debt for Coke and Pepsi as does the operating cash flow to cash interest cost ratio. These two ratios tend to correlate highly. They differ under the following conditions:

1. The firm experiences rapid growth, with additional working capital investments causing income from continuing operations to exceed cash flow from operations.

2. The firm issues debt that does not require periodic cash interest payments (for example, zero-coupon debt or payment-in-kind debt).

3. The firm experiences significant timing differences between financial reporting and tax reporting, so that income tax expense differs from income tax payments.

In cases in which these three conditions are not present, the interest coverage ratio usually serves as a useful surrogate for the operating cash flow to cash interest costs ratio. When the conditions are present and when the interest coverage ratio is less than approximately 2.0, the analyst should use the cash-flow version of the ratio to assess short-term liquidity risk.

Summary of Short-Term Liquidity Risk Analysis. The short-term liquidity risk ratios suggest that Coke has slightly more short-term liquidity than Pepsi. However, neither firm's ratios are at levels that should cause the analyst alarm. Both companies have established brand names and dominate the soft drink industry. Previous sections of this chapter discussed their healthy profitability picture, suggesting that both firms could obtain short-term financing if needed. Their established lines of credit provide a cushion if short-term liquidity becomes a problem.

LONG-TERM SOLVENCY RISK

Analysts use measures of long-term liquidity, or solvency, risk to examine a firm's ability to meet interest and principal payments on long-term debt and similar obligations as they come due. If the firm cannot make payments on time, it becomes insolvent and may require reorganization or liquidation.

Perhaps the best indicator for assessing long-term solvency risk is a firm's ability to generate earnings over a period of years. Profitable firms either generate sufficient cash from operations or obtain needed cash from creditors or owners. The measures of profitability discussed in this chapter therefore apply for this purpose as well. Four other measures used in examining long-term solvency risk are (1) debt ratios, (2) interest converage ratio, (3) operating cash flow to total liabilities ratio, and (4) operating cash flow to capital expenditures ratio.

Debt Ratios. Analysts use debt ratios to measure the amount of long-term debt financing in a firm's capital structure. The higher this proportion, the higher the long-term solvency risk. Several variations in debt ratios exist. Three commonly encountered measures are:

$$\text{Long-Term Debt Ratio} = \frac{\text{Long-Term Debt}}{\text{Long-Term Debt} + \text{Shareholders' Equity}}$$

$$\text{Debt/Equity Ratio} = \frac{\text{Long-Term Debt}}{\text{Shareholders' Equity}}$$

$$\text{Long-Term Debt to Assets Ratio} = \frac{\text{Long-Term Debt}}{\text{Total Assets (Equities)}}$$

The debt ratios for Coke and Pepsi for Year 8 are as follows:

	Coke		**Pepsi**	
Long-Term Debt Ratio	$\dfrac{\$1,428}{\$1,428 + \$4,584}$	$= 23.8\%$	$\dfrac{\$7,442.6}{\$7,442.6 + \$6,338.7}$	$= 54.0\%$
Debt/Equity Ratio	$\dfrac{\$1,428}{\$4,584}$	$= 31.2\%$	$\dfrac{\$7,442.6}{\$6,338.7}$	$= 117.4\%$
Long-Term Debt to Assets Ratio	$\dfrac{\$1,428}{\$12,021}$	$= 11.9\%$	$\dfrac{\$7,442.6}{\$23,705.8}$	$= 31.4\%$

Exhibit 3.10 shows the debt ratios for Coke and Pepsi during the last three years. Pepsi has substantially higher debt ratios than Coke. The high debt ratios relate in part to Pepsi's greater involvement in capital-intensive restaurant operations. Pepsi also used debt to finance acquisitions in previous years. Note the high correlation between changes in these three debt ratios over time. This result is not surprising since they use essentially the same financial statement data. The analyst can generally select one of these ratios and use it consistently over time. Because different debt ratios exist, the analyst should use caution when reading financial periodicals and discussing debt ratios with others to be sure of the particular version of the debt ratio being used. A debt/equity ratio higher than 1.0 (that is, more long-term debt than shareholders' equity) is not unusual, but a long-term debt ratio or long-term debt to assets ratio higher than 1.0 is highly unusual (requiring a negative shareholders' equity).

Interest Coverage Ratio.   The interest coverage ratio indicates the number of times that net income before interest expense and income taxes exceeds interest expense. The interest coverage ratios for Coke and Pepsi for Year 8 are:

$$\text{Interest Coverage Ratio}^8 = \frac{\text{Net Income} + \text{Interest Expense} + \text{Income Tax Expense}}{\text{Interest Expense}}$$

$$\text{Coke} \qquad 20.0 = \frac{\$2,188 + \$168 + \$997}{\$168}$$

$$\text{Pepsi} \qquad 5.2 = \frac{\$1,587.9 + \$572.7 + \$834.6}{\$572.7}$$

The interest coverage ratios for Coke were 13.4 in Year 6 and 17.1 in Year 7 and for Pepsi were 3.7 in Year 6 and 4.2 in Year 7. Analysts typically view coverage ratios of less than approximately 2.0 as risky situations. Thus, neither Coke nor Pepsi appears to have much long-term solvency risk by this measure.

---

[8]Increased precision suggests that the denominator include total interest cost for the year, not just the amount recognized as interest expense. If a firm self-constructs fixed assets, it must capitalize a portion of its interest cost each year and add it to the cost of the self-constructed assets. The analyst should probably apply this refinement of the interest coverage ratio only to electric utilities, which engage in heavy borrowing to construct their capital-intensive plants.

EXHIBIT 3.10

Debt Ratios for Coke and Pepsi, Year 6 to Year 8

	Coke			Pepsi		
	Year 6	Year 7	Year 8	Year 6	Year 7	Year 8
Long-Term Debt Ratio	18.2%	22.4%	28.3%	58.5%	59.8%	54.0%
Debt/Equity Ratio . .	22.3%	28.8%	31.2%	140.8%	148.7%	117.4%
Long-Term Debt to Assets Ratio	9.6%	10.1%	11.9%	41.6%	38.0%	31.4%

If a firm must make other required periodic payments (for example, pensions, leases), then the analyst could include these amounts in the calculation as well. If so, the analyst refers to the ratio as the *fixed charges coverage ratio*.

One criticism of the interest or fixed charges coverage ratios as measures of long-term solvency risk is that they use earnings rather than cash flows in the numerator. Firms pay interest and other fixed charges with cash, not with earnings. When the value of the ratio is relatively low (that is, less than approximately 2.0), the analyst should use the cash-flow version of this ratio discussed under short-term liquidity risk.

Operating Cash Flow to Total Liabilities Ratio.   The debt and interest coverage ratios do not recognize a firm's ability to generate cash flow from operations to service debt. The ratio of cash flow from operations to total liabilities overcomes this deficiency. This cash flow ratio is similar to the one used in assessing short-term liquidity, but here the denominator includes all liabilities (current and noncurrent).

The operating cash flow to total liabilities ratios for Year 8 for Coke and Pepsi using their reported amounts are as follows:

$$\frac{\text{Operating Cash Flow to}}{\text{Total Liabilities Ratio}} = \frac{\text{Cash Flow from Continuing Operations}}{\text{Average Total Liabilities}}$$

$$\text{Coke} \quad .34 = \frac{\$2,508}{.5(\$7,164 + \$7,437)}$$

$$\text{Pepsi} \quad .19 = \frac{\$3,134.4}{.5(\$15,595.5 + \$17,367.1)}$$

The ratio for Coke was .37 in Year 6 and .34 in Year 7 and for Pepsi was .19 in Year 6 and .19 in Year 7. A ratio of 20 percent or more is common for a financially healthy company. Thus, both companies appear to have low long-term solvency risk by this measure, although Pepsi's ratio warrants continuing scrutiny.

Operating Cash Flow to Capital Expenditures Ratio.   A final ratio for assessing long-term solvency risk is the operating cash flow to capital expenditures ratio. This ratio provides information about a firm's ability to generate cash flow from operations in excess of the capital expenditures needed to maintain and build plant capacity. The firm can use any excess cash flow to service debt. The analyst calculates this ratio as follows:

$$\text{Operating Cash Flow to Capital Expenditures Ratio} = \frac{\text{Cash Flow from Continuing Operations}}{\text{Capital Expenditures}}$$

$$\text{Coke} \quad 3.14 = \frac{\$2,508}{\$800}$$

$$\text{Pepsi} \quad 1.58 = \frac{\$3,134.4}{\$1,981.6}$$

The corresponding ratios for Year 6 and Year 7 were 2.63 and 2.06 for Coke and 1.67 and 1.58 for Pepsi. Thus, both of these firms are generating more than enough cash from operations to finance capital expenditures and have amounts remaining to service debt. Recall that consumer foods products are in the maturity stage of their product life cycles and thus the analyst should expect a ratio higher than 1.0.

The operating cash flow to capital expenditures ratio indicates the ability to service debt but does not explicitly consider the future level of debt that a firm must repay. Also, management's discretionary latitude to alter the level of capital expenditures each year affects the ratio. A firm experiencing a poor year in terms of profitability may cut back its capital expenditures sufficiently to induce an increase in the ratio. Thus, the analyst should interpret trends in the ratio cautiously.

Summary of Long-Term Solvency Risk Analysis.   The debt, interest coverage, and cash flow ratios indicate that Pepsi has more long-term solvency risk than Coke, but neither firm has significant risk overall. Both firms are profitable and generate the needed cash flow to service their debt.

INTERPRETING FINANCIAL STATEMENT RATIOS

The analyst can compare financial ratios for a particular firm with similar ratios for the same firm for earlier periods (time-series analysis) or with those of other firms for the same period (cross-section analysis). This section discusses some of the issues involved in making such comparisons.

COMPARISONS WITH CORRESPONDING RATIOS OF EARLIER PERIODS

A time-series analysis of a particular firm's financial statement ratios permits a historical tracking of the trends and variability in the ratios over time. The analyst can study the impact of economic conditions (recession, inflation), industry conditions (shift in regulatory status, new technology), and firm-specific conditions (shift in corporate strategy, new management) on the time-series pattern of these ratios.

Some of the questions that the analyst should raise before using ratios of past financial statement data as a basis for interpreting ratios for the current period include these:

1. Has the firm made a significant change in its product, geographical, or customer mix that affects the comparability of financial statement ratios over time?
2. Has the firm made a major acquisition or divestiture?
3. Has the firm changed its methods of accounting over time? For example, does the firm now consolidate a previously unconsolidated entity?

One major concern with using past performance as a basis for comparison is that the earlier performance might have been at an unsatisfactory level. Any improvement during the current year still leaves the firm at an undesirable level. An improved profitability ratio may mean little if a firm ranks last in its industry in terms of profitability in all years.

Another concern involves interpreting the rate of change in a ratio over time. The analyst's interpretation of a 10 percent increase in profit margin differs, depending on whether other firms in the industry experienced a 15 percent versus a 5 percent increase. Comparing a particular firm's ratios with those of similar firms lessens the concerns discussed above.

COMPARISONS WITH CORRESPONDING RATIOS OF OTHER FIRMS

The major task confronting the analyst in performing a cross-section analysis is identifying the other firms to use for comparison. The objective is to select firms with similar products, strategies, size, and age. Few firms may meet these criteria. One common approach is to use average industry ratios, such as those published by Dun & Bradstreet and Robert Morris Associates or those derived from computerized databases. Exhibit 3.11 summarizes the information provided in two of these published surveys. These published ratios provide an overview of the performance of an industry.

The analyst should consider the following issues when using industry ratios:

1. *Definition of an Industry.*   Publishers of average industry ratios generally classify diversified firms into the industry of their major product. General Mills, for example, appears as a consumer foods company, even though it generates almost one-fourth of its sales from restaurants. General Mills has two of the largest restaurant chains in the United States (Red Lobster and Olive Garden), but the Restaurant category in these publications does not include amounts for General Mills' restaurants. The industry also excludes privately held and foreign firms. If these types of firms are significant for a particular industry, the analyst should recognize the possible impact of their absence from the published data.
2. *Calculation of Industry Average.*   Is the published ratio a simple (unweighted) average of the ratios of the included firms, or is it weighted by size of firm? Is the weighting based on sales, assets, market value, or some other factor? Is the median of the distribution used instead of the mean?

EXHIBIT 3.11

Description of Published Industry Ratios

Robert Morris Associates, *Annual Statement Studies*

1. Presents common size balance sheets and income statements and 16 financial statement ratios by four-digit standard industrial classification (SIC) code.
2. Provides data for all firms within each four-digit industry code for each of the last five years.
3. Provides data for the most recent year only by size of firm, using assets as the size variable. Data include only firms with assets less than $100 million.
4. Common size statements represent the average for each industry category (not clear whether this is a simple or a weighted average).
5. The summaries present the median and upper and lower quartiles for each ratio.

Dun and Bradstreet, *Industry Norms and Key Financial Ratios*

1. Presents common size balance sheets and income statements and 14 financial statement ratios by four-digit SIC code.
2. Presents data for the most recent year only.
3. Gives no breakdown by size of company.
4. Common size statements constructed for the industry using total assets (balance sheet) and sales (income statement) as the base. The common size percentages times the median level of assets and sales for the industry result in a balance sheet and income statement for the median-size firm.
5. The summaries present the median and upper and lower quartiles for each ratio.

3. *Distribution of Ratios around the Mean.* To interpret a deviation of a particular firm's ratio from the industry average requires information on the distribution around the mean. The analyst interprets a ratio that is 10 percent higher than the industry mean differently, depending on whether the standard deviation is 5 percent versus 15 percent higher or lower than the mean. The published sources of industry ratios give either the quartiles or the range of the distribution.
4. *Definition of Financial Statement Ratios.* The analyst should examine the definition of each published ratio to ensure that it is consistent with that calculated by the analyst. For instance, is the rate of return on common shareholders' equity based on average or beginning-of-the-period common shareholders' equity? Does the debt/equity ratio include all liabilities or just long-term debt?

Average industry ratios serve as a useful basis of comparison as long as the analyst recognizes their possible limitations.

SUMMARY

This chapter presents various financial statement ratios for assessing profitability and risk. The large number of financial ratios discussed is probably overwhelming at this point. Enhanced understanding of these financial ratios results from using and interpreting the ratios, not from memorizing them.

Exhibit 3.12 summarizes the financial ratios discussed in this chapter. Profitability analysis proceeds through four levels of depth. Level 1 involves measures of profitability for a firm as a whole: the rate of return on assets and the rate of return on common shareholders' equity. Level 2 disaggregates ROA and ROCE into important components. ROA disaggregates into profit margin and assets turnover. ROCE disaggregates into ROA and leverage components. Level 3 disaggregates the profit margin into various expense-to-sales percentage and disaggregates the assets turnover into individual asset turnovers. Level 4 uses product and geographical segment data to study ROA, profit margin, and assets turnover more fully.

EXHIBIT 3.12

Summary of Profitability and Risk Ratios

Profitability Ratios

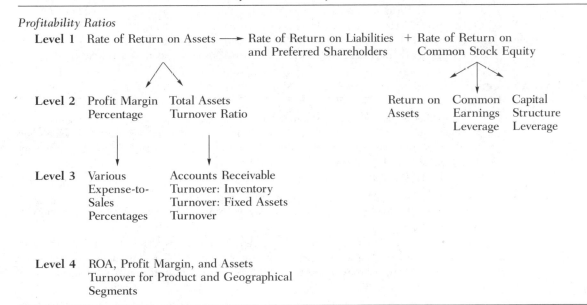

| **Level 1** | Rate of Return on Assets ⟶ Rate of Return on Liabilities and Preferred Shareholders + Rate of Return on Common Stock Equity |

| **Level 2** | Profit Margin Percentage | Total Assets Turnover Ratio | | Return on Assets | Common Earnings Leverage | Capital Structure Leverage |

| **Level 3** | Various Expense-to-Sales Percentages | Accounts Receivable Turnover: Inventory Turnover: Fixed Assets Turnover |

Level 4 ROA, Profit Margin, and Assets Turnover for Product and Geographical Segments

---

Risk Analysis

Short-Term Liquidity Risk	**Ability**	**Needs**
Current Ratio	Current Assets	Current Liabilities
Quick Ratio	Quick Assets	Current Liabilities
Operating Cash Flow to Current Liabilities Ratio	Cash Flow from Operations	Current Liabilities
Working Capital Activity Ratios	Receivable and Inventory Turnovers	
Operating Cash Flow to Cash Interest Costs	Cash Flow from Operations before Cash Outflow for Interest and Income Taxes	Accounts Payable Turnover Cash Outflow for Interest
Long-Term Solvency Risk		
Debt Ratios		Debt Service
Interest Coverage Ratio	Income before Interest and Taxes	Interest Expense
Operating Cash Flow to Total Liabilities Ratio	Cash Flow from Operations	Total Liabilities
Operating Cash Flow to Capital Expenditures Ratio	Cash Flow from Operations	Capital Expenditures

The analysis of risk involves a comparison of (1) a firm's *ability* to generate or obtain cash with (2) its *need* for cash to pay obligations as they come due. This matching must occur with respect to both the amount and timing of cash flows. With the exception of the debt ratios, each of the risk ratios discussed in this chapter relates ability to needs, as the lower portion of Exhibit 3.12 shows. Because the ability to generate cash and the need for cash can differ, depending on the time horizon, the analyst assesses both short-term liquidity risk and long-term solvency risk.

APPENDIX 3.1

EARNINGS PER COMMON SHARE

A second financial statement ratio in addition to ROCE that common equity investors frequently use to assess profitability is earnings per common share (EPS). As Chapter 12 discusses more fully, analysts and investors frequently use EPS to value firms. This section describes briefly the calculation of EPS and discusses some of its uses and limitations.[9]

CALCULATING EPS

Firms that do not have (1) outstanding convertible bonds or convertible preferred stock that holders can exchange for shares of common stock or (2) options or warrants that holders can use to acquire common stock have *simple capital structures*. For such firms, the accountant calculates basic EPS as follows:

$$\frac{\text{Basic EPS}}{\text{(Simple Capital Structure)}} = \frac{\text{Net Income} - \text{Preferred Stock Dividends}}{\text{Weighted Average Number of Common Shares Outstanding}}$$

The numerator of basic EPS for a simple capital structure is identical to the numerator of ROCE. The denominator is a weighted average of common shares outstanding during the period, reflecting new stock issues, treasury stock acquisitions, and similar transactions.

Example 1. Brown Corporation had the following capital structure during its most recent year.

	January 1	December 31
Preferred Stock, $20 par Value, 500 Shares Issued and Outstanding	$ 10,000	$ 10,000
Common Stock, $10 par Value, 4,000 Shares Issued...	40,000	40,000
Additional Paid-in Capital	50,000	50,000
Retained Earnings	80,000	85,600
Treasury Shares—Common (1,000 shares)	—	(30,000)
Total Shareholders' Equity	$180,000	$155,600

---

[9]The calculations of earnings per common share discussed in this section conform to an exposure draft of a proposed reporting standard that the Financial Accounting Standards Board expects to issue as a final standard early in 1996.

Retained earnings changed during the year as follows:

Retained Earnings, January 1	$80,000
Plus Net Income	7,500
Less Dividends:	
Preferred Stock	(500)
Common Stock	(1,400)
Retained Earnings, December 31	$85,600

The preferred stock is not convertible into common stock. The firm acquired the treasury stock on July 1. There are no stock options or warrants outstanding. The calculation of basic earnings per share for Brown Corporation appears below:

$$\text{Basic EPS} = \frac{\$7,500 - \$500}{(.5 \times 4,000) + (.5 \times 3,000)} = \frac{\$7,000}{3,500} = \$2 \text{ per share}$$

Firms that have either convertible securities or stock options or warrants outstanding have *complex capital structures*. Such firms must present two EPS amounts: basic EPS and diluted EPS. Diluted EPS reflects the dilution potential of convertible securities, options, and warrants. Dilution refers to the reduction in basic EPS that would result if convertible securities were exchanged for shares of common stock or holders of stock options or warrants exercised them. This section describes the calculation of diluted EPS in general terms.

Accountants calculate diluted EPS as follows:

$$\frac{\text{Diluted EPS}}{\text{(Complex Capital Structure)}} = \frac{\text{Net Income} - \text{Preferred Stock Dividends} + \text{Adjustments for Dilutive Securities}}{\text{Weighted Average Number of Common Shares Outstanding} + \text{Weighted Average Number of Shares Issuable from Dilutive Securities}}$$

For purposes of calculating diluted EPS only, the accountant assumes the conversion of convertible bonds and convertible preferred stock and the exercise of stock options and warrants. The accountant adds back any interest expense (net of taxes) on convertible bonds and dividends on convertible preferred stock that the firm subtracted in computing net income to common. The accountant also adds back any amount recognized as compensation expense on stock options to the numerator. The additional common shares issuable upon conversion of bonds and preferred stock and exercise of stock options and warrants are added to the denominator. The computation of the additional shares to be issued upon the exercise of stock options assumes that the firm would use any cash proceeds from such exercise to repurchase common shares on the open market. Only the net incremental shares issued (shares issued under options minus assumed shares repurchased) enter the computation of diluted EPS.

Example 2. Assume that Brown Corporation's preferred stock is convertible into 1,000 shares of common stock. Also assume that Brown Corporation has stock options outstanding that holders can currently exchange for 300 incremental shares of common stock. Brown Corporation recognized $600 of compensation expense (net of taxes) related to these stock options during the current year. The calculation of diluted EPS is as follows:

$$\text{Diluted EPS} = \frac{\$7,500 - \$500 + \$500 + \$600}{(.5 \times 4,000) + (.5 \times 3,000) + (1.0 \times 1,000) + (1.0 \times 300)} = \frac{\$8,100}{4,800}$$

$$= \$1.69 \text{ per share}$$

The calculation assumes the conversion of the convertible preferred stock into common stock as of January 1. If conversion had taken place, the firm would not have paid preferred dividends during the year. Thus, the analyst adds back the $500 preferred dividends, which the accountant subtracted in computing net income available to common stock, to the numerator of fully diluted earnings per share. The weighted average number of shares in the denominator increases for the 1,000 common shares that the firm would issue upon conversion of the preferred stock. The accountant likewise adds back to net income the after-tax cost of stock options initially recognized as expense in computing net income. The weighted average number of shares in the denominator increases for the incremental shares issuable.

The accountant makes these adjustments to EPS for complex capital structures only if their effect is dilutive (that is, the adjustments reduce basic EPS) and only if diluted EPS differs by at least 3 percent from basic EPS for a simple capital structure. Both EPS amounts appear on the income statement.

Refer to the income statements and notes on accounting policies of Coke and Pepsi. Both companies show only a single EPS (although both companies separate continuing operations and adjustments for changes in accounting principles). Both companies have stock options outstanding, but neither company has convertible debt or preferred stock outstanding. Coke and Pepsi report in Note 1 to their financial statements that their EPS uses the weighted average number of common shares outstanding in the denominator, implying that the dilutive effect of options is immaterial.

CRITICISMS OF EPS

Critics of EPS as a measure of profitability point out that EPS does not consider the amount of assets or capital required to generate a particular level of earnings. Two firms with the same earnings and EPS are not equally profitable if one firm requires twice the amount of assets or capital to generate those earnings as does the other firm. The number of shares of common stock outstanding serves as a poor measure of the amount of capital in use. The number of shares outstanding usually relates to a firm's attempts to achieve a desirable trading range for its common stock. For example, suppose that a firm has an aggregate market value for its common shares of $10 million. If the firm has 500,000 shares outstanding, the shares will sell for $20 per share. If the firm has 1,000,000 shares outstanding, the shares will sell for $10 per share. The amount of capital in place is the same in both instances, but the number of shares outstanding and, therefore, EPS are different.

For similar reasons, analysts cannot compare EPS amounts across firms. Two firms can have identical earnings, common shareholders' equities, and ROCEs, but their EPSs will differ if they have different numbers of shares outstanding.

EPS is also an ambiguous measure of profitability because it reflects (1) operating performance in the numerator and (2) capital structure decisions in the denominator. For example, a firm can experience reduced earnings during the year but report a higher EPS than the previous year if it has repurchased sufficient shares during the period. When assessing earnings performance, the analyst must separate the impact of these two factors on EPS.

PROBLEMS

3.1 ANALYZING OPERATING PROFITABILITY. Wal-Mart Stores is the largest retailing firm in the world. Its sales mix for Year 11, Year 12, and Year 13 is as follows:

	Year 11	Year 12	Year 13
Discount Stores	78.8%	72.8%	72.6%
Warehouse Clubs.............	20.2	21.5	22.2
Food Distribution	1.0	5.7	5.2
	100.0%	100.0%	100.0%

Exhibit 3.13 presents an abbreviated income statement for Wal-Mart Stores.

REQUIRED

 a. Prepare a common size income statement for Wal-Mart Stores for Year 11, Year 12, and Year 13, with sales equal to 100 percent.
 b. What are the likely reasons for the change in the cost of goods sold to sales percentage?
 c. What are the likely reasons for the change in the selling and administrative expense to sales percentage?
 d. What are the likely reasons for the change in the income tax expense on operating income to sales percentage?

3.2 CALCULATING AND INTERPRETING OPERATING PROFITABILITY RATIOS. Sony Corporation, a Japanese company, manufactures and markets consumer electronics products (video and audio equipment, televisions) and produces and distributes entertainment products (music, motion pictures) worldwide. Exhibit 3.14 presents a partial income statement for Sony Corporation for Year 3, Year 4, and Year 5. Exhibit 3.15 presents selected product and geographical segment data.

REQUIRED

 a. Prepare a common size income statement for Sony Corporation for Year 3, Year 4, and Year 5, with sales equal to 100 percent.

EXHIBIT 3.13

Wal-Mart Stores
Abbreviated Income Statement
(amounts in millions)
(Problem 3.1)

	Year 11	Year 12	Year 13
Sales	$ 32,624	$ 43,915	$ 55,520
Other Revenues	240	374	465
Cost of Goods Sold......................	(25,500)	(34,786)	(44,175)
Selling and Administrative Expenses	(5,152)	(6,684)	(8,320)
Operating Income before Income Taxes......	$ 2,212	$ 2,819	$ 3,490
Income Tax Expense on Operating Income...	(809)	(1,038)	(1,282)
Operating Income	$ 1,403	$ 1,781	$ 2,208

EXHIBIT 3.14

Sony Corporation
Partial Income Statement
(amounts in billions of yen)
(Problem 3.2)

	Year 3	Year 4	Year 5
Sales	¥ 3,929	¥ 3,993	¥ 3,734
Other Revenues	80	57	72
Cost of Goods Sold	(2,838)	(2,929)	(2,756)
Selling and Administrative Expenses	(911)	(938)	(878)
Operating Income before Income Taxes	¥ 260	¥ 183	¥ 172
Income Tax Expense on Operating Income	(145)	(97)	(115)
Operating Income	¥ 115	¥ 86	¥ 57

EXHIBIT 3.15

Sony Corporation
Segment Data
(Problem 3.2)

	Sales Mix			Profit Margin		
	Year 3	Year 4	Year 5	Year 3	Year 4	Year 5
Electronics	80%	79%	79%	4.0%	2.5%	3.1%
Entertainment . . .	20	21	21	8.4%	7.2%	3.2%
	100%	100%	100%			
Japan	38%	36%	37%	3.2%	3.8%	4.0%
United States	26	27	32	4.4%	3.3%	(0.4%)
Europe	26	25	19	8.4%	6.0%	5.6%
Other	10	12	12	9.8%	5.5%	7.7%
	100%	100%	100%			

b. Suggest likely reasons for the changes in the profitability of Sony Corporation during this three-year period. The statutory income tax rate in Japan was 52 percent each year.

3.3 CALCULATING AND INTERPRETING ACCOUNTS RECEIVABLE TURNOVER RATIOS.
Champion International Corporation (Champion) and Scott Paper Company (Scott) are forest products companies. Champion derives the majority of its revenues from supplying printing paper and newsprint for a variety of business and publishing needs. Scott derives the majority of its revenues from supplying personal care and cleaning papers for consumer needs. Champion derives approximately 80 percent of its revenues from within the United States; the comparable percentage for Scott is 65 percent. Data for these two companies for Year 7, Year 8, and Year 9 follow (amounts in millions).

	December 31			
	Year 6	Year 7	Year 8	Year 9
Accounts Receivable				
Champion................	$487	$ 477	$ 470	$ 494
Scott	$702	$ 546	$ 556	$ 491
		Year 7	Year 8	Year 9
Sales				
Champion................		$4,786	$4,926	$5,069
Scott		$4,977	$4,886	$4,749

REQUIRED

a. Calculate the accounts receivable turnover ratio for Champion and Scott for Year 7, Year 8, and Year 9.
b. Suggest possible reasons for the difference in the accounts receivable turnovers of Champion versus Scott during the three-year period.
c. Suggest possible reasons for the significant decrease in the accounts receivable of Scott between Year 6 and Year 7. Sales for Scott during Year 6 were $5,356 million.
d. Suggest possible reasons for the trend in the accounts receivable turnover of these two companies during the three-year period.

3.4 CALCULATING AND INTERPRETING INVENTORY TURNOVER RATIOS. Eli Lilly and Merck develop, manufacture, and market prescription drugs worldwide. Lilly derives approximately 38 percent of its sales from outside the United States; Merck derives approximately 25 percent of sales from abroad. Both firms use the same cost-flow assumptions for inventories and cost of goods sold. Selected data for each firm appear below (amounts in millions):

	Year 6	Year 7	Year 8
Eli Lilly			
Sales	$5,192	$5,726	$6,167
Growth Rate in Sales	24.3%	10.3%	7.7%
Cost of Goods Sold..........	$1,523	$1,718	$1,897
Average Inventories	$ 637	$ 735	$ 868
	Year 6	Year 7	Year 8
Merck			
Sales	$7,671	$8,603	$9,663
Growth Rate in Sales	17.1%	12.1%	12.2%
Cost of Goods Sold..........	$1,778	$1,935	$2,096
Average Inventories	$ 837	$ 942	$1,087

REQUIRED

a. Calculate the inventory turnover ratio for each firm for Year 6, Year 7, and Year 8.
b. Suggest reasons for the changes in the inventory turnover ratios of these two firms during the three-year period.
c. Suggest reasons for the differences in the inventory turnover ratios of Lilly versus Merck.

d. Calculate the inventory turnover ratio for each firm for Year 6, Year 7, and Year 8 using sales instead of cost of goods sold in the numerator.

e. Why does the relative ranking of inventory turnover ratios of Lilly versus Merck computed in part (*a*) differ from those in part (*d*)?

3.5 CALCULATING AND INTERPRETING FIXED ASSET TURNOVER. USX primarily produces steel and petroleum products. Selected data from the financial statements of USX appear below (amounts in millions):

	Sales	**Capital Expenditures**	**Average Fixed Assets**
Year 6	$18,825	$1,392	$11,589
Year 7	$17,813	$1,505	$11,676
Year 8	$18,064	$1,151	$11,681

REQUIRED

a. Calculate the fixed asset turnover for USX for each year.

b. What factors might explain the change in the fixed asset turnover between Year 6 and Year 7?

c. What factors might explain the change in the fixed asset turnover between Year 7 and Year 8?

3.6 CALCULATING AND INTERPRETING THE RATE OF RETURN ON COMMON SHAREHOLDERS' EQUITY AND ITS COMPONENTS. The following data relate to Wal-Mart Stores for Year 11, Year 12, and Year 13 (amounts in millions):

	Year 11	**Year 12**	**Year 13**
Net Income	$1,608	$1,995	$2,333
Interest Expense	$ 266	$ 323	$ 517
Income Tax Rate	34%	34%	35%

	December 31			
	Year 10	**Year 11**	**Year 12**	**Year 13**
Total Assets	$11,388	$15,543	$20,565	$26,441
Total Common Shareholders' Equity ..	$ 5,366	$ 6,989	$ 8,759	$10,753

REQUIRED

a. Calculate the rate of return on common shareholders' equity for Year 11, Year 12, and Year 13. Disaggregate ROCE into rate of return on assets, common earnings leverage, and capital structure leverage components.

b. Suggest reasons for the change in the ROCE over the three years.

3.7 INTERPRETING THE RATE OF RETURN ON COMMON SHAREHOLDERS' EQUITY AND ITS COMPONENTS. Selected financial data for UAL, parent company of United Airlines, appear in Exhibit 3.16.

		EXHIBIT 3.16			

UAL
Selected Data
(Problem 3.7)

	Year 6	Year 7	Year 8	Year 9	Year 10
Rate of Return on Common					
Shareholders' Equity........	23.2%	5.8%	(20.3%)	(36.2%)	(6.8%)
Rate of Return on Assets......	6.3%	2.3%	(2.8%)	(2.4%)	1.3%
Common Earnings Leverage ...	74.4%	54.1%	131.0%	159.6%	(38.0%)
Capital Structure Leverage.....	5.0	4.7	5.5	9.6	13.4
Growth Rate in Sales.........	9.0%	12.7%	5.7%	10.5%	12.6%
Growth Rate in Assets........	7.6%	10.9%	23.5%	24.1%	4.8%

REQUIRED

a. In which years did financial leverage work to the advantage of the common shareholders and in which years did it work to their disadvantage? Explain.

b. Identify possible reasons for the increasing capital structure leverage ratios during the five-year period.

c. What is the likely reason for the increasing common earnings leverage ratio between Year 6 and Year 9?

d. What is the interpretation of a common earnings leverage ratio exceeding 100 percent (Year 8 and Year 9)?

e. What is the interpretation of a negative common earnings leverage ratio (Year 10)?

3.8 CALCULATING AND INTERPRETING THE RATE OF RETURN ON COMMON SHARE-HOLDERS' EQUITY AND EARNINGS PER COMMON SHARE. Selected data for General Mills for Year 2, Year 3, and Year 4 appear below (amounts in millions):

	Year 2	Year 3	Year 4
Net Income	$472.7	$ 505.6	$ 506.1
Weighted Average Number of Common			
Shares Outstanding....................	164.5	165.7	163.1
Average Common Shareholders' Equity	$961.6	$1,242.2	$1,294.7

REQUIRED

a. Compute the rate of return on common shareholders' equity (ROCE) for Year 2, Year 3, and Year 4.

b. Compute basic earnings per common share (EPS) for Year 2, Year 3, and Year 4.

c. Interpret the changes in ROCE versus EPS over the three-year period.

3.9 CALCULATING AND INTERPRETING SHORT-TERM LIQUIDITY RATIOS. Hewlett Packard manufactures and markets electronic products and services for a wide range of business, government, and consumer needs. Net income and cash flow from operations for three recent years appear below (amounts in millions):

	Year 5	Year 6	Year 7
Sales	$14,494	$16,410	$20,317
Cost of Goods Sold	$ 7,858	$ 9,158	$12,123
Net Income	$ 755	$ 881	$ 1,177
Cash Flow from Operations	$ 1,552	$ 1,288	$ 1,142

Exhibit 3.17 presents partial balance sheets for Hewlett Packard on December 31, Year 4, Year 5, Year 6, and Year 7.

REQUIRED

a. Compute the following short-term liquidity ratios for Hewlett Packard for the Year 5, Year 6, and Year 7:
   (1) Current Ratio (year end).
   (2) Quick Ratio (year end).
   (3) Cash Flow from Operations to Average Current Liabilities Ratio.
   (4) Days Accounts Receivable.
   (5) Days Inventory.
   (6) Days Accounts Payable.
b. Assess the changes in the short-term liquidity risk of Hewlett Packard during the three-year period.

EXHIBIT 3.17

Hewlett Packard Corporation
Partial Balance Sheet
(amounts in millions)
(Problem 3.9)

	December 31			
	Year 4	Year 5	Year 6	Year 7
Current Assets				
Cash	$1,077	$ 625	$ 641	$ 889
Marketable Securities	—	495	394	755
Accounts Receivable	2,883	2,976	3,497	4,208
Inventories	2,092	2,273	2,605	3,691
Prepayments	458	347	542	693
Total Current Assets	$6,510	$6,716	$7,679	$10,236
Current Liabilities				
Accounts Payable	$ 660	$ 686	$ 925	$ 1,223
Bank Loans	1,896	1,201	1,384	2,190
Other Current Liabilities	1,887	2,176	2,785	3,455
Total Current Liabilities	$4,443	$4,063	$5,094	$ 6,868

3.10 CALCULATING AND INTERPRETING PROFITABILITY AND RISK RATIOS. Hasbro is one of the leading firms in the toy, games, and amusements industry. Its promoted brands group includes products from Jurassic Park™, Batman®, Nerf®, and Easy Bake® Oven. Its games and puzzles group includes Monopoly®, Scrabble®, Trivial Pursuit®, Cootie®, and Sorry®. Its infant and preschool group includes Mr. Potato Head®, Barney®, G. I. Joe®, Tinkertoys®, and Play-Doh® products.

Exhibit 3.18 presents the balance sheet for Hasbro for the years ended December 31, Year 5 through Year 8. Exhibit 3.19 presents the income statement, and Exhibit 3.20 presents the statement of cash flows for Year 6 through Year 8. Hasbro acquired Tonka Corporation on May 7, Year 6. Hasbro immediately commenced major promotional efforts to revive the brand name products of Tonka.

EXHIBIT 3.18

Hasbro
Balance Sheets
(amounts in millions)
(Problem 3.10)

	December 31			
	Year 5	Year 6	Year 7	Year 8
Assets				
Cash	$ 289	$ 120	$ 126	$ 186
Accounts Receivable	353	551	638	721
Inventories	138	208	218	250
Prepayments	82	146	135	144
Total Current Assets	$ 862	$1,025	$1,117	$1,301
Property, Plant, and Equipment (net)	169	225	251	280
Other Assets	254	700	715	712
Total Assets	$1,285	$1,950	$2,083	$2,293
Liabilities and Shareholders' Equity				
Accounts Payable	$ 85	$ 152	$ 184	$ 174
Short-Term Borrowing	29	36	64	62
Other Current Liabilities	244	406	453	512
Total Current Liabilities	$ 358	$ 594	$ 701	$ 748
Long-Term Debt	57	380	206	200
Other Noncurrent Liabilities	3	21	70	68
Total Liabilities	$ 418	$ 995	$ 977	$1,016
Common Stock	$ 29	$ 43	$ 44	$ 44
Additional Paid-in Capital	286	277	287	297
Retained Earnings[a]	512	580	742	921
Foreign Currency Translation Adjustment	58	60	33	15
Treasury Stock	(18)	(5)	0	0
Total Shareholders' Equity	$ 867	$ 955	$1,106	$1,277
Total Liabilities and Shareholders' Equity	$1,285	$1,950	$2,083	$2,293

[a]The change in retained earnings does not equal net income (Exhibit 3.19) minus dividends (Exhibit 3.20) because of adjustments to net income for nonrecurring items discussed in later chapters.

EXHIBIT 3.19

Hasbro
Income Statements
(amounts in millions)
(Problem 3.10)

	For the Year Ended December 31		
	Year 6	Year 7	Year 8
Sales	$2,141	$ 2,541	$ 2,747
Other Revenues	10	4	4
Cost of Goods Sold	(967)	(1,094)	(1,183)
Selling and Administrative Expenses:			
Advertising	(325)	(377)	(384)
Research and Development and Royalties	(193)	(250)	(281)
Amortization of Intangibles	(29)	(34)	(35)
Other Selling and Administrative	(389)	(462)	(498)
Interest Expense	(43)	(36)	(30)
Income Tax Expense	(84)	(113)	(130)
Net Income	$ 121	$ 179	$ 210

Geographical segment data from Hasbro indicate the following:

	Year 6	Year 7	Year 8
Sales Mix			
United States	59%	59%	61%
Foreign	41	41	39
	100%	100%	100%

	Year 6	Year 7	Year 8
Rate of Return on Assets			
United States	8.8%	13.3%	15.7%
Foreign	20.3%	20.8%	16.6%

	Year 6	Year 7	Year 8
Profit Margin			
United States	9.4%	12.8%	14.5%
Foreign	13.5%	12.7%	11.6%

	Year 6	Year 7	Year 8
Assets Turnover			
United States	0.92	1.04	1.08
Foreign	1.51	1.64	1.43

EXHIBIT 3.20

Hasbro
Statements of Cash Flows
(amounts in millions)
(Problem 3.10)

	For the Year Ended January 31		
	Year 6	Year 7	Year 8
Operations			
Net Income	$ 121	$ 179	$ 210
Depreciation and Amortization	82	96	100
Addbacks and Subtractions—Net	(60)	2	(8)
(Increase) Decrease in Accounts Receivable	(54)	(133)	(91)
(Increase) Decrease in Inventories	24	(15)	(34)
(Increase) Decrease in Prepayments	(8)	10	(8)
Increase (Decrease) in Accounts Payable and			
Other Current Liabilities	15	91	48
Cash Flow from Operations.................	$ 120	$ 230	$ 217
Investing			
Property, Plant, and Equipment Acquired	$ (56)	$ (90)	$(100)
Other Investing Transactions	(348)	(4)	(26)
Cash Flow from Investing	$(404)	$ (94)	$(126)
Financing			
Increase in Short-Term Borrowing	0	$ 38	0
Increase in Long-Term Borrowing	$ 300	0	0
Increase in Common Stock	17	16	$ 10
Decrease in Short-Term Borrowing	(68)	0	(9)
Decrease in Long-Term Borrowing.............	(113)	(161)	(12)
Dividends	(13)	(16)	(20)
Other Financing Transactions	(8)	(7)	0
Cash Flow from Financing	$ 115	$(130)	$ (31)
Change in Cash............................	$(169)	$ 6	$ 60
Cash—Beginning of Year.....................	289	120	126
Cash—End of Year..........................	$ 120	$ 126	$ 186

REQUIRED

a. Exhibit 3.21 presents profitability and risk ratios for Hasbro for Year 6 and Year 7. Calculate the amounts of these financial ratios for Year 8. The income tax rate was 34 percent for Year 6 and Year 7 and 35 percent for Year 8.

b. Assess the changes in the profitability of Hasbro over the three-year period, suggesting reasons for the changes observed.

c. Assess the short-term liquidity and long-term solvency risk of Hasbro.

3.11 CALCULATING AND INTERPRETING PROFITABILITY AND RISK RATIOS. Lands' End Corporation sells men's, women's, and children's clothing through catalogs. Financial statements for Lands' End for Year 2, Year 3, and Year 4 appear in Exhibit 3.22 (balance

EXHIBIT 3.21

Hasbro
Financial Statement Ratio Analysis
(Problem 3.10)

	Year 6	Year 7	Year 8
Profit Margin for Rate of Return on Assets	7.0%	8.0%	
Assets Turnover	1.32	1.26	
Rate of Return on Assets	9.2%	10.1%	
Common Earnings Leverage	81.0%	88.3%	
Capital Structure Leverage.	1.8	2.0	
Rate of Return on Common Shareholders' Equity	13.3%	17.4%	
Cost of Goods Sold ÷ Sales	45.2%	43.1%	
Selling and Administrative Expense ÷ Sales.	43.7%	44.2%	
Income Tax Expense (excluding tax effects of interest expense) ÷ Sales	4.6%	4.9%	
Accounts Receivable Turnover.	4.7	4.3	
Inventory Turnover	5.6	5.1	
Fixed Asset Turnover	10.9	10.7	
Current Ratio.	1.7	1.6	
Quick Ratio	1.1	1.1	
Operating Cash Flow ÷ Average Current Liabilities . . .	25.2%	35.5%	
Days Accounts Receivable	77	85	
Days Inventory.	65	71	
Days Accounts Payable	42	56	
Long-Term Debt Ratio	28.5%	15.7%	
Debt-Equity Ratio	39.8%	18.6%	
Long-Term Debt ÷ Total Assets	19.5%	9.9%	
Operating Cash Flow ÷ Average Total Liabilities.	17.0%	23.3%	
Interest Coverage Ratio.	5.8	9.1	
Operating Cash Flow ÷ Capital Expenditures	2.1	2.6	

sheet), Exhibit 3.23 (income statement), and Exhibit 3.24 (statement of cash flows). Exhibit 3.25 presents financial statement ratios for Lands' End for Year 2 and Year 3. The income tax rate during these two years was 34 percent.

REQUIRED

a. Calculate the ratios in Exhibit 3.25 for Year 4. The income tax rate for Year 4 is 35 percent.

b. Assess the changes in the profitability of Lands' End during the three-year period, offering possible explanations for the changes observed.

c. Assess the short-term liquidity risk and long-term solvency risk of Lands' End.

3.12 INTERPRETING PROFITABILITY AND RISK RATIOS. Microsoft Corporation is one of the largest and fastest-growing software development firms in the world. It sells both operating systems for computers (including MS-DOS and MS Windows) and applications software (including *Excel, Word, PowerPoint, Office,* and *Access*). It also sells mouse pointing devices in its hardware group. Exhibit 3.26 presents financial statement ratios for Microsoft for Year 4, Year 5, and Year 6.

EXHIBIT 3.22

Lands' End—Balance Sheets
(amounts in thousands)
(Problem 3.11)

	December 31			
	Year 1	Year 2	Year 3	Year 4
Assets				
Cash	$ 27,264	$ 1,390	$ 22,754	$ 21,569
Accounts Receivable	1,209	830	465	3,644
Inventories	73,863	122,558	106,057	149,688
Prepayments..............................	5,488	6,495	8,255	17,375
Total Current Assets......................	$107,824	$131,273	$137,531	$192,276
Property, Plant, and Equipment (net)..........	77,576	74,527	74,229	79,691
Other Assets..............................	—	—	43	1,863
Total Assets	$185,400	$205,800	$211,803	$273,830
Liabilities and Shareholders' Equity				
Accounts Payable..........................	$ 37,797	$ 28,351	$ 36,976	$ 54,855
Short-Term Borrowing	0	13,000	0	0
Current Portion of Long-Term Debt..........	1,682	1,682	0	40
Other Current Liabilities	21,295	31,515	30,339	36,154
Total Current Liabilities...................	$ 60,774	$ 74,548	$ 67,315	$ 91,049
Long-Term Debt	3,349	1,667	0	40
Other Noncurrent Liabilities	4,451	2,953	5,100	6,756
Total Liabilities	$ 68,574	$ 79,168	$ 72,415	$ 97,845
Common Stock	$ 201	$ 201	$ 201	$ 201
Additional Paid-in Capital	31,136	31,296	31,577	31,287
Retained Earnings..........................	98,381	123,418	153,324	192,406
Treasury Stock............................	(12,892)	(28,283)	(45,714)	(47,909)
Total Shareholders' Equity.................	$116,826	$126,632	$139,388	$175,985
Total Liabilities and Shareholders' Equity	$185,400	$205,800	$211,803	$273,830

EXHIBIT 3.23

Lands' End—Income Statements
(amounts in thousands)
(Problem 3.11)

	For the Year Ended December 31		
	Year 2	Year 3	Year 4
Sales	$ 683,427	$ 733,623	$ 869,975
Cost of Goods Sold...................	(395,302)	(427,292)	(512,521)
Selling and Administrative Expenses ...	(239,083)	(250,968)	(287,225)
Interest Expense	(1,550)	(1,330)	(359)
Income Tax Expense..................	(18,760)	(20,533)	(27,441)
Net Income	$ 28,732	$ 33,500	$ 42,429

EXHIBIT 3.24

Lands' End
Statements of Cash Flows
(amounts in thousands)
(Problem 3.11)

	For the Year Ended January 31		
	Year 2	Year 3	Year 4
Operations			
Net Income	$ 28,732	$ 33,500	$ 42,429
Depreciation and Amortization	7,428	7,900	8,286
Addbacks and Subtractions—Net	(926)	510	(757)
(Increase) Decrease in Accounts Receivable ..	379	365	(3,179)
(Increase) Decrease in Inventories	(48,695)	16,501	(43,631)
(Increase) Decrease in Prepayments	(1,007)	999	(6,291)
Increase (Decrease) in Accounts Payable	(9,446)	8,625	17,879
Increase (Decrease) in Other Current			
Liabilities	10,220	(1,176)	6,317
Cash Flow from Operations..............	$(13,315)	$ 67,224	$ 21,053
Investing			
Property, Plant, and Equipment Acquired	$ (4,791)	$ (8,576)	$(15,997)
Cash Flow from Investing	$ (4,791)	$ (8,576)	$(15,997)
Financing			
Increase in Short-Term Borrowing	$ 13,000	0	$ 80
Increase in Common Stock	0	$ 2,551	132
Decrease in Short-Term Borrowing	0	(13,000)	0
Decrease in Long-Term Borrowing..........	(1,682)	(3,349)	0
Decrease in Common Stock................	(15,391)	(20,792)	(2,861)
Dividends	(3,695)	(3,589)	(3,592)
Other Financing Transactions	0	895	0
Cash Flow from Financing	$ (7,768)	$(37,284)	$ (6,241)
Change in Cash..........................	$(25,874)	$ 21,364	$ (1,185)
Cash—Beginning of Year..................	27,264	1,390	22,754
Cash—End of Year.......................	$ 1,390	$ 22,754	$ 21,569

REQUIRED (Problem 3.12)

a. What are the likely reasons for the increased profit margin for rate of return on assets between Year 4 and Year 5?

b. What are the likely reasons for the decreased profit margin for rate of return on assets between Year 5 and Year 6?

c. What are the likely reasons for the decreased total assets turnover during the three years?

d. Suggest reasons for the increased accounts receivable turnover during the three years.

EXHIBIT 3.25

Lands' End
Financial Statement Ratio Analysis
(Problem 3.11)

	Year 2	Year 3	Year 4
Profit Margin for Rate of Return on Assets	4.4%	4.7%	
Assets Turnover................................	3.5	3.5	
Rate of Return on Assets	15.2%	16.5%	
Common Earnings Leverage	96.6%	97.4%	
Capital Structure Leverage.....................	1.6	1.6	
Rate of Return on Common Shareholders' Equity ..	23.6%	25.2%	
Cost of Goods Sold ÷ Sales	57.8%	58.2%	
Selling and Administrative Expense ÷ Sales.......	35.0%	34.2%	
Income Tax Expense (excluding tax effects of			
interest expense) ÷ Sales	2.8%	2.9%	
Accounts Receivable Turnover..................	670.4	1133.0	
Inventory Turnover	4.0	3.7	
Fixed Asset Turnover	9.0	9.9	
Current Ratio.................................	1.8	2.0	
Quick Ratio	0	.3	
Days Accounts Receivable	1	0	
Days Inventory................................	91	98	
Days Accounts Payable	27	29	
Operating Cash Flow ÷ Average Current			
Liabilities	(19.7%)	94.8%	
Total Liabilities ÷ Total Assets	38.5%	34.2%	
Long-Term Debt ÷ Total Assets	0.8%	0	
Debt-Equity Ratio	1.3%	0	
Operating Cash Flow ÷ Average Total Liabilities...	(18.0%)	88.7%	
Interest Coverage Ratio........................	31.6	41.6	
Operating Cash Flow ÷ Capital Expenditures	(2.8)	7.8	

e. Suggest reasons for the decrease in the inventory turnover ratio between Year 5 and Year 6.

f. What are the likely reasons for the increases in the current and quick ratios during the three years?

g. Suggest reasons for the fact that Microsoft carries no long-term debt.

3.13 INTERPRETING PROFITABILITY AND RISK RATIOS. NIKE maintains a leading market position in athletic footwear and sports apparel. It emphasizes performance over fashion. Most of the ideas for NIKE's technological innovations come from its Sport Research Laboratory, which conducts extensive studies on a wide variety of basic and applied research projects, from children's foot morphology to the problem of turf toe in football to apparel aerodynamics. The rationale for its performance-driven strategy has come under increasing attack in recent years as the athletic footwear industry in the United States has matured and the European markets are viewed as being not too far behind. The principal growth market is East Asia.

EXHIBIT 3.26

Microsoft Corporation
Financial Statement Ratio Analysis
(Problem 3.12)

	Year 4	Year 5	Year 6
Profit Margin for Rate of Return on Assets	25.3%	25.7%	25.4%
Assets Turnover...................................	1.34	1.29	1.16
Rate of Return on Assets	33.9%	33.1%	29.6%
Common Earnings Leverage	99.3%	99.8%	100.0%
Capital Structure Leverage......................	1.2	1.2	1.2
Rate of Return on Common Shareholders' Equity ...	40.8%	40.0%	35.1%
Cost of Goods Sold ÷ Sales	19.6%	16.9%	16.9%
Selling and Administrative Expense ÷ Sales........	33.2%	34.6%	35.5%
Research and Development Expense ÷ Sales	12.8%	12.8%	12.5%
Income Tax Expense (excluding tax effects of interest expense) ÷ Sales	11.4%	12.1%	11.9%
Accounts Receivable Turnover....................	8.7	10.8	12.3
Inventory Turnover	7.0	7.0	5.9
Fixed Asset Turnover	4.3	4.3	4.6
Current Ratio...................................	3.5	4.0	5.1
Quick Ratio	3.2	3.6	4.7
Operating Cash Flow ÷ Average Current Liabilities .	237.9%	242.2%	212.7%
Days Accounts Receivable	42	34	30
Days Inventory..................................	52	52	61
Days Accounts Payable	71	102	118
Long-Term Debt Ratio	0	0	0
Debt-Equity Ratio	0	0	0
Long-Term Debt ÷ Total Assets	0	0	0
Operating Cash Flow ÷ Average Total Liabilities....	237.9%	242.2%	212.7%
Interest Coverage Ratio..........................	135.2	521.5	N/A
Operating Cash Flow ÷ Capital Expenditures	2.2	2.8	4.6
Sales (Year 3 = 100).............................	155.8	233.2	317.7
Sales—United States (Year 3 = 100)	141.2	219.0	309.6
Sales—Europe (Year 3 = 100)	178.1	268.5	339.6
Sales—Other International (Year 3 = 100).........	153.3	213.1	309.5

Sales Mix

	Year 4	Year 5	Year 6
Operating Systems Software	37	41	35
Applications Software..........................	51	50	59
Hardware	12	9	6
	100%	100%	100%

Sales Mix

	Year 4	Year 5	Year 6
United States	57%	59%	61%
Europe	34	32	30
Other International............................	9	9	9
	100%	100%	100%

Rate of Return on Assets

	Year 4	Year 5	Year 6
United States	29.2%	35.7%	32.6%
Europe	48.4%	37.7%	31.8%
Other International............................	5.8%	3.8%	5.8%

Exh. 3.26—Continued	Year 4	Year 5	Year 6
Profit Margin			
United States	30.8%	35.4%	36.2%
Europe	39.5%	32.3%	27.9%
Other International	6.4%	4.0%	4.6%
Assets Turnover			
United States	.9	1.0	.9
Europe	1.2	1.2	1.1
Other International	.9	.9	1.3

Nearly 99 percent of the footwear sold worldwide is manufactured in East Asia. Athletic footwear companies do not own the manufacturing facilities but place personnel in the factories to oversee the manufacturing process. The manufacturing process is labor intensive, with sewing machines used as the primary equipment. U.S. athletic footwear companies typically price their purchases of footwear from these factories in U.S. dollars. Footwear and sportswear companies sell their products through various department, specialty, and discount stores. Their sales forces function to educate retailers on new product innovations, store display design, and similar activities. Advertising and promotion expenditures, including endorsements by nationally known athletes and entertainers, create demand and pull products through the distribution channel.

Exhibit 3.27 presents financial statement ratios and other data for NIKE for Year 5, Year 6, and Year 7.

REQUIRED

a. What are the likely reasons for the decreasing profit margin for the rate of return on assets during the three years?

b. What is the likely reason for the decrease in the assets turnover between Year 6 and Year 7?

c. What is the likely reason for the increasing common earnings leverage ratio during the three years?

d. What are the likely reasons for the decrease in the cash flow from operations to average current liabilities ratio between Year 5 and Year 6?

e. What are the likely reasons for the increase in the interest coverage ratio between Year 6 and Year 7?

f. What is the likely reason for the rapid fixed asset turnover in all three years?

g. What is the likely reason for the relatively small amount of long-term debt in the capital structure in all three years?

h. What evidence do you see that the U.S. market for athletic footwear has matured, that the European market is rapidly maturing, and that East Asia is the rapid growth area?

3.14 INTERPRETING PROFITABILITY AND RISK RATIOS. Texas Instruments is a high-technology company with sales or manufacturing operations in more than 30 countries. Its products include semiconductors, printers and consumer electronics products, defense electronics systems, software productivity tools, and metallurgical materials. Exhibit 3.28 presents financial statement ratios and other data for Texas Instruments for Year 4, Year 5, and Year 6.

EXHIBIT 3.27

NIKE
Financial Statement Ratio Analysis
(Problem 3.13)

	Year 5	Year 6	Year 7
Profit Margin for Rate of Return on Assets	10.3%	9.7%	8.1%
Assets Turnover................................	1.9	1.9	1.7
Rate of Return on Assets	19.5%	18.8%	13.5%
Common Earnings Leverage	94.2%	95.5%	96.8%
Capital Structure Leverage......................	1.5	1.4	1.3
Rate of Return on Common Shareholders' Equity ...	27.8%	24.5%	17.6%
Cost of Goods Sold ÷ Sales	61.3%	60.7%	60.7%
Selling and Administrative Expense ÷ Sales........	22.4%	23.5%	25.7%
Income Tax Expense (excluding tax effects of interest expense) ÷ Sales	6.0%	6.1%	5.2%
Accounts Receivable Turnover....................	6.1	6.2	5.5
Inventory Turnover	3.9	4.5	4.3
Fixed Asset Turnover	10.7	10.9	9.7
Current Ratio..................................	3.30	3.58	3.15
Quick Ratio	2.04	2.12	2.18
Operating Cash Flow ÷ Average Current Liabilities .	83.1%	60.8%	113.6%
Days Accounts Receivable	60	59	66
Days Inventory.................................	92	81	84
Days Accounts Payable	28	20	29
Long-Term Debt Ratio	4.6%	.9%	.7%
Debt-Equity Ratio	5.2%	.9%	.7%
Long-Term Debt ÷ Total Assets	3.7%	.7%	.5%
Operating Cash Flow ÷ Average Total Liabilities....	71.6%	49.0%	98.2%
Interest Coverage Ratio.........................	18.0	24.1	33.1
Operating Cash Flow ÷ Capital Expenditures	4.1	2.7	6.1
Total Sales (Year 4 = 100)......................	113.4	130.9	126.1
Sales in United States (Year 4 = 100)	106.0	118.0	113.5
Sales in Europe (Year 4 = 100)..................	138.4	163.4	139.6
Sales in Other Countries (Year 4 = 100)...........	108.7	160.3	217.7
Sales Mix			
United States	67%	64%	64%
Europe	27	28	24
Other International	6	8	12
	100%	100%	100%
Rate of Return on Assets			
United States	32.6%	29.8%	29.4%
Europe	38.2%	41.4%	25.3%
Other International	64.6%	50.9%	24.1%
Profit Margin			
United States	15.7%	15.9%	14.2%
Europe	18.8%	16.4%	13.4%
Other International	24.0%	20.6%	15.3%
Assets Turnover			
United States	2.1	1.9	2.1
Europe	2.0	2.5	1.9
Other International	2.7	2.5	1.6

EXHIBIT 3.28

Texas Instruments
Financial Statement Ratio Analysis
(Problem 3.14)

	Year 4	Year 5	Year 6
Profit Margin for Rate of Return on Assets	(5.6%)	3.8%	5.9%
Assets Turnover................................	1.3	1.5	1.5
Rate of Return on Assets	(7.6%)	5.5%	9.1%
Common Earnings Leverage	116.0%	74.8%	90.0%
Capital Structure Leverage......................	2.9	3.1	2.8
Rate of Return on Common Shareholders' Equity ..	(25.9%)	12.7%	22.6%
Cost of Goods Sold ÷ Sales	83.5%	76.9%	73.6%
Selling and Administrative Expense ÷ Sales.......	20.2%	17.5%	17.8%
Income Tax Expense (excluding tax effects of interest expense) ÷ Sales	1.8%	1.9%	2.8%
Accounts Receivable Turnover...................	7.3	7.9	7.8
Inventory Turnover	6.7	7.4	8.1
Fixed Asset Turnover	2.8	3.3	3.9
Current Ratio.................................	1.5	1.6	1.7
Quick Ratio	1.0	1.1	1.1
Operating Cash Flow ÷ Average Current Liabilities	27.4%	49.6%	51.0%
Days Accounts Receivable	50	46	47
Days Inventory................................	55	49	45
Days Accounts Payable	93	94	85
Long-Term Debt Ratio	31.4%	31.8%	23.1%
Debt-Equity Ratio	45.8%	46.7%	30.0%
Long-Term Debt ÷ Total Assets	17.9%	17.5%	11.6%
Operating Cash Flow ÷ Average Total Liabilities...	14.5%	25.5%	27.0%
Interest Coverage Ratio........................	(6.4)	8.2	15.8
Operating Cash Flow ÷ Capital Expenditures	.8	1.9	1.3
Sales (Year 3 = 100)...........................	103.3	113.3	129.8
Sales—Components (Year 3 = 100)..............	110.2	128.3	164.0
Sales—Defense Electronics (Year 3 = 100)	102.9	105.9	98.0
Sales—Information Technologies (Year 3 = 100)...	103.0	106.1	114.7

Sales Mix

	Year 4	Year 5	Year 6
Components..................................	50%	53%	60%
Defense Electronics...........................	29	27	22
Information Technologies.......................	19	18	17
Metallurgical Materials........................	2	2	1
	100%	100%	100%

Rate of Return on Assets

	Year 4	Year 5	Year 6
Components..................................	(6.7%)	12.6%	22.8%
Defense Electronics...........................	11.7%	23.0%	22.9%
Information Technologies.......................	(9.3%)	4.3%	4.7%
Metallurgical Materials........................	2.7%	5.3%	(5.9%)

Profit Margin

	Year 4	Year 5	Year 6
Components..................................	(5.5%)	8.5%	13.5%
Defense Electronics...........................	5.7%	9.7%	10.2%
Information Technologies.......................	(4.0%)	2.0%	2.3%
Metallurgical Materials........................	1.7%	2.6%	(3.1%)

Exh. 3.28—Continued	Year 4	Year 5	Year 6
Assets Turnover			
Components	1.2	1.5	1.7
Defense Electronics............................	2.0	2.4	2.2
Information Technologies........................	2.3	2.1	2.0
Metallurgical Materials..........................	1.6	2.0	1.9

REQUIRED

a. What are the likely reasons for the increasing profit margin for rate of return on assets during the three years?
b. What is the likely reason for the increase in the inventory and fixed asset turnover ratios during the three years?
c. Did financial leverage work to the benefit of the common shareholders each year? Explain.

EXHIBIT 3.29

Boise Cascade
Financial Statement Ratio Analysis
(Problem 3.15)

	Year 8	Year 9	Year 10
Profit Margin for Rate of Return on Assets	7.6%	3.6%	.9%
Assets Turnover	1.1	.9	.8
Rate of Return on Assets	8.5%	3.4%	.8%
Common Earnings Leverage	77.6%	34.8%	(276.7%)
Capital Structure Leverage......................	2.4	2.9	3.2
Rate of Return on Common Shareholders' Equity ..	15.9%	3.4%	(6.8%)
Cost of Goods Sold ÷ Sales	78.8%	84.4%	90.9%
Selling and Administrative Expense ÷ Sales.......	9.4%	10.0%	10.4%
Income Tax Expense (excluding tax effects of interest expense) ÷ Sales	4.6%	2.0%	.3%
Accounts Receivable Turnover....................	10.6	10.0	10.1
Inventory Turnover	8.3	7.8	7.4
Fixed Asset Turnover	1.6	1.3	1.1
Current Ratio.................................	1.4	1.3	1.4
Quick Ratio	.7	.6	.6
Operating Cash Flow ÷ Average Current Liabilities	72.8%	35.1%	9.8%
Days Accounts Receivable	34	36	36
Days Inventory................................	44	47	49
Days Accounts Payable	40	37	32
Long-Term Debt Ratio	48.7%	55.1%	60.2%
Debt-Equity Ratio	95.1%	122.8%	151.3%
Long-Term Debt ÷ Total Assets	36.2%	40.4%	46.3%
Operating Cash Flow ÷ Average Total Liabilities...	22.0%	8.7%	2.1%
Interest Coverage Ratio.........................	5.6	2.0	.3
Operating Cash Flow ÷ Capital Expenditures	.7	.3	.2
Sales (Year 7 = 100)..........................	105.9	102.2	96.4

d. What is the likely reason for the increasing current ratio over the three years?

e. Assess the changes in the long-term solvency risk of Texas Instruments during the three years.

3.15 INTERPRETING PROFITABILITY AND RISK RATIOS. Boise Cascade processes wood pulp into paper products for a wide variety of business and consumer uses. Its paper-processing facilities are capital intensive. Exhibit 3.29 presents profitability and risk ratios for Boise Cascade for Year 8, Year 9, and Year 10.

REQUIRED

a. What is the likely reason for the declining rate of return on assets during the three years?

b. Did financial leverage work to the advantage of the common shareholders each year?

c. What is the likely reason for the decline in the cash flow from operations to current liabilities ratio during the three years?

d. Assess the changes in the long-term solvency risk of Boise Cascade during the three years.

SPECIALTY RETAILING INDUSTRY ANALYSIS: THE GAP AND THE LIMITED

The GAP and The Limited compete in the specialty retailing segment of the retail industry. This segment experienced its most significant growth during the 1980s. During previous decades, department stores maintained a leadership position in retailing. Department stores offered the advantage of one-stop shopping by carrying a broad line of clothing, household, furniture, and other products. The size and product line breadth of department stores provided them with certain economies of scale (purchasing, storage, transportation). The two main disadvantages of department stores became the competitive weapons of specialty retailers: breadth and depth of a specialty product line and expertise in services offered in support of that product line. The specialty retailers tended to locate in shopping centers anchored by established department stores, benefiting from shopping center traffic without incurring much of the promotion cost to attract customers.

The 1990s witnessed a change in the economics of specialty retailing. Competition among specialty retailers increased significantly as the number of specialty retailers reached the saturation point in many locales. In addition, department stores adopted a "mini-boutique" strategy, whereby their stores became a collection of specialty retail shops under one roof. A second factor affecting specialty retailers was the recession that occurred in the United States in 1991 and 1992. Many consumers "traded down" and purchased from outlet malls and discount stores. Retailers selling fashion-oriented products such as The GAP and The Limited were especially hard hit during this period. A third factor affecting specialty retailing is the movement toward at-home shopping. This movement results in part from the scarcity of time for shopping (catalogs and home shopping television networks responded to this need) and in part from concerns about personal safety.

The GAP and The Limited entered the specialty retailing market with clothing designed for teenage and young working female customers. The GAP subsequently expanded its product line to include children's apparel. It operates stores under the names of The GAP, GAP

Kids, Banana Republic, and GAP Warehouse. The Limited expanded its product line to include men's, women's and children's apparel as well as personal care products. It operates stores under the names of The Limited, Express, Lerner, Lane Bryant, Victoria's Secret, Structure, The Limited Too, Abercrombie & Fitch, Henri Bendel, Bath & Body, Cacique, and Panhaligon. The Limited gives the managers of each of these chains considerable freedom to make strategic and operating decisions.

Both firms locate their stores almost exclusively in shopping malls. They lease their retail space. The Limited has adopted the strategy of locating stores from several of its chains in the same shopping mall. This strategy provides The Limited with bargaining power on lease terms and with possible economies of scale in transportation, information processing, and other support services.

Exhibit 1 presents selected data for The GAP and The Limited. Exhibits 2 to 4 present the financial statements of The GAP for Year 2 through Year 4, and Exhibits 5 to 7 present the financial statements for The Limited for these same years. These financial statements reflect the capitalization of lease commitments for store space. (Chapter 6 discusses the procedure for capitalizing such leases.) Exhibits 8 and 9 present financial ratios for The GAP and The Limited, respectively, for Year 2 and Year 3. Year 2 was the last year before a recession in the United States, and Year 3 and Year 4 were recession years.

REQUIRED

a. Calculate the values of each of the ratios in Exhibits 8 and 9 for Year 4. The income tax rate for all years is 35 percent.
b. Assess the changes in the profitability and risk of The GAP during the three-year period, offering possible reasons for the changes observed.
c. Repeat part (*b*) for The Limited.
d. Compare the profitability and risk of The GAP versus The Limited during the three-year period, suggesting possible reasons for the differences observed.

EXHIBIT 1

The GAP and The Limited
Selected Data
(Case 3.1)

	The GAP			The Limited		
	Year 2	Year 3	Year 4	Year 2	Year 3	Year 4
Number of Stores	1,216	1,307	1,370	4,194	4,425	4,623
Total Square Footage (000s)	5,638	6,509	7,546	20,355	22,863	24,426
Sales per Square Foot.............	$481	$489	$463	$288	$285	$278
Comparable Store Sales Growth	13%	5%	1%	3%	2%	(1%)

EXHIBIT 2

The GAP
Balance Sheets
(amounts in millions)
(Case 3.1)

	January 31			
	Year 1	Year 2	Year 3	Year 4
Assets				
Cash	$ 66	$ 192	$ 243	$ 460
Marketable Securities	0	0	0	84
Accounts Receivable	10	8	10	15
Inventories	247	314	366	331
Prepayments	42	52	72	66
Total Current Assets	$ 365	$ 566	$ 691	$ 956
Property, Plant, and Equipment (net)	1,086	1,367	1,638	2,464
Other Assets	28	34	38	66
Total Assets	$1,479	$1,967	$2,367	$3,486
Liabilities and Shareholders' Equity				
Accounts Payable	$ 115	$ 158	$ 193	$ 214
Short-Term Borrowing	0	0	0	8
Current Portion of Long-Term Debt	13	3	0	0
Other Current Liabilities	136	169	142	240
Total Current Liabilities	$ 264	$ 330	$ 335	$ 462
Long-Term Debt	707	897	1,063	1,798
Other Noncurrent Liabilities	43	62	81	99
Total Liabilities	$1,014	$1,289	$1,479	$2,359
Common Stock	$ 8	$ 8	$ 8	$ 8
Additional Paid-in Capital	91	125	210	240
Retained Earnings	457	637	762	971
Treasury Stock	(91)	(92)	(92)	(92)
Total Shareholders' Equity	$ 465	$ 678	$ 888	$1,127
Total Liabilities and Shareholders' Equity	$1,479	$1,967	$2,367	$3,486

The GAP
Income Statements
(amounts in millions)
(Case 3.1)

	For the Year Ended January 31		
	Year 2	Year 3	Year 4
Sales	$ 2,519	$ 2,960	$ 3,296
Other Revenues	4	4	7
Cost of Goods Sold	(1,499)	(1,873)	(2,023)
Selling and Administrative Expenses	(575)	(661)	(748)
Interest Expense	(78)	(90)	(107)
Income Tax Expense	(141)	(129)	(167)
Net Income	$ 230	$ 211	$ 258

The GAP
Statements of Cash Flows
(amounts in millions)
(Case 3.1)

	For the Year Ended January 31		
	Year 2	Year 3	Year 4
Operations			
Net Income	$ 230	$ 211	$ 258
Depreciation	82	114	142
Addbacks and Subtractions—Net	7	17	(16)
(Increase) Decrease in Accounts Receivable	2	(2)	(5)
(Increase) Decrease in Inventories	(67)	(52)	34
(Increase) Decrease in Prepayments	(6)	(9)	(2)
Increase (Decrease) in Accounts Payable	43	36	24
Increase (Decrease) in Other Current Liabilities	43	(8)	116
Cash Flow from Operations	$ 334	$ 307	$ 551
Investing			
Property, Plant, and Equipment Acquired	$(237)	$(206)	$(212)
Investments Acquired	0	0	(84)
Other Investing Transactions	(9)	(10)	(4)
Cash Flow from Investing	$(246)	$(216)	$(300)
Financing			
Increase in Short-Term Borrowing	0	0	$ 8
Increase in Long-Term Borrowing	$ 75	0	0
Increase in Common Stock	20	$ 9	11
Decrease in Short-Term Borrowing	0	0	0
Decrease in Long-Term Borrowing	(13)	(5)	0
Decrease in Common Stock	(1)	—	—

	For the Year Ended January 31		
Exh. 4—Continued	**Year 2**	**Year 3**	**Year 4**
Financing—continued			
Dividends	(41)	(44)	(53)
Other Financing Transactions	(2)	0	0
Cash Flow from Financing	$ 38	$ (40)	$ (34)
Change in Cash.	$ 126	$ 51	$ 217
Cash—Beginning of Year.	66	192	243
Cash—End of Year	$ 192	$ 243	$ 460

EXHIBIT 5

The Limited
Balance Sheets
(amounts in millions)
(Case 3.1)

	January 31			
	Year 1	**Year 2**	**Year 3**	**Year 4**
Assets				
Cash	$ 13	$ 34	$ 41	$ 320
Marketable Securities	0	0	0	0
Accounts Receivable	670	736	837	1,057
Inventories	585	730	804	734
Prepayments.	96	105	102	110
Total Current Assets	$1,364	$1,605	$1,784	$2,221
Property, Plant, and Equipment (net) . .	3,411	4,373	5,281	5,019
Other Assets.	112	157	248	248
Total Assets	$4,887	$6,135	$7,313	$7,488
Liabilities and Shareholders' Equity				
Accounts Payable.	$ 200	$ 200	$ 309	$ 250
Short-Term Borrowing	0	0	0	16
Current Portion of Long-Term Debt. . .	0	0	0	0
Other Current Liabilities	281	320	411	441
Total Current Liabilities	$ 481	$ 520	$ 720	$ 707
Long-Term Debt	2,556	3,430	4,009	4,003
Other Noncurrent Liabilities	290	308	316	336
Total Liabilities	$3,327	$4,258	$5,045	$5,046
Common Stock	$ 190	$ 190	$ 190	$ 190
Additional Paid-in Capital	99	101	128	129
Retained Earnings.	1,481	1,783	2,137	2,397
Treasury Stock.	(210)	(197)	(187)	(274)
Total Shareholders' Equity	$1,560	$1,877	$2,268	$2,442
Total Liabilities and Shareholders' Equity	$4,887	$6,135	$7,313	$7,488

The Limited
Income Statements
(amounts in millions)
(Case 3.1)

	For the Year Ended January 31		
	Year 2	Year 3	Year 4
Sales	$ 6,149	$ 6,944	$ 7,245
Other Revenues	12	19	7
Cost of Goods Sold.....................	(4,154)	(4,682)	(4,939)
Selling and Administrative Expenses	(1,081)	(1,202)	(1,257)
Interest Expense	(266)	(334)	(411)
Income Tax Expense....................	(257)	(290)	(254)
Net Income	$ 403	$ 455	$ 391

The Limited
Statement of Cash Flows
(amounts in millions)
(Case 3.1)

	For the Year Ended January 31		
	Year 2	Year 3	Year 4
Operations			
Net Income	$ 403	$ 455	$ 391
Depreciation.....................................	223	247	271
Addbacks and Subtractions—Net	0	0	(3)
(Increase) Decrease in Accounts Receivable	(65)	(101)	(219)
(Increase) Decrease in Inventories	(145)	(74)	70
(Increase) Decrease in Prepayments	(9)	3	(6)
Increase (Decrease) in Accounts Payable	0	109	(59)
Increase (Decrease) in Other Current Liabilities	69	115	3
Cash Flow from Operations....................	$ 476	$ 754	$ 448
Investing			
Property, Plant, and Equipment Acquired	$(523)	$(430)	$(296)
Investments Acquired	(19)	(60)	0
Other Investing Transactions......................	0	0	220
Cash Flow from Investing	$(542)	$(490)	$ (76)
Financing			
Increase in Short-Term Borrowing................	0	0	0
Increase in Long-Term Borrowing	$ 223	$ 150	$ 250

Exh. 7—Continued	For the Year Ended January 31		
	Year 2	Year 3	Year 4
Increase in Common Stock	15	17	7
Decrease in Short-Term Borrowing	0	(322)	(26)
Decrease in Long-Term Borrowing.................	(50)	0	(100)
Decrease in Common Stock.......................	0	0	(93)
Dividends	(101)	(102)	(131)
Other Financing Transactions	0	0	0
Cash Flow from Financing	$ 87	$(257)	$ (93)
Change in Cash.................................	$ 21	$ 7	$ 279
Cash—Beginning of Year.........................	13	34	41
Cash—End of Year.............................	$ 34	$ 41	$ 320

EXHIBIT 8

The GAP
Ratio Analysis
(Case 3.1)

	Year 2	Year 3	Year 4
Profit Margin for ROA	11.1%	9.1%	
Assets Turnover..................................	1.5	1.4	
Rate of Return on Assets	16.3%	12.4%	
Common Earnings Leverage	81.9%	78.3%	
Capital Structure Leverage........................	3.0	2.8	
Rate of Return on Common Shareholders' Equity	40.2%	26.9%	
Cost of Goods Sold ÷ Sales	59.5%	63.3%	
Selling and Administrative Expense ÷ Sales.........	22.8%	22.3%	
Income Tax Expense ÷ Sales[a].....................	6.7%	5.4%	
Accounts Receivable Turnover.....................	279.9	328.9	
Inventory Turnover	5.3	5.5	
Fixed Asset Turnover	2.1	2.0	
Current Ratio....................................	1.7	2.1	
Quick Ratio	.6	.8	
Cash Flow from Operations ÷ Current Liabilities	112.5%	92.3%	
Days Accounts Receivable	1	1	
Days Inventory...................................	68	66	
Days Accounts Payable	32	33	
Long-Term Debt Ratio	57.0%	54.5%	
Debt-Equity Ratio	132.3%	119.7%	
Long-Term Debt ÷ Assets.........................	45.6%	44.9%	
Cash Flow from Operations ÷ Total Liabilities	29.0%	22.2%	
Interest Coverage Ratio...........................	5.8	4.8	
Cash Flow from Operations ÷ Capital Expenditures..	1.4	1.5	

[a]Excluding tax effects of interest expense.

EXHIBIT 9

The Limited
Ratio Analysis
(Case 3.1)

	Year 2	Year 3	Year 4
Profit Margin for ROA..........................	9.4%	9.7%	
Assets Turnover.................................	1.1	1.0	
Rate of Return on Assets........................	10.5%	10.0%	
Common Earnings Leverage	70.0%	67.4%	
Capital Structure Leverage......................	3.2	3.2	
Rate of Return on Common Shareholders' Equity	23.5%	22.0%	
Cost of Goods Sold ÷ Sales	67.6%	67.4%	
Selling and Administrative Expense ÷ Sales.........	17.6%	17.3%	
Income Tax Expense ÷ Sales[a]...................	5.7%	5.9%	
Accounts Receivable Turnover....................	8.7	8.8	
Inventory Turnover	6.3	6.1	
Fixed Asset Turnover	1.6	1.4	
Current Ratio..................................	3.1	2.5	
Quick Ratio	1.5	1.2	
Cash Flow from Operations ÷ Current Liabilities	95.1%	121.6%	
Days Accounts Receivable	42	41	
Days Inventory.................................	58	60	
Days Accounts Payable	17	20	
Long-Term Debt Ratio	64.6%	63.9%	
Debt-Equity Ratio..............................	182.7%	176.8%	
Long-Term Debt ÷ Assets.......................	55.9%	54.8%	
Cash Flow from Operations ÷ Total Liabilities	12.6%	16.2%	
Interest Coverage Ratio..........................	3.5	3.2	
Cash Flow from Operations ÷ Capital Expenditures..	.9	1.8	

[a]Excluding tax effects of interest expense.

CHAPTER 4

DATA ISSUES IN ANALYZING FINANCIAL STATEMENTS

Learning Objectives

1. Understand the role of net income as a measure of the past profitability of a firm and the necessary adjustments for nonrecurring items to enhance its usefulness as a predictor of future profitability.
2. Review the accounting standards for classification of income items as related to (a) continuing operations, (b) discontinued operations, (c) extraordinary items, and (d) changes in accounting principles and the analyst's adjustments to eliminate nonrecurring income items in these categories.
3. Understand the issues in using financial statement data as originally reported versus as restated in subsequent years' financial statements and the analysts' adjustments to transform one set of data to the other.
4. Use quarterly earnings data to measure profit margins for different yearly reporting periods.
5. Obtain an overview of differences in accounting principles across major industrialized countries around the world.

The financial statement ratios discussed in Chapter 3 use data from the financial statements as inputs. The financial statement data should reflect comparable measurement and reporting procedures both across time and across firms so that the analyst can identify economic, strategic, and other important differences. This chapter discusses several financial statement data issues that the analyst should consider before calculating financial statement ratios, including:

1. Nonrecurring income items.
2. Restated financial statements.
3. Account classification differences.
4. Reporting period differences.
5. Accounting principles differences.

NONRECURRING INCOME ITEMS

Net income, or earnings, plays a central role in the analysis of a firm's profitability. The levels of earnings and changes in those levels over time should relate closely to the levels and changes in a firm's stock prices. Lev examined numerous research studies relating reported earnings and stock prices and concluded that "the correlation between earnings and stock returns is very low, sometimes negligible."[1] Lev then concludes: "The low information content is probably due to biases introduced by accounting measurement and valuation principles and in some cases to manipulation of reported data by management."[2]

One possible source of bias is the inclusion of nonrecurring items in net income. One would expect a low correlation between *reported* earnings and stock prices if investors eliminate nonrecurring, or transitory, components of net income and price a firm's common stock based on recurring, or "permanent," earnings. The task of the analyst is to identify and eliminate income items that are not expected to affect the ongoing profitability of a firm.

Generally accepted accounting principles, or GAAP, in the United States require firms to report income items in four categories:[3]

1. Income from continuing operations.
2. Income, gains, and losses from discontinued operations.
3. Extraordinary items.
4. Effects of changes in accounting principles.

The following sections discuss issues related to each of these four categories of income.

INCOME FROM CONTINUING OPERATIONS

GAAP defines continuing operations in terms of a *business* in which a firm expects to continue an involvement rather than in terms of whether a particular revenue or

---

[1]Baruch Lev, "On the Usefulness of Earnings and Earnings Research: Lessons and Directions from Two Decades of Empirical Research," *Journal of Accounting Research—Supplement,* 1989, p. 155.

[2]Ibid, p. 185.

[3]Accounting Principles Board, *Opinion No. 30,* "Reporting the Results of Operations," 1973.

expense item is likely to recur. Income from continuing operations includes revenues and expenses directly related to manufacturing and selling a firm's principal products and services. It also includes gains and losses from activities peripherally related to this principal business.

Example 1.   Income from continuing operations of Delta Air Lines for three recent years included gains from the disposition of flight equipment of $18 million, $17 million, and $35 million. Such gains relate, although indirectly, to providing transportation services. Thus, Delta includes the gains in income from continuing operations. Because Delta will likely sell aircraft each year, the analyst should include these gains in income from continuing operations when assessing Delta's ongoing profitability.

Because GAAP defines continuing operations in terms of a firm's continuing involvement in a business, this income statement category may include nonrecurring revenues, gains, expenses, and losses related to this continuing business. The analyst should search for such nonrecurring items and decide whether to exclude them when assessing profitability.

Example 2.   H. J. Heinz, a consumer foods company, regularly acquires and disposes of branded food products companies as it shifts its product line to high growth markets. Gains and losses from divestitures appear in "other income" in the Income from Continuing Operations section of the income statement and are generally not material in amount. In a recent year, however, Heinz sold its investment in a cornstarch business at a pretax gain of $221 million, which represented 22 percent of income before taxes from continuing operations. Although divestitures recur, a divestiture of this size had not occurred for Heinz for several years. The analyst should probably eliminate this gain from income related to continuing operations when assessing Heinz' ongoing profitability.

Firms report nonrecurring items in income from continuing operations on a *pretax* basis. Income tax expense includes the tax effects of the nonrecurring item. The analyst should eliminate both the pretax income item and any related tax effect. Heinz does not disclose the tax effect of this gain either in its income statement or in notes to the financial statements. The analyst must assume, therefore, that the tax effect equals the statutory tax rate times the amount of the gain. The income tax note indicates that the statutory tax rate was 35 percent. Thus, the analyst eliminates the $221 million gain, reduces income tax expense by $77 million ($= .35 \times \$221$), and reduces income from continuing operations by $144 million ($= \$221 - \$77$).

To achieve consistency with the income statement, it appears desirable that the analyst eliminate the assets of this cornstarch business from total assets at the beginning of the year when calculating ROA. Firms seldom, however, report separately the individual assets and liabilities of businesses sold during the year, so such an adjustment is not possible. Furthermore, assets at the end of the year include either the proceeds of sale or other assets that the firm subsequently acquired with the proceeds of sale. Thus, it is similarly not feasible to eliminate from total assets at the end of the year the portion relating to disposition of the cornstarch business. Unless the firm clearly discloses the assets of disposed businesses, the analyst generally cannot adjust the balance sheet. This omission overstates average assets in the denominator of ROA and thereby understates ROA. The analyst should consider this downward bias when interpreting ROA.

To achieve consistency with the income statement, it also appears desirable that the analyst eliminate the after-tax gain from retained earnings when computing ROCE. This adjustment is more feasible than the adjustment to total assets discussed above because it involves simply eliminating the after-tax gain (or loss). The argument against adjusting retained earnings is that the gain (or loss) is a component of *accumulated* earnings, which the balance sheet attempts to portray, even though a gain of this magnitude is not expected to recur in income from continuing operations in the future.

The statement of cash flows reports the proceeds of sale as an investing activity, which the analyst can either eliminate or deemphasize when assessing a firm's cash-generating ability. The Operations section of the statement of cash flows includes a subtraction in the amount of the gain. This subtraction offsets the gain included in income from continuing operations and eliminates its effect on cash flow from operations.

Although it might appear desirable to eliminate the effects of nonrecurring income items from all three financial statements so that they properly articulate, firms seldom provide the necessary information. The analyst can make certain assumptions to accomplish this articulation, but the level of bias injected into the resulting measures might be intolerably high. Eliminating their effect on income from continuing operations at least removes them from the principal measure used to assess ongoing profitability.

Example 3. The income statement of McDonnell Douglas for a recent year included a $600 million pension settlement gain, which represents 153 percent of income from continuing operations. The notes to the financial statements indicate that McDonnell Douglas used pension fund assets to purchase single premium annuity contracts for retired employees. The purchase of these annuity contracts settled the firm's obligation to those retired employees for $600 million less than the market value of the associated assets in the pension fund. Providing retirement benefits to employees is a normal component of compensation, hence, the classification in income from continuing operations. However, this pension settlement gain appears only once in the last 10 years. Thus, the settlement gain is both nonrecurring and material in amount. The analyst should probably exclude the gain and its tax effects from income related to continuing operations.

Example 4. Income from continuing operations of Digital Equipment Corporation (DEC) for three recent years included restructuring charges of $550 million, $1,100 million, and $1,500 million. DEC reports that these charges relate to plant closings and employee separations. DEC has downsized its computer operations in light of a maturing of the computer industry worldwide and recessionary conditions. Because DEC remains in the computer business, these restructuring charges appear in income from continuing operations. The issue for the analyst is whether to include these charges in an ongoing assessment of DEC's profitability.

The case for including them in income from continuing operations is as follows: (1) DEC has made a charge for three years in a row and (2) it is not clear that DEC has completed its downsizing; DEC's charges increased during each of the three years. The case for excluding these charges and their related tax effects from income from continuing operations is that it permits the analyst to assess more easily DEC's past profitability from manufacturing and selling computer products, its principal business activity.

Example 5. Income from continuing operations of Bristol-Myers Squibb includes an $890 million provision for restructuring for its most recent year. A note to the financial statements indicates that the firm recorded the restructuring charge "in connection with various restructuring actions taken by the company to strengthen its four core businesses in recognition of changing worldwide health care trends." Unlike the case with DEC, this is the only such restructuring charge reported by Bristol-Myers Squibb in the last decade. On the other hand, this restructuring charge may be the first of several recurring charges as changes continue to occur in the health-care arena.

Example 6. Refer to Note 18 to Coke's financial statements in Appendix A. Coke characterizes the following income items as "nonrecurring" (amounts are pretax in millions):

	Year 6	Year 8
Litigation Provision and Reversal	$(21)	$ 23
Provision to Increase Efficiencies	—	(63)
Restructuring Charge in Unconsolidated Affiliate	(44)	(42)
Gain on Sale of Assets	96	84
Total	$ 31	$ 2

Coke's $21 million provision in Year 6 for litigation losses rests on the conservatism convention in accounting. A favorable court ruling in Year 8 eliminated the need for this provision. The analyst might consider adding $21 million to pretax earnings for Year 6 and subtracting $23 million from pretax earnings for Year 8 to gain a better perspective on the trend in profitability. The amounts involved, however, are sufficiently small that such adjustment would not likely alter significantly the time-series trend of earnings.

The $63 million provision in Year 8 to increase efficiencies appears to be nonrecurring. However, Coke's unconsolidated affiliates made similar charges in Year 6 ($44 million) and Year 8 ($42 million). Thus, these provisions appear to be recurring. Similarly, the gains on sales of assets are recurring and a normal element of ongoing operations. Also, the amounts involved for these items are relatively small compared to Coke's income before income taxes.

Example 7. Refer to Note 3 to Pepsi's financial statements in Appendix B. Pepsi characterizes as "unusual" restructuring charges the $170 million pretax in Year 6 and $193.5 million pretax in Year 7. These charges are 10.2 percent of income before income taxes each year. Thus, these charges appear to be material in amount. Pepsi's provisions in two of the last three years raise questions as to their recurring versus nonrecurring nature. Pepsi's profitability ratios including and excluding these restructuring charges are as follows:

	Including Restructuring Charges			Excluding Restructuring Charges		
	Year 6	Year 7	Year 8	Year 6	Year 7	Year 8
Profit Margin..........	7.6%	7.7%	7.8%	8.2%	8.3%	7.8%
Return on Assets.......	8.3%	8.5%	8.8%	8.9%	9.2%	8.8%
Return on Common Shareholders' Equity..	20.7%	23.9%	27.2%	23.0%	26.3%	27.2%

Pepsi's profitability appeared to continually increase during the three-year period when earnings include the restructuring charges. A different picture emerges when the analyst excludes the restructuring charges. Operating profitability increased between Year 6 and Year 7 but declined in Year 8. The increased ROCE in Year 8 results from increased financial leverage.

SUMMARY OF RESTRUCTURING CHARGES

The treatment of restructuring charges in assessments of profitability has gained increasing importance in recent years for the following reasons:

1. Recent worldwide recessionary conditions have led an increasing number of firms to include restructuring charges in their reported earnings.
2. The Financial Accounting Standards Board has not yet issued a pronouncement regarding how firms should measure restructuring charges and when firms should include such charges in measuring income.

Interpreting a particular firm's restructuring charge is difficult because firms vary in their treatment of these items:

1. Some firms apply their accounting principles conservatively (for example, use relatively short lives for depreciable assets, expense immediately expenditures for repairs of equipment, use relatively short amortization lives for intangible assets). Such firms have smaller amounts to write off as restructuring charges than if they had applied their accounting principles less conservatively.
2. Some firms attempt to minimize the amount of the restructuring charge each year so as not to penalize reported earnings too much. Such firms (such as DEC in Example 4) often must take restructuring charges for several years in order to provide adequately for restructuring costs.
3. Some firms attempt to maximize the amount of the restructuring charge in a particular year. This approach communicates the "bad news" all at once (referred to as the "big bath" approach) and reduces or eliminates the need for additional restructuring charges in the future. If the restructuring charge later turns out to

have been too large, income from continuing operations in a later period includes a restructuring credit that increases reported earnings.

Elliott and Shaw studied discretionary restructuring changes that exceeded 1 percent of end-of-year assets during the period 1982 to 1985.[4] They found that (1) the firms making the restructuring charges tended to be larger and carry more debt than other firms in their industry, (2) experienced declining ROAs and ROCEs during the three years preceding the write-offs, (3) experienced lower ROAs and ROCE than other firms in their industry, and (4) experienced lower security returns based on market prices for the three years before, coincident with, and 18 months following the announcement of the write-off than the median returns of their industries. These findings suggest that firms made restructuring changes in response to long-term operating difficulties. Whether one can extrapolate these findings to more recent restructuring charges remains to be studied.

The lack of definitive guidance from the FASB regarding the measurement of restructuring charges and the latitude of management to time the recognition of such charges should lead the analyst to interpret restructuring charges carefully.

INCOME, GAINS, AND LOSSES FROM DISCONTINUED OPERATIONS

A second category of income relates to discontinued operations. When a firm decides to exit a particular segment of its business, it classifies that business as a *discontinued business*.

Example 8. McDonnell Douglas has engaged historically in three principal business activities: (1) aerospace, (2) financial services, and (3) information systems. It recently decided to sell its information services segment. McDonnell Douglas classified this business as a discontinued business.

Example 9. The Mead Corporation has engaged historically in three principal business activities: (1) paper products, (2) electronic publishing, and (3) insurance. Mead recently decided to divest its insurance operations, which it immediately classified as a discontinued business.

GAAP stipulates that a discontinued business must be separable, or distinguishable, both physically and operationally.[5] That is, a firm must be able to identify the particular assets of the discontinued business and that business must not be integrated operationally with ongoing businesses. Refer to Example 1 involving Delta Airlines. The sale of aircraft does not represent a discontinued business because such aircraft are integrally related to Delta's continuing involvement in providing transportation services. Refer also to Example 2 for Heinz. The sale of the cornstarch business likewise does not represent a discontinued business because cornstarch is integrally related to the manufacture of ongoing food products of Heinz. The degree to which a particular divested business operationally integrates with

---

[4]John A. Elliott and Wayne H. Shaw, "Write-Offs as Accounting Procedures to Manage Perceptions," *Journal of Accounting Research—Supplement,* 1988, pp. 91–119.

[5]Accounting Principles Board, *Opinion No. 30,* "Reporting the Results of Operations," 1973, par. 13.

ongoing businesses likely varies across firms, depending on their organizational structures and operating policies. Thus, the gain or loss from the sale of a business might appear in income from continued operations for one firm (that is, the divested business is operationally integrated) and in discontinued operations for another firm (that is, the divested business is not operationally integrated).

Two dates are important in measuring the income effects of discontinued operations. The *measurement date* is the date on which a firm commits itself to a formal plan to dispose of a segment. The *disposal date* is the date of closing the sale, if the firm intends to sell the segment, or the date operations cease, if the firm intends to abandon the segment.

A firm reports net income or loss of the discontinued segment prior to the measurement date as a separate item in the discontinued operations section of the income statement. Most U.S. firms include three years of income statement information in their income statements. A firm that decides during the current year to divest a business includes the net income or loss of this business in discontinued operations, not only for the current year but also for the preceding two years in comparative income statements, even though the firm had previously reported the latter income in continuing operations in the income statements originally prepared for those two years.

At the measurement date, the firm estimates (1) the net income or loss it expects the discontinued business to generate between the measurement date and the disposal date and (2) the gain or loss it expects from the sale or abandonment of the segment. The firm then nets these two amounts. If the net amount is an estimated *loss,* the firm recognizes the loss in the year that includes the measurement date. It simultaneously increases an account, Estimated Losses from Discontinued Operations, which appears among liabilities on the balance sheet. Realized losses (or gains) subsequent to the measurement date from either (1) or (2) above reduce (increase) this account instead of appearing in the income statements of those years. If the net amount from netting (1) and (2) above is a *gain,* the firm recognizes the income and gains only when realized in subsequent years. These provisions rest on the conservatism convention of recognizing losses as soon as they become evident but postponing the recognition of gains until realization occurs.

Example 10. The discontinued operations section of the income statement of McDonnell Douglas appears as follows (in millions):

	Year 9	Year 10	Year 11
Discontinued Operations			
Earnings (loss) from Operations Net of Taxes.....	$ (7)	$21	$ (6)
Gain on Disposals, Net of Taxes................	78	16	74
Total	$71	$37	$68

McDonnell Douglas decided in Year 8 to divest its information services business. It continued to operate this business while it sold off various parts. The portions retained operated at a net loss in Year 9 and Year 11 and at a net profit in Year 10. The disposed portions were sold at a gain each year and were included in income from discontinued operations. This reporting suggests that McDonnell Douglas expected a net gain after netting (1) and (2) above at the measurement date. It therefore reports all net losses, net profits, and gains in the period realized.

Example 11. The discontinued operations section of the income statement of The Mead Corporation appears as follows (in millions):

	Year 10	Year 11	Year 12
Discontinued Operations			
Loss from Discontinued Operations, Net of Taxes . . .	($74.8)	($10.0)	—

During Year 10, Mead decided to dispose of its insurance operations. It included an estimated loss of $74.8 million in discontinued operations during that year, reflecting the net effects of estimating (1) and (2) above. Actual losses during Year 11 from operating and selling the insurance unit totaled $84.8 million. Mead charged $74.8 million of the realized loss against the Estimated Losses from Discontinued Operations account established during Year 10, and an additional $10 million appears in the Discontinued Operations section of the income statement for Year 11. If the actual loss realized had been less than $74.8 million, Mead Corporation would have reported a gain in the Discontinued Operations section of the income statement for Year 11.

Similar to restructuring charges included in income from continuing operations, the analyst must decide whether to include or exclude income from discontinued operations in assessments of profitability. The corporate strategy of some firms is to buy and sell businesses continuously. For such firms, income from discontinued operations is an ongoing source of profitability, and the analyst might decide to include this income in assessments of profitability. For most firms, however, income from discontinued operations represents a nonrecurring source of earnings. Recall that the definition of a discontinued operation envisions a firm's exit from a major area of business as opposed to divesting a portion of an ongoing business, such as a plant or a geographical division. Most firms do not change the major areas of business in which they are involved on a sufficiently regular basis to justify considering income from discontinued operations as a recurring source of profitability.

A second argument for excluding income from discontinued operations relates to its measurement. The amount reported as income from discontinued operations for a particular year may represent (a) an estimated amount applicable to the current and future years, if the netting of (1) and (2) above at the measurement date is an estimated loss, or (b) an actual, or realized, amount applicable to the current year only if the netting of (1) and (2) above at the measurement date is an estimated gain. These measurement and reporting procedures cloud the interpretation of the time-series behavior of income from discontinued operations.

Thus, in most cases, the analyst should exclude income from discontinued operations when assessing profitability. The analyst faces similar balance sheet issues to those discussed previously for restructuring and other nonrecurring items included in income from continuing operations. Some firms disclose the net assets of discontinued businesses on a separate line in the balance sheet. The analyst can achieve consistency with the exclusion of income from discontinued operations from the income statement by excluding the net assets of these businesses from the balance sheets. Many firms, however, do not disclose these assets separately.

Cash flow from operations in the statement of cash flows includes the cash flows related to operating, as opposed to selling, a discontinued business. Consistency with the income statement suggests eliminating this source of operating cash flows if firms disclose the necessary information. The proceeds from the sale of a discontinued business appear as an investing activity. The analyst can either eliminate or deemphasize this source of cash when assessing the ongoing cash-generating ability of a firm.

The analyst will likely encounter difficulties preparing an articulated set of financial statements that fully exclude discontinued operations. The desirable approach is to exclude the effects of discontinued operations to the extent that firms provide the necessary information but keep the lack of articulation in mind when making interpretations.

EXTRAORDINARY ITEMS

A third section of the income statement includes extraordinary gains and losses. An income item classified as extraordinary must meet all three of the following criteria:[6]

1. Unusual in nature.
2. Infrequent in occurrence.
3. Material in amount.

A firm applies these criteria as they relate to its own operations and to similar firms in the same industry, taking into consideration the environment in which the entities operate. Thus, an item might be extraordinary for some firms but not for others.

Income items that meet all three of these criteria are rarely found in corporate annual reports in the United States. The most frequently encountered item classified as "extraordinary" is a gain or loss on the retirement of debt prior to maturity. With wide variations in interest rates in recent years, it is not unusual for a firm to issue new debt and use the proceeds to retire existing debt prior to maturity. Firms may not engage in such transactions every year, but they often do so on a recurring basis. Thus, this item does not appear to satisfy the criteria for an extraordinary item. Accounting standard setters, however, desired to alert the user of financial statements to the existence of these gains and losses.[7] Including them among extraordinary items instead of as a part of income from continuing operations increases the likelihood that they will not be overlooked.

The question for the analyst is whether to include or exclude gains and losses from early retirement of debt in assessments of profitability. The response depends

---

[6]Ibid., pp. 20 and 24.

[7]Financial Accounting Standards Board, *Statement of Financial Accounting Standards No. 4,* "Reporting Gains and Losses from Extinguishment of Debt," 1975.

on the recurring versus nonrecurring nature of these gains and losses for a particular firm. A firm that reports such gains in, say, two of three years will likely continue to engage in early debt retirements. The analyst might consider including the gains and losses in earnings in this case when assessing profitability. On the other hand, a firm that reports such items in, say, one of five years will not likely engage in early debt retirements on a recurring basis. The analyst should consider excluding the extraordinary gain or loss in this case. The cash outflow to retire debt appears as a financing transaction on the statement of cash flows. The operations section of the statement of cash flows will show an addback (subtraction) for an extraordinary loss (gain) that did not use operating cash flows.

Adjustments for Changes in Accounting Principles

A fourth section of the income statement reports the effects of changes in accounting principles. Firms may voluntarily change their accounting principles, such as shift from a first-in, first-out (FIFO) to a last-in, first-out (LIFO) cost-flow assumption for inventories or from an accelerated to the straight-line depreciation method. More frequently, new FASB pronouncements mandate a change in accounting principles. Recent pronouncements requiring the reporting of changes in accounting principles involve health-care benefits for retired employees,[8] income taxes,[9] and postemployment benefits.[10] Chapter 6 discusses these items more fully.

Firms that change their accounting principles must calculate, as of the *beginning* of the year of the change, the cumulative difference between net income under the accounting principle used previously and under the new accounting principle. The firm reports this cumulative difference (net of taxes) in this fourth section of the income statement.[11]

Example 12. The income statement of Ford for a recent year reveals the following (in millions):

	Year 10	Year 11	Year 12
Ford			
Income from Continuing Operations	$860.1	($2,258.0)	($ 501.8)
Cumulative Effect of Changes in			
Accounting Principles:			
Adoption of FASB *Statement No. 106*	—	—	(7,540.2)
Adoption of FASB *Statement No. 109*	—	—	657.0
Net Income (loss)	$860.1	($2,258.0)	($7,385.0)

---

[8]Financial Accounting Standards Board, *Statement of Financial Accounting Standards No. 106*, "Employers' Accounting for Postretirement Benefits Other Than Pensions," 1990.

[9]Financial Accounting Standards Board, *Statement of Financial Accounting Standards No. 109*, "Accounting for Income Taxes," 1992.

[10]Financial Accounting Standards Board, *Statement of Financial Accounting Standards No. 112*, "Employers' Accounting for Postemployment Benefits," 1992.

[11]Accounting Principles Board, *Opinion No. 20*, "Accounting Changes," 1971, p. 18.

The $7.5 billion charge related to FASB *Statement No. 106* represents the obligation (net of taxes) as of the beginning of Year 12 to provide health-care benefits to employees during retirement. Prior to *Statement No. 106,* firms recognized an expense each year as they paid health insurance premiums on behalf of retired employees, a so-called "pay-as-you-go" system. This new reporting standard requires firms to recognize an expense each year *during the employees' working years* for a portion of the present value of the health insurance premiums expected to be paid during the employees' retirement years. The adoption of *Statement No. 106* results in an immediate obligation for health-care benefits already earned by employees but not previously recognized as either an expense or a liability by the employer. This reporting standard gives firms the option of either recognizing the full amount of the health-care obligation immediately, as Ford does, or recognizing it piecemeal over the remaining working lives of employees. The reporting standard also gives firms flexibility as to when they adopt *Statement No. 106* (Chapter 6 discusses this reporting standard more fully.)

The case for excluding the effect of adopting *Statement No. 106* from net income in the year of adoption includes the following: (1) the charge results because the firm did not recognize health-care benefits expenses in prior years; one might view the charge as a correction of cumulative misstatements of previously reported expenses; (2) a charge of this magnitude is nonrecurring; and (3) the amount of the obligation and timing of its recognition will vary across firms, depending on the reporting option selected.

Excluding the charge from net income in the year of adoption but allowing it to flow through to retained earnings results in a reduction in retained earnings and a recognition of an unfunded health-care obligation and a deferred tax asset on the balance sheet at the beginning of the year of adoption. The amounts taken from Ford's financial statements are as follows (in millions):

Health Care Benefits Liability	$12,040
Deferred Tax Asset Related to Above	(4,500)
Cumulative Effect of Change in Accounting Principle	$ 7,540

The analyst obtains a consistent comparative balance sheet at the beginning and end of the year of adoption of *Statement No. 106* by reflecting this obligation on the balance sheet as of the end of the year preceding the year of adoption (that is, Year 11 for Ford). The journal entry to reflect this health-care obligation on Ford's balance sheet at the end of Year 11 is:

December 31, Year 11

Deferred Tax Asset	$4,500	
Retained Earnings	7,540	
Health-Care Liabilities		12,040

The debit of $7,540 million to Retained Earnings reflects the cumulative reduction in retained earnings that would have occurred if Ford had applied *Statement No. 106* in all years prior to Year 12.

Income from continuing operations for Year 12 will include an expense for the increase in the present value of the health-care benefits obligation as a result of employees working an additional year and perhaps generating increased health-care benefits. The amount reported in the notes to Ford's financial statements for Year 12 is $723 million pretax and $455 million after taxes. Charges of this nature will continue in future years as employees render services, so including the $455 million after-tax amount in income related to continuing operations seems appropriate.

The inclusion of this $455 million in net income for Year 12 results in an inconsistency with prior years, however. The analyst needs to know the expense actually recognized on a pay-as-you-go basis in each prior year analyzed relative to the amount that the firm would have recognized if it had applied *Statement No. 106* each year. Firms do not disclose this information.

Thus, the adjustment for adoption of *Statement No. 106* involves (1) eliminating the cumulative effect of the change in accounting principles from net income in the year of adoption and (2) reflecting the health-care benefits obligation on the balance sheet at the end of the year preceding the year of adoption. The analyst should consider the effects of omitting the health-care obligation from financial statements of earlier years when making interpretations of profitability and risk ratios.

The $657 million credit to earnings for Ford related to FASB *Statement No. 109* represents a restatement of deferred tax assets and deferred tax liabilities. Prior to *Statement No. 109*, firms used the income tax rate in effect each year when providing deferred taxes for that year. *Statement No. 109* requires firms to use the enacted tax rate for the year that the firm expects the deferred taxes to be paid. Because income tax rates have declined during the past decade, most firms find that their deferred tax assets and deferred tax liabilities overstate the amounts required by *Statement No. 109*. Adoption of *Statement No. 109* increases earnings for Ford by $657 million for Year 12.

The case for excluding the effect of adoption of *Statement No. 109* from net income is the same as for recognition of health-care benefits: (1) the charge or credit represents a correction of amounts previously reported for prior years, (2) a charge of this magnitude is nonrecurring, and (3) firms have flexibility as to when they adopt this reporting standard.

The adjustment to the financial statements is also similar. (1) eliminate the charge or credit from net income in the year of adoption and (2) adjust the deferred tax asset or liability at the end of the preceding year in the amount of the cumulative effect. The journal entry to reflect the latter adjustment for Ford is:

December 31, Year 11

Deferred Tax Liability	657	
Retained Earnings		657

Example 13. Refer to the income statement for Coke in Appendix A. Coke reports adjustments for changes in accounting principles as follows (amounts are net of

taxes in millions of U.S. dollars):

	Year 6	Year 7	Year 8
Postretirement Benefits:			
Consolidated Operations...........	—	$(146)	—
Equity Investments	—	(73)	—
Postemployment Benefits	—	—	$(12)

Coke recorded the postretirement benefits (health-care) obligation as of January 1, Year 7. Thus, its income statements for Year 7 and Year 8 include expenses for such benefits measured consistently under the new reporting standard, and its balance sheets at the end of Year 7 and Year 8 include unfunded amounts for its health-care obligation. The income statement for Year 6 includes health-care benefits measured on a pay-as-you-go basis instead of the accrual basis, and the balance sheet on December 31, Year 6, excludes the health-care obligation. The analyst might attempt to estimate the change in health-care benefits expense for Year 6 and adjust net income accordingly. The analyst can adjust the December 31, Year 6, balance sheet to include the health-care obligation. Note 14 to Coke's financial statements provides the necessary information:

Retained Earnings..................................	146	
Deferred Tax Asset	92	
Health-Care Obligation.........................		238

    To record health-care obligation related to
    consolidated operations.

Retained Earnings..................................	73	
Investments in Affiliates........................		73

    To record proportionate share of health-care
    obligation of investments accounted for using the
    equity method.

Coke also provided for an unfunded postemployment benefits obligation to former and inactive employees during Year 8. FASB *Statement No. 112* requires firms to accrue an expense and an obligation during employees' working years. Thus, this provision represents a cumulative correction of amounts recognized on a pay-as-you-go basis in prior years. Coke discloses in Note 1 to its financial statements that the income effect of this charge for Year 8 was immaterial. One might conclude that earnings of prior years would also not change materially. The analyst can record the obligation on the balance sheet of December 31, Year 7:

Retained Earnings..................................	12	
Deferred Tax Asset	8	
Employee Benefits Obligation....................		20

This adjustment provides comparable balance sheet amounts relating to this obligation for December 31, Year 7 and Year 8. However, the December 31, Year 6, balance sheet will not include a similar liability. The analyst can either (1) assume that a similar liability applies to the Year 6 balance sheet or (2) recognize no liability on the Year 6 balance sheet but incorporate its omission into interpretations of debt and other financial statement ratios. The $20 million obligation is sufficiently small in this case that conclusions about Coke's profitability and risk would not likely change by including an amount for this obligation on the December 31, Year 6, balance sheet.

Example 14.   Refer to Pepsi's income statement in Appendix B. Pepsi reports adjustments for changes in accounting principles as follows (amounts are net of income taxes in millions of U.S. dollars):

	Year 6	Year 7	Year 8
Postretirement Benefits...........	—	$(356.7)	—
Income Taxes....................	—	(570.7)	—

The rationale for eliminating these charges from earnings for Year 7 and adjusting Pepsi's December 31, Year 6, balance sheet are the same as for Coke. The adjustments, using information from Notes 10 and 13 to Pepsi's financial statements, are:

December 31, Year 6

Retained Earnings.................................	356.7	
Deferred Tax Asset	218.6	
Postretirement Benefit Obligation		575.3

To accrue unfunded postretirement benefits obligation on December 31, Year 6.

December 31, Year 6

Retained Earnings.................................	570.7	
Deferred Tax Liability.........................		570.7

To adjust deferred tax liability in accordance with FASB *Statement No. 109* as of December 31, Year 6.

Pepsi reports in Note 12 to its financial statements that it has delayed adoption of FASB *Statement No. 112* until Year 9.

SUMMARY OF ADJUSTMENTS FOR CHANGES IN ACCOUNTING PRINCIPLES

The FASB continues to issue new reporting standards that require recognition as a change in accounting principle. The nature of any adjustments depends on the particular reporting item but follows the general procedures discussed for health-care benefits and income taxes.

CHANGES IN ACCOUNTING ESTIMATES

Applying various generally accepted accounting principles requires firms to make estimates. Example include the uncollectible rate for accounts receivable; the depreciable lives for fixed assets; the amortization period for intangibles; the return rate for warranties; and interest, compensation, and inflation rates for pensions, health-care, and other retirement benefits.

Firms periodically make changes in these estimates. The amounts reported in prior years for various revenues and expenses will be misstated, given the new estimates. Firms might conceivably (1) retroactively restate prior years' revenues and expenses to reflect the new estimates, (2) include the cumulative effect of the change in estimate in income in the year of the change (similar to a change in accounting principle), or (3) spread the effect of the prior years' misstatement over the current and future years.

GAAP requires firms to follow the third procedure described above.[12] Standard setters view the making of estimates and the revising of those estimates as an integral and ongoing part of applying accounting principles. Standard setters are concerned about the credibility of financial statements if firms revise their financial statements each time they change an accounting estimate. Standard setters are also concerned that users of the financial statements will overlook a change in an estimate if its effect does not appear in the income statement of the current and future years.

Some changes in accounting estimates result from changed economic conditions. For example, recessionary conditions might increase uncollectible accounts receivable and necessitate a change in the uncollectibles rate. Technological improvements or increased intensity of use may reduce the useful lines of depreciable assets. The analyst, however, should be alert to situations in which a firm changes its accounting estimates with no apparent reason other than to increase earnings. For example, a major airline operated at a net loss of $113 million in a recent year. The notes to its financial statements state that the airline "increased the estimated useful lives and salvage values of certain of its aircraft types to better reflect current estimates. The change reduced depreciation expense by $80 million for the year and reduced the net loss by $27 million." The analyst should compare the new depreciable lives used by this airline with those of other airlines to assess whether the change in estimate appears motivated primarily by a desire to increase reported earnings.

SUMMARY OF THE NONRECURRING ITEMS

Previous sections discussed the reporting of various types of income items. When analyzing a firm's profitability, the analyst strives to eliminate nonrecurring income items. By doing so, the analyst can better predict a firm's likely future profitability. The nature of any adjustment made to the reported data requires an understanding of GAAP's requirements for reporting various income items. The examples presented in previous sections suggest that the analyst may choose to eliminate certain items included in income from continuing operations and may choose not to eliminate certain items included in discontinued operations or extraordinary items. The examples illustrate some of the issues the analyst should consider when making these decisions.

---

[12]Ibid., par. 31.

RESTATED FINANCIAL STATEMENT DATA

There are several situations in which GAAP requires firms to restate retroactively the financial statements of prior years when the current year's annual report includes prior years' financial statements for comparative purposes:

1. A firm that decides during the current year to discontinue its involvement in a particular line of business reclassifies the income of that business for prior years as a discontinued operation, even though the firm had included this income in continuing operations in income statements originally prepared for these years. The firm may also reclassify the net assets of the discontinued business as of the end of the preceding year to a single line, "Net assets of discontinued business," even though these net assets appeared among individual assets and liabilities in the balance sheet originally prepared for the preceding year.
2. If a firm merges with another firm in a transaction accounted for as a pooling of interests (discussed in Chapter 7), it must restate prior years' financial statements to reflect the results for the two entities combined.
3. Certain changes in accounting principles (for example, change from a LIFO cost-flow assumption for inventories to any other cost-flow assumption, change in the method of income recognition on long-term contracts) require the restatement of prior years' financial statements to reflect the new method.

The analyst must decide whether to use the financial statement data as originally reported for each year or as restated to reflect the new conditions. Because the objective of most financial statement analysis is to evaluate the past as a guide for projecting the future, the logical response is to use the restated data.

The analyst encounters difficulties, however, in using restated data. Most companies include balance sheets for two years and income statements and statements of cash flows for three years in their annual reports. Analysts can calculate ratios based on balance sheet data only (for example, current assets/current liabilities, long-term debt/shareholders' equity) for two years at most on a consistent basis. Analysts can calculate ratios based on data from the income statement (for example, cost of goods sold/sales) or from the statement of cash flows (for example, cash flow from operations/capital expenditures) for three years at most on a consistent basis. However, many important ratios rely on data from both the balance sheet and either the income statement or the statement of cash flows. For example, the rate of return on common shareholders' equity equals net income to common stock divided by average common shareholders' equity. The denominator of this ratio requires two years of balance sheet data. Thus, it is possible to calculate ratios based on average data from the balance sheet and one of the other two financial statements for only one year under the new conditions. The analysts could obtain balance sheet amounts for prior years from earlier annual reports, but this results in comparing restated income statement or statement of cash flow data for those earlier years with nonrestated balance sheet data.

To illustrate this issue, refer to the financial statements of General Mills (Mills) in Exhibits 4.1 (income statement) and 4.2 (balance sheet). The notes to Mills' financial statements indicate that Mills decided in Year 5 to dispose of its toy and fashion segments and the nonapparel retailing businesses within its specialty retailing segment. It reported a loss of $188.3 million from these discontinued operations in its income statement for Year 5 (see first column of Exhibit 4.1). In its comparative income statements for Year 4 and Year 3 (second and third columns), the income from these discontinued operations appears on the line, "Discontinued operations after tax." Exhibit 4.1 also shows the amounts as originally reported for Year 4 and Year 3

EXHIBIT 4.1

General Mills, Inc., and Subsidiaries
Consolidated Statement of Earnings
(amounts in millions, except per share data)

	Fiscal Year Ended			As Originally Reported	
	May 26, Year 5 (52 weeks)	May 27, Year 4 (52 weeks)	May 29, Year 3 (52 weeks)	May 27, Year 4 (52 weeks)	May 29, Year 3 (52 weeks)
Continuing operations					
Sales	$4,285.2	$4,118.4	$4,082.3	$5,600.8	$5,550.8
Costs and Expenses: Cost of sales, exclusive of items below	2,474.8	2,432.8	2,394.8	3,165.9	3,123.3
Selling, general and administrative expenses	1,368.1	1,251.5	1,288.3	1,849.4	1,831.6
Depreciation and amortization expenses	110.4	99.0	94.2	133.1	127.5
Interest expense	60.2	31.5	39.5	61.4	58.7
Total Costs and Expenses.	$4,013.5	$3,814.8	$3,816.8	$5,209.8	$5,141.1
Earnings from Continuing Operations—Pretax.	$ 271.7	$ 303.6	$ 265.5	$ 391.0	$ 409.7
Gain (Loss) from Redeployments	(75.8)	53.0	2.7	7.7	—
Earnings from Continuing Operations after Redeployments—Pretax	195.9	356.6	268.2	398.7	409.7
Income Taxes	80.5	153.9	106.1	165.3	164.6
Earnings from Continuing Operations after Redeployments	115.4	202.7	162.1	233.4	245.1
Earnings per Share—Continuing Operations after Redeployments	2.58	4.32	3.24	4.98	4.89
Discontinued Operations after Tax	(188.3)	30.7	83.0	—	—
Net Earnings (loss)	(72.9)	233.4	245.1	233.4	245.1
Net Earnings (loss) per Share	(1.63)	4.98	4.89	4.98	4.89
Average Number of Common Shares . .	44.7	46.9	50.1	46.9	50.1

EXHIBIT 4.2

General Mills, Inc., and Subsidiaries
Consolidated Balance Sheets
(in millions)

	Fiscal Year Ended	
	May 26, Year 5	May 27, Year 4
Assets		
Current Assets		
Cash and Short-Term Investments	$ 66.8	$ 66.0
Receivables, Less Allowance for Doubtful Accounts of $4.0 in		
Yr. 5 and $18.8 in Yr. 4	284.5	550.6
Inventories	377.7	661.7
Investments in Tax Leases	—	49.6
Prepaid Expenses	40.1	43.6
Net Assets of Discontinued Operations and Redeployments	517.5	18.4
Total Current Assets	$1,286.6	$1,389.9
Land, Buildings, and Equipment at Cost		
Land	93.3	125.9
Buildings	524.4	668.6
Equipment	788.1	904.7
Construction in Progress	80.2	130.0
Total Land, Buildings and Equipment	$1,486.0	$1,829.2
Less Accumulated Depreciation.	(530.0)	(599.8)
Net Land, Buildings, and Equipment	$ 956.0	$1,229.4
Other Assets		
Net Noncurrent Assets of Businesses to Be Spun Off	$ 206.5	$ —
Intangible Assets, Principally Goodwill	50.8	146.0
Investments and Miscellaneous Assets	162.7	92.8
Total Other Assets.	$ 420.0	$ 238.8
Total Assets	$2,662.6	$2,858.1
Liabilities and Stockholders' Equity		
Current Liabilities		
Accounts Payable.	$ 360.8	$ 477.8
Current Portion of Long-Term Debt.	59.4	60.3
Notes Payable.	379.8	251.0
Accrued Taxes	1.4	74.3
Accrued Payroll.	91.8	119.1
Other Current Liabilities	164.0	162.9
Total Current Liabilities.	$1,057.2	$1,145.4
Long-Term Debt	449.5	362.6
Deferred Income Taxes.	29.8	76.5
Deferred Income Taxes—Tax Leases	60.8	—
Other Liabilities and Deferred Credits.	42.0	49.0
Total Liabilities	1,639.3	1,633.5

Exh. 4.2—Continued	Fiscal Year Ended	
	May 26, Year 5	May 27, Year 4
Stockholders' Equity		
Common Stock	$ 213.7	$ 215.4
Retained Earnings.	1,201.7	1,375.0
Less Common Stock in Treasury, at Cost	(333.9)	(291.8)
Cumulative Foreign Currency Adjustment.	(58.2)	(74.0)
Total Stockholders' Equity	$1,023.3	$1,224.6
Total Liabilities and Stockholders' Equity	$2,662.6	$2,858.1

(columns four and five) in which Mills included the revenues and expenses from these operations in continuing operations. Exhibit 4.2 shows the comparative balance sheets for Year 5 and Year 4. Note that the net assets of these discontinued businesses appear on a separate line in the Year 5 balance sheet. However, individual asset and liability accounts include the amounts for these discontinued activities in the Year 4 balance sheet. Thus, Mills provides income statements for three years with the operations of these discontinued businesses set out separately but only one balance sheet. The analyst cannot even calculate ratios using income statement and average balance sheet data for one year on a consistent basis in this case.

In cases in which the firm provides sufficient information to restate prior years' financial statements without injecting an intolerable number of assumptions, the analyst should use retroactively restated financial statement data. In cases in which the firm does not provide sufficient information to do the restatements, the analysts should use the amounts as originally reported for each year. When making *interpretations* of the resulting ratios, the analyst attempts to assess how much of the change in the ratios results from the new reporting condition and how much relates to other factors.

ACCOUNT CLASSIFICATION DIFFERENCES

Firms frequently classify items in their financial statements in different ways. For example, one firm might report Depreciation and Amortization Expense as a separate item in its income statement, whereas another firm might include it in Cost of Goods Sold and Selling and Administrative Expenses. The analyst cannot compare directly the financial statement ratios involving these accounts across the two firms. The analyst must either allocate the amounts for depreciation for the first firm to Cost of Goods Sold and Selling and Administrative Expenses or extract the amounts for Depreciation and Amortization Expense for the second firm from Cost of Goods Sold and Selling and Administrative Expenses and report them separately.

The goal when comparing two or more companies is to obtain comparable data sets. A scan of the financial statements should permit the analyst to identify significant differences that might affect the analysis and interpretations. When the analyst can easily and unambiguously reclassify accounts, the reclassified data should serve as the basis for analysis. If the reclassifications require numerous assumptions, it is probably better not to make them. The analyst should note the differences in account classification for further reference when interpreting the financial statement analysis.

REPORTING PERIOD DIFFERENCES

Although the majority of publicly held corporations in the United States use a December year end, in several industries the principal competitors use different year ends. Consider the following example of the consumer foods industry:

Company	Year End
Campbell Soup	August
General Mills	May
Heinz	April
Kellogg	December
Quaker Oats	June

The question arises as to whether the analyst should place firms on a comparable reporting period before performing financial statement analysis.

The response depends on (1) the length of the time period by which the year ends differ and (2) the occurrence of events during that time period that precludes reasonable comparisons between companies. If the year ends differ by three months or fewer, the analyst generally need not make adjustments. If the year ends differ by more than three months and the industry is either cyclical or subject to major strikes, raw materials shortages, or similar problems in the intervening period, the analyst should examine the impact of different year ends. Note that the analyst need not make adjustments when sales are seasonal (as opposed to cyclical), because the fiscal year for each firm will include a full set of seasonal and nonseasonal quarters.

The analyst obtains the data needed to make adjustments for different year ends from quarterly reports. Publicly held firms provide certain income statement and balance sheet data quarterly, although they do not need to present a full set of financial statements. Also, quarterly financial statements are typically not audited by independent accountants.

The annual report usually includes summary information from these quarterly reports. Exhibit 4.3 presents quarterly information from a recent annual report for Campbell Soup Company. Campbell shows various income statement items for each of the quarters of the last two fiscal years. With this information, the analyst can compute sales or earnings for various periods as follows (amounts in millions):

Year Ended May Year 8

Sales ($998.8 + $1,179.1 + $1,336.1 + $1,207.4) = $4,721.4

Net Earnings ($70.1 + $94.9 + $84.6 + $22.4) = $ 272.0

EXHIBIT 4.3

Campbell Soup Company
Quarterly Data
(amounts in millions)

	Year 7			
	First	Second	Third	Fourth
Net Sales	$1,114.6	$1,248.6	$1,128.3	$ 998.8
Cost of Products Sold	798.7	872.8	812.0	697.0
Net Earnings	58.7	70.4	48.1	70.1
Per Share				
Net Earnings	.45	.54	.37	.54
Dividends	.16	.18	.18	.18
Market Price				
High	33.25	31.88	35.38	34.88
Low	26.38	28.00	29.44	30.13

	Year 8			
	First	Second	Third	Fourth
Net Sales	$1,179.1	$1,336.1	$1,207.4	$1,146.3
Cost of Products Sold	830.7	920.3	857.8	784.0
Earnings before Cumulative Effect of Accounting Change	62.4	84.6	22.4	72.2
Cumulative Effect of Change in Accounting for Income Taxes	32.5			
Net Earnings	94.9	84.6	22.4	72.2
Per Share				
Earnings before Cumulative Effect of Accounting Change	.48	.65	.17	.56
Cumulative Effect of Change in Accounting for Income Taxes	.25			
Net Earnings	.73	.65	.17	.56
Dividends	.18	.21	.21	.21
Market Price				
High	34.19	30.00	31.25	26.88
Low	22.75	24.38	25.75	23.88

Year Ended February Year 8

Sales ($1,128.3 + $998.8 + $1,179.1 + $1,336.1) = $4,642.3

Net Earnings ($48.1 + $70.1 + $94.9 + $84.6) = $ 297.7

Year Ended November Year 7

Sales ($1,248.6 + $1,128.3 + $998.8 + $1,179.1) = $4,554.8

Net Earnings ($70.4 + $48.1 + $70.1 + $94.9) = $ 283.5

Because each of these time periods represents the end of a quarter in Campbell's fiscal year, the quarterly report will include the balance sheet for that period end. Thus, the analyst would use the May data when comparing Campbell and General Mills. The analyst would use the November year-end data when comparing Campbell with Kellogg because the year ends are sufficiently close. Coke and Pepsi use a December year end, so no adjustment is necessary.

ACCOUNTING PRINCIPLES DIFFERENCES

Business firms use a particular set of accounting principles, or methods, in preparing their financial statements. A note to the financial statement usually describes the accounting method followed. Differences in accounting principles may affect both time-series and cross-sectional comparisons of financial statement ratios.

1. *Time-Series Analysis.*   A firm may change its accounting principles either voluntarily (such as a change from FIFO to LIFO for inventories and cost of goods sold) or involuntarily (such as the FASB–mandated changes in accounting for retirement benefits or income taxes). The changes affect the comparability of the financial statement data over time.
2. *Cross-Sectional Analysis.*   Firms may differ in their accounting principles, thereby affecting cross-sectional comparisons of financial statement data, for the following reasons:
   a. Firms select different accounting principles from the set of acceptable methods. The first column of Exhibit 4.4 summarizes acceptable accounting methods in the United States. Firms have a choice as to the cost-flow assumption for inventories and the depreciation method for fixed assets. The method of structuring particular transactions affects the accounting for leased assets and corporate acquisitions. Chapter 5, 6, and 7 discuss each of these accounting principles more fully.
   b. Firms vary as to when they adopt new FASB–mandated accounting principles. For example, Ford (see Example 12) adopted the provisions of FASB *Statement No. 109* in Year 12, whereas General Motors adopted this reporting standard during the preceding year.
   c. Firms operate in different countries where the set of acceptable accounting principles differ. Exhibit 4.4 compares and contrasts acceptable accounting principles in the United States with those in five major industrialized countries. The required methods of accounting for marketable securities, investments in securities, deferred taxes, corporate acquisitions, and goodwill amortization differ across countries.

REPORTING STRATEGIES AND SELECTION OF ACCOUNTING PRINCIPLES

Numerous research studies during the last three decades have examined the following questions: Why do firms select particular accounting principles rather than alternative, generally accepted methods? Do the particular methods selected make any difference to the users of financial statements? Researchers have addressed these questions by examining particular selection decisions (for example, FIFO versus

EXHIBIT 4.4

Summary of Generally Accepted Accounting Principles for Major Industrialized Countries

	United States	Canada	France	Japan	Great Britain	Germany
Marketable Securities (current asset)	Market value	Lower of cost or market	Lower of cost or market	Cost (unless price declines considered permanent)	Lower of cost or market	Lower of cost or market
Bad Debts	Allowance method	Allowance method	Allowance method for identifiable uncollectible accounts	Allowance method	Allowance method	Allowance method for identifiable uncollectible accounts
Inventories—Valuation	Lower of cost or market	Lower of cost or market	Lower of cost or market	Lower of cost or market	Lower of cost or market	Lower of cost or market
—Cost-Flow Assumption	FIFO, LIFO, average	FIFO, average	FIFO, average	FIFO, LIFO, average	FIFO, average	Average (unless physical flow is FIFO or LIFO
Fixed Assets—Valuation	Acquisition cost less depreciation	Acquisition cost less depreciation	Acquisition cost less depreciation[a]	Acquisition cost less depreciation	Acquisition cost less depreciation[b]	Acquisition cost less depreciation
—Depreciation	Straight line, declining balance, sum of the years' digits	Straight line, accelerated	Straight line, accelerated	Straight line, declining balance, sum of the years' digits	Straight line, declining balance, sum of the years' digits	Straight line, accelerated
Research and Development	Expensed when incurred	Expensed when incurred	Generally expensed when incurred but may be capitalized and amortized	Expensed when incurred or capitalized and amortized	Expensed when incurred	Expensed when incurred
Leases	Operating and capital lease methods	Operating and capital lease methods	Operating and capital lease methods	Operating and capital lease methods	Operating and capital lease methods	Operating and capital lease methods
Deferred Taxes	Deferred tax accounting required	Deferred tax accounting required	Book/tax conformity generally required, so deferred tax accounting not an issue	Book/tax conformity generally required, so deferred tax accounting not an issue	Deferred tax accounting required based on probability that liability or asset will crystallize	Book/tax conformity generally required, so deferred tax accounting not an issue

	United States	Canada	France	Japan	Great Britain	Germany
Investments in Securities						
0%–20%	Market value	Cost (unless price declines considered permanent)	Lower of cost or market[a]	Cost (unless price declines considered permanent)	Lower of cost or market	Cost (unless price declines considered permanent)
20%–50%	Equity	Equity	Equity	Cost (unless price declines considered permanent)	Equity	Cost (unless price declines considered permanent)
more than 50%	Consolidation required	Consolidation generally required	Consolidation required	Consolidation not required (except in certain filings with the Ministry of Finance)	Both parent company and group (consolidated) financial statements presented	Consolidation required
Corporate Acquisitions Accounting Method	Purchase and pooling of interests methods	Purchase method[c]	Purchase method	Purchase method	Purchase and pooling of interests methods	Purchase method
Amortization of Goodwill	Amortized over maximum of 40 years	Amortized over maximum of 40 years	Amortization required	Amortized over maximum of 5 years	Goodwill either written off immediately against a retained earnings reserve or capitalized and amortized over its expected useful life	Amortized over period of 5 to 15 years

[a]Generally accepted accounting principles in France permit periodic revaluations of tangible fixed assets and investments to current market values. However, the book/tax conformity requirement in France results in immediate taxation of unrealized gains. As a consequence, revaluations are unusual.

[b]Generally accepted accounting principles in Great Britain permit periodic revaluations of land, buildings, and certain intangibles to current market values. The firm credits a revaluation reserve account, a component of shareholders' equity.

[c]Generally accepted accounting principles in Canada permit the pooling of interests method when the accountant cannot identify which firm is the acquiror and which firm is the acquiree.

LIFO for inventories, straight-line versus accelerated methods for depreciable assets), rather than the aggregate effect of all accounting principles chosen by firms.

The literature suggests three reporting strategies that might motivate firms' selection decisions: profit maximization, conservatism, and income smoothing. Each of these reporting strategies focuses on the income effect of alternative accounting principles rather than on their balance sheet effect. Chapter 1 pointed out that income over sufficiently long time periods equals cash inflows less cash outflows from operating, investing, and financing (except dividends and capital stock transactions) activities. Thus, the total income under each of these reporting strategies is the same; only the timing of the income recognition differs.

1. *Profit Maximization.*   Firms might select those accounting principles that maximize cumulative reported earnings. Such firms would likely use the percentage-of-completion method for long-term contracts, a first-in, first-out (FIFO) cost-flow assumption for inventories, and the straight-line depreciation method for depreciable assets (later chapters discuss each of these accounting principles). Management might select this reporting strategy with the intent of placing the firm in the most favorable light before shareholders. Also, management might maximize its compensation if the firm ties bonuses or other compensation to reported earnings. The shareholders of a publicly held firm are too numerous and detached from the firm to monitor its day-to-day operations. The shareholders therefore hire managers as their agents to conduct and monitor these operations. Shareholders must implement incentive schemes to ensure that managers act in the best interests of shareholders. A bonus-based compensation scheme tied to earnings might serve as such an incentive arrangement. Increased earnings beyond those already anticipated by the market should increase stock prices and thereby reward shareholders. Increased earnings should also increase management's compensation. Thus, properly designed incentive schemes help both shareholders and management. Note that the firm could base the bonus arrangement on objectives other than maximizing earnings, such as maximizing cash flow or rates of return on assets or shareholders' equity.[13] Note also that the profit maximization strategy focuses on reported earnings to shareholders, not the profit maximization dictum of microeconomics. The latter uses economic values, not accounting values, in measuring net income.

2. *Conservatism.*   Firms might also select those accounting principles that minimize cumulative reported earnings. Such firms would likely use the completed-contract method for long-term contracts, a last-in, first-out (LIFO) cost-flow assumption for inventories, and an accelerated depreciation method for depreciable assets. Minimizing cumulative taxable income usually results in the smallest present value of tax payments to governmental bodies. Some firms might pursue the same reporting strategy in preparing financial statements for shareholders. Such an action eliminates the need to keep two sets of books, one for tax reporting and one for financial reporting. Management might wish to

---

[13]A rich literature on agency theory has developed during the last decade. For a summary of its principal concepts, see Ross L. Watts and Jerold L. Zimmerman, *Positive Accounting Theory* (Englewood Cliffs, NJ: Prentice-Hall, 1986).

portray a conservative, controlled image to shareholders, perhaps thereby reducing the risk that future earnings levels will disappoint shareholders. In some countries (France, Germany, Japan) tax-reporting rules heavily influence financial reporting to banks and shareholders. Regulators may even require conformity between tax- and financial reporting methods (as is the case in the United States with LIFO). In these cases, firms adopt conservatism as a reporting strategy.

3. *Income Smoothing.* Later chapters discuss the relation between earnings and stock prices. Empirical evidence indicates that unexpected changes in earnings correlate with unexpected changes in stock prices. We might expect, therefore, that a firm with wide fluctuations in its reported earnings would also experience wide fluctuations in its stock prices. Analysts often view fluctuations in stock prices as an indicator of risk. Increased risk should lead to a higher cost of funds. The rationale for an income-smoothing strategy is that firms can reduce market-perceived risk by selecting accounting methods that smooth reported earnings. Such firms would probably use the percentage-of-completion method rather than the completed-contract method for long-term contracts and a LIFO cost-flow assumption for inventories. (Chapter 5 discusses why LIFO generally results in smoother earnings over time than does FIFO or weighted average.) Firms would select either the straight-line or an accelerated depreciation method to smooth earnings, depending on whether maintenance and other costs of maintaining depreciable assets are level over the life of the assets (use straight-line method) or whether such costs increase with age (use an accelerated depreciation method). Note that the income-smoothing reporting strategy focuses on net income, not necessarily on individual revenues and expenses. Note also that firms can accomplish income smoothing in ways other than by their selection of accounting principles. For example, firms can make conservative or nonconservative estimates of uncollectible accounts, depreciable lives, warranty claims, and similar items requiring estimates. Firms can also time their expenditures on maintenance, advertising, research and development, and similar costs to smooth earnings.[14]

ANALYSTS' TREATMENT OF ALTERNATIVE ACCOUNTING PRINCIPLES

Questions similar to those raised earlier for nonrecurring income items and restated data apply to differences in accounting principles. Should the analyst restate the financial statement data of the companies so that they are comparable? Or should the analyst use the reported amounts in performing the ratio analysis and consider the impact of different accounting methods at the interpretation stage? The response to this question again depends on whether the financial statements and notes provide sufficient information to make reasonably reliable restatements. Chapters 5, 6, and 7 discuss the adjustments that the analyst can make for inventory cost-flow assumptions, depreciation methods, leases, deferred taxes, corporate acquisition method,

---

[14]For a summary of the principal concepts underlying income smoothing, see Joshua Ronen and S. Sadan, *Smoothing Income Numbers: Objectives, Means, and Implications* (Reading, MA: Addison-Wesley, 1981). Also see Brett Trueman and Sheridan Titman, "An Explanation for Accounting Income Smoothing," *Journal of Accounting Research—Supplement*, 1988, pp. 127–139.

and consolidation policy.[15] Foreign firms whose bonds or common stock trade in U.S. capital markets must present in filings with the Securities and Exchange Commission a reconciliation of net income and shareholders' equity under GAAP in their own country and GAAP in the United States. This information permits the analyst to restate the financial statements of foreign firms into U.S. accounting principles.

SUMMARY

Making meaningful interpretations of financial statement ratios requires the analyst to study the financial statements and notes for data issues that affect the comparability of financial data across time and across firms. When firms provide sufficient information, the analyst should adjust, or restate, the financial statements before calculating financial statement ratios. Such adjustments are particularly important for nonrecurring income items. When firms do not provide the necessary information to make adjustments, the analyst should note the data issue and attempt to incorporate it into interpretations of the financial ratios.

Chapters 5, 6, and 7 explore important financial reporting issues in greater depth. Chapter 5 focuses on asset valuation and income measurement. Chapter 6 examines the recognition and valuation of liabilities. Chapter 7 explores topics that have pervasive effects on all three principal financial statements, including corporate acquisitions, intercorporate investments, and foreign currency translation.

PROBLEMS

4.1 ADJUSTING FOR UNUSUAL INCOME ITEMS. H. J. Heinz Company engages in the processed food products business. It derives approximately 58 percent of its sales from within the United States and 42 percent from other countries. Exhibit 4.5 presents an income statement for Heinz for Year 2, Year 3, and Year 4. Notes to the financial statements reveal the following information:

1. *Gain on Sale of Cornstarch Business.* In Year 2, Heinz sold The Hubinger Company, a major worldwide producer of cornstarches, for $325 million. Other Year 2 sales did not materially affect earnings.
2. *Gain on Sale of Confectionery and Specialty Rice Businesses.* In Year 4, Heinz sold its Near East specialty rice business for $80 million. Also in Year 4, Heinz sold its confectionery business in Italy for $133 million. These sales include trademarks, brand names, inventory, and fixed assets.
3. *Restructuring Charges.* Heinz provided restructuring charges of $88 million in Year 2 for consolidation of functions, staff reductions, organizational reform, and plant

---

[15]A study of the effect of restating financial statements for inventory cost-flow assumptions, depreciation methods, consolidation policy, pension accounting, and deferred tax accounting revealed rank-order correlations of the reported and the restated data generally above 95 percent on 16 different profitability and risk ratios. These results should at least lead the analyst to think carefully about the need to make adjustments for differences in accounting principles unless it appears that the differences materially affect the financial statements. See James P. Dawson, Peter M. Neupert, and Clyde P. Stickney, "Restating Financial Statements for Alternative GAAPs: Is It Worth the Effort?" *Financial Analysts Journal,* November–December 1980, pp. 3–11.

EXHIBIT 4.5

H. J. Heinz Company
Income Statement
(amounts in millions)
(Problem 4.1)

	Year 2	Year 3	Year 4
Sales	$ 6,582	$ 7,103	$ 7,047
Gain on Sale of Cornstarch Business..........	221		
Gain on Sale of Confectionery and Specialty			
Rice Businesses			127
Other Income.............................	13	1	3
Cost of Goods Sold........................	(4,103)	(4,530)	(4,382)
Selling and Administrative Expenses	(1,594)	(1,712)	(1,724)
Interest Expense	(135)	(146)	(149)
Income before Income Taxes.................	$ 984	$ 716	$ 922
Income Tax Expense.......................	(346)	(186)	(319)
Net Income	$ 638	$ 530	$ 603

modernizations and closures. Heinz included $66 million of this charge in cost of goods sold and $22 million in selling and administrative expenses. Heinz provided restructuring charges of $192 million ($143 million in cost of goods sold and $49 million in selling and administrative expenses) in Year 3 relating to employee severance and relocation costs and facilities consolidation and closure costs. These charges resulted from a decision to reduce employment levels by 3,000. As of the end of Year 4, Heinz reduced employment levels by 2,000 and anticipated completion of the reductions in Year 5.

   4. The statutory income tax rate was 34 percent in Year 2 and Year 3 and 35 percent in Year 4.

REQUIRED
a. Discuss whether or not you would eliminate each of the following items when assessing the operating profitability of Heinz:
   (1) Gain on sale of cornstarch business.
   (2) Gain on sale of confectionery and specialty rice businesses.
   (3) Restructuring charges.
b. Indicate the adjustment you would make to net income to eliminate each of the items in part (a).
c. Prepare a common size income statement for Year 2, Year 3, and Year 4 using the amounts in Exhibit 4.5. Set sales equal to 100 percent.
d. Repeat part (c) using amounts that exclude the effects of the items in part (a).
e. Assess the changes in the profitability of Heinz during the three-year period.

4.2 ADJUSTING FOR UNUSUAL INCOME ITEMS. Eli Lilly and Company (Lilly) maintains a leading market position in the ethical (prescription) drug industry. It derives approximately 62 percent of its revenues from within the United States and the remainder from other countries. Exhibit 4.6 presents Lilly's income statement for Year 5, Year 6, and Year 7. The notes to its financial statements reveal the following information.

EXHIBIT 4.6

Eli Lilly and Company
Income Statement
(amounts in millions)
(Problem 4.2)

	Year 5	Year 6	Year 7
Sales	$ 5,726	$ 6,167	$ 6,452
Other Income.........................	151	99	120
Cost of Goods Sold....................	(1,718)	(1,897)	(1,959)
Research and Development	(767)	(925)	(954)
Selling and Administrative..............	(1,473)	(1,624)	(1,713)
Restructuring and Special Charges.......	—	(566)	(1,173)
Interest Expense	(40)	(72)	(71)
Income before Income Taxes............	$ 1,879	$ 1,182	$ 702
Income Taxes.........................	(564)	(354)	(211)
Net Income	$ 1,315	$ 828	$ 491

Restructuring and Special Charges.   In Year 6 and Year 7, Lilly took actions to enhance its competitiveness in the changing health-care environment, reduce expenses, and improve efficiencies. It recognized restructuring charges as a direct result of revised strategic actions. Its special charges represent unusual, generally nonrecurring expense items. The principal components of restructuring and special charges appear below (amounts in millions):

	Restructuring	Special Charges
Year 6		
Global Manufacturing Strategy	$218.9	
Provision for Redirection—Medical Devices	161.3	
Legal, Environmental, and Asbestos Abatement		$139.4
Research Investment Expenses....................		46.1
Total..	$380.2	$185.5

	Restructuring	Special Charges
Year 7		
Work Force Reductions.........................	$545.4	
Manufacturing Consolidations and Closings	249.9	
Revised Distribution Strategies...................	71.7	
Pharmaceutical Streamlining.....................	35.3	
Intangibles Write-Downs	18.7	$ 56.5
Asset Write-Downs, Legal Accruals, Other	2.4	192.8
Total..	$923.4	$249.3

Other Unusual Items.   In Year 6 and Year 7, Lilly recognized other charges of $204 million and $30 million, respectively, representing miscellaneous unusual items covering a variety of other operational matters. These charges are reflected in the applicable operating expense items in the income statement.

REQUIRED

a. Discuss the appropriate treatment of (1) restructuring charges, (2) special charges, and (3) other unusual items in an assessment of the profitability of Lilly.

b. Prepare a common size income statement for Lilly for Year 5, Year 6, and Year 7 using the reported amounts in Exhibit 4.6. Set sales revenue equal to 100 percent.

c. Compute the net income to sales percentage for each year, assuming the elimination of restructuring and special charges. The income tax rate was 34 percent in Year 5 and Year 6 and 35 percent in Year 7.

d. Repeat part (c) also excluding the other unusual items.

e. The statement of cash flow shows an addback to net income for restructuring and special charges of $566 million in Year 6 and $1,041 in Year 7. What is the interpretation of these addbacks?

f. Assess the changes in the profitability of Lilly during the three-year period.

4.3 ADJUSTING FOR UNUSUAL INCOME ITEMS. The Upjohn Company (Upjohn) is a leading pharmaceutical company, deriving approximately 82 percent of its revenues from human health-care products and 18 percent from agricultural and animal care products. Upjohn derives approximately 75 percent of its revenues from within the United States and 25 percent from other countries. Exhibit 4.7 presents an income statement and Exhibit 4.8

EXHIBIT 4.7

The Upjohn Company
Income Statement
(amounts in millions)
(Problem 4.3)

	Year 8	Year 9	Year 10
Continuing Operations			
Sales	$ 3,320	$ 3,549	$ 3,611
Other Revenues	50	80	97
Cost of Goods Sold	(805)	(905)	(920)
Research and Development	(523)	(582)	(642)
Selling and Administrative	(1,301)	(1,390)	(1,409)
Restructuring Charges	(5)	(24)	(216)
Interest	(20)	(31)	(31)
Income before Taxes and Minority Interest	$ 716	$ 697	$ 490
Income Taxes	(179)	(153)	(89)
Minority Interest	(3)	1	1
Income from Continuing Operations	$ 534	$ 545	$ 402
Discontinued Operations			
Earnings from Operations (net of taxes)	$ 3	$ 2	$ 4
Gain on Sale (net of taxes)	—	—	5
Income from Discontinued Operations	$ 3	$ 2	$ 9
Accounting Changes	—	$ (223)	$ (19)
Net Income	$ 537	$ 324	$ 392

EXHIBIT 4.8

The Upjohn Company
Statement of Cash Flows
(amounts in millions)
(Problem 4.3)

	Year 8	Year 9	Year 10
Operations			
Net Income	$ 537	$ 324	$ 392
Depreciation and Amortization	142	166	174
Deferred Income Taxes	(52)	23	(82)
Restructuring Charges	5	24	216
Accounting Changes	—	223	19
Other	(12)	(15)	5
Changes in Working Capital Accounts	67	(148)	56
Cash Flow from Operations	$ 687	$ 597	$ 780
Investing			
Proceeds from Disposal of Property, Plant, and Equipment	$ 3	$ 6	$ 18
Sale of Marketable Securities	184	227	184
Sale of Discontinued Operations	—	—	31
Property, Plant, and Equipment Additions	(258)	(295)	(324)
Purchase of Marketable Securities	(423)	(437)	(249)
Other	(2)	3	(1)
Cash Flow from Investing	$(496)	$(496)	$(341)
Financing			
Proceeds from Issuance of Debt	$ 48	$ 122	$ 340
Repayment of Debt	(27)	(16)	(216)
Debt Maturing in Three Months or Less	49	133	(191)
Dividends	(223)	(252)	(265)
Purchase of Treasury Stock	(97)	(49)	(54)
Other	32	13	(1)
Cash Flow from Financing	$(218)	$ (49)	$(387)
Change in Cash	$ (27)	$ 52	$ 52
Cash—Beginning of Year	215	188	240
Cash—End of Year	$ 188	$ 240	$ 292

presents a statement of cash flows for Upjohn for Year 8, Year 9, and Year 10. The notes to the financial statements reveal the following information.

Restructuring Charges.   Upjohn incurred restructuring charges totaling $5 million ($3 million after tax) to write down certain facilities and equipment in Year 8. In Year 9, it incurred restructuring charges totaling $24 million ($15 million after tax) for a special voluntary early retirement program in the United States and Puerto Rico. In Year 10, it incurred restructuring charges of $216 million ($159 million after tax) for a worldwide work force reduction of 1,500 employees and elimination of excess manufacturing capacity.

Discontinued Operations. Upjohn sold its agricultural chemical business in December Year 10. It retained the vegetable and agronomic seed sales activities of this business.

Accounting Changes. Upjohn adopted Financial Accounting Standards Board *Statement No. 106* (postretirement benefits other than pensions) in Year 9, reducing net income by $236 million. It also adopted *Statement No. 109* (income taxes), increasing earnings by $13 million in Year 9. Upjohn adopted *Statement No. 112* (postemployment benefits) in Year 10, reducing earnings by $19 million.

REQUIRED

a. Discuss the appropriate treatment of (1) restructuring charges, (2) income from discontinued operations, and (3) accounting changes in an assessment of the profitability of Upjohn.
b. Indicate the adjustments to the income statement of Upjohn to eliminate each of the items in part (*a*).
c. Interpret the reporting of each of the items in part (*a*) in the statement of cash flows.
d. Prepare a common size income statement for Upjohn for Year 8, Year 9, and Year 10 based on the reported amounts. Set sales equal to 100 percent.
e. Repeat part (*d*) but eliminate the effects of each of the items in part (*a*).
f. Assess the changes in the profitability of Upjohn during the three-year period.

4.4 ADJUSTING FOR UNUSUAL ITEMS. Borden, Inc., derives approximately 67 percent of its revenues from branded food products and 33 percent from packaging and industrial products. The geographical sales mix comprises approximately 67 percent from the United States and 33 percent from other countries. Exhibit 4.9 presents an income statement and Exhibit 4.10 presents a statement of cash flow for Borden for Year 13, Year 14, and Year 15. The notes to the financial statements reveal the following additional information.

Restructuring Charges and Discounted Operations. Prior to Year 11, Borden reported continually increasing sales while maintaining a profit margin of approximately 4 percent. Borden regularly purchased branded food products companies and other businesses with the cash flows generated by its mature food products business. Sales and earnings started declining in Year 11, however, the result of deteriorating market positions in certain branded food products segments and difficulties in managing the diverse set of businesses in which Borden competed. Borden embarked on a major restructuring program in Year 11. The restructuring program involved both organizational changes and divestiture of its North American snacks, seafood, jams and jellies, and other businesses. The restructuring charges in Year 13, Year 14, and Year 15 relate to employee severances and relocations and plant closings, part of which Borden includes in continuing operations and part of which it includes in income from discontinued operations. The loss on disposal recognized in Year 15 represents a pretax charge of $637 million ($490 million after taxes) to provide for disposal of the North American businesses described above.

REQUIRED

a. Why do the amounts for restructuring charges in the income statement in Exhibit 4.9 differ from the amounts for restructuring charges reported in the Operations section of the statement of cash flows in Exhibit 4.10?
b. Why does the amount for loss on disposal of discontinued operations in the income statement in Exhibit 4.9 differ from the amount reported in the Operations section of the statement of cash flows in Exhibit 4.10?

EXHIBIT 4.9

Borden, Inc.
Income Statement
(amounts in millions)
(Problem 4.4)

	Year 13	Year 14	Year 15
Continuing Operations			
Sales	$ 5,924	$ 5,872	$ 5,506
Other Income (Expense)—Net	37	24	(6)
Cost of Goods Sold.........................	(4,269)	(4,302)	(4,079)
Selling and Administrative...................	(1,024)	(1,164)	(1,224)
Restructuring..............................	(67)	(298)	(115)
Interest	(167)	(117)	(125)
Minority Interest	(3)	(40)	(41)
Income Taxes..............................	(151)	(14)	27
Income (Loss) from Continuing Operations	$ 280	$ (39)	$ (57)
Discontinued Operations			
Income (Loss) from Operations...............	$ 15	$ (86)	$ (66)
Loss on Disposal...........................	—	—	(490)
Income (Loss) from Discontinued Operations...	$ 15	$ (86)	$ (556)
Extraordinary Item			
Loss on Early Retirement of Debt.............	—	$ (11)	—
Accounting Changes			
Postemployment Benefits	—	—	$ (18)
Postretirement Benefits Other than Pensions ...	—	$ (189)	—
Income Taxes..............................	—	(40)	—
Total Accounting Changes.................	—	$ (229)	$ (18)
Net Income	$ 295	$ (365)	$ (631)

c. Why do the amounts for accounting changes reported in the income statement in Exhibit 4.9 differ from the amounts reported in the Operations section of the statement of cash flows in Exhibit 4.10?

d. Discuss whether or not you would eliminate each of the following items when assessing the operating profitability of Borden: (1) restructuring charges, (2) discontinued operations, (3) loss on early retirement of debt, and (4) accounting changes.

e. Assume that for this part that you have decided to eliminate each of the four items in part (*d*). Indicate the change in net income as a result of such eliminations. The income tax rate is 34 percent for Year 13 and Year 14 and 35 percent for Year 15.

f. Prepare a common size income statement for Borden reflecting the eliminations in part (*e*). Set sales equal to 100 percent.

g. Assess the changes in the profitability of Borden during the three-year period.

EXHIBIT 4.10

Borden, Inc.
Statement of Cash Flows
(amounts in millions)
(Problem 4.4)

	Year 13	Year 14	Year 15
Operations			
Net Income	$ 295	$(365)	$(631)
Depreciation and Amortization	217	228	224
Loss on Disposal—Discontinued Operations	—	—	637
Restructuring.................................	(65)	317	147
Nonpension Postemployment Benefits Obligation ...	—	318	36
(Increase) Decrease in Accounts Receivable	20	(30)	48
(Increase) Decrease in Inventories	8	1	21
Increase (Decrease) in Accounts Payable	(15)	(4)	(1)
Increase (Decrease) in Current and Deferred Taxes.	63	(175)	(242)
Other Changes in Working Capital Accounts	(174)	3	(87)
Cash Flow from Operations..................	$ 349	$ 293	$ 152
Investing			
Capital Expenditures...........................	$(376)	$(286)	$(177)
Divestiture of Businesses	94	123	53
Purchase of Businesses.........................	(29)	(20)	(9)
Cash Flow from Investing	$(311)	$(183)	$(133)
Financing			
Increase (Decrease) in Short-Term Debt	$(310)	$ 255	$(536)
Increase in Long-Term Debt	223	45	275
Issuance of Capital Stock	507	4	12
Reduction in Long-Term Debt...................	(244)	(266)	(129)
Dividends	(165)	(170)	(127)
Other..	(3)	—	400
Cash Flow from Financing	$ 8	$(132)	$(105)
Change in Cash...............................	$ 46	$ (22)	$ (86)
Cash—Beginning of Year......................	162	208	186
Cash—End of Year...........................	$ 208	$ 186	$ 100

4.5   USING ORIGINALLY REPORTED VERSUS RESTATED DATA. Prior to Year 8, General Dynamics Corporation engaged in a wide variety of industries, including weapons manufacturing under government contracts, information technologies, commercial aircraft manufacturing, missile systems, coal mining, material service, ship management, and ship financing. During Year 8, General Dynamics sold its information technologies business. During Year 9, General Dynamics sold its commercial aircraft manufacturing business. During Year 9, it also announced its intention to sell its missile systems, coal mining, material service, ship management, and ship-financing businesses. These strategic moves would leave General

Dynamics with only its weapons manufacturing business. Financial statements for General Dynamics for Year 8 as originally reported, Year 8 as restated in the Year 9 annual report for discontinued operations, and Year 9 as originally reported appear in Exhibit 4.11 (balance sheet), Exhibit 4.12 (income statement), and Exhibit 4.13 (statement of cash flows).

REQUIRED

a. Refer to the balance sheets of General Dynamics in Exhibit 4.11. Why does the restated amount for total assets for Year 8 of $4,672 million differ from the originally reported amount of $6,207 million?

b. Refer to the income statement for General Dynamics in Exhibit 4.12. Why are the originally reported and restated net income amounts for Year 8 the same (that is, $505 million) when each of the individual revenues and expenses decreased upon restatement?

EXHIBIT 4.11

General Dynamics Corporation
Balance Sheets
(amounts in millions)
(Problem 4.5)

	Year 8 as Originally Reported	Year 8 as Restated in Year 9 Annual Report	Year 9 as Reported
Assets			
Cash and Cash Equivalents	$ 513	$ 507	$ 513
Marketable Securities	307	307	432
Accounts Receivable	444	99	64
Contracts in Process	2,606	1,474	1,550
Net Assets of Discontinued Businesses	—	1,468	767
Current Assets	449	145	329
Total Current Assets	$4,319	$4,000	$3,655
Property, Plant, and Equipment (net)	1,029	372	322
Other Assets	859	300	245
Total Assets	$6,207	$4,672	$4,222
Liabilities and Shareholders' Equity			
Accounts Payable and Accruals	$2,593	$ 642	$ 553
Current Portion of Long-Term Debt	516	450	145
Other Current Liabilities	—	1,174	1,250
Total Current Liabilities	$3,109	$2,266	$1,948
Long-Term Debt	365	163	38
Other Noncurrent Liabilities	753	263	362
Total Liabilities	$4,227	$2,692	$2,348
Common Stock	$ 55	$ 55	$ 42
Additional Paid-in Capital	25	25	—
Retained Earnings	2,651	2,651	2,474
Treasury Stock	(751)	(751)	(642)
Total Shareholders' Equity	$1,980	$1,980	$1,874
Total Liabilities and Shareholders' Equity	$6,207	$4,672	$4,222

EXHIBIT 4.12

General Dynamics Corporation
Income Statement
(amounts in millions)
(Problem 4.5)

	Year 8 as Originally Reported	Year 8 as Restated in Year 9 Annual Report	Year 9 as Reported
Continuing Operations			
Sales	$8,751	$3,322	$3,472
Operating Costs and Expenses	(8,359)	(3,207)	(3,297)
Interest Income (Expense), Net	(34)	4	25
Other Expense, Net	(27)	(27)	27
Earnings before Income Taxes	$ 331	$ 92	$ 227
Income Tax Credit	43	114	21
Income from Continuing Operations	$ 374	$ 206	$ 248
Discontinued Operations			
Earnings from Operations	$ 131	$ 299	$ 193
Gain on Disposal..........................	—	—	374
Net Income	$ 505	$ 505	$ 815

c. Refer to the statement of cash flows for General Dynamics in Exhibit 4.13. Why is the restated amount of cash flow from operations for Year 9 of $609 million less than the originally reported amount of $673 million?

d. If the analyst wished to analyze changes in the structure of assets and equities between Year 8 and Year 9, which columns and amounts in Exhibit 4.11 would the analyst use? Explain.

e. If the analyst wished to analyze changes in the operating profitability between Year 8 and Year 9, which columns and amounts in Exhibit 4.12 would the analyst use? Explain.

f. If the analyst wished to use cash flow ratios to assess short-term liquidity and long-term solvency risk, which columns and amounts in Exhibit 4.13 would the analyst use? Explain.

4.6 USING ORIGINALLY REPORTED VERSUS RESTATED DATA. INTERCO is a manufacturer and retailer of a broad line of consumer products, including London Fog, Florsheim Shoes, Converse, Ethan Allen Furniture, and Lane Furniture. During Year 9, INTERCO became the target of an unfriendly takeover attempt. In an effort to defend itself against the takeover, INTERCO declared a special dividend of $1.4 billion. It financed the dividend by issuing long-term debt and preferred stock. INTERCO planned to dispose of certain businesses to repay a portion of this debt. Exhibits 4.14, 4.15, and 4.16 present balance sheets, income statements, and statements of cash flows, respectively, for INTERCO. The first column of each exhibit shows the amounts as originally reported for Year 8. The second column shows the restated amounts for Year 8 to reflect the decision to dispose of certain businesses that the Company had previously included in continuing operations. The third column shows the amounts reported for Year 9.

EXHIBIT 4.13

General Dynamics Corporation
Statements of Cash Flows
(amounts in millions)
(Problem 4.5)

	Year 8 as Originally Reported	Year 8 as Restated in Year 9 Annual Report	Year 9 as Reported
Operations			
Income from Continuing Operations	$ 374	$ 206	$ 248
Depreciation and Amortization	303	140	56
(Increase) Decrease in Accounts Receivable	(91)	4	35
(Increase) Decrease in Contracts in Process	237	(83)	(76)
(Increase) Decrease in Other Current Assets	13	8	(6)
Increase (Decrease) in Accounts Payable and Accruals	262	51	(66)
Increase (Decrease) in Other Current Liabilities .	(469)	(41)	11
Cash Flow from Continuing Operations	$ 629	$ 285	$ 202
Cash Flow from Discontinued Operations.	44	324	288
Cash Flow from Operations.	$ 673	$ 609	$ 490
Investing			
Proceeds from Sale of Discontinued Operations. .	$ 184	$ 184	$ 1,039
Capital Expenditures.	(82)	(29)	(18)
Purchase of Marketable Securities	(307)	(307)	(125)
Other.	56	3	32
Cash Flow from Investing	$(149)	$(149)	$ 928
Financing			
Issue of Common Stock	—	—	$ 57
Repayment of Debt	$ (61)	$ (11)	(454)
Purchase of Common Stock.	—	—	(960)
Dividends	(42)	(42)	(55)
Other.	(17)	—	—
Cash Flow from Financing	$(120)	$ (53)	$(1,412)
Change in Cash.	$ 404	$ 407	$ 6
Cash—Beginning of Year.	109	100	507
Cash—End of Year	$ 513	$ 507	$ 513

REQUIRED

a. Refer to the balance sheets of INTERCO in Exhibit 4.14. Why is the restated amount for total assets for Year 8 of $1,830,400 different from the originally reported amount for total assets of $1,985,586?

b. Refer to the income statement of INTERCO in Exhibit 4.15. Why is the originally reported and restated net income the same ($145,003) when each of the company's individual revenues and expenses decreased upon restatement?

EXHIBIT 4.14

INTERCO
Balance Sheets
(amounts in thousands)
(Problem 4.6)

	Year 8 as Originally Reported	Year 8 as Restated in Year 9 Annual Report	Year 9 as Originally Reported
Cash and Marketable Securities	$ 31,882	$ 23,299	$ 77,625
Receivables	486,657	310,053	329,299
Inventories	805,095	514,193	490,967
Prepayments	35,665	24,984	41,625
Net Assets of Discontinued Businesses	—	521,644	346,372
Total Current Assets	$1,359,299	$1,394,173	$ 1,285,888
Property, Plant, and Equipment (net)	479,499	317,238	327,070
Other Assets	146,788	118,989	162,344
Total Assets	$1,985,586	$1,830,400	$ 1,775,302
Current Liabilities	$ 373,343	$ 269,315	$ 736,268
Long-Term Debt	299,140	266,191	1,986,837
Other Noncurrent Liabilities	61,766	43,557	57,947
Total Liabilities	$ 734,249	$ 579,063	$ 2,781,052
Contributed Capital	$ 256,740	$ 256,740	$ 339,656
Retained Earnings	1,179,964	1,179,964	(1,208,250)
Treasury Stock	(185,367)	(185,367)	(137,156)
Total Shareholders' Equity	$1,251,337	$1,251,337	$(1,005,750)
Total Liabilities and Shareholders' Equity	$1,985,586	$1,830,400	$ 1,775,302

EXHIBIT 4.15

INTERCO
Income Statements
(amounts in thousands)
(Problem 4.6)

	Year 8 as Originally Reported	Year 8 as Restated in Year 9 Annual Report	Year 9 as Originally Reported
Sales	$3,341,423	$1,995,974	$2,011,962
Other Income	29,237	13,714	18,943
Total Revenues	$3,370,660	$2,009,688	$2,030,905
Cost of Goods Sold	$2,284,640	$1,288,748	$1,335,678
Selling and Administrative	799,025	493,015	537,797
Interest	33,535	29,188	141,735
Income Taxes	108,457	85,303	19,977
Total Expenses	$3,225,657	$1,896,254	$2,035,187
Income from Continuing Operations	$ 145,003	$ 113,434	$ (4,282)
Income from Discontinued Operations	—	31,569	74,432
Net Income	$ 145,003	$ 145,003	$ 70,150

EXHIBIT 4.16

INTERCO
Statements of Cash Flows
(amounts in thousands)
(Problem 4.6)

	Year 8 as Originally Reported	Year 8 as Restated in Year 9 Annual Report	Year 9 as Originally Reported
Operations			
Income (Loss) from Continuing Operations	$ 145,003	$ 113,434	$ (4,282)
Depreciation.....................................	62,772	40,570	40,037
Other Addbacks (Subtractions)	13,957	8,750	(24,230)
Change in Operating Working Capital Accounts	(103,958)	(96,271)	29,015
Cash Flow from Continuing Operations	$ 117,774	$ 66,483	$ 40,540
Cash Flow from Discontinued Operations..........	—	27,964	249,704
Cash Flow from Operations....................	$ 117,774	$ 94,447	$ 290,244
Investing			
Sale of Fixed Assets	$ 8,102	$ 1,145	$ 4,134
Acquisition of Fixed Assets	(65,880)	(45,925)	(50,966)
Cash Flow from Investing	$ (57,778)	$ (44,780)	$ (46,832)
Financing			
Increase in Short-Term Borrowing................	$ 1,677	$ 1,677	$ —
Increase in Long-Term Borrowing	205,673	205,533	1,967,500
Increase in Capital Stock	4,606	4,606	19,994
Decrease in Long-Term Borrowing.................	(95,841)	(85,570)	(617,401)
Decrease in Capital Stock	(160,442)	(160,442)	(102,341)
Dividends	(64,219)	(64,219)	(1,456,162)
Other..	54	252	(676)
Cash Flow from Financing	$(108,492)	$ (98,163)	$ (189,086)
Net Change in Cash...........................	$ (48,496)	$ (48,496)	$ 54,326

c. Refer to the statement of cash flows for INTERCO in Exhibit 4.16. Why is the restated amount of cash flow from operations for Year 8 of $94,447 less than the originally reported amount of $117,774?

d. If the analyst wished to analyze changes in the structure of assets and equities between Year 8 and Year 9, which columns and which amounts in Exhibit 4.14 would the analyst use? Explain.

e. If the analyst wishes to compare the change in operating performance between Year 8 and Year 9, which columns and which amounts in Exhibit 4.15 would the analyst use? Explain.

f. Describe briefly how INTERCO's actions during Year 9 might thwart an unfriendly takeover attempt.

4.7 ADJUSTING FINANCIAL STATEMENTS FOR DIFFERENT ACCOUNTING PRINCIPLES.
Glaxo Holdings (Glaxo) is the largest pharmaceutical company in the United Kingdom.

Financial statements for Glaxo prepared in accordance with generally accepted accounting principles (GAAP) in the United Kingdom appear in Exhibit 4.17 (balance sheet), Exhibit 4.18 (income statement), and Exhibit 4.19 (statement of cash flows). Exhibit 4.20 presents a reconciliation of shareholders' equity and net income from U.K. accounting principles to U.S. accounting principles. A description of the reconciling items appears below.

Deferred Taxation.   U.K. GAAP requires the recognition of deferred taxes only when it is probable that deferred tax benefits or liabilities will crystallize. U.S. GAAP requires the recognition of deferred taxes for all temporary differences between financial and tax reporting.

EXHIBIT 4.17

Glaxo
Balance Sheet
(amounts in millions)
(Problem 4.7)

	June 30		
	Year 2	Year 3	Year 4
Assets			
Cash	£ 225	£ 390	£ 119
Marketable Securities	1,524	2,107	2,644
Accounts Receivable	720	916	908
Inventories	475	595	575
Other Current Assets	211	234	234
Total Current Assets	£3,155	£4,242	£4,480
Investments in Securities	32	61	55
Property, Plant, and Equipment (net)	2,341	2,959	3,184
Other Assets	154	196	168
Total Assets	£5,682	£7,458	£7,887
Liabilities and Shareholders' Equity			
Accounts Payable	£ 162	£ 178	£ 188
Short-Term Debt	366	597	400
Other Current Liabilities	1,040	1,425	1,542
Total Current Liabilities	£1,568	£2,200	£2,130
Long-Term Debt	137	243	298
Deferred Income Taxes	179	193	139
Other Noncurrent Liabilities	159	165	154
Total Liabilities	£2,043	£2,801	£2,721
Minority Interests in Subsidiaries	£ 67	£ 111	£ 123
Common Stock	£ 753	£ 758	£ 762
Additional Paid-in Capital	77	151	229
Retained Earnings	2,742	3,637	4,052
Total Shareholders' Equity	£3,572	£4,546	£5,043
Total Liabilities and Shareholders' Equity	£5,682	£7,458	£7,887

EXHIBIT 4.18

Glaxo
Income Statements
(amounts in millions)
(Problem 4.7)

	Year Ended June 30	
	Year 3	Year 4
Sales	£ 4,930	£ 5,656
Other Revenues	206	65
Cost of Goods Sold..........................	(871)	(1,007)
Selling and Administrative....................	(1,795)	(1,972)
Research and Development	(739)	(858)
Interest	(56)	(44)
Income Taxes................................	(461)	(525)
Minority Interest in Net Income	(7)	(12)
Net Income	£ 1,207	£ 1,303

Postretirement Benefits Other Than Pensions. U.K. GAAP allows recognition of postretirement benefits other than pensions on a cash basis. U.S. GAAP requires recognition of this benefit obligation on an accrual basis. The postretirements benefit obligation was £26 million pounds on July 1, Year 3.

Goodwill. U.K. GAAP allows firms to write off goodwill against retained earnings. U.S. GAAP requires firms to capitalize and amortize goodwill over a maximum period of 40 years.

Dividends. U.K. GAAP provides for the recognition of a liability when the board of directors recommends a dividend to shareholders for their approval. U.S. GAAP does not recognize a dividend until declared by the board of directors, which occurs in the United Kingdom after shareholders' approval.

REQUIRED

a. Indicate the adjustments to Glaxo's balance sheet, income statement, and statement of cash flows to convert its financial statements from U.K. GAAP to U.S. GAAP. Glaxo includes the dividend recommended to shareholders in other current liabilities.
b. Compute the rate of return on common shareholders' equity using the reported amounts (U.K. GAAP) and the adjusted amounts (U.S. GAAP). Disaggregate ROCE into ROA, common earnings leverage, and capital structure leverage components. The income tax rate is 33 percent.
c. Why are ROCE and ROA larger and the capital structure leverage ratio smaller using the reported amounts (U.K. GAAP) than using the adjusted amounts (U.S. GAAP)?

4.8 ADJUSTING FINANCIAL STATEMENTS FOR DIFFERENT ACCOUNTING PRINCIPLES.
Benetton, headquartered in Italy, operates women's retail apparel stores worldwide. Financial

EXHIBIT 4.19

Glaxo
Statement of Cash Flows
(amounts in millions)
(Problem 4.7)

	Year Ended June 30	
	Year 3	Year 4
Operations		
Net Income	£1,207	£ 1,303
Depreciation and Amortization	225	282
Other Addbacks	86	120
Other Subtractions	(29)	(11)
	£1,489	£ 1,694
(Increase) Decrease in Accounts Receivable	(196)	8
(Increase) Decrease in Inventories	29	5
(Increase) Decrease in Other Current Assets	102	0
Increase (Decrease) in Accounts Payable	16	10
Increase (Decrease) in Other Current Liabilities	30	41
Cash Flow from Operations	£1,470	£ 1,758
Investing		
Property, Plant, and Equipment Sold	£ 84	£ 22
Property, Plant, and Equipment Acquired	(608)	(575)
Investments Acquired	(337)	(814)
Other Investing Transactions	3	4
Cash Flow from Investing	£ (858)	£(1,363)
Financing		
Increase (Decrease) in Short-Term Borrowing	£ 27	£ (12)
Issue of Common Stock	69	51
Dividends	(543)	(705)
Cash Flow from Financing	£ (447)	£ (666)
Change in Cash	£ 165	£ (271)
Cash—Beginning of Year	225	390
Cash—End of Year	£ 390	£ 119

statements for Benetton prepared in accordance with Italian generally accepted accounting principles (GAAP) appear in Exhibit 4.21 (balance sheet), Exhibit 4.22 (income statement), and Exhibit 4.23 (statement of cash flows). Exhibit 4.24 presents a reconciliation of shareholders' equity and net income from Italian accounting principles to U.S. accounting principles. A description of the reconciling items appears below.

Revaluation of Fixed Assets. Prior to Year 4, Italian law permitted firms to revalue fixed assets to market values, increasing a shareholders' equity account for the write-up. Depreciation on the revalued amounts appears in depreciation expense in subsequent years.

EXHIBIT 4.20

Glaxo
Reconciliation of U.K. and U.S. GAAP
(amounts in millions)
(Problem 4.7)

	June 30		
	Year 2	Year 3	Year 4
Shareholders' Equity, U.K. GAAP	£3,572	£4,546	£5,043
Deferred Taxation	(218)	(279)	(307)
Postretirement Benefits Other than Pensions	—	—	(26)
Goodwill.	23	27	35
Dividends	330	455	549
Shareholders' Equity, U.S. GAAP	£3,707	£4,749	£5,294

	Year Ended June 30	
	Year 3	Year 4
Net Income, U.K. GAAP	£1,207	£1,303
Deferred Taxation	(61)	(28)
Postretirement Benefits Other than Pensions	—	(26)
Goodwill Amortization	(1)	(1)
Net Income, U.S. GAAP	£1,145	£1,248

EXHIBIT 4.21

Benetton
Balance Sheet
(amounts in millions of Italian Lire)
(Problem 4.8)

	Year 5	Year 6	Year 7
Assets			
Cash	L 322,180	L 451,269	L 459,888
Marketable Securities	150,985	125,721	394,489
Accounts Receivable	882,475	1,077,000	1,304,878
Inventories	327,638	403,668	440,059
Other Current Assets	21,167	47,258	105,503
Total Current Assets	L1,704,445	L2,104,916	L2,704,817
Investments in Securities	172,916	120,257	49,409
Property, Plant, and Equipment (net) . .	270,808	533,975	590,546
Other Assets.	78,825	58,620	49,247
Total Assets	L2,226,994	L2,817,768	L3,394,019

Exh. 4.21—Continued	Year 5	Year 6	Year 7
Liabilities and Shareholders' Equity			
Accounts Payable..................	L 513,181	L 530,797	L 531,196
Short-Term Debt..................	272,291	671,245	710,118
Other Current Liabilities	106,808	156,356	233,955
Total Current Liabilities..........	L 892,280	L1,358,398	L1,475,269
Long-Term Debt	486,618	356,584	664,015
Deferred Income Taxes..............	22,838	29,231	1,410
Other Noncurrent Liabilities	43,911	83,173	126,041
Total Liabilities	L1,445,647	L1,827,386	L2,266,735
Minority Interests in Subsidiaries	L 64,815	L 67,621	L 64,006
Common Stock	L 81,777	L 81,777	L 81,777
Additional Paid-in Capital	186,661	186,661	186,661
Surplus from Revaluation of Assets ...	46,222	46,222	46,222
Retained Earnings.................	401,872	608,101	748,618
Total Shareholders' Equity.........	L 716,532	L 922,761	L1,063,278
Total Liabilities and Shareholders' Equity......................	L2,226,994	L2,817,768	L3,394,019

EXHIBIT 4.22

Benetton
Income Statements
(amounts in millions of Italian Lire)
(Problem 4.8)

	Year Ended June 30	
	Year 6	Year 7
Sales	L2,512,641	L2,751,458
Other Revenues	75,533	147,737
Cost of Goods Sold.....................	(1,526,913)	(1,591,403)
Selling and Administrative...............	(629,089)	(752,129)
Interest	(158,673)	(205,804)
Income Taxes..........................	(83,017)	(138,217)
Minority Interest in Net Income	(5,773)	(3,604)
Net Income	L 184,709	L 208,038

Goodwill Write-Off.   Italian GAAP allows firms to write off goodwill from corporate acquisitions against retained earnings in the year of acquisition. U.S. GAAP requires the capitalization and subsequent amortization of goodwill.

Deferred Taxes.   The reconciling items for deferred taxes represent the deferred income tax effects of other reconciling adjustments.

EXHIBIT 4.23

Benetton
Statement of Cash Flows
(amounts in millions of Italian Lire)
(Problem 4.8)

	Year Ended June 30	
	Year 6	Year 7
Operations		
Net Income	L 184,709	L 208,038
Depreciation and Amortization	82,120	90,885
Other Addbacks	224,508	309,154
Other Subtractions	(25,529)	(1,875)
	L 465,808	L 606,202
(Increase) Decrease in Accounts Receivable	(163,210)	(252,168)
(Increase) Decrease in Inventories	(34,201)	(19,764)
(Increase) Decrease in Other Current Assets	(28,651)	21,811
Increase (Decrease) in Accounts Payable	13,130	(17,569)
Increase (Decrease) in Other Current Liabilities	(67,605)	(111,412)
Cash Flow from Operations	L 185,271	L 227,100
Investing		
Property, Plant, and Equipment Sold	L 13,794	L 13,364
Investments Sold	92,901	73
Property, Plant, and Equipment Acquired	(93,730)	(116,415)
Investments Acquired	(108,978)	(45,081)
Other Investing Transactions	(6,724)	(26,399)
Cash Flow from Investing	L(102,737)	L(174,458)
Financing		
Increase (Decrease) in Short-Term Borrowing	L (37,619)	L 113,419
Increase (Decrease) in Long-Term Borrowing	29,494	154,633
Dividends	(53,132)	(67,776)
Other Financing Translations	12,675	1,641
Cash Flow from Financing	L (48,582)	L 201,917
Effect of Translation Adjustment	L 69,061	L (7,790)
Change in Cash	L 103,013	L 246,769
Cash—Beginning of Year	463,283	566,296
Cash—End of Year	L 566,296	L 813,065

REQUIRED

a. Indicate the effect on the balance sheet, income statement, and statement of cash flows of adjusting Benetton's financial statements to U.S. GAAP.

b. Compute Benetton's rate of return on common shareholders' equity using the reported amounts (Italian GAAP) and the restated amounts (U.S. GAAP). Disaggregate ROCE

EXHIBIT 4.24

Benetton
Reconciliation of U.K. and U.S. GAAP
(amounts in millions of Italian lire)
(Problem 4.8)

	June 30		
	Year 5	Year 6	Year 7
Shareholders' Equity, Italian GAAP.....	L716,532	L922,761	L1,063,278
Elimination of Revaluations of Fixed Assets Net of Depreciation...........	(19,494)	(16,919)	(13,785)
Reinstatement of Goodwill Previously Written Off	57,101	7,295	6,043
Deferred Taxes.......................	(17,886)	5,668	5,611
Shareholders' Equity, U.S. GAAP.......	L736,253	L918,805	L1,061,147

	Year Ended June 30	
	Year 6	Year 7
Net Income, Italian GAAP	L184,709	L208,038
Reduction in Depreciation on Revalued Fixed Assets....	2,575	3,134
Amortization of Goodwill	(338)	(1,252)
Deferred Taxes..................................	23,554	(57)
Net Income, U.S. GAAP	L210,500	L209,863

into ROA, common earnings leverage, and capital structure leverage components. The income tax rate is 36 percent.

c. Discuss the effect of the restatements to U.S. GAAP on your assessments of Benetton's profitability.

INTERNATIONAL PAPER: A RECURRING DILEMMA

International Paper Company is the largest forest products company in the world. It operates in five segments of the forest products industry:

1. *Printing Paper.* Uncoated and coated papers used for reprographic and printing, envelopes, writing tablets, file folders, and magazines.
2. *Packaging.* Liner board used for corrugated boxes and bleached packaging board used for food, pharmaceutical, cosmetic, and other consumer products.
3. *Distribution.* Sale of printing, graphic, packaging, and similar products through wholesale and retail outlets. Sales of these outlets comprise approximately 20 percent of International Paper products and 80 percent of other manufacturers' products.

4. *Specialty Products.* Film, door facings, and wood siding, fabrics, and chemicals used for adhesives and paints.
5. *Forest Products.* Logs, lumber, plywood, and wood panels. International Paper has the largest timber holdings of any private-sector entity in the United States.

The sales mix for four recent years appears below.

	Year 4	Year 5	Year 6	Year 7
Printing Papers	34%	31%	29%	27%
Packaging...............	26	26	26	22
Distribution	18	19	21	22
Specialty Products........	13	15	14	17
Forest Products	9	9	10	12
	100%	100%	100%	100%
United States	77%	76%	76%	79%
Europe	21	22	22	19
Other..................	2	2	2	2
	100%	100%	100%	100%

The financial statements for International Paper for Year 4 through Year 7 appear in Exhibit 1 (income statement), Exhibit 2 (balance sheet), and Exhibit 3 (statement of cash

EXHIBIT 1

International Paper
Income Statements
(amounts in millions)
(Case 4.1)

	Year Ended December 31			
	Year 4	Year 5	Year 6	Year 7
Sales	$12,960	$ 12,703	$ 13,598	$ 13,685
Cost of Goods Sold.......................	(9,930)	(10,041)	(10,987)	(11,089)
Selling and Administrative Expenses	(1,595)	(1,649)	(1,760)	(1,786)
Restructuring Charges	(212)	(60)	(398)	—
Interest Expense	(277)	(315)	(247)	(310)
Income Taxes............................	(377)	(239)	(64)	(211)
Income from Continuing Operations	$ 569	$ 399	$ 142	$ 289
Extraordinary Loss on Debt Retirement......	—	—	(6)	—
Changes in Accounting Principles	—	(215)	(50)	—
Net Income	$ 569	$ 184	$ 86	$ 289

International Paper
Balance Sheets
(amounts in millions)
(Case 4.1)

	December 31				
	Year 3	Year 4	Year 5	Year 6	Year 7
Assets					
Cash	$ 102	$ 256	$ 238	$ 225	$ 242
Accounts Receivable	1,517	1,798	1,841	1,861	1,856
Inventories	1,355	1,638	1,780	1,938	2,024
Prepayments	122	247	272	342	279
Total Current Assets	$ 3,096	$ 3,939	$ 4,131	$ 4,366	$ 4,401
Investments in Securities	467	103	383	599	631
Property, Plant, and Equipment (net)	7,002	8,038	8,591	9,643	9,658
Other Assets	1,017	1,589	1,836	1,851	1,941
Total Assets	$11,582	$13,669	$14,941	$16,459	$16,631
Liabilities and Shareholders' Equity					
Accounts Payable	$ 934	$ 1,094	$ 1,110	$ 1,259	$ 1,089
Notes Payable	1,017	1,087	1,699	2,356	2,089
Other Current Liabilities	779	974	918	916	831
Total Current Liabilities	$ 2,730	$ 3,155	$ 3,727	$ 4,531	$ 4,009
Long-Term Debt	2,324	3,096	3,351	3,096	3,601
Deferred Income Taxes	1,020	1,135	1,044	1,417	1,614
Other Noncurrent Liabilities	361	651	1,080	1,226	1,182
Total Liabilities	$ 6,435	$ 8,037	$ 9,202	$10,270	$10,406
Common Stock	$ 117	$ 117	$ 118	$ 127	$ 127
Additional Paid-in Capital	1,161	1,243	1,264	1,792	1,704
Retained Earnings	4,195	4,581	4,592	4,472	4,553
Treasury Stock	(326)	(309)	(235)	(202)	(159)
Total Shareholders' Equity	$ 5,147	$ 5,632	$ 5,739	$ 6,189	$ 6,225
Total Liabilities and Shareholders' Equity	$11,582	$13,669	$14,941	$16,459	$16,631

flows). Exhibit 4 presents financial statement ratios based on the amounts in Exhibits 1 through 3. Exhibit 5 presents profitability ratios for the product segments of International Paper, both including and excluding the restructuring charges discussed below.

The notes to the financial statements reveal the following information.

Restructuring Charges.   In December Year 4, the Company completed a review of operations in the context of its ongoing programs to emphasize value-added products in growing markets and improve the efficiency of its facilities. As a result, the Company

EXHIBIT 3

International Paper
Statements of Cash Flows
(amounts in millions)
(Case 4.1)

	Year Ended December 31			
	Year 4	Year 5	Year 6	Year 7
Operations				
Net Income	$ 569	$ 184	$ 86	$ 289
Depreciation	667	725	850	898
Restructuring Charges	212	60	398	—
Changes in Accounting Principles	—	215	50	—
Other Addbacks and Subtractions	58	75	(194)	32
	$ 1,506	$ 1,259	$ 1,190	$ 1,219
(Increase) Decrease in Accounts Receivable	(59)	79	2	78
(Increase) Decrease in Inventories	(55)	(74)	(127)	(93)
(Increase) Decrease in Prepayments	(125)	(25)	(70)	63
Increase (Decrease) in Accounts Payable	160	16	149	(170)
Increase (Decrease) in Other Current Liabilities	(42)	(78)	(66)	(168)
Cash Flow from Operations	$ 1,385	$ 1,177	$ 1,078	$ 929
Investing				
Capital Expenditures	$(1,409)	$(1,328)	$(1,531)	$ (971)
Investments Acquired	(2)	(640)	(341)	(151)
Cash Flow from Investing	$(1,411)	$(1,968)	$(1,872)	$(1,122)
Financing				
Increase in Long-Term Borrowing	$ 967	$ 1,583	$ 1,852	$ 1,276
Issue of Common Stock	40	45	703	225
Decrease in Long-Term Borrowing	(634)	(589)	(1,458)	(1,016)
Dividends	(183)	(186)	(206)	(208)
Other Financing Transactions	(10)	(80)	(110)	(67)
Cash Flow from Financing	$ 180	$ 773	$ 781	$ 210
Change in Cash	$ 154	$ (18)	$ (13)	$ 17
Cash—Beginning of Year	102	256	238	225
Cash—End of Year	$ 256	$ 238	$ 225	$ 242

recorded a pretax charge of $212 million ($137 million after taxes), principally related to the planned sale or closure of certain wood products and converting facilities, the estimated cost of environmental remediation, and severance and other personnel expenses associated with the business improvement program.

In December Year 5, the Company recorded a $60 million ($37 million after taxes) reduction in work force charge to cover severance costs associated with the elimination of more than 1,000 positions from its worldwide work force.

EXHIBIT 4

International Paper
Financial Statement Ratios
(Case 4.1)

	Year 4	Year 5	Year 6	Year 7
Profit Margin for ROA	5.8%	3.1%	1.8%	3.6%
Assets Turnover	1.0	.9	.9	.8
Rate of Return on Assets	6.0%	2.7%	1.6%	3.0%
Common Earnings Leverage	75.7%	47.0%	34.5%	58.9%
Capital Structure Leverage	2.3	2.5	2.6	2.7
Rate of Return on Common Shareholders' Equity	10.6%	3.2%	1.4%	4.7%
Cost of Goods Sold ÷ Sales	76.6%	79.0%	80.8%	81.0%
Selling and Administrative Expense ÷ Sales	12.3%	13.0%	12.9%	13.1%
Interest Expense ÷ Sales	2.1%	2.5%	1.8%	2.3%
Income Tax Expense ÷ Sales	4.3%	3.5%	1.7%	3.1%
Accounts Receivable Turnover	7.8	7.0	7.3	7.4
Inventory Turnover	6.6	5.9	5.9	5.6
Fixed Asset Turnover	1.7	1.5	1.5	1.4
Current Ratio	1.3	1.1	1.0	1.1
Quick Ratio	.7	.6	.5	.5
Cash Flow from Operations ÷ Average Current Liabilities	47.1%	34.2%	26.1%	21.8%
Days Accounts Receivable	47	52	50	50
Days Inventory	55	62	62	65
Days Accounts Payable	36	40	39	38
Liabilities ÷ Assets	58.8%	61.6%	62.4%	62.6%
Long-Term Debt ÷ Assets	22.6%	22.4%	18.8%	21.7%
Long-Term Debt ÷ Shareholders' Equity	55.0%	58.4%	50.0%	57.8%
Cash Flow from Operations ÷ Average Total Liabilities	19.1%	13.7%	11.1%	9.0%
Interest Coverage Ratio	4.4	3.0	1.8	2.6
Cash Flow from Operations ÷ Capital Expenditures	1.0	.9	.7	1.0

In November Year 6, the Company recorded a pretax charge of $398 million ($263 million after taxes) to establish a productivity improvement reserve. Over 80 percent of this charge represents asset write-downs for facility closings or realignments and related severance and relocation costs. The balance covers one-time costs of environmental clean-up, remediation, and legal costs.

Extraordinary Item.   The Company recorded a loss of $6 million on the early extinguishment of high-interest rate debt during Year 6.

Accounting Changes.   The Company adopted the provisions of FASB *Statement No. 106,* "Employer's Accounting for Postretirement Benefits Other Than Pensions," on January 1, Year 5. The Company recognized a pretax charge of $350 million ($215 million after taxes). The Company adopted the provisions of FASB *Statement No. 109,* "Accounting for Income Taxes," on January 1, Year 6, resulting in a charge of $50 million.

REQUIRED

a. For each of the three categories of income items described above, discuss (1) whether you would eliminate it when assessing the profitability of International Paper and, if so,

EXHIBIT 5

International Paper
Product Line Segment Profitability Analysis
(Case 4.1)

	ROA				Profit Margin				Assets Turnover			
	Year 4	Year 5	Year 6	Year 7	Year 4	Year 5	Year 6	Year 7	Year 4	Year 5	Year 6	Year 7
Profitability Analysis (including restructuring charges)												
Printing Paper	13.3%	5.5%	(1.1%)	(1.9%)	14.1%	7.3%	(1.7%)	(3.1%)	.94	.75	.62	.60
Packaging	13.3%	11.0%	9.9%	6.2%	12.3%	11.1%	9.3%	6.1%	1.08	.99	1.06	1.03
Distribution	.9%	5.3%	4.9%	5.3%	.3%	2.0%	1.7%	1.8%	3.03	2.57	2.81	2.89
Specialty Products . .	11.1%	9.4%	2.8%	10.1%	12.7%	9.5%	3.1%	10.7%	.87	.99	.92	.94
Forest Products	1.8%	7.0%	12.3%	27.8%	2.6%	10.3%	13.2%	26.2%	.70	.68	.93	1.06
Profitability Analysis (excluding restructuring charges)												
Printing Paper	13.8%	5.8%	.7%	(1.9%)	14.6%	7.8%	1.2%	(3.1%)	.94	.75	.62	.60
Packaging	15.0%	11.4%	10.7%	6.2%	13.9%	11.5%	10.1%	6.1%	1.08	.99	1.06	1.03
Distribution	5.2%	5.4%	6.0%	5.3%	1.7%	2.1%	2.1%	1.8%	3.03	2.57	2.81	2.89
Specialty Products . .	11.9%	10.2%	9.6%	10.1%	13.6%	10.4%	10.5%	10.7%	.87	.99	.92	.94
Forest Products	5.1%	7.0%	16.7%	27.8%	7.2%	10.3%	17.9%	26.2%	.70	.68	.93	1.06

(2) the adjustments you would make to the income statement, balance sheet, and statement of cash flows.

b. Taking into consideration the adjustments from part (*a*), analyze and interpret the changes in the profitability and risk of International Paper during this four-year period. Year 5 and Year 6 were years of economic recession in the United States. The statutory tax rate was 34 percent in Year 4 to Year 6 and 35 percent in Year 7.

TANAGUCHI CORPORATION: PART A

Dave Ando and Yoshi Yashima, recent business school graduates, work as research security analysts for a mutual fund specializing in international equity investments. Based on several strategy meetings, senior managers of the fund decided to invest in the machine tool industry. One international company under consideration is Tanaguchi Corporation, a Japanese manufacturer of machine tools. As staff analysts assigned to perform fundamental analysis on all new investment options, Ando and Yashima obtain a copy of Tanaguchi Corporation's unconsolidated financial statements and notes (Appendix A) and set out to calculate its usual spreadsheet of financial statement ratios. Exhibit 1 presents the results of their efforts. As a basis for comparison, Exhibit 1 also presents the median ratios for U.S. machine tool companies for a comparable year. The following conversation ensues.

Dave: Tanaguchi Corporation does not appear to be as profitable as comparable U.S. firms. Its operating margin and rate of return on assets are significantly less than the median ratios for U.S. machine tool operators. Its rate of return on common equity is only slightly less than its U.S. counterparts, but this is at the expense of assuming much more financial leverage and therefore risk. Most of this leverage is in the form of short-term borrowing. You can see this in its higher total liabilities to total assets ratio combined with its lower long-term debt ratio. This short-term borrowing and higher risk are also evidenced by the lower current and quick ratios. Finally, the market price of Tanaguchi Corporation's shares are selling at a higher multiple of net income and stockholders' equity than U.S. machine tool companies. I can't see how we can justify paying more for a company that is less profitable and more risky than comparable U.S. companies. It doesn't seem to me that it is worth exploring this investment possibility any further.

Yoshi: You may be right, Dave. However, I wonder if we are not comparing apples and oranges. As a Japanese company, Tanaguchi Corporation operates in an entirely different institutional and cultural environment than U.S. machine tool companies. Furthermore, it prepares its financial statements in accordance with Japanese generally accepted accounting principles (GAAP), which differ from those in the United States.

Dave: Well, I think we need to explore this further. I recall seeing a report on an associate's desk comparing U.S. and Japanese accounting principles. I will get a copy for us (Appendix B).

SOURCE: Paul R. Brown of New York University coauthored this case. It appeared in *Issues in Accounting Education,* Spring 1992, pp. 57–59, and is reproduced with permission of the American Accounting Association.

		EXHIBIT 1

Tanaguchi Corporation and U.S. Machine Tool Companies
Comparative Financial Ratio Analysis
(Case 4.2)

	Tanaguchi Corporation	Median Ratio for U.S. Machine Tool Companies[a]
Profitability Ratios		
Operating Margin after Taxes (before interest expense and related tax effects)..	2.8%	3.3%
× Total Assets Turnover................	1.5	1.8
= Return on Assets	4.2%	5.9%
× Common Earnings Leverage Ratio......	0.83	0.91
× Capital Structure Leverage	3.8	2.6
= Return on Common Equity............	13.3%[b]	13.9%[b]
Operating Margin Analysis		
Sales	100.0%	100.0%
Other Revenue/Sales....................	0.4	—
Cost of Goods Sold/Sales...............	(73.2)	(69.3)
Selling and Administrative/Sales..........	(21.0)	(25.8)
Income Taxes/Sales....................	(3.4)	(1.6)
Operating Margin (excluding interest and related tax effects)....................	2.8%	3.3%
Asset Turnover Analysis		
Receivable Turnover	5.1	6.9
Inventory Turnover	6.3	5.2
Fixed Asset Turnover	7.5	7.0
Risk Analysis		
Current Ratio.........................	1.1	1.6
Quick Ratio	0.7	0.9
Total Liabilities/Total Assets	73.8%	61.1%
Long-Term Debt/Total Assets	4.7%	16.1%
Long-Term Debt/Stockholders' Equity	17.9%	43.2%
Times Interest Covered.................	5.8	3.1
Market Price Ratios (per common share)		
Market Price/Net Income	45.0	9.0
Market Price/Stockholders' Equity	5.7	1.2

[a]**SOURCE:** Robert Morris Associates, *Annual Statement Studies* (except price-earnings ratio).

[b]The amounts for return on common equity may not precisely equal the product of return on assets, common earnings leverage, and capital structure leverage due to rounding.

REQUIRED

Using the report comparing U.S. and Japanese accounting principles (Appendix B) and Tanaguchi Corporation's financial statements and notes (Appendix A), identify the most important differences between U.S. and Japanese GAAP. Consider both the differences in acceptable methods and in the methods commonly used. For each major difference, indicate the likely effect (increase, decrease, or no effect) of converting Tanaguchi's financial statements to U.S. GAAP (1) on net income, (2) on total assets, and (3) on the ratio of liabilities divided by stockholders' equity.

CASE 4.2, APPENDIX 4.1

UNCONSOLIDATED FINANCIAL STATEMENTS FOR TANAGUCHI CORPORATION

Tanaguchi Corporation
Balance Sheet
(in billions of yen)
(Case 4.2)

	March 31	
	Year 4	Year 5
Assets		
Current Assets		
Cash	¥ 30	¥ 27
Marketable Securities (Note 1)	20	25
Notes and Accounts Receivable (Note 2)		
Trade Notes and Accounts	200	210
Affiliated Company	30	45
Less: Allowance for Doubtful Accounts	(5)	(7)
Inventories (Note 3)	130	150
Other Current Assets	25	30
Total Current Assets	¥ 430	¥ 480
Investments		
Investment in and Loans to Affiliated Companies (Note 4)	¥ 110	¥ 140
Investments in Other Companies (Note 5)	60	60
Total Investments	¥ 170	¥ 200
Property, Plant, and Equipment (Note 6)		
Land	¥ 25	¥ 25
Buildings	110	130
Machinery and Equipment	155	180
Less: Depreciation to Date	(140)	(165)
Total Property, Plant, and Equipment	¥ 150	¥ 170
Total Assets	¥ 750	¥ 850
Liabilities and Stockholders' Equity		
Current Liabilities		
Short-Term Bank Loans	¥ 185	¥ 200
Notes and Accounts Payable		
Trade Notes and Accounts	140	164
Affiliated Company	25	20
Other Current Liabilities	40	50
Total Current Liabilities	¥ 390	¥ 434
Long-Term Liabilities		
Bonds Payable (Note 7)	¥ 20	¥ 20
Convertible Debt	20	20
Retirement and Severance Allowance (Note 8)	122	153
Total Long-Term Liabilities	¥ 162	¥ 193

| | March 31 | |
Balance Sheet—Continued	Year 4	Year 5
Stockholders' Equity		
Common Stock, 10 par value	¥ 15	¥ 15
Capital Surplus	40	40
Legal Reserve (Note 9).............................	16	17
Retained Earnings (Note 9).........................	127	151
Total Stockholders' Equity	¥ 198	¥ 223
Total Liabilities and Stockholders' Equity	¥ 750	¥ 850

Tanaguchi Corporation
Statement of Income and Retained Earnings for Fiscal Year 5
(in billions of yen)
(Case 4.2)

Revenues	
Sales (Note 10)	¥1,200
Interest and Dividends (Note 11)......................................	5
Total Revenues...	¥1,205
Expenses	
Cost of Goods Sold..	¥ 878
Selling and Administrative..	252
Interest	13
Total Expenses...	¥1,143
Income before Income Taxes...	¥ 62
Income Taxes (Note 12)	(34)
Net Income	¥ 28
Retained Earnings	
Balance, Beginning of Fiscal Year 5...................................	¥ 127
Net Income	28
Deductions:	
Cash Dividends	(3)
Transfer to Legal Reserve (Note 9)...................................	(1)
Balance, End of Fiscal Year 5	¥ 151

NOTES TO FINANCIAL STATEMENTS FOR TANAGUCHI CORPORATION

Note 1: Marketable securities appear on the balance sheet at acquisition cost.

Note 2: Accounts and notes receivable are noninterest bearing. Within 15 days of sales on open account, customers typically sign noninterest-bearing, single-payment notes. Customers usually pay these notes within 60 to 180 days after signing. When Tanaguchi Corporation needs cash, it discounts these notes with Menji Bank. Tanaguchi Corporation remains contingently liable in the event customers do not pay these notes at maturity. Receivables from (and payables to) affiliated company are with Takahashi Corporation (see Note 4) and are noninterest bearing

Note 3: Inventories appear on the balance sheet at lower of cost or market. The measurement of acquisition cost uses a weighted average cost-flow assumption.

Note 4: Intercorporate investments appear on the balance sheet at acquisition cost. The balances in this account at the end of Year 4 and Year 5 comprise the following:

	Year 4	Year 5
Investments in Tanaka Corporation (25%)	¥ 15	¥ 15
Investment in Takahashi Corporation (80%)	70	70
Loans to Takahashi Corporation	25	55
	¥110	¥140

Note 5: Other investments represent ownership shares of less than 20 percent and appear at acquisition cost.

Note 6: Fixed assets appear on the balance sheet at acquisition cost. The firm capitalizes expenditures that increase the service lives of fixed assets, whereas it expenses immediately expenditures that maintain the originally expected useful lives. It computes depreciation using the declining-balance method. Depreciable lives for buildings are 30 to 40 years and for machinery and equipment are 6 to 10 years.

Note 7: Bonds payable comprises two bond issues as follows:

	Year 4	Year 5
12% semiannual, ¥10 billion face value bonds, with interest payable on March 31 and September 30 and the principal payable at maturity on March 31, Year 20; the bonds were initially priced on the market to yield 10%, compounded semiannually..	¥11.50	¥11.45
8% semiannual, ¥10 billion face value bonds, with interest payable on March 31 and September 30 and the principal payable at maturity on March 31, Year 22; the bonds were initially priced on the market to yield 10%, compounded semiannually..	¥ 8.50	¥ 8.55
	¥20.00	¥20.00

Note 8: The firm provides amounts as a charge against income each year for estimated retirement and severance benefits but does not fund these amounts until it makes actual payments to former employees.

Note 9: The firm reduces retained earnings and increases the Legal Reserve account for a specified percentage of dividends paid during the year. The following plan for appropriation of retained earnings was approved by shareholders at the annual meeting held on June 29, Year 5:

Transfer to Legal Reserve..	¥(1)
Cash Dividend	(3)
Directors' and Statutory Auditors' Bonuses...........................	(1)
Elimination of Special Tax Reserve Relating to Sale of Equipment	1

Note 10: The firm recognizes revenues from sales of machine tools at the time of delivery. Reported sales for Year 5 are net of a provision for doubtful accounts of ¥50 billion.

Note 11: Interest and Dividend Revenue includes ¥1.5 billion from loans to Takahashi Corporation, an unconsolidated subsidiary.

Note 12: The firm computes income taxes based on a statutory tax rate of 55 percent for Year 5. Deferred tax accounting is not a common practice in Japan.

CASE 4.2, APPENDIX 4.2

COMPARISON OF U.S. AND JAPANESE GAAP

1. STANDARD SETTING PROCESS

U.S.   The U.S. Congress has the legal authority to prescribe acceptable accounting principles, but it has delegated that authority to the Securities and Exchange Commission (SEC). The SEC has stated that it will recognize pronouncements of the Financial Accounting Standard Board (FASB), a private-sector entity, as the primary vehicle for specifying generally accepted accounting standards.

Japan   The Japanese Diet has the legal authority to prescribe acceptable accounting principles. All Japanese corporations (both publicly and privately held) must periodically issue financial statements to their stockholders following provisions of the Japanese Commerical Code. This code is promulgated by the Diet. The financial statements follow strict legal entity concepts.

Publicly listed corporations in Japan must also file financial statements with the Securities Division of the Ministry of Finance following accounting principles promulgated by the Diet in the Securities and Exchange Law. The Diet, through the Ministry of Finance, obtains advice on accounting principles from the Business Advisory Deliberations Council (BADC), a body composed of representatives from business, the accounting profession,

SOURCES: The Japanese Institute of Certified Public Accountants, *Corporate Disclosure in Japan* (July 1987); KPMG Peat Marwick, *Comparison of Japanese and U.S. Reporting and Financial Practices* (1989); Price Waterhouse, *Doing Business in Japan* (1993).

and personnel from the Ministry of Finance. The BADC has no authority on its own to set acceptable accounting principles. The financial statements filed with the Securities Division of the Ministry of Finance tend to follow economic entity concepts, with intercorporate investments either accounted for using the equity method or consolidated.

All Japanese corporations file income tax returns with the Taxation Division of the Ministry of Finance. The accounting principles followed in preparing tax returns mirror closely those used in preparing financial statements for stockholders under the Japanese Commercial Code. The minister of finance will sometimes need to reconcile conflicting preferences of the Securities Division (desiring financial information better reflecting economic reality) and the Taxation Division (desiring to raise adequate tax revenues to run the government).

2. PRINCIPAL FINANCIAL STATEMENTS

Balance sheet, income statement, statement of cash flows. *U.S.*

Balance sheet, income statement, proposal for appropriation of profit or disposition of loss. *Japan* The financial statements filed with the Ministry of Finance contain some supplemental information on cash flows.

3. INCOME STATEMENT

Accrual basis. *U.S.*

Accrual basis. *Japan*

4. REVENUE RECOGNITION

Generally at time of sale; percentage-of-completion method usually required on long-term *U.S.* contracts; installment and cost-recovery-first methods permitted when there is high uncertainty regarding cash collectibility.

Generally at time of sale; percentage-of-completion method permitted on long-term contracts; *Japan* installment method common when collection period exceeds two years regardless of degree of uncertainty of cash collectibility.

5. UNCOLLECTIBLE ACCOUNTS

Allowance method. *U.S.*

Allowance method. *Japan*

6. INVENTORIES AND COST OF GOODS SOLD

Inventories valued at lower of cost or market. Cost determined by FIFO, LIFO, weighted *U.S.* average, or standard cost. Most firms use LIFO for domestic inventories and FIFO for non-domestic inventories.

Japan   Inventories valued at lower of cost or market. Cost determined by specific identification, FIFO, LIFO, weighted average, or standard cost. Most firms use weighted average or specific identification.

7. FIXED ASSETS AND DEPRECIATION EXPENSE

U.S.   Fixed assets valued at acquisition cost. Depreciation computed using straight-line, declining-balance, and sum-of-the-years'-digits methods. Permanent declines in value are recognized. Most firms use straight line for financial reporting and an accelerated method for tax reporting.

Japan   Fixed assets valued at acquisition cost. Depreciation computed using straight-line, declining-balance, and sum-of-the-years'-digits methods. Permanent declines in value are recognized. Most firms use a declining-balance method for financial and tax reporting.

8. INTANGIBLE ASSETS AND AMORTIZATION EXPENSE

U.S.   Internally developed intangibles expensed when expenditures are made. Externally purchased intangibles capitalized as assets and amortized over expected useful life (not to exceed 40 years). Goodwill cannot be amortized for tax purposes.

Japan   The cost of intangibles (both internally developed and externally purchased) can be expensed when incurred or capitalized and amortized over the period allowed for tax purposes (generally 5 to 20 years). Goodwill is amortized over 5 years. Some intangibles (for example, property rights) are not amortized.

9. LIABILITIES RELATED TO ESTIMATED EXPENSES (WARRANTIES, VACATION PAY, EMPLOYEE BONUSES)

U.S.   Estimated amount recognized as an expense and as a liability. Actual expenditures are charged against the liability.

Japan   Estimated amount recognized as an expense and as a liability. Actual expenditures are charged against the liability. Annual bonuses paid to members of the board of directors and to the Commercial Code auditors are not considered expenses but a distribution of profits. Consequently, such bonuses are charged against retained earnings.

10. LIABILITIES RELATED TO EMPLOYEE RETIREMENT AND SEVERANCE BENEFITS

U.S.   Liability recognized for unfunded accumulated benefits.

Japan   Severance benefits more common than pension benefits. An estimated amount is recognized each period as an expense and as a liability for financial reporting. The maximum liability recognized equals 40 percent of the amount payable if all eligible employees were terminated currently. There is wide variability in the amount recognized. Benefits are deducted for tax purposes only when actual payments are made to severed employees. Such benefits are seldom funded beforehand.

11. Liabilities Related to Income Taxes

Income tax expense based on book income amounts. Deferred tax expense and deferred tax asset or liability recognized for temporary (timing) differences between book and taxable income.   *U.S.*

Income tax expense based on taxable income amounts. Deferred tax accounting not practiced. In consolidated statements submitted to the Ministry of Finance by listed companies (see No. 18), deferred tax accounting is permitted.   *Japan*

12. Noninterest Bearing Notes

Notes stated at present value of future cash flows and interest recognized over term of the note.   *U.S.*

Notes stated at face amount and no interest recognized over term of the note. Commonly used as a substitute for Accounts Payable.   *Japan*

13. Bond Discount or Premium

Subtracted from or added to the face value of the bond and reported among liabilities on the balance sheet. Amortized over the life of the bond as an adjustment to interest expense.   *U.S.*

Bond discount usually included among intangible assets and amortized over the life of the bonds. Bond discount and premium may also be subtracted from or added to face value of bonds on the balance sheet and amortized as an adjustment of interest expense over the life of the bonds.   *Japan*

14. Leases

Distinction made between operating leases (not capitalized) and capital leases (capitalized).   *U.S.*

All leases treated as operating leases.   *Japan*

15. Legal Reserve (part of shareholders' equity)

Not applicable   *U.S.*

When dividends are declared and paid, unappropriated retained earnings and cash are reduced by the amount of the dividend. In addition, unappropriated retained earnings are reduced, and the legal reserve account is increased by a percentage of this dividend, usually 10 percent, until such time as the legal reserve equals 25 percent of stated capital. The effect of the latter entry is to capitalize a portion of retained earnings to make it part of permanent capital.   *Japan*

16. APPROPRIATIONS OF RETAINED EARNINGS

U.S. Not a common practice in the United States. Appropriations have no legal status when they do appear.

Japan Stockholders must approve each year the "proposal for appropriation of profit or disposition of loss." Four items commonly appear: dividend declarations, annual bonuses for directors and Commercial Code auditors, transfers to legal reserves, and changes in reserves.

The income tax law permits certain costs to be deducted earlier for tax than for financial reporting and permits certain gains to be recognized later for tax than for financial reporting. To obtain these tax benefits, the tax law requires that these items "be reflected on the company's books." The *pretax effects* of these timing differences *do not appear* on the income statement. Instead, an entry is made decreasing Unappropriated Retained Earnings and increasing special Retained Earnings Reserves (a form of appropriated retained earnings). When the timing difference reverses, the above entry is reversed. The *tax effects* on these timing differences *do appear* on the income statement, however. In the year that the timing difference originates, Income Tax Expense and Income Tax Payable are reduced by the tax effect of the timing difference. When the timing difference reverses, Income Tax Expense and Income Tax Payable are increased by a corresponding amount.

17. TREASURY STOCK

U.S. Shown at acquisition cost as a subtraction from total shareholders' equity. No income recognized from treasury stock transactions.

Japan Reacquired shares are either canceled immediately or shown as a current asset on the balance sheet.

18. INVESTMENTS IN SECURITIES

A. Marketable Securities (Current Asset)

U.S. Market value method.

Japan Reported at acquisition cost, unless price declines are considered permanent, in which case lower of cost or market.

B. Investments (Noncurrent Asset)

U.S. Accounting depends on ownership: Less than 20 percent, market value method; 20 percent to 50 percent, equity method; more than 50 percent, consolidated.

Japan The principal financial statements are those of the parent company only (that is, unconsolidated statements). Intercorporate investments are carried at acquisition cost. Listed companies must provide consolidated financial statements as supplements to the principal statements in filings to the Ministry of Finance. The accounting for investments in securities in these supplementary statements is essentially the same as in the United States.

19. CORPORATE ACQUISITIONS

Purchase method or pooling of interests method.

U.S.

Purchase method.

Japan

20. FOREIGN CURRENCY TRANSLATION

The translation method depends on whether the foreign unit operates as a self-contained entity (all-current method) or as an extension of the U.S. parent (monetary/nonmonetary method).

U.S.

For branches, the monetary/nonmonetary translation method is used, with any translation adjustment flowing through income. For subsidiaries, current monetary items are translated using the current rate, other balance sheet items use the historical rate, and the translation adjustment is part of shareholders' equity.

Japan

21. SEGMENT REPORTING

Segment information (sales, operating income, assets) disclosed by industry segment, geographical location, and type of customer.

U.S.

Sales data by segment (industry, geographical location).

Japan

CASE 4.3

TANAGUCHI CORPORATION: PART B[1]

Dave Ando and Yoshi Yashima spend the next several days converting the financial statements of Tanaguchi Corporation from Japanese to U.S. GAAP. Although their conversions required them to make several estimates, Dave and Yoshi felt comfortable that they had largely filtered out the effects of different accounting principles. Exhibit 2 of this case presents the profitability and risk ratios for Tanaguchi Corporation based on Japanese GAAP (column 1) and as restated to U.S. GAAP (column 2). Column 3 shows the median ratios for U.S. machine tool companies (the same as those reported in Exhibit 1). After studying the financial statement ratios in Exhibit 2, the following conversation ensues.

SOURCE: Paul R. Brown of New York University coauthored this case. It appeared in *Issues in Accounting Education,* Spring 1992, pp. 57–59, and is reproduced with permission of the American Accounting Association.

[1] Refer to Case 4.2, Tanaguchi Corporation: Part A, for background for this case.

EXHIBIT 2

Tanaguchi Corporation and U.S. Machine Tool Companies
Comparative Financial Ratio Analysis
(Case 4.3)

	Tanaguchi Corp. (Japanese GAAP) (1)	Tanaguchi Corp. (U.S. GAAP) (2)	Median Ratio for U.S. Machine Tool Companies (3)
Profitability Ratios			
Operating Margin after Taxes (before interest expense and related tax effects)...	2.8%	2.9%	3.3%
× Total Assets Turnover..................	1.5	1.5	1.8
= Return on Assets	4.2%	4.5%	5.9%
× Common Earnings Leverage Ratio.......	.83	.83	.91
× Capital Structure Leverage	3.8	4.0	2.6
= Return on Common Equity.............	13.3%[b]	14.8%[b]	13.9%[a]
Operating Margin Analysis			
Sales	100.0%	100.0%	100.0%
Other Revenue/Sales......................	.4	.4	—
Cost of Goods Sold/Sales.................	(73.2)	(73.4)	(69.3)
Selling and Administrative/Sales...........	(21.0)	(20.6)	(25.8)
Income Taxes/Sales......................	(3.4)	(3.5)	(1.6)
Operating Margin (excluding interest and related tax effects).....................	2.8%	2.9%	3.3%
Asset Turnover Analysis			
Receivable Turnover	5.1	5.0	6.9
Inventory Turnover	6.3	6.5	5.2
Fixed Asset Turnover	7.5	7.2	7.0
Risk Analysis			
Current Ratio............................	1.1	1.0	1.6
Quick Ratio	.7	.7	.9
Total Liabilities/Total Assets	73.8%	74.5%	61.1%
Long-Term Debt/Total Assets	4.7%	5.1%	16.1%
Long-Term Debt/Stockholders' Equity	17.9%	18.3%	43.2%
Times Interest Covered...................	5.8	5.7	3.1
Market Price Ratios (per common share)			
Market Price/Net Income	45.0	30.9	9.0
Market Price/Stockholders' Equity	5.7	4.6	1.2

[a]**SOURCE:** Robert Morris Associates, *Annual Statement Studies* (except price-earnings ratio).

[b]The amounts for return on common equity may not precisely equal the product of return on assets, common earnings leverage, and capital structure leverage due to rounding.

> **Dave:**   The operating profitability of Tanaguchi Corporation, as evidenced by the rate of return on assets, is still lower than comparable U.S. firms, even after adjusting for differences in accounting principles. Although Tanaguchi's rate of return on common equity is now higher than its U.S. counterparts, the higher return occurs at the expense of taking on substantially more debt and therefore more risk. A significant portion of the difference

in price-earnings ratios between Tanaguchi Corporation and U.S. companies results from differences in accounting principles. However, large differences still remain. I'm still not convinced that investing in Tanaguchi Corporation makes sense. Yoshi, am I on track with my interpretations or am I missing something?

Yoshi: I'm not sure we are yet to the point where we can make a recommendation regarding an investment in the shares of Tanaguchi Corporation. We need to develop a better understanding of why the restated financial ratios for Tanaguchi Corporation still differ so much from those for U.S. machine tool companies.

One possible explanation might relate to the practice of many Japanese companies to operate in corporate groups, which the Japanese call *keiretsus*. Tanaguchi Corporation is a member of the Menji *keiretsu*. Each *keiretsu* typically comprises firms in 8 or 10 different industries (for example, one *keiretsu* might include firms in the steel, chemicals, forest products, retailing, insurance, and banking industries). The companies usually hold stock in each other; investments in the 25 percent to 30 percent range are common. These investments are not made for the purpose of controlling or even significantly influencing other members of the corporate group. Rather, they serve as a mechanism for providing operating links between the entities. It is common for one corporation in the *keiretsu* to source many of its raw materials from another group member and to sell a substantial portion of its products to entities within the group. Each *keiretsu* includes a bank that provides needed funds to group members. It is rare that the bank would allow a member of the group to experience significant operating problems or to go bankrupt due to lack of funds.

A second, but related, institutional difference between the United States and Japan concerns stock ownership patterns. Roughly one-third of Japanese companies' shares is held by members of its *keiretsu* and another one-third is held by financial institutions, typically banks and insurance companies not affiliated with the *keiretsu*. This leaves only one-third of the shares held by individuals. The large percentage of intercorporate stock holdings has historically lessened the concern about keeping investors happy by paying large dividends or reporting ever-increasing earnings per share, as seems to be the case in the United States.

Instead, the emphasis of Japanese companies has been on serving new or growing markets, increasing market share, and strengthening the members of the *keiretsu*. The Japanese economy has grown more rapidly than the U.S. economy during the last several decades. In addition, Japanese companies have built their export markets and added operations abroad. The strategic emphasis has been on gaining market dominance in this growth environment, not on attaining particular levels of profit margin, rates of return, or earnings per share.

Finally, stock price changes in Japan appear related more to changes in real estate values than to the operating performance of individual companies. Real estate values and stock prices moved dramatically upward during the 1980s, although significant decreases have occurred recently. The increasing stock prices appeared to keep investors happy, leading them to deemphasize the kinds of profitability performance evaluation common in the United States. (*Note:* Your instructor may assign additional references in conjunction with this case that elaborate on strategic, institutional, and cultural differences between the United States and Japan.)

REQUIRED

After studying the financial statements and notes for Tanaguchi Corporation, develop explanations for the differences in the profitability and risk ratios for Tanaguchi Corporation reported in column 2 of Exhibit 2 as compared to those reported in column 3 for U.S. machine tool companies.

CHAPTER 5

GENERALLY ACCEPTED ACCOUNTING PRINCIPLES: INCOME RECOGNITION AND ASSET VALUATION

Learning Objectives

1. Review the criteria for recognizing income and expenses under the accrual basis of accounting and apply these criteria to various types of businesses.
2. Calculate the income statement, balance sheet, and statement of cash flow effects of recognizing income prior to the point of sale, at the time of sale, and subsequent to sale.
3. Analyze and interpret the effects of FIFO versus LIFO on profit margin and asset turnover measures and convert the financial statements of a firm from a LIFO to a FIFO basis.
4. Use financial statement disclosures on depreciable assets to calculate average depreciable lives and age of such assets and convert the financial statements of a firm from a straight-line to an accelerated depreciation basis.
5. Understand the alternative ways that firms account for research and developments costs and software development costs and the difficulties that these alternatives present when analyzing the profitability of high-technology firms.
6. Understand the distinction between changes in the general purchasing power of the monetary unit and changes in the prices of specific assets and liabilities and the accounting methods designed to adjust financial statements for these two types of changing prices.

The particular accounting principles, or methods, that a firm selects from the set of alternative methods deemed acceptable by the accounting profession (that is, GAAP) can significantly impact the financial statements and affect the appropriateness of their interpretations. This chapter and the next two describe alternative accounting methods commonly encountered in corporate annual reports. This chapter examines income recognition, inventory cost-flow assumptions, and depreciable and intangible asset accounting. The focus is on GAAP in the United States, although the chapter notes differences between the United States and other countries. Appendix 5.1 discusses issues of income recognition and asset valuation in highly inflationary or deflationary environments.

INCOME RECOGNITION

Figure 5.1 depicts the operating process for a typical manufacturing firm. The *amount* of income from operating activities equals the difference between the cash a firm ultimately receives from customers and the cash it pays to suppliers, employees, and others to manufacture and sell a product. To obtain an appropriate matching of revenues (outputs) and expenses (inputs) in the income statement, firms use the accrual basis rather than the cash basis of accounting.

Use of the accrual basis, however, does not settle the question of *when* firms recognize revenues (and matching expenses). Firms could recognize revenues (1) during the period of production, (2) at the completion of production, (3) at the time of sale, (4) during the period while receivables are outstanding, or (5) at the time of cash collection.

CRITERIA FOR REVENUE RECOGNITION

GAAP requires the recognition of revenue under the accrual basis of accounting when a firm:

1. Has provided all, or a substantial portion, of the services to be performed.
2. Has received either cash, a receivable, or some other asset susceptible to reasonably precise measurement.

FIGURE 5.1

Operating Process for a Manufacturing Firm

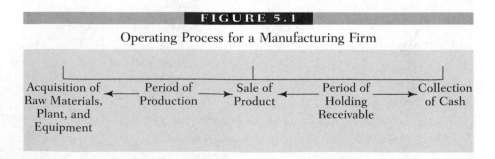

A firm incurs costs as it performs services. To justify revenue recognition, a firm needs to have performed sufficient services so that it can measure or estimate the total costs it expects to incur. Such measurement of total costs permits an appropriate matching of expenses with revenues.

The benefit that a firm obtains from providing services is the cash or cash equivalent value of other consideration it expects to receive. To justify revenue recognition, a firm needs to have a reasonably precise measurement of the amount of this expected benefit. Receiving cash provides such measurement. Receiving other assets may also provide such measurement if the firm can ascertain the cash-equivalent value of these assets in a reasonably reliable manner.

Most firms recognize revenues at the time of sale (delivery). At that time, the firm transfers the goods to a buyer or performs the required services. Its obligation for future services, such as for warranties, is either insignificant or, if significant, is subject to reasonably precise measurement. An exchange between an independent buyer and seller provides an objective measure of the amount of revenue. If the firm makes the sale on account, its past experience and assessment of the credit standing of customers provide a basis for predicting the amount of cash it will collect. Thus, the firm usually meets the criteria for revenue recognition at the time of sale.

CRITERIA FOR EXPENSE RECOGNITION

GAAP requires the recognition of expenses under the accrual basis of accounting as follows:

1. Costs directly associated with revenues become expenses in the period in which a firm recognizes the revenues.
2. Costs not directly associated with revenues become expenses in the period in which a firm consumes the services or benefits of the costs in operations.

Most of the costs of manufacturing and selling a product closely relate to particular revenues. The firm matches expense recognition with revenue recognition for such items. Other costs, such as insurance and property taxes on administrative facilities, salaries of corporate officers, and depreciation on computer equipment, bear only an indirect relation to revenues generated during the period. Such costs become expenses in the period in which the firm consumes the benefits of insurance or of governmental, administrative, and computer services. Accountants refer to such costs as *period expenses*.

Although most firms recognize revenues and expenses at the time of sale, the analyst should assess whether this timing of income recognition is appropriate in particular cases. The next section illustrates some of the issues that the analyst should address.

APPLICATION OF REVENUE AND EXPENSE RECOGNITION CRITERIA

This section illustrates the application of the criteria for revenue and expense recognition for various types of businesses.

Example 1.   Paramount Communications produces movies. It incurs production costs in filming the movies, advertising costs in promoting the films, and royalty costs for the principal actors and actresses, producers, directors, and others. Paramount generates revenues from movie theaters based on the number of tickets sold. It may also generate revenues from the sale of videos and residual rights to the movies, television or cable networks, or to foreign licensees. The amount of revenues generated from the sale of videos and residual movie rights depends in part on the success of the films in their initial theater run.

The movie studio can easily measure the amount of revenues from theater ticket sales and can recognize it as sales occur. The amount of revenues that a film will generate from video sales and the sales of residual rights is highly uncertain as of the time of the movie's initial release. The criteria for the recognition of revenue are therefore not met until sales of videos and residual rights occur in later periods. The movie studio can easily match royalty expense with revenues because the royalty amount is usually a percentage of the revenues. The principal income recognition issue for movie studios is determining how much of the costs of filming and promoting the movie should the studio match with theater ticket revenues and how much should it leave on the balance sheet as an asset and match with revenues from video sales and residual rights in later periods. The revenue pattern of previous movies may provide a basis for projecting the likely total revenues from new releases. Also, one would expect (hope) that the movie studio considered revenue projections in establishing the cost budget for the movie. When examining the financial statements of a movie studio, the analyst should study carefully the profit margin on movies reported in the income statement and the amount of deferred production costs remaining on the balance sheet.

Example 2.   Columbia Records runs periodic promotions to enlist subscribers to its tape or compact disc-of-the-month programs. For a nominal fee, new subscribers receive a set of tapes or compact discs and promise to purchase a certain minimum number of such items over some future time period. The firm sends subscribers cards each month that list the tapes or compact discs available for that month. Subscribers return the cards if they wish to purchase one of the selections. Similar arrangements apply to book-of-the-month or craft-of-the-month programs.

The principal income measurement issue in these settings is the timing of revenue recognition. Should Columbia recognize the revenues from selling the minimum number of required tapes or compact discs when customers commit to such purchases upon subscription? Or should Columbia recognize a portion of the revenues each month when it sends out the cards? The return rate from customers desiring to purchase the tape or compact disc selection is relatively low each month. If the return rate were highly predictable, such as 20 percent or 30 percent, the firms could simply recognize revenue for that portion of customer orders. The return rate, however, is not only low but unpredictable. The selection in one month may have a 20 percent customer order rate and the next month's selection may experience a 50 percent customer demand rate. Furthermore, several months might elapse before the size of customer orders becomes clear. Columbia does not meet the criteria for revenue recognition either at the time customers subscribe or at the time it sends out cards each month because the amount of cash that the firm will ultimately receive and its date of receipt are not measurable with sufficient precision. Columbia should delay recognition until it ships products to customers.

Additional income recognition issues arise with respect to the initial promotional offer. Should Columbia recognize the costs of the promotional tapes or compact discs as an expense in the period when the customer subscribes to the program, or should it spread such costs over the future periods when customers purchase the additional items required by the program? Firms that defer such costs report a deferred asset, such as Deferred Subscription Costs, on their balance sheet.

Example 3.   Automotive and appliance manufacturers typically provide warranty or maintenance services for products sold. Some companies include such services automatically in the sale of their products; the selling price includes a charge for the automobile or appliance and its related warranty. Other companies provide a very limited warranty with the product and sell a more comprehensive warranty or maintenance agreement separately. Customers can decide whether to purchase the extended protection. This protection may cover a period of three to five years.

These firms typically receive cash for both the product sold and any related warranty at the time they sell the main product. Thus, little uncertainty exists regarding the amount of revenue. The principal income recognition issue regards the amount of expense to match against the revenue. These firms must provide future services, the cost of which the firms will not know with certainty for several years. If these firms will perform only minimal future services or can predict the costs of such services with a reasonably high degree of precision, they can recognize the warranty revenue in the period when they sell the main product. Such firms would also recognize an estimated warranty expense to match against such revenues. A Warranty Liability account reflecting the expected costs of future warranty claims appears on the balance sheet. If these firms must provide substantial future services or if the cost of the future services is highly uncertain, they should delay the recognition of warranty revenue. A Warranty Advances account appears among liabilities for such firms. These firms recognize warranty revenue and warranty expense each period as time passes and customers make warranty claims.

Example 4.   Metropolitan Life Insurance Company sells life insurance policies to customers. The firm receives premium payments each year and invests the cash in stocks, bonds, real estate, and other income-producing assets. The premiums received from customers plus the income from investments over the life of insured individuals provide the funds to pay the required death benefits.

Life insurance companies receive cash from premiums and from investments each period. They invest in readily marketable securities for the most part, so that they can measure the changes in the market value of their investments. Measuring the amount of revenue each period while the life insurance policy is outstanding presents few difficulties. The only issue on the revenue side is whether these firms should recognize as revenue the unrealized gains and losses from changes in the market value of investments. Common practice in the insurance industry is to recognize such gains and losses each year in computing net income.

There is usually little question about the total expense on a life insurance policy. Other than administrative costs, the only expense is the face value of the policy.

The income recognition issue is determining how much of this total cost life insurance companies should recognize as an expense each year to match against premium and investment revenues. The objective is to spread these costs over the life of the insured. Determining the length of this period and the pattern of expense recognition requires actuarial calculations of expected life, investment returns, and similar factors. Note that allocating an equal portion of the total cost to each year of expected life does not necessarily provide an appropriate matching of revenues and expenses. Although insurance premiums typically remain level over the contract period, investment revenues increase over time as premiums and investment returns accumulate. Life insurance companies increase a liability each period, often called Policyholder Reserves, for the amount of expense recognized. They reduce this account when they pay insurance claims. An analyst examining the financial statements of a life insurance company should study carefully the amount shown for Policyholder Reserves and the change in this account each year. Such an assessment provides information about both the adequacy of investments to cover potential claims and the amount of net income each period.

These four examples illustrate situations in which firms in certain industries do not necessarily meet the criteria for revenue and expense recognition at the time of sale. An underlying theme in each instance is uncertainty: uncertainty about the amount of cash that the firm will ultimately receive and uncertainty about the amount of cash it will ultimately disburse. Analysts sometimes use the concept of *quality of earnings* to refer to how well reported earnings amounts reflect cash flows ultimately received or paid. Earnings amounts that require significant estimates of future cash flows, as in the four examples discussed above, are of lower quality than the earnings of firms that do not require such estimations (consider, for example, a service business for which the timing of earnings and cash flows closely coincide). In addition to the selection of accounting principles (such as the timing of income recognition), the application of accounting principles (such as the depreciable lives used for plant and equipment) and managerial discretion in timing costs (such as maintenance, advertising, research and development) affect earnings quality. The lower the quality of earnings, the higher is the *potential* for a firm to manage reported earnings and possibly mislead investors.[1] The analyst assesses earnings quality subjectively rather than measuring it in a precise manner.

The next section explores more fully the financial statements' impact of recognizing income either earlier than the time of sale (a common practice among long-term contractors) or later than the time of sale (a common practice when firms sell goods on an installment payment basis and experience high uncertainty regarding the collectibility of cash).

INCOME RECOGNITION FOR LONG-TERM CONTRACTORS

The operating process for a long-term contractor (for example, building contractor, aerospace manufacturer, shipbuilder) differs from that of a manufacturing firm (depicted in Figure 5.1) in three important respects:

---

[1]For an excellent discussion of earnings management, see Katherine Schipper, "Earnings Management," *Accounting Horizons,* December 1989, pp. 91–102.

1. The period of construction (production) may span several accounting periods.
2. Contractors identify customers and agree on a contract price in advance (or at least in the early stages of construction).
3. Customers often make periodic payments of the contract price as work progresses.

The operating activities of long-term contractors often satisfy the criteria for the recognition of revenue during the period of construction. The existence of a contract indicates that the contractor has identified a buyer and agreed on a price. The contractor either collects cash in advance or concludes, based on an assessment of the customer's credit standing, that it will receive cash equal to the contract price after completion of construction. Although the contract may obligate the contractor to perform substantial future services, the contractor should be able to estimate the cost of these services with reasonable precision. In agreeing to a contract price, the firm must have some confidence in the estimates of the total costs it will incur on the contract.

When contractors meet the criteria for revenue recognition as construction progresses, they usually recognize revenue during the period of construction using the *percentage-of-completion method*. Under the percentage-of-completion method, contractors recognize a portion of the total contract price, based on the degree of completion of the work during the period, as revenue for the period. They base this proportion either on engineers' or architects' estimates of the degree of completion or on the ratio of costs incurred to date to the total expected costs for the contract. The actual schedule of cash collections is *not* a determining factor in measuring the amount of revenue recognized each period under the percentage-of-completion method. Even if a contractor expects to collect the entire contract price at the completion of construction, it still uses the percentage-of-completion method as long as it can make reasonable estimates as construction progresses of the amount of cash it will collect and of the costs it will incur.

As contractors recognize portions of the contract price as revenues, they recognize corresponding proportions of the total estimated costs of the contract as expenses. The percentage-of-completion method, following the principles of the accrual basis of accounting, matches expenses with related revenues.

Example 5. To illustrate the percentage-of-completion method, assume that a firm agrees to construct a bridge for $5,000,000. Estimated costs are as follows: Year 1, $1,500,000; Year 2, $2,000,000; and Year 3, $500,000. Thus, the expected gross margin from the contract is $1,000,000 ($5,000,000 − $1,500,000 − $2,000,000 − $500,000).

When the contractor bases the degree of completion on the percentage of total costs incurred to date and incurs actual costs as anticipated, revenue and expense from the contract are as follows:

Year	Degree of Completion	Revenue	Expense	Gross Margin
1	$1,500,000/$4,000,000 = 37.5%	$1,875,000	$1,500,000	$ 375,000
2	$2,000,000/$4,000,000 = 50.0%	2,500,000	2,000,000	500,000
3	$ 500,000/$4,000,000 = 12.5%	625,000	500,000	125,000
		$5,000,000	$4,000,000	$1,000,000

Actual costs on contracts seldom coincide precisely with expectations. As new information on expected total costs becomes available, contractors must adjust reported income on the contract. They make the adjustment to reported income for this change in estimated total costs during the current and future periods rather than retroactively restating income of prior periods.

Example 6.   Refer to Example 5. Assume now that actual costs incurred in Year 2 for the contract were $2,200,000 instead of $2,000,000 and that total expected costs on the contract are now $4,200,000. Revenue, expense, and gross margin from the contract are as follows:

Year	Cumulative Degree of Completion	Revenue	Expense	Gross Margin
1	$1,500,000/$4,000,000 = 37.5%	$1,875,000	$1,500,000	$375,000
2	$3,700,000/$4,200,000 = 88.1%	2,530,000[a]	2,200,000	330,000
3	$4,200,000/$4,200,000 = 100%	595,000[b]	500,000	95,000
		$5,000,000	$4,200,000	$800,000

[a](0.881 × $5,000,000) − $1,875,000 = $2,530,000
[b]$5,000,000 − $1,875,000 − $2,530,000 = $595,000

Example 7.   If it appears that the contractor will realize a loss on the completion of a contract, the contractor must recognize the loss in full as soon as it becomes evident. For example, if at the end of Year 2, the contractor expects to realize a loss of $200,000 on the contract, it must recognize a loss of $575,000 in Year 2. The $575,000 amount offsets the income of $375,000 recognized in Year 1 plus a loss of $200,000 anticipated on the overall contract.

Contractors report actual contract costs on the balance sheet in the Contracts in Process account. This account includes not only accumulated costs to date but any income or loss recognized on the contract. Exhibit 5.1 shows the Contracts in Process account for the bridge contract. If the contractor periodically bills the customer for portions of the contract price, it reports the amount billed as a subtraction from the amount in the Contracts in Process account.

Some long-term contractors postpone the recognition of revenue until they complete the construction project. Such firms use the *completed-contract method* of recognizing revenue. If the firm in Example 6 had used the completed-contract method, it would have recognized no revenue or expense from the contract during Year 1 or Year 2. It would recognize contract revenue of $5,000,000 and contract expenses of $4,200,000 in Year 3. Note that total income is $800,000 under both the percentage-of-completion and completed-contract methods, equal to cash inflows of $5,000,000 less cash outflows of $4,200,000. If the contractor anticipates a loss on a contract, the contractor recognizes the loss as soon as it becomes evident, even if the contract is incomplete.

The Contracts in Process account under the completed-contract method shows a balance of $1,500,000 on December 31, Year 1, the accumulated costs to date. This

EXHIBIT 5.1

Calculation of Balance in Contracts in Process Account
Using the Percentage-of-Completion Method

	Accumulated Costs	Accumulated Income	Amount in Contracts in Process Account
Example 5 (Profit = $1,000,000)			
During Year 1	$ 1,500,000	$ 375,000	$ 1,875,000
Balance, December 31, Year 1..............	$ 1,500,000	$ 375,000	$ 1,875,000
During Year 2	2,000,000	500,000	2,500,000
Balance, December 31, Year 2..............	$ 3,500,000	$ 875,000	$ 4,375,000
During Year 3	500,000	125,000	625,000
Completion of Contract during Year 3	(4,000,000)	(1,000,000)	(5,000,000)
Balance, December 31, Year 3..............	$ 0	$ 0	$ 0
Example 6 (Profit = $800,000)			
During Year 1	$ 1,500,000	$ 375,000	$ 1,875,000
Balance, December 31, Year 1..............	$ 1,500,000	$ 375,000	$ 1,875,000
During Year 2	2,200,000	330,000	2,530,000
Balance, December 31, Year 2..............	$ 3,700,000	$ 705,000	$ 4,405,000
During Year 3	500,000	95,000	595,000
Completion of Contract during Year 3	(4,200,000)	(800,000)	(5,000,000)
Balance, December 31, Year 3..............	$ 0	$ 0	$ 0
Example 7 (Loss = $200,000)			
During Year 1	$ 1,500,000	$ 375,000	$ 1,875,000
Balance, December 31, Year 1..............	$ 1,500,000	$ 375,000	$ 1,875,000
During Year 2	2,200,000	(575,000)	1,625,000
Balance, December 31, Year 2..............	$ 3,700,000	$ (200,000)	$ 3,500,000
During Year 3	1,500,000	—	1,500,000
Completion of Contract during Year 3	(5,200,000)	200,000	(5,000,000)
Balance, December 31, Year 3..............	$ 0	$ 0	$ 0

account shows a balance on December 31, Year 2, of $3,500,000 under Example 5, $3,700,000 under Example 6, and $3,500,000 under Example 7. These amounts reflect accumulated cost to date minus, in Example 7, the estimated loss on the contract. These amounts are less than the amounts shown in the Contracts in Process account for Examples 5 and 6 under the percentage-of-completion method (see Exhibit 5.1) by the amount of accumulated income recognized under the latter method. Accelerating the recognition of income under the percentage-of-completion method increases both assets and net income (part of retained earnings). Thus, income recognition and asset valuation closely interrelate.

In some cases, contractors use the completed-contract method because the contracts are of such short duration (a few months) that earnings reported with the percentage-of-completion method and the completed-contract method are not significantly different. In these cases, the lower costs of implementing the completed-contract method explain its use. Contractors also use the completed-contract method when they have not obtained a specific buyer during the construction phase, as is sometimes the case in the construction of residential housing. These cases require future selling efforts. Substantial uncertainty may exist regarding the ultimate contract price and the amount of cash that the contractor will receive.

The primary reason that a contractor would not use the percentage-of-completion method when a contract exists is that there is substantial uncertainty regarding the total costs it will incur in completing the project. If the contractor cannot estimate the total costs, it will be unable to estimate the percentage of total costs incurred as of a given date and, thereby, the percentage of services already rendered. It will also be unable to estimate the total income from the contract.

Contractors must use the percentage-of-completion method for income tax purposes. Although most firms would prefer to use the completed-contract method for tax purposes, thereby delaying the recognition of income and payment of income taxes, the Internal Revenue Code does not permit it.

A statement of the International Accounting Standards Committee (IASC) provides only for the percentage-of-completion method. Wide variation exists, however, among member countries with respect to implementing this IASC standard. For example, Canada, France, Germany, Japan, and the United States permit both methods, the United Kingdom and the Netherlands allow only the percentage-of-completion method, and Austria allows only the completed-contract method.

REVENUE RECOGNITION WHEN CASH COLLECTIBILITY IS UNCERTAIN

Occasionally, estimating the amount of cash or cash equivalent value of other assets that a firm will receive from customers is difficult. This may occur because the customer's future financial condition is highly uncertain or because the customer may have the right to return the items purchased, thereby avoiding the obligation to make cash payments. This uncertainty regarding future cash flows may prevent the selling firm from measuring at the time of sale the present value of the cash it expects to receive. The firm therefore recognizes revenue at the time it collects cash using either the installment method or the cost-recovery-first method. Unlike the cash method of accounting, these revenue recognition methods attempt to match expenses with associated revenues.

Installment Method. Under the *installment method,* a firm recognizes revenue as it collects portions of the selling price in cash. At the same time, it recognizes corresponding portions of the cost of the good or service sold as an expense. For example, assume that a firm sells for $100 merchandise costing $60. The buyer agrees to pay (ignoring interest) $20 each month for five months. The firm recognizes revenue of $20 each month as it receives cash. Likewise, it recognizes cost of goods sold of $12 ($20/$100 × $60) each month. By the end of five months, the firm recognizes total income of $40 [5 × ($20 − $12)].

Land development companies, which typically sell undeveloped land and promise to develop it over several future years, sometimes use the installment method. The buyer makes a nominal down payment and agrees to pay the remainder of the purchase price in installments over 10, 20, or more years. In these cases, future devel-

EXHIBIT 5.2

Illustration of Income Recognition Methods from Installment Sales

Amortization Schedule for Note Receivable

Year	Note Receivable January 1 (1)	Interest Revenue at 12 Percent (2)	Cash Payment Received (3)	Repayment of Principal (4)	Note Receivable, December 31 (5)
1	$20,000,000	$2,400,000	$ 5,548,195	$ 3,148,195	$16,851,805
2	16,851,805	2,022,217	5,548,195	3,525,978	13,325,827
3	13,325,827	1,599,099	5,548,195	3,949,096	9,376,731
4	9,376,731	1,125,208	5,548,195	4,422,987	4,953,744
5	4,953,744	594,449	5,548,193	4,953,744	0
		$7,740,973	$27,740,973	$20,000,000	

Column (2) = 0.12 × Column (1)
Column (3) = Given
Column (4) = Column (3) − Column (2)
Column (5) = Column (1) − Column (4)

Income Recognition from Sale of Computer

Year	Time of Sale — (6) Revenue	Time of Sale — (7) Expense	Installment Method — (8) Revenue	Installment Method — (9) Expense	Cost-Recovery-First Method — (10) Revenue	Cost-Recovery-First Method — (11) Expense	All Three Methods (12) Interest Revenue
1	$20,000,000	$16,000,000	$ 3,148,195	$ 2,518,556	$ 3,148,195	$ 3,148,195	$2,400,000
2	—	—	3,525,978	2,820,782	3,525,978	3,525,978	2,022,217
3	—	—	3,949,096	3,159,277	3,949,096	3,949,096	1,599,099
4	—	—	4,422,987	3,538,390	4,422,987	4,422,987	1,125,208
5	—	—	4,953,744	3,962,995	4,953,744	953,744	594,449
	$20,000,000	$16,000,000	$20,000,000	$16,000,000	$20,000,000	$16,000,000	$7,740,973

Column (8) = Column (4)
Column (9) = 0.80 × Column (8)
Column (10) = Column (4)

Column (11) = Column (10) until Cumulative Revenues = $16,000,000
Column (12) = Column (2)

Notes Receivable (Net) Reported on Balance Sheet

	Time of Sale (13) Notes Receivable	Installment Method (14) Notes Receivable	Installment Method (15) Less Deferred Gross Margin	Installment Method (16) Notes Receivable (net)	Cost-Recovery-First Method (17) Notes Receivable	Cost-Recovery-First Method (18) Less Deferred Gross Margin	Cost-Recovery-First Method (19) Notes Receivable (net)
Income Recognition							
January 1, Year 1	$20,000,000	$20,000,000	$4,000,000	$16,000,000	$20,000,000	$4,000,000	$16,000,000
December 31, Year 1	16,851,805	16,851,805	3,370,361	13,481,444	16,851,805	4,000,000	12,851,805

opment of the land is a significant aspect of the earnings process. Also, substantial uncertainty often exists as to the ultimate collectibility of the installment notes, particularly those not due until many years in the future. The customer can always elect to stop making payments, losing the right to own the land.

Cost-Recovery-First Method. When firms experience substantial uncertainty about cash collection, they can also use the *cost-recovery-first method* of income recognition. The cost-recovery-first method matches the costs of generating revenues dollar for dollar with cash receipts until the firm recovers all such costs. Revenues equal expenses in each period until full cost recovery occurs. Only when cumulative cash receipts exceed total costs does a firm show profit (that is, revenue without any matching expenses) in the income statement.

To illustrate the cost-recovery-first method, refer to the previous example relating to the sale of merchandise for $100. During the first three months, the firm recognizes revenue of $20 and expense of $20. By the end of the third month, cumulative cash receipts of $60 exactly equal the cost of the merchandise sold. During the fourth and fifth months, the firm recognizes revenue of $20 each month but without an offsetting expense. For the five months as a whole, total income is again $40 (equal to cash inflow of $100 less cash outflow of $60), but the income recognition pattern differs from that of the installment method.

Comprehensive Illustration of Income Recognition Methods for Installment Sales. Digital Equipment Corporation (DEC) sold a computer costing $16,000,000 to the city of Boston for $20,000,000 on January 1, Year 1. The city of Boston agreed to make annual payments of $5,548,195 on December 31, Year 1, to December 31, Year 5 (five payments in total, with fifth payment being $5,548,193). The top panel of Exhibit 5.2 shows an amortization table for the note receivable underlying this transaction. The five payments when discounted at 12 percent have a present value equal to the $20,000,000 selling price. Thus, 12 percent is the interest rate implicit in the note. Column (2) shows the interest revenue that DEC recognizes each year from providing financing services to the city of Boston (that is, permitting the city to delay payment of the $20,000,000 selling price).

The middle panel shows the revenue and expense that DEC recognizes under three income recognition methods. Columns (6) and (7) assume that DEC recognizes income from the sale of the computer at the time of sale. Such immediate recognition rests on the premise that the city of Boston will pay the amounts due under the note with a high probability.

If substantial uncertainty exists regarding cash collectibility of the notes, DEC should use either the installment or cost-recovery-first methods. Columns (8) and (9) show the amounts for the installment period. Revenues in column (8) represent collections of the $20,000,000 principal amount of the note (that is, the portion of each cash payment made by the city that does not represent interest). Column (9) shows the expense each year, which represents 80 percent (= $16,000,000 ÷ $20,000,000) of the revenue recognized. Columns (10) and (11) show the amounts for the cost-recovery-first method. Note that DEC recognizes no income until Year 5, when cumulative cash receipts exceed the $16,000,000 cost of manufacturing the computer.

Exh. 5.2—Continued   **Notes Receivable (Net) Reported on Balance Sheet**

| | Time of Sale | Installment Method | | | Cost-Recovery-First Method | | |
	(13) Notes Receivable	(14) Notes Receivable	(15) Less Deferred Gross Margin	(16) Notes Receivable (net)	(17) Notes Receivable	(18) Less Deferred Gross Margin	(19) Notes Receivable (net)
December 31, Year 2	13,325,827	13,325,827	2,665,165	10,660,662	13,325,827	4,000,000	9,325,827
December 31, Year 3	9,376,731	9,376,731	1,875,346	7,501,385	9,376,731	4,000,000	5,376,731
December 31, Year 4	4,953,744	4,953,744	990,749	3,962,995	4,953,744	4,000,000	953,744
December 31, Year 5	—	—	—	—	—	—	—

Column (13), Column (14), Column (17) = Column (1)
Column (15) = $4,000,000 − Cumulative Income Recognized = Column (8) − Column (9) for the current and prior years.
  For example, $3,370,361 = $4,000,000 − ($3,148,195 − $2,518,556).
Column (16) = Column (14) − Column (15)
Column (18) = $4,000,000 − Cumulative Income Recognized = Column (10) − Column (11) for the current and prior years.
Column (19) = Column (17) − Column (18).

Note that total cash inflows of $27,740,973 (column 3) equal total revenue (sales revenue—columns 6, 8, and 10—plus interest revenue—column 12—and total cash outflows of $16,000,000 equal total total expense—columns 7, 9, and 11).

The lower panel of Exhibit 5.2 shows the amounts that DEC reports on its balance sheet for each of the three income recognition methods. Recognizing income at the time of sale results in the largest cumulative income through the first four years and the largest assets. Recognizing income using the installment method results in the next largest cumulative income and the next largest assets. The cost-recovery-first method results in the smallest cumulative income and the smallest assets. The differences in assets equal the differences in cumulative income recognized. Thus, we see again that asset valuation closely relates to income recognition. Note also that at the end of five years, cumulative income and assets are identical for all three income recognition methods.

Use of Installment and Cost-Recovery-First Methods.   GAAP permits firms to use the installment method and the cost-recovery-first method only when substantial uncertainty exists about cash collection. For most sales of goods and services, past experience and an assessment of customers' credit standing provide a sufficient basis for estimating the amount of cash that firms will receive. GAAP does not permit firms to use the installment method and the cost-recovery-first method in these cases for financial reporting. These firms must generally recognize revenue at the time of sale.

Income tax laws allow the installment method for income tax reporting under some circumstances, even when no uncertainty exists regarding cash collections. Manufacturing firms selling on extended payment plans often use the installment method for income tax reporting (while recognizing revenue at the time of sale for financial reporting). Firms seldom use the cost-recovery-first method for tax reporting.

DISCLOSURE OF REVENUE RECOGNITION METHOD

The notes to the financial statements include a note on the accounting policies that a firm follows. If a firm recognizes a significant amount of revenue at times other than the time of sale, this note indicates the methods followed. The notes on accounting policies for Coke and Pepsi do not include information on revenue recognition, implying that both firms recognize revenue at the time of sale.

INVENTORY COST-FLOW ASSUMPTION

Firms selling relatively high dollar-valued items, such as automobiles, trailers, and real estate, can ascertain from the accounting records the specific cost of the items sold. These firms recognize this amount as an expense, cost of goods sold, and match it against sales revenue in measuring net income.

In most cases, firms cannot identify the cost of the specific items sold. Inventory items are sufficiently similar and their unit costs sufficiently small that firms cannot justify economically the cost of designing an accounting system to track specific unit costs. To measure cost of goods sold in these cases, firms must make some assumption about the *flow of costs* (not the flow of units, since firms usually sell the oldest goods first). GAAP permits three cost-flow assumptions:

1. First-in, first-out (FIFO).
2. Weighted average.
3. Last-in, first-out (LIFO).

FIFO assigns the cost of the earliest purchases to the units sold and the cost of the most recent purchases to ending inventory. LIFO assigns the cost of the most recent purchases to the cost of goods sold and the earliest purchases to inventory. Weighted average assigns the average cost of all units available for sale during the period (units in beginning inventory plus units purchased) to both units sold and units in ending inventory. Figure 5.2 depicts these relationships graphically, assuming that a firm purchases units evenly over the year.

FIGURE 5.2

Cost-Flow Assumptions

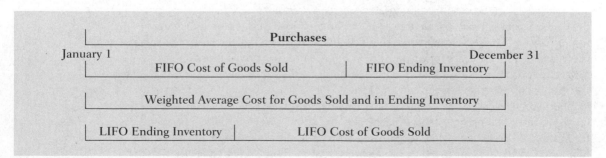

FIFO

FIFO results in balance sheet amounts for ending inventory that are closest to current replacement cost. The cost of goods sold tends to be somewhat out of date, however, because FIFO charges to expense the earlier prices of beginning inventory and the earliest purchases during the year. When prices are rising, FIFO leads to the highest reported net income of the three methods. When prices fall, it leads to the smallest.

LIFO

LIFO results in amounts for cost of goods sold that closely approximate current costs. Balance sheet amounts, however, can contain the cost of acquisitions made many years previously. Consider the diagram in Figure 5.3 that shows purchases, LIFO ending inventory, and LIFO cost of goods sold over several periods for a firm.

During each of the first four periods, the firm purchases more units than it sells. Thus, the number of physical units in ending inventory increases each year. The firm assigns costs to the units in inventory at the end of Year 1 based on the earliest purchases in Year 1. We refer to the costs assigned to these units as the *base LIFO layer* (denoted with the letter *a* in Figure 5.3). LIFO prices the units in inventory at the end of Year 2 in two layers. Units equal to those on hand at the end of Year 1 carry unit costs based on purchase prices paid at the beginning of Year 1. Units *added* to ending inventory during Year 2 carry unit costs based on purchase prices paid at the beginning of Year 2 (denoted with the letter *b* in Figure 5.3). The balance sheet at the end of Year 2 states the inventory at the sum of the costs assigned to these two layers. Note that LIFO does not assume that the actual physical flow of units sold will track a LIFO assumption. LIFO is a *cost flow,* or cost assignment, method, not a means of tracking the physical movement of goods.

As the quantity of units in ending inventory continues to increase in Year 3 and Year 4, the firm adds new LIFO layers. At the end of Year 4, LIFO assigns costs to

FIGURE 5.3

Illustration of LIFO Ending Inventory Layers

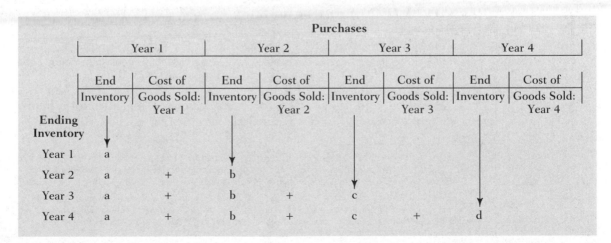

		Purchases						
	Year 1		Year 2		Year 3		Year 4	
	End Inventory	Cost of Goods Sold: Year 1	End Inventory	Cost of Goods Sold: Year 2	End Inventory	Cost of Goods Sold: Year 3	End Inventory	Cost of Goods Sold: Year 4
Ending Inventory								
Year 1	a							
Year 2	a	+	b					
Year 3	a	+	b	+	c			
Year 4	a	+	b	+	c	+	d	

ending inventory based on purchases made at the beginning of Year 1, Year 2, Year 3, and Year 4. Thus, the longer a firm remains on LIFO, the more its ending inventory valuation differs from current replacement costs.

During periods of rising prices, LIFO generally results in the highest cost of goods sold and the lowest net income of the three cost-flow assumptions. For this reason, firms usually prefer LIFO for income tax purposes. If a firm chooses a LIFO cost-flow assumption for tax purposes, the income tax law requires the firm to use LIFO for financial reporting to shareholders.

LIFO LIQUIDATION

One exception to the generalization that LIFO produces the lowest net income during periods of rising prices can occur when a firm sells more units during a period than it purchases (referred to as a *LIFO layer liquidation*). In this case, LIFO assigns the cost of all the current period's purchases plus the costs assigned to the most recent LIFO layers to the cost of goods sold. For example, assume that sales exceeded purchases in Year 5 in the preceding example. The firm assigns the cost of all of Year 5's purchases to the units sold. LIFO then assigns the cost of Year 4's LIFO layer (reflecting purchase prices at the beginning of Year 4) to the excess units sold, then assigns Year 3's LIFO layer (reflecting purchase prices at the beginning of Year 3) to any remaining excess units, and so on until it has assigned a cost to all units sold. Because LIFO assigns older, lower costs to a portion of the units sold, LIFO cost of goods sold may not exceed FIFO costs of goods sold, despite experiencing rising prices during the current period.

When firms experience LIFO liquidations, two cash-flow effects likely occur. First, firms delay purchasing inventory items, thereby delaying a cash outflow. Second, firms increase their taxable income and the required cash outflow for taxes. Researchers have examined the effect of LIFO liquidations on abnormal stock price behavior at the time firms disclose such liquidations. No abnormal stock price reaction was observed on average in these studies when those firms' tax positions (for example, availability of net operating loss carry forwards) were ignored. However, when this tax position was considered, low tax-paying firms had a higher abnormal price reaction to a LIFO liquidation than other firms had.[2]

CHARACTERISTICS OF LIFO ADOPTERS

Researchers have examined the characteristics of firms that do and do not adopt LIFO. Although these research studies do not always show consistent results, the following factors appear related to the decision to adopt LIFO:[3]

1. *Direction and Rate of Factor Price Changes for Inventory Items.*
   Firms experiencing rapidly increasing factor prices for raw materials, labor, or

---

[2]Thomas L. Stober, "The Incremental Information Content of Financial Statement Disclosures: The Case of LIFO Inventory Liquidations," *Journal of Accounting Research,* Supplement 1986, pp. 138–160; Sen Yo Tse, "LIFO Liquidations," *Journal of Accounting Research,* Spring 1990, pp. 229–238.

[3]For a review of these studies, see Frederick W. Lindahl, "Dynamic Analysis of Inventory Accounting Choice," *Journal of Accounting Research,* Autumn 1989, pp. 201–226, and Nicholas Dopuch and Morton Pincus, "Evidence on the Choice of Inventory Accounting Methods: LIFO versus FIFO," *Journal of Accounting Research,* Spring 1988, pp. 28–59.

other product costs obtain greater tax benefits from LIFO than do firms experiencing smaller factor price increases or price decreases.

2. *Variability in the Rate of Inventory Growth.*   LIFO adopters show more variable rates of inventory growth before adopting LIFO than do firms that remain on FIFO. The variability of inventory growth declines after adopting LIFO. Because LIFO tends to match more recent inventory costs with sales than does FIFO or weighted average (these methods use costs that are six to fifteen months old relative to current replacement costs), LIFO tends to result in less variability in the gross margin percentage over the business cycle. Firms with variable rates of inventory growth (perhaps because of cyclicality in their industry) can more easily accomplish an income-smoothing reporting objective using LIFO than if they use FIFO or average cost.

3. *Tax Savings Opportunities.*   LIFO adopters tend not to have tax loss carry-forwards available to offset future taxable income. These firms instead adopt LIFO to provide future tax savings. LIFO adopters also realize larger tax savings in the year of adoption than in the surrounding years, suggesting that the decision is in part motivated by tax rather than financial reporting considerations.

4. *Industry Membership.*   Firms in certain industries are more likely to adopt LIFO than are firms in other industries. Since firms in an industry face similar factor price changes and variability in their inventory growth rates, one would expect similar choices concerning cost-flow assumptions.

5. *Asset Size.*   Larger firms are more likely to adopt LIFO than are smaller firms. LIFO increases record-keeping costs, relative to FIFO, both in the year of adoption and in subsequent years. Larger firms realize larger amounts of tax savings than do smaller firms to absorb the adoption and on-going record-keeping costs of LIFO.

One hypothesis examined in this research is the relation between LIFO adoption and managerial compensation. Because LIFO usually results in lower earnings, one would expect managerial compensation of LIFO adopters to be either less than compensation of non-LIFO adopters or to include a lower component of compensation based on earnings. Studies have found no difference in managerial compensation of LIFO and non-LIFO adopters, although adopters had a smaller earnings component to their compensation.

WEIGHTED AVERAGE

The weighted average cost-flow assumption falls between the other two in its effect on the balance sheet and the income statement. It is, however, much more like FIFO than like LIFO in its effects on the balance sheet. When inventory turns over rapidly, purchases during the current period receive a heavy weight in the weighted average unit cost. The weighted average assumption therefore reflects current prices almost as much as FIFO.

CONVERSION FROM LIFO TO FIFO

No cost-flow assumption based on historical cost can simultaneously report current cost data in both the income statement and the balance sheet. If a firm reports current costs in the income statement under LIFO, its balance sheet amount for ending inventory contains some very old costs. The out-of-date LIFO inventory valuation provides potentially misleading information to users of financial statements. Consequently, the Securities and Exchange Commission requires firms using LIFO to disclose in notes to the financial statements the amounts by which LIFO inventories are less than they would be if the firm had reported inventories at FIFO or current cost. Analysts sometimes refer to the difference in ending inventory valuation between LIFO and FIFO or current cost as the *LIFO reserve*. From this disclosure, it is possible to restate a LIFO firm's income to a FIFO basis. In this way, the analyst can place firms using LIFO on a basis more comparable to firms using FIFO.

Refer to the financial statements of Coke and Pepsi in Appendices A and B, respectively. Note 1 to Coke's financial statements indicates that it uses a combination of FIFO, LIFO, and average cost-flow assumptions for inventories and cost of goods sold. This note also indicates that the current cost of inventories exceeds their LIFO amounts by $24 million at the end of Year 7 and $9 million at the end of Year 8. The top panel of Exhibit 5.3 shows the conversion of Coke's inventories and cost of goods sold from a combination of three cost-flow assumptions to a combination of FIFO and average costs. Because reporting standards do not require the disclosure of the

---

EXHIBIT 5.3

Restatement of Inventories and Cost of Goods Sold for Differences in Cost-Flow Assumptions

	FIFO/LIFO/ Average Cost	Excess of Current Cost over LIFO Cost	FIFO/ Average Cost
Coke—Restatement to a Combination of FIFO and Average Cost			
Beginning Inventory	$1,019[a]	$24[c]	$1,043[d]
Purchases	5,190		5,190
Available	$6,209		$6,233
Less Ending Inventory	1,049[a]	(9)[c]	1,058[e]
Cost of Goods Sold	$5,160[b]	$15	$5,175

[a]As reported in the balance sheet.
[b]As reported in the income statement.
[c]As reported in Note 1 to Coke's financial statements.
[d]$1,043 = $1,019 + $24.
[e]$1,058 = $1,049 − (−$9).

Pepsi—Restatement to a Combination of FIFO and Average Cost			
Beginning Inventory	$ 768.8[a]	$ 3.4[c]	$ 772.2[d]
Purchases	12,102.0		12,102.0
Available	$12,870.8		$12,874.2
Less Ending Inventory	924.7[a]	8.9[c]	915.8[e]
Cost of Goods Sold	$11,946.1[b]	$12.3	$11,958.4

[a]As reported in the balance sheet.
[b]As reported in the income statement.
[c]As reported in Pepsi's note on inventories.
[d]$772.2 = $768.8 + $3.4.
[e]$915.8 = $924.7 − $8.9.

excess of current cost over average cost of inventories, it is not possible to restate inventories and cost of goods sold fully to a FIFO basis. Coke does not report the liquidation of a LIFO layer during Year 8. Thus, the quantity of inventory items under LIFO likely increased. Yet the excess of current cost over LIFO cost decreased, suggesting that the acquisition costs of inventory items valued under LIFO decreased during the year. As one would expect during a period of decreasing prices, cost of goods sold on a FIFO/average cost basis is higher than when a firm uses LIFO for a portion of its inventories. Coke's gross margin percentage (sales minus cost of goods sold divided by sales) on a combination of FIFO, LIFO, and average costs is 63.0 percent [($13,957 − $5,160) ÷ $13,957] and on a combination of FIFO and average cost is 62.9 percent [($13,957 − $5,175) ÷ $13,957]. Thus, Coke's use of LIFO for a portion of its inventories had virtually no effect on measures of its operating profitability.

Pepsi indicates in Note 5 on inventories that it also uses a combination of FIFO, LIFO, and average costs. The lower panel of Exhibit 5.3 shows the conversion of Pepsi's inventories and cost of goods sold to a combination of FIFO and average costs. The excess of current cost over LIFO cost was positive at the beginning but negative at the end of Year 8, suggesting that prices decreased during Year 8 for the inventories valued at LIFO cost (Pepsi does not report that it dipped into its LIFO layers during the year). As with Coke, the restatement had virtually no effect on cost of goods sold and gross margin percentages.

Example 8. Bethlehem Steel Company uses a LIFO cost-flow assumption. A recent annual report reveals the following (amounts in millions):

	December 31	
	Year 8	Year 9
Inventories at FIFO Cost	$ 899.1	$ 972.8
Excess of FIFO Cost over LIFO Cost	(530.1)	(562.5)
Inventories at LIFO Cost	$ 369.0	$ 410.3
Current Assets (LIFO)	$1,439.8	$1,435.2
Current Liabilities	870.1	838.0
		For Year 9
Sales		$5,250.9
Cost of Goods Sold (LIFO)		4,399.1
Net Income		245.7
Income Tax Rate		35%

Exhibit 5.4 shows the conversion of Bethlehem Steel Company from a LIFO to a FIFO cost-flow assumption for Year 9.

The gross margin percentage under LIFO is 16.2 percent [($5,250.9 − $4,399.1) ÷ $5,250.9] and under FIFO is 16.8 percent [($5,250.9 − $4,366.7) ÷ $5,250.9]. The lower gross margin value under LIFO suggests that the manufacturing costs of steel increased during Year 9.

EXHIBIT 5.4

Conversion of Bethlehem Steel Company from LIFO to FIFO

	LIFO	Excess of FIFO Cost over LIFO Cost	FIFO
Beginning Inventory	$ 369.0	$ 530.1	$ 899.1
Purchases	4,440.4	—	4,440.4
Available	$4,809.4	$ 530.1	$5,339.5
Less Ending Inventory	(410.3)	(562.5)	(972.8)
Cost of Goods Sold	$4,399.1	$ (32.4)	$4,366.7

The calculation of the inventory turnover ratio, a measure that indicates the efficiency with which a firm manages its inventory, appears below:

$$\text{LIFO:} \quad \$4,399.1 \div 0.5(\$369.0 + \$410.3) = 11.3$$
$$\text{FIFO:} \quad \$4,366.7 \div 0.5(\$899.1 + \$972.8) = 4.7$$

The dramatic difference in the inventory turnover ratio under LIFO and FIFO reflects the many years that have elapsed since Bethlehem Steel Company adopted LIFO. Its inventory under the current (FIFO) cost is more than twice as large as its book (LIFO) value. The inventory turnover ratio based on LIFO amounts gives a poor indication of the actual physical turnover of inventory items because it divides a cost of goods sold amount reflecting current costs by an average inventory amount reflecting very old costs. The inventory turnover ratio under FIFO provides a better indication of the physical turnover of inventory items because it divides a cost of goods sold reflecting only slightly out-of-date costs by an average inventory reflecting relatively recent costs. Although the *trend* in the inventory turnover ratio for a particular firm is likely to be similar under LIFO and FIFO, cross-sectional comparisons are inappropriate if one firm uses LIFO and another uses FIFO. Also, the LIFO measure of the inventory turnover ratio does not accurately reflect the number of days that inventories are held.

The inventory cost-flow assumption also affects the current ratio, a measure commonly used to assess short-term liquidity risk. The conversion from LIFO to FIFO increases inventories at the end of Year 9 by $562.5 million, increasing the current ratio. However, *cumulative* pretax income and taxable income would have been $562.5 million higher under FIFO. Income tax laws do not permit a firm to use LIFO for taxes if it uses FIFO for financial reporting. Thus, Bethlehem Steel Company would have paid $196.9 million (= 0.35 × $562.5) more in income taxes under FIFO than under LIFO. The income taxes saved by adopting LIFO are now partly in cash and partly in other assets (for example, inventories, equipment). Assuming that the $196.9 million reduces cash on the December 31, Year 9, balance sheet, the current ratio under LIFO and FIFO appears below:

$$\text{LIFO:} \quad \$1,435.2 \div \$838.0 \dots\dots\dots\dots\dots\dots\dots\dots\dots\dots\dots 1.71$$
$$\text{FIFO:} \quad \$1,435.2 + (1 - 0.35)(\$562.5) \div \$838.0 \dots\dots\dots 2.15$$

Thus, the current ratios differ significantly. The assumption that the extra income taxes paid under FIFO reduce cash only, not other assets, moderates the differences in the current ratios. The current ratio on December 31, Year 9, under FIFO would likely exceed 2.15.

Conversion of Bethlehem Steel Company's financial statements from LIFO to FIFO requires the following adjustments:

	December 31	
	Year 8	**Year 9**
Balance Sheet		
Cash: 0.35 × $530.1; 0.35 × $562.5	$−185.5	$−196.9
Inventories	+530.1	+562.5
Retained Earnings: 0.65 × $530.1; 0.65 × $562.5......	$+344.6	$+365.6
Income Statement		
Cost of Goods Sold..		$ −32.4
Income Tax Expense: 0.35 × $32.4		+11.3
Net Income: 0.65 × $32.4..		$ +21.1
Statement of Cash Flows		
Net Income		$ +21.1
Increase in Inventories: ($410.3 − $369.0) − ($972.8 − $899.1)........		(+32.4)
Cash Flow from Operations.......................................		$ −11.3

Cash flow from operations decreases for the extra income taxes paid under FIFO.

The conversion procedure illustrated in Exhibits 5.3 and 5.4 is especially useful when comparing U.S. and non-U.S. firms. Most industrialized countries do not permit the use of LIFO for financial reporting. One important exception is Japan, but even most Japanese firms use specific identification or average costs rather than LIFO. Thus, the analyst should restate inventories and cost of goods sold for U.S. firms using LIFO to make them more comparable to cost-flow assumptions used outside the United States.

STOCK PRICE REACTION TO CHANGES IN INVENTORY COST-FLOW ASSUMPTION

The required conformity of tax and financial reporting for firms choosing a LIFO cost-flow assumption provides fertile ground for researchers studying the efficiency of capital markets. LIFO saves taxes and therefore increases cash. A switch to LIFO should result in a positive stock price reaction if capital markets react intelligently to information about the switch. The switch also results in lower reported earnings to shareholders. A negative stock price reaction suggests an inefficient stock market that fails to examine the underlying economic effects of accounting principles decisions.

Numerous research studies have examined this question, some observing positive price reactions and other observing negative price reaction at the time of the switch.[4] Refinements to the research methodology to provide for different earnings expectation models, tax positions, and other factors have not yet resulted in a definitive answer to the question about the intelligence of the market's reaction. Recent research studies have examined the characteristics of firms that remain on FIFO versus firms that switch to LIFO (see the discussion earlier in this section) in an attempt to sort out these conflicting results.

ACCOUNTING FOR FIXED ASSETS

Virtually all firms report some amount of property, plant, and equipment on their balance sheets. The higher the degree of a firm's capital intensity, the higher is the proportion of its total assets represented by property, plant, and equipment. Among the questions analysts should raise about property, plant, and equipment are the following:

1. At what amount does the balance sheet report gross property, plant, and equipment?
2. Over what useful lives does the firm depreciate its plant and equipment?
3. What depreciation method does the firm use to write off the cost of property, plant, and equipment?

The following sections consider each of these questions.

ASSET VALUATION

Fixed assets by their nature have useful lives that extend over several years. Consequently, the extent to which the amounts reported on the balance sheet for fixed assets reflect current replacement costs versus acquisition costs becomes a concern both in judging the profitability of operations and in valuing a company.

Generally accepted accounting principles in the United States and virtually all other countries require the valuation of fixed assets at acquisition costs. Exceptions include Great Britain and the Netherlands; GAAP in those countries permits periodic revaluations to current replacement cost. (Appendix 5.1 discusses the accounting for such revaluations.) Accounting's use of acquisition cost valuations rests on the presumption that such amounts are more objectively measurable than are the current market values of fixed assets. Difficulties encountered in determining current market values include (1) the absence of active markets for many used fixed assets, particularly those specific to a particular firm's needs, (2) the need to identify comparable assets currently available in the market to value assets in place, and (3) the need to make assumptions about the effect of technological and other improvements when using the prices of new assets currently available on the market in the valuation process.

---

[4]See Dopuch and Pincus, "Evidence on the Choice of Inventory Accounting Measures," for a summary of this research.

The disclosures of property, plant, and equipment on the balance sheet or in the notes permit the analyst to estimate the relative age of depreciable assets and get some sense of the extent to which acquisition costs reflect outdated valuations. Appendices A and B disclose the following information for Coke and Pepsi, respectively, at the end of Year 8:

	Coke	Pepsi
Depreciable Assets (excluding land)	$ 5,399	$13,063.6
Accumulated Depreciation	(1,867)	(5,394.4)
Net Depreciable Assets	$ 3,532	$ 7,669.2
Depreciation Expense	$ 333	$ 1,100.0

Both companies use the straight-line depreciation method. At the end of Year 8, Coke's depreciable assets were 5.6 years old on average ($1,867 ÷ $333), and Pepsi's were 4.9 years old on average ($5,394.4 ÷ $1,100.0). Pepsi's somewhat newer assets reflect its heavy acquisition activity in recent years. Given relatively low inflation rates in the United States in recent years, the historical cost values shown on Coke's and Pepsi's balance sheets are probably not significantly out of date.

A different picture emerges in the steel industry. At the end of a recent year, Bethlehem Steel's depreciable assets were 16.3 years old and Inland Steel's depreciable assets were 20.1 years old. These amounts represent average ages of such assets. Thus, the historical cost amounts likely differ significantly from their current market value. Ascertaining the current market value of such assets is particularly difficult because new steel-making facilities currently available on the market are technologically superior to existing depreciable assets.

A second issue related to the amount shown for the gross amount of fixed assets is the treatment of expenditures to add to or improve existing plant and equipment. GAAP stipulates that firms should capitalize (that is, add to the asset's cost) expenditures that increase the service potential (either in quantity or quality) of an asset beyond that originally anticipated. Firms should expense immediately those expenditures that merely maintain the originally expected service potential. A firm's capitalization versus expense policy with respect to such expenditures affects its reported earnings and provides management with some flexibility to manage earnings. Unfortunately, firms do not provide sufficient information to permit the analyst to assess the quality of earnings with respect to such expenditures. Examples of typical disclosures follow.

Bristol Myers-Squibb. Expenditures for additions, renewals, and betterments are capitalized at cost.

Georgia-Pacific. Replacements of major units of property are capitalized and the related properties are retired. Replacements of minor units of property and repairs and maintenance costs are charged to expense as incurred.

American Airlines. Maintenance and repair costs for owned and leased equipment and property are charged to operating costs as incurred.

DEPRECIABLE LIFE

Depreciation is a process of allocating the historical cost of depreciable assets to the periods of their use in a reasonably systematic manner. One factor in this depreciation process is the expected useful life. Both physical wear and tear and technological obsolescence affect this life. Firms make estimates of this expected total life, a process that again offers management an opportunity to manage reported earnings.

The disclosures that firms make about depreciable lives is usually not very helpful to the analyst in assessing a firm's aggressiveness in lengthening depreciable lives to increase earnings. Consider the following typical disclosures:

American Airlines.   The depreciable lives used for the principal asset classifications are as follows:
   Jet aircraft: 6–20 years.
   Commuter aircraft: 5–15 years.
   Major parts and assemblies: Life of equipment.
   Buildings and improvements: 10–30 years.
   Other equipment: 3–15 years.

Delta Airlines.   Flight equipment is depreciated over a 15-year period from dates placed in service. Ground property and equipment are depreciated over their estimated service lives, which range from 3 to 30 years.

United Airlines.   Estimated useful lives range from 5 to 15 years for flight equipment and 3 to 32 years for other property and equipment.

Because most firms in the United States use the straight-line depreciation method, the analyst can measure the average total life of depreciable assets by dividing average depreciable assets (gross) by depreciation expense for the year. The calculations for Coke and Pepsi follow:

	Coke	Pepsi
Depreciable Assets (Gross):		
December 31, Year 7......................	$5,040.0	$11,085.2
December 31, Year 8......................	5,399.0	13,063.6
Average Depreciable Assets (Gross) for Year 8...	$5,219.5	$12,074.4
Depreciation Expense, Year 8	$ 333.0	$ 1,100.0
Average Total Depreciable Life	15.7 years	11.0 years

This difference is somewhat surprising given the following components of depreciable assets:

	Coke		Pepsi	
Average Buildings and Improvements..	$1,572.5	30.1%	$ 5,010.1	41.5%
Average Equipment	3,647.0	69.9	7,064.3	58.5
Average Depreciable Assets	$5,219.5	100.0%	$12,074.4	100.0%

One would expect Coke, with its higher proportion of equipment, to have a smaller average total life. It is difficult to conclude, however, whether Coke uses unusually long lives or Pepsi uses unusually short lives.

DEPRECIATION METHOD

The third factor in the calculation of depreciation (in addition to the acquisition cost and expected useful life of depreciable assets) is the depreciation method. GAAP permits firms to write off assets evenly over their useful lives (straight-line method) or to write off larger amounts during the early years and smaller amounts in later years (accelerated depreciation methods). Note that total depreciation over an asset's life cannot exceed acquisition costs (unless firms revalue such assets to current market values). Thus, straight-line and accelerated depreciation methods differ only in the timing of depreciation expense, not in its total amount over time.

Virtually all firms in the United States use the straight-line method for financial reporting. They use accelerated depreciation methods for tax reporting based on depreciable lives specified in the income tax law. These lives are usually shorter than the depreciable lives firms use for financial reporting.

GAAP in most countries other than the United States also permits both accelerated and straight-line depreciation methods. In countries in which tax laws heavily influence financial reporting (Germany, France, Japan), most firms use accelerated depreciation methods for both financial and tax reporting. Thus, comparisons of U.S. firms with those of some other countries require the analyst to assess the effect of different depreciation methods. The analyst must either restate reported U.S. amounts to an accelerated basis or convert reported amounts for other countries to a straight-line basis.

The analyst can place U.S. firms on an accelerated depreciation basis using information in the income tax note. FASB *Statement No. 109* requires firms to report in notes to the financial statements the deferred tax liability related to depreciation timing differences at the beginning and end of the year.[5] Pepsi, for example, reports in Note 13 (see Appendix B) that its deferred tax liability related to property, plant, and equipment was $526.8 million on December 31, Year 7, and $552.3 million on December 31, Year 8. These deferred taxes relate to differences in both depreciable lives and depreciation methods. Converting Pepsi's financial statements to amounts reported for tax purposes requires the following adjustments (assuming a 35 percent income tax rate):

---

[5]Financial Accounting Standards Board, *Statement No. 109*, "Accounting for Income Taxes," 1992.

| | December 31 | |
	Year 7	Year 8
Balance Sheet		
Property, Plant, and Equipment (net):		
$526.8 ÷ 0.35; $552.3 ÷ 0.35	$−1,505.1	$−1,578.0
Deferred Tax Liability	−526.8	−552.3
Retained Earnings	−978.3	−1,025.7
Income Statement		
Depreciation Expense: ($552.3 − $526.8) ÷ 0.35		$ +72.9
Income Tax Expense: 0.35 × $72.9		−25.5
Net Income: 0.65 × $72.9		$ −47.4
Statement of Cash Flows		
Net Income		$ −47.4
Depreciation Expense		+72.9
Change in the Increase in Deferred Tax Liability for Depreciation		
Timing Difference ($552.3 − $526.8)		−25.5
Cash Flow from Operations		$ 0

Various financial statement ratios based on reported (straight-line) and restated (accelerated) depreciation amounts appear below:

	Reported	Restated
Rate of Return on Assets		
$1,587.9 + 0.65($572.7) ÷ 0.5($20,951.2 + $23,705.8)	8.8%	
$1,587.9 − $47.4 + 0.65($572.7) ÷ 0.5($20,951.2		
− $1,505.1 + $23,705.8 − $1,578.0)		9.2%
Rate of Return on Common Shareholders' Equity		
$1,587.9 ÷ 0.5($5,355.7 + $6,338.7)	27.2%	
$1,587.9 − $47.4 ÷ 0.5($5,355.7 − $978.3 + $6,338.7		
− $1,025.7)		31.8%
Profit Margin for ROA		
$1,587.9 + 0.65($572.7) ÷ $25,020.7	7.8%	
$1,587.9 − $47.4 + 0.65($572.7) ÷ $25,020.7		7.6%
Total Assets Turnover		
$25,020.7 ÷ 0.5($20,951.2 + $23,705.8)	1.12	
$25,020.7 ÷ 0.5($20,951.2 − $1,505.1 + $23,705.8		
− $1,578.0)		1.20
Fixed Asset Turnover		
$25,020.7 ÷ 0.5($7,442.0 + $8,855.6)	3.07	
$25,020.7 ÷ 0.5($7,442.0 − $1,505.1 + $8,855.6		
− $1,578.0)		3.79

Predicting whether the conversion from straight line to accelerated will increase or decrease rates of return is difficult because both the numerator and denominator of each ratio decrease. For Pepsi, the increased asset turnover ratio more than offsets the decline in the profit margin ratio.

ACCOUNTING FOR INTANGIBLE ASSETS

Intangible assets include patents, copyrights, trademarks, trade names, franchise rights, customer lists, and goodwill. Two characteristics distinguish intangible assets: their intangibility (that is, lack of physical attributes) and their multiple-period useful life. GAAP in the United States accounts for intangible assets as follows:

1. Firms expense in the period incurred the cost of developing intangibles. The rationale for immediate expensing of such costs is the difficulty in ascertaining whether a particular expenditure results in a future benefit (that is, an asset) or not (an expense). Accountants provide more conservative measures of earnings by expensing such costs immediately. Thus, Coke and Pepsi spend millions of dollars each year promoting their name and products. The names *Coke* and *Pepsi* represent one of the most valuable "assets" of these firms. Yet GAAP does not permit these firms to recognize an asset for the expenditures made to develop and maintain these trade names.

2. Firms recognize as an asset expenditures made to acquire intangible assets from others. In this case, the firm makes an expenditure on a specifically identifiable intangible asset. The existence of an external market transaction provides evidence of the value of the intangible asset. The acquiring firm must consider the future benefits of the intangible to at least equal the price paid. Financial statement preparers and users have criticized the differing treatment of internally developed versus externally purchased intangibles. They point out that internally developed intangibles also result from external market exchanges (payments to advertising agencies for promotion services, payments to employees for research and development services). Supporters of GAAP point out that the market exchange in the case of externally acquired intangibles validates the existence of a "completed asset," whereas the market exchange in the case of internally developed intangibles validates only that the firm has made an expenditure. It does not validate the existence and value of future benefits.

3. Firms must amortize intangible assets over their expected useful lives. If the firm cannot estimate the useful life, GAAP permits a maximum amortization period of 40 years. Common practice uses straight-line amortization.

ACCOUNTING FOR RESEARCH AND DEVELOPMENT COSTS

The application of these principles of intangible asset accounting to research and development (R&D) costs is particularly controversial. Consider the following examples involving biotechnology companies.

Example 9. Biogen develops biotechnology products internally in its research laboratories. GAAP requires Biogen to expense R&D costs each year as incurred.[6] Its R&D expense/sales percentage was 29.7 percent in Year 8. It shows no asset on its balance sheet related to this research.

Example 10. Genzyme Corporation follows a strategy of both internal development of technology and acquisition of other companies involved in biotechnology research. GAAP requires Genzyme to expense R&D costs incurred internally. It must also expense in the year incurred any portion of the acquisition price of other companies related to *in-process technology* but capitalize and subsequently amortize any portion of the acquisition price of these companies related to completed technologies.[7] Its R&D expense/sales percentage for internal R&D costs and amortization of previously capitalized costs was 18.1 percent for Year 8. However, because it made an acquisition of another company during the year, it also expensed the portion of the purchase price related to in-process technology. The total R&D expense/sales percentage for the year was 41.4 percent.

Example 11. Amgen follows a strategy of both internal development of biotechnology and external development through a series of joint ventures and partnerships. Amgen contributes preliminary research findings for its interest in these joint ventures and partnerships. The other participants provide funding to continue development of this preliminary research. In some cases, Amgen contracts with the joint venture or partnership to perform the continued development in its own laboratories. In this case, Amgen receives a fee each period in an amount approximately equal to the R&D costs incurred in conducting the research. In other cases, the joint venture or partnership entity conducts the research, in which case Amgen may show no R&D expense on its books. Amgen generally maintains the right of first refusal to any products developed, in which case it must pay the owners of the joint venture a periodic royalty. Amgen's R&D expense/sales percentage for Year 8 was 16.7 percent, the lowest of the three firms. It shows only minor amounts on its balance sheet for investments in joint ventures and partnerships, relating to cash advances. Because Amgen must expense initial development costs when incurred, its contribution of preliminary research findings for an interest in these joint ventures and partnerships does not result in increasing an asset.

The different strategies that these firms pursue in developing biotechnologies and the required accounting for their R&D costs complicate any cross-sectional analysis of their financial statements. To the extent that the economic substance of these arrangements differ, different accounting treatments may be appropriate. If, on the other hand, the economic substance is similar and the principal aim is to keep R&D costs out of the income statement, the differing accounting treatments seem unwarranted.

---

[6]Financial Accounting Standards Board, *Statement No. 2,* "Accounting for Research and Development Costs," 1974.

[7]Financial Accounting Standards Board, *Interpretation No. 4,* "Applicability of FASB Statement No. 2 to Business Combinations Accounted for by the Purchase Method," 1975.

The economic characteristics of R&D arrangements suggest a twofold approach to dealing with these different reporting standards:

1. Capitalize and subsequently amortize all expenditures on R&D that have future service potential, whether a firm incurs the R&D cost internally or whether it purchases in-process or completed technology externally. Expense immediately all R&D costs that have no future service potential.
2. Consolidate the firm's share of the assets, liabilities, revenues, and expenses of R&D joint ventures or partnerships with its own financial statements.

Unfortunately, current financial statement disclosures do not permit the analyst to implement the twofold approach. The analyst must either study the past R&D suc cess of a firm to assess the historical relation between R&D expenditures and sales or have specific technical knowledge of current R&D endeavors to implement the first element above. Implementing the second element requires financial statements for the joint ventures or partnerships. Firms currently disclose condensed financial statement information only for significant joint ventures and partnerships. With- out adequate disclosures, the analyst must proceed with caution when analyzing R&D–intensive businesses.

ACCOUNTING FOR SOFTWARE DEVELOPMENT COSTS

GAAP treats the cost of developing computer software somewhat differently than R&D costs. A firm must expense when incurred all costs incurred internally in de- veloping computer software until such development proceeds to the point that the firm establishes the technological feasibility of a product. Thereafter, the firm must capitalize and subsequently amortize additional development costs.[8] The FASB de- fines *technological feasibility* as the completion of a detailed program design or, in its absence, of a working model. A key issue in applying this reporting standard is the treatment of costs to improve an existing product.

Example 12.   Lotus Development Corporation introduced its first version of *Lo- tus 1-2-3* in 1983. It continually revises this software to increase its capabilities and adapt to changes in hardware capabilities and design. Lotus also develops new soft- ware on an ongoing basis. The income statement for Year 8 reports software develop ment expense of $118 million (13.1 percent of sales). In addition, the firm reports 19.2 million of amortization expense (2.1 percent of sales) relating to previously cap- italized software development costs. Its balance sheet shows $99.3 million of capital- ized software costs and other intangibles, which represents 13 percent of total assets.

Example 13.   Microsoft Corporation introduced its first version of *Word* in 1983. Microsoft also continually revises this software to enhance its capabilities. In con- trast to Lotus, Microsoft expenses all software development costs as incurred. It re- ports software development expense of $352 million (12.8 percent of sales) for Year 8 and shows no asset on its balance sheet for capitalized software development costs.

---

[8]Financial Accounting Standards Board, *Statement No. 86,* "Accounting for the Costs of Computer Software to Be Sold, Leased, or Otherwise Marketed," 1985.

Example 14. Aldus Corporation maintains a leading market position in publishing and graphics software. It develops new software internally and through aggressive external acquisitions of other software companies. Aldus expenses initial software development costs incurred internally. It capitalizes such costs once a program attains technological feasibility. It also capitalizes the cost of software acquired in corporate acquisitions to the extent that the software has achieved technological feasibility. Its Year 8 income statement reports internal software development expense of $17.7 million (10.2 percent of sales) and amortization of previously capitalized software development costs of $13.9 million (8.9 percent of total assets).

The flexibility that firms enjoy in defining when a product reaches technological feasibility and whether updated versions of existing products represent newly developed products (development costs expensed when incurred) or further development of current products (development costs capitalized and amortized) should cause the analyst to proceed cautiously when analyzing computer software development companies. An added concern in this regard is the small size of many such companies and the rapid pace of technological change in this industry.

ACCOUNTING FOR GOODWILL

The most common setting in which intangibles arise is in corporate acquisitions. As Chapter 7 discusses more fully, acquiring firms must allocate the purchase price to the assets acquired and liabilities assumed when purchasing another entity. Acquiring firms usually allocate the purchase price to identifiable, tangible assets (inventories, land, equipment) first. They then allocate any excess purchase price to identifiable, intangible assets such as patents, customer lists, or trade names, with the remainder allocated to goodwill. Goodwill is a residual and effectively represents all intangibles that are not specifically identifiable.

Firms seldom disclose much information about their intangible assets. For example, Coke shows Goodwill and Other Intangible Assets on its balance sheet. Coke's Note 1 on accounting policies states only that it values these intangibles at cost and amortizes them on a straight-line basis over estimated periods of benefit (not exceeding 40 years). Coke gives no information about the type of intangibles included. Pepsi lists a similar account on its balance sheet. Note 7 to its financial statements indicates that the largest portion of this asset represents the value of franchise rights reacquired in the acquisition of franchised bottling and restaurant operations.

The income tax law in the United States follows GAAP as described above with one important exception: firms generally cannot amortize goodwill and other intangibles that have an indefinite useful life.

GAAP in countries outside of the United States likewise requires amortization of goodwill, but the amortization period is usually less than 40 years. Some of these countries have a shorter amortization period because of the close conformity of tax and financial reporting (for example, France, Germany, Japan).

How should an analyst treat goodwill that appears on a firm's balance sheet? One approach is to follow GAAP, leaving goodwill among total assets and amortization of goodwill among total expenses. The justification for this approach is that the initial valuation of goodwill arose from an exchange between an independent buyer and a seller of another corporate entity and simply represents valuable resources that accountants cannot separately identify. These valuable resources enable the firm to generate profits. The analyst should include these resources in the asset base on which management should be expected to generate a reasonable return. These valuable resources will not likely last forever, so amortization of their cost over some period of years seems appropriate.

Another approach eliminates goodwill from assets and subtracts its amount from retained earnings or other common shareholders' equity accounts. The analyst adds back to net income the amortization of goodwill reflected in the accounts. The justification for this approach is twofold.

1. The amount allocated to goodwill from a corporate acquisition may simply occur because the firm paid too much but may not necessarily indicate the presence of resources with future service potential. Subtracting the amount allocated to goodwill from retained earnings suggests that the excess purchase price is a loss for the firm.
2. Immediate subtraction of goodwill from retained earnings treats goodwill arising from an acquisition similar to goodwill developed internally. In the latter case, firms expense advertising, training, and other costs when incurred, so no asset appears on the balance sheet.

SUMMARY

The unifying concept for the various GAAP discussed in this chapter (income recognition, inventory cost-flow assumption, depreciable asset accounting, and intangible asset accounting) is the link between income recognition and asset valuation. The recognition of revenue usually coincides with an increase in assets (usually cash or a receivable). The recognition of expense usually coincides with a decrease in assets (cash, inventories, depreciable, or intangible assets) or an increase in liabilities (which will require a decrease in assets in a later period). Thus, the income statement and balance sheet closely interrelate.

APPENDIX 5.1

ACCOUNTING FOR THE EFFECTS OF CHANGING PRICES

Changing prices affect the measurement of operating performance and financial position in two principal ways:

1. Changes in the *general* level of prices in an economy (as measured by the prices of a broad basket of goods and services) affect the purchasing power of the monetary unit (for example, the U.S. dollar). During periods of inflation (deflation), the measuring unit loses (gains) purchasing power. Because the measuring unit does not reflect a constant amount of purchasing power over time, accounting measurements of assets, liabilities, revenues, and expenses made with this measuring unit are not comparable. Adding the acquisition

cost of land acquired ten years ago for $10 million to the acquisition cost of land acquired this year for $10 million is as inappropriate as adding the cost of land acquired in the United States for $10 million to the cost of land acquired by a subsidiary in the United Kingdom for £10 million. We refer to the accounting issues created by changes in the general level of prices as a *measuring unit problem.*

2. Changes in the *specific* prices of individual assets and liabilities (for example, inventories, fixed assets) affect the measurement of revenues and expenses on the income statement and the valuation of assets and liabilities on the balance sheet. Land acquired last year for $10 million may now have a market value of $14 million. Should the accountant report this land on the balance sheet at its acquisition cost of $10 million or at its current market value of $14 million? Should net income include an unrealized holding gain of $4 million? We refer to the accounting issues created by changes in the prices of specific assets and liabilities as a *valuation problem.*

Summarizing,

1. Accounting can use either a *nominal* measuring unit (that is, one that gives no recognition to the changing value of the measuring unit) or a *constant* measuring unit (that is, one that restates measurements made over time to reflect a constant measuring unit).
2. Accounting can use either *acquisition cost* valuations or *current* (replacement) *cost* valuations for assets and liabilities; changes in current cost valuations over time affect the measurement of net income and shareholders' equity.

The combination of alternative measuring units and valuation methods presents four possible treatments of the effects of changing prices:

	Measuring Unit	
	Nominal	*Constant*
Acquisition Cost		
Valuation Method		
Current Cost		

We illustrate each of these four combinations using a simple example. Exhibit 5.5 summarizes the data used in the illustration. A firm begins its first year of operations, Year 1, with $400 in cash and contributed capital. On January 1, Year 1, the Consumer Price Index (CPI) is 200. The firm immediately acquires two widgets for $100 each and a piece of equipment for $100. During the first six months of Year 1, general price inflation is 5 percent. Thus, the CPI increases from 200 to 210. On June 30, Year 1, the firm sells one widget for $240 and replaces it at the new higher replacement cost of $115. The firm also pays other expenses totaling $100 on June 30, Year 1. During the second six months of the year, general price inflation is 10 percent (the CPI increases from 210 to 231). On December 31, Year 1, the re-

EXHIBIT 5.5

Data for Inflation Accounting Illustration

Balance Sheet as of Jan. 1, Year 1

Cash: $400		Contributed Capital: $400	

Date:	January 1, Year 1	June 30, Year 1	December 31, Year 1
CPI	200	210 (5% increase)	231 (10% increase)
Cost of One Widget	$100	$115	$140
Cost of Equipment	$100	$110	$120
Transactions	1. Buy 2 widgets at $100 each, $200	1. Sell 1 widget for $240; replace widget at $115	Closed books and prepare statements
	2. Purchase equipment (5-year life) for $100	2. Pay other expenses of $100	

placement cost of the widget is $140, and the replacement cost of the equipment in new condition is $120.

Financial statements prepared under each of the four combinations of measuring units and valuation methods appear in Exhibit 5.6. The following sections discuss each of these approaches to accounting for changing prices.

ACQUISITION COST/NOMINAL DOLLAR ACCOUNTING

Column 1 of Exhibit 5.6 shows the results for Year 1 as they would appear in the conventional financial statements prepared in the United States. These financial statements give no explicit consideration to the effects of changing prices, either in general or for specific assets and liabilities.

Sales appear at the nominal dollars received when the firm sold the widget on June 30. Other expenses appear at the nominal dollars expended on June 30. Cost of goods sold, depreciation, and equipment reflect the nominal dollars expended on January 1. Inventories on the balance sheet reflect the nominal dollars expended on January 1 and June 30. Thus, the financial statements use a measuring unit of unequal size (purchasing power).

Likewise, the financial statements do not reflect the increase in the replacement cost of the inventory and the equipment during Year 1. Is the firm better off by the $20 of net income if it must replace the widget for a higher current cost? Is $20 of depreciation a sufficient measure of the cost of the equipment used during Year 1? Might the firm be better off by more than the $20 of net income because it held inventories and equipment while their replacement costs increased?

One might justify the use of nominal dollars as the measuring unit when the rate of general price inflation is relatively low (for example, less than 5 percent per year). The rapid turnover of assets for most businesses does not result in serious distortions in financial statement measurements. Likewise, the use of a last-in, first-out cost-flow assumption for cost of goods sold and accelerated depreciation for fixed assets provides at least a partial solution to the problems created by changes in specific prices (these accounting principles provide measures of expenses that approximate current replacement costs but result in balance sheet valuations for assets that can deviate widely from current costs).

EXHIBIT 5.6

Illustration of Financial Statements Reflecting Inflation Accounting

	(1) Acquisition Cost/ Nominal Dollars		(2) Acquisition Cost/ Constant Dollars		(3) Current Cost/ Nominal Dollars		(4) Current Cost/ Constant Dollars	
Income Statement								
Sales		$240		$264.0[a]		$240		$264.0
Cost of Goods Sold	$100		$115.5[b]		$115		$126.5[n]	
Depreciation	20		23.1[c]		22[i]		24.2[o]	
Other Expenses	100	220	110.0[d]	248.6	100	237	110.0	260.7
Operating Income		$ 20		$ 15.4		$ 3	$	3.3
Realized Holding Gains								
Goods Sold		—		—		15[j]		11.0[p]
Depreciable Assets Used . .		—		—		2[k]		1.1[q]
Unrealized Holding Gains								
Inventory		—		—		65[l]		38.0[r]
Depreciable Assets		—		—		16[m]		3.6[s]
Purchasing Power Loss		—		(18.0)[e]		—		(18.0)[e]
Net Income		$ 20		$ (2.6)		$101		$ 39.0
Balance Sheet								
Cash		$125		$125.0		$125		$125
Inventory		215		242.0[f]		280		280
Equipment	$100		$115.5[g]		$120		$120	
Accumulated Depreciation . .	(20)	80	(23.1)	92.4	(24)	96	(24)	96
Total Assets		$420		$459.4		$501		$501
Contributed Capital		$400		$462.0[h]		$400		$462[h]
Retained Earnings		20		(2.6)		101		39
Total Equity		$420		$459.4		$501		$501

[a] $240 × (231/210) = $264.0
[b] $100 × (231/200) = $115.5
[c] $100 × (231/200) = $115.5; $115.5/5 = $23.1
[d] $100 × (231/210) = $110
[e] [$100 × (10/200) × (231/210)] + $125 × (21/210) = $5.50 + $12.50 = $18
[f] $100 × (231/200) + $115 × (231/210) = $242
[g] $100 × (231/200) = $115.5
[h] $400 × (231/200) = $462
[i] $110/5 = $22
[j] $115 − $100 = $15

[k] $22 − $20 = $2
[l] $280 − $215 = $65
[m] $96 − $80 = $16
[n] $115 × (231/210) = $126.5
[o] $22 × (231/210) = $24.2
[p] $126.5 − $115.5 = $11
[q] $24.2 − $23.1 = $1.1
[r] $280 − $242 = $38
[s] $96 − $92.4 = $3.6

ACQUISITION COST/CONSTANT DOLLAR ACCOUNTING

Column 2 of Exhibit 5.6 shows financial statements restated to dollars of constant general purchasing power. Acquisition cost valuations still underlie the measurement of revenues, expenses, assets and liabilities. However, the nominal dollars underlying these measurements are restated to dollars of constant purchasing power at the end of Year 1. Other constant-dollar measuring units are also possible (for example, January 1, Year 1, constant dollars or June 30, Year 1, constant dollars).

Sales revenue was originally measured in dollars of June 30, Year 1, purchasing power. The restatement expresses the $240 of sales revenue in terms of dollars of December 31, Year 1, purchasing power. Likewise, inventories and equipment reflect restatements of nominal dollar, acquisition-cost valuations to dollars of constant December 31, Year 1, purchasing power. Thus, an equivalent measuring unit underlies the amounts in column 2. Note that these restated amounts do not represent the current replacement costs of the specific assets and liabilities. The specific prices of assets and liabilities could have changed in an entirely different direction and pattern than prices in general.

One new element in column 2 of Exhibit 5.6 is the *purchasing power gain or loss on monetary items*. A firm that holds cash and claims to a fixed amount of cash (for example, accounts receivable, marketable debt securities) during a period of inflation loses general purchasing power. The dollars held or received later have less general purchasing power after the period of inflation than they had before. A firm that borrows from others, promising to pay a fixed amount in cash at a later time (for example, accounts payable, income taxes payable, bonds payable), gains general purchasing power. The dollars paid later have less general purchasing power after the period of inflation than they had before. The purchasing power gain or loss is a measure of the increase or decrease in general purchasing power during a period due to being in a net lending position (purchasing power loss) or net borrowing position (purchasing power gain). The accountant calculates the purchasing power gain or loss on *monetary items*. Monetary items include cash and claims receivable or payable in a fixed amount of cash regardless of changes in the general price level.

In the illustration, the firm held $100 of cash during the first six months of the year while the general purchasing power of the dollar decreased 5 percent. It therefore lost $5 of general purchasing power. This $5 loss is measured in terms of dollars of June 30, Year 1, purchasing power. Measured in dollars of December 31, Year 1, constant dollars, the purchasing power loss for the first six months of Year 1 is $5.50. The firm held $125 of cash during the second six months of the year. With 10 percent inflation during this six-month period, an additional loss in purchasing power of $12.50 occurs. Note *e* of Exhibit 5.6 shows the calculations. This illustration is simplified in that the firm has no receivables or payables. In more typical settings, firms that engage in long-term borrowing often are in a net monetary liability position (that is, monetary liabilities exceed monetary assets). During periods of inflation, these firms experience purchasing power gains.

Constant dollar accounting, in contrast to current cost accounting discussed next, carries a higher level of objectivity. Independent accountants can examine canceled checks, invoices, and other documents to verify acquisition cost valuations. The restatements to constant dollars use general price indexes published by governmental bodies.

The user of constant dollar financial statements must remember, however, that the amounts reported for individual assets and liabilities do not reflect the current costs of these items. Also, the firm is not necessarily better or worse off in an amount equal to the purchasing power gain or loss on monetary items. Lenders and borrowers incorporate the *expected* rate of inflation into the interest rate charged for delayed payments. Conceptually, purchasing power gains should offset interest expense, and purchasing power losses should offset interest revenue. Whether a firm is better or worse off depends on the actual rate of inflation relative to the expected rate incorporated into the interest rate.

CURRENT COST/NOMINAL DOLLAR ACCOUNTING

Column 3 of Exhibit 5.6 reports amounts in terms of the current replacement cost of specific assets and liabilities. Matched against sales are the current costs of replacing the widget sold and the services of the equipment used. Operating income (sales minus expenses measured at current replacement cost) reports the firm's ability to maintain its operating capacity. If sales revenue is not large enough to cover the cost of replacing goods and services used up, the firm must cut back its level of operations (unless it secures outside financing).

Current cost income also includes *realized and unrealized holding gains and losses*. A holding gain or loss arises from holding an asset (or liability) while its replacement cost changes. The widget purchased on January 1, Year 1, for $100 was held during the first six months of the year while its replacement cost increased to $115. When the firm sold the widget on June 30, it realized a holding gain of $15 ($115 − $100). Likewise, the two widgets in ending inventory give rise to unrealized holding gains of $65: $40 ($140 − $100) on the other widget acquired on January 1 and $25 ($140 − $115) on the widget acquired on June 30.

Whether holding gains constitute an increase in the value of a firm is a subject of controversy. Proponents argue that firms that purchase assets early in anticipation of increases in replacement costs are better off than firms that delay purchases and must pay the higher replacement costs. Opponents argue that firms cannot use such holding gains as the basis for dividend payments without impairing the ability to replace those assets used or sold.

Current cost/nominal dollar accounting is subject to two other criticisms. First, current replacement cost valuations are not as easy to verify or audit as acquisition cost valuations. Different appraisers likely provide different replacement cost valuations for various assets. The variation in appraisal values is particularly wide in the case of assets specific to a firm for which active secondhand markets do not exist. Second, the use of nominal dollars means that the measuring unit underlying current replacement cost valuations is not constant across time. Revenues and expenses reflect the purchasing power of the monetary unit during the year, whereas assets and liabilities reflect year-end purchasing power. Distortions caused by changes in the general purchasing power of the measuring unit are less severe in current cost/nominal dollar accounting than in acquisition cost/nominal dollar accounting because current replacement costs reflect more recent measurements.

CURRENT COST/CONSTANT DOLLAR ACCOUNTING

Column 4 of Exhibit 5.6 shows the result of accounting for changes in both general and specific prices. Sales, cost of goods sold, and other expenses measured in terms of replacement costs on June 30, Year 1 (column 3 amounts), are restated from dollars of June 30 purchasing power to dollars of December 31 purchasing power in column 4. Balance sheet amounts for assets reflect current replacement cost valuations and constant dollars on December 31, Year 1.

Perhaps the most interesting disclosures in column 4 are the holding gains. The reported amounts indicate the extent to which changes in prices of the firm's specific assets exceed (or fall short of) the change in the general price level. Economists refer to such holding gains (or losses) as *real holding gains and losses*. Column 4 also includes the purchasing power gain on monetary items.

Current cost/constant dollar accounting deals with both accounting problems caused by changing prices: the measuring unit problem and the valuation problem. Although current cost/constant dollar accounting provides a comprehensive solution to these problems, the user of financial statements based on this approach should keep in mind the concerns discussed previously: (1) current cost valuations are less objective than acquisition cost valuations, (2) the firm is not necessarily better or worse off in an amount equal to the purchasing power gain or loss on monetary items, and (3) the firm cannot distribute to shareholders an amount equal to the holding gains on nonmonetary items (for example, inventories, equipment) if it is to maintain its operating capacity.

PROBLEMS

5.1 INCOME RECOGNITION FOR VARIOUS TYPES OF BUSINESSES. Discuss when each of the following types of businesses is likely to recognize revenues and expenses.

  a. A savings and loan association that loans money for home mortgages.
  b. A seller of trading stamps to food stores; food store customers can redeem the stamps for various household products.
  c. A travel agency that books hotels, transportation, and similar services for customers and earns a commission from the providers of these services.
  d. A major league baseball team that sells season tickets before the season begins and signs multiyear contracts with players. These contracts typically defer the payment of a significant portion of the compensation provided by the contract until the player retires.
  e. A firm that manufactures and sells limited edition figurines. The firm agrees to repurchase the figurines at any time during the twenty years after sale if the market value of the figurine does not increase by at least 10 percent annually.
  f. A producer of fine whiskey that ages twelve years before sale.
  g. A timber-growing firm that contracts to sell all timber in a particular tract when it reaches twenty years of age. Each year the firm harvests another tract. The price per board foot of timber equals the market price when the customer signs the purchase contract plus 10 percent for each year until harvest.
  h. An airline that provides transportation services to customers. Each flight grants frequent-flier miles to customers. Customers earn a free flight when they accumulate sufficient frequent-flier miles.

5.2 MEASURING INCOME FROM LONG-TERM CONTRACTS. Turner Construction Company agreed on January 1, Year 1, to construct an observatory for Dartmouth College for $120 million. Dartmouth College must pay $30 million on signing and $30 million at the end of Year 1, Year 2, and Year 3. Expected construction costs are $10 million for Year 1, $60 million for Year 2, and $30 million for Year 3. Assume that these cash flows occur at the end of each year. Also assume that an appropriate interest rate for this contract is 10 percent. Amortization schedules for the deferred cash flows appear below.

Amortization Schedule for Cash Received

Year	Balance January 1	Interest Revenue	Payment	Reduction in Principal	Balance December 31
1	$74,606	$7,460	$30,000	$22,540	$52,066
2	52,066	5,207	30,000	24,793	27,273
3	27,273	2,727	30,000	27,273	—

Amortization Schedule for Cash Disbursed

Year	Balance January 1	Interest Expense	Payment	Reduction in Principal	Balance December 31
1	$81,217	$8,122	$10,000	$ 1,878	$79,339
2	79,339	7,934	60,000	52,066	27,273
3	27,273	2,727	30,000	27,273	—

REQUIRED

a. Indicate the amount and nature of income (revenue and expense) that Turner would recognize during Year 1, Year 2, and Year 3 if it uses the completed-contract method. Ignore income taxes.

b. Repeat part (*a*), using the percentage-of-completion method.

c. Repeat part (*a*), using the installment method.

d. Indicate the balance in the Construction-in-Process account on December 31, Year 1, Year 2, and Year 3 (just prior to completion of the contract) under the completed-contract and the percentage-of-completion methods.

5.3   ANALYZING FINANCIAL STATEMENT DISCLOSURES REGARDING INVENTORIES AND FIXED ASSETS. USX derives revenues from the manufacture of steel and the refining and marketing of petroleum products. USX uses a LIFO cost-flow assumption for inventories, straight-line depreciation for financial reporting, and accelerated depreciation for tax reporting. Exhibit 5.7 presents selected data for USX for Year 5 and Year 6. The income tax rate is 35 percent.

REQUIRED

a. The excess of FIFO over LIFO inventories was $380 million on December 31, Year 4, $390 million on December 31, Year 5, and $340 million on December 31, Year 6. Compute the cost of goods sold for USX for Year 5 and Year 6, assuming that it had used a FIFO cost-flow assumption.

b. Compute the inventory turnover ratio for USX for Year 5 and Year 6 using (1) a LIFO cost-flow assumption and (2) a FIFO cost-flow assumption.

EXHIBIT 5.7

USX
Financial Statement Data
(amounts in millions)
(Problem 5.3)

	December 31		
	Year 4	Year 5	Year 6
Inventories (LIFO).....................	$ 1,858	$ 1,930	$ 1,626
Property, Plant, and Equipment (net)......	11,593	11,759	11,603
Total Assets	17,039	17,252	17,374
Deferred Tax Liability Relating to Temporary Depreciation Differences	2,594	2,556	2,680
Common Shareholders' Equity	4,987	3,709	3,864

	Year Ended December 31	
	Year 5	Year 6
Sales	$17,813	$18,064
Cost of Goods Sold........................	14,140	13,793
Depreciation Expense......................	1,091	1,077
Interest Expense	485	630
Net Income (loss)	(78)	86

c. Compute the amount of depreciation expense that USX recognized for income tax purposes for Year 5 and Year 6. Note that the amount reported as the deferred tax liability relating to temporary depreciation differences represents the cumulative income taxes delayed as of each balance sheet date because USX uses accelerated depreciation for tax purposes and straight-line depreciation for financial reporting.

d. Compute the fixed asset turnover ratio for Year 5 and Year 6, assuming the use of (1) straight-line depreciation and (2) accelerated (tax) depreciation.

e. Compute the rate of return on assets for Year 5 and Year 6 based on the reported amounts (that is, LIFO for inventories and straight-line depreciation). Disaggregate ROA into profit margin and assets turnover.

f. Repeat part (e) using FIFO for inventories and accelerated (tax) depreciation. Assume that USX uses FIFO for both financial and tax reporting. Any tax effects reduce or increase cash. Disaggregate ROA into profit margin and assets turnover components.

g. Compute the rate of return on common shareholders' equity for Year 5 and Year 6 based on the reported amounts. Disaggregate ROCE into ROA, common earnings leverage, and capital structure leverage components.

h. Repeat part (g) using FIFO for inventories and accelerated (tax) depreciation.

i. Interpret the changes in the profitability and risk of USX between Year 5 and Year 6 in light of the preceding analyses.

5.4 ANALYZING DISCLOSURES REGARDING FIXED ASSETS. Exhibit 5.8 presents selected financial statement data for three chemical companies: Ethyl Corporation, Monsanto, and Olin Corporation.

EXHIBIT 5.8

Three Chemical Companies
Selected Financial Statement Data on Depreciable Assets
(amounts in millions)
(Problem 5.4)

	Ethyl Corporation	Monsanto	Olin Corporation
Depreciable Assets at Cost			
December 31, Year 4.........................	$1,639	$7,662	$2,492
December 31, Year 5.........................	1,909	7,382	2,509
Accumulated Depreciation			
December 31, Year 4.........................	809	4,597	1,558
December 31, Year 5.........................	910	4,580	1,624
Net Income, Year 5	90	494	(65)
Depreciation Expense, Year 5	113	469	131
Deferred Tax Liability Relating to Depreciable Assets			
December 31, Year 4.........................	98	43	129
December 31, Year 5.........................	130	49	133
Income Tax Rate	35%	35%	35%
Depreciation Method for Financial Reporting.......	Straight Line	Straight Line	Straight Line
Depreciation Method for Tax Reporting............	Accelerated	Accelerated	Accelerated

REQUIRED

a. Compute the average total depreciable life of assets in use for each firm during Year 5.
b. Compute the average age to date of depreciable assets in use for each firm at the end of Year 5.
c. Compute the amount of depreciation expense recognized for tax purposes for each firm for Year 5 using the amount of the deferred tax liability related to depreciation timing differences.
d. Compute the amount of net income for Year 5 for each firm, assuming that depreciation expense for financial reporting equals the amount computed in part (c) for tax reporting.
e. Compute the amount each company would report for property, plant, and equipment (net) on December 31, Year 5, if it had used accelerated (tax reporting) depreciation instead of straight-line depreciation.
f. What factors might explain the difference in average total life of Olin Corporation relative to the other two firms?
g. What factors might explain the older average age for depreciable assets of Olin Corporation relative to the other two firms?
h. What factors might explain the proportionally larger adjustment for Ethyl Corporation to convert to accelerated (tax) depreciation relative to the other two firms?

5.5 INTERPRETING FINANCIAL STATEMENT DISCLOSURES RELATING TO INCOME RECOGNITION. Deere & Company manufactures agricultural and industrial equipment and provides financing and insurance services for its independent dealers and their retail customers. Exhibit 5.9 presents an income statement and Exhibit 5.10 presents a balance sheet for Deere for Year 10 and Year 11.

EXHIBIT 5.9

Deere & Company
Income Statement
(amounts in millions)
(Problem 5.5)

	Year Ended October 31	
	Year 10	Year 11
Revenues		
Equipment Sales Revenue (Note 1)	$6,779	$5,848
Finance Revenue (Note 2)	593	654
Insurance Premium Revenue (Note 3)	384	444
Investment Revenue	119	109
Total Revenues	$7,875	$7,055
Expenses		
Cost of Goods Sold	$5,424	$4,894
Insurance Claims	335	406
Selling and Administrative Expenses	1,094	1,330
Interest Expense	435	450
Income Tax Expense	181	(5)
Total Expenses	$7,469	$7,075
Net Income (loss)	$ 406	$ (20)

EXHIBIT 5.10

Deere & Company
Balance Sheet
(amounts in millions)
(Problem 5.5)

	October 31	
	Year 10	Year 11
Assets		
Cash	$ 185	$ 279
Marketable Securities	857	801
Accounts and Notes Receivable (Note 2)	7,140	7,839
Inventories (Note 4)	678	538
Property, Plant, and Equipment (Note 5)	1,331	1,420
Other Assets	473	772
Total Assets	$10,664	$11,649
Liabilities and Shareholders' Equity		
Short-Term Borrowing	$ 2,893	$ 3,471
Accounts Payable and Accrued Expenses	1,751	1,809
Insurance Claims Payable	444	491
Long-Term Borrowing	1,786	2,206
Deferred Income Taxes	172	75
Pension Liability	611	762
Total Liabilities	$ 7,657	$ 8,814
Common Stock	$ 831	$ 839
Retained Earnings	2,176	1,996
Total Shareholders' Equity	$ 3,007	$ 2,835
Total Liabilities and Shareholders' Equity	$10,664	$11,649

NOTE 1: Deere recognizes income from equipment sales for financial reporting at the time of shipment to dealers. Provisions for sales incentives to dealers, returns and allowances, and uncollectible accounts are made at the time of sale. There is a time lag, which varies based on the timing and level of retail demand, between when Deere records sales to dealers and when dealers sell equipment to retail customers. Deere recognizes income from equipment sales using the installment method for tax reporting.

NOTE 2: Deere provides financing to independent dealers and retail customers for Deere products. Accounts and notes receivable appear net of unearned finance income. Deere recognizes the unearned finance income as finance revenue over the period that dealer and customer notes are outstanding.

NOTE 3: Deere provides property and casualty insurance to purchasers of Deere products. Deere recognizes premium revenues evenly over the term of insurance coverage and recognizes expenses for actual and expected future claims arising from losses sustained by policyholders each year.

NOTE 4: Deere uses a LIFO cost-flow assumption for inventories and cost of goods sold. The excess of FIFO over LIFO cost of inventories was $1,121 million on October 31, Year 10, and $1,217 million on October 31, Year 11.

NOTE 5: Property, plant, and equipment is outlined in the following table. Deere depreciates fixed assets using the straight-line method for financial reporting. Depreciation expense was $177 million in Year 10 and $190 million in Year 11. Deere uses accelerated depreciation for tax reporting.

	October 31	
	Year 10	Year 11
Land	$ 39	$ 40
Buildings	763	771
Machinery and Equipment	2,279	2,387
Dies, Patterns, Tools....................	364	359
Total	$ 3,445	$ 3,557
Less Accumulated Depreciation	(2,114)	(2,137)
	$ 1,331	$ 1,420

REQUIRED (Problem 5.5 continued)

a. Using the criteria for revenue recognition, justify the timing of revenue recognition by Deere for its equipment sales. Consider why recognition of revenue either earlier or later than the time of shipment to dealers would not be more appropriate.

b. Describe briefly how the following balance sheet accounts of Deere & Company would change if it recognized revenues during the period of production using the percentage-of-completion method. You need not give amounts but indicate the likely direction of the change and describe the computation of its amount.

> Accounts and Notes Receivable
>
> Inventories
>
> Retained Earnings

c. Respond to question (*b*), assuming that Deere & Company recognized revenue using the installment method.

> Accounts and Notes Receivable
>
> Inventories
>
> Retained Earnings

d. Compute the amount of cost of goods sold for Year 11, assuming that Deere & Company had used a FIFO instead of a LIFO cost-flow assumption.

e. Did the number and costs of inventory items likely increase or decrease during Year 11? Explain.

f. Compute the average age of Deere's depreciable assets at the end of Year 11.

g. The statement of cash flows reports the following information for Year 11 (amounts in millions):

> Proceeds from sale of property, plant, and equipment ..... $ 32
> Acquisition of property, plant, and equipment $352

Compute the gain or loss recognized on the sale of property, plant, and equipment.

5.6 INTERPRETING DISCLOSURES REGARDING CHANGING PRICES. Chilgener S.A. is the second largest provider of electric transmission services in Chile. Exhibit 5.11 presents

EXHIBIT 5.11

Chilgener, S.A.
Balance Sheet
(amounts in millions of constant December 31, Year 13 pesos)
(Problem 5.6)

	December 31	
	Year 12	Year 13
Assets		
Cash	P 4,031	P 30,140
Accounts Receivable	7,121	10,923
Inventories	8,664	8,622
Other Current Assets	15,053	50,746
Total Current Assets.........................	P 34,869	P 100,431
Fixed Assets at Cost	P 436,595	P 438,067
Technical Revaluation of Fixed Assets	29,075	29,075
Accumulated Depreciation	(165,394)	(171,353)
Net Fixed Assets	P 300,276	P 295,789
Other Assets..................................	P 37,606	P 93,840
Total Assets	P 372,751	P 490,060
Liabilities and Shareholders' Equity		
Short-Term Borrowing	P 11,068	P 50,800
Accounts Payable..............................	10,127	15,860
Other Current Liabilities	5,839	6,233
Total Current Liabilities......................	P 27,034	P 72,893
Long-Term Debt	87,360	96,482
Other Noncurrent Liabilities	5,347	9,245
Total Liabilities	P 119,741	P 178,620
Paid-in Capital................................	P 190,233	P 238,818
Technical Revaluation of Fixed Assets	29,075	29,075
Retained Earnings..............................	33,702	43,547
Total Shareholders' Equity....................	P 253,010	P 311,440
Total Liabilities and Shareholders' Equity	P 372,751	P 490,060

the balance sheet for Chilgener on December 31, Year 12 and Year 13. Exhibit 5.12 presents the income statement for Chilgener for Year 12 and Year 13. Excerpts from the notes to its financial statements appear below.

SUMMARY OF SIGNIFICANT ACCOUNTING PRINCIPLES

General. The consolidated financial statements have been prepared in conformity with generally accepted accounting principles in Chile and with the regulations issued by the Superintendency of Corporations and Insurance Companies.

EXHIBIT 5.12

Chilgener S.A.
Income Statement
(amounts in millions of constant December 31, Year 13 pesos)
(Problem 5.6)

	December 31	
	Year 12	**Year 13**
Operating Revenues	P 70,514	P 90,030
Operating Costs.............................	(38,871)	(53,556)
Operating Margin	P 31,643	P 36,474
Selling and Administrative Expense	(10,114)	(11,809)
Operating Income	P 21,529	P 24,665
Financial Income............................	P 3,258	P 10,415
Share of Profits of Investees	1,123	4,278
Financing Expenses	(7,136)	(7,263)
Other Nonoperating Expenses..................	(1,544)	(1,584)
Price-Level Restatement	3,471	(1,250)
Nonoperating Income	P (828)	P 4,596
Income before Tax..........................	P 20,701	P 29,261
Income Tax................................	(3,264)	(4,030)
Net Income	P 17,437	P 25,231

Price Level Restatement. These consolidated financial statements have been restated through the application of an adjustment based on the change in the consumer price index in order to reflect the effect of fluctuations in the purchasing power of the Chilean peso. Restatements have been based on the official index published by the Chilean Institute of Statistics which amounts to a 12.1 percent increase for the year ended December 31, Year 13 (in Year 12, 14 percent). Moreover, income and expenses were also restated so as to express them at year-end purchasing power. The Year 12 financial statements and their relevant notes have been adjusted (without being reflected in the accounting records) by 12.1 percent with the only purpose of allowing their comparison with the Year 12 financial statements in constant pesos of December Year 13.

Inventories. Inventories consist of raw materials and spares which are valued at their replacement cost. The values thus determined do not exceed their net realizable value in accordance with generally accepted accounting principles.

Fixed Assets. Fixed assets are presented according to contribution values or at cost, as the case may be, plus price-level restatement. The value of fixed assets was adjusted on June 30, Year 6 in accordance with the Technical Appraisal Circulars of the Superintendency of Corporations and Insurance Companies. Depreciation has been calculated on a straight-line basis on the adjusted value of assets, in accordance with their remaining useful life. Depreciation for Year 13 amounted to P10,206 and to P9,941 for Year 12. It is included in operating costs and includes additional depreciation for technical reappraisal of fixed assets amounting to P1,166 in Year 13 and P1,195 in Year 12.

Bonds. Bonds are shown at nominal year-end value plus accrued interest.

REQUIRED

a. Does Chilgener's reporting most closely resemble (1) acquisition cost/constant peso reporting, (2) current cost/nominal peso reporting, or (3) current cost/constant peso reporting? Explain.

b. Interpret the last sentence in the note on the price-level restatement.

c. What is the likely reason that Chilgener reported a price-level restatement gain on its income statement for Year 12 but a price-level restatement loss for Year 13?

d. Assume that sales and price-level changes occurred evenly during Year 12 and Year 13. Compute the *nominal* peso change in sales between Year 12 and Year 13.

e. Have the current replacement costs of Chilgener's fixed assets increased at a faster or slower rate than the general price level? Explain your reasoning. If you do not think that the disclosures permit an answer to this question, explain your reasoning.

f. Why does the amount in the account Technical Revaluation of Fixed Assets remain at P29,075 during Year 13 if the note on fixed assets indicates that Chilgener recognized depreciation on the revalued fixed asset amount?

CASE 5.1

ARIZONA LAND DEVELOPMENT COMPANY

Joan Locker and Bill Dasher organized the Arizona Land Development Company (ALDC) on January 2, Year 1. They contributed land with a market value of $300,000 and cash of $100,000 for all of the common stock of the corporation. The land served as the initial inventory of property sold to customers.

ALDC sells undeveloped land, primarily to individuals approaching retirement. Within a period of nine years from the date of sale, ALDC promises to develop the land so that it is suitable for the construction of residential housing. ALDC makes all sales on an installment basis. Customers pay 10 percent of the selling price at the time of sale and remit the remainder in equal installments over the next nine years.

ALDC estimates that development costs will equal 50 percent of the selling price of the land and that development work will take nine years to complete from the date of sale. Actual development costs have coincided with expectations. The firm incurs 10 percent of the development costs at the time of sale and incurs the remainder evenly over the next nine years.

ALDC remained a privately held firm for its first six years. Exhibits 1 through 3 present the firm's income statement, balance sheet, and statement of cash flows, respectively, for Year 1 to Year 6. ALDC recognizes income from sales of undeveloped land at the time of sale. The amount shown for sales each year in Exhibit 1 represents the gross amount ALDC ultimately expects to collect from customers for land sold in that year. The amount shown for estimated development costs each year is the gross amount that ALDC expects ultimately to disburse to develop land sold in that year. The firm treats selling expenses as a period expense. It is subject to a 34 percent income tax rate. ALDC uses the installment method of income recognition for income tax purposes.

ALDC contemplates making its initial public offering of common stock early in Year 7. The firm asks you to assess whether its income recognition method, as reflected in Exhibits 1 to 3, accurately reflects its operating performance and financial position. To assist you, the firm has prepared financial statements following three other income recognition methods as described next.

Income Recognition at Time of Sale but with Discounting of Future Cash Flows to Their Present Value.

Exhibits 4 to 6 present the financial statements following this income recognition method. This method discounts

EXHIBIT 1

Arizona Land Development Company
Income Statements
Income Recognition at Time of Sale—No Discounting of Cash Flows
(Case 5.1)

	Year 1	Year 2	Year 3	Year 4	Year 5	Year 6
Sales...............	$ 650,000	$ 900,000	$1,500,000	$2,500,000	$1,200,000	$ 400,000
Less						
Cost of Land Inventory Sold.....	(65,000)	(90,000)	(150,000)	(250,000)	(120,000)	(40,000)
Estimated Development Costs.....	(325,000)	(450,000)	(750,000)	(1,250,000)	(600,000)	(200,000)
Gross Profit............	$ 260,000	$ 360,000	$ 600,000	$1,000,000 $	480,000	$ 160,000
Selling Expenses.........	(65,000)	(90,000)	(150,000)	(250,000)	(120,000)	(40,000)
Net Income before Taxes......	$ 195,000	$ 270,000	$ 450,000	$ 750,000	$ 360,000	$ 120,000
Income Taxes						
Current............	—	—	(9,778)	(26,091)	(73,009)	(94,902)
Deferred...........	(66,300)	(91,800)	(143,222)	(228,909)	(49,391)	54,102
Net Income...........	$ 128,700	$ 178,200	$ 297,000	$ 495,000	$ 237,600	$ 79,200

EXHIBIT 2

Arizona Land Development Company
Balance Sheets
Income Recognition at Time of Sale—No Discounting of Cash Flows
(Case 5.1)

	Year 1	Year 2	Year 3	Year 4	Year 5	Year 6
Assets						
Cash	$100,000	$ 132,500	$ 100,222	$ 126,631	$ 131,122	$ 273,720
Notes Receivable	520,000	1,175,000	2,220,000	3,915,000	4,320,000	3,965,000
Land Inventory	235,000	145,000	95,000	45,000	125,000	185,000
Total Assets	$855,000	$1,452,000	$2,415,222	$4,086,631	$4,576,122	$4,423,720
Liabilities and Shareholders' Equity						
Estimated Development Cost Liability	$260,000	$ 587,500	$1,110,000	$1,957,500	$2,160,000	$1,982,500
Deferred Income Taxes.	66,300	158,100	301,322	530,231	579,622	525,520
Common Stock	400,000	400,000	400,000	500,000	500,000	500,000
Retained Earnings.	128,700	306,900	603,900	1,098,900	1,336,500	1,415,700
Total Liabilities and Shareholders' Equity	$855,000	$1,452,500	$2,415,222	$4,086,631	$4,576,122	$4,423,720

EXHIBIT 3

Arizona Land Development Company
Statements of Cash Flows
Income Recognition at Time of Sale—No Discounting of Cash Flows
(Case 5.1)

	Year 1	Year 2	Year 3	Year 4	Year 5	Year 6
Operations						
Net Income	$ 128,700	$ 178,200	$ 297,000	$ 495,000	$ 237,600	$ 79,200
(Increase) Decrease in Notes Receivable	(520,000)	(655,000)	(1,045,000)	(1,695,000)	(405,000)	355,000
(Increase) Decrease in Land Inventory	65,000	90,000	50,000	50,000	(80,000)	(60,000)
Increase (Decrease) in Estimated Development Cost Liability	260,000	327,500	522,500	847,500	202,500	(177,500)
Increase (Decrease) in Deferred Income Taxes	66,300	91,800	143,222	228,909	49,391	(54,102)
Cash Flow from Operations	$ 0	$ 32,500	$ (32,278)	$ (73,591)	$ 4,491	$ 142,598
Financing						
Common Stock Issued	—	—	—	100,000	—	—
Change in Cash	$ 0	$ 32,500	$ (32,278)	$ 26,409	$ 4,491	$ 142,598

EXHIBIT 4

Arizona Land Development Company
Income Statements
Income Recognition at Time of Sale—With Discounting of Cash Flows
(Case 5.1)

	Year 1	Year 2	Year 3	Year 4	Year 5	Year 6
Sales	$ 411,336[a]	$ 569,543	$ 865,737	$1,442,895	$ 759,390	$ 253,130
Less						
Cost of Land Inventory Sold	(65,000)	(90,000)	(150,000)	(250,000)	(120,000)	(40,000)
Estimated Development Costs	(205,668)[b]	(284,771)	(432,869)	(721,448)	(379,695)	(126,565)
Gross Profit	$ 140,668	$ 194,772	$ 282,868	$ 471,447	$ 259,695	$ 86,565
Selling Expenses	(65,000)	(90,000)	(150,000)	(250,000)	(120,000)	(40,000)
Interest Revenue	41,560[c]	96,293	196,609	361,257	411,130	400,899
Interest Expense	(20,780)[d]	(48,147)	(98,304)	(180,628)	(205,566)	(200,449)
Net Income before Taxes	$ 96,448	$ 152,918	$ 231,173	$ 402,076	$ 345,259	$ 247,015
Income Taxes						
Current	—	(9,778)	(68,821)	(26,091)	(73,009)	(94,902)
Deferred	(32,792)	(51,992)	(68,821)	(110,615)	(44,379)	10,917
Net Income	$ 63,656	$ 100,926	$ 152,574	$ 265,370	$ 227,871	$ 163,030

[a]Represents the present value of $65,000 received on January 1, Year 1, plus the present value of a series of $65,000 cash inflows on December 31, Year 1 to Year 9, discounted at 12 percent.

[b]Represents the present value of $32,500 paid on January 1, Year 1, plus the present value of a series of $32,500 cash outflows on December 31, of Year 1 to Year 9, discounted at 12 percent.

[c]0.12($41,336 − $65,000) = $41,560.
[d]0.12($205,668 − $32,500) = $20,780.

EXHIBIT 5

Arizona Land Development Company
Balance Sheets
Income Recognition at Time of Sale—With Discounting of Cash Flows
(Case 5.1)

	Year 1	Year 2	Year 3	Year 4	Year 5	Year 6
Assets						
Cash	$100,000	$ 132,500	$ 100,222	$ 126,631	$ 131,122	$ 273,720
Notes Receivable	322,896[a]	743,732	1,351,078	2,350,230	2,725,750	2,624,779
Land Inventory	235,000	145,000	95,000	45,000	125,000	185,000
Total Assets	$657,896	$1,021,232	$1,546,300	$2,521,861	$2,981,872	$3,083,499
Liabilities and Shareholders' Equity						
Estimated Development Cost Liability	$161,448[b]	$ 371,866	$ 675,539	$1,175,115	$1,362,876	$1,312,390
Deferred Income Taxes	32,792	84,784	153,605	264,220	308,599	297,682
Common Stock	400,000	400,000	400,000	500,000	500,000	500,000
Retained Earnings	63,656	164,582	317,156	582,526	810,397	973,427
Total Liabilities and Shareholders' Equity	$657,896	$1,021,232	$1,546,300	$2,521,861	$2,981,872	$3,083,499

[a]$411,336 − $65,000 + $41,560 − $65,000 = $322,896 (see Notes a and c to Exhibit 4).

[b]$205,668 − $32,500 + $20,780 − $32,500 = $161,448 (see Notes b and d to Exhibit 4).

EXHIBIT 6

Arizona Land Development Company
Statements of Cash Flows
Income Recognition at Time of Sale—With Discounting of Cash Flows
(Case 5.1)

	Year 1	Year 2	Year 3	Year 4	Year 5	Year 6
Operations						
Net Income	$ 63,656	$ 100,926	$ 152,574	$ 265,370	$ 227,871	$163,030
(Increase) Decrease in Notes Receivable	(322,896)	(420,836)	(607,346)	(999,152)	(375,520)	100,971
(Increase) Decrease in Land Inventory. . . .	65,000	90,000	50,000	50,000	(80,000)	(60,000)
Increase (Decrease) in Estimated Development						
Cost Liability.	161,448	210,418	303,673	499,576	187,761	(50,486)
Increase (Decrease) in Deferred Income Taxes.	32,792	51,992	68,821	110,615	44,379	(10,917)
Cash Flow from Operations.	$ 0	$ 32,500	$ (32,278)	$ (73,591)	$ 4,491	$142,598
Financing						
Common Stock Issued	—	—	—	100,000	—	—
Change in Cash.	$ 0	$ 32,500	$ (32,278)	$ 26,409	$ 4,491	$142,598

future cash inflows from customers and future cash outflows for development work to their present values. The gross profit recognized at the time of sale equals the present value of cash inflows net of the present value of cash outflows. One might view this gross profit as the current cash equivalent value of the gross profit that the firm will ultimately realize over the nine-year period. As time passes, this method reports the increase in the present value of cash inflows as interest revenue each year and the increase in the present value of cash outflows as interest expense. Thus, this income recognition method results in reporting two types of income: a gross profit from selling land and interest from delayed cash flows. The computations of present values underlying the financial statements in Exhibits 4 to 6 rest on the following assumptions.

1. ALDC makes all sales on January 1 of each year. It receives 10 percent of the gross selling price at the time of sale and pays 10 percent of the gross development costs immediately.
2. The firm receives 10 percent of the gross selling price from customers and pays 10 percent of the gross development costs on December 31 of each year, beginning with the year of sale.
3. The interest rates used in discounting are as follows:

Sales In	Interest Rate
Year 1	12%
Year 2	12
Year 3	15
Year 4	15
Year 5	12
Year 6	12

Income Recognition Using the Installment Method—With Discounting of Cash Flows.

Exhibits 7 to 9 present the financial statements following this income recognition method. ALDC uses this income recognition method for tax reporting.

Income Recognition Using the Percentage-of-Completion Method.

Exhibits 10 to 12 present the financial statements following this income recognition method. The presumption underlying this method is that ALDC is primarily a developer of real estate and that its income should reflect its development activity, not its sales activity. The difference between the contract price and the total estimated costs of the land and development work represents the total income from development of the land. The percentage-of-completion method uses actual costs incurred to date as a percentage of estimated total costs to determine the degree of completion each period. Multiplying this percentage times the contract price yields sales revenue each year. Multiplying this percentage times the total expected costs yields cost of goods sold.

REQUIRED

a. For each of the four income recognition methods illustrated in Exhibits 1 through 12, show the supporting calculations for each of the following items for Year 2:
(1) Sales revenue for Year 2.
(2) Cost of goods sold for Year 2.

EXHIBIT 7

Arizona Land Development Company
Income Statements
Income Recognition Using Installment Method—With Discounting of Cash Flows
(Case 5.1)

	Year 1	Year 2	Year 3	Year 4	Year 5	Year 6
Sales Revenue	$ 38,440[a]	$148,707	$ 249,802	$ 427,243	$ 377,706	$ 347,017
Cost of Goods Sold	(58,195)[a]	(97,852)	(164,374)	(281,133)	(248,537)	(228,343)
Gross Profit	$ 30,245[a]	$ 50,855	$ 85,428	$ 146,110	$ 129,169	$ 118,674
Selling Expenses	(65,000)	(90,000)	(150,000)	(250,000)	(120,000)	(40,000)
Interest Revenue	41,560[b]	96,293	196,609	361,257	411,130	400,899
Interest Expense	(20,780)[c]	(48,147)	(98,304)	(180,628)	(205,566)	(200,449)
Net Income before Taxes	$(13,975)	$ 9,001	$ 33,733	$ 76,739	$ 214,733	$ 279,124
Income Taxes						
Current	—[d]	—[d]	(9,778)[d]	(26,091)	(73,009)	(94,902)
Deferred	—	—	—	—	—	—
Net Income	$(13,975)	$ 9,001	$ 23,955	$ 50,648	$ 141,724	$ 184,222

[a]Exhibit 4 indicates that the total gross profit from land sold in Year 1 is $140,668. The present value of the amounts that ALDC will receive from customers is $411,336 (see Exhibit 4). Thus, for each dollar of the $411,336 collected, the firm recognizes 34.2 cents (= $140,668 ÷ $411,336) of gross profit. During Year 1, ALDC collects $130,000 from sales of land made in Year 1 ($65,000 on January 1 and $65,000 on December 31). However, only $23,440 (= $65,000 − $41,560) of the December 31 payment represents payment of a portion of the $411,336 selling price. The remainder ($41,560) represents interest. Thus, the gross profit recognized in Year 1 is $30,245 [0.342($65,000 + $23,440)].

[b]See Note c to Exhibit 4.

[c]See Note d to Exhibit 4.

[d]ALDC carries forward the $13,975 loss in Year 1 to offset net income before taxes in future years ($9,001 in Year 2 and $4,974 in Year 3).

EXHIBIT 8

Arizona Land Development Company
Balance Sheets

Income Recognition Using Installment Method—With Discounting of Cash Flows

(Case 5.1)

	Year 1	Year 2	Year 3	Year 4	Year 5	Year 6
Assets						
Cash	$100,000	$132,500	$ 100,222	$ 126,631	$ 131,122	$ 273,720
Notes Receivable	212,473[a]	489,392	899,298	1,573,113	1,818,107	1,749,245
Land Inventory	235,000	145,000	95,000	45,000	125,000	185,000
Total Assets	$547,473	$766,892	$1,094,520	$1,744,744	$2,074,229	$2,207,965
Liabilities and Shareholders' Equity						
Estimated Development Cost Liability	$161,448[b]	$371,866	$ 675,539	$1,175,115	$1,362,876	$1,312,390
Deferred Income Taxes	—	—	—	—	—	—
Common Stock	400,000	400,000	400,000	500,000	500,000	500,000
Retained Earnings	(13,975)	(4,974)	18,981	69,629	211,353	395,575
Total Liabilities and Shareholders' Equity	$547,473	$766,892	$1,094,520	$1,744,744	$2,074,229	$2,207,965

[a]The derivation of this amount is as follows:

	Notes Receivable—Gross	Deferred Gross Profit	Notes Receivable—Net
January 1, Year 1	$411,336	$140,668	$270,668
Less Cash Received, January 1, Year 1	(65,000)	—	(65,000)
Plus Interest Revenue, Year 1	41,560	—	41,560
Less Cash Received, December 31, Year 1	(65,000)	—	(65,000)
Gross Profit Recognized, Year 1	—	(30,245)	30,245
Totals	$322,896	$110,423	$212,473

[b]See Note b to Exhibit 5.

EXHIBIT 9

Arizona Land Development Company
Statements of Cash Flows
Income Recognition Using Installment Method—With Discounting of Cash Flows
(Case 5.1)

	Year 1	Year 2	Year 3	Year 4	Year 5	Year 6
Operations						
Net Income (Loss)............	$ (13,975)	$ 9,001	$ 23,955	$ 50,648	$ 141,724	$184,222
(Increase) Decrease in Notes Receivable	(212,473)	(276,919)	(409,906)	(673,815)	(244,994)	68,862
(Increase) Decrease in Land Inventory...........	65,000	90,000	50,000	50,000	(80,000)	(60,000)
Increase (Decrease) in Estimated Development Cost Liability............	161,448	210,418	303,673	499,576	187,761	(50,485)
Increase (Decrease) in Deferred Income Taxes	—	—	—	—	—	—
Cash Flow from Operations........	$ 0	$ 32,500	$ (32,278)	$ (73,591)	$ 4,491	$142,598
Financing						
Common Stock Issued	—	—	—	100,000	—	—
Change in Cash........	$ 0	$ 32,500	$ (32,278)	$ 26,409	$ 4,491	$142,598

EXHIBIT 10

Arizona Land Development Company
Income Statements
Income Recognition Using Percentage-of-Completion Method
(Case 5.1)

	Year 1	Year 2	Year 3	Year 4	Year 5	Year 6
Sales	$ 216,667[a]	$ 354,167	$ 629,167	$1,087,500	$ 862,500	$ 695,833
Cost of Goods Sold	(130,000)[a]	(212,500)	(377,500)	(652,500)	(517,500)	(417,500)
Gross Profit	$ 86,667[a]	$ 141,667	$ 251,667	$ 435,000	$ 345,000	$ 278,333
Selling Expenses	(65,000)	(90,000)	(150,000)	(250,000)	(120,000)	(40,000)
Net Income before Taxes	$ 21,667	$ 51,667	$ 101,667	$ 185,000	$ 225,000	$ 238,333
Income Taxes						
Current	—	—	(9,778)	(26,091)	(73,009)	(94,902)
Deferred	(7,367)	(17,567)	(24,789)	(36,809)	(3,491)	13,869
Net Income	$ 14,300	$ 34,100	$ 67,100	$ 122,100	$ 148,500	$ 157,300

[a]Land sold under contract in Year 1 had a contract price of $650,000 and estimated contract cost of $390,000 (= $65,000 + $325,000) (see Exhibit 1). ALDC incurred development costs of $130,000 (= $65,000 for land + $32,500 on January 1, Year 1, + $32,500 on December 31, Year 1) during Year 1. Thus, the percentage of completion as of the end of Year 1 is 33.3 percent (= $130,000 ÷ $390,000). Sales are 33.3 percent of $650,000 and cost of goods sold is 33.3 percent of $390,000.

EXHIBIT 11

Arizona Land Development Company
Balance Sheets
Income Recognition Using Percentage-of-Completion Method
(Case 5.1)

	Year 1	Year 2	Year 3	Year 4	Year 5	Year 6
Assets						
Cash	$100,000	$132,500	$100,222	$126,631	$131,122	$273,720
Contracts in Process	216,667[a]	570,834	1,200,001	2,287,501	3,150,001	3,845,834
Less Progress Billings	(130,000)[b]	(375,000)	(830,000)	(1,635,000)	(2,430,000)	(3,185,000)
Contracts in Process (net)	$186,667	$328,334	$470,223	$779,132	$851,123	$934,554
Land Inventory	235,000	145,000	95,000	45,000	125,000	185,000
Total Assets	$421,667	$473,334	$565,223	$824,132	$976,123	$1,119,554
Liabilities and Shareholders' Equity						
Deferred Income Taxes	$ 7,367	$ 24,934	$ 49,723	$ 86,532	$ 90,023	$ 76,154
Common Stock	400,000	400,000	400,000	500,000	500,000	500,000
Retained Earnings	14,300	48,400	115,500	237,600	386,100	543,400
Total Liabilities and Shareholders' Equity	$421,667	$473,334	$565,223	$824,132	$976,123	$1,119,554

[a]Accumulated costs of $130,000 + gross profit recognized in Year 1 of $86,667 (see Note *a* to Exhibit 10).

[b]Down payment of $65,000 received on January 1, Year 1, plus $65,000 installment payment received on December 31, Year 1.

EXHIBIT 12

Arizona Land Development Company
Statements of Cash Flows
Income Recognition Using Percentage-of-Completion Method
(Case 5.1)

	Year 1	Year 2	Year 3	Year 4	Year 5	Year 6
Operations						
Net Income	$ 14,300	$ 34,100	$ 67,100	$ 122,100	$ 148,500	$ 157,300
(Increase) Decrease in Contracts in Process	(216,667)	(354,167)	(629,167)	(1,087,500)	(862,500)	(695,833)
Increase (Decrease) in Progress Billings	130,000	245,000	455,000	805,000	795,000	755,000
(Increase) Decrease in Land Inventory	65,000	90,000	50,000	50,000	(80,000)	(60,000)
Increase (Decrease) in Deferred Income Taxes . . .	7,367	17,567	24,789	36,809	3,491	(13,869)
Cash Flow from Operations	$ 0	$ 32,500	$ (32,278)	$ (73,591)	$ 4,491	$ 142,598
Financing						
Common Stock Issued	—	—	—	100,000	—	—
Change in Cash	$ 0	$ 32,500	$ (32,278)	$ 26,409	$ 4,491	$ 142,598

(3) Gross profit for Year 2.

(4) Notes receivable on December 31, Year 2, under the first three income recognition methods and the Contracts in Process account on December 31, Year 2, under the fourth income recognition method.

(5) Estimated Development Costs Liability on December 31, Year 2, under the first three income recognition methods and the Progress Billings account on December 31, Year 2, under the fourth income recognition method.

b. Evaluate each of the four income recognition methods described in the case relative to the criteria for revenue and expense recognition. Which method do you think best portrays the operating performance and financial position of ALDC? Discuss your reasoning?

c. Which income recognition method is ALDC likely to prefer in reporting to shareholders?

d. Why did ALDC choose the installment method for tax reporting?

e. With respect to maximizing cumulative reported earnings, the four income recognition methods rank order as follows: (1) income recognition at time of sale—no discounting of cash flows, (2) income recognition at time of sale—with discounting of cash flows, (3) income recognition using the percentage-of-completion method, (4) income recognition using the installment method—with discounting of cash flows. What is the reason behind this rank ordering?

f. The difference in cumulative reported earnings between any two income recognition methods equals (1) the difference in Notes Receivable or Contracts in Process (net) minus (2) the difference in the Estimated Development Cost Liability minus (3) the difference in the Deferred Income Taxes Liability. What is the rationale behind this relation?

g. Why is the amount shown on the income statement for "current" income taxes the same in each year for all four income recognition methods but the amount of total income tax expenses (current plus deferred) in each year different across income recognition methods?

h. Given that net income each year differs across the four income recognition methods, why is the amount of cash provided by operations the same? Under what conditions would a firm report different amounts of cash flow from operations for different income recognition methods?

CHIRON CORPORATION: AN R&D PUZZLE

Chiron Corporation is in the human health-care industry, applying genetic engineering and other tools of biotechnology to develop products that diagnose, prevent, and treat human diseases, Exhibit 1 for this case presents an income statement for Chiron for Year 5, Year 6, and Year 7. Total revenues increased from $141 million in Year 5 to $318 million in Year 7, a 49.8 percent compound annual growth rate. Net income increased from a $445 million loss in Year 5 to a $18 million profit in Year 7. The analyst encounters difficulties understanding the reasons for the increased profitability because of the following:

1. The company has grown both internally and through corporate acquisitions.
2. The company uses joint ventures and collaborative research agreements to develop and market new products.
3. Sales to related parties represent 41 percent of total revenues in Year 5, 38 percent in Year 6, and 43 percent in Year 7.

The following sections elaborate on these complicating factors.

Chiron operates in four major product markets:

1. *Therapeutics.*   The product emphasis in this segment is oncology.
2. *Ophthalmic Surgical.*   The two principal products in this segment are equipment for removing cataracts using ultrasound technology and intraocular lenses for cataract surgeries.
3. *Diagnostics.*   The primary product for this market is a blood screening device for hepatitis C virus. The company engages in research applying DNA probe-testing technologies to develop new diagnostic products.
4. *Vaccines.*   This segment offers immunizations for adult and pediatric diseases.

THERAPEUTICS

The company's involvement in therapeutics is through its wholly owned, consolidated subsidiary, Cetus Corporation (Cetus). Chiron acquired Cetus on December 28, Year 5, by exchanging shares of its common stock with a market value of $887.8 million. The acquisition was accounted for using the purchase method. Chiron restated the assets and liabilities of Cetus to their market values on December 28, Year 5. The difference between the $887.8 million purchase price and the market value of identifiable assets and liabilities was allocated $442 million to in-process technologies and $44.8 million to base technologies. Amortization expense on the capitalized amount was $3.9 million in Year 6 and Year 7 and is included in other operating expenses in Exhibit 1. The amounts allocated to in-process and base technologies are not deductible for tax purposes. Under the purchase method used in this acquisition, Chiron recognizes the earnings of Cetus subsequent to the date of acquisition.

OPHTHALMIC SURGICAL

The company's involvement in Ophthalmic Surgical is through its wholly owned, consolidated subsidiary, Intra Optics. Chiron acquired Intra Optics on January 5, Year 6, by exchanging shares of its common stock. Chiron accounted for the acquisition using the pooling of interest method. Under a pooling of interests, the book values of Intra Optic's assets and liabilities carry over after the acquisition. Chiron's earnings are retroactively restated to include the earnings of Intra Optics for all years presented.

DIAGNOSTICS

The company's involvement in diagnostics is through a joint venture with Ortho Diagnostic Systems, a subsidiary of Johnson & Johnson. Chiron conducts research, development, and manufacturing for the Chiron/Ortho joint venture. The joint venture reimburses Chiron at cost for these services, which were as follows:

	Research and Development	Manufacturing
Year 5	$8.0	$ 9.3
Year 6	$9.2	$10.6
Year 7	$9.8	$11.3

Chiron's 50 percent share of the earnings of this joint venture totaled $49.8 million in Year 5, $73.6 million in Year 6, and $77.1 million in Year 7.

EXHIBIT 1

Chiron Corporation
Income Statement
(amounts in thousands)
(Case 5.2)

	Year 5	Year 6	Year 7
Revenues			
Product Sales			
Related Parties.....................	$ 10,576	$ 11,801	$ 23,156
Unrelated Parties..................	40,696	99,779	124,737
	$ 51,272	$111,580	$147,893
Research Revenues			
Related Parties.....................	$ 18,331	$ 24,486	$ 54,552
Unrelated Parties..................	12,144	16,017	14,391
	$ 30,475	$ 40,503	$ 68,943
License Fees—Unrelated Parties	9,906	19,939	22,960
Equity in Earnings of Joint Ventures	49,845	74,238	77,739
Total Revenues.....................	$ 141,498	$246,260	$317,535
Expenses			
Research and Development	$ 80,001	$142,265	$140,030
Cost of Goods Sold..................	28,423	54,692	68,484
Selling and Administrative Expenses	44,068	99,707	95,790
Write-off of In-Process Technologies	442,484	—	—
Other Operating Expenses............	2,287	7,499	(1,907)
Total Expenses.....................	$ 597,263	$304,163	$302,397
Income (Loss) from Operations.........	$(455,765)	$ (57,903)	$ 15,138
Interest Income	12,997	6,973	7,949
Income (Loss) before Income Taxes	$(442,768)	$ (50,930)	$ 23,087
Income Tax Expense..................	(1,882)	(4,024)	(4,703)
Net Income	$(444,650)	$ (54,954)	$ 18,384

VACCINES

The company's involvement in vaccines is through a joint venture with CIBA-GEIGY. Chiron conducts research, development, and manufacturing services for the Chiron/CIBA-GEIGY joint venture. The joint venture reimburses Chiron at cost for these services, which were as follows:

	Research and Development	Manufacturing
Year 5	$10.3	$ 1.3
Year 6	$15.3	$ 1.2
Year 7	$44.8	$11.9

Chiron's equity in the earnings of the Chiron/CIBA-GEIGY joint venture were zero in Year 5, $.638 million in Year 6, and $.639 million in Year 7.

REQUIRED

a. Recast the income statement of Chiron Corporation for Year 5, Year 6, and Year 7 into a format that enhances understanding of the changes in its profitability during the three-year period. Give particular consideration to the presentation of each of the following items:

(1) The appropriate measure of total revenues and the classification of its components.

(2) The measurement of research and development expense, particularly with respect to the treatment of cost-reimbursed research and development services and the cost of in-process purchased technologies.

b. Identify the principal reasons for the changes in the profitability of Chiron during the three-year period.

CASE 5.3

CORPORACION INDUSTRIAL SANLUIS: COPING WITH CHANGING PRICES

Corporacion Industrial Sanluis (Sanluis) is a leading conglomerate firm in Mexico. It derives revenues from the manufacture of auto parts (springs and drums), the mining of precious metals (gold and silver), and the provision of hotel services (owner of several Hyatt resort hotels). Sanluis is the first Mexican company to have its shares traded in the United States through American Depository Receipts.

Sanluis follows generally accepted accounting principles in Mexico to prepare its financial statements. Its Year 8 financial statements and notes are attached as Exhibit 1 (balance sheet), Exhibit 2 (statement of income), and Exhibit 3 (statement of changes in financial position). This case examines financial disclosures in Mexico with respect to changing prices and assesses Sanluis' success in coping with inflation.

REQUIRED

a. Which of the methods of accounting for changing prices discussed in Appendix 5.1 does Sanluis apparently use? Indicate the clues supporting your conclusion.

b. Prepare a balance sheet for Sanluis as of December 31, Year 8, under each of the three methodologies indicated in the following columns. Aggregate individual assets in preparing this analysis. You may find it useful to begin with liabilities and shareholders' equity and work backward toward total assets.

	Historical Cost/ Nominal Pesos	Historical Cost/ Constant Pesos	Current Cost/ Constant Pesos
Assets			
Liabilities			
Preferred Stock			
Common Stock			
Other Equity Accounts . .			
Retained Earnings			
Deficit in Restatement of Capital			
Total Equities			

EXHIBIT 1

Corporacion Industrial Sanluis, S.A. DE C.V. and Subsidiaries
Consolidated Balance Sheet
(in thousands of constant December 31, Year 8, Mexican Pesos)
(Case 5.3)

	December 31	
	Year 7	Year 8
Assets		
Cash and Short-Term Investment	P 177,670	P 219,490
Accounts Receivable	82,017	79,866
Inventories	68,027	64,075
Prepayments.	2,282	9,856
Total Current Assets	P 329,996	P 373,287
Property, Plant, and Equipment	P 854,628	P 810,026
Accumulated Depreciation	(294,622)	(240,632)
Total Property, Plant, and Equipment	P 560,006	P 569,394
Other Assets.	P 27,193	P 28,395
Total Assets	P 917,195	P 971,076
Liabilities and Shareholders' Equity		
Bank Loans	P 195,090	P 308,323
Accounts Payable.	37,115	56,639
Accrued Liabilities	27,275	38,960
Total Current Liabilities	P 259,480	P 403,922
Long-Term Debt	184,993	125,957
Total Liabilities	P 444,473	P 529,879
Preferred Stock—Nominal Value	P 59,796	P 59,796
Restatement Increase.	7,134	7,134
	P 66,930	P 66,930
Common Stock—Nominal Value	P 15,000	P 15,000
Restatement Increase.	188,902	188,902
	P 203,902	P 203,902
Other Equity Accounts—Nominal Value.	P 27,702	P 17,301
Restatement Increase.	58,729	62,725
	P 86,431	P 80,026
Retained Earnings—Nominal Value.	P 278,492	P 317,505
Restatement Increase.	851,497	830,050
	P 1,129,989	P 1,147,555
Deficit in the Restatement of Capital	P(1,014,530)	P(1,057,216)
Total Shareholders' Equity	P 472,722	P 441,197
Total Liabilities and Shareholders' Equity	P 917,195	P 971,076

EXHIBIT 2

Corporacion Industrial Sanluis, S.A. DE C.V. and Subsidiaries
Consolidated Statement of Income
(in thousands of constant December 31, Year 8, Mexican Pesos)
(Case 5.3)

	Year 7	Year 8
Sales	P 411,213	P 429,471
Cost of Goods Sold	(327,489)	(334,198)
Depreciation and Depletion	(17,924)	(21,032)
Gross Profit	P 65,800	P 74,241
Distribution and Selling Expenses	(13,470)	(11,806)
General and Administrative Expenses	(36,355)	(29,100)
Exploration and Development Expenses	(2,364)	(1,320)
Operating Profit	P 13,611	P 32,015
Interest Expense, Net	(18,733)	(19,536)
Exchange Loss, Net	(16,540)	(7,514)
Gain on Net Monetary Position	29,263	19,481
Other Income—Net	8,390	3,463
Income from Continuing Operations before Tax and Statutory Employee Profit Sharing	P 15,991	P 27,909
Taxes and Statutory Employee Profit Sharing	(8,656)	(10,343)
Income from Continuing Operations	P 7,335	P 17,566

EXHIBIT 3

Corporacion Industrial Sanluis, S.A. DE C.V. and Subsidiaries
Consolidated Statement of Changes in Financial Position
(in thousands of constant December 31, Year 8, Mexican Pesos)
(Case 5.3)

	Year 7	Year 8
Operations		
Income from Continuing Operations	P 7,335	P 17,566
Depreciation and Depletion	17,925	21,032
Variation in Current Assets	3,642	17,631
Resources Provided by Operations	P 28,902	P 56,229
Financing		
Increase in Capital Stock	P 66,930	—
Bank Loans, Net	(15,643)	P 53,104
Resources Provided by Financing	P 51,287	P 53,104
Investing		
(Acquisition) Sale of Subsidiaries	P 16,590	P (9,963)
Acquisition of Property, Plant, and Equipment (net)	(63,965)	(57,550)
Resources Used for Investing	P (47,375)	P (67,513)
Increase in Cash and Short-Term Investments	P 32,814	P 41,820
Cash and Short-Term Investments at Beginning of Year	144,856	177,670
Cash and Short-Term Investments at End of Year	P177,670	P219,490

c. What is the likely explanation for Sanluis' recognition of a purchasing power gain on its monetary items during Year 8?

d. Did Sanluis experience a holding gain or a holding loss on its nonmonetary items (that is, inventories, fixed assets) during Year 8? What is the interpretation of this gain or loss?

e. How well has Sanluis coped with changing prices during Year 7 and Year 8? *Note:* Mexico's consumer price index increased 18.8 percent in Year 7 and 11.9 percent in Year 8.

EXCERPTS FROM NOTES TO THE FINANCIAL STATEMENTS

Note 1: Accounting Policies

a. The consolidated financial statements have been prepared in conformity with generally accepted accounting principles in Mexico and are stated in pesos of December 31, Year 8, purchasing power.

b. Marketable securities and other investments in shares are stated at market value.

c. Inventories are stated at estimated replacement cost. Cost of goods sold is determined by the last-in, first-out (LIFO) method.

d. Property, plant, and equipment are recorded at net replacement cost determined on the basis of appraisals made by independent experts registered at the National Securities Commission. Depreciation, amortization, and depletion are calculated by the straight-line method based on the estimated useful lives of the assets determined by the appraisers.

e. The restatement of capital stock represents the amount necessary to maintain the shareholders' investment in terms of purchasing power at the balance sheet date and is determined by applying to the historical amounts factors derived from the National Consumer Price Index (NCPI).

f. Retained earnings is expressed in pesos of purchasing power as of the latest balance sheet date and is determined by applying to the historical amounts factors derived from the NCPI.

g. The gain on net monetary position represents the effect of inflation, as measured by NCPI, on the company's monthly net monetary assets and liabilities during the year, restated in pesos of purchasing power as of the end of the most recent period.

h. The gain or loss from holding nonmonetary assets represents the amount by which the increases in the values of nonmonetary assets exceeds or falls short of the inflation rate measured in terms of the NCPI and is included in the deficit in the restatement of capital.

CHAPTER 6

GENERALLY ACCEPTED ACCOUNTING PRINCIPLES: LIABILITY RECOGNITION AND RELATED EXPENSES

Learning Objectives

1. Review the criteria for the recognition of an accounting liability and apply these criteria to various obligations of a firm, including financing arrangements structured to keep debt off of the balance sheet.
2. Understand the effect of the operating and capital lease methods on the financial statements and the adjustments required to convert operating leases to capital leases.
3. Understand the relation between the accounting records of the sponsoring employer of a pension or other retirement plan and the accounting records of the plan itself and the reasons for differences between the two sets of records. Adjust the financial statements of the sponsoring employer to incorporate information from the accounting records of the retirement plan with respect to any unrecognized obligation.
4. Understand the reasons for differences between the book values of assets and liabilities for financial reporting and their tax basis and the effect of such differences on the measurement of income tax expense.
5. Use information in the financial statement note on income taxes to identify reasons for changes in the income tax burden of a firm.
6. Understand the various uses of reserve accounts and their potential for managing earnings over time.

The recognition and valuation of liabilities affect the analysis of financial statements in two important ways:

1. *Profitability Analysis.*   In generating revenues during a period, firms use, or consume, various goods and services for which they may not make cash payments until future periods. Also, firms promise to provide goods or perform services in the future related to revenues recognized during the current period (for example, under warranty plans). The cost of these goods and services that the firm has already consumed or will consume in the future is an expense of the current period. Effective analysis of profitability requires that the analyst assess whether the firm has measured these expenses properly.
2. *Risk Analysis.*   The amount shown on the balance sheet for liabilities indicates the present value of the cash or other assets that the firm will need to discharge obligations coming due within the next year (current liabilities) and after one year (noncurrent liabilities). A firm with inadequate resources to satisfy these obligations runs the risk of insolvency or even bankruptcy. Effective analysis of risk requires the analyst to assess whether the firm has recognized and measured its liabilities properly. Recognition issues are particularly important because many firms engage in transactions that create financial risk but do not recognize a liability for such risks on the balance sheet. In fact, GAAP stipulates that the firm not recognize a liability in some cases.

This chapter discusses the accounting principles underlying liability recognition and valuation and illustrates their application to several financial reporting issues, including leases, retirement benefits, deferred taxes, and reserves. The chapter emphasizes GAAP in the United States but notes significant differences in accounting principles used in other countries.

PRINCIPLES OF LIABILITY RECOGNITION

Accounting recognizes an obligation as a liability if it satisfies three criteria:[1]

1. The obligation involves a probable future sacrifice of resources—a future transfer of cash, goods, or services or the forgoing of a future cash receipt—at a specified or determinable date. The firm can measure with reasonable precision the cash equivalent value of the resources needed to satisfy the obligation.
2. The firm has little or no discretion to avoid the transfer.
3. The transaction or event giving rise to the obligation has already occurred.

APPLICATION OF CRITERIA FOR LIABILITY RECOGNITION

The criteria for liability recognition may appear straightforward and subject to unambiguous interpretation. Unfortunately, this is not so. Various obligations of an

---

[1]Financial Accounting Standards Board, *Statement of Financial Accounting Concepts No. 6,* "Elements of Financial Statements," 1985, par. 36.

enterprise fall along a continuum with respect to how well they satisfy these criteria. Exhibit 6.1 classifies obligations into six groups. The following sections discuss each of these groups.

Obligations with Fixed Payment Dates and Amounts. The obligations that most clearly satisfy the liability recognition criteria are those with fixed payment dates and amounts (usually set by contract). Most obligations arising from borrowing arrangements fall into this category. A firm receives the benefit of having funds available for its use. The borrowing agreement specifies the timing and amount of interest and principal payments.

Obligations with Fixed Payment Amounts but Estimated Payment Dates. Most current liabilities fall into this category. Either oral agreements, written agreements, or legal statutes fix the amounts payable to suppliers, employees, and governmental agencies. Firms normally settle these obligations within a few months after incurring them. The firm can estimate the settlement date, although not precisely, with sufficient accuracy to warrant recognizing a liability.

Obligations with Estimated Payment Dates and Amounts. Obligations in this group require estimation because the firm cannot identify the specific future recipients of cash, goods, or services at the time the obligation becomes a liability. In addition, the firm cannot compute precisely the amount of resources it

---

EXHIBIT 6.1

Classification of Accounting Liabilities by Degree of Certitude

Obligations with Fixed Payment Dates and Amounts	Obligations with Fixed Payment Amounts but Estimated Payment Dates	Obligations for Which the Firm Must Estimate Both Timing and Amount of Payment	Obligations Arising from Advances from Customers on Unexecuted Contracts and Agreements	Obligations under Mutually Unexecuted Contracts	Contingent Obligations
Notes Payable Interest Payable Bonds Payable	Accounts Payable Salaries Payable Taxes Payable	Warranties Payable	Rental Fees Received in Advance Subscription Fees Received in Advance	Purchase Commitments Employment Commitments	Unsettled Lawsuits[a] Financial Instruments with Off-Balance-Sheet Risk[a]

Most Certain ⟵——————————————————————⟶ Least Certain

⟵———— Recognized as Accounting Liabilities ————⟶ | ⟵—— Not Generally Recognized as ——⟶ Accounting Liabilities

[a]If an obligation meets certain criteria for a loss contingency, firms must recognize the obligation as a liability. See the discussion later in this chapter.

will transfer in the future. For example, when a firm sells products under a warranty agreement, it promises to replace defective parts or perform certain repair services for a specified period of time. At the time of sale, the firm can neither identify the specific customers who will receive warranty benefits nor ascertain the amounts of their claims. Past experience, however, often provides the necessary information for estimating the likely proportion of customers who will make claims and the probable average amount of their claims. As long as the firm can estimate the probable amount of the obligation, it satisfies the first criterion for a liability. The selling price of goods sold under warranty includes an explicit or implicit charge for the warranty services. Thus, the receipt of cash or the right to receive cash in the sales transaction benefits the firm and creates the warranty liability.

Obligations Arising from Advances from Customers on Unexecuted Contracts and Agreements.   A firm sometimes receives cash from customers in advance for goods or services it will provide in a future period. For example, a rental firm may receive cash in advance of the rental period on rental property. A magazine publisher may receive subscription fees in advance of the subscription period. Organizations and associations may receive membership dues prior to the membership period. These firms could recognize revenue on the receipt of cash, as with the sale of products under warranty plans. In the case of advances from customers, however, all of the required transfer of resources (goods or services) will occur in the future. Revenue recognition generally requires that the firm deliver the goods or provide the services. Thus, the receipt of cash in advance creates a liability equal to the cash received. The firm might conceivably recognize a liability equal to the expected cost of delivering the promised goods or services, but doing so would result in recognizing the profit from the transaction before substantial performance had occurred.

Obligations under Mutually Unexecuted Contracts.   Mutually unexecuted contracts arise when two entities agree to make a transfer of resources but *neither* entity has yet made a transfer. For example, a firm may agree to supply its customers with specified amounts of merchandise over the next two years. Or a firm may agree to pay its president a certain sum as compensation over the next five years. A bank may agree to provide lines of credit to its business customers in the event that these firms need funds in the future. Because neither party has transferred resources, no accounting liability arises. This category of obligation, called *executory contracts,* differs from the preceding two, for which the contracts or agreements are partially executed. With warranty agreements, a firm receives cash but has not fulfilled its warranty obligation. With rental, subscription, and membership fees, a firm receives cash but has not provided the required goods or services.

Firms generally do not recognize obligations under mutually unexecuted contracts as accounting liabilities. If the amounts involved are material, the firm must disclose the nature of the obligation and its amount in notes to the financial statements.

Contingent Obligations.   An event whose outcome today is unknown may create an obligation for the future transfer of resources. For example, a firm may be a defendant in a lawsuit, the outcome of which depends on the results of legal proceedings. The obligation is *contingent* on future events.

Contingent obligations may or may not give rise to accounting liabilities. GAAP requires firms to recognize an estimated loss from a contingency (called a *loss contingency*) and a related liability only if both of the following conditions are met:

1. Information available prior to the issuance of the financial statements indicates that it is probable that an asset has been impaired or that a liability has been incurred.
2. The firm can estimate the amount of the loss with reasonable precision.[2]

The first criterion for recognition of a loss contingency rests on the probability, or likelihood, that an asset has been impaired or a liability has been incurred. GAAP does not provide clear guidance as to what probability cutoff defines *likely* or *probable*. The FASB has stated that "*probable* is used with its usual general meaning, rather in a specific accounting or technical sense, and refers to that which can be expected or believed on the basis of available evidence or logic but is neither certain or proved."[3]

The second criterion requires reasonable estimation of the amount of the loss. Again, GAAP does not define "reasonably estimated" in any precise terms. Instead, if the firm can narrow the amount of loss to a reasonable range, however large, GAAP presumes that the firm has achieved sufficient precision to justify recognition of a liability. The amount of the loss is the most likely estimate within the range. If no amount within the range is more likely than any other, the firm should use the amount at the lower end of the range.

GAAP refers to obligations meeting both of these two criteria as *loss contingencies*. One example suggested by the FASB relates to a toy manufacturer that sold toys later found to present a safety hazard. The toy manufacturer concludes that the likelihood of having to pay damages is high. The firm meets the second criterion if experience or other information enables the manufacturer to make a reasonable estimate of the loss. The toy manufacturer recognizes a loss and a liability in this case.

CONTROVERSIAL ISSUES IN LIABILITY RECOGNITION

Most obligations discussed in preceding sections clearly either were liabilities or were not liabilities. Recently, firms have structured innovative financing arrangements in ways that may not satisfy the criteria for the recognition of a liability. A principal aim of such arrangements is to reduce the amount shown as liabilities on the balance sheet. Investors often use the proportion of debt in a firm's capital structure as a measure of risk and therefore as a factor in establishing the cost of funds. Other things being equal, firms prefer to obtain funds without showing a liability on the balance sheet in the hope that future lenders will ignore such financing in

---

[2]Financial Accounting Standards Board, *Statement of Financial Accounting Standards No. 5*, "Accounting for Contingencies," 1975, par. 8.

[3]Financial Accounting Standards Board, *Statement of Financial Accounting Concepts No. 6*, "Elements of Financial Statements," 1985, par. 35 (Note 21).

setting interest rates. Although there is little empirical evidence to support the notion that lenders ignore such financing in assessing a firm's risk, some firms *act* as if lenders do overlook such borrowing.

ISSUANCE OF HYBRID SECURITIES

One means of reducing the amount shown as liabilities is to issue securities that have both debt and equity characteristics (referred to as *hybrid securities*) but to classify them as equity on the balance sheet. For example, some firms have issued preferred stock that is subject to mandatory redemption after some period of time by the issuing firm. This preferred stock often has more debt than equity characteristics. Firms have also issued preferred stock that is subject to a call option by the issuing firm. The firm sets out provisions in the preferred stock agreement that make exercise of the call option highly probable. This preferred stock also has more debt than equity characteristics. On the other hand, some firms issue debt securities that have more equity than debt characteristics. For example, firms might issue bonds that are convertible into common stock. The firm sets out provisions in the debt instrument that make conversion into common stock highly probable. Or the firm might issue debt with interest payments tied to the firm's operating performance or dividend yield. (Firms treat these equity-like securities as debt to obtain a tax deduction for "interest expense.") Although accounting attempts to classify all financial instruments as either a liability or a shareholders' equity, the securities of most firms fall along a continuum from pure debt to pure equity. The accountant's dividing line is not always clear cut. The analyst should study the notes to the financial statements to assess whether the firm's classification of hybrid securities as debt versus equity seems reasonable.

OFF-BALANCE-SHEET FINANCING ARRANGEMENTS

Another way to reduce the amount shown as liabilities on the balance sheet is to structure a borrowing arrangement so that the firm does not recognize an obligation (referred to as *off-balance-sheet financing*). The following sections describe several off-balance-sheet financing arrangements. In several cases, the Financial Accounting Standards Board (FASB) has issued a reporting standard setting out how firms should treat such transactions for financial reporting purposes. In other cases, the FASB has not issued a financial reporting standard.

A general theme runs throughout the various off-balance-sheet financing arrangements: When firms leave liabilities off the balance sheet, they maintain the balance sheet equation either by reducing an existing asset or by not recognizing a newly acquired asset.

Sale of Receivables with Recourse.   Firms sometimes sell their accounts receivable with recourse as a means of obtaining short-term financing. If collections from customers are not sufficient to repay the amount borrowed plus interest, the firm must pay the difference (that is, the lender has recourse against the borrowing firm).

The question arises as to whether the recourse provision creates an accounting liability. Some argue that the arrangement is similar to a collateralized loan. The firm should leave the receivables on the books and recognize a liability in the amount of the cash received. Others argue that the firm has sold an asset; it should recognize a liability only if it is *probable* that collections from customers will be insufficient and the firm will be required to repay some portion of the amount received.

The FASB has ruled that firms should recognize transfers of receivables with recourse as sales if (1) the selling firm surrenders control of the future economic benefits and risks (for example, credit risk, interest-rate risk) of the receivables; (2) the buying firm cannot require the selling firm to repurchase the receivables except as set out in the recourse provisions; and (3) the selling firm can estimate any probable future obligation with reasonable accuracy.[4]

The principal refinement to the concept of an accounting liability brought out by *Statement No. 77* relates to identifying the party involved in the transaction that enjoys the economic benefits and sustains the economic risk of the *assets* (receivables in this case). If the selling (borrowing) firm controls the economic benefits/risks, the transaction is a collateralized loan. If the arrangement transfers these benefits/risks to the buying (lending) firm, the transaction is a sale.

Product Financing Arrangements.   Product financing arrangements occur when a firm (sponsor):

1. Sells inventory to another entity and, in a related transaction, agrees to repurchase the inventory at specified prices over specified times.
2. Arranges for another entity to purchase inventory items on the firm's behalf and, in a related transaction, agrees to purchase the inventory items from the other entity.

The first arrangement is similar to the sale of receivables with recourse except that greater certainty exists that the inventory transaction will require a future cash outflow. The second arrangement is structured to appear as a purchase commitment (recall that GAAP views purchase commitments as mutually unexecuted contracts, with a liability not normally recognized). In this case, however, the sponsoring firm usually creates the entity purchasing the inventory for the sole purpose of acquiring the inventory. The sponsoring firm usually guarantees the debt incurred by the other entity in acquiring the inventory. The other entity is often set up as a trust.

FASB *Statement No. 49* provides that firms recognize product financing arrangements as liabilities if they meet two conditions:

1. The arrangement requires the sponsoring firm to purchase the inventory, substantially identical inventory, or processed goods of which the inventory is a component, at specified prices.
2. The payments made to the other entity cover all acquisition, holding, and financing costs.[5]

---

[4]Financial Accounting Standards Board, *Statement of Financial Accounting Standards No. 77*, "Reporting for Transfers of Receivables with Recourse," 1983, par. 5.

[5]Financial Accounting Standards Board, *Statement of Financial Accounting Standards No. 49*, "Accounting for Product Financing Arrangements," 1981, par. 5.

The second criterion suggests that the sponsoring firm recognize a liability when it incurs the economic risks (changing costs, interest rates) of purchasing and holding inventory, even though it may not physically control the inventory or have a legal obligation to the supplier of the inventory. Thus, as with sales of receivables with recourse, a firm recognizes a liability when it enjoys the economic benefits and incurs the economic risks of the asset involved. It also recognizes an asset of equal amount, usually inventory.

Research and Development Financing Arrangements. When a firm borrows funds to carry out research and development work, it recognizes a liability at the time of borrowing and recognizes expenses as it incurs research and development costs.

Firms have engaged in innovative means of financing aimed at both keeping liabilities off the balance sheet and effectively excluding research and development expenses from the income statement. The arrangements vary somewhat but generally operate as follows:

1. The sponsoring firm contributes either preliminary development work or rights to future products to a partnership for a general interest in the partnership. It obtains limited partners (often corporate directors or officers) who contribute cash for their partnership interests.
2. The sponsoring firm conducts research and development work for the partnership for a fee. The sponsoring firm usually performs the research and development work on a best-efforts basis, with no guarantee of success. The sponsoring firm recognizes amounts received from the partnership for research and development services as revenues. The amount of revenue generally equals or exceeds the research and development costs it incurs.
3. The rights to any resulting products usually reside in the partnership. However, the partnership agreement usually constrains the returns and risks of the limited partners. The sponsoring firm can often acquire the limited partners' interests in the partnership if valuable products emerge. On the other hand, the sponsoring firm may have to guarantee certain minimum royalty payments to the partnership or agree to purchase the partnership's rights to the product.

In arrangements like these, the sponsoring firm attempts to obtain financing for its research and development work without having to recognize a liability.

FASB *Statement No. 68* establishes criteria for circumstances when firms must recognize such financing arrangements as liabilities.[6] The sponsoring firm recognizes a liability when either of the following conditions exists:

1. If the contractual agreement requires the sponsoring firm to repay any of the funds provided by the other parties regardless of the outcome of the research and development work.

---

[6]Financial Accounting Standards Board, *Statement of Financial Accounting Standards No. 68*, "Research and Development Arrangements," 1982.

indicate that the sponsoring firm bears the risk of fail-
velopment work, even though the contractual agree-
epay the other parties. For example, if a sponsoring
he partnership, must make minimum royalty pay-
st acquire the partnership's interest in any prod-
ne risk of the research and development work.

nce-sheet financing arrangements discussed above, firms
when they bear the risk associated with the asset or product in-
nancing.[7]

e-or-Pay or Throughput Contracts. A take-or-pay contract is an
agreement in which a purchaser agrees to pay specified amounts periodically to a
seller for products or services. A throughput contract is similar to a take-or-pay contract except that the "product" purchased is transportation or processing services.

To understand the rationale for such arrangements, consider the following case.
Suppose that two petroleum companies need additional refining capacity. If either
company builds a refinery, it records an asset and any related financing on its balance sheet. Suppose instead that the two companies form a joint venture to construct a refinery. The joint venture, an entity separate from the two petroleum
companies, obtains financing and constructs the refinery. To secure financing for
the joint venture, the two petroleum companies sign take-or-pay contracts agreeing
to make certain payments to the joint venture each period for refining services. The
payments are sufficient to cover all operating and financing costs of the refinery.
The joint owners must make the payments even if they acquire no refinery services.
The economic substance of this arrangement is that each petroleum company
half of the refinery and is obligated to the extent of half of the financing. The
us of the arrangement is that the two firms have simply signed noncan-
ase commitments (that is, executory contracts).
s not yet issued a reporting standard setting out when firms must
ay and throughput contracts as liabilities. FASB *Statement*
to disclose such commitments in the notes. The analyst should
hese commitments in notes to the financial statements to as-
urs the risks and rewards of the arrangement and should
y.

ce-Sheet Financing. The conventional ac-
cal cost is exchange or transaction oriented. Ac-
n exchange takes place. The criteria for liability
hapter illustrate this exchange orientation. Ac-
rm incurs an obligation to sacrifice resources
ved. GAAP has typically not recognized

pment through limited partnerships found that
firms have on research findings in the valu-
of these arrangements instead of recognition
ne Valuation of R&D Firms with R&D Limited
p. 1–21.

mutually unexecuted contracts as liabilities because the parties have changed promises to perform in the future. GAAP also does not genera the recognition of contingent obligations as liabilities because some futu must occur to establish the existence of a liability.

The evolving concept of an accounting liability recognizes that exchang promises can have economic substance even though a legal obligation to pay not immediately arise. When a firm enjoys the economic benefits and/or incurs th economic risks from an asset, the firm should recognize the asset and its related financing.

The FASB has examined the topic of off-balance-sheet financing for several years. Issues concerning the recognition and measurement of the obligations arising from transactions such as those described above are currently under consideration. In the meantime, the FASB requires firms to disclose in the notes to the financial statements information about material off-balance-sheet commitments or contingencies. A later section of this chapter illustrates such disclosures for lease commitments.

COMMITMENTS RELATED TO DERIVATIVE FINANCIAL INSTRUMENTS

One financial reporting area for which issues of off-balance-sheet commitments and their associated risk have surfaced in recent years relates to financial instruments. A financial instrument is a contractual right to receive or a contractual obligation to pay cash in the future. Firms already recognize some of these financial instruments as liabilities, such as bonds payable. Other financial instruments, such as financial guarantees, standby letters of credit, and commitments under interest or exchange rate swaps, do not appear as liabilities unless payment is highly likely. Each of these financial instruments is subject to credit risk; one party to the financial instrument may be unable to perform as stipulated by contract. These financial instruments are also subject to market risk. Changes in the market values of these instruments (arising, for example, from changes in interest rates or foreign exchange rates) may resul in a substantial shift in value from one party to the other party and affect the will ingness of the negatively affected party to perform as required. The FASB refers these risks as *off-balance-sheet risks* because they arise from events external to firm and not under its control. Firms holding financial instruments with mat off-balance-sheet risk must disclose the following information about the fina instruments.[8]

1. The face, contract, or notional principal amount.
2. The terms of the instruments and a discussion of their credit and mar cash requirements, and related accounting policies.
3. The *accounting loss* the entity would incur if any party to the finance ment failed completely to perform according to the terms of the contr collateral or other security, if any, for the amount due proved to be o the entity.

---

[8]Financial Accounting Standards Board, *Statement of Financial Accounting Stand* closure of Information about Financial Instruments with Off-Balance-Sheet Risk a ments with Concentrations of Credit Risk," 1990, par. 17 and 18.

4. The entity's policy for requiring collateral or other security on financial instruments it accepts and a description of collateral on instruments presently held.

Illustrations of these disclosures appear in Coke's Notes 4 and 8 and Pepsi's Notes 8, 16, and 17. More extensive disclosures typically appear in notes to the financial statements of commercial banks. Exhibit 6.2 summarizes disclosures appearing in a recent annual report of Bankers Trust. The amount disclosed in the Credit Risk Amount column is the accounting loss that Bankers Trust would recognize if any party to these financial instruments failed to perform and any collateral was without value. To provide some perspective, Bankers Trust shows total recorded liabilities of $68,639 million on this date.

The FASB issued *Statement No. 119* in 1994 in an effort to increase even more the disclosures regarding derivative financial instruments. Derivative financial instruments (such as interest-rate or foreign-exchange swaps) derive their value from changes in the prices of other financial contracts, such as interest rate or foreign exchange rates. Firms that hold or issue derivative financial instruments for trading purposes (typically commercial and investment banks) must disclose (1) the average and end-of-the-period market value of derivative financial instruments, distinguishing between assets and liabilities, and (2) the net gains and losses arising from trading activities during the reporting period, disaggregated by class, business activity, risk, or other category that is consistent with the management of those activities and where those net trading gains and losses appear in the income statement. Entities that hold or issue derivative financial instruments for purposes other than trading (for example, a manufacturing firm with foreign operations that hedges its foreign exchange risk using a forward contract) must disclose (1) the business or other

---

EXHIBIT 6.2

Disclosures by Bankers Trust of Financial Instruments with Off-Balance-Sheet Risk
(amounts in millions)

	Contract/ Notional Amount	Credit Risk Amount
Standby Letters of Credit	$ 5,199	$ 5,199
Commitments to Extend Credit	14,219	14,219
Custodian Securities Lent	11,628	11,628
Interest Rate Contracts		
Swaps	255,723	6,025
Options	194,795	1,017
Futures and Forwards	245,942	1,321
Foreign Exchange Rate Contracts		
Swaps	60,156	3,503
Options	99,595	1,660
Futures and Forwards	281,096	6,561
Other Contracts	28,565	2,496
Total Credit Risk Amount		$53,929

purpose for using a derivative financial instrument and (2) the accounting policies for reporting the derivative instrument in the financial statements.[9]

The analyst should view these disclosures as initial attempts by the FASB to require more information about off-balance-sheet obligations and off-balance-sheet risks. The disclosures assume a worst-case scenario regarding possible losses and financial risks. It is unlikely that firms will ultimately incur obligations or liabilities equal to the amount disclosed.

PRINCIPLES OF LIABILITY VALUATION

The general principles underlying the valuation of liabilities are as follows:

1. Liabilities requiring future cash payments (for example, bonds payable) appear at the present value of the required future cash flows discounted at an interest rate that reflects the uncertainty that the firm will be able to make these cash payments. The firm establishes this discount rate at the time it initially records a liability in the accounts (often referred to as the *historical interest rate*) and uses this interest rate in accounting for the liability in all future periods. For some liabilities due within the next year (for example, accounts payable, income taxes payable, salaries payable), the difference between the amount of the future cash flows and their present value is sufficiently small that accounting ignores the discounting process and reports the liabilities at the amounts ultimately payable.
2. Liabilities requiring the future delivery of goods or services (for example, Warranties Payable) appear at the estimated cost of those goods and services.
3. Liabilities representing advances from customers (for example, Rental Fees Received in Advance, Subscription Fees Received in Advance) appear at the amount of the cash advance.

The current market value of a liability may differ from the amount appearing on the balance sheet, particularly for long-term debt. The current market value reflects current interest rates and assessments of the firm's ability to make the required payments. The FASB requires firms to disclose the fair value of financial instruments, whether or not these financial instruments appear as liabilities (or assets) on the balance sheet.[10] Exhibit 6.3 illustrates these disclosures from Note 9 to Coke's financial statements in Appendix A.

Because interest rates have declined since Coke issued its long-term debt, the market value of the debt exceeds its book value. The hedging instruments contain an unrealized loss of $173 million [= $31 − ($142)].

---

[9]Financial Accounting Standards Board, *Statement of Financial Accounting Standard No. 119*, "Disclosure about Derivative Financial Instruments and Fair Value of Financial Instruments," 1994, par. 10 and 11.

[10]Financial Accounting Standards Board, *Statement of Financial Accounting Standards No. 107*, "Disclosures about Fair Values of Financial Instruments," 1991; Financial Accounting Standards Board, *Statement of Financial Accounting Standard No. 119*, "Disclosure about Derivative Financial Instruments and Fair Value of Financial Instruments," 1994, pars. 10 and 11.

EXHIBIT 6.3

Disclosures by Coke of the Fair Value of Financial Instruments
(amounts in millions)

	Carrying Value	Fair Value
December 31, Year 8		
Current Marketable Securities...............	$ 80	$ 82
Investments	88	88
Finance Subsidiary Receivables...............	259	265
Marketable Securities and Other Assets........	868	865
Long-Term Debt	(1,447)	(1,531)
Hedging Instruments	31	(142)

The next three sections of this chapter discuss more fully three particularly controversial liability recognition topics: leases, retirement benefits, and deferred income taxes. A final section considers the accounting for reserves.

LEASES

Many firms acquire rights to use assets through long-term leases. A company might, for example, agree to lease an office suite for five years or an entire building for forty years, promising to pay a fixed periodic fee for the duration of the lease. Leasing provides benefits to lessees such as the following:

1. Ability to shift the tax benefits of depreciation and other deductions from a lessee that has little or no taxable income (such as an airline) to a lessor that has substantial taxable income. The lessee expects the lessor to share some of the benefits of these tax deductions by allowing lower lease payments.
2. Flexibility to change capacity as needed without having to purchase or sell assets.
3. Ability to reduce the risk of technological obsolescence, relative to outright ownership, by maintaining the flexibility to shift to technologically more advanced assets.
4. Ability to finance the "acquisition" of an asset using lessor financing when alternative sources of financing are unavailable.

These potential benefits of leasing to lessees do not come without a cost. When the lessor assumes the risks of ownership, it requires the lessee to make larger lease payments than if the lessee incurs these risks. The party bearing the risks is a matter of negotiation between lessor and lessee.

Promising to make an irrevocable series of lease payments commits the firm just as surely as a bond indenture or mortgage, and the accounting is similar in many cases. This section examines two methods of accounting for long-term leases: the operating lease method and the capital lease method. The illustrations show the accounting by the lessee, the user of the leased asset. A later section discusses the accounting for the lessor, the owner of the asset.

To illustrate these two methods, suppose that Myers Company wants to acquire a computer that has a three-year life and costs $45,000. Assume that Myers must pay 10 percent per year to borrow money for three years. The computer manufacturer is willing to sell the equipment for $45,000 or to lease it for three years. Myers is responsible for property taxes, maintenance, and repairs of the computer whether it leases or purchases the computer.

Assume that Myers signs the lease on January 1, Year 1, and must make payments on the lease on December 31, Year 1, Year 2, and Year 3. (In practice, lessees usually make lease payments in advance, but the assumption of end-of-the-year payments simplifies the computations.) Compound interest computations show that each lease payment must be $18,095. (The present value of an annuity of $1 paid at the end of this year and each of the next two years is $2.48685 when the interest rate is 10 percent per year. Because the lease payments must have a present value equal to the current cash purchase price of $45,000 if the computer manufacturer is to be indifferent between selling and leasing the computer, each payment must be $45,000/2.48685 = $18,095.)

OPERATING LEASE METHOD

In an *operating lease,* the owner, or lessor, transfers only the rights to use the property to the lessee for specified periods of time. At the end of the lease period, the lessee returns the property to the lessor. For example, car rental companies lease cars by the day or week on an operating basis. Under leasing arrangements in which the lessee neither assumes the risks nor enjoys the rewards of ownership, the lessee treats the lease as an operating lease. Accounting gives no recognition to the signing of an operating lease (that is, the lessee reports neither the leased asset nor a lease liability on its balance sheet; the lease is simply a mutually unexecuted contract). The lessee recognizes rent expense in measuring net income each year. Myers Company makes the following journal entry on December 31, Year 1, Year 2, and Year 3:

Rent Expense	18,095	
Cash.		18,095

To recognize annual expense of leasing computer.

CAPITAL LEASE METHOD

Under leasing arrangements in which the lessee assumes the risks and enjoys rewards of ownership, the arrangement is a form of borrowing. GAAP treats such leases as *capital leases*. This treatment recognizes the signing of the lease as the simultaneous acquisition of a long-term asset and the incurring of a long-term liability for lease payments. At the time Myers Company signs the lease, it makes the following entry on its books:

Leased Asset..	45,000	
Lease Liability		45,000

To recognize acquisition of leased asset and the related liability.

Lessees recognize two expense items each year on capital leases. First, the lessee must amortize the leased asset over its useful life (that is, the term of the lease). Assuming that Myers uses straight-line depreciation, it recognizes depreciation expense of $15,000 (=$45,000 ÷ 3) each year as follows:

Depreciation Expense	15,000	
Accumulated Depreciation		15,000

To record depreciation of leased asset.

Second, the lease payment made each year is part interest expense on the lease liability and part reduction in the liability itself. Exhibit 6.4 shows the amortization schedule for this liability. Column (3) shows the amount of interest expense. The entries made at the end of Year 1, Year 2, and Year 3 are as follows:

December 31, Year 1:

Interest Expense...................................	4,500	
Lease Liability	13,595	
Cash.......................................		18,095

To recognize lease payment, interest on liability for year $(0.10 \times \$45,000 = \$4,500)$, and the plug for reduction in the liability. The present value of the liability after this entry is $\$31,405 = \$45,000 - \$13,595$.

EXHIBIT 6.4

Amortization Schedule for $45,000 Lease Liability,
Repaid in Three Annual Installments of $18,095 Each,
Interest Rate 10 Percent, Compounded Annually

Year (1)	Lease Liability, Start of Year (2)	Interest Expense for Year (3)	Payment (4)	Portion of Payment Reducing Lease Liability (5)	Lease Liability, End of Year (6)
1......	$45,000	$4,500	$18,095	$13,595	$31,405
2......	31,405	3,141	18,095	14,954	16,451
3......	16,451	1,644[a]	18,095	16,451	0

Column (2) = Column (6), Previous Period.
Column (3) = 0.10 × Column (2).
Column (4) is given.
Column (5) = Column (4) − Column (3).
Column (6) = Column (2) − Column (5).

[a]Does not equal 0.10 × $16,451 due to rounding.

December 31, Year 2:

Interest Expense...	3,141	
Lease Liability	14,954	
Cash..		18,095

To recognize lease payment, interest on liability for
year (0.10 × $31,405 = $3,141), and the plug for
reduction in the liability. The present value of the
liability after this entry is $16,451 = $31,405 − $14,954.

December 31, Year 3:

Interest Expense...	1,644	
Lease Liability	16,451	
Cash..		18,095

To recognize lease payment, interest on liability for
year (0.10 × $16,451 = $1,644), and the plug for
reduction in the liability. The present value of the
liability after this entry is zero (=$16,451 − $16,451).

Notice that, in the capital lease method, the total expense over the three years is
$54,285, comprising $45,000 (=$15,000 + $15,000 + $15,000) for depreciation expense and $9,285 (=$4,500 + $3,141 + $1,644) for interest expense. This total expense is exactly the same as that recognized under the operating lease method
described previously ($18,095 × 3 = $54,285). The capital lease method recognizes
expenses sooner than does the operating lease method, as Exhibit 6.5 summarizes,
but, over sufficiently long time periods, total expense equals the cash expenditure.
One difference between the operating lease method and the capital lease method is
the *timing* of the expense recognition. The other difference is that the capital lease
method recognizes both the asset and the liability on the balance sheet.

EXHIBIT 6.5

Comparison of Expense Recognized under Operating and Capital Lease Methods

	Expense Recognized Each Year under	
Year	**Operating Lease Method**	**Capital Lease Method**
1	$18,095	$19,500 (= $15,000 + $4,500)
2	18,095	18,141 (= 15,000 + 3,141)
3	18,095	16,644 (= 15,000 + 1,644)
Total	$54,285[a]	$54,285 (= $45,000[b] + $9,285[c])

[a]Rent expense.
[b]Depreciation expense.
[c]Interest expense.

CHOOSING THE ACCOUNTING METHOD

When a lessee treats a lease as a capital lease, it increases both an asset account and a liability account, thereby increasing total liabilities and making the company appear riskier. Given a choice, most managements prefer not to show the asset and a related liability on the balance sheet. These managements prefer an operating lease to either an installment purchase or a capital lease, for which both the asset and liability appear on the balance sheet. Many managements also prefer to recognize expenses later rather than sooner for financial reporting. These preferences have led managements to structure asset acquisitions so that the financing takes the form of an operating lease, thereby achieving off-balance-sheet financing.

Conditions Requiring Capital Lease Accounting. FASB *Statement No. 13* provides detailed rules of accounting for long-term leases. The lessor and lessee must account for a lease as a capital lease if it meets any one of four conditions.[11]

A lease is a capital lease (1) if it extends for at least 75 percent of the asset's life, (2) if it transfers ownership to the lessee at the end of the lease term, or (3) if it seems likely that the lessor will transfer ownership to the lessee because of a "bargain purchase" option. A bargain purchase option gives the lessee the right to purchase the asset for a price less than the expected fair market value of the asset when the lessee exercises its option. These first three conditions are relatively easy to avoid in lease contracts if lessors and lessees prefer to treat a lease as an operating lease rather than a capital lease.

The most difficult of the four conditions to avoid compares the contractual minimum lease payments discounted at an "appropriate" market interest rate with 90 percent of the fair market value of the asset at the time the lessee signs the lease. (The interest rate used must reflect the creditworthiness of the lessee.) (4) If the present value of the contractual minimum lease payments equals or exceeds 90 percent of the fair market value of the asset at the time of signing, the lease is a capital lease. In such cases, the lessor has less than or equal to 10 percent of the asset's value at risk to an uncertain residual value at the end of the lease term. The lease therefore transfers the major risks and rewards of ownership from the lessor (landlord) to the lessee. In economic substance, the lessee has acquired an asset and has agreed to pay for it under a long-term contract, which the lessee recognizes as a liability. When the present value of the minimum lease payments is less than 90 percent of the fair market value of the asset at the time of signing, the lessor bears the major risks and rewards of ownership and the lease is an operating lease.

Most other countries also set out criteria for distinguishing operating and capital leases. The particular criteria differ somewhat from those described above but attempt to identify the party enjoying the rewards and bearing the risks of ownership.

---

[11]Financial Accounting Standards Board, *Statement of Financial Accounting Standards No. 13*, "Accounting for Leases," 1976, par. 7.

EFFECTS ON LESSOR

The lessor (landlord) and the lessee (tenant) generally use the same criteria for classifying a lease as an operating lease or a capital lease. Under the operating lease method, the lessor recognizes rent revenue in the same amounts as the lessee recognizes rent expense. At the time of the signing of a capital lease, the lessor recognizes an asset, Lease Receivable, and revenue in an amount equal to the present value of all future cash flows ($45,000 in the Myers Company lease) and recognizes expense (analogous to cost of goods sold) in an amount equal to the book value of the leased asset. The difference between the revenue and expense is the lessor's gross margin from the "sale" of the asset. The lessor records the lease receivable like any other long-term receivable at the present value of the future cash flows. It recognizes interest revenue over the term of the lease in amounts that closely mirror interest expense by the lessee. Lessors tend to prefer capital lease accounting for financial reporting because it enables them to recognize income at the time of signing. The lessor's entries, assuming that it manufactured the computer for $39,000 are as follows:

Operating Lease Method
December 31 of each year:

Cash.	18,095	
Rent Revenue		18,095

To recognize annual revenue from renting computer.

Depreciation Expense	13,000	
Accumulated Depreciation		13,000

To recognize depreciation on rented computer
($13,000 = $39,000/3).

Capital Lease Method
January 1, Year 1:

Lease Receivable	45,000	
Sales Revenue.		45,000

To recognize the "sale" of a computer for a series of
future cash flows with a present value of $45,000.

Cost of Goods Sold	39,000	
Inventory.		39,000

To record the cost of the computer "sold" as
an expense.

December 31, Year 1:

Cash.	18,095	
Interest Revenue.		4,500
Lease Receivable		13,595

To recognize lease receipt, interest on receivable, and
reduction in receivable for Year 1. See supporting
calculations in the lessee's journal entries.

December 31, Year 2:

Cash.. 18,095

    Interest Revenue............................. 3,141

    Lease Receivable 14,954

  To recognize lease amounts for Year 2.

December 31, Year 3:

Cash.. 18,095

    Interest Revenue............................. 1,644

    Lease Receivable 16,451

  To recognize lease amounts for Year 3.

LEASE ACCOUNTING FOR TAX PURPOSES

An earlier section indicates that one of the benefits of leasing is that it permits the user of the property (the lessee) to shift the tax benefits of depreciation, interest, and other deductions to the lessor in the expectation of lowering the required lease payments. To achieve this benefit, the lease must satisfy all the criteria for an operating lease for tax purposes. These criteria differ somewhat from those that GAAP uses to classify leases for financial reporting. The five criteria for operating leases for tax reporting are:

1. Use of the property at the end of the lease term by someone other than the lessee is commercially feasible.
2. The lease does not have a bargain purchase option.
3. The lessor has a minimum 20 percent of its capital at risk.
4. The lessor has a positive cash flow and profit from the lease independent of tax benefits.
5. The lessee does not have an investment in the lease and has not lent any of the purchase price to the lessor.

These criteria attempt to identify the party to the lease that enjoys the rewards and bears the risks of ownership. Because the financial and tax-reporting criteria for leases differ, lessors and lessees may treat particular leases one way for financial reporting and another way for tax reporting.

CONVERTING OPERATING LEASES TO CAPITAL LEASES

Given the preference of lessees to structure leases as operating leases and the thin line that distinguishes operating and capital leases, the analyst may wish to restate the financial statements of lessees to convert all operating leases into capital leases. Such a restatement provides a more conservative measure of total liabilities.

To illustrate the procedure followed, refer to Pepsi's Note 9 on leases in Appendix B. Column (2) below shows Pepsi's commitments on noncancelable operating leases net of sublease revenues.

Year 1 (1)	Reported Lease Commitments (2)	Present Value Factor at 10%	Present Value
9	$237.5	0.90909	$ 215.9
10	$210.6	0.82645	174.1
11	$189.5	0.75131	142.4
12	$164.3	0.68301	112.2
13	$149.4	0.62092	92.8
after 13	$869.4	0.47097	409.5
			$1,146.9

The analyst must express the lease commitments in present value terms. The discount rate that the analyst uses is the lessee's incremental borrowing rate for secured debt with similar risk as the leasing arrangement. We assume a 10 percent rate in this case. To select a present value factor for payments after Year 13, we need to know in which years and what amounts that Pepsi will pay the $869.4 million. If we presume that payments after Year 13 will continue at the same amount as the $149.4 million payment in Year 13, Pepsi will pay the $869.4 million over 5.8 years (=$869.4 ÷ $149.4), or an average 2.9 years (=5.8 ÷ 2) after Year 13. The calculation above uses the present value factor for 7.9 years (that is, Pepsi will pay the $869.4 at the rate of $149.4 million at the end of Year 14, $149.4 million at the end of Year 15, $149.4 million at the end of Year 16, $149.4 million at the end of Year 17, $149.4 million at the end of Year 18, and $122.4 million at the end of Year 19; the elapsed time for Pepsi to pay the *average* dollar in this $869.4 million aggregate amount is at Year 15.9, which is 7.9 years from the beginning of Year 9).

The analyst adds the $1,146.9 million lease amount to property, plant, and equipment and to long-term debt on the December 31, Year 8, balance sheet. Similar calculations at the end of Year 7 (calculation not shown) result in a capitalized value of operating leases of $1,030.3 million and a remaining lease term of 10.6 years.

The analyst could also convert the income statement for Year 8 from the operating to the capital lease method:

Operating Lease Method (as reported)
  Lease Expense (see note on leases):
  Noncontingent Rents ($419.8 − $27.5 − ($16.6 − $4.4)) $380.1
  Contingent Rents ($27.5 − $4.4). 23.1
                                                                                                    $403.2

Capital Lease Method (as restated)
  Depreciation Expense ($1,030.3 ÷ 10.6) 97.2
  Interest Expense (0.10 × $1,030.3). 103.0
  Contingent Rents (see above). 23.1
    Total   223.3
Decrease in Reported Expenses $179.9

If the average lease is in the first half of its life, total expenses under the capital lease method tend to exceed total expense under the operating lease method. If the average lease is in the last half of its life, total expenses under the capital lease method tend to be less than under the operating lease method. The two expense amounts are approximately equal at the mid-life point (see Exhibit 6.5). In general, balance sheet restatements are more significant than income statement restatements. Consequently, the analyst can usually ignore restatements of the income statement.[12]

The analyst could restate the statement of cash flows for the capitalization of operating leases. Under the operating lease method, the lease payment for the year is an operating use of cash. Its inclusion as a subtraction in computing net income results in reporting its negative effect in the operating section of the statement of cash flows. Under the capital lease method, a portion of the cash payment represents a repayment of the lease liability, a financing instead of an operating use of cash. The analyst should reclassify this portion of the cash payment from the operating section to the financing section of the statement of cash flows. The analyst could also reduce net income for depreciation expense on the capitalized lease assets, but this same amount appears as an addback to net income for a noncash expense. Thus, the net effect of depreciation expense on cash flows is zero.

RETIREMENT BENEFITS

Employers typically provide two types of benefits to retired employees: (1) pension benefits and (2) health-care and life insurance coverage. GAAP, in both the United States and most other countries, requires that the employer recognize the cost of these benefits as an expense while the employees work and generate revenues rather than when they receive the benefits during retirement. Estimating the expected cost of the benefits requires assumptions about employee turnover, future compensation and health-care costs, interest rates, and other factors. Because the employer will not know the actual costs of these benefits until many years elapse, estimating their costs while the employees work involves imprecision.

A further issue relates to the pattern for recognizing the costs as an expense. Should the employer recognize an equal amount each year over the employee's working years? Or should the amount increase over time as compensation levels increase? FASB pronouncements on pension and health care benefits further complicate the question of the timing of expense recognition. These pronouncements do not require immediate recognition of an expense and a liability for benefits already earned by employees at the time firms adopt these reporting standards. Instead, the costs of benefits already earned can become expenses in future periods. One consequence of this reporting procedure is that the amount that firms show as pension or health-care liabilities on the balance sheet may understate the economic liability.

---

[12]For an alternative procedure for converting operating into capital leases, see Eugene A. Imhoff, Jr., Robert C. Lipe, and David W. Wright, "Operating Leases: Impact of Constructive Capitalization," *Accounting Horizons,* March 1991, pp. 51–63. In this study, the authors found that capitalizing operating leases decreased the rate of return on assets 34 percent for high lease firms and 10 percent for low lease firms and increased the debt/equity ratio 191 percent for high lease firms and 47 percent for low lease firms.

This section discusses the accounting issues related to pensions and to health-care and life insurance benefits.

PENSIONS

Pension plans work as follows:

1. Employers agree to provide certain pension benefits to employees. The arrangement may take the form of either a defined contribution plan or a defined benefit plan. Under a defined contribution plan, the employer agrees to contribute a certain amount to a pension fund each period (usually based on a percentage of employees' compensation), without specifying the benefits that employees will receive during retirement. The amounts that employees eventually receive depend on the performance of the pension fund. Under a defined benefit plan, the employer agrees to make pension payments to employees during retirement using a benefits formula based on wages earned and number of years of employment. The plan does not specify the amounts the employer will contribute to the pension fund. The employer must make contributions to the fund so that those amounts plus earnings from pension investments are sufficient to make the promised payments.

2. Employers periodically contribute cash to a pension trust. The trustee, or administrator, of the trust invests the cash received from the employer in stocks, bonds, and other investments. The assets in the pension trust accumulate each period from both employer contributions and income from investments. These assets appear on the balance sheet of the pension trust, not on the employer's balance sheet.

3. The employer satisfies its obligation under a defined contribution plan once it makes periodic contributions to the pension trust. The employer's obligation under a defined benefit plan increases each period as the result of two factors. First, employees' services during the period usually give them rights to increased benefits. Most defined benefit plans measure the pension benefit that employees will ultimately receive using the number of working years and their highest compensation levels (usually an average of their last several years of compensation before retirement). Employees earn increased benefits each period as they work an additional period at a higher compensation level. Second, the employer's obligation increases each period because time passes and the remaining time until employees begin receiving their pensions decreases. Thus, the present value of the pension obligation increases.

4. The pension trust makes pension payments to retired employees using assets in the pension fund. The employer's obligation under a defined benefit plan decreases by the amount paid.

The balance sheet of a defined benefit pension plan changes as follows each period:

Pension Fund Assets	Pension Fund Liabilities
Assets at Beginning of Period	Liabilities at Beginning of Period
± Actual Earnings on Investments	+ Increase in Liabilities due to Passage of Time
+ Contributions Received from the Employer	+ Increase in Liabilities from Employee Services
	± Actuarial Gains and Losses due to Changes in Assumptions
− Payments to Retirees	− Payments to Retirees
= Assets at End of Period	= Liabilities at End of Period

Pension assets will equal pension liabilities each period if a pension fund earns a return on pension investments exactly equal to the discount rate used in computing the present value of pension liabilities; receives pension contributions from the employer equal to the increase in pension liabilities from current employee services; and experiences employee turnover, compensation increases, and other factors exactly as assumed in computing pension liabilities. The employer will recognize pension expense equal to the cash contributed to the pension fund for current employee service.

Few firms experience this precise matching of pension assets and pension liabilities. Actual investment returns, employee turnover rates, and compensation cost increases seldom occur as expected. In addition, firms adopt or sweeten pension benefit plans, giving employees credit for services rendered prior to adoption or sweetening but do not immediately contribute cash to the pension fund equal to the newly created liability. Thus, most firms find that pension assets do not equal pension liabilities.

The employer's pension expense also differs from the cash contributed to the pension fund for current employee service. The firm may have to expense and fund additional amounts because of (1) underfunding of employee benefits earned prior to adoption or sweetening, (2) realization of investment returns less than expected, or (3) increases in pension liabilities due to changes in actuarial assumptions. The employer may be able to expense and fund less than the cost of current employee service if (1) excess contributions or investment returns in the past produce an excess of pension assets over pension liabilities or (2) pension liabilities decrease because of changes in actuarial assumptions.

Pension disclosures permit the analyst to assess the degree to which a firm has over- or underfunded its pension plan. These disclosures also permit an assessment of the performance of the pension fund during an accounting period.

Obligations under Defined Benefit Plans. Financial Accounting Standards Board *Statement No. 87* [13] requires firms to disclose certain information about defined benefit pension plans in notes to the financial statements. Refer to Pepsi's

---

[13]Financial Accounting Standards Board, *Statement of Financial Accounting Standards No. 87,* "Employer's Accounting for Pensions," 1985.

Note 11 on retirement plans in Appendix B. Exhibit 6.6 summarizes the pension disclosures. The top portion of Exhibit 6.6 shows assets and liabilities of the pension plan. The last two lines show the amounts that Pepsi records on its books related to the pension plan. The unrecognized items represent amounts reflected in the accounting records of the pension plan but not yet recognized on the employers' books. Interpreting these disclosures requires several definitions:

Accumulated Benefit Obligation. The present value of amounts the employer expects to pay to retired employees (taking into consideration actuarial assumptions concerning employee turnover and mortality) based on employees' service to date and current-year compensation levels. The accumulated benefit obligation indicates the present value of the benefits earned to date, excluding any future salary increases that will serve as the base for computing the pension payment and excluding future years of service prior to retirement. Vested benefits usually represent the largest portion of the accumulated benefit obligation, meaning that employees will not lose the right to their pension benefit if they leave the employer prior to retirement. Employees lose nonvested benefits if they terminate employment prior to vesting. Most nonvested benefits vest after an employee works for five to ten years.

Projected Benefit Obligation. The actuarial present value of amounts the employer expects to pay to retired employees based on employees' service to date

---

EXHIBIT 6.6

Pension Disclosures by Pepsi
(amounts in millions)

	December 31, Year 7	December 31, Year 8
Accounting Records of Pension Plan		
Actuarial Present Value of Benefit Obligations		
Vested..	$ (853.4)	$(1,085.6)
Nonvested..	(80.7)	(136.1)
Accumulated Benefit Obligation............................	$ (934.1)	$(1,221.7)
Effect of Projected Future Salary Increases	(166.3)	(214.6)
Projected Benefit Obligation	$(1,100.4)	$(1,436.3)
Plan Assets at Market Value	1,299.2	1,442.9
Projected Benefit Obligation (in excess of) or less than Plan Assets	$ 198.8	$ 6.6
Unrecognized Net (gain) Loss................................	(53.8)	61.7
Unrecognized Prior Service Cost	52.2	65.3
Unrecognized Net Assets at July 29, Year 5	(114.2)	(86.3)
Accounting Records of Employer		
Adjustment to Recognize Minimum Liability	—	(37.3)
Prepaid Pension Asset......................................	$ 83.0	$ 10.0

but using the expected future salaries that will serve as the base for computing the pension payment. The difference between the accumulated and projected benefit obligations is the effect of future salary increases. Consequently, the projected benefit obligation exceeds the accumulated benefit obligation. The projected benefit obligation is also closer in amount to what one might view as an economic measure of the pension obligation: the present value of amounts the employer expects to pay to employees during retirement based on total expected years of service (past and future) and expected future salaries. FASB *Statement No. 87* does not require disclosure of this economic obligation.

The required disclosures show the relationship between the market value of pension fund assets and the projected benefit obligation at each valuation date. Pepsi's pension plan is overfunded as of the end of Year 8 by $6.6 million. There are several implications of an overfunded pension plan:

1. Pepsi can reclaim the excess assets for corporate uses. The amount reclaimed becomes immediately subject to income taxes. Corporate raiders have sometimes used excess pension assets to help finance the leveraged buyout of a firm.
2. Pepsi can discontinue contributions to the pension fund until such time as the assets in the pension fund equal the projected benefit obligation.
3. Pepsi can continue its historical pattern of funding on the presumption that the overfunded status is due to temporary market appreciation of investments that could easily reverse in the future.

Although one might argue that an excess of pension fund assets over the projected benefit obligation represents an asset of the employer, FASB *Statement No. 87* does not permit firms to recognize this resource on the balance sheet.

In like manner, one might view an excess of the projected benefit obligation over pension fund assets as a liability that firms should report on the balance sheet. Refer to Note 13 to Coke's financial statements in Appendix A. Coke has certain pension plans for which the projected benefit obligation exceeds the assets in the pension fund by $175 million (=$100 + $75) at the end of Year 7 and $214 million (=$131 + $83) at the end of Year 8. The FASB, responding to criticisms that the measurement of the projected benefit obligation requires subjective projections of future salary increases, stipulates instead that firms show an excess of the *accumulated* benefit obligation over pension fund assets on the balance sheet as a liability (referred to as the *minimum liability*). Note that Coke has an accumulated benefit obligation of $237 million (=$111 + $126) at the end of Year 8 for certain underfunded U.S. and international plans but assets of $96 million (=$2 + $94) in its pension funds related to this obligation. Coke includes $159 million (=$109 + $50) in Other Liabilities on its balance sheet related to these plans. It reports similar amounts for Year 7. Because the accumulated benefit obligation is usually smaller than the projected benefit obligation, relatively few firms report a liability for underfunded benefits by this measure.

The only asset or liability that normally appears on the balance sheet occurs when the cumulative amounts recognized as pension expense differ from the cumulative amounts of cash contributed to the pension fund. This asset or liability is a relatively small amount compared to the aggregate pension assets and obligations.

Note, for example, that Pepsi has a Prepaid Pension Asset of $69.9 million at the end of Year 8 (=$.8 + $69.1) included among its assets for certain overfunded pension plans. For reasons discussed below, Pepsi has contributed more to its pension fund than it has recognized as an expense, resulting in a Prepaid Pension Asset on the balance sheet.

Measurement of Pension Expense. Firms must calculate net pension expense each year based on the projected benefit cost method, which means that actuarial calculations use accumulated service to date and projected future salaries. Exhibit 6.7 summarizes the seven elements included in net pension expense.

We noted earlier that if (1) pension assets equal pension liabilities, (2) the rate of return on pension assets equals the interest rate used to compute the present value of the pension liability, and (3) actuarial assumptions turn out as expected, the

---

EXHIBIT 6.7

Components of Pension Expense

	Effect on Pension Expense	
	Debit (Increase)	**Credit (Decrease)**
1. Service Cost—the increase in the projected benefit obligation because employees worked an additional year	X	
2. Interest Cost—the increase in the projected benefit obligation because of the passage of time	X	
3. Actual Return on Plan Assets—the change in the market value of plan assets due to interest, dividends, and changes in the market value of investments		X
4. Difference between Actual Return and Expected Return on Plan Assets		
Actual Return > Expected Return	X	
Actual Return < Expected Return		X
5. Amortization of net pension asset (pension fund assets exceed projected benefit obligation) or net pension liability (pension fund assets are less than projected benefit obligation) as of the date of initial adoption of *Statement No.* 87. The firm amortizes the net asset or net obligation straight line over the average remaining service life of employees.		
Net Pension Liability.....................................	X	
Net Pension Asset		X
6. Amortization of increases in the projected benefit obligation that arise because the firm sweetens the pension benefit formula and gives employees credit for their prior service under the sweetened benefit arrangement. The amortization period is generally the average remaining service life of employees, although a shorter period may be required if an employer regularly sweetens its pension plan	X	
7. Amortization of gains and losses because actual experience differs from actuarial assumptions (e.g., salary, interest rate, turnover, mortality, asset returns).		
Actuarial Loss	X	
Actuarial Gain		X

employer's pension expense equals the current employee service cost (item 1 in Exhibit 6.7). Items 2 and 3 net to zero and items 4, 5, 6, and 7 are zero. The lack of equality of pension assets and liabilities and the realization of a different rate of return on assets than the interest rate used to compute the pension liability result in unequal offsetting of items 2 and 3. This inequality plus changes in the pension benefit formula and an inability to realize actuarial assumptions create the need for larger or smaller employer contributions to the pension fund in the future. Because the employer's total expenses must ultimately equal the cash contributed to the pension fund, pension expense must increase or decrease as well. *Statement No.* 87 requires firms to smooth the effect of these excess or deficient amounts (items 4 through 7), rather than including them in the calculation of pension expense immediately.

Pepsi discloses these seven components of pension expense on six lines (Pepsi combines items 6 and 7 on the line Net Other Amortization), as follows:

	Year 6	Year 7	Year 8
Service Cost-Benefits Earned during the Year ..	$ 46.7	$ 60.9	$ 69.5
Interest Cost on Projected Benefit Obligation ...	69.3	82.9	90.6
Actual Return on Plan Assets	(224.1)	(97.3)	(202.3)
Deferred Gain	128.7	(7.6)	91.3
Amortization of Net Transition Gain	(19.0)	(19.0)	(18.7)
Net Other Amortization	5.5	1.7	10.5
Net Pension Expense	$ 7.1	$ 21.6	$ 40.9

Note the following aspects about net pension expense:

1. The effect of combining the third and fourth components of pension expense is that pension expense decreases by the *expected* return on pension assets each period. The disclosure of this expected return appears in two steps: (a) the actual return plus or minus (b) the difference between the actual and the expected return. This method of disclosure permits the financial statement user to assess the actual performance of the pension fund during the period, but it smooths out the effect of unexpected gains and losses by including them as part of the amortization of actuarial gains and losses (seventh component of pension expense). Pepsi's actual return on investments during Year 6 and Year 8 exceeded expectations. Pepsi deferred a portion of this return each year. The actual return during Year 7 was less than expectations, so Pepsi deferred the shortfall. Pepsi's disclosure practice of combining items 6 and 7 of pension expense on the line Net Other Amortization makes it difficult to disaggregate the portion of the net amount due to amortization of differences between the actual and expected rate of return on pension assets (line 4) and amortization of deferred amounts from prior years (lines 6 and 7).

2. In addition to amortization of actuarial gains and losses, amortization of any net pension asset or net pension liability when the firm adopted FASB *Statement No.* 87 affects pension expense. The objective in amortizing this item is to smooth its effect on pension expense.

3. The seven components of pension expense may net to a pension expense or a pension credit.

Relation of Pension Expense to Pension Funding.   The amount that a firm recognizes as pension expense each period does not necessarily equal the amount the firm contributes to its pension fund. The firm measures the amount for pension expense in accordance with the provisions of FASB *Statement No. 87.* The amount that the firm contributes to its pension fund relies on actuaries' recommendations concerning the needed level of funding plus decisions by the firm regarding investments of its financial resources. For example, a firm with a significantly over-funded pension plan might delay additional contributions for a few years and use the cash for other corporate purposes. In this case, the firm recognizes pension expense each year but does not contribute cash to the pension fund. Alternatively, a firm might contribute more than the amount of pension expense. Earnings on pension investments are not subject to income taxation, whereas earnings on cash left within a firm are subject to taxation. Within prescribed limits, firms can make excess pension contributions and delay or avoid taxes on investment earnings.

When a firm recognizes more pension expense that it contributes to the pension fund, a pension liability appears on the balance sheet. When pension expense is less than pension funding, a pension asset appears on the balance sheet. Pepsi, for example, reports a prepaid pension asset of $101.4 million at the end of Year 7 (=$29.1 + $72.3) and $69.9 million at the end of Year 8 (=$.8 + $69.1) relating to certain overfunded pension plans, suggesting that it has funded some pension plans faster than it has recognized pension expense. Note that this pension asset (or pension liability) on the balance sheet bears no necessary relation to the more important measure of the status of a pension plan: the difference between the total assets in the pension fund and the projected benefit obligation, which is usually a much larger amount.

Refer now to Note 13 to the financial statements of Coke in Appendix A. The combined assets of $927 million (=$631 + $2 + $200 + $94) in Coke's pension plans at the end of Year 8 are less than the projected benefit obligation of $1,104 million (=$598 + $133 + $196 + $177) by $177 million (=$1,104 − $927). Similar amounts for Year 7 result in an underfunded pension obligation of $87 million. The increase in the net underfunded pension obligation results primarily from the decrease in the discount rate used to calculate the projected benefit obligation. Note that the reduction in the assumed level of compensation increases reduces the projected benefit obligation. Note also that the actual return on investments of $104 million (=$77 + $27) exceeded the expected return for Year 8 of $81 million [0.095 × (=$587 + $1 + $188 + $73)]. Thus, poor investment performance does not account for the increase in the net unfunded pension liability.

Analysts' Treatment of Pensions.   Exhibit 6.8 presents an analysis of Pepsi's pension plan disclosures for Year 8. The assets in the pension fund at the beginning and the end of Year 8 exceeded the projected benefit obligation. Thus, Pepsi has an overfunded pension plan.

Pension plan investments generated earnings of $202.3 million during Year 8 (Pepsi discloses this amount in the components of its pension expense for the year). The earnings include interest, dividends, realized gains and losses from sales of

EXHIBIT 6.8

Analysis of Pension Plan Disclosures of Pepsi for Year 8
(amounts in millions)

Accounting Records of Pension Plan

Assets at Beginning of Year.........	$1,299.2	Liability at Beginning of Year	$1,100.4
Plus Earnings from Investments	202.3	Plus Service Cost	69.5
Plus Contribution from Pepsi	5.2[a]	Plus Interest Cost	90.6
Less Payments to Retirees (Plug)	(63.8)	Less Payments to Retirees	(63.8)
Assets at End of Year	$1,442.9	Plus (Minus) Actuarial Loss (Gain).....	239.6[b]
		Liability at End of Year..............	$1,436.3

[a]Pension Expense...	$ 40.9
Decrease in Prepaid Pension Asset ($83.0 − $10.0)..	(73.0)
Increase in Adjustment for Minimum Liability...	37.3
Pension Contribution	$ 5.2
[b]Unrecognized Net Gain, Prior Service Cost, and Net Transition Asset, Beginning of Year: ($53.8) + 52.2 + ($114.2)..	$(115.8)
Plus Actuarial Loss for Year 8 Plug...	239.6
Less Excess of Actual over Expected Earnings for Year 8...	(91.3)
Less Amortization for Year 8 ($18.7) + $10.5	8.2
Unrecognized Net Loss, Prior Service Cost, and Net Transition Asset, End of Year: ($61.7 + $65.3 + ($86.3)........	$ 40.7

investments, and unrealized gains and losses from changes in the market value of investments. The portions of the $202.3 million of earnings that were realized during Year 8 and that are unrealized at the end of Year 8 are not a required disclosure.

Pepsi makes the following journal entry on its books during Year 8 relating to pension expense and pension funding:

Pension Expense	40.9	
Shareholders' Equity Account (minimum Pension		
Liability)	37.3	
Prepaid Pension Asset		73.0
Cash..		5.2

The excess assets in the pension fund probably led Pepsi to curtail its cash contribution during Year 8.

The projected benefit obligation increased because of service cost and interest cost during Year 8. Pepsi discloses the amounts for these items in the components of pension expense. The actuarial loss occurs for two reasons: Pepsi (1) reduced the discount rate it uses to compute the projected benefit obligation (see the disclosures in Pepsi's Note 11 in Appendix B), which increases the liability and the unrecognized loss, and (2) sweetened the pension benefit formula, which gave employees credit for prior years of service. Pepsi also reduced the assumed rate of compensation increases (see Pepsi's Note 11 in Appendix B), which reduced the projected benefit obligation. However, the two items above dominated the effect of the compensation assumption and resulted in an actuarial loss for the year.

An analyst assessing a firm's profitability and risk might treat a difference between pension assets and pension liabilities in various ways:

1. Make no adjustment to the employer's balance sheet for an under- or overfunded pension plan. The rationale for this approach is that the under- or overfunding is a temporary condition that will work itself out over a longer time period.
2. Recognize an underfunded projected benefit obligation as a liability. The employer may have to contribute an amount to the pension fund in the future equal to the underfunding. Including the obligation among liabilities provides better measures for assessing financial structure risk. Coke's underfunded projected benefit obligation is $214 million (=$131 + $83) at the end of Year 8. The income tax rate is 35 percent. Coke already reports a liability related to these underfunded pension plans of $159 million (=$109 + $50) at the end of Year 8. The entry to reflect the additional underfunded projected benefit obligation of $55 million (=$214 − $159) is as follows (in millions):

Deferred Tax Asset (0.35 × $55)	19	
Retained Earnings (0.65 × $55)	36	
Pension Liability................................		55

3. Recognize an overfunded projected benefit obligation as an asset and an underfunded projected benefit obligation as a liability. This approach shows the potential benefit of accessing excess pension assets as well as the potential cost of an underfunded obligation. The entry to record the underfunded obligation appears under item 2 above. Coke's pension plans that have assets in excess of the projected benefit obligation total $37 million (=$33 + $4) at the end of Year 8. The balance sheet currently shows an accrued pension liability of $17 million and a prepaid pension asset of $16 million related to these plans. The entry to reflect the net $37 million asset of these plans is as follows:

Accrued Pension Liability............................	17	
Prepaid Pension Asset ($37 − $16)	21	
Deferred Tax Asset (0.35 × $17)		6
Deferred Tax Liability (0.35 × $21)...............		7
Retained Earnings		25

    To eliminate accrued pension liability related to overfunded pension plans and establish prepaid pension asset.

4. Include both the assets and liabilities of the pension fund on the employer's balance sheet. Include the return on pension assets as an interest and dividend revenue and the interest cost component of pension expense as interest expense on the employer's income statement. This approach consolidates the financial statements of the pension fund with those of the employer, much like those for a parent company and majority-owned subsidiaries. The case for consolidation rests on the employer's right to access pension assets and obligation to provide for pension liabilities. The counterargument for consolidation is that federal pension law constrains significantly the operational relationship between the employer and its pension fund as compared to most parent/subsidiary relationships.

POSTRETIREMENT BENEFITS OTHER THAN PENSIONS

In addition to pensions, most employers provide health care and life insurance benefits to retired employees. This benefit may take the form of a fixed dollar amount to cover part or all of the cost of health and life insurance (analogous to the defined contribution type of pension plan), or the benefit may specify the level of health care or life insurance provided (analogous to the defined benefit type of pension plan).

The accounting issues related to these postretirement obligations are similar to those discussed previously for pensions. The employer must recognize the cost of the postretirement benefits during the employees' years of service. The employer may or may not set aside funds to cover the cost of these benefits. Health and life insurance expense each period includes an amount for current service plus interest on the health care or life insurance benefits obligation at the beginning of the period. Expected earnings on investments in a postretirement benefits fund, if any, reduce these expenses. The employer defers and then amortizes actuarial gains and losses due to changes in employee turnover, health care costs, interest rates, and similar factors. The major difference between the accounting for pensions and the accounting for other postretirement benefits is that firms need not report an excess of the accumulated benefits obligation over assets in a postretirement benefits fund as a liability on the balance sheet.[14] Firms must report this amount in the notes to the financial statements. During the deliberation process on the reporting standard for postretirement benefits, business firms exerted pressure on the FASB not to require recognition of the underfunded accumulated benefits obligation, particularly for health care benefits. These business firms argued that the amount of this obligation was both large, relative to other liabilities and shareholders' equity, and uncertain because of uncertainties regarding future health care inflation rates. Some firms indicated that they would eliminate health care retirement benefits if the FASB required recognition of the liability. As a compromise, the FASB allows firms to recognize the obligation either in full on adoption of *Statement No. 106* or piecemeal over employees' working years.

Refer to Note 14 to Coke's financial statements in Appendix A. Coke adopted the provisions of FASB *Statement No. 106* in Year 7. It elected to recognize the full obligation for health care and life insurance benefits on adoption. By the end of Year 7, its balance sheet includes a liability of $234 million. This liability grew to $256 million by the end of Year 8. Coke includes a liability of $233 million in its December 31, Year 8, balance sheet. The remaining $23 million (=$256 − $233) is an unrecognized actuarial loss arising during Year 8, which Coke will amortize over future years. The actuarial loss occurred primarily because during Year 8 Coke reduced the discount rate that it uses to measure its obligation. Any increase in the discount rate in future years could turn the unrecognized loss into an unrecognized gain. The analyst might conclude, therefore, that the postretirement benefit obligation already recognized by Coke satisfactorily reflects its obligation.

---

[14]The accumulated benefits obligation for health care incorporates health care costs expected when employees receive benefits and is therefore more similar to the projected benefit pension obligation than the accumulated benefit pension obligation. See Financial Accounting Standards Board, *Statement of Financial Accounting Standards No. 106,* "Employer's Accounting for Postretirement Benefits Other than Pensions," 1990.

Refer now to Note 10 to Pepsi's financial statements in Appendix B. Pepsi likewise adopted the provisions of FASB *Statement No. 106* in Year 7. It elected to recognize the full obligation for postretirement benefits at the time of adoption. Except for the effects of sweetening the benefit formula in Year 8 and actuarial losses in Year 7 and Year 8, its balance sheet likewise already reflects its obligation for postretirement benefits.

Analysts' concerns with postretirement benefits other than pensions are similar to those for pensions. Should the analyst add the underfunded postretirements benefit obligation to liabilities in assessing risk? How reasonable are the firm's assumptions regarding health care cost increases, discount rates, and amortization periods? Is the postretirement benefit fund, if any, generating returns consistent with the expected rate of return?

INCOME TAXES

Income taxes affect the analysis of a firm's profitability (income tax expense is a subtraction when computing net income) and its cash flows (income taxes currently payable require cash). Deferred tax assets and deferred tax liabilities on the balance sheet affect future cash flows. The note to the financial statements on income taxes contains useful information for assessing a firm's income tax position. This section presents an overview of the required income tax disclosures and a discussion of how the analyst might use this information when analyzing a firm's financial statements.

OVERVIEW OF INCOME TAX ACCOUNTING

Standard-setting bodies in the United States have taken the position for many years that income tax expense for a particular year is not simply the amount of income taxes currently payable to governmental bodies on the taxable income of that year. Firms must also recognize the benefits of future tax deductions and the obligations related to future taxable incomes to the extent that revenues and expenses affect income for financial reporting during the current period but will affect taxable income in future periods. The underlying concept is matching: matching income tax expense with the income reported for financial reporting, even though the associated cash flows for income taxes will not occur until future periods.

Prior to the issuance of Financial Accounting Standards Board *Statement No. 109*[15] in February 1992, the accounting for income taxes followed an *income statement approach*. The following diagram summarizes the approach previously followed:

(1) Income before Income Taxes for Financial Reporting
± (2) Additions or Subtractions to Eliminate Permanent Differences between Income for Financial and Tax Reporting
= (3) Base for Income Tax Expense

---

[15]Financial Accounting Standards Board, *Statement of Financial Accounting Standards No. 109*, "Accounting for Income Taxes," 1992.

± (4) Additions or Subtractions for Temporary Differences between Income for Financial and Tax Reporting

= (5) Taxable Income

The journal entry to record income tax expense was:

Income Tax Expense (Tax Rate × Line 3)	x	
Deferred Tax Asset or Deferred Tax Liability (Tax Rate × Line 4)	x	x
Income Tax Payable (Tax Rate × Line 5)		x

FASB *Statement No. 109* now requires firms to follow a *balance sheet approach* when computing income tax expense. The following description summarizes the approach:

1. Identify at each balance sheet date all differences between the *book basis* (that is, the book value for financial reporting) of assets, liabilities, and tax loss carryforwards and the *tax basis* of assets, liabilities, and tax loss carryforwards.
2. Eliminate differences from Step 1 that will not have a future tax consequence. Terminology prior to *Statement No. 109* referred to these differences as *permanent differences*. An example is goodwill. Firms must amortize goodwill for financial reporting but generally cannot deduct this amortization for tax purposes. Thus, the book basis and tax basis of goodwill will differ. Note that the eliminations in this step reflect the cumulative effect of permanent differences as of the date of the balance sheet, not just the current year's permanent difference included in line (2) above following an income statement approach.
3. Separate the remaining differences after the first two steps into those that give rise to future tax deductions and those that give rise to future taxable income. GAAP refers to these differences as *temporary differences*. Exhibit 6.9 summarizes the possibilities. Multiply differences between the book and tax bases of assets and liabilities that give rise to future tax deductions by the *enacted* marginal tax rate expected to apply in those future periods. The result is a *deferred tax asset*. Multiply differences between the book and tax bases of assets and liabilities that give rise to future taxable income by the *enacted* marginal tax rate expected to apply in those future periods. The result is a *deferred tax liability*.

Firms may have unused net operating loss and tax credit carryforwards as of a balance sheet date. These items have the potential to reduce future taxable income (operating loss carryforwards) or future taxes payable (tax credit carryforwards). The firm includes the tax effect of these carryforwards in deferred tax assets at each balance sheet date.

4. Assess the likelihood that the firm will realize the benefits of deferred tax assets in the future. This assessment should consider the nature (for example, cyclical or noncyclical) and characteristics (for example, growing, mature, or declining) of the firm's business and its tax-planning strategies for the future. If realization of the benefits of deferred tax assets is "more likely than not" (that is, exceeds 50 percent), then deferred tax assets equal the amounts computed in Step 3 above. However, if it is more likely than not that a firm will not realize some or all of the deferred tax assets, the firm must reduce the deferred tax assets for a

EXHIBIT 6.9

Examples of Temporary Differences

	Assets	Liabilities
Future Tax Deduction	Tax Basis of Assets Exceeds Book (Financial Reporting) Basis[a]	Tax Basis of Liabilities Is Less than Book (Financial Reporting) Basis[b]
Future Taxable Income	Tax Basis of Assets Is Less than Book (Financial Reporting) Basis[c]	Tax Basis of Liabilities Exceeds Book (Financial Reporting) Basis[d]

Examples

[a]Accounts receivable using the direct charge-off method for uncollectible accounts for tax purposes exceeds accounts receivable (net) using the allowance method for financial reporting.

[b]Tax reporting does not recognize an estimated liability for warranty claims (firms can deduct only actual expenditures on warranty claims), whereas firms must recognize such a liability for financial reporting to match warranty expense with sales revenue in the period of sale.

[c]Depreciable assets using accelerated depreciation for tax purposes exceed depreciable assets using straight-line depreciation for financial reporting.

[d]Leases recognized by a lessee as capital leases for tax reporting and operating leases for financial reporting.

valuation allowance (similar in concept to the allowance for uncollectible accounts). The valuation allowance reduces the deferred tax assets to the amounts the firm expects to realize by way of reduced taxes in the future.

The results of following this four-step procedure are a deferred tax asset and a deferred tax liability at each balance sheet date. Income tax expense each period equals:

1. Income taxes currently payable on taxable income.
2. Plus a net credit change in the deferred tax asset or liability and minus a net debit change in the deferred tax asset or liability between the beginning and the end of the period.

A comparison between the components of income tax expense using the income statement approach prior to *Statement No. 109* and the balance sheet approach appears below.

Income Statement Approach (Pre-*Statement No. 109*)	**Balance Sheet Approach** (*Statement No. 109*)
(1) Taxes Current Payable on Taxable Income	(4) Taxes Current Payable on Taxable Income
(2) Taxes Potentially Saved or Payable in the Future from Timing Differences between Current Period Income for Financial and Tax Reporting	(5) Change in Deferred Tax Assets and Deferred Tax Liabilities during the Current Period
(3) Income Tax Expense = (1) + (2)	(6) Income Tax Expense = (4) + (5)

The principal difference between these two approaches relates to item (2) versus item (5). Item (2) includes only temporary differences for the current year between financial and tax-reporting incomes, whereas item (5) includes temporary differences, enacted changes during a period in future income tax rates, and changes in the valuation allowance as a result of new information regarding the realizability of deferred tax assets. When tax rates do not change and a firm recognizes no valuation allowance, the income statement and balance sheet approaches yield identical amounts for income tax expense.

REQUIRED INCOME TAX DISCLOSURES

The amount reported as income tax expense in the income statement is the net result of applying (1) a lengthy list of rules for measuring taxable income and tax liabilities according to the *Internal Revenue Code* (gives the "current" portion of income tax expense) and (2) the seemingly complex procedure discussed above to measure the deferred portion. The notes to the financial statements provide additional information to help the analyst understand better the makeup of income tax expense. Four specific disclosures are particularly useful for assessing a firm's tax position. The sections below discuss and illustrate these disclosures.

Components of Income Tax Expense. Firms must disclose the amount of income taxes currently payable and the amount deferred, broken down by governmental entity (federal, foreign, state, and local).

	Components of Income Tax Expense		
	Year 1	Year 2	Year 3
Current—Federal	$123	$105	$191
—Foreign	61	75	128
—State and Local	13	12	18
Total Current	$197	$192	$337
Deferred—Federal	$ 70	$ 40	$ 35
—Foreign	19	30	38
Total Deferred	$ 89	$ 70	$ 73
Total Income Tax Expense	$286	$262	$410

The journal entries made to record income taxes each year appear below:

	Year 1		Year 2		Year 3	
Income Tax Expense	286		262		410	
Income Tax Payable		197		192		337
Deferred Tax Asset or Deferred Tax Liability		89		70		73

Components of Income before Taxes. Assessing a firm's tax position over time or relative to other firms requires some base for scaling the amount of income tax expense. Income before taxes serves this purpose.

	Components of Income before Taxes		
	Year 1	Year 2	Year 3
United States	$600	$450	$ 700
Foreign	200	250	350
Total	$800	$700	$1,050

The average, or effective, tax rates for the three years on total income before taxes are:

Year 1: $286/$800 = 35.7%

Year 2: $262/$700 = 37.4%

Year 3: $410/$1,050 = 39.0%.

Thus, the effective tax rate increased over the three-year period.

Reconciliation of Income Taxes at Statutory Rate with Income Tax Expense. The third required disclosure explains why the effective tax rates shown above differ from the statutory federal tax rate on income before taxes. Firms can express reconciling items in either dollar amounts or percentage terms.

Reconciliation of Income Taxes at Statutory Rate with Income Tax Expense			
	Year 1	Year 2	Year 3
(1) Income Taxes on Income before Taxes at Statutory Rate............................	35.0%	35.0%	35.0%
(2) Foreign Tax Rates Greater (Less) than Statutory Federal Rate......................	1.3	2.5	4.1
(3) State and Local Taxes	1.1	1.1	1.1
(4) Dividend Deduction........................	(0.5)	(0.5)	(0.6)
(5) Tax-Exempt Income........................	(0.5)	(0.4)	(0.4)
(6) Goodwill Amortization	0.2	0.4	0.6
(7) Percentage Depletion in Excess of Cost........	(0.7)	(0.7)	(0.8)
Income Tax Expense	35.9%	37.4%	39.0%

The statutory federal tax rate was 35 percent in each year. The effective tax rates were greater than the statutory rates. The reconciliation includes two types of reconciling items: (1) tax rate differences and (2) permanent differences. The sections below discuss each of these reconciling items more fully.

Foreign Tax Rates Greater (Less) than Statutory Federal Rate.   The denominator of the effective tax rate computation combines both U.S.–source and foreign-source income for financial reporting. The initial assumption on line (1) is that all of this income is subject to taxes at a rate equal to the U.S. federal statutory rate. Foreign tax rates are usually different from the U.S. federal rate, however. This line indicates how much the overall effective tax rate increased or decreased because of these foreign rate differences.

Refer to the first two types of income tax disclosures discussed earlier. Foreign tax expense for Year 3 totaled $166 (=$128 + $38). Pretax book income from foreign sources was $350. If this income were subject to tax at the federal rate of 35 percent, foreign income tax expense would have been $123 (=0.35 × $350). Foreign tax expense of $166 exceeded the amount at the federal statutory rate by $43 (=$166 − $123). The excess taxes as a percentage of *total* pretax book income, the denominator of the effective tax rate, is 4.1 percent (=$43/$1,050). Foreign-source income was taxed at a rate of 47.4 percent (=$166/$350).

It would be desirable to have a breakdown of total foreign income and foreign taxes by individual countries, but firms rarely disclose such information.

State and Local Taxes.   The statutory tax rate on line (1) reflects federal taxes only. The reconciliation adds state and local taxes on income for financial reporting since such taxes are part of income tax expense. The amount of the reconciling item is state and local taxes net of their federal tax benefit. State and local taxes are deductible in determining taxable income for federal purposes, so the incremental effect of state and local taxes beyond the federal statutory rate appears on line (3).

Refer to the disclosure of the components of income tax expense discussed previously. State and local taxes for Year 3 were $18. Net of the federal tax benefit of 35 percent, state and local taxes are $12 [=(1 − 0.35)($18)]. This $12 amount increases the effective tax rate by 1.1 percent (=$12/$1,050) for Year 3.

As with foreign taxes, the income tax note to the financial statements does not give any further detail on the income and taxes by jurisdictional unit within the United States.

Dividends Received Deduction.   Depending on the investor's ownership percentage, only 20 percent or 30 percent of dividends received from *unconsolidated domestic* subsidiaries and affiliates is subject to federal taxation. The dividend deduction is intended to reduce the effect of triple taxation of the corporate organization form. The full dividend received is included in income for financial reporting. The calculation on line (1) presumes that the dividend is subject to tax at the statutory rate. The reduction on line (4) indicates the tax savings due to the 70 percent or 80 percent dividends received deduction.

Tax-Exempt Income.   Income for financial reporting includes interest revenue on state and municipal obligations. Such interest revenue, however, is never included in taxable income. The income tax savings from this permanent difference appears on line (5).

Goodwill Amortization.   A firm that acquires another firm and pays a higher price than the market value of its identifiable assets must allocate the excess to goodwill. The firm must amortize goodwill over a period not exceeding 40 years for financial reporting purposes, but it generally cannot amortize goodwill for tax purposes. By subtracting goodwill amortization in computing book income before taxes, line (1) presumes a tax benefit equal to the amortization times the statutory tax rate. The addition on line (6) reflects the fact that no tax benefit accrues to this permanent difference.

Percentage Depletion in Excess of Cost. The *Internal Revenue Code* permits firms involved in mineral extraction to claim a depletion deduction equal to a specified percentage times the gross income from the property each year. Over the life of a mineral property, total percentage depletion will likely exceed the acquisition cost of the property. For financial reporting purposes, total depletion cannot exceed acquisition cost under generally accepted accounting principles. The excess of percentage depletion over book depletion represents a permanent difference that reduces the effective tax rate.

The foregoing discussion illustrates the reconciling items most commonly encountered in corporate annual reports. Other items reported have characteristics similar to those discussed above.

Components of Deferred Tax Assets and Liabilities. The fourth disclosure item in the income tax note is a list of the components of the deferred tax asset and the deferred tax liability at the beginning and the end of each year. Exhibit 6.10 presents the required disclosure. The change in deferred tax asset and

---

EXHIBIT 6.10

Disclosures Related to Deferred Taxes

	Components of Deferred Tax Assets and Liabilities			
	December 31			
	Year 0	Year 1	Year 2	Year 3
Deferred Tax Asset				
(8) Uncollectible Accounts Receivable....	$ 15	$ 17	$ 19	$ 16
(9) Warranties........................	76	89	105	91
(10) Pensions	53	67	83	71
(11) Leases	32	42	54	62
(12) Net Operating Losses	—	—	13	—
Total Deferred Tax Asset............	$176	$215	$274	$240
Deferred Tax Liability				
(13) Depreciable Assets	$275	$355	$421	$476
(14) Inventories.......................	41	49	58	59
(15) Installment Receivables.............	149	171	205	193
(16) Intangible Drilling and Development Costs	58	76	96	91
Total Deferred Tax Liability	$523	$651	$780	$819

deferred tax liability each year represents deferred income tax expense for that year. Note that Deferred Tax Assets experienced a net credit change of $34 (=$240 − $274) between Year 2 and Year 3 and Deferred Tax Liabilities experienced a net credit change of $39 (=$819 − $780). The total credit change in these accounts of $73 (=$34 + $39) equals the deferred component of income tax expense for Year 3 (see the first income tax disclosure item).

The following sections discuss the components of deferred taxes.

Uncollectible Accounts.   Firms provide for estimated uncollectible accounts in the year of sale for financial reporting but cannot recognize bad debt expense for tax purposes until an actual customer's account becomes uncollectible. Thus, the book value of accounts receivable is less than its tax basis. The difference represents the future tax deductions for bad debt expense. These future tax benefits times the tax rate give rise to a deferred tax asset. The deferred tax asset relating to uncollectible accounts increased between Year 0 and Year 2, suggesting that bad debt expense for financial reporting continued to exceed bad debt expense for tax reporting. Such a relation characterizes a firm with increasing sales. The decrease in the deferred tax asset during Year 3 suggests that sales declined, causing bad debt expense for tax reporting to exceed the amount for financial reporting.

Warranties.   Firms provide for estimated warranty costs in the year of sale for financial reporting but cannot recognize warranty expense for tax reporting until the firm makes actual expenditures to provide warranty services. Thus, the book value of the warranty liability (a positive amount) exceeds the tax basis of the warranty liability (zero, because the income tax law does not permit recognition of a warranty liability). The difference represents the future tax deductions for warranty expense. The increase in the deferred tax asset relating to warranties between Year 0 and Year 2 is consistent with a growing firm, whereas the decrease in Year 3 indicates a firm whose sales of product under warranty plans probably declined.

Pensions.   Firms recognize pension expense each year as employees render services for financial reporting and when the firm contributes cash to the pension fund for tax reporting. The income tax law limits a firm's ability to claim tax deductions when a pension fund is overfunded (that is, pension fund assets exceed pension fund liabilities). Thus, firms may curtail making pension fund contributions even though they must recognize pension expense each year. The book basis of the pension liability (a positive amount) exceeds the tax basis (not recognized). The future tax deductions for pension expense result in a deferred tax asset. For our illustrative firm, pension expense for financial reporting exceeded the amount for tax reporting during Year 1 and Year 2, and the deferred tax asset relating to pensions increased. The deferred tax asset decreased in Year 3, indicating a larger expense for tax reporting than for financial reporting (that is, the book basis of the pension liability decreased during the year). Several explanations might account for such a decrease. First, the firm resumed funding the pension obligation and made a multiyear contribution. Second, the firm curtailed employment during Year 3 in light of the decrease in sales, reducing pension expense, but made a pension contribution sufficient to reduce the pension liability. Third, the firm experienced a negative pension expense during Year 3 because of an overfunded pension plan. The negative pension expense reduces the pension liability and thereby the amount of future tax deductions previously considered available.

Leases. Our illustrative firm leases equipment from other entities (lessors). Firms may treat leases as either operating leases or as capital leases for financial and tax reporting. If the leases qualify as operating leases, the lessor recognizes rent revenue and depreciation expense and the lessee recognizes rent expense. If leases qualify as capital leases, the lessor recognizes a gain on the "sale" of the leased property at the inception of the lease and recognizes interest revenue each year from financing the lessee's "purchase" of the property. The lessee depreciates the assets each period and recognizes interest expense on its borrowing from the lessor.

Leasing arose as an industry in part to shift tax deductions on property from firms that needed the use of property but did not have sufficient taxable income to take advantage of the tax deductions to other entities with higher tax rates that could take advantage of the deductions. If a lease qualifies as an operating lease for tax-purposes, the lessor gets the tax deductions for depreciation and can possibly pass through some of these benefits to the lessee in the form of lower lease payments.

An earlier section of this chapter indicated that the criteria for an operating lease and a capital lease for financial reporting are not identical to those for tax reporting. It is possible to structure leases that are operating leases for tax reporting, even though they qualify as capital leases for financial reporting. Our illustrative firm shows a deferred tax asset relating to leases. The likely scenario is that this firm treats leases as capital leases for financial reporting and as operating leases for tax reporting. Thus, the book basis of the leased asset and the lease liability (a positive amount) exceeds the tax basis of the asset and liability (not recognized). Depreciation and interest expense recognized for financial reporting exceed rent expense recognized for tax reporting. In later years, rent expense for tax reporting will exceed depreciation and interest expense. These future tax deductions give rise to a deferred tax asset. The deferred tax asset increased each year, suggesting that this firm increased its involvement in leasing during the three-year period (that is, the firm has more leased assets in the early years of the lease period when the book expenses exceed the tax deduction than in the later years when the tax deduction exceeds the book expenses).

Net Operating Losses. A firm may operate for both financial and tax reporting at a net loss for the year. The firm can carry back this net loss to offset taxable income of the three preceding years and receive a refund for income taxes paid in those years. The firm recognizes the refund as an income tax credit in the year of the net loss.

If the firm either has no positive taxable income in the three preceding years against which to carry back the net loss or if the net loss exceeds the taxable income of those three preceding years, the firm must carry forward the net loss. This carryforward provides future tax benefits in that it can offset positive taxable incomes and thereby reduce income taxes otherwise payable. The benefits of the net operating loss carryforward give rise to a deferred tax asset.

Our illustrative firm recognized a deferred tax asset during Year 2 and realized the benefits of the net operating loss carryforward during Year 3. Referring back to the disclosure of the components of income tax expense, we see that this firm paid taxes to all three governmental units during Year 2. Thus, the firm must have been unable to offset the net operating loss incurred by some subunit during the year against the taxable income of the overall entity. One possibility is that the firm owns a majority interest in a subsidiary and therefore consolidates it for financial reporting. Its ownership percentage, however, is less than the 80 percent required to include the subsidiary in a consolidated tax return. Thus, the net loss of the subsidiary can offset net income of only that subsidiary in a later year. The firm recognizes this future benefit as a deferred tax asset. This firm shows no valuation allowance related to the deferred tax asset, indicating a greater than 50 percent probability of realizing the tax benefits in the future.

Depreciation. Firms claim depreciation on their tax returns using accelerated methods over periods shorter than the expected useful lives of depreciable assets. Most firms depreciate assets for financial reporting using the straight-line method over the expected useful lives of such assets. Thus, the book value of depreciable assets will likely exceed their tax basis. Depreciation expense for tax reporting in future years will be less than the amounts for financial reporting, giving rise to a liability for future tax payments. The deferred tax liability relating to depreciable assets increased each year, suggesting that this firm has more assets in their early years when tax depreciation exceeds book depreciation. The deferred tax liability increased, however, at a decreasing rate, suggesting a slowdown in the growth rate in capital expenditures.

Inventories. The book value of inventories for our illustrative firm exceeds their tax basis, giving rise to future tax liabilities. Perhaps this firm includes certain elements of cost as part of manufacturing overhead for financial reporting but deducts them when incurred for tax reporting.

Installment Receivables. Firms that sell assets on account and permit customers to pay over two or more future years often recognize revenue at the time of sale for financial reporting and when they collect cash using the installment method for tax reporting. The book basis of these receivables exceeds their tax basis and gives rise to deferred tax liabilities. The deferred tax liability relating to installment sales increased between Year 0 and Year 2, characteristic of a growing firm (that is, revenues from sales during the current period exceed collections this period from sales made in prior periods). The deferred tax liability on installment sales decreased during Year 3, consistent with the decline in sales noted above in the discussion of deferred taxes related to uncollectible accounts and warranties.

Intangible Drilling and Development Costs. Firms can deduct for tax purposes in the year of the cash expenditure certain costs of acquiring rights to drill and for drilling a property to ascertain the existence of mineral resources. These firms must capitalize and amortize such costs for financial reporting. The book basis of the property exceeds the tax basis and gives rise to a deferred tax liability. The deferred tax liability for this item increased between Year 0 and Year 2, indicating a growth in drilling and development activity. The decrease in the liability during Year 3 suggests a cutback in such expenditures.

ASSESSING A FIRM'S TAX POSITION

The note to the financial statements on income taxes defines the effective tax rate as follows:

$$\text{Effective Tax Rate} = \frac{\text{Income Tax Expense}}{\text{Book Income before Income Taxes}}$$

Exhibit 6.11 presents an analysis of effective tax rates. This analysis separates the amounts for each year into domestic and foreign components.

The combined effective tax rate based on income tax expense increased each year. The effective tax rate on the domestic portion remained relatively steady at a rate near the 35 percent federal statutory tax rate. Differences in the domestic tax position due to rate differences and permanent differences offset each other. On the other hand, the effective tax rate on the foreign portion exceeded 35 percent and that rate increased each year. The analyst should explore the reasons for this increase in the foreign effective tax rate more fully with management. Perhaps foreign markets are growing more rapidly than domestic markets and the firm's overall profit margin increased as a result of a strategic shift toward these foreign markets. Alternatively, the firm may need to search for more tax-effective ways to operate abroad. For example, the firm might:

1. Shift some operations (manufacturing, marketing) to the United States where the effective tax rate is lower.
2. Assess whether transfer prices or cost allocations can be adjusted to shift income from high to low tax rate jurisdictions.

EXHIBIT 6.11

Analysis of Effective Tax Rates

	Year 1 Domestic	Year 1 Foreign	Year 2 Domestic	Year 2 Foreign	Year 3 Domestic	Year 3 Foreign
(1) Net Income before Income Taxes..	$600	$200	$450	$250	$700	$350
Income Taxes at 35% Statutory Federal Rate	$210	$ 70	$157	$ 87	$245	$123
Foreign Tax Rates Greater than 35%.........................	—	10	—	18	—	43
State and Local Taxes	9	—	8	—	11	—
Dividends Deduction	(4)	—	(3)	—	(6)	—
Tax Exempt Income	(4)	—	(3)	—	(4)	—
Goodwill Amortization	1	—	3	—	6	—
Percentage Depletion	(6)	—	(5)	—	(8)	—
(2) Income Tax Expense	$206	$ 80	$157	$105	$244	$166
Effective Tax Rates: (2) ÷ (1)	34.3%	40.0%	34.9%	42.0%	34.9%	47.4%
Combined Effective Tax Rates........	35.7%		37.4%		39.0%	

3. Shift from domestic to foreign borrowing to increase deductions for interest against foreign-source income.

4. Shift from an equity to debt financing of foreign operations to increase interest deductions against foreign-source income.

The increasing tax rates abroad and an increasing proportion of income derived from abroad suggest a continuing increase in the combined effective tax rate that could hurt future profitability unless the firm takes counter actions.

INCOME TAX DISCLOSURES FOR COKE AND PEPSI

Refer to the income tax disclosures for Coke in Note 15 to its financial statements in Appendix A. The entry to record income tax expense for Year 8 is as follows (amounts in millions):

Income Tax Expense ($1,059 − $62)...................	997	
Deferred Tax Assets ($661 − $538)....................	123	
Deferred Tax Liabilities ($635 − $620)............		15
Income Tax Payable...........................		1,059
Income Tax Expense (Changes in Accounting Principles).................................		8
Income Tax Expense (Other Accounts)............		38

Coke's income tax expense includes taxes currently payable of $1,059 million minus a net $108 million (=$123 − $15) debit change in deferred tax assets and liabilities. Thus, total income tax expense is $951 million (=$1,059 − $108). Coke reports $997 million as related to continuing operations, an $8 million credit related to changes in accounting principles, and $38 million related to other income accounts. The $38 million probably relates to equity in earnings of unconsolidated bottling operations. The relation between income tax expense and income tax payable in the preceding journal entry suggests that Coke's taxable income for Year 8 exceeded book income before taxes. This same relationship occurred in Year 6 and Year 7.

The largest component of deferred tax assets is for benefit plans. A deferred tax asset suggests that Coke recognized expenses for financial reporting that it has not yet recognized for tax reporting. Note 13 indicates that Coke has an accrued pension liability of $160 million (=$17 + $109 − $16 + $50), and Note 14 indicates that Coke has an accrued postretirement benefits liability of $233 million at the end of Year 8. A liability for these employee benefits is consistent with the recognition of expenses earlier than funding. Coke reports a deferred tax asset for benefits of net operating loss carryforwards of certain international subsidiaries but also includes a valuation allowance to reflect the probability of realizing these and other deferred tax assets. Coke shows deferred tax liabilities related to the use of accelerated depreciation for tax purposes and straight-line depreciation for financial reporting. It also reports deferred taxes for the recognition of equity method income for financial reporting earlier than the recognition of dividend revenue for tax purposes from these investments.

The income tax rate changed from 34 percent to 35 percent during Year 8. Coke computed its deferred tax assets and liabilities at the end of Year 8 using this new rate. Thus, the change in the net deferred tax assets includes temporary differences, tax rate changes, and a change in the valuation allowance.

Coke's effective tax rate remained in the range of 31 percent to 32 percent during the three-year period. The tax savings that Coke realizes from operating in certain lower tax rate countries, principally Puerto Rico, largely accounts for an effective tax rate lower than the statutory tax rate.

Refer now to Note 13 to Pepsi's financial statements in Appendix B. The journal entry to record Pepsi's income taxes for Year 8 is as follows:

Income Tax Expense ($751.3 + $83.3)	834.6	
Deferred Tax Assets [($1,289.0 − $249.0) − ($896.5 − $181.3)]	324.8	
Income Tax Expense (Other Accounts)	191.4	
Deferred Tax Liabilities ($2,933 − $2,333.8)		599.5
Income Tax Payable		751.3

Pepsi's income tax expense includes taxes currently payable of $751.3 million plus a net $274.7 million credit change (=$559.5 − $324.8) in deferred tax assets and liabilities. Thus, Pepsi's income before taxes for financial reporting exceeded its taxable income. Pepsi includes $834.6 million of income tax expense in continuing operations and $191.4 million in other accounts.

Pepsi's largest component of deferred tax liabilities relates to intangible assets other than goodwill. Note 7 indicates that Pepsi acquired franchised bottling and restaurant operations and assigned a portion of the purchase price to franchise rights and trademarks. Pepsi amortizes these amounts over a period of 20 to 40 years for financial reporting. The recognition of a deferred tax liability for these items suggests that Pepsi is deducting the cost of these items for tax purposes earlier than for financial reporting.

Pepsi reports a deferred tax asset for postretirement benefits, principally related to the recognition of a liability for health care benefits under FASB *Statement No. 106*. Pepsi shows a valuation allowance for deferred tax assets that exceeds in amount the benefit of net operating loss carryforwards, suggesting uncertainty regarding the realizability of other deferred tax assets.

Pepsi's effective tax rate exceeds that of Coke but is still less than the statutory U.S. federal tax rate of 35 percent. Pepsi derives a higher proportion of its income from within the United States, relative to Coke, and therefore has a larger percentage increase in the effective tax rate for state income taxes. Pepsi, like Coke, operates in certain countries, principally Puerto Rico and Ireland, that have tax rates lower than those in the United States.

IS THE DEFERRED TAX LIABILITY REALLY A LIABILITY?

Considerable controversy has surrounded the accounting for deferred income taxes for decades, particularly with respect to whether the Deferred Income Tax Liability account is a liability. Proponents of the required accounting point out that temporary differences eventually reverse. When they do, taxable income will likely exceed income before taxes for financial reporting, and the firm's cash payment for taxes will exceed income tax expense. Thus, a future cash outflow in the amount of the Deferred Tax Liability will occur.

Opponents point out that, for a growing firm, temporary differences originating in a period exceed temporary differences reversing in the period, so that the Deferred Tax Liability account continually increases. Opponents therefore argue that net timing differences never require future cash flows. They further point out that the Deferred Tax Liability account does not represent a legal obligation of a firm. If the firm files for bankruptcy, it will not owe the amount in the Deferred Tax Liability account to governmental bodies. The firm pays the required taxes to governmental bodies each year based on its taxable income. The amount in the Deferred Tax Liability account arises only because accountants attempt to smooth income tax expense so that it matches income before taxes for financial reporting.

The analyst obtains a more conservative measure of liabilities by leaving the Deferred Income Tax Liability account on the balance sheet as a liability. An alternative approach involves studying the behavior of deferred income taxes during recent years. If the Deferred Tax Liability account has increased continually, the analyst might eliminate it from liabilities and add it to retained earnings. This treatment presumes that the firm should not have provided deferred taxes to begin with. If the Deferred Tax Liability account increases in some years and decreases in other years, the analyst can leave the account among liabilities.

The treatment of deferred taxes assumes even greater importance when comparing U.S. with non-U.S. firms. Firms in France, Germany, and Japan use similar accounting methods for financial and tax reporting so that the issue of deferred tax accounting does not arise. Firms in Great Britain provide deferred taxes for timing differences only when a high probability exists that a liability will become due. Deferred tax accounting in Canada closely mirrors U.S. reporting practices.

UNDERSTANDING RESERVES IN THE FINANCIAL STATEMENTS

Chapters 5 and 6 emphasize two important concepts underlying the financial statements:

1. Income over sufficiently long time periods equals cash inflows minus cash outflows from operating, investing, and financing activities (except dividends and capital transactions).
2. Because accountants prepare financial statements for discrete periods of time shorter than the life of a firm, the recognition of revenues does not necessarily coincide with the receipt of cash, and the recognition of expenses does not necessarily coincide with the disbursement of cash.

Assets such as inventories, investments, property, plant, equipment, and intangibles result from past cash outflows. The costs of these assets become expenses in future periods when the firm uses the services of these assets in operations or through sale. Liabilities, such as salaries payable, interest payable, taxes payable, and pensions payable reflect the cost of services already received by a firm. They generally require a future cash outflow. Thus, most asset and liability accounts result from efforts to match revenues with expenses for discrete periods of time.

Because revenues must ultimately equal the total cash inflows and expenses must ultimately equal the total cash outflows (except for dividends and capital transactions), firms in the long run cannot alter the total *amount* of revenues and expenses. In the short run, however, firms can only estimate ultimate cash flows. In addition, the accountant allocates benefits received in the form of revenues and services consumed in the form of expenses to discrete accounting periods with some imprecision. As Chapter 4 discussed, management may have incentives to shift revenues or expenses between accounting periods to accomplish certain reporting objectives. Audits by the firm's independent accountants, taxing authorities, and government regulators serve as control mechanisms on management's behavior.

The analyst should develop a sensitivity to financial reporting areas for which firms enjoy flexibility in measuring revenues, expenses, assets, and liabilities. The last two chapters discussed reporting areas that allow management to select from among alternative GAAP to influence reported earnings (for example, FIFO versus LIFO). These chapters also discussed reporting areas that require firms to make estimates in applying accounting principles (for example, useful lives for depreciable assets, future salary increases for pensions). Management's latitude for influencing reported earnings correlates directly with the role or significance of estimates in applying accounting principles.

In the United States, all revenues, gains, expenses, and losses eventually flow through the income statement. The analyst can study the time-series pattern of earnings to assess the extent to which firms attempt to shift income through time. In some countries, certain income items do not flow through the income statement but instead increase or decrease a shareholders' equity account directly. In addition, common practice in certain countries permits liberal shifting of income between accounting periods either to minimize income taxes or to smooth earnings. The accounting mechanism used to accomplish these reporting results is called a *reserve*. This section discusses briefly the nature and use of reserves.

NATURE OF A RESERVE ACCOUNT

As the following sections discuss, reserve accounts may appear on the balance sheet as a deduction from an asset, as a liability, or as a component of shareholders' equity. (Thus, reserve accounts always carry a credit balance.) They may appear for a limited period of time or represent a permanent account. Firms may use reserve accounts to shift earnings between periods, or they may not affect earnings in any period. These multiple uses of reserve accounts and the implication that firms have set aside assets equal to the reserve result in considerable confusion among financial statement users. Using the term *reserve* in the title of an account in the United States is generally unacceptable. When firms use an account that functions similar to a reserve, U.S. firms must use more descriptive terminology. Reserve accounts commonly appear in the financial statements of non-U.S. firms. The next section illustrates some of the ways that firms in the United States and other countries use reserve accounts and the issues that these uses raise for analysts.

USES OF RESERVE ACCOUNTS

1. *Matching Expenses with Associated Revenues.* The recognition of an expense during the current period could result in an increase in a reserve account. The reserve account might appear on the balance sheet as a reduction in an asset. For example, firms provide for bad debt expense and increase the account Reserve for Bad Debts (U.S. firms use the account Allowance for Uncollectible Accounts). This reserve account appears as a subtraction from Accounts Receivable on the balance sheet. Likewise, firms recognize depreciation expense and increase the account Reserve for Depreciation (U.S. firms use the account Accumulated Depreciation). The reserve account appears as a reduction from fixed assets on the balance sheet. Alternatively, the reserve account might appear as a liability on the balance sheet. For example, a firm might provide for warranty expense or pension expense and increase the accounts Reserve for Warranties (Estimated Warranty Liability in the United States) or Reserve for Retirement Benefits (Accrued Retirement Liability in the United States). When used properly, these reserve accounts serve the same functions as the corresponding accounts that U.S. firms use: to permit an appropriate matching of revenues and expenses and an appropriate valuation of assets and liabilities. Of course, firms in both the United States and other countries can misuse these accounts (that is, under- or overstating the provisions each year) to shift earnings between periods. In addition to searching for situations in which such shifting has occurred, the analyst's main concern with these reserves is understanding the nature of the reserve account in each case. In the United States, there is usually an analogous account that helps the analyst in this interpretation.

2. *Keeping Expenses out of the Income Statement.* A practice in some countries is to create a reserve account by reducing the Retained Earnings account. For example, a firm might debit Retained Earnings and credit Reserve for Price Increases or Reserve for Contingencies. These accounts appear among the shareholders' equity accounts and may carry a title such as Retained Earnings Appropriated for Price Increases or Retained Earnings Appropriated for Contingencies. When firms later experience the price increase or contingency, they charge the cost against the reserve account rather than include it in expenses. These costs therefore bypass the income statement and usually result in an overstatement of earnings. Note that this use of reserves does not misstate total shareholders' equity because all of the affected accounts (Retained Earnings, reserve accounts, expense accounts) are components of shareholders' equity. Thus, the analyst's primary concern with these reserves is interpreting net income as a measure of operating performance. The analyst can study the shareholders' equity portion of the balance sheet to ascertain whether firms have used reserve accounts to avoid sending legitimate expenses through the income statement.

3. *Revaluing Assets but Delaying Income Recognition Effect.* Firms might use reserves in situations when they revalue assets but do not desire the income effect of the revaluation to affect income of the current period. Chapter 7 points out that firms in the United States account for investments in equity securities using the market value method. When market value differs from

acquisition costs, U.S. firms write up or write down the investment account. GAAP in the United States does not generally permit the immediate recognition of this increase or decrease in market value in measuring income (except for securities held for trading purposes; see the discussion in Chapter 7). Instead, these firms increase or decrease an account titled Unrealized Gain or Loss in Market Value of Investments and include it as an element among shareholders' equity accounts. When the firm sells the securities, it eliminates the unrealized gain or loss account and recognizes a realized gain or loss in measuring net income. Another example of this use of the reserve account relates to foreign currency translation (discussed in Chapter 7). U.S. firms with foreign operations usually translate the financial statements of their foreign entities into U.S. dollars each period using the exchange rate at the end of the period. Changes in the exchange rate cause an unrealized foreign currency gain or loss. Firms do not recognize this gain or loss in measuring income each period but instead use a shareholders' equity account titled Unrealized Foreign Currency Adjustment (see the balance sheets of Coke and Pepsi in Appendix A and B, respectively). When the firm disposes of the foreign unit, it eliminates the unrealized foreign currency adjustment account and recognizes a gain or loss on disposal. U.S. firms could use titles such as Reserve for Price Declines in Investments or Reserves for Foreign Currency Gains and Losses, as is common practice in some countries, but U.S. GAAP requires a more descriptive title.

GAAP in the United Kingdom permits periodic revaluations of fixed assets and intangible assets to their current market value. The increased valuation of assets that usually occurs leads to an increase in a revaluation reserve account included in the shareholders' equity section of the balance sheet. Depreciation or amortization of the revalued assets may appear fully on the income statement each period as an expense or split between the income statement (depreciation or amortization based on acquisition cost) and a reduction in the revaluation reserve (depreciation or amortization based on the excess of current market value over acquisition cost).

The analyst's concern with this type of reserve is the appropriateness of revaluing the asset and delaying the recognition of its income effect. Note that total shareholders' equity is the same regardless of whether the unrealized gain or loss immediately affects net income or whether it affects another shareholders' equity account and later affects net income. This use of reserves does affect net income of the current period. The analyst may wish to restate reported net income of the current period to incorporate changes in these reserves.

4. *Permanently Reclassifying Retained Earnings.* Local laws or practices may dictate that firms transfer an amount from retained earnings, which is available for dividends, to a more permanent account, which is not available for dividends. U.S. firms typically "capitalize" a portion of retained earnings when they issue a stock dividend. Several other countries require firms to report a certain amount of legal capital on the balance sheet. Such firms reduce retained earnings and increase an account titled Legal Capital or Legal Reserve. The implication of such disclosures is that assets equal to the amount of this legal capital are not available for dividends. This use of reserves has no effect on net income of the current or future periods.

The quality of disclosures regarding reserves varies considerably across countries. Analysts often encounter difficulties attempting to understand, much less adjust for, the effect of changes in reserves. An awareness of the ways that firms might use reserve accounts should help the analyst know the kinds of questions to raise when studying the financial statements. Until greater standardization occurs across countries in the use of reserves, the analyst must recognize the lack of comparability of net income and balance sheet amounts and perhaps the increased importance of a statement of cash flows.

SUMMARY

This chapter explored various reporting areas in which expense measurement and liability recognition interact. These reporting areas therefore affect both profitability analysis and risk analysis. The desire of many firms to keep debt off the balance sheet, with the hope of lowering their cost of financing, should put the analyst on guard for the existence of unreported liabilities. The lack of physical existence of liabilities (unlike most assets) increases the difficulty experienced by both the independent auditor and the analyst in identifying the existence of unreported liabilities. This chapter described some of the areas that the analyst should consider when engaging in this search.

PROBLEMS

6.1 ACHIEVING OFF-BALANCE-SHEET FINANCING (ADAPTED FROM MATERIALS BY R. DIETER, D. LANDSITTEL, J. STEWART, AND A. WYATT). Brion Company wishes to raise $50 million cash but, for various reasons, does not wish to do so in a way that results in a newly recorded liability. Brion is sufficiently solvent and profitable that its bank is willing to lend up to $50 million at the prime interest rate. Brion's financial executives have devised six different plans, described in the following sections.

Transfer of Receivables with Recourse. Brion will transfer to Credit Company its long-term accounts receivable, which call for payments over the next two years. Credit Company will pay an amount equal to the present value of the receivables less an allowance for uncollectibles as well as a discount because it is paying now but will collect cash later. Brion must repurchase from Credit Company at face value any receivables that become uncollectible in excess of the allowance. In addition, Brion may repurchase any of the receivables not yet due at face value less a discount specified by formula and based on the prime rate at the time of the initial transfer. (This option permits Brion to benefit if an unexpected drop in interest rates occurs after the transfer.) The accounting issue is whether the transfer is a sale (in which case Brion increases Cash, reduces Accounts Receivable, and recognizes expense or loss on transfer) or whether the transfer is merely a loan collateralized by the receivables (in which case Brion increases Cash and increases Notes Payable at the time of transfer).

Product Financing Arrangement. Brion will transfer inventory to Credit Company, which will store the inventory in a public warehouse. Credit Company may use the inventory as collateral for its own borrowings, whose proceeds will be used to pay Brion. Brion will pay storage costs and will repurchase all the inventory within the next four years at contractually fixed prices plus interest accrued for the time elapsed between the transfer and later repurchase. The accounting issue is whether the inventory is sold to Credit Company, with later repurchases treated as new acquisitions for Brion's inventory, or whether the transaction is merely a loan, with the inventory remaining on Brion's balance sheet.

Throughput Contract.   Brion wants a branch line of a railroad built from the main rail line to carry raw material directly to its own plant. It could, of course, borrow the funds and build the branch line itself. Instead, it will sign an agreement with the railroad to ship specified amounts of material each month for 10 years. Even if it does not ship the specified amounts of material, it will pay the agreed shipping costs. The railroad will take the contract to its bank and, using it as collateral, borrow the funds to build the branch line. The accounting issue is whether Brion would increase an asset for future rail services and increase a liability for payments to the railroad. The alternative is to make no accounting entry except when Brion makes payments to the railroad.

Construction Partnership.   Brion and Mission Company will jointly build a plant to manufacture chemicals both need in their own production processes. Each will contribute $5 million to the project called Chemical. Chemical will borrow another $40 million from a bank, with Brion only guaranteeing the debt. Brion and Mission are each to contribute equally to future operating expenses and debt service payments of Chemical, but, in return for its guaranteeing the debt, Brion will have an option to purchase Mission's interest for $20 million four years hence. The accounting issue is whether Brion should recognize a liability for the funds borrowed by Chemical. Because of the debt guarantee, debt service payments will ultimately be Brion's responsibility. Alternatively, the debt guarantee is a commitment merely to be disclosed in notes to Brion's financial statements.

Research and Development Partnership.   Brion will contribute a laboratory and preliminary finding about a potentially profitable gene-splicing discovery to a partnership called Venture. Venture will raise funds by selling the remaining interest in the partnership to outside investors for $2 million and borrowing $48 million from a bank with Brion guaranteeing the debt. Although Venture will operate under Brion's management, it will be free to sell the results of its future discoveries and development efforts to anyone, including Brion. Brion is not obligated to purchase any of Venture's output. The accounting issue is whether Brion would recognize the liability. (Would it make any difference if Brion has either the *option* to purchase or an *obligation* to purchase the results of Venture's work?)

Hotel Financing.   Brion owns and operates a profitable hotel. It could use the hotel as collateral for a conventional mortgage loan. Instead, it considers selling the hotel to a partnership for $50 million cash. The partnership will sell ownership interests to outside investors for $5 million and borrow $45 million from a bank on a conventional mortgage loan, using the hotel as collateral. Brion guarantees the debt. The accounting issue is whether Brion would record the liability for the guaranteed debt of the partnership.

REQUIRED

Discuss the appropriate treatment of each of these proposed arrangements from the viewpoint of the auditor (who must decide whether the transaction will result in a liability to be recorded or whether footnote disclosure will suffice) and from the viewpoint of an investment banker (who must assess the financing structure of Brion in order to make a competitive bid on a proposed new underwriting of Brion company's common shares).

6.2 Accounting for Attempted Off-Balance-Sheet Financing Arrangements

a. International Paper Company (IP) needs $100 million of additional financing but, because of restrictions in existing debt convenants, cannot place any more debt on its balance sheet. To obtain the needed funds, it plans to transfer cutting rights to a mature timber tract to a newly created trust as of January 1, Year 8. The trust will use the cutting rights to obtain a $100 million, five-year, 10 percent interest rate bank loan due in five equal installments with interest on December 31 of each year.

The timber will be harvested each year and sold to obtain funds to service the loan and pay operating costs. Based on current prices, 10 percent more standing wood is available for cutting than should be needed to service the loan and pay ongoing operating costs of the tract (including wind, fire, and erosion insurance). If the selling price of timber decreases in the future, the volume of timber harvested will be increased sufficiently to service the debt. If the selling price of timber increases in the future, the volume harvested will remain as originally anticipated but any cash left over after debt service and coverage of operating costs will be invested by the trust to provide a cushion for possible future price decreases. The value of any cash or uncut timber at the end of five years will revert to IP. IP will not guarantee the debt. The bank, however, has the right to inspect the tract at any time and to replace IP's forest management personnel with managers of its own choosing if it believes the tract is being mismanaged.

REQUIRED

Discuss the appropriate accounting for this transaction by IP in light of other FASB pronouncements on off-balance-sheet financing.

b. On June 24, Year 4, Delta Airlines entered into a revolving accounts receivable facility (Facility) providing for the sale of $489 million of a defined pool of accounts receivable (Receivables) through a wholly owned subsidiary to a trust in exchange for a senior certificate in the principal amount of $300 million (Senior Certificate) and a subordinate certificate in the principal amount of $189 million (Subordinate Certificate). The subsidiary retained the Subordinate Certificate and the company received $300 million in cash from the sale of the Senior Certificate to a third party. The principal amount of the Subordinate Certificate fluctuates daily, depending on the volume of Receivables sold, and is payable to the subsidiary only to the extent that the collections received on the Receivables exceed amounts due on the Senior Certificate. The full amount of the allowance for doubtful accounts related to the Receivables sold has been retained, as the company has substantially the same credit risk as if the Receivables had not been sold. Under the terms of the Facility, the company is obligated to pay fees that approximate the purchaser's cost of issuing a like amount of commercial paper plus certain administrative costs.

REQUIRED

Delta requests your advice on the appropriate accounting for this transaction. How would you respond?

c. In Year 2, a wholly owned subsidiary of the Sun Company became a one-third partner in Belvieu Environmental Fuels (BEF), a joint venture formed for the purpose of constructing, owning, and operating a $220 million methyl tertiary butyl ether (MTBE) production facility in Mont Belvieu, Texas. As of December 31, Year 3, BEF had borrowed $128 million against a construction loan facility of which Sun guarantees one-third, or $43 million. The plant, which has a designed capacity of 12,600 barrels daily of MTBE, is expected to begin production in mid-Year 4. When production commences, the construction loan will be converted into a five-year, nonrecourse term loan with a first priority lien on all project assets.

To obtain a secure supply of oxygenates for the manufacture of reformulated fuels, Sun has entered into a 10-year take-or-pay agreement with BEF, which commences when the plant becomes operational. Pursuant to this agreement, Sun will purchase all of the MTBE production from the plant. The minimum per unit price to be paid for the MTBE production while the nonrecourse term loan is outstanding will equal BEF's annual raw material and operating costs and debt service payments divided by the plant's annual designed capacity. Notwithstanding this minimum price, Sun has agreed to pay BEF a price during the first three years of the off-take agreement, which approximates prices included in current MTBE long-term sales agreements in the marketplace. This price is expected to exceed the minimum price required by the loan agreement. Sun will negotiate a new pricing arrangement with BEF for the remaining years that the take-or-pay agreement is in effect, which will be based on the expected market conditions existing at such time.

REQUIRED

How should Sun account for this transaction?

6.3 ACCOUNTING FOR A LEASE BY THE LESSOR AND THE LESSEE. Delta Airlines needs to acquire computer equipment from Hewlett-Packard (HP) as of January 1, Year 4. Delta can borrow the necessary funds to purchase the computer for $2,000,000. Delta desires to keep debt off of its balance sheet, however, and wishes to structure an operating lease with HP. The computer has an estimated life to HP of eight years. Delta will lease the computer for five years, at which time the computer reverts back to HP. The cost to HP to manufacture the computer is $1,600,000. Delta's borrowing rate for five-year, secured financing is 10 percent.

REQUIRED

a. Assume that Delta must make rental payments on December 31 of Year 4 through December 31 of Year 8. What is the maximum annual rental (to the nearest dollar) that Delta can make and still permit this lease to qualify as an operating lease?

b. Assume that Delta must make rental payments on January 1, Year 4, through January 1, Year 8. What is the maximum annual rental (to the nearest dollar) that Delta can make and still permit this lease to qualify as an operating lease?

c. Assume for the remaining parts of this problem that Delta will make annual payments of $527,595 on December 31, Year 4, through December 31, Year 8. Indicate the nature and amount of revenues and expenses (excluding income taxes), that each company would report for each of the Years 4 through 8, assuming that they accounted for the lease as an operating lease.

d. Repeat part (c), assuming that each company accounted for the lease as a capital lease.

e. Assume that these firms treat the lease as a capital lease for financial reporting and as an operating lease for tax reporting. Compute the amount of deferred tax asset or deferred tax liability each firm would report related to the lease on December 31, Year 4, through December 31, Year 8. The income tax rate is 35 percent.

6.4 ACCOUNTING FOR CAPITAL LEASES. Wal-Mart leases most of its office, warehouse, and retail space under a combination of capital and operating leases. The disclosures related to *capital leases* for its fiscal year ending January 31, Year 7, appear below (amounts in millions):

	January 31	
	Year 6	Year 7
Property, Plant, and Equipment under Capital Leases........	$1,724	$1,986
Less Accumulated Depreciation.........................	(369)	(448)
Net Property, Plant, and Equipment under Capital Leases	$1,355	$1,538
Capitalized Lease Obligation	$1,591	$1,818

Fully depreciated leased assets originally capitalized for $24 million were written off during fiscal Year 7. The weighted average discount rate used to compute the present value of the capitalized lease obligation was 11 percent. Assume that new leases capitalized and lease payments occur evenly throughout the year.

REQUIRED

a. Prepare an analysis that explains the change in the following accounts during the Year 7 fiscal year.
   (1) Property, Plant, and Equipment under Capital Leases.
   (2) Accumulated Depreciation.
   (3) Capitalized Lease Obligation.
b. Assume that Wal-Mart treats these capitalized leases as operating leases for income tax purposes. The income tax rate is 35 percent. Compute the total amount of pretax expenses related to these leased assets for financial and tax reporting for the Year 7 fiscal year.
c. Compute the amount of deferred tax asset and/or deferred tax liability that Wal-Mart would report on its January 31, Year 7, balance sheet related to these leases.

6.5 EFFECT OF CAPITALIZING OPERATING LEASES ON BALANCE SHEET RATIOS. Some retailing companies own their own stores or acquire their premises under capital leases. Other retailing companies acquire the use of store facilities under operating leases, contracting to make future payments. An analyst comparing the capital structure risks of retailing companies may wish to make adjustments to reported financial statement data to put all firms on a comparable basis.

Certain data from the financial statements of The Gap and The Limited appear here (amounts in millions):

	The Gap	Limited
Balance Sheet as of End of Year 3		
Current Liabilities............................	$ 462	$ 707
Long-Term Debt	75	650
Other Noncurrent Liabilities	99	336
Shareholders' Equity........................	1,127	2,442
Total	$1,763	$4,135
Minimum Payments under Operating Leases		
Year 4	$ 233	$ 568
Year 5	235	559
Year 6	234	542
Year 7	227	523
Year 8	218	504
After Year 8	2,231	2,695
Total	$3,378	$5,391

REQUIRED

a. Compute the present value of operating lease obligations using a 10 percent discount rate for The Gap and The Limited at the end of Year 3. Assume that all cash flows occur at the end of each year.

b. Compute each of the following ratios for The Gap and The Limited as of the end of Year 3 using the amounts as originally reported in their balance sheets for the year.

Liabilities to Assets Ratio = Total Liabilities/Total Assets

Long-Term Debt Ratio = Long-Term Debt/(Long-Term Debt + Shareholders' Equity)

c. Repeat part (*b*) but assume that these firms capitalize operating leases.

d. Comment on the results from parts (*b*) and (*c*).

6.6 FINANCIAL STATEMENT EFFECTS OF CAPITAL AND OPERATING LEASES. Delta Airlines leases aircraft used in its operations. Information taken from its financial statements and notes for Year 3 and Year 4 appear below (amounts in millions).

Balance Sheet	December 31, Year 3	December 31, Year 4
Property Rights under Capital leases (net of accumulated depreciation)	$ 45	$31
Capitalized Lease Obligation	$109	$97

NOTES TO THE FINANCIAL STATEMENTS

Leases. Minimum lease payments under *capital leases* as of December 31, Year 3 and Year 4, are (assume all cash flows occur at the end of each year):

	December 31, Year 3	December 31, Year 4
Lease Payments on December 31 of		
Year 4	$ 21	$ —
Year 5	18	18
Year 6	18	18
Year 7	18	18
Year 8	15	15
After Year 8	58	58
Total	$148	$127
Less Discount	(39)	(30)
Present Value...................	$109	$ 97

Minimum lease payments under *operating leases* as of December 31, Year 3 and Year 4, appear below:

	December 31, Year 3	December 31, Year 4
Lease Payment on December 31 of		
Year 4	$ 905	—
Year 5	916	$ 952
Year 6	941	965
Year 7	940	961
Year 8	923	940
After Year 8	13,202	13,558
Total	$17,827	$17,376

REQUIRED

a. Complete the following analyses relating to capital leases for Year 4:

Property Rights under Capital Leases, December 31, Year 3	
New Capital Leases Entered into during Year 4....................	
Amortization of Property Rights for Year 4.......................	
Property Rights under Capital Leases, December 31, Year 4	
Capitalized Lease Obligation, December 31, Year 3..................	
Increase in Capitalized Lease Obligation for Interest during Year 4 ...	
New Capitalized Lease Obligations Entered into during Year 4.......	
Cash Payments under Capital Leases during Year 4	
Capitalized Lease Obligation, December 31, Year 4.................	

b. Compute the average interest rate for leases capitalized as of December 31, Year 4.

c. Determine the amount that Delta would have reported as rent expense for Year 4 if it had treated all capital leases as operating leases.

    d.   Determine the amount reported as rent expense for Year 4 for all operating leases.

    e.   Compute the present value of commitments under operating leases on December 31, Year 3 and Year 4, assuming that 10 percent is an appropriate discount rate.

    f.   Assume that Delta had capitalized all operating leases using the amounts computed in part (*e*). Complete the following analysis for year 4:

Capitalized Value of Operating Leases, December 31, Year 3 . . . .

Increase in Capitalized Value for Interest during Year 4 . . . .

New Operating Leases Capitalized during Year 4 . . . .

Cash Payments under Capitalized Operating Leases during Year 4 . . . .   _____

Capitalized Value of Operating Leases, December 31, Year 4 . . . .   ========

---

    g.   Delta Airlines treats *all* of its leases as operating leases for tax purposes. The income tax rate is 35 percent, and Delta expects this rate to continue into the foreseeable future. Compute the amount of deferred tax asset or liability that Delta will recognize at the end of Year 3 and the end of Year 4. Indicate whether the change in the deferred tax asset or liability during Year 4 increases or decreases income tax expense for the year.

6.7   ANALYZING PENSION AND POSTRETIREMENT BENEFIT DISCLOSURES. Exhibit 6.12 presents pension plan disclosures for Scott Paper Company (Scott). Exhibit 6.13 presents similar information for its postretirements (health-care) benefits plan.

REQUIRED

    a.   Complete the following analysis of the pension plan for Year 7:

Pension Fund Assets, Beginning of Year 7 . . . .

Plus Earnings on Pension Fund Investments during Year 7 . . . .

Plus Contributions Received from Scott during Year 7 . . . .

Less Pension Payments to Retirees during Year 7 . . . .   _____

Pension Fund Assets, End of Year 7 . . . .   ========

Projected Benefit Obligation, Beginning of Year 7 . . . .

Plus Service Cost for Year 7 . . . .

Plus Interest Cost for Year 7 . . . .

Less Pension Payments to Retirees during Year 7 . . . .

Plus (Minus) Actuarial Loss (Gain) for Year 7 . . . .   _____

Projected Benefit Obligation, End of Year 7 . . . .   ========

---

    b.   Did the return on pension fund investments exceed or fall short of expectations during Year 6 and Year 7? Explain.

    c.   What is the likely reason for the actuarial gain or loss during Year 7?

    d.   Give the journal entry that the analyst would make to recognize the underfunded projected benefit obligation at the end of Year 6 and Year 7. The income tax rate is 35 percent.

    e.   Complete the following analysis of the postretirement benefits plan for Year 7:

EXHIBIT 6.12

Scott Paper Company
Pension Disclosures
(amounts in millions)
(Problem 6.7)

	Year 6	Year 7
Net Pension Expense		
Service Cost..	$ 33.3	$ 33.8
Interest Cost..	108.9	111.3
Earnings on Pension Investments		
Actual..	(68.9)	(242.1)
Deferral of Difference between Actual and Expected Return..........	(52.0)	120.3
Amortization of Items Not Previously Recognized		
Net Transition Asset..	(5.6)	(5.4)
Prior Service Cost..	5.8	8.2
Net Actuarial and Investment Losses...........................	1.0	1.3
Net Pension Expense..	$ 22.5	$ 27.4
Status of Pension Plan		
Accumulated Benefit Obligation.....................................	$ 1,222.9	$ 1,394.7
Effect of Salary Increases..	174.1	166.5
Projected Benefit Obligation..	$ 1,397.0	$ 1,561.2
Fair Value of Plan Assets...	(1,181.1)	(1,360.1)
Underfunded Projected Benefit Obligation...........................	$ 215.9	$ 201.1
Unamortized Net Transition Asset...................................	49.4	43.5
Unamortized Prior Service Cost.....................................	(45.1)	(44.4)
Unamortized Net Actuarial and Investment Losses....................	(135.2)	(132.7)
Adjustment for Minimum Liability...................................	46.4	61.8
Accrued Pension Liability on Balance Sheet..........................	$ 131.4	$ 129.3
Actuarial Assumptions		
Expected Return on Plan Assets.....................................	10.5%	10.5%
Discount Rate..	8.2%	7.1%
Rate of Compensation Increases.....................................	5.6%	4.6%

Accumulated Benefit Obligation, Beginning of Year 7................	
Plus Service Cost for Year 7.......................................	
Plus Interest Cost for Year 7......................................	
Less Health-Care Premiums Paid during Year 7.....................	
Plus (Minus) Increase (Decrease) in Transition Obligation during	
Year 7...	
Plus (Minus) Actuarial Loss (Gain) for Year 7.....................	_____
Accumulated Benefit Obligation, End of Year 7....................	========

f. What is the likely reason for the actuarial loss during Year 7?

g. What is the likely reason for the change in the transition obligation during Year 7?

EXHIBIT 6.13		

Scott Paper Company
Postretirement Benefit Disclosures
(amounts in millions)
(Problem 6.7)

	Year 6	Year 7
Net Postretirement Benefits Expense		
Service Cost..................................	$ 8.2	$ 9.3
Interest Cost.................................	23.2	23.5
Amortization of Items Not Previously Recognized		
Transition Obligation.........................	18.4	17.1
Net Actuarial Losses.........................	—	.8
Net Postretirement Benefits Expense	$ 49.8	$ 50.7
Status of Postretirement Benefits Plan		
Accumulated Benefit Obligation	$ 313.0	$ 329.5
Unrecognized Transition Obligation	(263.7)	(224.1)
Unrecognized Actuarial Loss.....................	(4.8)	(27.3)
Accrued Postretirement Benefits Liability	$ 44.5	$ 78.1
Actuarial Assumptions		
Discount Rate	8.0%	7.0%
Health-Care Cost Trend Rate	12.4%	10.9%

h. Give the journal entry that the analyst would make to recognize the underfunded postretirement benefits obligation at the end of Year 6 and Year 7. The income tax rate is 35 percent.

i. The projected benefit obligation of the pension plan ($1,397 million at the end of Year 6 and $1,561.2 million at the end of Year 7) exceeds the accumulated benefit obligation for postretirement benefits ($313 million at the end of Year 6 and $329.5 million at the end of Year 7). Pension expense of $27.4 million for Year 7, however, is less than postretirement benefits expense of $50.7 million for Year 7. Explain this apparent paradox.

6.8 ANALYZING PENSION DISCLOSURES. The note on pensions for Westinghouse for Year 9 appears in Exhibit 6.14. Westinghouse used a 9 percent discount rate and a 6 percent rate of increase in future compensation levels to compute the projected benefit obligation and an 11 percent expected long-term rate of return on assets for all three years. The income tax rate was 35 percent.

REQUIRED

a. Complete the following analysis of changes in the Accrued Pension Asset (Liability) account on the books of Westinghouse for Year 9.

Accrued Pension Asset on Balance Sheet, Beginning of Year 9 ....
Minus Pension Expense for Year 9................................
Plus Pension Contribution for Year 9.............................
Minus Increase in Adjustment to Recognize Minimum Liability
during Year 9...
Accrued Pension Liability on Balance Sheet, End of Year 9 ....

EXHIBIT 6.14

Westinghouse
Pension Disclosures
(amounts in millions)
(Problem 6.8)

	Year 7	Year 8	Year 9
Net Periodic Cost			
Service Cost.............................	$ 65	$ 65	$ 68
Interest Cost.............................	438	436	432
Amortization of			
Unrecognized Net Obligation	44	48	44
Unrecognized Prior Service Cost	11	8	6
Unrecognized Net Loss	—	3	19
	$ 558	$ 560	$ 569
Return on Plan Assets			
Actual Return	$ 53	$(699)	$(107)
Unrecognized Return on Plan Assets.......	(525)	216	(376)
Recognized Return on Plan Assets.........	$(472)	$(483)	$(483)
Net Periodic Pension Cost	$ 86	$ 77	$ 86

	Year 8	Year 9
Funded Status of Pension Plan		
Accumulated Benefit Obligation	$ 4,774	$ 4,568
Effect of Projected Compensation Levels.................	324	389
Projected Benefit Obligation	$ 5,098	$ 4,957
Plan Assets at Fair Value	(4,856)	(4,265)
Projected Benefits Obligation in Excess of Plan Assets	$ 242	$ 692
Unrecognized Transition Obligation	(385)	(341)
Unrecognized Prior Service Cost	(13)	(7)
Unrecognized Net Loss	(708)	(1,140)
Adjustment to Recognize Minimum Liability	—	1,099
Accrued Pension (Asset) Liability on Balance Sheet	$ (864)	$ 303

b. Complete the following analysis of changes in pension fund assets during Year 9.

Pension Fund Assets, Beginning of Year 9	
Plus Earnings on Pension Fund Investments during Year 9	
Plus Contributions Received from Westinghouse during Year 9	
Less Pension Payments to Retirees during Year 9	_____
Pension Fund Assets, End of Year 9.............................	======

c. Complete the following analysis of changes in the projected benefit obligation of the pension plan during Year 9.

Projected Benefit Obligation, Beginning of Year 9 . . . .
Plus Service Cost for Year 9 . . . .
Plus Interest Cost for Year 9 . . . .
Less Pension Payments to Retirees during Year 9 . . . .
Plus (Minus) Actuarial Loss (Gain) for Year 9 . . . .   _____
Projected Benefit Obligation, End of Year 9 . . . .   =======

---

d. Complete the analysis below of changes in the unrecognized net loss during Year 9.

Unrecognized Net Loss, Beginning of Year 9 . . . .
Plus (Minus) Actuarial Loss (Gain) during Year 9 . . . .
Plus (Minus) Unrecognized Deficient (Excess) Returns on Plan
    Assets during Year 9 . . . .
Less Amortization of Unrecognized Net Loss during Year 9 . . . .   _____
Unrecognized Net Loss, End of Year 9 . . . .   =======

---

e. Did Westinghouse sweeten its pension plan during Year 9 and make the benefits retroactive? Explain.
f. What is the likely reason for the increase in the unrecognized net loss from $708 million at the end of Year 8 to $1,140 million at the end of Year 9?
g. Suggest two reasons for the decrease in the accumulated and projected benefit obligations during Year 9.
h. Give the journal entry that you would make as an analyst to recognize the underfunded projected benefit obligation at the end of Year 8. The income tax rate is 35 percent.
i. Repeat part (*a*) for Year 9.

6.9 INTERPRETING PENSION DISCLOSURES. Exhibit 6.15 reveals information with respect to Chrysler Corporation's pension plan. Chrysler contributed $3,530 million to its pension fund during Year 7.

REQUIRED

a. Complete the following analysis of changes in pension fund assets during Year 7.

Pension Fund Assets, Beginning of Year 7 . . . .
Plus Earnings on Pension Fund Investments . . . .
Plus Contributions Received from Chrysler . . . .
Less Pension Payments to Retirees. . . . .   _____
Pension Fund Assets, End of Year 7. . . . .   =======

---

b. Complete the following analysis of changes in the projected benefit obligation during Year 7.

EXHIBIT 6.15

Chrysler Corporation
Pension Disclosures
(amounts in millions)
(Problem 6.9)

	Year 6	Year 7
Components of Pension Expense		
Service Cost.....................................	$ 189	$ 238
Interest Cost.....................................	813	858
Return on Plan Assets		
Actual Return	(865)	(1,318)
Deferred Gain	336	577
Expected Return on Plan Assets....................	(473)	(355)
Net Amortization.................................	364	401
Total	$ 837	$ 756
Actuarial Assumptions		
Discount Rate	8.38%	7.38%
Rate of Increase in Compensation	6.00%	6.00%
Long-Term Rate of Return on Plan Assets	10.00%	10.00%
Funded Status of Pension Plan		
Accumulated Benefit Obligation	$10,088	$12,368
Effect of Salary Increases	211	262
Projected Benefit Obligation	$10,299	$12,630
Plan Assets at Market Value	6,441	10,428
Projected Benefit Obligation in Excess of Plan Assets ...	$ 3,858	$ 2,202
Unrecognized Net Loss	(1,128)	(1,714)
Unrecognized Prior Service Cost	(1,029)	(1,707)
Unamortized Net Obligation at Date of Adoption	(1,293)	(1,147)
Adjustment to Recognize Minimum Liability	3,373	3,089
Net Pension Liability on Balance Sheet	$ 3,781	$ 723

Projected Benefit Obligation, Beginning of Year 7	
Plus Service Cost for Year 7	
Plus Interest Cost for Year 7	
Minus Pension Payments to Retirees for Year 7	
Plus (Minus) Actuarial Loss (Gain) for Year 7	
Projected Benefit Obligation, End of Year 7	

c. Complete the following analysis of changes in the unrecognized net loss, unrecognized prior service cost, and unamortized net obligation at date of adoption.

Unrecognized Net Loss, Prior Service Cost and Net Obligation at Beginning of Year 7	
Plus (Minus) Actuarial Gain (Loss) for Year 7	
Plus (Minus) Deferred Loss (Gain) from Pension Fund Investments for Year 7	
Minus Net Amortization for Year 7 Included in Pension Expense.....	———
Unrecognized Net Loss, Prior Service Cost and Net Obligation at End of Year 7	═══

d. Prepare an analysis that explains the change in the net pension liability on the balance sheet of Chrysler between the beginning and end of Year 7.

e. What is the likely reason for the decrease in pension expense between Year 6 and Year 7?

f. What is the likely reason for the change in the unrecognized net loss between Year 6 and Year 7?

g. What is the likely reason for the change in the unrecognized prior service cost between Year 6 and Year 7?

h. Give the journal entry that the analyst would make to recognize the underfunded pension obligation on December 31, Year 7. The income tax rate is 35 percent.

6.10 INTERPRETING POSTRETIREMENT BENEFITS DISCLOSURES. The notes to the financial statements of Chrysler Corporation reveal the following information with respect to its postretirement benefit plan (amounts in millions):

	Year 7
Components of Postretirement Benefits Expense	
Benefits Attributed to Employees' Service	$142
Interest on Accumulated Postretirement Benefit Obligation	626
Total	$768

	Year 6	Year 7
Discount Rate	8.6%	7.5%
Average Health-Care Inflation Rate	6.3%	6.3%
Accumulated Postretirement Benefits Obligation	$7,645	$9,111
Assets in Postretirement Benefit Fund	—	—
Net Obligation	$7,645	$9,111
Unrecognized Net Loss	—	(1,126)
Postretirement Benefit Obligation Recognized in Balance Sheet	$7,645	$7,985

Chrysler adopted the provisions of *Statement No. 106* at the end of Year 6.

REQUIRED

a. Give the journal entry that Chrysler made at the end of Year 6 to adopt *Statement No. 106*. The income tax rate is 35 percent.

b. Give the journal entry that Chrysler made to recognize postretirement benefits expense and funding during Year 7. Be sure to consider any deferred tax effect.

c. What is the likely reason for the increase in the unrecognized net loss during Year 7?

d. Why does Chrysler not include in postretirement benefits expense for Year 7 a reduction for the expected return on assets and an increase for amortization of the net loss?

e. Give the journal entry that the analyst would make at the end of Year 7 to recognize any unrecognized postretirement benefit obligations.

6.11 INTERPRETING INCOME TAX DISCLOSURES. Exhibit 6.16 presents information from the income tax note of Borden, Inc., for Year 5.

EXHIBIT 6.16

Borden, Inc.
Income Tax Disclosures
(amounts in millions)
(Problem 6.11)

	Year 4	Year 5
Income Tax Expense		
Current...	$ 58.8	$ (1.9)
Deferred.......................................	(89.7)	(208.9)
Income Tax Expense (credit).........................	$ (30.9)	$(210.8)
Income Tax Reconciliation		
Income Taxes at Statutory Rate of 35%................	$ (52.8)	$(280.0)
State and Local Taxes (net of Federal tax benefit).......	(2.2)	(22.6)
Foreign Tax Differentials............................	1.7	0.1
Capital Loss Benefit................................	(17.9)	—
Restructuring Programs.............................	40.0	4.3
Loss on Disposal of Discontinued Operation...........	—	81.3
Other (net)..	0.3	6.1
	$ (30.9)	$(210.8)
Component of Deferred Tax Assets		
Postemployment Benefits Other than Pensions..........	118.4	131.7
Restructuring Programs.............................	113.8	140.1
Loss Carryforwards................................	42.9	108.6
Divestiture Reserve................................	—	147.4
Other...	95.7	130.7
	370.8	658.5
Valuation Reserve..................................	(42.9)	(58.7)
Deferred Tax Asset.................................	$327.9	$ 599.8
Components of Deferred Tax Liabilities		
Property, Plant, and Equipment.....................	$212.5	$ 236.5
Pension Contributions..............................	22.9	26.5
Deferred Charges..................................	50.8	52.4
Other...	67.2	62.1
Deferred Tax Liability..............................	$353.4	$ 377.5

REQUIRED

a. Was taxable income greater or less than book income before taxes for Year 4? Explain.

b. Was taxable income greater or less than book income before taxes for Year 5? Explain.

c. Compute the amount of state and local income tax expense (credit) for Year 5?

d. What is the likely reason that amounts for restructuring programs appear in both the income tax reconciliation and in deferred tax assets?

e. Was postemployment benefits expense (other than pensions) greater or less than the contribution to this benefits fund during Year 5? Explain.

f. Depreciation expense for financial reporting was $224 million during Year 5. Compute the amount of depreciation expense for tax reporting.

g. Has Borden's funding of its pension plan been faster or slower than its recognition of pension expense? Explain.

6.12 ANALYZING INCOME TAX DISCLOSURES. Exhibit 6.17 presents information from the income tax notes of TRW, Inc., for Year 6.

REQUIRED

a. Give the journal entry to record income tax expense for Year 5.

b. Was taxable income greater or less than book income before income taxes for Year 5? Explain.

c. Why is there a positive amount for income tax expense for Year 5 if earnings before income taxes is negative for the year?

d. Give the journal entry to record income tax expense for Year 6.

e. Was taxable income greater or less than book income before income taxes for Year 6? Explain.

f. Why do restructuring charges appear in both the income tax reconciliation and in deferred tax assets?

g. What is the likely reason for the change in the deferred tax asset for postretirement benefits other than pensions?

h. What is the likely reason for the change in deferred taxes related to pensions from a deferred tax asset at the end of Year 4 to a deferred tax liability at the end of Year 5?

i. What is the likely reason for the valuation allowance related to deferred tax assets?

j. What is the likely explanation for the behavior of the deferred tax liability related to depreciation?

6.13 ANALYZING INCOME TAX DISCLOSURES. Exhibit 6.18 presents income tax disclosures for Sun Company for Year 12 and Year 13.

REQUIRED

a. Give the journal entry to record the provision for income taxes for Year 12. Use a single deferred tax asset or deferred tax liability account.

b. What is the relation between the amount of income before taxes for financial reporting and taxable income for Year 12?

c. Give the journal entry to record the provision for income taxes for Year 13. Use separate deferred tax asset and deferred tax liability accounts.

d. What is the relation between the amount of income before taxes for financial reporting and taxable income for Year 13?

e. What is the likely event that gave rise to the deferred tax asset for retirement benefit obligations?

EXHIBIT 6.17

TRW, Inc.
Income Tax Disclosures
(amounts in millions)
(Problem 6.12)

	Year 4	Year 5	Year 6
Earnings before Income Taxes			
U.S..	$178	$(156)	$213
Non–U.S.....................................	165	27	135
	$343	$(129)	$348
Provision for Income Taxes			
Current			
U.S.......................................	$ 97	$ 25	$ 81
Foreign..................................	75	39	59
Deferred			
U.S.......................................	(44)	(39)	11
Foreign..................................	7	(14)	3
	$135	$ 11	$154
Effective Tax Rate Reconciliation			
U.S. Statutory Tax Rate	35.0%	(35.0%)	35.0%
U.S. State and Local Taxes	4.2	0.3	3.6
Non–U.S. Tax Rate Variances	3.0	14.9	4.2
Losses on Restructuring without Income Tax			
Benefit	—	23.1	3.6
Other......................................	(2.8)	4.9	(2.1)
Effective Income Tax Rate....................	39.4%	8.2%	44.3%
Components of Deferred Taxes			
Deferred Tax Assets			
Postretirement Benefits Other than Pensions	—	$ 232	$244
Restructuring Charges	$ 50	121	124
Pensions	115	—	—
Non–U.S. Net Operating Loss Carryforwards ...	—	30	36
Valuation Allowance	—	(30)	(36)
Total	$165	$ 353	$368
Deferred Tax Liabilities			
Depreciation...............................	$351	$ 431	$470
Pensions	—	55	45
Total	$351	$ 486	$515

f. Why do restructuring charges give rise to a deferred tax asset?

g. What does the increase in the deferred tax liability for depreciation and depletion suggest about Sun's capital expenditures?

h. Why does the investment in leases give rise to a deferred tax liability?

EXHIBIT 6.18

Sun Company
Income Tax Disclosures
(amounts in millions)
(Problem 6.12)

	Year 12	Year 13
Components of Income before Taxes		
U.S.	$ (174)	$ 138
Foreign	(258)	288
Total	$(432)	$ 426
Income Tax Expense (Credit)	**Year 12**	**Year 13**
Current		
U.S.	$ 36	$ 29
Foreign	114	55
Total Current	$ 150	$ 84
Deferred		
U.S.	$(124)	$ 11
Foreign	(141)	48
Total Deferred	$(265)	$ 59
Total Income Tax Expense	$(115)	$ 143

	December 31	
	Year 12	**Year 13**
Components of Deferred Taxes		
Deferred Tax Assets		
Retirement Benefit Obligations	$ 156	$ 162
Estimated Expenses Not Yet Deductible	278	252
Tax Loss Carryforwards	79	53
Restructuring Charges	104	100
Other	43	70
Valuation Allowance	(98)	(92)
Total Deferred Tax Assets	$ 562	$ 545
Deferred Tax Liabilities		
Depreciation and Depletion	$(598)	$(655)
Investment in Foreign Subsidiaries	(27)	(24)
Investment in Leases	(58)	(45)
Other	(64)	(65)
Total Deferred Tax Liabilities	$(747)	$(789)
Net Deferred Tax Liability	$(185)	$(244)
Tax Rate Reconciliation		
Income Taxes at U.S. Statutory Rate	$(147)	$ 149
Foreign Tax Rates in Excess of (less than) U.S. Tax Rate	32	(2)
Other	—	(4)
Income Tax Provision	$(115)	$ 143

AMERICAN AIRLINES AND UNITED AIRLINES: A PENSION FOR DEBT

American Airlines and United Airlines maintain dominant market positions in the airline market in the United States. Airlines carry heavy investments in fixed assets. Their high proportions of fixed operating costs provide potential benefits and risks of economies and diseconomies of scale. The commodity nature of air travel and the excess capacity in this highly competitive industry have resulted in operating losses for many airlines in recent years.

Airlines rely heavily on debt financing for their fixed asset investments. The financing may take the form of borrowing to purchase fixed assets or leasing under a capital lease arrangement. Airlines have turned increasingly in recent years to operating leases as a means to keep debt off of their balance sheets. The fixed costs of servicing on-balance-sheet debt and off-balance-sheet leasing commitments add to the potential scale economies and diseconomies.

Airlines are unionized and provide pension, health care, and other postretirement benefits to employees. The obligations under various benefit plans are not fully reflected in liabilities on the balance sheet.

An effective analysis of the risk of airlines requires consideration of the effects of commitments under operating leases and underfunded retirement benefit obligations. This case analyzes the disclosures of American and United with respect to leases, pensions, and health care benefits. Data for American and United appear in the following exhibits:

Exhibit 1: Balance sheet data.

Exhibit 2: Income and cash flow data.

Exhibit 3: Capital and operating lease data.

Exhibit 4: Pension data.

Exhibit 5: Postretirement benefits data.

CAPITAL LEASES

REQUIRED

a. Complete the following analysis of changes in the capitalized lease assets and capitalized lease obligation of American for Year 3.

Capitalized Lease Assets (Net), December 31, Year 2 . . . .
Plus New Leases Capitalized during Year 3 . . . .
Less Depreciation Recognized for Year 3 . . . .
Capitalized Lease Assets (Net), December 31, Year 3 . . . .

Capitalized Lease Liability, December 31, Year 2[a] . . . .
Plus Interest on Lease Liability for Year 3 . . . .
Plus New Leases Capitalized During Year 3 . . . .
Less Cash Payments Made on Capital Leases during Year 3 . . . .
Capitalized Lease Liability, December 31, Year 3 . . . .

---

[a]Be sure to include current and noncurrent portions.

b. Repeat part (*a*) for United for Year 3.

American Airlines and United Airlines
Balance Sheet Data
(Case 6.1)

| | American | | United | |
| | December 31 | | December 31 | |
	Year 2	Year 3	Year 2	Year 3
Assets				
Current Assets.....................................	$ 2,868	$ 2,690	$ 3,298	$ 3,713
Property, Plant, and Equipment				
Cost...	$15,908	$17,175	$10,600	$11,161
Accumulated Depreciation	(4,529)	(4,914)	(4,205)	(4,691)
Net	$11,379	$12,261	$ 6,395	$ 6,470
Property, Plant, and Equipment under Capital Leases				
Cost...	$ 2,459	$ 2,476	$ 1,060	$ 1,131
Accumulated Depreciation	(644)	(760)	(344)	(395)
Net	$ 1,815	$ 1,716	$ 716	$ 736
Other Assets.....................................	$ 2,644	$ 2,659	$ 1,848	$ 1,921
Total Assets	$18,706	$19,326	$12,257	$12,840
Liabilities and Shareholders' Equity				
Current Operating Liabilities........................	$ 4,058	$ 4,107	$ 4,225	$ 4,375
Short-Term Borrowing	380	—	450	315
Current Maturities of Long-Term Debt	183	200	116	144
Current Maturities of Capital Leases	99	110	54	62
Total Current Liabilities...........................	$ 4,720	$ 4,417	$ 4,845	$ 4,896
Long-Term Debt	5,643	5,431	2,801	2,702
Capital Leases	2,195	2,123	812	827
Other Noncurrent Liabilities	2,799	3,079	3,093	3,177
Total Liabilities	$15,357	$15,050	$11,551	$11,602
Preferred Stock	—	$ 1,081	—	$ 65
Common Stock	$ 2,093	2,111	$ 393	994
Retained Earnings.................................	1,256	1,084	313	179
Total Shareholders' Equity	$ 3,349	$ 4,276	$ 706	$ 1,238
Total Liabilities and Shareholders' Equity	$18,706	$19,326	$12,257	$12,840

OPERATING LEASES

c. Assume for this part that 10 percent is the appropriate interest rate to capitalize the operating lease commitments of American and United. Also assume that all lease payments occur at the end of each year. Compute the present value of the operating lease commitments of each airline as of December 31, Year 2 and Year 3.

d. Compare the total expenses for operating leases for Year 3, assuming that American and United accounted for these leases as operating leases (that is, as reported) versus as capital leases.

EXHIBIT 2

American Airlines and United Airlines
Income and Cash Flow Data
(Case 6.1)

	American		United	
	Year 2	Year 3	Year 2	Year 3
Operating Revenues	$ 14,396	$ 15,816	$ 12,890	$ 14,511
Operating Expenses	(14,421)	(15,126)	(13,428)	(14,248)
Operating Income	$ (25)	$ 690	$ (538)	$ 263
Interest Expense	(651)	(668)	(328)	(358)
Other Income (expense)	(21)	(135)	210	48
Income before Taxes........	$ (697)	$ (113)	$ (656)	$ (47)
Income Taxes Benefit	222	17	239	16
Net Income	$ (475)	$ (96)	$ (417)	$ (31)
Cash Flow from				
Operations	$ 843	$ 1,377	$ 575	$ 858
Investing...............	(2,954)	(1,754)	(537)	(740)
Financing	2,062	395	35	(203)
Change in Cash...........	$ (49)	$ 18	$ 73	$ (85)
Capital Lease Obligations				
Incurred	$ 418	$ 21	$ 276	$ 71
Rent Expense.............	$ 1,300	$ 1,300	$ 1,060	$ 1,211

EXHIBIT 3

American Airlines and United Airlines
Capital and Operating Lease Data
(Case 6.1)

	American		United	
	Year 2	Year 3	Year 2	Year 3
Commitments under Capital Leases				
Payable In				
Year 3	$ 268	—	$ 136	—
Year 4	267	$ 268	136	$ 144
Year 5	280	281	137	145
Year 6	264	268	138	147
Year 7	248	250	133	141
Year 8	a	245	a	145
Subsequent............	2,629	2,404	611	552
Total	$ 3,956	$ 3,716	$ 1,291	$ 1,274
Less Inputed Interest......	(1,662)	(1,483)	(425)	(385)
	$ 2,294	$ 2,233	$ 866	$ 889
Current Portion..........	(99)	(110)	(54)	(62)
Long-Term Portion	$ 2,195	$ 2,123	$ 812	$ 827

Exh. 3—Continued	American		United	
	Year 2	Year 3	Year 2	Year 3

Commitments under Operating Leases

Payable In

	American		United	
Year 3	$ 932	—	$ 1,107	—
Year 4	864	$ 982	1,214	$ 1,275
Year 5	837	967	1,200	1,288
Year 6	819	939	1,201	1,269
Year 7	797	954	1,170	1,251
Year 8	a	961	a	1,294
Subsequent	15,592	16,420	20,074	19,824
Total	$19,841	$21,223	$25,966	$26,201

[a]Amounts included on next line.

EXHIBIT 4

American Airlines and United Airlines
Pension Data
(Case 6.1)

	American		United	
	Year 2	Year 3	Year 2	Year 3
Net Periodic Pension Cost				
Service Cost	$ 152	$ 167	$ 180	$ 186
Interest Cost	268	285	320	356
Actual Return on Plan Assets	(229)	(638)	(289)	(310)
Net Amortization and Deferral	(52)	356	24	19
Total	$ 139	$ 170	$ 235	$ 251
	December 31		December 31	
	Year 2	Year 3	Year 2	Year 3
Status of Pension Plan				
Accumulated Benefit Obligation	$2,709	$3,283	$3,267	$4,200
Effect of Salary Increases	659	721	794	825
Projected Benefit Obligation	$3,368	$4,004	$4,061	$5,025
Plan Assets at Fair Value	2,928	3,550	3,052	3,589
Underfunded Projected Benefit Obligation	$ 440	$ 454	$1,009	$1,436
Unrecognized Net Loss	(845)	(957)	(55)	(624)
Unrecognized Prior Service Cost	(23)	35	(557)	(455)
Unrecognized Transition Asset	81	70	73	16
Adjustment for Minimum Liability ...	—	—	255	346
Prepaid Pension Cost	$ (347)	$ (398)		
Accrued Pension Liability			$ 725	$ 719
Actuarial Assumptions				
Expected Return on Assets	11.3%	10.5%	10.3%	9.8%
Discount Rate	9.0%	7.5%	8.8%	7.5%
Salary Inflation	4.9%	4.4%	4.3%	4.0%

EXHIBIT 5

American Airlines and United Airlines
Postretirement Benefits Data
(Case 6.1)

	American		United	
	Year 2	Year 3	Year 2	Year 3
Net Postretirement Benefits Cost				
Service Cost......................................	$ 43	$ 47	$ 28	$ 38
Interest Cost.....................................	83	87	83	92
Net Amortization and Deferral	—	(4)	—	3
Total	$ 126	$ 130	$ 111	$ 133

	December 31		December 31	
	Year 2	Year 3	Year 2	Year 3
Status of Postretirement Benefit Plan				
Accumulated Postretirement Benefits Obligation	$ 987	$1,209	$1,135	$1,331
Plan Assets at Fair Value	—	(7)	(86)	(91)
Underfunded Postretirement Benefits Obligation	$ 987	$1,202	$1,049	$1,240
Unrecognized Net Gain (Loss)	19	(111)	(49)	(149)
Accrued Postretirement Benefits Obligation	$1,006	$1,091	$1,000	$1,091
Actuarial Assumptions				
Discount Rate	9.0%	7.5%	8.8%	7.5%
Health Care Inflation Rate				
Initial Year...................................	11.0%	11.0%	12.0%	11.0%
Steady State	4.0%	4.0%	4.0%	4.0%

e. Compute the long-term debt ratio (Long-Term Debt ÷ Long-Term Debt + Shareholders' Equity) as of December 31, Year 3, with and without capitalization of operating leases. Assume no change in retained earnings as a result of capitalizing operating leases.

PENSIONS

f. Prepare an analysis that accounts for the change in pension fund assets and the projected benefit obligation during Year 3 for each airline's pension fund using the following format:

Pension Fund Assets
Balance, December 31, Year 2...................................
Plus Return on Pension Investments during Year 3.................
Plus Contributions Received from the Employer during Year 3.......
Less Payments to Retirees during Year 3..........................
Balance, December 31, Year 3..................................

Projected Benefit Obligation

Balance, December 31, Year 2. . . . .

Plus Service Cost for Year 3 . . . .

Plus Interest Cost for Year 3 . . . .

Less Payments to Retirees during Year 3. . . . .

Plus or Minus Actuarial Gains or Losses for Year 3 . . . .

Balance, December 31, Year 3. . . . .

g. Evaluate the investment performance of each airline's pension fund during Year 3.

h. Present the journal entry that the analyst would make to recognize the net under-funded projected benefit obligation of each airline as of December 31, Year 3. The income tax rate is 35 percent.

POSTRETIREMENT BENEFIT OBLIGATION OTHER THAN PENSIONS

i. Repeat part (*f*) for the postretirement benefits obligation (other than pensions) for American and United.

j. Give the journal entry that the analyst would make to recognize the underfunded, un-recognized liability for postretirement benefits other than pensions as of December 31, Year 3.

SYNTHESIS

k. Compute the long-term debt ratio (Long-Term Debt/Long-Term Debt + Shareholders' Equity) for American and United on December 31, Year 3, based on (1) reported data and (2) restated data that include operating leases, underfunded pension obligations, and underfunded postretirement benefits obligations. Include the pension and postretirement benefit obligations in long-term debt.

CASE 6.2

SUN MICROSYSTEMS: A NOT-TOO-TAXING EXPERIENCE

Sun Microsystems designs, manufactures, and sells computer hardware and software aimed primarily at engineers, architects, and others with sophisticated graphic needs. Sun's income statement for Year 11, Year 12, and Year 13 reveal the following (amounts in millions):

	Year 11	Year 12	Year 13
Sales			
Domestic.	$1,584	$1,783	$2,321
Foreign	1,637	1,806	1,788
Total Sales	$3,221	$3,589	$4,109

Income before Income Taxes			
Domestic..............................	$ 214	$ 207	$ 130
Foreign................................	62	41	88
Total Income before Income Taxes......	$ 276	$ 248	$ 218
Net Income............................	$ 182	$ 166	$ 151

The notes to the financial statements reveal the following information with respect to income taxes.

	Year 11	Year 12	Year 13
Provision for Income Taxes			
Current			
U.S. federal................................	$ 55	$ 38	$ 38
State......................................	15	11	6
Foreign....................................	49	25	38
Total Current...........................	$119	$ 74	$ 82
Deferred			
U.S. federal................................	$ (14)	$ 12	$ (14)
State......................................	(2)	2	3
Foreign....................................	(9)	(6)	(4)
Total Deferred..........................	$ (25)	$ 8	$ (15)
Provision for Income Taxes....................	$ 94	$ 82	$ 67
Components of Deferred Taxes			
Deferred Tax Assets			
Inventory Valuation..........................	$ 39	$ 38	$ 34
Warranty Reserves...........................	30	31	42
Foreign Loss Carryforwards..................	41	45	41
Fixed Asset Basis Differences.................	25	23	23
Compensation Not Currently Deductible........	10	12	19
Other......................................	12	13	5
Gross Deferred Tax Assets....................	$157	$162	$164
Valuation Allowance.........................	(16)	(20)	(14)
Deferred Tax Assets.........................	$141	$142	$150
Deferred Tax Liabilities			
Depreciation of Fixed Assets.................	(5)	(14)	(7)
Net Deferred Tax Assets......................	$136	$128	$143
Income Tax Reconciliation			
Expected Tax at 35 percent...................	$ 97	$ 87	$ 76
State Income Tax, Net of Federal Tax Benefit....	8	8	6
Foreign Earnings Taxed at Higher Rate.........	3	2	4
Interest on State and Municipal Securities......	(27)	(19)	(16)
Incurrence (Utilization) of Foreign Losses.......	16	4	(4)
Other......................................	(3)	—	1
Provision for Income Taxes..................	$ 94	$ 82	$ 67

REQUIRED

a. Give the journal entries to record income tax expense for Year 12 and Year 13.

b. Did income before taxes for financial reporting exceed or fall short of taxable income for Year 12? for Year 13? Explain.

c. Discuss briefly the major factors that caused the relation between income before taxes for financial reporting and taxable income—see part (b)—to change between Year 12 and Year 13.

d. Prepare a tax reconciliation analysis similar to Exhibit 6.11 in the text. Include a total column (that is, domestic and foreign) for each year.

e. Analyze the level and changes in Sun's effective tax rate on domestic income between Year 11 and Year 13.

f. Repeat part (e) for foreign-source income.

g. Compute the pretax and after-tax profit margin for Sun's domestic, foreign, and overall operations for Year 11, Year 12, and Year 13. How does the change in Sun's effective tax rates affect the interpretations of its changing profit margin?

CASE 6.3

CIFRA: REMODELING THE FINANCIAL STATEMENTS

CIFRA, S.A. DE C.V., and Subsidiaries is a leading retailer in Mexico. At the end of Year 8, Year 9, and Year 10, it operated the following retailing establishments:

	Year 8		Year 9		Year 10	
	No. of Stores	Square Feet	No. of Stores	Square Feet	No. of Stores	Square Feet
Self-Service Stores	38	2,775,508	33	2,253,788	33	2,285,800
Discount Warehouse Stores	29	1,308,127	39	1,821,193	45	2,216,577
Supermarkets . .	34	479,030	35	505,176	37	568,371
Department Stores	29	1,545,771	28	1,501,578	31	1,698,075
Restaurants	78	16,616[a]	89	18,274[a]	106	21,818[a]
Hypermarkets .	—	—	2	361,832	5	871,819
Membership Clubs	—	—	3	291,704	7	688,788

[a]Seating capacity.

CIFRA follows an "everyday-low-price" strategy in its stores.

CIFRA commenced a major remodeling effort in all of its retailing establishments in Year 8. It expects to complete these renovations by the end of Year 11. CIFRA created an account, Fund for Remodeling, which it uses to cover the cost of remodeling. Financial statements for CIFRA for Year 8, Year 9, and Year 10 appear as Exhibit 1 (balance sheet); Exhibit 2 (statement of earnings); and Exhibit 3 (statement of changes in financial position). Selected notes follow these financial statements.

EXHIBIT 1

CIFRA, S.A. DE C.V., and Subsidiaries
Consolidated Balance Sheet
(in millions of constant December 31, Year 10 Mexican Pesos)
(Case 6.3)

	December 31			
	Year 7	**Year 8**	**Year 9**	**Year 10**
Assets				
Current Assets				
Cash and Short-Term Investments	P 942	P 1,382	P2,180	P 1,940
Accounts Receivable	144	231	152	234
Inventories	814	804	1,080	1,319
Prepayments.	8	15	47	38
Total Current Assets	P1,908	P 2,432	P3,459	P 3,531
Property, Plant, and Equipment	P3,668	P 4,188	P5,389	P 7,378
Accumulated Depreciation	(930)	(1,013)	(1,079)	(1,298)
Net Property, Plant, and Equipment.	P2,738	P 3,175	P4,310	P 6,080
Investments in Securities	—	P 69	—	—
Surplus Pension Funds.	—	—	—	P 593
Total Assets	P4,646	P 5,676	P7,769	P10,204
Current Liabilties				
Accounts Payable—Trade.	P1,336	P 1,494	P1,882	P 2,279
Other Accounts Payable	496	570	627	571
Fund for Remodeling (Note 1).	—	111	261	51
Total Current Liabilities.	P1,832	P 2,175	P2,770	P 2,901
Reserve for Seniority Premiums (Note 2).	—	—	P 21	P 22
Shareholders' Equity				
Capital Stock	P 900	P 900	P 900	P 900
Legal Reserve	201	229	264	264
Retained Earnings.	1,469	1,995	2,678	3,726
Surplus on Restatement of Fixed Assets and				
Capital Stock	410	501	782	1,447
Treasury Stock.	(166)	(124)	(38)	(124)
Majority Shareholders' Equity	P2,814	P 3,501	P4,586	P 6,213
Minority Shareholders' Equity.	—	—	392	1,068
Total Shareholders' Equity	P2,814	P 3,501	P4,978	P 7,281
Total Liabilities and Shareholders' Equity	P4,646	P 5,676	P7,769	P10,204

REQUIRED

a. Prepare an analysis of the changes in the Funds for Remodeling account during Year 8,
Year 9, and Year 10.

b. Which of the amounts from part (*a*) did CIFRA charge against earnings for each year?

c. Which amounts (if any) related to remodeling do you think CIFRA should have charged
against earnings each year? Explain your reasoning.

EXHIBIT 2

CIFRA, S.A. DE C.V., and Subsidiaries
Consolidated Statement of Earnings
(in millions of constant December 31, Year 10 Mexican Pesos)
(Case 6.3)

	Year 8	Year 9	Year 10
Net Sales	P10,287	P12,417	P 14,231
Cost of Goods Sold	(7,870)	(9,525)	(11,135)
Operating Expenses	(1,859)	(2,154)	(2,306)
Operating Income	P 558	P 738	P 790
Comprehensive Financing Income			
Financial Income	P 239	P 338	P 324
Gain on Monetary Position	91	42	9
Other Income (Expenses)—Net	16	(39)	(17)
Earnings before Taxes	P 904	P 1,079	P 1,106
Income Taxes and Employees' Statutory Profit Sharing (Note 3)	(250)	(309)	(308)
Earnings before Special Items	P 654	P 770	P 798
Special Items Net of Applicable Income Taxes			
Net Effect of Bulletin D-3 on Labor Obligations (Note 2)	—	—	233
Reversion of Surplus in Pension Funds (Note 2)	309	549	—
Fund for Remodeling (Note 1)	(179)	(270)	—
Reserve for Seniority Premiums (Note 2)	—	(21)	—
Net Earnings	P 784	P 1,028	P 1,031
Minority Interest in Earnings	—	(15)	3
Majority Share	P 784	P 1,013	P 1,034

d. What adjustments must be made to the financial statements for Year 8, Year 9, and Year 10 to conform to the accounting suggested in your response to part (*c*)?

e. Suggest reasons for the fact that CIFRA chose to account for remodeling costs at it did.

f. Using your restated financial statements from part (*d*), assess CIFRA's profitability and risk for Year 8 through Year 10.

NOTES TO EXHIBITS 1—3

Note 1: CIFRA commenced a major remodeling effort of its retailing establishments in Year 8. It created the Fund for Remodeling account on its balance sheet, which CIFRA increased by provisions of P179 million (net of taxes) in Year 8 and P270 million (net of taxes) in Year 9. CIFRA charges a portion of remodeling expenditures (net of taxes) each year against the Fund for Remodeling account and capitalizes a portion in fixed assets.

Note 2: The Mexican government instituted a mandatory pension program on May 1, Year 9. All CIFRA employees participate in this program from the effective date forward. Retirement benefits earned in CIFRA's retirement plans prior to the effective date remain the responsibility of CIFRA. CIFRA's pension plan for nonsenior employees had pension assets in excess of pension liabilities. CIFRA reverted part of the excess back to the company during Year 8 and Year 9. Its pension plan for senior employees had pension liabilities in excess of pension assets on May 1, Year 9. CIFRA

EXHIBIT 3

CIFRA, S.A. DE C.V., and Subsidiaries
Consolidated Statement of Changes in Financial Position
(in millions of constant December 31, Year 10 Mexican Pesos)
(Case 6.3)

	Year 8	Year 9	Year 10
Net Earnings before Special Items	P 654	P 770	P 798
Depreciation and Amortization	174	199	237
Other Addbacks...	—	—	3
Change in			
Accounts Receivable	(87)	77	(83)
Inventories	19	(285)	(245)
Prepayments...	(8)	(32)	11
Accounts Payable—Trade..............................	158	388	397
Other Accounts Payable	(17)	15	(41)
Resources Provided by Operations	P 893	P 1,132	P 1,077
Reimbursement of Pension Surplus (Note 2).................	P 309	P 549	P —
Investment of Minority Shareholders	—	P 446	P 676
Other Investments..	P (69)	—	—
Payment of Dividends.....................................	(210)	(289)	(323)
Premium on Sale of Shares...............................	5	71	279
Resources Provided by Financing	P (274)	P 228	P 632
Acquisition of Property and Equipment	P (420)	P (991)	P(1,739)
Application of Fund for Remodeling (Note 1)	(68)	(120)	(210)
Resources Used for Investing.............................	P (488)	P(1,111)	P(1,949)
(Decrease) Increase in Cash and Short-Term Investments	P 440	P 798	P (240)
Cash and Short-Term Investments—Beginning of Year	942	1,382	2,180
Cash and Short-Term Investments—End of Year.............	P1,382	P 2,180	P 1,940

recognized a liability for the excess. On December 31, Year 10, the pension plan for nonsenior employees had pension assets in excess of pension liabilities of P593 million. CIFRA recognized this excess as an asset on this date. It credited retained earnings for P360 million (relating to returns on pension fund investments for years prior to Year 10) and earnings for Year 10 for P233 million (relating to returns on pension fund investments during Year 10).

Note 3: CIFRA recognizes deferred taxes for *nonrecurring* timing differences between income before taxes for financial reporting and taxable income. There were no *recurring* timing differences qualifying for the recognition of deferred taxes under Mexican accounting principles in Year 8, Year 9, or Year 10.

CHAPTER 7

GENERALLY ACCEPTED ACCOUNTING PRINCIPLES: INTERCORPORATE ENTITIES

Learning Objectives

1. Apply the criteria for the purchase and pooling of interests methods of accounting for a corporate acquisition and understand the effects of each method on the financial statements at the time of the acquisition and in subsequent years.
2. Understand the financial statement effects of the market value, equity, proportionate consolidation, and full consolidation methods and the conditions when each method best portrays the operating relationships between two entities.
3. Prepare a set of translated financial statements using the all-current method and the monetary/nonmonetary method and understand the conditions when each method best portrays the operating relationship between a U.S. parent firm and its foreign subsidiary.
4. Understand the accounting issues in preparing financial statement data for segments of a firm and the appropriate use of segment data when analyzing a firm's profitability.

This chapter continues the discussion of generally accepted accounting principles (GAAP). As was the case in Chapters 5 and 6, the objective is to develop a sufficient understanding of the effects of alternative accounting methods so that the analyst can analyze and meaningfully interpret the financial statements. The focus, as before, is on GAAP in the United States, with significant differences from other countries noted. This chapter considers the following:

1. Corporate acquisitions.
2. Investments in securities.
3. Foreign currency translation.
4. Segment reporting.

CORPORATE ACQUISITIONS

Corporate acquisitions occur when one corporation acquires all, or substantially all, of another corporation's common stock in a single transaction. GAAP permits two methods of accounting for corporate acquisitions, depending on the structure of the transaction: the purchase method and the pooling of interests method.[1]

Exhibit 7.1 shows financial statement information for Company P and Company S, which we use to illustrate these two accounting methods. Company P acquires 100 percent of the outstanding common stock of Company S. Management estimates that the combination will save $50,000 a year in operating expenses before income taxes. Columns (1) and (2) of Exhibit 7.1 show abbreviated single-company financial statements of each company prior to the combination. Column (3) shows the market values of the assets, liabilities, and shareholders' equity of Company S. Company S has 22,000 shares of common stock outstanding that sell for $84 per share in the market. The market value of Company S's shareholders' equity is therefore $1,848,000 (= 22,000 × $84). The market value ($1,848,000) exceeds the book value ($450,000) of shareholders' equity by $1,398,000. There are three reasons for this difference.

1. Long-term depreciable assets have a market value of $850,000 but a book value of only $450,000. The lower book value of depreciable assets results from the accounting use of historical cost valuations for assets. Company S initially recorded its depreciable assets at acquisition cost. Over time, Company S recognized a portion of this acquisition cost as depreciation expense. GAAP does not permit the firm to recognize increases in the market values of these assets. The market value of Company S, as measured by the market value of its common stock, reflects the economic values, not book values, of assets.
2. Deferred income taxes of $140,000 arise because the firm cannot deduct the $400,000 excess of the market value over the book value of depreciable assets as depreciation expense for income tax purposes in future years ($400,000 × 0.35 = $140,000). This $140,000 amount represents the extra income taxes that the firm will pay in future years because taxable income will exceed book income before income taxes. Stated another way, the $140,000 represents the loss in future tax benefits because the company cannot base depreciation on the $850,000 market value of depreciable assets. We might show the $140,000 as a

---

[1] Accounting Principles Board, *Accounting Principles Board Opinion No. 16,* "Business Combinations," 1970.

EXHIBIT 7.1

Consolidated Statements Comparing Purchase and Pooling of Interests Methods

	Historical Cost		S Shown at Current Market Values	Companies P and S Consolidated at Date of Acquisition	
	P (1)	S (2)	(3)	Purchase (4)	Pooling of Interests (5)
Balance Sheets					
Assets:					
Current Assets..............	$1,500,000	$450,000	$ 450,000	$1,950,000	$1,950,000
Depreciable Assets less Accum. Depreciation..............	1,700,000	450,000	850,000	2,550,000	2,150,000
Goodwill...................	—	—	1,138,000	1,138,000	—
Total Assets	$3,200,000	$900,000	$2,438,000	$5,638,000	$4,100,000
Equities:					
Liabilities	$1,300,000	$450,000	$ 450,000	$1,750,000	$1,750,000
Deferred Income Tax Liability.	—	—	140,000	140,000	—
Shareholders' Equity.........	1,900,000	450,000	1,848,000	3,748,000	2,350,000
Total Equities.............	$3,200,000	$900,000	$2,438,000	$5,638,000	$4,100,000
Income Statements					
Precombination Income before Income Taxes..............	$ 300,000	$160,000		$ 460,000	$ 460,000
From Combination					
Cost Savings	—	—		50,000	50,000
Extra Depreciation Expense...	—	—		(80,000)	—
Base for Income Tax Expense ...	$ 300,000	$160,000		$ 430,000	$ 510,000
Income Tax Expense...........	(105,000)	(56,000)		(150,500)	(178,500)
Goodwill Amortization.........	—	—		(28,450)	—
Net Income	$ 195,000	$104,000		$ 251,050	$ 331,500
Number of Common Shares Outstanding...............	100,000	22,000		144,000	144,000
Earnings per Share............	$ 1.95	$ 4.73		$ 1.74	$ 2.30

reduction in the market value of depreciable assets ($850,000 − $140,000 = $710,000) on the premise that the market value of these assets *to* P is only $710,000, not $850,000. As discussed later, GAAP includes the $140,000 in the Deferred Income Tax Liability account.

3. Goodwill of $1,138,000 exists. The $1,138,000 amount for goodwill equals the difference between the acquisition cost ($1,848,000) and the market value of identifiable assets and liabilities ($450,000 + $850,000 − $450,000 − $140,000 = $710,000). Goodwill includes intangible attributes that a firm cannot separately identify (for example, well-trained labor force, reputation for high-quality products, superior managerial skills), as well as any merger premium that the acquirer had to pay to consummate the corporate acquisition.

Company P, the acquiring company, has 100,000 shares of common stock outstanding, which sell for $42 each in the market.

PURCHASE METHOD

Under the purchase method, the acquirer records the assets and liabilities of the acquired company at the amount of cash or market value of other consideration given in the exchange. The purchase method therefore follows the principles of acquisition cost accounting (that is, the acquiring company records assets and liabilities at the price it pays for them). To illustrate, assume that P issues (sells) 44,000 additional common shares on the market for $42 each, or $1,848,000 in total, and uses the proceeds to purchase 100 percent of the outstanding common shares of S. When cash is the only consideration used in a corporate acquisition, GAAP requires the use of the purchase method (discussed more fully below). Column (4) of Exhibit 7.1 shows the combined, or consolidated, balance sheet of P and S on the date of the combination under the purchase method. The accountant combines the book values of P's assets and equities with the market values of S's assets and equities in applying the purchase method.

The lower panel of Exhibit 7.1 shows the effect of using the purchase method for the acquisition on income statements of subsequent years. The consolidated income statement starts with the combined pretax incomes of P and S, assuming no acquisition had occurred. We add the $50,000 of cost savings resulting from more efficient operations after the combination. We subtract the additional depreciation arising from the asset revaluation. The additional depreciation expense of $80,000 reflects a five-year life and the use of the straight-line depreciation method [$80,000 = 0.20($850,000 − $450,000)]. The $430,000 of book income before taxes and before amortization of goodwill is the basis for income tax *expense* of $150,500. Taxable income of $510,000 (= $460,000 + $50,000) is the basis for income taxes *payable* of $178,500. The combined companies report the difference between income tax expense of $150,500 and income tax payable of $178,500, or $28,000, as a reduction in Deferred Income Tax Liability established at the date of acquisition. This $28,000 amount equals the income tax rate of 35 percent times the extra depreciation expense of $80,000. Goodwill amortization of $28,450 assumes straight-line amortization over 40 years ($28,450 = $1,138,000 ÷ 40).

POOLING OF INTERESTS METHOD

The pooling of interests method accounts for a corporate acquisition as the uniting of the ownership interests of two companies by an exchange of common stock. The pooling of interests method views the exchange of common shares as a change in *form,* not in *substance;* that is, the shareholders of the predecessor companies become shareholders in the new combined enterprise. Each of the predecessor companies continues its operations as before. Because no change occurs in either the ownership interests or the nature of the activities of the enterprises involved, no new basis of accountability arises. The accountant merely adds the book values of the assets and liabilities of both companies when accounting for a "corporate acquisition" as a pooling of interests. Unlike the purchase method, the consolidated balance sheet does not reflect the market values of the acquired company's assets and liabilities on the date of acquisition.

To illustrate the pooling of interests method, assume that P issues the 44,000 shares of its common stock directly to the shareholders of S in return for their shares. Previous shareholders of P and S now own the outstanding shares of P and S combined. The consolidated balance sheet in column (5) of Exhibit 7.1 is the sum of the separate company amounts in columns (1) and (2). The pooling of interests method requires no revaluations of assets, nor does it result in the recognition of goodwill.

The consolidated income statement is likewise the sum of the amounts for the separate companies (except for recognizing the projected cost savings). Because the balance sheet does not reflect asset revaluations and goodwill under the pooling of interests method, the accountant records no additional depreciation or amortization. For this reason, income under the pooling of interests method is usually higher than under the purchase method. Furthermore, assets and shareholders' equities are usually less under the pooling of interests method than under the purchase method. Rates of return on assets and on shareholders' equity will likely exceed those under the purchase method.

CRITERIA FOR POOLING OF INTERESTS

The concept of a pooling of interests envisions two independent companies agreeing to combine their shareholder groups and their operations and continuing to operate in a new combined form. It does not view the transaction as one company buying out the other.

To qualify for the pooling of interests method, the transaction must meet the twelve criteria set out in Exhibit 7.2. Unless the transaction satisfies all twelve criteria, the combining firms cannot use the pooling method. On the other hand, if the transaction satisfies all criteria, the combining firms must use the pooling method.

The first two criteria attempt to operationalize the notion that the combining companies acted independently in their decision to combine. The next seven criteria attempt to ensure that the shareholders of the predecessor companies become common equity holders in the new combined enterprise. GAAP includes several of these criteria to circumvent abuses of the pooling method. The aim of the last three criteria is to ensure continuity of the shareholder groups and of operations after the combination.

MANAGING FUTURE EARNINGS

Critics of the pooling of interests method argue that it not only keeps reported expenses from increasing after the merger, but also it may allow the management of the pooled companies to manage reported earnings in an arbitrary way. Suppose, as has happened, that Company P merges with an old, established firm, Company F, which has produced commercial movie films. Company F has amortized these films, made in the 1940s and 1950s, so that by the 1990s, their book value is close to zero. But the market value of the films is much larger than zero because television stations and cable networks find that old movies please their audiences. If Company P acquires Company F and uses the purchase method, the old films appear on

---

EXHIBIT 7.2

Criteria for Pooling of Interests Method

Prior to the Combination

1. Each of the combining companies is autonomous and has not been a subsidiary or division of another corporation within two years before initiation of the plan to combine.
2. Each of the combining companies is independent of the other combining companies.

At the Time of the Combination

3. The combination occurs in a single transaction or in accordance with a specific plan that the combining entities complete within one year.
4. A corporation issues only common stock with rights identical to the majority of its outstanding voting stock in exchange for substantially all (at least 90 percent) of the voting stock of another company.
5. None of the combining companies changes the equity interest of the voting common stock in contemplation of the combination either within two years before initiating the plan of combination or between the initiation and consummation dates; changes in contemplation of the combination may include distributions to shareholders and additional issuances, exchanges, and retirements of securities.
6. Each of the combining companies acquires shares of voting common stock only for purposes other than business combinations, and no company reacquires more than a normal number of shares between the initiation and consummation dates.
7. The ratio of the interest of an individual common shareholder to those of other common shareholders in a combining company remains the same as a result of the exchange of stock in the combination.
8. Shareholders can exercise the voting rights to which the common stock in the combined corporation entitle them; the combined company can neither deprive nor restrict the shareholders from exercising those rights.
9. The combining entities resolve all issues at the consummation date of the plan; no provisions of the plan relating to the issue of securities or other consideration are pending.

Subsequent to the Combination

10. The combined corporation does not agree directly or indirectly to retire or reacquire all or part of the common stock issued in the combination.
11. The combined corporation does not make special financial arrangements for the benefit of the former shareholders of a combining company, such as guaranteeing loans secured by stock issued in the combination, which in effect negate the exchange of equity securities.
12. The combined corporation does not intend or plan to dispose of a significant part of the assets of the combining companies within two years after the combination other than disposals in the ordinary course of business of the formerly separate companies or to eliminate duplicate facilities or excess capacity.

SOURCE: Accounting Principles Board, *Accounting Principles Board Opinion No. 16*, "Business Combinations," 1970, pp. 45–49.

---

the consolidated balance sheet at the films' current market values. If Company P merges with Company F and uses the pooling of interests method, the films appear on the consolidated balance sheet at their near-zero book values. Then, when Company P wants to boost reported earnings for the year, it can sell some old movies to a television or cable network and report a large gain. Actually, of course, the owners of Company F enjoyed this gain when they "sold" the films to Company P for current asset values, not the obsolete book values.

Those who defend pooling of interests accounting argue that the management of the pooled enterprise has no more opportunity to manage earnings than did the management of Company F before the pooling. Management of Company F can sell old movies any time it chooses and report handsome gains. The use of the historical cost basis of accounting creates the opportunities for managing earnings. Defenders of pooling argue that there is no reason to penalize the management of a merged company relative to the management of an established company with many under-valued assets on its books. Opponents of pooling reply that the management of Company F earned the holding gains, whereas the management of Company P can report them as realized gains under pooling.

Proponents of the pooling of interests method point out that the purchase method also provides opportunities for managing future earnings. Under the purchase method, the combining companies allocate the aggregate purchase price to identifi-able assets and liabilities based on their market values. The market values of many assets, particularly depreciable assets, patents, copyrights, and similar items, are dif-ficult to measure objectively because of the absence of well-organized, used asset markets. Thus, the combining companies can allocate relatively low amounts to as-sets that the firm will write off quickly as expenses (such as machinery) and rela-tively large amounts to assets that it will write off over longer periods (such as buildings) or not write off at all (such as land). The combining companies must use appraisals or other independent evidence of market values to validate the purchase price allocation, but there is considerable latitude in selecting appraisers!

One common practice in applying the purchase method is the establishment of *acquisition "reserves."* At the time that one company acquires another company, it may not know fully the potential losses inherent in the acquired assets or the poten-tial liabilities of the acquired company. The acquiring company will allocate a por-tion of the purchase price to various types of acquisition reserves (for example, estimated losses on long-term contracts, estimated liabilities for unsettled lawsuits). An acquiring company has up to one year after the date of acquisition to revalue these acquisition reserves as new information becomes available. After that, the ac-quisition reserve amounts remain in the accounts and absorb losses as they occur. That is, the firm charges actual losses against the acquisition reserves instead of against income for the period of the loss.

To illustrate, assume that at the date of acquisition, there is unsettled litigation involving an acquired company. The acquiring company, based on the information it has available, estimates that a pretax loss of $3 million will ultimately result. It allo-cates $3 million to an acquisition reserve (liability account) and debits Deferred Tax Assets for the $1.05 million ($0.35 \times \$3$ million) tax effect. The acquiring firm would presumably pay less for this company because of this potential liability. As-sume that settlement of the lawsuit occurs three years after the date of the acquisi-tion for $2 million (pretax). The accountant charges the $2 million loss against the $3 million reserve instead of against net income for the year and reduces Deferred Tax Assets by $.7 million ($0.35 \times \$2$ million). Furthermore, the accountant elimi-nates the $1 million remaining in the acquisition reserve and the $.35 million remaining in Deferred Tax Assets, increasing net income by $.65 million ($1 mil-lion $-$ .35 million) in the year of the settlement.

When used properly, acquisition reserves are an accounting mechanism that helps ensure that the assets and liabilities of an acquired company reflect market values. However, given the estimates required in establishing such reserves, manage-ment has some latitude in managing earnings under the purchase method.

CORPORATE ACQUISITIONS AND INCOME TAXES

Most corporate acquisitions involve a transaction between the acquiring corporation and the *shareholders* of the acquired corporation. Although the board of directors and management of the acquired company may closely monitor the discussions and negotiations, the acquisition usually takes place with the acquiring corporation giving some type of consideration to the shareholders of the acquired corporation in exchange for their stock. From a legal viewpoint, the acquired corporation remains a legally separate entity that has simply had a change in the makeup of its shareholder group.

The income tax treatment of corporate acquisitions follows these legal-entity notions. In most acquisitions, the acquired company does not restate its assets and liabilities for tax purposes to reflect the amount that the acquired corporation paid for the shares of common stock. Instead, the tax basis of assets and liabilities of the acquired company before the acquisition carries over after the acquisition.[2] In this sense, the tax treatment of a corporate acquisition is analogous in concept to a pooling of interests. Thus, even if the combining entities use the purchase method for financial reporting, they treat the transaction like a pooling for tax purposes (actually called a *nontaxable reorganization*).

INTERPRETING CORPORATE DISCLOSURES ON ACQUISITIONS

Refer to Pepsi's Note 4 on acquisitions and investments in affiliates in Appendix B. Pepsi made acquisitions totaling $1.4 billion in Year 8, $1.4 billion in Year 7, and $.8 billion in Year 6. It used a combination of cash, Pepsi common stock, and assumption of debt as consideration. Because Pepsi common stock represents a minor proportion of the total consideration, Pepsi used the purchase method of accounting for these acquisitions. These acquisitions involved franchised bottling operations and consumer foods companies. Pepsi allocated a large portion of the purchase prices to intangible assets (franchise rights and goodwill). Note that goodwill and other intangibles compose 33.4 percent (= $7,929.5 ÷ $23,705.8) of total assets at the end of Year 8, largely resulting from these acquisitions. Coke, in contrast, made fewer acquisitions during this period (see Note 17 to its financial statements). Its goodwill and other intangibles compose 4.6 percent (= $549 ÷ $12,021) of total assets. A large portion of the difference in the total assets of Pepsi and Coke represents a difference in the amount of recorded intangibles. These companies must amortize the intangibles, thereby reducing net income. Pepsi reports $303.7 million of amortization for Year 8, whereas Coke's amortization totals $27 million. The firms cannot deduct the portion representing amortization of goodwill for tax purposes. Thus, Pepsi shows an increase in its effective tax rate each year (see Pepsi's Note 13 on income tax) for "nondeductible amortization of goodwill and other intangibles."

The analyst should examine carefully the financial statements of firms engaging in a merger accounted for as a pooling of interests. The market values of assets and liabilities often far exceed their recorded values. For example, May Department

---

[2]An acquiring company can elect to liquidate the acquired company under Section 338 of the Internal Revenue Code and thereby record assets and liabilities at their market values for tax purposes. However, the acquired company must pay taxes immediately on differences between these market values and the tax basis of assets and liabilities.

Stores merged with Associated Dry Goods in a transaction treated as a pooling of interests. The book values for Associated at the time of the merger were as follows (in millions):

Assets	$2,489
Liabilities	$1,589
Shareholders' Equity	900
	$2,489

May used these amounts to record the merger. The financial statements indicate that May exchanged 69.7 million shares of its common stock for all of Associated's outstanding common stock. Based on a market price per share for May of approximately $38 on the date of the merger, the market value of Associated's shareholders' equity was $2,648.6 million (= 69.7 × $38). The book value of shareholders' equity was $900 million. The excess of market value over book value of shareholders' equity of $1,748.6 million (= $2,648.6 − $900.0) represents undervalued or nonrecorded assets and liabilities. If the analyst assumes that all of the difference is goodwill and amortizes it over 40 years, then goodwill amortization of the merged enterprise increases $43.7 million (= $1,748.6 ÷ 40) using the purchase method instead of the pooling of interests method. Reported earnings of the combined enterprise for the year of the merger were $381 million. If the entities had used the purchase method, net income would be no more than $337.3 million (= $381.0 − $43.7), an 11.5 percent decrease. If a portion of the excess purchase price were allocated to assets with lives shorter than the 40-year amortization period for goodwill, net income would be even less than $337.3 million.

The analyst should also exert care when comparing U.S. and non-U.S. firms engaged in corporate acquisitions. In most other countries, the pooling of interests method is either disallowed or allowed only under unusual circumstances (such as an inability to identify which company is the purchaser when the merging firms are of similar size). Furthermore, considerable diversity exists in accounting for goodwill. Firms in the United Kingdom can charge off goodwill directly against shareholders' equity accounts, bypassing the income statement. Firms in Japan amortize goodwill over five years, whereas firms in Germany use a period between five and fifteen years. These differences in accounting methods for corporate acquisitions will likely increase in importance as international acquisition activity accelerates in the 1990s.

INVESTMENTS IN SECURITIES

Firms invest in the securities (debt, preferred stock, common stock) of other entities (corporations, government units) for a variety of reasons:

1. Short-term investments of temporarily excess cash.
2. Long-term investments to:
    a. Lock in high yields on debt securities.

b. Exert significant influence on an important raw materials supplier, customer, technological innovator, or other valued entity.

c. Gain voting control of another entity whose operations mesh well strategically with those of the investing firm.

Firms report investments of the first type in the Current Assets section of the balance sheet under the title Marketable Securities. These investments tend to be in government securities. Firms report investments of the second type under Investments in the Noncurrent Assets section of the balance sheet. These longer-term investments tend to be in equity, rather than debt, securities.

TYPES OF INVESTMENTS

The accounting for investments depends on the purpose of the investment and on the percentage of voting stock that one firm owns of another. Figure 7.1 identifies three types of investments:

1. *Minority, Passive Investments.* Firms view debt securities or shares of capital stock of another corporation as a good investment and acquire them for their anticipated interest or dividends and capital gains (increases in the market prices of the securities). The percentage owned of another corporation's voting shares is not so large that the acquiring company can control or exert significant influence over the other company. GAAP views investments in debt securities, preferred stock, or common stock when the firm holds less than 20 percent of the voting stock as minority passive investments.

2. *Minority, Active Investments.* Firms acquire shares of another corporation so that the acquiring corporation can exert significant influence over the other

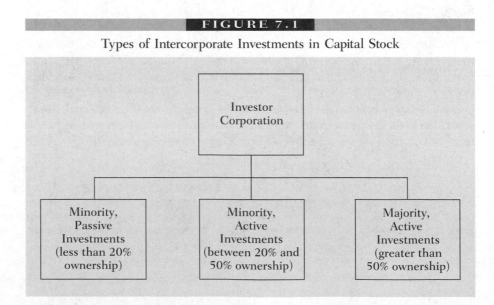

FIGURE 7.1

Types of Intercorporate Investments in Capital Stock

company's activities. This significant influence is usually at a broad policy-making level through representation on the other corporation's board of directors. Because of the wide dispersion of ownership of most publicly held corporations, many of whose shareholders do not vote their shares, firms can exert significant influence over another corporation with ownership of less than a majority of the voting stock. GAAP views investments of between 20 and 50 percent of the voting stock of another company as a minority, active investment unless evidence indicates that the acquiring firm cannot exert significant influence.

3. *Majority, Active Investments.*   Firms acquire shares of another corporation so that the acquiring corporation can control the other company. This control is typically at both the broad policy-making level and at the day-to-day operational level. Ownership of more than 50 percent of the voting stock of another company implies an ability to control unless available evidence indicates the contrary.

The accounting for these three types of investments attempts to reflect the different purpose of each. Exhibit 7.3 summarizes the reporting for each type of investment in the financial statements.

MINORITY, PASSIVE INVESTMENTS

If a firm does not own a sufficient percentage of the voting stock of another corporation to control or significantly influence it, the management of the investment involves two activities: awaiting the receipt of interest or dividends and deciding when to sell the investment for a capital gain or loss. GAAP requires firms to account for minority, passive investments using either amortized acquisition cost or the market value method.[3] A summary of the accounting follows:

1. Firms initially record investments at acquisition cost.
2. Revenues each period equal interest and dividends received or receivable.
3. The accounting at the end of each period depends on the type of security and the firm's reason for holding it. *Statement No. 115* classifies securities into three categories:
   a. Debt securities for which a firm has a positive intent and ability to hold to maturity.
   b. Debt and equity securities held as *trading securities*.
   c. Debt and equity securities held as *available for sale*.
   Firms must account for debt securities expected to be held until maturity at amortized acquisition cost. That is, the firm must amortize any difference between the acquisition cost and maturity value of these debt securities as an adjustment to interest revenue over the life of the debt. Firms report all other debt and equity securities at market value at the end of each period. The reporting of any unrealized holding gain or loss depends on the purpose of holding the securities. If firms actively buy and sell securities to take advantage of short-term differences or changes in market values, these firms classify the securities as

---

[3]Financial Accounting Standards Board, *Statement of Financial Accounting Standards No. 115,* "Accounting for Certain Investments in Debt and Equity Securities," 1993.

EXHIBIT 7.3

Reporting Investments in Securities in the Financial Statements

Financial Statement	Minority Passive Investments	Minority Active Investments	Majority Active Investments
Income Statement	Interest and dividend revenue Unrealized increases and decreases in the market value of securities classified as trading securities Realized gains and losses on sales of securities	Investor's share of investee's net income minus amortization of any excess of the purchase price over the book value of the investee's shareholders' equity at the time of acquisition	Individual revenues and expenses of investee minus the minority interest's share of investee's net income included in consolidated net income
Balance Sheet	Marketable securities and investments in securities reported at market value (except that debt securities held to maturity appear at amortized acquisition cost) Unrealized increases and decreases in the market value of securities classified as available for sale included in shareholders' equity section of the balance sheet	Investments reported at acquisition cost plus investor's cumulative share of investee's net income minus cumulative amortization of excess purchase price over book value acquired minus dividends received from investee since acquisition	Investment in securities account eliminated and replaced by investee's individual assets and liabilities in preparing consolidated balance sheet Minority interest's claim on investee's net assets shown in the shareholders' equity section of consolidated balance sheet
Statement of Cash Flows	Cash received from interest and dividends included in cash flow from operations; cash flows associated with purchases and sales included in cash flows from investing	Cash received from interest and dividends included in cash flow from operations. Cash flows associated with purchases and sales included in cash flows from investing	Individual cash flows from operating, investing, and financing activities of investee included in consolidated statement of cash flows

trading securities, a current asset on the balance sheet. Commercial banks, for example, often trade securities in different capital markets worldwide to take advantage of temporary differences in market prices. Manufacturers, retailers, and other nonfinancial firms occasionally invest funds for trading purposes, but such situations are unusual. Firms include unrealized holding gains and losses on trading securities in the calculation of net income each period. Firms classify debt and equity securities that do not fit one of these first two categories as securities *available for sale,* including them as either current assets or noncurrent assets, depending on the expected holding period. Unrealized holding "gains" or "losses" on securities available for sale are not included in income each period but instead appear in a separate shareholders' equity account, Unrealized Holding Gain or Loss on Securities Available for Sale.

4. When a firm sells trading securities, it recognizes the difference between the selling price and the book value (that is, the market value at the end of the most recent accounting period prior to sale) as a gain or loss. When a firm sells a security classified as available for sale, it recognizes the difference between the selling prices and the *acquisition cost* of the security as a realized gain or loss. At the time of sale, the firm must eliminate any amount related to that security in the shareholders' equity account Unrealized Holding Gain or Loss on Securities Available for Sale.

INTERPRETING FINANCIAL STATEMENT DISCLOSURES FOR INVESTMENTS IN SECURITIES

Coke and Pepsi both show investments in marketable securities in the current assets section of their balance sheets. Coke reports these securities "at cost" and Pepsi reports them "at cost, which approximates market." Although this reporting appears to violate the required use of the market value method, GAAP permits departures when the results are not materially different. Coke reports in Note 9 that the cost of its marketable securities is $80 million and the market value is $82 million. Pepsi discloses in Note 16 that the "carrying value of all financial instruments was not materially different from fair value."

Because firms invest in marketable securities with temporarily excess cash, the analyst can generally presume that firms could sell these securities for an amount at least equal to the amount shown on the balance sheet. This is a reasonable presumption for firms located in countries that require the market method, such as France and the United Kingdom. Certain countries, such as Canada, Japan, and Germany, require the valuation of marketable securities at acquisition cost unless the firms consider a price decline to be permanent. Firms in the latter countries seldom disclose the market value of their marketable securities. If interest rates have increased or stock prices have declined materially in one of these countries during the last several months of the accounting period, the analyst should interpret the reported amounts for these securities cautiously.

MINORITY, ACTIVE INVESTMENTS

When a firm owns less than a majority of the voting stock of another corporation, the accountant must exercise judgment in ascertaining whether the firm can exert significant influence. For the sake of uniformity, GAAP presumes that one company can significantly influence another company when it owns 20 percent or more of the voting stock of the other company. Ownership of less than 20 percent may permit a firm to exert significant influence, but in these cases management must demonstrate to the independent accountants that exerting significant influence is possible (for example, by placing individuals on the investee's board of directors).

GAAP requires firms to account for minority, active investments, generally those in which ownership is between 20 and 50 percent, using the *equity method*.[4] Under

---

[4]Accounting Principles Board, *Accounting Principles Board Opinion No. 18,* "The Equity Method of Accounting for Investments in Common Stock," 1971.

the equity method, the firm owning shares in another firm recognizes as revenue (expense) in each period its share of the net income (loss) of the other firm. See, for example, the income statement of Coke. The line Equity Income includes Coke's share of the earnings from 20 percent- to 50 percent-owned affiliates. If the investor pays more for the shares of an investee than the book value of the common share-holders' equity underlying the shares, the investor must amortize the excess purchase price over a period not exceeding 40 years. The investor treats dividends received from the investee as a return of investment, not as income. In the discussion that follows, we designate the firm owning shares as P and the firm whose shares P owns as S.

The rationale for using the equity method when significant influence is present is best understood by considering the financial statement effects of using the market value method for securities classified as available for sale in these circumstances. Under the market value method, P recognizes income or loss on the income state-ment only when it receives a dividend or sells all or part of the investment. Suppose, as often happens, that S follows a policy of financing its own growing operations through the retention of earnings and consistently declares dividends significantly less than its net income. The market price of S's shares will probably increase to re-flect the retention of assets generated by earnings. Under the market value method, P's only reported income from the investment will be the modest dividends received. P, because of its ownership percentage, can influence the dividend policy of S and thereby the amount of income recognized under the market value method. Under these conditions, the market value method may not reasonably reflect the earnings of S generated under P's influence. The equity method provides a better measure of a firm's earnings and of its investment when, because of its ownership interest, it can significantly influence the operations and dividend policy of another firm.

Under the equity method, firms report investments on the balance sheet at acqui-sition cost plus (minus) the investor's share of the investee's net income (loss) each period minus amortization of any excess purchase price minus the dividends re-ceived from the investee each period.

The statement of cash flows reports cash flows, not equity method earnings. Thus, in deriving cash flow from operations, the statement of cash flows subtracts the investor's share of the investee's earnings from net income and adds the cash dividends received. Most firms report this adjustment as a subtraction for the in-vestor's share of the *undistributed* earnings (net income minus dividends) of the investee.

INTERPRETING FINANCIAL STATEMENT DISCLOSURES FOR EQUITY METHOD INVESTMENTS

Refer to the financial statements for Coke in Appendix A. Its balance sheet shows investments in Coca-Cola Enterprises, Coca-Cola Amatil, and Other, principally bottling operations. Note 3 sets out additional information about these investments. Coca-Cola Enterprises is a 44 percent-owned bottler. Coca-Cola Amatil is a more than 50 percent-owned bottler, but Coke intends to reduce its ownership below 50 percent. Thus, Coke's investments represent minority, active investments for which it uses the equity method. The note indicates that these investees generated earnings of $243 million (= −$15 + $258) during Year 8. Coke's share of this income is $91 million (= −$6 + $97), which agrees with the amount that Coke shows as equity income on its income statement for Year 8. Coke's statement of cash flows shows a subtraction from net income of $35 million for "equity income, net of dividends" in deriving cash flow from operations. Coke therefore received cash dividends of $56 million (= $91 − $35) from these investments during Year 8.

One might wonder why Coke chooses to own less than a controlling interest in these bottlers, a critical component of its operating activities. A possible explanation is that this arrangement permits Coke to keep debt off its balance sheet. Note 3 indicates that these bottlers carry liabilities of $11.714 billion (= $7.422 + $4.292) on assets of $15.756 billion (= $8.682 + 7.074). Thus, the ratio of liabilities to total assets for the bottlers is 74.3 percent (= $11.714 ÷ $15.756). The corresponding percentage ratio of liabilities to total assets for Coke with these investments reported using the equity method is 61.9 percent. If Coke owned a majority interest, GAAP would require Coke to consolidate its financial statements with those of the bottlers (see discussion in the next section of this chapter), and Coke's debt/equity ratio would increase. Note that the total assets of these investees exceed those of Coke ($15.756 billion versus $12.021 billion).

Refer now to the financial statements of Pepsi in Appendix B. Pepsi shows Investments in Affiliates on its balance sheet. Note 1 on accounting policies indicates that Pepsi accounts for these investments using the equity method. It nets equity income from these investments against selling, general, and administrative expenses, perhaps because the amounts are not sufficiently material to warrant a separate line in the income statement. Pepsi owns most of its bottling operations.

The analyst should address two questions in particular when examining the financial statements of firms with significant equity-method intercorporate investments:

1. What is the relation between equity-method income and cash flows received from the investees?
2. Are assets and liabilities essential to a firm's operations submerged in the intercorporate investment account?

The analyst answers the first question by comparing equity-method income on the income statement with the adjustment to net income for undistributed earnings of investees in the statement of cash flows. Coke, for example, derived only 2.9 percent of its pretax earnings during Year 8 from equity-method investees and received only a minor amount of cash from these investments.

The analyst answers the second question by studying the notes on intercorporate investments. Firms must disclose partial balance sheet and income statement information for significant intercorporate investments. As an earlier section discussed, Coke maintains less than a controlling interest in its major bottling operations. The assets and liabilities of these bottlers do not appear on Coke's balance sheet. A later section demonstrates the procedure an analyst might follow to incorporate amounts for such investments on the balance sheet.

The analyst should also exert caution when examining the financial statements of firms in other countries. In Canada, France, Great Britain, and in certain filings with the Ministry of Finance in Japan, firms commonly use the equity method for minority, active investments. Countries that follow a strict legal definition of the entity, such as Germany, tend to report these intercorporate investments at acquisition cost, even when significant influence is present.

MAJORITY, ACTIVE INVESTMENTS

When one firm, P, owns more than 50 percent of the voting stock of another company, S, P can control the activities of S. This control may occur at both a broad policy-making level and a day-to-day operational level. The majority investor in this case is the *parent* and the majority-owned company is the *subsidiary*. GAAP requires the combining or *consolidating* of the financial statements of majority-owned companies with those of the parent (unless the parent cannot for legal or other reasons exercise control).[5]

Reasons for Legally Separate Corporations.   There are many reasons for a business firm's preference to operate as a group of legally separate corporations rather than as a single legal entity. From the viewpoint of the parent company, the more important reasons for maintaining legally separate subsidiary companies include the following:

1. *To Reduce Financial Risk.*   Separate corporations may mine raw materials, transport them to a manufacturing plant, produce the product, and sell the finished product to the public. If any one part of the total process proves to be unprofitable or inefficient, losses from insolvency fall only on the owners and creditors of the one subsidiary corporation. Furthermore, creditors have a claim on the assets of the subsidiary corporation only, not on the assets of the parent company.
2. *To Meet More Effectively the Requirements of State Corporation Laws and Tax Legislation.*   If a firm does business in many states, it must often contend with overlapping and inconsistent taxation, regulations, and requirements. Organizing separate corporations to conduct the operations in the various states may reduce administrative costs.
3. *To Expand or Diversify with a Minimum of Capital Investment.*   A firm may absorb another company by acquiring a controlling interest in its voting stock. It may accomplish this result with a substantially smaller capital investment, as well as with less difficulty, inconvenience, and risk, than if it had constructed a new plant or geared up for a new line of business.

Purpose of Consolidated Statements.   For a variety of reasons, then, a parent and several legally separate subsidiaries may exist as a single economic entity. A consolidation of the financial statements of the parent with those of each of its subsidiaries presents the results of operations, financial position, and changes in cash flows of an affiliated group of companies under the control of a parent, essentially as if the group of companies were a single entity. The parent and each subsidiary are legally separate entities, but they operate as one centrally controlled *economic entity*.

---

[5]Financial Accounting Standards Board, *Statement of Financial Accounting Standards No. 94,* "Consolidation of Majority-Owned Subsidiaries," 1987.

Consolidated financial statements generally provide more useful information to the sharcholders of the parent corporation than would separate financial statements of the parent and each subsidiary.

Consolidated financial statements also generally provide more useful information than does the equity method. The parent, because of its voting interest, can effectively control the use of the subsidiary's individual assets. Consolidation of the individual assets, liabilities, revenues, and expenses of both the parent and the subsidiary provides a more realistic picture of the operations and financial position of the single economic entity.

In a legal sense, consolidated statements merely supplement, but do not replace, the separate statements of the individual corporations, although it is common practice in the United States to present only the consolidated statements in published annual reports.

Consolidation Policy. GAAP requires that firms prepare consolidated financial statements when they meet the following two criteria:

1. The parent owns more than 50 percent of the voting stock of the subsidiary.
2. There are no important restrictions on the ability of the parent to exercise control of the subsidiary.

Ownership of more than 50 percent of the subsidiary's voting stock implies an ability to exert control over the activities of the subsidiary. For example, the parent can control the subsidiary's corporate policies and dividend declarations. There may be situations in which the parent cannot control the subsidiary's activities, despite the ownership of a majority of the voting stock. For example, the subsidiary may reside in a foreign country that severely restricts the withdrawal of funds from that country. Or the subsidiary may be in bankruptcy and under the control of a court-appointed group of trustees. In these cases, the parent will probably not consolidate its financial statements with those of the subsidiary. When the parent owns more than 50 percent of the shares but cannot exercise control, it uses the market value method.

Disclosure of Consolidation Policy. The note to the financial statements that describes significant accounting policies includes a statement about the consolidation policy of the parent. If a parent does not consolidate a significant majority-owned subsidiary, the notes will disclose that fact. The notes to the financial statements of Coke and Pepsi indicate that they consolidate all majority-owned subsidiaries. The one exception is Coke's investments in Coca-Cola Amatil Limited. Coke states that its controlling interest is temporary because it intends to reduce its interest below 50 percent. Thus, it accounts for this investment using the equity method.

Understanding Consolidated Statements. This section discusses several concepts essential for understanding consolidated financial statements:

1. The Need for Intercompany Eliminations.
2. Eliminating Double Counting of Intercompany Payables.

3. Eliminating Double Counting of Investment.
4. Eliminating Double Counting of Income.
5. Eliminating Intercompany Sales.
6. The Meaning of Consolidated Net Income.
7. The Nature of the External Minority Interest in Consolidated Subsidiary.

The Need for Intercompany Eliminations.   State corporation laws typically require each legally separate corporation to maintain its own set of books. Thus, during the accounting period, the accounting system of each corporation records transactions of that entity with all other entities (both affiliated and nonaffiliated). At the end of the period, each corporation prepares its own set of financial statements. The consolidation of these financial statements involves summing the amounts for various financial statement items across the separate company statements. The amounts resulting from the summation require adjustments, however, to eliminate double counting resulting from *intercompany transactions.* Consolidated financial statements reflect the results of an affiliated group of companies operating as a single company. Thus, consolidated financial statements include only the transactions between the consolidated entity and others outside the group.

The eliminations to remove intercompany transactions typically appear on a *consolidation worksheet,* not on the books of any of the legal entities in the consolidated group. The accountant prepares the consolidated financial statements directly from the worksheet. The consolidated entity generally maintains no separate set of books.

To illustrate the need for, and the nature of, *elimination entries,* refer to the data for Company P and Company S in Exhibit 7.4. Column (1) shows the balance sheet and income statement data for Company P taken from its separate company books. Column (2) shows similar data for Company S. Column (3) sums the amounts from columns (1) and (2). The amounts in column (3) include the effects of several intercompany items and, therefore, do not represent the correct amounts for *consolidated* assets, equities, revenues, or expenses.

Eliminating Double Counting of Intercompany Payables.   Separate company records indicate that $12,000 of Company S's accounts receivable represent amounts payable by Company P. The amounts in column (3) count the current assets underlying this transaction twice: once as part of Accounts Receivable on Company S's books and a second time as Cash (or Other Assets) on Company P's books. Also, Accounts Payable in column (3) includes the liability shown on Company P's books, even though the amount is not payable to an entity external to the consolidated group. To eliminate double counting on the asset side and to report Accounts Payable at the amount payable to external entities, the elimination entry reduces the amounts for Accounts Receivable and Accounts Payable in column (3) by $12,000.

Eliminating Double Counting of Investment.   Company P's balance sheet shows an asset, Investment in Stock of Company S. The subsidiary's balance sheet shows its individual assets and liabilities. The combined balance sheets in column (3) include both Company P's investment in Company S's net assets and the assets and liabilities themselves. We must eliminate Company P's account, Investment in Stock of Company S, from the sum of the balance sheets. Because the consolidated

EXHIBIT 7.4

Illustrative Data for Preparation of Consolidated Financial Statements

| | Single-Company Statements | | |
	Company P (1)	Company S (2)	Combined (3) = (1) + (2)
Condensed Balance Sheets on December 31			
Assets			
Accounts Receivable	$ 200,000	$ 25,000	$ 225,000
Investment in Stock of Company S (at equity)	705,000	—	705,000
Other Assets.	2,150,000	975,000	3,125,000
Total Assets	$3,055,000	$1,000,000	$4,055,000
Equities			
Accounts Payable.	$ 75,000	$ 15,000	$ 90,000
Other Liabilities.	70,000	280,000	350,000
Common Stock	2,500,000	500,000	3,000,000
Retained Earnings.	410,000	205,000	615,000
Total Equities.	$3,055,000	$1,000,000	$4,055,000
Condensed Income Statement for Current Year			
Revenues			
Sales	$ 900,000	$ 250,000	$1,150,000
Equity in Earnings of Company S	48,000	—	48,000
Total Revenues.	$ 948,000	$ 250,000	$1,198,000
Expenses			
Cost of Goods Sold (excluding depreciation)	$ 440,000	$ 80,000	$ 520,000
Depreciation Expense	120,000	50,000	170,000
Administrative Expense	80,000	40,000	120,000
Income Tax Expense.	104,000	32,000	136,000
Total Expenses.	$ 744,000	$ 202,000	$ 946,000
Net Income	$ 204,000	$ 48,000	$ 252,000
Dividend Declarations.	50,000	13,000	63,000
Increase in Retained Earnings for the Year.	$ 154,000	$ 35,000	$ 189,000

balance sheet must maintain the accounting equation, we must make corresponding eliminations on the right-hand, or equities, side as well. To understand the eliminations from the right-hand side of the balance sheet, recall that the right-hand side shows the sources of the firm's financing. Creditors (liabilities) and owners (shareholders' equity) finance Company S. Company P owns 100 percent of Company S's voting shares. Thus, the creditors of both companies and Company P's shareholders finance the assets on the consolidated balance sheet of the single economic entity. In other words, the equities of the consolidated entity are the liabilities of both companies but the shareholders' equity of Company P alone. If we added the shareholders' equity accounts of Company S to those of Company P, we would count twice the financing from Company P's shareholders (once on the parent's books and once on the subsidiary's books). Hence, when we eliminate Company P's investment account from the sum of the two companies' assets, we maintain the accounting equation by eliminating the shareholders' equity accounts of Company S.

Eliminating Double Counting of Income.   Similarly, we must eliminate certain intercompany items from the sum of income statement accounts to present meaningfully the operating performance of the consolidated entity. Company P's accounts show Equity in Earnings of Company S of $48,000. Company S's records show individual revenues and expenses that net to $48,000. If we merely summed the revenues and expenses of the two companies, as column (3) of Exhibit 7.4 illustrates, we would double count Company S's earnings. We must eliminate the account Equity in Earnings of Company S in preparing consolidated statements.

Eliminating Intercompany Sales.   Another example of an intercompany item involves intercompany sales of inventory. Separate company records indicate that Company S sold merchandise to Company P for $40,000 during the year. None of this inventory remains in Company P's inventory on December 31. The sale of the merchandise inventory increases Sales Revenue on both Company S's books (sale to Company P for $40,000) and on Company P's books (sale to an external entity for probably a higher price). Thus, the combined amounts for Sales Revenue overstate sales from the standpoint of the consolidated entity by $40,000. Likewise, Cost of Goods Sold of both companies includes the separate-company costs of the goods sold. To eliminate double counting, we must eliminate $40,000 from consolidated Cost of Goods Sold.

The Meaning of Consolidated Net Income.   The amount of consolidated net income for a period exactly equals the amount that the parent shows on its separate company books from applying the equity method; that is, consolidated net income equals

Parent Company's Net Income from Its Own Activities	+	Parent Company's Share of Subsidiary's Net Income	−	Profit (or + Loss) on Intercompany Transactions	−	Amortization of Goodwill from the Acquisition

A consolidated income statement differs from an equity method income statement in the *components* presented. When using the equity method for an unconsolidated subsidiary, the parent's share of the subsidiary's net income minus gain (or plus loss) on intercompany transactions and minus amortization of goodwill appears on a single line, Equity in Earnings of Unconsolidated Subsidiary. In a consolidated income statement, we combine the individual revenues and expenses of the subsidiary (less intercompany adjustments) with those of the parent and eliminate the account Equity in Earnings of Unconsolidated Subsidiary shown on the parent's books. Some accountants refer to the equity method as a *one-line consolidation* because it nets the individual revenues and expenses of the subsidiary into the one account, Equity in Earnings of Unconsolidated Subsidiary.

The Nature of External Minority Interest in Consolidated Subsidiary.
The parent does not always own 100 percent of the voting stock of a consolidated

subsidiary. Accountants refer to the owners of the remaining shares of voting stock as the *minority interest*. These shareholders have a proportionate interest in the net assets (= total assets − total liabilities) of the subsidiary as shown on the subsidiary's separate corporate records. These shareholders also have a proportionate interest in the earnings of the subsidiary.

One issue that the accountant must confront in preparing consolidated statements is whether the statements should show only the parent's share of the assets and liabilities of the subsidiary or whether they should show all of the subsidiary's assets and liabilities along with the minority interests' claim on them. GAAP shows all of the assets and liabilities of the subsidiary because the parent, with its controlling voting interest, effectively directs the use of all the assets and liabilities, not merely an amount equal to the parent's percentage of ownership. The consolidated balance sheet and income statement in these instances, however, must disclose the interest of the minority shareholders in the consolidated subsidiary.

The amount of the minority interest appearing on the balance sheet results from multiplying the common shareholders' equity of the subsidiary by the minority's percentage of ownership. For example, if the common shareholders' equity (or assets minus liabilities) of a consolidated subsidiary totals $500,000 and the minority owns 20 percent of the common stock, the minority interest appears on the consolidated balance sheet at $100,000 (= 0.20 × $500,000). The consolidated balance sheet shows the minority interest as part of shareholders' equity. The financial statements of Coke and Pepsi give no indication that a minority interest exists in any of its consolidated subsidiaries.

The amount of the minority interest in the subsidiary's income results from multiplying the subsidiary's net income by the minority's percentage of ownership. The consolidated income statement shows the proportion of consolidated income applicable to the parent company and the proportion of the subsidiary's income applicable to the minority interest. Typically, the minority interest in the subsidiary's income appears as a subtraction in calculating consolidated net income.

Limitations of Consolidated Statements.   The consolidated statements do not replace those of individual corporations; rather, they supplement those statements and aid in their interpretation. Creditors must rely on the resources of one corporation and may be misled if forced to rely entirely on consolidated statements that combine the data of a company in good financial condition with one verging on insolvency. Firms can legally declare dividends only from their own retained earnings. When the parent company does not own all of the shares of the subsidiary, the outside or minority shareholders can judge the dividend constraints, both legal and financial, only by inspecting the subsidiary's statements.

Consolidation of Unconsolidated Subsidiaries and Affiliates.
The analyst may wish to assess the financial position of a firm with all important majority-owned subsidiaries and minority-owned affiliates consolidated. Coke, for example, has significant investments in bottlers that are integral to its operations. Consolidation of the financial statements of these affiliates with those of Coke presents a more realistic picture of the assets and liabilities of Coke as an operating enterprise. Consolidation also places Coke on a more comparable basis with Pepsi, which owns most of its bottling operations.

Exhibit 7.5 presents a consolidation worksheet for Coke and its bottlers. Coke's balance sheet provides the amounts in column (1). Note 3 to Coke's financial statements provides the amounts for columns (2) and (3). The amounts in column (4) eliminate amounts in the intercorporate investment accounts on Coke's books against the shareholders' equity accounts of the affiliates. The column also shows the reclassification of a portion of the shareholders' equity accounts of the affiliates to recognize the minority or external interests' claims. The amount that Exhibit 7.5 shows for the minority interest equals the total shareholders' equity of the affiliates times the minority interests' ownership percentage. This percentage is 56 percent for Coca-Cola Enterprises. Coke does not disclose its ownership percentage in Other Equity Investments. We can approximate this percentage by comparing Coke's equity income from these investments ($97 million in Note 3) to the total net income of the investees ($258 million in Note 3). Coke appears to own 37.6 percent (= $97 ÷ $258) and the external interests own 62.4 percent.

This procedure probably includes some measurement error. The amounts that Coke shows for its intercorporate investments ($498 and $1,629) do not equal its share (44 percent and 37.6 percent) of the shareholders' equity of the investees. The difference represents negative or positive goodwill of $56 million and $583 million. Exhibit 7.5 includes this goodwill in noncurrent assets. The consolidated amounts in Column (5) provide a better sense of the assets and obligations under Coke's influence and integral to its operations. Net income for Coke remains the same regardless

---

EXHIBIT 7.5

Coke and Equity Method Affiliates
Consolidation Worksheet

	Coke (1)	Coca-Cola Enterprises (2)	Other Equity Investments (3)	Eliminations (4)	Consolidated (5)
Current Assets............	$ 4,434	$ 746	$2,294		$ 7,474
Investments in Securities ...	3,309	—	—	(A) − 498[a]	
				(B) −1,629[a]	1,182
Noncurrent Assets........	4,278	7,936	4,780	(A) − 56[c]	
				(B) + 583[e]	17,521
Total Assets	$12,021	$8,682	$7,074		$26,177
Current Liabilities........	$ 5,171	$1,007	$1,926		$ 8,104
Noncurrent Liabilities......	2,269	6,415	2,366		11,047
External Interests.........	—	—	—	(A) + 706[b]	
				(B) +1,736[d]	2,442
Shareholders' Equity.......	4,581	1,260	2,782	(A) −1,260[a]	
				(B) −2,782[a]	4,584
	$12,021	$8,682	$7,074		$26,177

[a]Given in Coke's Note 3.

[b]$706 = 0.56 × $1,260.

[c]−$56 = [$498 − (0.44 × $1,260)].

[d]$1,736 = (1 − 0.376) ($2,782).

[e]$583 = [$1,629 − (0.376 × $2,782)]

of whether Coke accounts for these investments using the equity method or consolidates them. The components of net income (that is, sales, cost of goods sold) do change, but not net income.

Consider now the effect of consolidating Coke's bottlers on its rate of return on assets. Coke's ROA based on its reported amounts is as follows:

$$ROA = \frac{\$2,188 + (1 - 0.35)(\$168)}{0.5(\$11,052 + \$12,021)} = 19.9\%$$

Operating income in the numerator of ROA does not change as a result of consolidation. To exclude the effect of financing from the numerator of ROA, we must add back the interest expense (net of taxes) recognized by Coke's bottlers. Coke's Note 3 does not provide the amount of interest expense for those entities. We might approximate this amount by assuming that the noncurrent liabilities represent interest-bearing debt. Using the disclosures in Coke's Note 8, the weighted average interest rate on its long-term debt was 6.9 percent for Year 8. Using an assumed interest rate of 7 percent on the debt of Coke's investees and amounts for noncurrent liabilities from Note 3 for Year 8 and corresponding disclosures from its Year 7 annual report yields interest expense of \$561 million [$= 0.07 \times 0.5(\$5,527 + \$6,415 + \$1,720 + \$2,366)$] for Year 8. We inject some error into the calculation of ROA to the extent that some of the current liabilities of these entities bear interest, that some of the noncurrent liabilities do not bear interest, and that 7 percent is not a reasonable interest rate.

The final adjustment to the numerator of ROA to consolidate these bottlers is to add the external interest in earnings. This adjustment permits the numerator to include 100 percent of the operating income of Coke and its bottlers and the denominator to include 100 percent of the assets of these entities. Coke's Note 3 shows the total income or loss of these bottlers for Year 8 ($-\$15 + \$258 = \$243$), as well as Coke's equity share ($-\$6 + \$97 = \$91$). The share of the external interest is therefore \$152 million ($= \$243 - \$91$). Consolidating Coke's bottlers results in the following recomputed ROA for Year 8:

$$ROA = \frac{\$2,188 + (1 - 0.35)(\$168 + \$561) + \$152}{0.5(\$23,883 + \$26,177)} = \frac{\$2,814}{\$25,030} = 11.2\%$$

Thus, Coke's ROA for Year 8 still exceeds that of Pepsi (8.8 percent), but consolidation of the bottlers eliminates most of the differences observed when using Coke's reported amounts.

The consolidation of majority-owned subsidiaries is a relatively recent phenomenon in some countries (Germany, Japan). These countries tended to follow strict legal definitions of the reporting entity. GAAP in these countries now generally requires the preparation of consolidated financial statements, although the requirement in Japan applies only to filings with the Ministry of Finance.

JOINT VENTURE INVESTMENTS

Firms frequently come together in joint ventures to carry out their business activities. For example, two chemical firms may join together to construct a chemical-processing plant. Each firm agrees to purchase 50 percent of the output of the plant and to pay 50 percent of the operating and debt service costs. When the firms sell the plant, each firm receives one-half of the net cash proceeds. By joining together, they can perhaps construct a larger, more efficient plant than if each firm built its own smaller plant.

Joint ventures are unique in that joint control is present. Neither firm has a majority, voting position. Both firms must generally agree to make significant policy changes. These investments therefore fall between minority, active investments and majority, active investments.

Firms account for joint ventures using the equity method. They include the investment in the joint venture in the noncurrent asset section, Investments, on the balance sheet. The assets and liabilities of the joint venture do not appear on the balance sheet of either owner. Long-term debt typically finances most joint ventures. By accounting for the joint venture using the equity method, firms keep this debt off the balance sheet. As Chapter 6 discusses, firms commonly attempt to keep debt off the balance sheet in an effort to present a less-risky position to potential lenders. Joint ventures have increased in popularity in recent years.

The Financial Accounting Standards Board is currently studying the accounting for joint ventures. At issue is whether firms should use the equity method or whether proportionate consolidation is more appropriate. Under proportionate consolidation, the investor's share of the assets and liabilities of the joint venture appear in separate sections on the asset and liabilities sides of the balance sheet, with the investment account eliminated. Some accountants argue that proportionate consolidation better captures the economics of these transactions when joint control is present.

INCOME TAX CONSEQUENCES OF INVESTMENTS IN SECURITIES

For income tax purposes, investments fall into two categories:

1. *Investments in Debt Securities, Preferred Stock, and Less than 80 Percent of the Common Stock of Another Entity.* Firms recognize interest or dividends received or receivable each period as taxable income (subject to a partial dividend exclusion), as well as gains or losses when they sell the securities.

2. *Investments in 80 Percent or More of the Common Stock of Another Entity.* Firms can prepare consolidated tax returns for these investments.

As is evident, the methods of accounting for investments for financial and tax reporting do not overlap precisely. Thus, temporary differences for which firms must recognize deferred taxes will likely arise. Coke, for example, cannot file consolidated tax returns with Coca-Cola Enterprises or other equity investments because its ownership percentage is less than 80 percent. Coke reports in Note 15 deferred tax liabilities relating to these equity investments because it includes its share of the investees' earnings each year for financial reporting but recognizes dividends received as income on its tax return.

FOREIGN CURRENCY TRANSLATION

U.S. parent companies must translate the financial statements of foreign branches and subsidiaries into U.S. dollars before preparing consolidated financial statements for shareholders and creditors. This section describes and illustrates the translation methodology and discusses the implications of the methodology both for managing international operations and for interpreting financial statement disclosures regarding such operations.

Two general issues arise in translating the financial statements of a foreign branch or subsidiary.

1. Should the firm translate individual financial statement items at the exchange rate at the time of the transaction (referred to as the *historical exchange rate*) or at the exchange rate during or at the end of the current period (referred to as the *current exchange rate*)? Financial statement items that firms translate using the historical exchange rates appear in the financial statements at the same U.S. dollar equivalent amount each period regardless of changes in the exchange rate. For example, land acquired in France for 10,000 French francs when the exchange rate was $.40 per French francs appears on the balance sheet at $4,000 each period. Financial statement items that firms translate using the current exchange rate appear in the financial statements at a different U.S. dollar amount each period when exchange rates change. Thus, a change in the exchange rate to $.60 per French franc results in reporting the land at $6,000 in the balance sheet. Financial statement items for which firms use the current exchange rate give rise to a *foreign exchange adjustment* each period.
2. Should the firm recognize the foreign exchange adjustment as a gain or loss in measuring net income each period as it arises or should the firm defer its recognition until a future period? The foreign exchange adjustment represents an unrealized gain or loss, much the same as changes in the market value of marketable securities, inventories, or other assets. Should GAAP require realization of the gain or loss through sale of the foreign operation before recognizing it, or should the unrealized gain or loss flow directly to the income statement as the exchange rate changes?

The foreign currency translation methods differ across countries primarily with regard to the answers to these two questions. The following section describes GAAP in the United States. A later section considers GAAP in other countries.

FUNCTIONAL CURRENCY CONCEPT

Central to the translation of foreign currency items is the *functional currency concept.*[6]

---

[6]Financial Accounting Standards Board, *Statement of Financial Accounting Standards No. 52,* "Foreign Currency Translation," 1981.

Foreign entities (whether branches or subsidiaries) are of two general types:

1. A foreign entity operates as a relatively self-contained and integrated unit within a particular foreign country. The functional currency for these operations is the currency of that foreign country.
2. The operations of a foreign entity are a direct and integral component or extension of the parent company's operations. The functional currency for these operations is the U.S. dollar.

FASB *Statement No. 52* sets out characteristics for determining whether the currency of the foreign unit or the U.S. dollar is the functional currency. Exhibit 7.6 summarizes these characteristics. The operating characteristics of a particular foreign operation may provide mixed signals regarding which currency is the functional currency. Management must exercise judgment in determining which functional currency best captures the economic effects of a foreign entity's operations and financial position. As a subsequent section discusses, management may wish to structure certain financings or other transactions to swing the balance to favor selecting either the foreign currency or the U.S. dollar as the functional currency. Once a firm determines the functional currency of a foreign entity, it must use it consistently over time unless changes in economic circumstances clearly indicate a change in the functional currency.

EXHIBIT 7.6

Factors for Determining Functional Currency of Foreign Unit

	Foreign Currency Is Functional Currency	**U.S. Dollar Is Functional Currency**
Cash Flows of Foreign Entity	Receivables and payables denominated in foreign currency and not usually remitted to parent currently	Receivables and payables denominated in U.S. dollars and readily available for remittance to parent
Sales Prices	Influenced primarily by local competitive conditions and not responsive on a short-term basis to exchange rate changes	Influenced by worldwide competitive conditions and responsive on a short-term basis to exchange rate changes
Cost Factors	Foreign unit obtains labor, materials, and other inputs primarily from its own country	Foreign unit obtains labor, materials, and other inputs primarily from the United States
Financing	Financing denominated in currency of foreign unit or generated internally by the foreign unit	Financing denominated in U.S. dollars or ongoing fund transfers by the parent
Relations between Parent and Foreign Unit	Low volume of intercompany transactions and little operational interrelations between parent and foreign unit	High volume of intercompany transactions and extensive operational interrelations between parent and foreign unit

SOURCE: Financial Accounting Standards Board, *Statement of Financial Accounting Standards No. 52,* "Foreign Currency Translation," 1981.

to the guidelines in Ex-
reign entity operates in a
o be too unstable to serve
. dollar instead. A highly
tive inflation of at least
countries and many de-
lar problems for the U.S.

DOLOGY — FOREIGN CURRENCY
IS FUNCTIONAL CURRENCY

n unit, GAAP requires
d column of Exhibit 7.7
method.

Principles: Intercorporate Entities

es at the average exchange rate during the
of-the-period exchange rate. Net income
losses of the foreign unit. That is, a
nominated in a currency other than
ment of the account. The gain or
e the account originated and
recognize this gain or loss
though it is not yet real-

f the U.S. parent,
unit is subject
ges on this
a sepa-
in

rency (FC)

7

Summary of Translation Methodology

U.S. Dollars

cy Is the Functional (urrent method)	U.S. Dollar Is the Functional Currency (monetary/non-monetary method)
venues and expenses as n currency into U.S. rage exchange rate come includes ized transaction realized translation e firm sells the	Firms translate revenues and expenses using the exchange rate in effect when the firm made the original measurements underlying the valuations. Firms translate revenues and most operating expenses using the average exchange rate during the period. However, they translate cost of goods sold and depreciation using the historical exchange rate appropriate to the related asset (inventory, fixed assets). Net income includes (1) realized and unrealized transaction gains and losses and (2) unrealized translation gains and losses on the net monetary position of the foreign unit each period.

.0:1FC $ 20.0
.0:1FC   40.0
.0:1FC   60.0
.0:1FC   80.0
            $200.0

	as U.S. eriod les	Firms translate monetary assets and liabilities using the end-of-the-period exchange rate. They translate nonmonetary assets and equities using the historical exchange rate.

$2.0:1FC $ 80.0
$2.0:1FC   40.0
              $120.0

$1.0:1FC $ 30.0[a]
              12.5[b]
              37.5[b]
           $ 80.0
           $200.0

Firms translate revenues and expen
period and balance sheet items at the end
includes only *transaction* exchange gains an
foreign unit that has receivables and payables d
its own must make a currency conversion on settle
loss from changes in the exchange rate between the t
the time of settlement is a transaction gain or loss. Firm
during the periods while the account is outstanding, even
ized or settled.

When a foreign unit operates more or less independently
GAAP assumes that only the parent's equity investment in the foreig
to exchange rate risk. The firm measures the effect of exchange rate cl
investment each period but includes the resulting "translation adjustment
rate account in the shareholders' equity section of the balance sheet rath
net income. GAAP's rationale for this treatment is that the firm's investr
foreign unit is for the long term; short-term changes in exchange ates
therefore, affect periodic net income. Firms recognize the cumulativ a
translation adjustment account when measuring any gain or loss fr dis
the foreign unit.

Illustration.   Exhibit 7.8 illustrates the all-current method for a foreig
ing its first year of operations. The exchange rate was $1:1 functional cur

---

EXHIBIT 7.8

Illustration of Translation Methodology when the Foreign Currency Is the Functional Currency

	Foreign Currency	
Balance Sheet		
Assets		
Cash	FC	10
Receivables		20
Inventories		30
Fixed Assets (net)		40
Total	FC	100
Liabilities and Shareholders' Equity		
Accounts Payable	FC	40
Bonds Payable		20
Total	FC	60
Common Stock	FC	30
Retained Earnings		10
Unrealized Translation Adjustment		—
Total	FC	40
Total	FC	100

Exh. 7.8—Continued	Foreign Currency	U.S. Dollars	

Income Statement

Sales Revenue	FC 200	$1.5:1FC	$300.0
Realized Transaction Gain..............	2[c]	$1.5:1FC	3.0[c]
Unrealized Transaction Gain...........	1[d]	$1.5:1FC	1.5[d]
Cost of Goods Sold...................	(120)	$1.5:1FC	(180.0)
Selling & Administrative Expense	(40)	$1.5:1FC	(60.0)
Depreciation Expense..................	(10)	$1.5:1FC	(15.0)
Interest Expense	(2)	$1.5:1FC	(3.0)
Income Tax Expense...................	(16)	$1.5:1FC	(24.0)
Net Income	FC 15		$ 22.5

	Foreign Currency	U.S. Dollars	
[a]Retained Earnings, Jan. 1...............	FC 0.0		$ 0.0
Plus Net Income	15.0		22.5
Less Dividends	(5.0)	$2.0:1FC	$(10.0)
Retained Earnings, Dec. 31	FC 10.0		$ 12.5
[b]Net Asset Position, Jan. 1...............	FC 30.0	$1.0:1FC	$ 30.0
Plus Net Income	15.0		22.5
Less Dividends	(5.0)	$2.0:1FC	$(10.0)
Net Asset Position, Dec. 31	FC 40.0		$ 42.5
Net Asset Position, Dec. 31	⌐———————→	$2.0:1FC	80.0
Unrealized Translation "Gain"			$ 37.5

[c]The foreign unit had receivables and payables denominated in a currency other than its own. When it settled these accounts during the period, the foreign unit made a currency conversion and realized a transaction gain of FC2.

[d]The foreign unit has receivables and payables outstanding that will require a currency conversion in a future period when the foreign unit settles the accounts. Because the exchange rate changed while the receivables/payables were outstanding, the foreign unit reports an unrealized transaction gain for financial reporting.

on January 1, $2:1 FC on December 31, and $1.5:1 FC on average during the year. Thus, the foreign currency increased in value relative to the U.S. dollar during the year. The firm translates all assets and liabilities on the balance sheet at the exchange rate on December 31. It translates common stock at the exchange rate on the date of issuance; the translation adjustment account includes the effects of changes in exchange rates on this investment. The translated amount of retained earnings results from translating the income statement and dividends. Note that the firm translates all revenues and expenses of the foreign unit at the average exchange rate. The foreign unit realized a transaction gain during the year and recorded it on its books. In addition, the translated amounts for the foreign unit include an unrealized transaction gain arising from exposed accounts that are not yet settled. Note (a) to Exhibit 7.8 shows the computation of translated retained earnings. The foreign unit paid the dividend on December 31. Note (b) shows the calculation of the translation adjustment. By investing $30 in the foreign unit on January 1 and allowing the $22.5 of earnings to remain in the foreign unit throughout the year while the foreign currency was increasing in value relative to the U.S. dollar, the parent has a potential exchange "gain" of $37.5. It reports this amount in the separate shareholders' equity account on the balance sheet.

TRANSLATION METHODOLOGY — U.S. DOLLAR IS FUNCTIONAL CURRENCY

When the functional currency is the U.S. dollar, GAAP requires firms to use the *monetary/nonmonetary translation method*. The right-hand column of Exhibit 7.7 summarizes the translation procedure under the monetary/nonmonetary method.

The underlying premise of the monetary/nonmonetary method is that the translated amounts reflect amounts that the firm would have reported if it had originally made all measurements in U.S. dollars. To implement this underlying premise, GAAP makes a distinction between monetary items and nonmonetary items.

A monetary item is an account whose maturity amount does not change as the exchange rate changes. From a U.S. dollar perspective, these accounts give rise to exchange gains and losses because the number of U.S. dollars required to settle the fixed foreign currency amounts fluctuates over time with exchange rate changes. Monetary items include cash, receivables, accounts payable, and other accrued liabilities and long-term debt. Firms translate these items using the end-of-the-period exchange rate and recognize translation gains and losses. These translation gains and losses increase or decrease net income each period, whether or not the foreign unit must make an actual currency conversion to settle the monetary item.

A nonmonetary item is any account that is not monetary and includes inventories, fixed assets, common stock, revenues, and expenses. Firms translate these accounts using the historical exchange rate in effect when the foreign unit initially made the measurements underlying these accounts. Inventories and cost of goods sold translate at the exchange rate when the foreign unit acquired the inventory items. Fixed assets and depreciation expense translate at the exchange rate when the foreign unit acquired the fixed assets. Most revenues and operating expenses other than cost of goods sold and depreciation translate at the average exchange rate during the period. The objective is to state these accounts at their U.S. dollar-equivalent historical cost amounts. In this way, the translated amounts reflect the U.S. dollar perspective that is appropriate when the U.S. dollar is the functional currency.

Illustration.   Exhibit 7.9 shows the application of the monetary/nonmonetary method to the data considered in Exhibit 7.8. Net income again includes both realized and unrealized transaction gains and losses. Net income under the monetary/nonmonetary translation method also includes a $22.5 translation loss. As Exhibit 7.9 shows, the firm was in a net monetary liability position during a period when the U.S. dollar decreased in value relative to the foreign currency. The translation loss arises because the U.S. dollars required to settle these foreign-denominated net liabilities at the end of the year exceed the U.S. dollar amount required to settle the net liability position before the exchange rate changed.

EXHIBIT 7.9

Illustration of Translation Methodology when the U.S. Dollar Is the Functional Currency

	Foreign Currency		U.S. Dollars	
Balance Sheet				
Assets				
Cash	FC	10	$2.0:1FC	$ 20.0
Receivables.		20	$2.0:1FC	40.0
Inventories		30	$1.5:1FC	45.0
Fixed Assets (net)		40	$1.0:1FC	40.0
Total	FC	100		$ 145.0
Liabilities and Shareholders' Equity				
Accounts Payable.	FC	40	$2.0:1FC	$ 80.0
Bonds Payable		20	$2.0:1FC	40.0
Total	FC	60		$ 120.0
Common Stock	FC	30	$1.0:1FC	$ 30.0
Retained Earnings.		10		(5.0)[a]
Total	FC	40		$ 25.0
Total	FC	100		$ 145.0
Income Statement				
Sales Revenue	FC	200	$1.5:1FC	$ 300.0
Realized Transaction Gain.		2	$1.5:1FC	3.0
Unrealized Transaction Gain.		1	$1.5:1FC	1.5
Unrealized Translation Loss		—		(22.5)[b]
Cost of Goods Sold.		(120)	$1.5:1FC	(180.0)
Selling & Administrative Expense		(40)	$1.5:1FC	(60.0)
Depreciation Expense.		(10)	$1.0:1FC	(10.0)
Interest Expense		(2)	$1.5:1FC	(3.0)
Income Tax Expense.		(16)	$1.5:1FC	(24.0)
Net Income	FC	15		$ 5.0

	Foreign Currency		U.S. Dollars	
[a]Retained Earnings, Jan. 1.	FC	0	—	$ 0.0
Plus Net Income		15		5.0
Less Dividends		(5)	$2.0:1FC	$(10.0)
Retained Earnings, Dec. 31	FC	10		$ (5.0)

[b]Income for financial reporting includes any unrealized translation gain or loss for the period. The net monetary position of a foreign unit during the period serves as the basis for computing the translation gain or loss. The foreign unit was in a net monetary liability position during a period when the U.S. dollar decreased in value relative to the foreign currency. The translation loss arises because the U.S. dollars required to settle the net monetary liability position at the end of the year exceed the U.S. dollars required to settle the obligation at the time the firm initially recorded the transactions giving rise to change in net monetary liabilities during the period. The calculations follow:

Exh. 7.9—Continued	Foreign Currency		U.S. Dollars	
Net Monetary Position, Jan. 1	FC 0.0	—	$	0.0
Plus				
Issue of Common Stock	FC 30.0	$1.0:1FC	$	30.0
Sales for Cash and on Account	200.0	$1.5:1FC		300.0
Settlement of Exposed Receivable/Payable at a Gain	2.0	$1.5:1FC		3.0
Unrealized Gain on Exposed Receivable/Payable	1.0	$1.5:1FC		1.5
Less				
Acquisition of Fixed Assets	(50.0)	$1.0:1FC		(50.0)
Acquisition of Inventory	(150.0)	$1.5:1FC		(225.0)
Selling & Admin. Costs Incurred	(40.0)	$1.5:1FC		(60.0)
Interest Cost Incurred	(2.0)	$1.5:1FC		(3.0)
Income Taxes Paid	(16.0)	$1.5:1FC		(24.0)
Dividend Paid	(5.0)	$2.0.1FC		(10.0)
Net Monetary Liability Position, Dec. 31	FC (30.0)		$	(37.5)
		$2.0.1FC		−(60.0)
Unrealized Translation Loss			$	22.5

IMPLICATIONS OF FUNCTIONAL CURRENCY DETERMINATION

As these illustrations demonstrate, the functional currency and related translation method can significantly affect translated financial statement amounts for a foreign unit. Some summary comparisons follow:

	Functional Currency Is:	
	Foreign Currency	**U.S. Dollar**
Net Income	$ 22.5	$ 5.0
Total Assets	200.0	145.0
Shareholders' Equity	80.0	25.0
Return on Assets	11.3%	3.4%
Return on Equity	28.1%	20.0%

These differences arise for two principal reasons:

1. The all-current translation method (foreign currency is the functional currency) uses current exchange rates, while the monetary/nonmonetary translation method (U.S. dollar is the functional currency) uses a mixture of current and historical rates. Not only are net income and total asset amounts different, but also the relative proportions of receivables, inventories, and fixed assets to total assets, debt/equity ratios, and gross and net profit margins differ. When firms use the all-current translation method, the translated amounts reflect the same financial statement relationships (for example, debt/equity ratios) as when measured in the foreign currency. When the U.S. dollar is the functional currency, financial statement relationships get measured in U.S. dollar-equivalent amounts and financial ratios differ from their foreign currency amounts.

2. The other major reason for differences between the two translation methods is the inclusion of unrealized translation gains and losses in net income under the monetary/nonmonetary method. Much of the debate with respect to the predecessor to FASB *Statement No. 52,* which was *Statement No. 8,* involved the inclusion of this unrealized translation gain or loss in net income. Many companies argued that the gain or loss was a bookkeeping adjustment only and lacked economic significance, particularly when the transaction required no currency conversion to settle a monetary item. Also, its inclusion in net income often caused wide, unexpected swings in earnings, particularly in quarterly reports.

As discussed earlier, the organization structure and operating policies of a particular foreign unit determine its functional currency. When these operating characteristics provide mixed signals, management must exercise judgment in identifying the functional currency. For reasons discussed above, most firms prefer to use the foreign currency as the functional currency because the all-current method generally results in fewer earnings surprises. Some actions that management might consider to swing the balance of factors toward use of the foreign currency as the functional currency include these:

1. *Decentralize Decision Making into the Foreign Unit.* The greater the degree of autonomy of the foreign unit, the more likely that its currency will be the functional currency. The U.S. parent company can design effective control systems to monitor the activities of the foreign unit while at the same time permitting the foreign unit to operate with considerable freedom.
2. *Minimize Remittances/Dividends.* The greater the degree of earnings retention by the foreign unit, the more likely its currency will be the functional currency. The parent may obtain cash from a foreign unit indirectly rather than directly through remittances or dividends. For example, a foreign unit with mixed signals about its functional currency might, through loans or transfer prices for goods or services, send cash to another foreign unit whose functional currency is clearly its own currency. This second foreign unit can then remit it to the parent. Other possibilities for interunit transactions are possible to ensure that *some* foreign currency rather than the U.S. dollar is the functional currency.

INTERPRETING FINANCIAL STATEMENT DISCLOSURES

Refer to the financial statements for Coke in Appendix A. Coke's Note 1 on accounting policies does not indicate the foreign currency translation method it uses for foreign operations. Note 20 discloses that Coke has substantial foreign involvements (67 percent of sales and 60 percent of assets in Year 8). Coke conducts a portion of these operations in Latin America and Africa, where high inflation rates often dictate the use of the monetary/nonmonetary translation method.

Coke's balance sheets shows the account, Foreign Currency Translation Adjustment, in the shareholders' equity section, suggesting that Coke uses the all-current translation method for a portion of its foreign operations. These operations resulted in a negative translation adjustment of $271 million at the end of Year 7 and a negative adjustment of $420 million at the end of Year 8, an increase of $149 million during Year 8. The all-current translation method assumes that Coke's net asset position (that is, assets minus liabilities, or shareholders' equity) is at risk to exchange rate changes. The reporting of a larger negative amount in the translation adjustment at the end of Year 8 than at the beginning suggests that, on average, foreign currencies decreased in value relative to the U.S. dollar during Year 8.

Refer now to Pepsi's financial statements in Appendix B. Note 18 indicates that Pepsi also has major foreign operations, although not as significant as those of Coke. Pepsi discloses no information about the foreign currency translation method it uses for foreign operations. Its balance sheet shows a Currency Translation Adjustment account in the shareholders' equity section. This adjustment account reflects an increase in the negative balance during Year 8, the same as for Coke, suggesting that Pepsi also operated in countries whose currency on average decreased in value relative to the U.S. dollar.

Both Coke and Pepsi have significant foreign operations. Changes in exchange rates can significantly affect interpretations of their profitability, independent of the translation method used. Consider the example in Exhibit 7.10.

Under the first scenario, the average exchange rate was $10:1FC during the period. Foreign sales represent 40 percent of consolidated sales (= $1,000 ÷ $2,500) and the consolidated profit margin is 28 percent. Under the second scenario, foreign operations as measured in the local currency are identical to those above. In this case, however, the average exchange rate was $15:1FC. After translation, foreign sales represent 50 percent of consolidated sales (= $1,500 ÷ $3,000) and the profit margin is now 26.7 percent. Although the operations of this foreign unit are largely self-contained within the foreign country and, on an operational level at least, not affected by exchange rate changes, the extent to which the exchange rate changed did have an effect on consolidated financial statements in U.S. dollars.

EXHIBIT 7.10

Effect of Foreign Sales on Consolidated Profit Margin

	Foreign Subsidiary			U.S. Parent	Consolidated
	Foreign Currency	$10:1FC	U.S. Dollars	U.S. Dollars	
Scenario 1					
Sales	FC 100	$10:1FC	$1,000	$1,500	$2,500
Expenses.	80	$10:1FC	800	1,000	1,800
Net Income	FC 20	$10:1FC	$ 200	$ 500	$ 700
Profit Margin.			20%	33%	28%
Scenario 2					
Sales	FC 100	$15:1FC	$1,500	$1,500	$3,000
Expenses.	80	$15:1FC	1,200	1,000	2,200
Net Income	FC 20	$15:1FC	$ 300	$ 500	$ 800
Profit Margin.			20%	33%	26.7%

Coke's and Pepsi's disclosures regarding foreign operations, though sparse, are not unusual. Most firms aggregate information for all foreign operations so that the analyst encounters difficulties trying to interpret the impact of international activities on profitability and risk. The interpretive difficulties increase when comparing U.S. companies with non-U.S. companies. Reporting practices vary widely. In addition to the all-current and monetary/nonmonetary translation methods, some countries permit the current/noncurrent method (current assets and liabilities translate at the current exchange rate; noncurrent assets and liabilities translate at the historical exchange rate). In addition to recognizing translation adjustments in income immediately or in a separate shareholders' equity account, some countries require firms to amortize this adjustment into income over a period of future years. As capital markets become more integrated internationally, one would hope that greater uniformity in translation methods will evolve.

FOREIGN CURRENCY TRANSLATION AND INCOME TAXES

Income tax laws make a distinction between a foreign branch of a U.S. parent and a subsidiary of a U.S. parent. A subsidiary is a legally separate entity from the parent, but a branch is not. The translation procedure of foreign branches is essentially the same as for financial reporting (except that taxable income does not include translation gains and losses until realized). That is, a firm selects a functional currency for each foreign branch and uses the all-current or monetary/nonmonetary translation method as appropriate.

For foreign subsidiaries, taxable income includes only dividends received each period (translated at the exchange rate on the date of remittance). Because parent companies typically consolidate foreign subsidiaries for financial reporting but cannot consolidate them for tax reporting, temporary differences that require the provision of deferred taxes likely arise.

SEGMENT REPORTING

Each of the three topics discussed thus far in this chapter (corporate acquisitions, investments in securities, and foreign currency translation) involve the aggregation of information about various entities or units into a single set of financial statements. When these entities or units operate in an integrated or coordinated manner, it is useful to examine the results of operations and financial position for the combined entities as a whole.

The process of combining or aggregating information for various entities, however, can hinder the analyst in making judgments about the returns and risks of the subunits. For example, General Electric Company (GE) manufactures and distributes a wide line of industrial and consumer products. Its wholly owned, consolidated subsidiary, General Electric Financial Services (GEFS), operates in leasing, venture capital, investment banking, and other financial services. The consolidated financial statements merge these different activities. Yet the assets of GE are primarily inventories and fixed assets; those of GEFS are largely receivables. The capital structure of GEFS includes considerably more debt than that of GE.

To provide useful information about its subunits, GAAP requires firms to provide certain segment information.[7] This section describes these disclosures, which Chapter 3 used in analyzing the profitability of Coke and Pepsi.

DEFINITION OF SEGMENTS

GAAP requires firms to report segment data in three ways, according to (1) product/industry, (2) geographical location (foreign versus domestic), and (3) major customers (for example, U.S. government). However, firms provide segment data only for those segments that make up 10 percent or more of total sales, income, or assets.

Statement No. 14 does not prescribe a list of acceptable segment classes. Instead, firms are free to determine the segment groupings that best characterize their operations. Both Coke (Note 19) and Pepsi (Note 18) indicate that they operate in soft drinks and consumer foods, and Pepsi also operates in restaurants. Both firms have significant foreign operations but break out their segment data differently. Coke, for example, includes Canadian with Pacific operations; Pepsi includes Canadian with Mexican operations.

TRANSFER PRICING AND TREATMENT OF CENTRAL CORPORATE EXPENSES

Most firms operate with some degree of integration. As a consequence, most segments sell a portion of their output to other segments within the firm. Two questions arise with respect to intersegment sales:

1. Should segment sales include intersegment sales or should firms eliminate intersegment sales from the segment data?
2. At what transfer price should segments report intersegment sales (cost, market price)?

Statement No. 14 requires firms to disclose material intercompany sales in their segment reports. They must also disclose the transfer price used. Coke indicates in Note 19 that intersegment transfers are not material. Pepsi makes no such disclosure, implying that its intersegment transfers are also immaterial.

A second reporting issue is the treatment of central corporate costs (president's salary, corporate office expenses). Should firms allocate these costs to segments in measuring segment operating income or should they remain unallocated? FASB *Statement No. 14* does not prescribe one treatment or the other but requires firms to disclose the nature and amount of corporate expenses and indicate clearly how they treat such costs in the segment report.

Coke includes a Corporate column in its segment disclosures. This column includes amounts that Coke chooses not to allocate to the segments. It does not disclose the items included in the $396 million on the operating income line for Year 8. An examination of Coke's income statement suggests that it primarily includes interest expense. Note that the consolidated operating income reported in the segment

---

[7]Financial Accounting Standards Board, *Statement of Financial Accounting Standard No. 14,* "Financial Reporting for Segments of a Business Enterprise," 1976.

disclosures is pretax income. Pepsi's segment note indicates that it allocated some corporate expenses to segments but provides no further detail.

SEGMENT ITEMS DISCLOSED

For each identifiable product or industry segment, firms must disclose five items of information:

1. Sales.
2. Operating income.
3. Identifiable assets.
4. Capital expenditures.
5. Depreciation expense.

For geographic segments, firms must report only segment sales, operating income, and identifiable assets. For segment disclosures by major customers, firms need only report sales.

The required segment disclosures in Canada closely parallel those in the United States. European countries and Japan tend to require the reporting of sales by major industry grouping and by geographic location. Firms in these countries seldom disclose information about segment operating income or assets.

The analyst gains additional insight into the profitability and risk of a firm using these segment disclosures.

1. *Profitability Analysis.* Chapter 3 discussed the rate of return on assets and its disaggregation into profit margin and asset turnover components. The segment disclosures permit similar calculations at a segment level:

$$\text{Rate of Return on Assets} = \text{Profit Margin} \times \text{Asset Turnover}$$

$$\frac{\text{Operating Income}}{\text{Identifiable Assets}} = \frac{\text{Operating Income}}{\text{Sales}} \times \frac{\text{Sales}}{\text{Identifiable Assets}}$$

2. *Cash-Generating Ability of Operations.* Chapters 2 and 3 discussed the analysis of a firm's cash-generating ability. We focused on cash flow from operations. A measure of a firm's ability to finance itself internally is cash flow from operations divided by capital expenditures. Operating income plus depreciation and amortization expense is roughly equivalent to working capital provided by operations. Although this is not the same as cash flow from operations, it does provide some information about the liquidity characteristics of the segments. When we divide this amount by capital expenditures, the result is a rough measure of the segment's ability to finance itself from operations.

The segment data for Pepsi for Year 8 in Note 18 permits the calculation of the "cash flow" to capital expenditures ratio for Pepsi's three industry segments. As Exhibit 7.11 demonstrates, all three segments produce an excess of operating cash flow over capital expenditures. However, the capital-intensive restaurant segment has the smallest excess. Pepsi probably uses excess cash flow from its beverage and snack foods segments to finance its growing restaurant segment.

EXHIBIT 7.11

Calculation of Cash Flow to Capital Expenditures Ratio for Pepsi's Industry Segments

	Beverages	Snack Foods	Restaurants
Operating Income	$1,109.0	$1,189.6	$ 778.0
Depreciation	358.5	279.2	457.2
Amortization	157.4	40.9	105.4
Cash Flow from Operations	$1,624.9	$1,509.7	$1,340.6
Capital Expenditures	$ 491.3	$ 491.4	$1,004.4
Cash Flow to Capital Expenditures	3.3	3.1	1.3

SUMMARY

Unlike reporting topics such as inventories, leases, and deferred taxes (covered in Chapters 5 and 6), which affect one or only a few lines in the financial statements, the topics discussed in this chapter tend to affect many line items in the financial statements. The accounting for corporate acquisitions, intercorporate investments, foreign currency translation, and segment reporting are therefore more pervasive in their financial statement effects. This situation both increases their potential significance to the financial analyst and provides a source for concern. Full disclosure of the effects of using the purchase method instead of the pooling of interests method or translating the financial statements of a foreign unit using the all-current method instead of the monetary/nonmonetary method is cumbersome and possibly confusing. The analyst must often contend with less than sufficient disclosures when interpreting financial statements affected by the topics considered in this chapter.

PROBLEMS

7.1   EFFECT OF THE PURCHASE METHOD AND THE POOLING OF INTERESTS METHOD ON THE BALANCE SHEET AND THE INCOME STATEMENT. Condensed balance sheet data for Moran Corporation and Walther Corporation as of January 1, Year 8, follow.

	Book Values		Market Values
	Moran (1)	Walther (2)	Walther (3)
Current Assets	$1,200	$ 800	$ 900
Fixed Assets	1,800	1,200	1,500
Goodwill	—	—	
	$3,000	$2,000	$
Current Liabilities	$1,000	$ 600	$ 600
Noncurrent Liabilities	1,400	1,000	1,000
Shareholders' Equity	600	400	
	$3,000	$2,000	$

The shares of Moran currently sell on the market for $40 per share. Moran wishes to acquire all of the common stock of Walther as of January 1, Year 8, and is considering two ways to structure the acquisition.

> *Alternative A.*   Moran will issue at par 10 percent, 20-year bonds for $1,200. It will use the proceeds to acquire all of the common stock of Walther. The firms will account for the transaction using the purchase method for financial reporting. This transaction is a taxable exchange to the shareholders of Walther but a nontaxable exchange for Walther.
>
> *Alternative B.*   Moran will issue 25 shares of its common stock for all of the common stock of Walther. The firms will account for the transaction using the pooling of interests method for financial reporting. This transaction is a nontaxable exchange to both Walther Corporation and its shareholders.

REQUIRED
a. Prepare pro forma balance sheets under Alternative A and Alternative B as of January 1, Year 8. The income tax rate is 40 percent.
b. Before considering the effects of the acquisition, Moran projects net income of $300 and Walther projects net income of $200 for Year 8. Compute the amount of pro forma net income for Year 8 for the merged firm under each alternative. Both firms use a LIFO cost-flow assumption for inventories and do not expect to liquidate a LIFO layer during Year 8. Depreciable assets have a 10-year remaining life as of January 1, Year 8. Both firms use the straight-line depreciation method. Amortize any goodwill over 20 years.

7.2   EFFECT OF THE PURCHASE METHOD AND THE POOLING OF INTERESTS METHOD ON CONSOLIDATED BALANCE SHEET AND INCOME STATEMENT. AT&T launched a hostile takeover bid for NCR early in Year 6. AT&T was successful in acquiring all of the common stock of NCR for $7,800 million of AT&T common stock. Financial statement data for these companies for Year 5, taken from their most recent annual reports prior to the transaction, reveal the following (amounts in millions):

	AT&T	NCR
December 31, Year 5 (before takeover)		
Total Assets	$43,775	$4,547
Total Liabilities	29,682	2,757
Total Shareholders' Equity.........	14,093	1,790
	$43,775	$4,547

REQUIRED
a. Assume for this part that AT&T used the purchase method to account for its acquisition of NCR. Also assume that $2 billion of any excess purchase price relates to depreciable assets with a market value in excess of their book value. These depreciable assets have an average remaining life of 10 years at the date of acquisition. AT&T uses the straight-line depreciation method and amortizes goodwill over 40 years. The income tax rate is 34 percent. Prepare a consolidated balance sheet as of January 2, Year 6.
b. Repeat part (*a*) but assume that all of any excess purchase price relates to goodwill.
c. Assume for this part that AT&T accounted for the transaction using the pooling of interests method. Prepare a consolidated balance sheet as of January 2, Year 6.

d. AT&T actually accounted for this transaction using the pooling of interests method. It reported consolidated net income for Year 6 of $2,880 million (excluding a restructuring charge). Compute the amount of consolidated net income for Year 6 if AT&T had accounted for the acquisition following the assumptions in part (*a*).

e. Repeat the requirements in part (*d*) following the assumptions in part (*b*).

7.3   EFFECT OF THE PURCHASE METHOD AND THE POOLING OF INTERESTS METHOD ON BALANCE SHEET AND INCOME STATEMENT. Bristol-Myers Company and Squibb Company, both pharmaceutical firms, agreed to merge as of October 1, Year 9. Bristol-Myers exchanged 234 million shares of its common stock for the outstanding shares of Squibb. The shares of Bristol-Myers sold for $55 per share on the merger date, resulting in a transaction with a market value of $12.87 billion. The firms accounted for the merger as a pooling of interests.

REQUIRED

a. The most recent balance sheets of Bristol-Myers and Squibb prior to the merger reveal the following (amounts in millions):

	Bristol-Myers	Squibb
Assets	$5,190	$3,083
Liabilities	$1,643	$1,682
Shareholders' Equity.	3,547	1,401
	$5,190	$3,083

Prepare a summary consolidated balance sheet such as those above for Bristol-Myers and Squibb, assuming that the firms accounted for the merger using (1) the pooling of interests method and (2) the purchase method. Assume that any excess of market value over book value relates to goodwill.

b. Net Income of Bristol-Myers and Squibb prior to and subsequent to the merger appear below (amounts in millions). The amounts for Year 9 exclude a special charge for merger-related expenses.

	Pre merger			Post merger	
	Year 7	Year 8	First Nine Months of Year 9	Last Three Months of Year 9	Year 10
Bristol-Myers	$710	$829	$716	—	—
Squibb	$358	$425	$384	—	—
Combined	—	—	—	$340	$1,748

Compute the amount of net income that Bristol-Myers Squibb would report for Year 9 using the pooling of interests method.

c. Compute the amount of net income that Bristol-Myers Squibb would report for Year 9 using the purchase method. Assume that the firm amortizes goodwill over 40 years. Note that net income under the purchase method excludes earnings of Squibb prior to the merger.

d. Compute the amount of net income that Bristol-Myers Squibb would report for Year 10 using the purchase method.

e. Complete the following schedule of net income:

	Bristol-Myers Company		Bristol-Myers Squibb Company	
	Year 7	Year 8	Year 9	Year 10
Pooling of Interests Method				
Purchase Method				

f. Refer to the analysis in part (*e*). Compare the levels and growth rates in net income for the purchase and pooling of interests methods.

7.4 EFFECT OF THE PURCHASE METHOD AND THE POOLING OF INTERESTS METHOD ON BALANCE SHEET AND INCOME STATEMENT. Ormond Company acquired all of the outstanding common stock of Daytona Company on January 1, Year 5. Ormond gave shares of its common stock with a market value of $312 million in exchange for the Daytona common stock. Daytona will remain a legally separate entity after the exchange, but Ormond will prepare consolidated financial statements each period with Daytona. The transaction qualifies as a nontaxable exchange for income tax purposes. Exhibit 7.12 presents the balance sheets of Ormond and Daytona on January 1, Year 5, just prior to the acquisition. The income tax rate is 40 percent. The following information applies to Daytona.

1. The market value of Daytona's fixed assets exceeds their book value by $50 million.
2. Daytona owns a patent with a market value of $40 million.

EXHIBIT 7.12

Ormond Company and Daytona Company
Balance Sheets
January 1, Year 5
(amounts in millions)
(Problem 7.4)

	Ormond Company	Daytona Company
Cash	$ 25	$ 15
Accounts Receivable	60	40
Fixed Assets (net)	250	170
Patent	—	—
Deferred Tax Asset	10	—
Goodwill........................	—	—
Total Assets	$345	$225
Accounts Payable & Accruals	$ 60	$ 40
Long-Term Debt	120	60
Deferred Tax Liability.............	40	—
Other Noncurrent Liabilities	30	—
Common Stock	80	50
Retained Earnings................	15	75
Total Equities...................	$345	$225

3. Daytona is a defendant in a lawsuit that it expects to settle during Year 5 at a pretax cost of $25 million. The firm carries no insurance against such lawsuits. If permitted, Ormond desires to establish an acquisition reserve for this lawsuit.
4. Daytona has an unrecognized and unfunded retirement health care benefits obligation totaling $20 million on January 1, Year 5.

REQUIRED

a. Prepare a consolidated balance sheet for Ormond and Daytona on January 1, Year 5, assuming that Ormond accounts for the acquisition using the purchase method.
b. Repeat part (*a*) assuming that Ormond accounts for the acquisition using the pooling of interests method.
c. Exhibit 7.13 presents income statements and balance sheets taken from the separate company books at the end of Year 5, assuming that Ormond had accounted for its

---

EXHIBIT 7.13

Ormond Company and Daytona Company
Consolidation Worksheet
Year 5
(in millions)
(Problem 7.4)

	Ormond Company	Daytona Company
Income Statement for Year 5		
Sales	$ 600	$ 450
Equity in Earnings of Daytona Co.	18	—
Operating Expenses	(550)	(395)
Interest Expense	(10)	(5)
Loss on Lawsuit	—	(20)
Income Tax Expense	(23)	(12)
Net Income	$ 35	$ 18
Balance Sheet on December 31, Year 5		
Cash	$ 45	$ 25
Accounts Receivable	80	50
Investment in Daytona Co.	327[a]	—
Fixed Assets	280	195
Patent	—	—
Deferred Tax Asset	15	—
Goodwill	—	—
Total Assets	$ 747	$ 270
Accounts Payable & Accruals	$ 85	$ 55
Long-Term Debt	140	75
Deferred Tax Liability	50	—
Other Noncurrent Liabilities	40	—
Common Stock	392	50
Retained Earnings	40	90
Total Equities	$ 747	$ 270

[a]$312 initial investment + $18 equity in earnings − $3 dividend received = $327.

acquisition of Daytona using the *purchase method*. The following information applies to these companies.

(1) The fixed assets of Daytona had an average remaining life of five years on January 1, Year 5. The firms use the straight line depreciation method.

(2) Daytona's patent had a remaining life of ten years on January 1, Year 5.

(3) Daytona settled the lawsuit during Year 5 and expects no further liability.

(4) Daytona will amortize and fund its retirement health care benefits obligation over twenty years. It included $1 million in operating expenses during Year 5 related to amounts unrecognized and unfunded as of January 1, Year 5.

(5) Amortize goodwill straight-line over 40 years.

Prepare a consolidated income statement for Year 5 and a consolidated balance sheet on December 31, Year 5, following the purchase method of accounting.

7.5   EFFECT OF MARKET VALUE AND EQUITY METHODS ON BALANCE SHEET AND INCOME STATEMENT. Seagram acquired 11.7 percent of Time Warner on January 2, Year 3. Financial statement data for these firms at the end of Year 3 reveal the following (amounts in millions):

Seagram

Assets—December 31, Year 3

Investment in Time Warner at Market Value (11.7% ownership)	$ 1,769
All Other Assets	9,949
Total Assets	$11,718

Liabilities	$ 6,717

Shareholders' Equity

Unrealized Appreciation in Market Value of Time Warner (pretax)	13
All Other Shareholders' Equity	4,988
Total Liabilities and Shareholders' Equity	$11,718

Income Statement for Year 3

Dividend Revenue from Time Warner (net of taxes)	$ 8
All Other Revenue and Expenses (net of taxes)	371
Net Income	$ 379

Time Warner—December 31, Year 3

Assets	$16,892

Liabilities	$15,522
Shareholders' Equity	1,370
	$16,892

Net Loss for Year 3	$ (339)

REQUIRED

a. The total common shareholders' equity of Time Warner on January 1, Year 3, was $1,810. Assume that any excess purchase price relates to goodwill. Compute the amount of goodwill related to Seagram's investment in Time Warner on the date of acquisition.

b. Assume for this part that Seagram had used the equity method instead of the market value method to account for its investment in Time Warner during Year 3. Compute the maximum amount of net income that Seagram would report for Year 3. The income tax rate is 35 percent.

c. Compute the total assets for Seagram on December 31, Year 3, if it had used the equity method instead of the market value method throughout Year 3.

7.6 APPLYING THE EQUITY, PROPORTIONATE CONSOLIDATION, AND FULL CONSOLIDATION METHODS. Mylan Laboratories is a leading firm in the generic pharmaceutical industry. Generic drugs have chemical compositions similar to ethical drugs but sell for a significantly lower price. Once the patent period ends on an ethical drug, generic drug companies break down the drug into its basic chemical elements. They then submit an applica-

---

EXHIBIT 7.14

Mylan Laboratories
Financial Statement Data
(amounts in thousands)
(Problem 7.6)

	Year 5	Year 6	Year 7	Year 8
Balance Sheet				
Current Assets.............................	$ 94,502	$ 120,014	$ 180,482	$ 209,572
Investment in and Advances to Somerset.......	18,045	13,674	14,844	17,964
Noncurrent Assets.........................	74,408	93,032	155,779	175,789
Total Assets	$186,955	$ 226,720	$ 351,105	$ 403,325
Current Liabilities..........................	$ 12,931	$ 17,909	$ 26,482	$ 17,926
Noncurrent Liabilities.......................	6,493	5,359	7,348	5,430
Shareholders' Equity.......................	167,531	203,452	317,275	379,969
Total Liabilities and Shareholders' Equity	$186,955	$ 226,720	$ 351,105	$ 403,325
Income Statement				
Sales		$ 131,936	$ 211,964	$ 251,773
Costs and Expenses		(100,458)	(135,759)	(188,304)
Operating Income		$ 31,478	$ 76,205	$ 63,469
Equity in Earnings of Somerset.............		18,664	21,136	23,596
Income before Taxes......................		$ 50,142	$ 97,341	$ 87,065
Income Tax Expense.......................		(10,028)	(26,720)	(13,998)
Net Income		$ 40,114	$ 70,621	$ 73,067
Cash-Flow Statement				
Net Income		$ 40,114	$ 70,621	$ 73,067
Equity in Earnings of Somerset.............		(18,664)	(21,136)	(23,596)
Cash Received from Somerset..............		23,035	19,966	20,676
Other Addbacks and Subtractions...........		5,962	7,959	14,690
Changes in Working Capital Accounts........		(4,519)	(9,073)	(49,204)
Cash Flow from Operations.................		$ 45,928	$ 68,337	$ 35,633

tion to the Food and Drug Administration to sell a generic equivalent of the ethical drug. The ability to sell generic drugs at a lower price results from lower research and development, marketing, and other costs.

Mylan owns 50 percent of the common stock of Somerset Pharmaceuticals (Somerset). Somerset sells an ethical drug for Parkinson's disease. Exhibit 7.14 presents financial statement data for Mylan, which accounts for its investment in Somerset using the equity method. Equity in earnings of Somerset includes Mylan's 50 percent share of Somerset's earnings minus amortization of intangible assets resulting from the acquisition of Somerset. Such intangible assets are amortized over 15 years. Amortization expense totaled $924,000 in each of the Years 6 through 8. Additionally, Mylan charges Somerset a management services fee each year and includes it in the Equity in Earnings of Somerset account. Somerset records this fee as an expense in measuring earnings. Exhibit 7.15 presents financial statement data for Somerset.

REQUIRED

a. Prepare an analysis of the changes in the shareholders' equity of Somerset for each of the Years 6 through 8.
b. Prepare an analysis of the changes in the Investment in and Advances to Somerset account on Mylan's books for each of the Years 6 through 8. Be sure to indicate the

---

EXHIBIT 7.15

Somerset Pharmaceuticals
Financial Statement Data
(amounts in thousands)
(Problem 7.6)

	Year 5	Year 6	Year 7	Year 8
Balance Sheet				
Current Assets	$22,801	$ 24,597	$ 30,409	$ 27,931
Noncurrent Assets	2,802	2,791	2,670	6,043
Total Assets	$25,603	$ 27,388	$ 33,079	$ 33,974
Current Liabilities	$ 7,952	$ 15,413	$ 20,675	$ 14,918
Payable to Owners	7,274	1,490	1,796	1,002
Other Noncurrent Liabilities	3,302	975	808	642
Shareholders' Equity	7,075	9,510	9,800	17,412
Total Liabilities and Shareholders' Equity	$25,603	$ 27,388	$ 33,079	$ 33,974
Income Statement				
Sales		$ 93,513	$108,518	$111,970
Costs and Expenses		(42,041)	(49,872)	(50,465)
Income before Taxes		$ 51,472	$ 58,646	$ 61,505
Income Tax Expense		(18,806)	(21,789)	(19,547)
Net Income		$ 32,666	$ 36,857	$ 41,958

amounts for equity in earnings of Somerset, management fee, goodwill amortization, dividend received, and other cash payments received.

c. Does the equity method, proportionate consolidation method, or full consolidation method best reflect the operating relationships between Mylan and Somerset? Explain.

d. Prepare an income statement for Mylan and Somerset for Year 6, Year 7, and Year 8 using the proportionate consolidation method.

e. Repeat part (d) using the full consolidation method.

f. Compute the ratio of operating income before income taxes to sales for Year 6, Year 7, and Year 8 using the equity method, proportionate consolidation method, and full consolidation method.

g. Why do the ratios computed in part (f) differ across the three methods of accounting for the investment in Somerset?

h. Compute the effective tax rate (that is, income tax expense divided by income before income taxes) for Year 6, Year 7, and Year 8 using the equity method, proportionate consolidation method, and full consolidation method.

i. Why do the measures of the effective tax rate computed in part (h) differ across the three methods of accounting for the investment in Somerset?

7.7 CALCULATING THE TRANSLATION ADJUSTMENT UNDER THE ALL-CURRENT METHOD AND THE MONETARY/NONMONETARY METHOD. Foreign Sub is a wholly-owned

---

EXHIBIT 7.16

Foreign Sub
Financial Statement Data
(Problem 7.7)

	December 31	
	Year 3	Year 4
Cash	FC 100	FC 150
Accounts Receivable	300	350
Inventories	350	400
Land	500	700
	FC1,250	FC1,600
Accounts Payable	FC 150	FC 250
Long-Term Debt	200	300
Common Stock	500	600
Retained Earnings	400	450
	FC1,250	FC1,600

	For Year 4
Sales	FC 4,000
Cost of Goods Sold	(3,200)
Selling and Administrative	(400)
Income Taxes	(160)
Net Income	FC 240
Dividend Declared and Paid on December 31	(190)
Increase in Retained Earnings	FC 50

subsidiary of U.S. Domestic Corporation, which acquired the subsidiary several years ago. The financial statements for Foreign Sub for Year 4 in its own currency appear in Exhibit 7.16.

The exchange rates between the U.S. dollar and the foreign currency of the subsidiary follow:

December 31, Year 3:	$10:1FC
Average—Year 4:	$8:1FC
December 31, Year 4:	$6:1FC

On January 1, Year 4, Foreign Sub issued FC100 of long-term debt and FC100 of common stock in the acquisition of land costing FC200. Operating activities occurred evenly over the year.

REQUIRED

a. Assume that Foreign Sub's currency is the functional currency. Compute the change in the cumulative translation adjustment for Year 4. Indicate whether the change increases or decreases shareholders' equity.
b. Assume that the U.S. dollar is the functional currency. Compute the amount of the translation gain or loss for Year 4. Indicate whether the amount is a gain or loss.

7.8 TRANSLATING THE FINANCIAL STATEMENTS OF A FOREIGN SUBSIDIARY; COMPARISON OF TRANSLATION METHODS. Stebbins Corporation established a wholly owned Canadian subsidiary on January 1, Year 6, by contributing 500,000 U.S. dollars for all of the subsidiary's common stock. The exchange rate on that date was C$1:US$.90 (that is, one Canadian dollar equaled 90 U.S. cents). The Canadian subsidiary invested 500,000 Canadian dollars in a building with an expected life of twenty years and rented it to various tenants for the year. The average exchange rate during Year 6 was C$1:U.S.$.85 and the exchange rate on December 31, Year 6, was C$1:U.S.$.80. Exhibit 7.17 shows the amounts taken from the books of the Canadian subsidiary at the end of Year 6 measured in Canadian dollars.

REQUIRED

a. Prepare a balance sheet, income statement, and retained earnings statement for the Canadian subsidiary for Year 6 in U.S. dollars, assuming that the Canadian dollar is the functional currency. Include a separate schedule showing the computation of the translation adjustment account.
b. Repeat part (a), but assume that the U.S. dollar is the functional currency. Include a separate schedule showing the computation of the translation gain or loss.
c. Why is the sign of the translation adjustment for Year 6 under the all-current translation method and the translation gain or loss for Year 6 under the monetary/nonmonetary translation method the same? Why do their amounts differ?
d. Assuming that the firm could justify either translation method, which method would the management of Stebbins Corporation likely prefer for Year 6?

7.9 TRANSLATING THE FINANCIAL STATEMENTS OF A FOREIGN SUBSIDIARY; SECOND YEAR OF OPERATIONS. Refer to Problem 7.8 for Stebbins Corporation for Year 6, its first year of operations. Exhibit 7.18 shows the amounts for the Canadian subsidiary for Year 7. The average exchange rate during Year 7 was C$1:U.S.$.82, and the exchange rate on December 31, Year 7, was C$1:U.S.$.84. The Canadian subsidiary declared and paid dividends on December 31, Year 7.

EXHIBIT 7.17

Canadian Subsidiary
Financial Statements
Year 6
(Problem 7.8)

Balance Sheet: December 31, Year 6

Assets

Cash	C$ 77,555
Rent Receivable	25,000
Building (net)	475,000
	C$577,555

Liabilities and Equity

Accounts Payable	6,000
Salaries Payable	4,000
Common Stock	555,555
Retained Earnings	12,000
	C$577,555

Income Statement for Year 6

Rent Revenue	C$125,000
Operating Expenses	(28,000)
Depreciation Expense	(25,000)
Translation Exchange Loss	—
Net Income	C$ 72,000

Retained Earnings Statement for Year 6

Balance, January 1, Year 6	—
Net Income	C$ 72,000
Dividends	(60,000)
Balance, December 31, Year 6	C$ 12,000

REQUIRED

a. Prepare a balance sheet, income statement, and retained earnings statement for the Canadian subsidiary for Year 7 in U.S. dollars, assuming that the Canadian dollar is the functional currency. Include a separate schedule showing the computation of the translation adjustment for Year 7 and the change in the translation adjustment account.

b. Repeat part (*a*), but assume that the U.S. dollar is the functional currency. Include a separate schedule showing the computation of the translation gain or loss.

c. Why is the sign of the translation adjustment for Year 7 under the all-current translation method and the translation gain or loss under the monetary/nonmonetary translation method the same? Why do their amounts differ?

d. Assuming that the firm could justify either translation method, which method would the management of Stebbins likely prefer for Year 7?

7.10 INTERPRETING FOREIGN CURRENCY TRANSLATION DISCLOSURES. Hewlett-Packard (HP) and Sun Microsystems derive similar proportions of their sales from the United States, Europe, and other locations. HP uses the U.S. dollar as its functional currency, and Sun uses the currency of each foreign operation as its functional currency.

EXHIBIT 7.18

Canadian Subsidiary
Financial Statements
Year 7
(Problem 7.9)

Balance Sheet

Assets

Cash	C$116,555
Rent Receivable	30,000
Building (net)	450,000
	C$596,555

Liabilities and Equity

Accounts Payable	7,500
Salaries Payable	5,500
Common Stock	555,555
Retained Earnings	28,000
	C$596,555

Income Statement

Rent Revenue	C$150,000
Operating Expenses	(34,000)
Depreciation Expense	(25,000)
Translation Exchange Gain	—
Net Income	C$ 91,000

Retained Earnings Statement

Balance, January 1, Year 7	C$ 12,000
Net Income	91,000
Dividends	(75,000)
Balance, December 31, Year 7	C$ 28,000

REQUIRED

a. The shareholders' equity section of Sun's balance sheet reveals the following (amounts in thousands):

	June 30	
	Year 5	**Year 6**
Common Stock	$ 928,934	$1,053,878
Retained Earnings	590,502	705,965
Cumulative Translation Adjustment	8,203	1,992
Treasury Stock	(42,557)	(119,052)
Total	$1,485,082	$1,642,783

Did the U.S. dollar likely increase or decrease in value on average during the year ended June 30, Year 6, against the foreign currencies of the countries in which Sun conducts its operations? Explain.

b. Sun uses a FIFO cost-flow assumption for inventories and cost of goods sold. Would the gross margin in U.S. dollars (that is, sales minus cost of goods sold) of Sun likely have increased or decreased for the year ended June 30, Year 6, if it had used the U.S. dollar as its functional currency instead of the currency of its foreign operations? Explain.

c. HP also uses a FIFO cost-flow assumption for inventories and cost of goods sold. Both companies maintain net monetary asset positions in their foreign operations. HP generated a pretax return from foreign operations of 7.9 percent for the year ended June 30, Year 6; Sun generated a pretax return of 2.9 percent. Would the profit margin of HP likely increase or decrease if it had used the currency of its foreign units as the functional currency? Explain.

7.11 Interpreting Foreign Currency Translation Disclosures. Bristol-Myers Squibb and Merck report the following data related to their European operations for two recent years (in millions):

	Bristol			Merck		
	Year 4	Year 5	Percentage Change	Year 4	Year 5	Percentage Change
Sales to Unaffiliated Entities....	$2,682	$2,923	+9.0%	$3,457	$3,803	+10.0%
Operating Income.............	$ 633	$ 647	+2.2%	$ 736	$ 742	+.8%
Profit Margin.................	23.6%	22.1%	−6.4%	21.3%	19.5%	−8.5%
Change in Sales between Year 4 and Year 5 Caused by:						
Volume Changes.........................			6%			7%
Price Changes..........................			1			1
Exchange Rate Changes...................			2			2
Total..................................			9%			10%

REQUIRED

a. Assume that the sales mixes and asset mixes among various European countries are identical for Bristol and Merck. Suggest reasons related to the way firms prepare segment data that may make it inappropriate to conclude that Bristol has a higher profit margin in Europe than does Merck.

b. Did the U.S. dollar increase or decrease in value on average relative to European currencies during Year 5? Explain.

c. Bristol uses the foreign currency as its functional currency; Merck uses the U.S. dollar as its functional currency for European operations. How might the foreign currency translation method affect the interpretation of the *change* in the profit margin for Bristol and Merck between Year 4 and Year 5?

7.12 Identifying the Functional Currency. Electronic Computer Systems (ECS) designs, manufactures, sells, and services networked computer systems, associated peripheral equipment, and related network, communications, and software products.

Exhibit 7.19 presents segment geographical data. ECS conducts sales and marketing operations outside the United States principally through sales subsidiaries in Canada, Europe, Central and South America, and East Asia by direct sales from the parent corporation and through various representative and distributorship arrangements. The company's interna-

EXHIBIT 7.19

Electronic Computer Systems
Geographical Segment Data
(amounts in thousands)
(Problem 7.12)

	Year 3	Year 4	Year 5
Revenues:			
Customers—United States	$ 4,472,195	$ 5,016,606	$ 5,810,598
Intercompany	1,354,339	1,921,043	2,017,928
Total	$ 5,826,534	$ 6,937,649	$ 7,828,526
Customers—Europe	2,259,743	3,252,482	4,221,631
Intercompany	82,649	114,582	137,669
Total	$ 2,342,392	$ 3,367,064	$ 4,359,300
Customers—Canada, East Asia,			
Americas.	858,419	1,120,356	1,443,217
Intercompany	577,934	659,204	912,786
Total	$ 1,436,353	$ 1,779,560	$ 2,356,003
Eliminations.	(2,014,922)	(2,694,829)	(3,068,383)
Net Revenue.	$ 7,590,357	$ 9,389,444	$11,475,446
Income			
United States	$ 342,657	$ 758,795	$ 512,754
Europe	405,636	634,543	770,135
Canada, East Asia, Americas.	207,187	278,359	390,787
Eliminations.	(126,771)	(59,690)	(38,676)
Operating Income	828,709	1,612,007	1,635,000
Interest Income	116,899	122,149	143,665
Interest Expense	(88,079)	(45,203)	(37,820)
Income before Income Taxes.	$ 857,529	$ 1,688,953	$ 1,740,845
Assets			
United States	$ 3,911,491	$ 4,627,838	$ 5,245,439
Europe	1,817,584	2,246,333	3,093,818
Canada, East Asia, Americas.	815,067	843,067	1,293,906
Corporate Assets (temporary cash			
investments)	2,035,557	1,979,470	2,057,528
Eliminations.	(1,406,373)	(1,289,322)	(1,579,135)
Total Assets	$ 7,173,326	$ 8,407,386	$10,111,556

tional manufacturing operations include plants in Canada, East Asia and Europe. These manufacturing plants sell their output to the company's sales subsidiaries, the parent corporation, or other manufacturing plants for further processing. .

ECS accounts for intercompany transfers between geographic areas at prices representative of unaffiliated party transactions.

Sales to unaffiliated customers outside the United States, including U.S. export sales, were $5,729,879,000 for Year 5, $4,412,527,000 for Year 4, and $3,179,143,000 for Year 3, which represented 50 percent, 47 percent, and 42 percent, respectively, of total operating revenues. The international subsidiaries have reinvested substantially all of their earnings to support operations. These accumulated retained earnings, before elimination of intercompany transactions, aggregated $2,793,239,000 at the end of Year 5, $2,070,337,000 at the end of Year 4, and $1,473,081,000 at the end of Year 3.

The company enters into forward exchange contracts to reduce the impact of foreign currency fluctuations on operations and the asset and liability positions of foreign subsidiaries. The gains and losses on these contracts increase or decrease net income in the same period as the related revenues and expenses, and for assets and liabilities, in the period in which the exchange rate changes.

REQUIRED

Discuss whether ECS should use the U.S. dollar or the currencies of its foreign subsidiaries as its functional currency.

CASE 7.1

FISHER CORPORATION[1]

Effective January 1, 1996, Weston Corporation and Fisher Corporation will merge their respective companies. Under the terms of the merger agreement, Weston will acquire all of Fisher's outstanding common shares. Fisher will remain a legally separate entity. However, Weston will consolidate its financial statements with those of Fisher at the end of each accounting period. According to the merger agreement, Weston can structure the transaction under any of the following three alternatives.

ALTERNATIVE A

Weston would acquire all of the outstanding common shares of Fisher for $58,500,000 in cash. To obtain the necessary cash, Weston would issue $59,000,000 of 10 percent, 20-year bonds on the open market. For financial reporting purposes, Weston would account for the merger using the purchase method. For tax purposes, the merger transaction is a taxable event to Fisher's shareholders. The tax basis of Fisher's net assets remains the same after the acquisition as before the acquisition; the tax law does not allow a revaluation of these net assets to market value.

ALTERNATIVE B

Weston would acquire all of the outstanding common shares of Fisher in exchange for the issuance of 1,800,000 shares of a new Weston preferred stock. The preferred stock would carry an annual dividend of $2 per share and would be convertible into .75 shares of Weston common stock at any time. The exchange ratio would be one share of the new preferred stock for each outstanding common share of Fisher. An independent investment banking firm has valued the preferred shares at $50,000,000. For financial reporting purposes, Weston would account for the merger using the purchase method. For tax purposes, the merger transaction is a nontaxable event to Fisher's shareholders. The tax basis of Fisher's net assets carry over after the acquisition.

---

[1]The author gratefully acknowledges the assistance of Gary M. Cypres in the preparation of this case.

ALTERNATIVE C

Weston would acquire all of the outstanding common shares of Fisher in exchange for 1,517,787 shares of Weston's $.30 par value common stock. Based on the market price at the merger date, these shares would have a market value of $48,000,000. For financial reporting purposes, Weston would account for the merger using the pooling of interests method. For tax purposes, the merger transaction is a nontaxable event to Fisher's shareholders. The tax basis of Fisher's net assets carry over after the acquisition.

The following summarizes the alternatives:

	Alternative A	Alternative B	Alternative C
Type of Consideration Given	Cash	Convertible Preferred Stock	Common Stock
Value of Consideration Given	$58,500,000	$50,000,000	$48,000,000
Financial Reporting Method	Purchase	Purchase	Pooling of Interests
Tax Reporting Method— Shareholders	Taxable	Nontaxable	Nontaxable
Tax Reporting Method—Fisher	Nontaxable	Nontaxable	Nontaxable

WESTON CORPORATION BACKGROUND (AS OF JANUARY 1, 1996)

Weston was formed on November 4, 1966, in a merger of four companies and has grown continually since that date. Weston is a worldwide Fortune 500 company with 1995 revenues of $482,000,000. The company designs and manufacturers environmental, energy, and engineered products and makes chemicals and specialty products.

Weston's long involvement with environmental protection systems began in 1937 with the development of the Weston machine for cleaning rust and scale from structural steel and other materials. Each Weston machine included air pollution controls to prevent the debris of the cleaning process from spreading. The Weston requires less time and less than one-tenth the energy of sandblasting. Further savings resulted from recycling the abrasive shot used in the cleaning process. As the Weston business grew, the company expanded its manufacturing capability. In addition to making Westons, spare parts, and associated pollution control equipment, the company began to produce consumables, such as the abrasives used by the Westons and the replacement filter bags that collected the fine particulate matter resulting from the cleaning process. Soon after the development of the Weston, growing customer interest in purchasing separately the pollution control devices utilized in the Weston machines resulted in the company's entry into the air pollution control business. By the early 1950s, it was offering a full range of fabric filter systems for a variety of industrial and utility uses. In the mid-1960s, the company became the North American licensee for certain European air pollution technologies, including Lurgi electrostatic precipitators.

To enable Weston to offer more comprehensive systems to solve environmental problems and to broaden its activities into related energy areas, the company sought an engineering and technological capability to complement its established manufacturing capacity. In 1988 it acquired Metallurgical Engineering Company. The company also increased its manufacturing capacity by constructing new facilities for its existing product lines and by acquiring additional facilities for the production of industrial fans and blowers and the means to design, erect, and service industrial chimneys. It further augmented its manufacturing capabilities in

1992 by purchasing BPM Corporation, a manufacturer of precision and industrial ball and roller bearings, motion transmission devices, and related products.

Weston is the exclusive licensee in the United States of certain European technology for the production of steam through the combustion of refuse. The same process permits the recovery of metal and other commercially valuable resources. The steam is used for a variety of purposes, including heating and generating electricity. In 1991, the company completed the construction of its first refuse-to-energy plant using such technology at Saugus, Massachusetts. The company is active in designing facilities and seeking to develop processes that allow the efficient and economical use of high-sulfur coal in an environmentally acceptable way on a commercial scale. The company also participates in developing other clean energy technologies such as the burning of biomass (primarily wood refuse).

Weston has another broad product category, chemicals and specialty products. The company manufactures chemicals, including urethane-based products, pigments, resins, varnishes, dispersions, and color flushes. The company offers various specialty products used in numerous printing processes including letterpress, offset, silk screen, flexographic, and gravure processes. The company also produces one-time carbon paper for business forms and for data processing as well as carbonless reproduction paper.

As Exhibit 1 illustrates, Weston's revenues, net income, and earnings per share had each grown for the years 1991 through 1995 at an average compounded annual rate of 23 percent.

EXHIBIT 1

Weston Corporation
Income Statements for the Years Ended December 31
(amounts in thousands)
(Case 7.1)

	1991	1992	1993	1994	1995	Estimated 1996[a]
Sales	$ 233,000	$ 321,300	$ 306,500	$ 361,500	$ 482,100	$ 560,000
Cost and Expenses						
Cost of Sales	(180,700)	(251,100)	(232,800)	(273,900)	(360,600)	(415,700)
Selling & Admin.	(36,500)	(51,600)	(51,900)	(58,300)	(86,921)	(105,632)
Operating Income	$ 15,800	$ 18,600	$ 21,800	$ 29,300	$ 34,579	$ 38,668
Equity in Net Income of Nonconsolidated Entities	2,300	3,800	3,600	2,600	3,200	4,000
Other Income (expense)..	(1,300)	(2,100)	(900)	(400)	(1,600)	(1,000)
Income before Taxes ...	$ 16,800	$ 20,300	$ 24,500	$ 31,500	$ 36,179	$ 41,668
Provision for Income Taxes................	(6,800)	(7,500)	(9,900)	(14,000)	(14,179)	(14,584)
Net Income	$ 10,000	$ 12,800	$ 14,600	$ 17,500	$ 22,000	$ 27,084
Earnings per Share......	$1.25	$1.60	$1.83	$2.22	$2.82	$3.47
Dividends per Share of Common Stock	$ .40	$ .40	$ .45	$ .63	$ .88	$1.20
Ave. Number of Shares of Common Stock Outstanding..........	8,000	8,000	8,000	7,900	7,800	7,800

[a]Before consideration of the merger with Fisher.

Growth in 1995 exceeded the average in all categories. These five-year growth rates include the recession year of 1993 when the company's net income increased by 14 percent despite a sales decline of 5 percent. Weston accomplished this growth rate from both operations and aggressive corporate acquisitions. The company intends to continue making acquisitions in the future.

Although Weston has exhibited strong financial growth, it has consistently maintained a conservative balance sheet (See Exhibit 2). The company's debt has steadily declined from

---

EXHIBIT 2

Weston Corporation
Consolidated Balance Sheets
December 31
(amounts in thousands)
(Case 7.1)

	1994	1995	Estimated 1996[a]
Assets			
Cash	$ 28,000	$ 28,000	$ 32,000
Accounts Receivable	84,000	90,000	100,000
Inventory	58,000	71,000	82,000
Other	4,000	13,000	13,000
Total Current Assets	$174,000	$202,000	$227,000
Property, Plant, and Equipment	$ 96,000	$116,000	$131,000
Less Accumulated Depreciation	(29,000)	(38,000)	(48,000)
Net	$ 67,000	$ 78,000	$ 83,000
Investment in Nonconsolidated Entities	42,000	45,000	47,000
Goodwill	8,400	8,000	7,800
Other Assets	6,000	7,000	7,200
Total Assets	$297,400	$340,000	$372,000
Liabilities			
Current Portion Long-Term Debt	$ 400	$ 2,000	$ —
Accounts Payable	23,000	30,000	40,000
Accrued Liabilities & Advances	67,000	78,000	91,000
Income Taxes	12,000	21,000	14,000
Total Current Liabilities	$102,400	$131,000	$145,000
Long-Term Debt	48,000	48,000	48,000
Deferred Taxes	9,000	10,000	10,000
Total Liabilities	$159,400	$189,000	$203,000
Shareholders' Equity			
Common Stock	$ 11,000	$ 11,000	$ 11,000
Capital Surplus	55,000	55,000	55,000
Retained Earnings	72,000	85,000	103,000
Total Shareholders' Equity	$138,000	$151,000	$169,000
Total Liabilities and Shareholders' Equity	$297,400	$340,000	$372,000

[a]Before consideration of the merger with Fisher.

EXHIBIT 3

Weston Corporation
Key Financial Highlights
1992–1996 Estimated
(Case 7.1)

	1992	1993	1994	1995	Estimated 1996 (E)[a]
Earnings per Share............	$ 1.60	$ 1.83	$ 2.22	$ 2.82	$ 3.53
Dividends per Share...........	$ .40	$ .45	$ .63	$ .88	$ 1.20
Current Ratio.................	1.8	2.0	1.7	1.5	1.6
Long-Term Debt as a Percentage of Long-Term Capital....................	28.9%	26.5%	25.8%	24.1%	22.1%
Return on Average Common Shareholders' Equity.........	12.4%	12.9%	13.6%	15.2%	16.9%
Book Value per Share..........	$ 13.50	$ 14.88	$ 17.69	$ 19.36	$ 21.68
Tangible Net Worth ($000)	$99,300	$111,600	$129,600	$143,000	$161,200
Times Interest Earned.........	5.7	7.8	9.8	10.9	10.0

[a]Before consideration of the merger with Fisher.

31 percent of long-term capital in 1991 to 24 percent in 1995 (See Exhibit 3). Dividends per share have ranged between 27 percent and 32 percent of earnings per share in each of the last five years.

Weston currently projects 25 percent growth in net income and earnings per share in 1996, with revenues increasing by 16 percent.

FISHER CORPORATION BACKGROUND (AS OF JANUARY 1, 1996)

Fisher is a leading designer and manufacturer of material handling and process equipment for heavy industry in the United States and abroad. Its sales have more than doubled, and its earnings have increased more than sixfold in the past five years. In material handling, Fisher is a major producer of electric overhead and gantry cranes, ranging from 5 tons in capacity to 600-ton giants, the latter used primarily in nuclear and conventional power-generating plants. It also builds underhung cranes and monorail systems for general industrial use carrying loads up to 40 tons, railcar movers, and railroad and mass transit shop maintenance equipment, plus a broad line of advanced package conveyors. Fisher is a world leader in evaporation and crystallization systems and furnishes dryers, heat exchangers, and filters to complete its line of chemical-processing equipment sold internationally to the chemical, fertilizer, food, drug, and paper industries. For the metallurgical industry, it designs and manufactures electric arc and induction furnaces, cupolas, ladles, and hot metal distribution equipment.

Exhibit 4 presents comparative income statements, and Exhibit 5 presents comparative balance sheets for Fisher.

Fisher's management estimates that revenues will remain approximately flat between 1995 and 1996 but that Fisher's net income for 1996 will decline to $2,500,000, compared with $6,602,000 in 1995. This decrease in net income results from a $1,000,000 increase in labor costs in 1996, a $3,000,000 loss in the construction of a crystallization system, a $1,000,000 expenditure to meet expected OSHA requirements, and a $1,000,000 expenditure to relocate one of its product lines to a new plant facility. Fisher has 1,800,000 shares outstanding on January 1, 1996. It currently pays a dividend of $1.22 per share.

EXHIBIT 4

Fisher Corporation—Income Statement
(amounts in thousands)
(Case 7.1)

	1991	1992	1993	1994	1995	Estimated 1996
Sales	$ 41,428	$ 53,541	$ 76,328	$109,373	$102,699	$100,000
Other Revenue & Gains	0	41	0	0	211	200
Cost of Goods Sold........	(33,269)	(43,142)	(60,000)	(85,364)	(80,260)	(85,600)
Sell. & Admin. Expense....	(6,175)	(7,215)	(9,325)	(13,416)	(12,090)	(10,820)
Other Expenses & Losses...	(2)	0	(11)	(31)	(1)	—
Earnings before Interest and Taxes	$ 1,982	$ 3,225	$ 6,992	$ 10,562	$ 10,559	$ 3,780
Interest Expense	(43)	(21)	(284)	(276)	(13)	—
Income Tax Expense.......	(894)	(1,471)	(2,992)	(3,703)	(3,944)	(1,323)
Income from Continual Operations	$ 1,045	$ 1,733	$ 3,716	$ 6,583	$ 6,602	$ 2,457

EXHIBIT 5

Fisher Corporation—Balance Sheet
(amounts in thousands)
(Case 7.1)

	1990	1991	1992	1993	1994	1995
Cash	$ 955	$ 961	$ 865	$ 1,247	$ 1,540	$ 3,100
Marketable Securities	0	0	0	0	0	2,900
Accounts/Notes Receivable.......	6,545	7,295	9,718	13,307	18,759	15,000
Inventories	7,298	8,686	12,797	20,426	18,559	18,000
Current Assets...............	$14,798	$16,942	$23,380	$34,980	$38,858	$39,000
Property, Plant, & Equipment	12,216	12,445	13,126	13,792	14,903	15,000
Less: Accumulated Depreciation ..	(7,846)	(8,236)	(8,558)	(8,988)	(9,258)	(9,000)
Other Assets..................	470	420	400	299	343	1,000
Total Assets	$19,638	$21,571	$28,348	$40,083	$44,846	$46,000
Accts. Payable—Trade	$ 2,894	$ 4,122	$ 6,496	$ 7,889	$ 6,779	$ 7,000
Notes Payable—Nontrade........	0	0	700	3,500	0	0
Current Part L-T Debt	170	170	170	170	170	0
Other Current Liabilities	550	1,022	3,888	8,624	12,879	8,000
Current Liabilities............	$ 3,614	$ 5,314	$11,254	$20,183	$19,828	$15,000
Long-Term Debt	680	510	340	170	0	0
Deferred Taxes................	0	0	5	228	357	1,000
Total Liabilities	$ 4,294	$ 5,824	$11,599	$20,581	$20,185	$16,000
Preferred Stock	$ 0	$ 0	$ 0	$ 0	$ 0	$ 0
Common Stock	2,927	2,927	2,927	5,855	7,303	9,000
Additional Paid-in Capital	5,075	5,075	5,075	5,075	5,061	5,000
Retained Earnings..............	7,342	7,772	8,774	8,599	12,297	16,000
Treasury Stock................	0	−27	−27	−27	0	0
Shareholders' Equity..........	$15,344	$15,747	$16,749	$19,502	$24,661	$30,000
Total Equities..............	$19,638	$21,571	$28,348	$40,083	$44,846	$46,000

ALLOCATION OF PURCHASE PRICE

Exhibit 6 shows the calculation of the purchase price and the allocation of any excess cost under each of the three alternatives for structuring the acquisition of Fisher.

EXHIBIT 6

Calculation of Purchase Price and Allocation of Excess Cost
(amounts in thousands)
(Case 7.1)

	Alternative A	Alternative B	Alternative C[a]
Purchase Price			
Base Price	$ 58,500	$ 50,000	$ 14,000
Acquisition Costs (Note 1)	500	500	500
Total	$ 59,000	$ 50,500	$ 14,500
Book Value of Contributed Capital of Fisher	(30,000)	(30,000)	(14,000)
Excess of Cost over Book Value to Be Allocated to Assets and Liabilities.	$ 29,000	$ 20,500	$ 500
Allocation of Excess Cost			
Recognition of "Reserve" for Losses on Long-Term Contracts (Note 2).	3,000 Cr.	3,000 Cr.	—
Write-up of Building and Equipment (Note 3).	17,000 Dr.	17,000 Dr.	—
Recognition of Unfunded Pension Liability (Note 4).	5,000 Cr.	5,000 Cr.	—
Recognition of Estimated Liability to Meet OSHA Requirements (Note 5)	1,000 Cr.	1,000 Cr.	—
Recognition of Estimated Costs to Relocate Facilities in Connection with Product Move (Note 6)	1,000 Cr.	1,000 Cr.	—
Total Allocated to Identifiable Assets and Liabilities.	7,000 Dr.	7,000 Dr.	—
Deferred Tax Effect (Note 7). . . .	2,450 Cr.	2,450 Cr.	—
Residual to Goodwill (Note 8). . .	24,450 Dr.	15,950 Dr.	—
Total Allocated.	$29,000 Dr.	$20,500 Dr.	—

---

[a]The pooling of interests method ignores the market value of Weston's common shares of $48,000,000. The shares exchanged receive a value equal to the book value of Fisher's contributed capital, $14,000,000. Weston must expense the acquisition costs in the year incurred.

Note 1: Acquisition costs consist of printing, legal, auditing, and finders fees and increase the cost of Fisher's shares acquired under alternatives A and B.

Note 2: The book value of certain of Fisher's long-term contracts (relating to a crystallization system) exceeds their market value by $3,000,000. Fisher expects to complete these contracts during 1996. Weston establishes a "reserve" for this loss as of the date of acquisition and includes it among current liabilities. When Fisher completes the contracts in 1996, the consolidated entity will charge the actual loss against the "reserve" for financial reporting. It will then claim a deduction for the loss in calculating taxable income.

Note 3: The market value of Fisher's property, plant, and equipment on January 1, 1996, is $23,000. Their book value and tax basis is $6,000. Thus, Weston allocates $17,000 (=$23,000 − $6,000) of the excess cost to property, plant, and equipment. The consolidated entity will depreciate the excess using the straight-line method over 10 years for financial reporting. It cannot depreciate the excess for tax purposes.

Note 4: Fisher has an unfunded pension obligation of $5,000 on January 1, 1996. It had planned to amortize this obligation straight line over 20 years from January 1, 1996. Weston allocates a portion of the purchase price to this obligation on the date of the acquisition.

Note 5: Fisher expects to incur $1,000 of costs during 1996 on its facilities to comply with various OSHA health and safety provisions. Weston allocates a portion of the purchase price to recognize this expected cost.

Note 6: Weston intends to relocate the manufacture of certain of Fisher's product lines to a new plant facility during 1996. The estimated costs of relocation total $1,000. Weston allocates a portion of the purchase price to recognize this expected cost.

Note 7: FASB *Statement No. 109* requires firms to provide deferred taxes for differences between the book basis and tax basis of assets and liabilities. Weston allocates the $7,000 amount of excess cost shown in Exhibit 6 to individual assets and liabilities for financial reporting. For tax reporting, the basis of these assets and liabilities remains the same as the amounts shown on Fisher's books before the acquisition. Thus, Weston provides deferred taxes of $2,450 (0.35 × $7,000), of which $1,750 [0.35 × ($3,000 Cr. + $1,000 Cr. + $1,000 Cr.)] is a current asset, $1,750 (0.35 × $5,000) is a noncurrent asset, and $5,950 (0.35 × $17,000) is a noncurrent liability. The consolidated entity eliminates these deferred taxes as it amortizes the related asset or liability.

Note 8: Weston allocates the remaining excess cost to goodwill. The consolidated entity amortizes goodwill over 40 years.

Exhibits 7 to 13 present pro forma consolidated financial statements for Weston and Fisher under each of the three alternatives.

REQUIRED

a. As a shareholder of Fisher, which alternative would you choose and why? The income tax rate on capital gains is 28 percent. Would your answer differ if you were an individual investor versus a pension fund?

b. As the chief financial officer of Weston, which alternative would you choose and why?

EXHIBIT 7

Weston Corporation and Fisher Corporation
Pro Forma Consolidated Balance Sheet as of January 1, 1996
Assuming Cash Exchange
(amounts in thousands)
(Case 7.1)

	Weston (before acquisition)	To Record Acquisition of Fisher's Shares		Weston (after acquisition)	Fisher (after acquisition)	Worksheet Consolidation Entries		Pro Forma Consolidated
	(1)	(2)	(3)	(4)	(5)	(6)	(7)	(8)
Assets								
Cash	$ 28,000	(A) 59,000	(B) 59,000	$ 28,000	$ 6,000			$ 34,000
Accounts Receivable	90,000			90,000	15,000			105,000
Inventory	71,000			71,000	18,000			89,000
Other	13,000			13,000	—	(C) 1,750		14,750
Total Current Assets	$202,000			$202,000	$39,000			$242,750
Property, Plant, and Equipment	$116,000			$116,000	$15,000	(C) 8,000		$139,000
Less: Accumulated Depreciation	(38,000)			(38,000)	(9,000)	(C) 9,000		(38,000)
Net Property, Plant, and Equipment	$ 78,000			$ 78,000	$ 6,000			$101,000
Investment in Nonconsolidated Entities	45,000	(B) 59,000		45,000	—			$ 45,000
Investment in Fisher	—			59,000	—		(C) 59,000	—
Goodwill	8,000			8,000	—	(C) 24,450		32,450
Other Assets	7,000			7,000	1,000	(C) 1,750		9,750
Total Assets	$340,000			$399,000	$46,000			$430,950

	Weston (before acquisition) (1)	To Record Acquisition of Fisher's Shares (2)	(3)	Weston (after acquisition) (4)	Fisher (after acquisition) (5)	Worksheet Consolidation Entries (6)	(7)	Pro Forma Consolidated (8)
Liabilities								
Current Portion Long-Term Debt...	$ 2,000			$ 2,000	$ —			$ 2,000
Accounts Payable	30,000			30,000	7,000		(C) 3,000	37,000
Accrued Liabilities & Advances	78,000			78,000	7,000		(C) 1,000	90,000
Income Taxes..............	21,000			21,000	1,000		(C) 1,000	22,000
Total Current Liabilities.........	$131,000			$131,000	$15,000			$151,000
Long-Term Debt	48,000		(A) 59,000	107,000	—			107,000
Other Liabilities	—			—	1,000		(C) 5,000	6,000
Deferred Taxes	10,000			10,000	—		(C) 5,950	15,950
Total Liabilities	$189,000			$248,000	$16,000			$279,950
Shareholders' Equity								
Preferred Stock............	$ —			$ —	$ —			$ —
Common Stock	11,000			11,000	9,000	(C) 9,000		11,000
Additional Paid-in Capital	55,000			55,000	5,000	(C) 5,000		55,000
Retained Earnings	85,000			85,000	16,000	(C) 16,000		85,000
Total Shareholders' Equity......	$151,000			$151,000	$30,000			$151,000
Total Liabilities and Shareholders' Equity........	$340,000			$399,000	$46,000			$430,950

(A) Issue of bonds for cash and payment of acquisition costs.

(B) Purchase of Fisher's outstanding common stock.

(C) Elimination of investment in Fisher and Fisher's shareholders' equity accounts and allocation of excess purchase price (see Exhibit 6 for amounts).

EXHIBIT 8

Weston Corporation and Fisher Corporation
Pro Forma Consolidated Income Statement for the Year Ending December 31, 1996
Assuming Cash Exchange
(amounts in thousands)
(Case 7.1)

	Weston	Fisher	Consolidation Worksheet Entries Dr.	Consolidation Worksheet Entries Cr.	Consolidated Pro Forma
Sales	$ 560,000	$100,000			$ 660,000
Cost of Sales					
Cost of Sales	(415,700)	(85,600)	(B) 1,700	(E) 5,000	(498,000)
Selling & Administrative	(105,632)	(10,820)	(C) 611	(D) 250	(116,813)
Operating Income	$ 38,668	$ 3,580			$ 45,187
Equity in Net Income of					
Nonconsolidated Entities	4,000	—			4,000
Other Income (expense)	(1,000)	200	(A) 5,900		(6,700)
Income before Taxes	41,668	3,780			$ 42,487
Provision for Income Taxes	(14,584)	(1,323)	(D) 88	(A) 2,065	(15,085)
			(E) 1,750	(B) 595	
Net Income	$ 27,084	$ 2,457			$ 27,402
Basic Earnings per Share	$ 3.47	$ 1.37			$ 3.51
Average Number Shares of					
Common Stock Outstanding . . .	7,800	1,800			7,800

(A) Interest on debt: 0.10 × $59,000 = $5,900, tax effect = $2,065

(B) Depreciation expense: $17,000 ÷ 10 = $1,700; deferred tax effects = 0.35 × $1,700 = $595

(C) Goodwill amortization: $24,450 ÷ 40 = $611; tax effect = 0

(D) Elimination of pension expense: $5,000 ÷ 20 = $250, deferred tax effect = 0.35 × $250 = $88

(E) Elimination of contract loss, OSHA cost, and relocation costs = $5,000; deferred tax effect: 0.35 × $5,000 = $1,750

EXHIBIT 9

Weston Corporation and Fisher Corporation
Pro Forma Consolidated Balance Sheet as of January 1, 1996
Assuming Preferred Stock Exchange
(amounts in thousands)
(Case 7.1)

	Weston (before acquisition)	To Record Acquisition of Fisher's Shares		Weston (after acquisition)	Fisher (after acquisition)	Consolidation Worksheet Entries		Pro Forma Consolidated
	(1)	(2)	(3)	(4)	(5)	(6)	(7)	(8)
Assets								
Cash	$ 28,000		(A) 500	$ 27,500	$ 6,000			$ 33,500
Accounts Receivable	90,000			90,000	15,000			105,000
Inventory	71,000			71,000	18,000			89,000
Other	13,000			13,000	—	(B) 1,750		14,750
Total Current Assets	$202,000			$201,500	$39,000			$242,250
Property, Plant, and Equipment	$116,000			$116,000	$15,000	(B) 3,000		$139,000
Less: Accumulated Depreciation	(38,000)			(38,000)	(9,000)	(B) 9,000		(38,000)
Net Property, Plant, and Equipment	$ 78,000			$ 78,000	$ 6,000			$101,000
Investment in Nonconsolidated Entities	45,000			$ 45,000	—			$ 45,000
Investment in Fisher		(A) 50,500		50,500	—		50,500 (B)	—
Goodwill	8,000			8,000	—	(B) 15,950		23,950
Other Assets	7,000			7,000	1,000	(B) 1,750		9,750
Total Assets	$340,000			$390,000	$46,000			$421,950

Exh. 9—Continued

Liabilities	Weston (before acquisition) (1)	To Record Acquisition of Fisher's Shares (2)	(3)	Weston (after acquisition) (4)	Fisher (after acquisition) (5)	Consolidation Worksheet Entries (6)	(7)	Pro Forma Consolidated (8)
Current Portion Long-Term Debt...	$ 2,000			$ 2,000	$ —			$ 2,000
Accounts Payable...	30,000			30,000	$ 7,000		3,000 (B)	37,000
Accrued Liabilities & Advances....	78,000			78,000	7,000		1,000 (B)	90,000
Income Taxes...	21,000			21,000	1,000		1,000 (B)	22,000
Total Current Liabilities...	$131,000			$131,000	$15,000			$151,000
Long-Term Debt...	48,000			48,000	—			48,000
Other Liabilities...	—			—	1,000		5,000 (B)	6,000
Deferred Taxes...	10,000			10,000	—		5,950 (B)	15,950
Total Liabilities...	$189,000			$189,000	$16,000			$220,950
Shareholders' Equity								
Preferred Stock...	$ —		(A) 50,000	$ 50,000	$ —			$ 50,000
Common Stock...	11,000			11,000	9,000	(B) 9,000		11,000
Additional Paid-in Capital...	55,000			55,000	5,000	(B) 5,000		55,000
Retained Earnings...	85,000			85,000	16,000	(B) 16,000		85,000
Total Shareholders' Equity...	$151,000			$201,000	$30,000			$201,000
Total Liabilities and Shareholders' Equity...	$340,000			$390,000	$46,000			$421,950

(A) Issue of preferred stock for the outstanding common shares of Fisher and payment of acquisition costs.

(B) Elimination of investment in Fisher and Fisher's shareholders' equity accounts and allocation of excess purchase price (see Exhibit 6 for amounts).

EXHIBIT 10

Weston Corporation and Fisher Corporation
Pro Forma Consolidated Income Statement for the Year Ending December 31, 1996
Assuming Preferred Stock Exchange
(amounts in thousands)
(Case 7.1)

	Weston	Fisher	Consolidation Worksheet Entries Dr.	Consolidation Worksheet Entries Cr.	Consolidated Pro Forma
Sales	$ 560,000	$100,000			$ 660,000
Cost of Sales					
Cost of Sales	(415,700)	(85,600)	(A) 1,700	(D) 5,000	(498,000)
Selling & Administrative	(105,632)	(10,820)	(B) 399	(C) 250	(116,601)
Operating Income	$ 38,668	$ 3,580			$ 45,399
Equity in Net Income of					
Nonconsolidated Entities	4,000	—			4,000
Other Income (expense)	(1,000)	200			(800)
Income before Taxes..........	$ 41,668	$ 3,780			$ 48,599
Provision for Income Taxes	(14,584)	(1,323)	(C) 88	(A) 595	(17,150)
			(D) 1,750		
Net Income	$ 27,084	$ 2,457			$ 31,449
Basic Earnings per Share........	$ 3.47	$ 1.37			(E)
Average Number Shares of					
Common Stock Outstanding ...	7,800	1,800			7,800

(A) Depreciation expense: $17,000 ÷ 10 = $1,700; deferred tax effect = 0.35 × $1,700 = $595.

(B) Goodwill amortization: $15,950 ÷ 40 = $399; tax effect = 0.

(C) Pension expense: $5,000 ÷ 20 = $250; deferred tax effect = 0.35 × $250 = $88.

(D) Loss on contract, OSHA, and relocation costs = $5,000; deferred tax effect = 0.35 × $5,000 = $1,750.

(E) Basic EPS: $\dfrac{(\$31,449 - \$3,600)}{7,800} = 3.57$

Diluted EPS: $\dfrac{\$31,449}{7,800 + 1,350} = 3.44$

EXHIBIT 11

Weston Corporation and Fisher Corporation
Pro Forma Consolidated Balance Sheet as of January 1, 1996
Assuming Common Stock Exchange
(amounts in thousands)
(Case 7.1)

	Weston (before acquisition)	To Record Acquisition of Fisher's Shares		Weston (after acquisition)	Fisher (after acquisition)	Worksheet Elimination Entries		Pro Forma Consolidated
	(1)	(2)	(3)	(4)	(5)	(6)	(7)	(8)
Assets								
Cash	$ 28,000		(B) 500	$ 27,500	$ 6,000			$ 33,500
Accounts Receivable	90,000			90,000	15,000			105,000
Inventory	71,000			71,000	18,000			89,000
Other	13,000			13,000	—			13,000
Total Current Assets	$202,000			$201,500	$39,000			$240,500
Property, Plant, and Equipment	$116,000			$116,000	$15,000			$131,000
Less: Accumulated Depreciation	(38,000)			(38,000)	(9,000)			(47,000)
Net Property, Plant, and Equipment	$ 78,000			$ 78,000	$ 6,000			$ 84,000
Investment in Nonconsolidated Entities	45,000			45,000	—			$ 45,000
Investment in Fisher	—	(A) 14,000		14,000	—		14,000 (C)	—
Goodwill	8,000			8,000	—			8,000
Other Assets	7,000			7,000	1,000			8,000
Total Assets	$340,000			$353,500	$46,000			$385,500

Exh. 11—Continued

	Weston (before acquisition) (1)	To Record Acquisition of Fisher's Shares (2)	(3)	Weston (after acquisition) (4)	Fisher (after acquisition) (5)	Worksheet Elimination Entries (6)	(7)	Pro Forma Consolidated (8)
Liabilities								
Current Portion Long-Term Debt...	$ 2,000			$ 2,000	—			$ 2,000
Accounts Payable	30,000			30,000	$ 7,000			37,000
Accrued Liabilities & Advances	78,000			78,000	7,000			85,000
Income Taxes..................	21,000			21,000	1,000			22,000
Total Current Liabilities.......	$131,000			$131,000	$15,000			$146,000
Long-Term Debt	48,000			48,000	—			48,000
Other Liabilities	—			—	1,000			1,000
Deferred Taxes	10,000			10,000	—			10,000
Total Liabilities	$189,000			$189,000	$16,000			$205,000
Shareholders' Equity								
Preferred Stock...............	$ —			$ —	$ —			$ C
Common Stock	11,000		(A) 455	11,455	9,000	(C) 9,000		11,455
Additional Paid-in Capital	55,000		(A) 13,545	68,545	5,000	(C) 5,000		68,545
Retained Earnings	85,000	(B) 500		84,500	16,000			100,500
Total Shareholders' Equity......	$151,000			$164,500	$30,000			$180,500
Total Liabilities and Shareholders' Equity........	$340,000			$353,500	$46,000			$385,500

(A) Issue of common stock for the outstanding common shares of Fisher.

(B) Immediate expensing of the acquisition costs of $500. See Exhibit 6 for the explanation. The same amount affects net income for 1996; see Exhibit 12.

(C) Elimination of investment in Fisher and Fisher's shareholders' equity accounts.

EXHIBIT 12

Weston Corporation and Fisher Corporation
Pro Forma Consolidated Income Statement for the Year Ending December 31, 1996
Assuming Common Stock Exchange
(amounts in thousands)
(Case 7.1)

	Weston	Fisher	Consolidation Worksheet Entries Dr.	Cr.	Consolidated Pro Forma
Sales	$ 560,000	$100,000			$ 660,000
Cost of Sales					
Cost of Sales	(415,700)	(85,600)			(501,300)
Selling & Administrative	(105,632)	(10,820)			(116,452)
Operating Income	$ 38,668	$ 3,580			$ 42,248
Equity in Net Income of					
Nonconsolidated Entities	4,000	—			4,000
Other Income (expense)	(1,000)	200	(A) 500		(1,300)
Income before Taxes	$ 41,668	$ 3,780			$ 44,948
Provision for Income Taxes	(14,584)	(1,323)		(A) 175	(15,732)
Net Income	$ 27,084	$ 2,457			$ 29,216
Basic Earnings per Share........	$ 3.47	$ 1.37			$ 3.14
Average Number Shares of					
Common Stock Outstanding ...	7,800	1,800			9,318

(A) Expensing the cost of acquisition = $500. Income tax effect = 0.35 × $500 = $170.

EXHIBIT 13

Weston Corporation and Fisher Corporation
Key Financial Highlights
(Case 7.1)

| | Actual for Weston Corporation | | | | Weston Corporation and Fisher Corporation Pro Forma for 1996 | | |
	1992	1993	1994	1995	Alternative A	Alternative B	Alternative C
Earnings per Common Share							
(basic)	$ 1.60	$ 1.83	$ 2.22	$ 2.82	$ 3.51	$ 3.57	$ 3.14
(diluted)	—	—	—	—	—	3.44	—
Dividends per Common Share	$ .40	$ .45	$ .63	$ .88	$ 1.20	$ 1.20	$ 1.20
Current Ratio[a]	1.8	2.0	1.7	1.5	1.6	1.6	1.6
Long-Term Debt as Percentage of Long-Term Capital[a]	28.9%	26.5%	25.8%	24.1%	41.5%	19.3%	21.0%
Return on Average Common Shareholders' Equity	12.4%	12.9%	13.6%	15.2%	17.1%	17.4%	15.4%
Book Value per Common Share	$ 13.50	$ 14.88	$ 17.69	$ 19.36	$ 19.36	$ 19.36	$ 19.37
Tangible Net Worth ($000)[a]	$99,300	$111,600	$129,600	$143,000	$118,550	$127,050	$172,500
Times Interest Earned	5.7	7.8	9.8	10.9	5.0	11.3	10.5
(with preferred dividend)	—	—	—	—	—	6.4	—

[a]Pro Forma amounts for these ratios are at date of acquisition of Fisher.

Calculation of Key Financial Ratios—Alternative A

Basic Earnings per Share: $27,402 ÷ 7,800 = $3.51

Current Ratio: $242,750 ÷ $151,000 = 1.6

Long-Term Debt to Long-Term Capital: $107,000 ÷ ($107,000 + $151,000) = 41.5%

Return on Common Equity: $27,402 ÷ 0.5[$151,000 + ($151,000 + $27,402 − $9,360)] = 17.1%

Common Dividend: 7,800 × $1.20 = $9,360

Book Value per Share: $151,000 ÷ 7,800 = $19.36

Tangible Net Worth: $430,950 − $32,450 − $279,950 = $118,550

Times Interest Earned: ($27,402 + $15,085 + $4,741 + $5,900) ÷ ($4,741 + $5,900) = 5.0

   Interest Expense with No Merger: ($27,084 + $15,584 + X) ÷ X = 10.0; X = $4,741

Calculation of Key Financial Ratios—Alternative B

Basic Earnings per Share: ($31,449 − $3,600) ÷ 7,800 = $3.57
   Preferred Dividend = 1,800 × $2 = $3,600

Diluted Earnings per Share: $31,449 ÷ (7,800 + 1,350) = 3.44
   Common Shares Issued upon Conversion of Preferred: 1.800 × 0.75 = 1,350.

Current Ratio: $242,250 ÷ $151,000 = 1.6

Long-Term Debt to Long-Term Capital: $48,000 ÷ ($48,000 + $201,000) = 19.3%

Return on Common Equity: ($31,449 − $3,600) ÷ 0.5[$151,000 + ($151,000 + $31,449 − $3,600 − $9,360)] = 17.4%

Book Value per Common Share: $151,000 ÷ 7,800 = $19.36

Tangible Net Worth: $421,950 − $23,950 − $220,950 − $50,000 = $127,050.

Times Interest Earned: ($31,449 + $17,150 + $4,741) ÷ $4,741 = 11.3
   With Preferred Dividend: ($31,449 + $17,150 + $4,741) ÷ ($4,741 + $3,600) = 6.4

Calculation of Key Financial Ratios—Alternative C

Basic Earnings per Share: $29,216 ÷ (7,800 + 1,518) = $3.14

Current Ratio: $240,500 ÷ $146,000 = 1.6

Long-Term Debt to Long-Term Capital: $48,000 ÷ ($48,000 + $180,500) = 21.0%

Return on Common Equity: $29,216 ÷ 0.5[$180,500 + ($180,500 + $29,216 − $11,182)] = 15.4%

Common Dividend: (7,800 + 1,518) × $1.20 = $11,182.

Book Value per Common Share: $180,500 ÷ (7,800 + 1,518) = $19.37

Tangible Net Worth: $385,500 − $8,000 − $205,000 = $172,500

Times Interest Earned: ($29,216 + $15,732 + $4,741) ÷ 4,741 = 10.5

CASE 7.2

CLARK EQUIPMENT COMPANY: ANALYZING A JOINT PROBLEM

Clark Equipment Company, through its wholly owned subsidiaries, operates in three principal product markets:

1. Small "lift and carry" products, including excavators for digging and loaders for hauling various materials. Its Bobcat® skid steer loader maintains a 50 percent worldwide market share.
2. Axles and transmissions for use by manufacturers of cranes and large material-handling machinery used in construction, mining, logging, and other industrial applications.
3. Axles and transmissions for use by manufacturers of automobiles, trucks, and tractors in the Brazilian market.

Sales for these product groups for Year 10 to Year 12 follow:

	Year 10		Year 11		Year 12	
Off Highway						
Lift-and-Carry Products....	$385	44%	$347	48%	$410	51%
Axles and Transmissions....	274	32	240	33	241	30
On Highway						
Axles and Transmissions....	205	24	140	19	152	19
	$864	100%	$727	100%	$803	100%

The geographical source of its product sales (that is, the location of its manufacturing facilities) for Year 10 to Year 12 follow:

	Year 10		Year 11		Year 12	
North America.............	$504	58%	$439	60%	$501	62%
Europe	165	19	153	21	157	20
South America.............	195	23	135	19	145	18
	$864	100%	$727	100%	$803	100%

Since Year 5, Clark has engaged in a 50 percent-owned joint venture with Volvo of Sweden. The joint venture, called VME Group, manufactures heavy earthmoving construction and mining equipment worldwide. Its principal competitors are Caterpillar, Komatsu, and, to a lesser extent, Deere & Company. Clark accounts for its investment in this joint venture using the equity method.

Key economic characteristics of the equipment manufacturing industry, which includes industrial, construction, and agricultural equipment, are as follows:

1. *Product Lines.* Products include tractors, excavators, loaders, haulers, cranes, compactors, and similar products. Manufacturers range from worldwide, full-line producers to regional niche players. There are currently more than 700 producers in the United States, yet six companies command more than 70 percent of the domestic market. Manufacturers compete on the basis of machine performance, price, aftermarket support, and parts availability. Approximately 20 to 30 percent of a manufacturer's sales typically come from the aftermarket. A large tractor, for example, usually consumes parts and service equal to the cost of the equipment within approximately two years of initial purchase.

2. *Production.* Equipment manufacturing is capital intensive. Manufacturers tend to centralize production around key machine components, such as engines, axles, transmissions, and hydraulics. Customizing products to particular customers' needs typically occurs at the assembly stage.
3. *Technology.* Electronic and computer-based technologies have played an increasingly important role in recent years, both in the design of the final product and its manufacturing. Robotics in particular has been applied successfully in the manufacturing process.
4. *Demand.* The relatively high cost of equipment and the cyclicality of many of the industries to which equipment manufacturers sell their products (for example, construction, mining, automotive) result in highly cyclical sales patterns. The level of interest rates, general conditions in the economy, and income tax considerations (for example, depreciation rates) significantly impact sales.
5. *Marketing.* Manufacturers use a distributor network to sell their products (original equipment and parts). The distributors usually sell a single manufacturer's products but complement the product offering with other products unique to the market that the manufacturer does not offer.

EXHIBIT 1

Condensed Financial Statement Data for
Clark Equipment Company with VME Group
Accounted for Using the Equity Method
(amounts in millions)
(Case 7.2)

	December 31			
	Year 9	**Year 10**	**Year 11**	**Year 12**
Balance Sheet				
Current Assets...............	$ 551	$ 468	$ 520	$396
Investment in VME Group......	142	166	135	119
Noncurrent Assets............	319	466	465	444
Total Assets	$1,012	$1,100	$1,120	$959
Current Liabilities............	$ 265	$ 282	$ 328	$187
Noncurrent Liabilities..........	255	238	554	519
Shareholders' Equity...........	492	580	238	253
Total Equities...............	$1,012	$1,100	$1,120	$959

	For the Year		
	Year 10	**Year 11**	**Year 12**
Income Statement			
Sales	$ 864	$ 727	$ 803
Equity in Earnings of VME.............	26	(29)	(47)
Cost of Goods Sold....................	(717)	(638)[a]	(664)
Interest Expense	(22)	(26)	(26)
Other Expenses, including Taxes	(111)	(87)	(94)
Net Income (loss)	$ 40	$ (53)	$ (28)

[a]Includes $20 million of charges for restructuring operations and environmental cleanup.

6. **Financing.** The capital-intensive nature of the manufacturing process leads these firms to rely on extensive long-term debt financing. Responsibility for arranging customer financing for equipment purchases may fall on the manufacturer, the distributor, or both.

Exhibit 1 presents condensed balance sheets for Clark as of December 31, Year 9, through December 31, Year 12, and condensed income statements for Year 10 through Year 12. These financial statements report Clark's investment in VME Group using the equity method. Exhibit 2 presents similar condensed financial statement data for VME Group.

REQUIRED

a. Prepare an analysis of the changes in the Investment in VME Group account on Clark's books for Year 9 through Year 11.
b. Exhibit 3 presents partial condensed balance sheets and income statements for Clark, assuming that it accounted for its investment in VME Group using the proportionate consolidation method (that is, Clark recognizes its 50 percent share of the assets, liabilities, revenues, and expenses of VME Group). Complete Exhibit 3 by preparing a balance sheet as of December 31, Year 12, and an income statement for Year 12 following the proportionate consolidation method.

EXHIBIT 2

VME Group
Condensed Financial Statement Data
(amounts in millions)
(Case 7.2)

	December 31			
	Year 9	Year 10	Year 11	Year 12
Balance Sheet				
Current Assets.............	$594	$665	$ 801	$649
Noncurrent Assets..........	177	231	392	321
Total Assets	$771	$896	$1,193	$970
Current Liabilities..........	$326	$354	$ 642	$516
Noncurrent Liabilities.......	187	232	299	230
Shareholders' Equity........	258	310	252	224
Total Equities............	$771	$896	$1,193	$970

	For the Year		
	Year 10	Year 11	Year 12
Income Statement			
Sales	$ 1,325	$ 1,368	$ 1,357
Cost of Goods Sold...............	(1,037)	(1,110)	(1,159)
Interest Expense	(20)	(33)	(29)
Other Expenses, including Taxes	(216)	(283)	(263)
Net Income (loss)	$ 52	$ (58)	$ (94)

c. Exhibit 4 presents partial condensed balance sheets and income statements for Clark, assuming that it accounted for its investment in VME Group using the full consolidation method (that is, Clark consolidated 100 percent of the assets, liabilities, revenues, and expenses of VME Group and reports Volvo's share of these items as a joint owners' interest. Complete Exhibit 4 by preparing a balance sheet as of December 31, Year 12, and an income statement for Year 12 following the full consolidation method.

d. Which of three methods of accounting for Clark's investment in VME Group (equity, proportionate consolidation, full consolidation) portrays better the economics of the relationship between the entities? Explain.

e. Exhibit 5 presents selected financial statement ratios for Clark and VME Group under each of the three methods of accounting. Calculate these ratios for Year 12. The income tax rate is 34 percent.

f. Identify the likely reasons for changes in Clark's profitability and risk during the period Year 10 to Year 12.

EXHIBIT 3

Condensed Financial Statement Data for Clark Equipment Company with VME Group Accounted for Using the Proportionate Consolidation Method
(amounts in millions)
(Case 7.2)

	December 31		
	Year 9	Year 10	Year 11
Balance Sheet			
Current Assets...............	$ 848.0	$ 800.5	$ 920.5
Noncurrent Assets............	407.5	581.5	661.0
Goodwill....................	13.0	11.0	9.0
Total Assets	$1,268.5	$1,393.0	$1,590.5
Current Liabilities............	$ 428.0	$ 459.0	$ 649.0
Noncurrent Liabilities.........	348.5	354.0	703.5
Shareholders' Equity..........	492.0	580.0	238.0
Total Equities..............	$1,268.5	$1,393.0	$1,590.5

	For the Year	
	Year 10	Year 11
Income Statement		
Sales	$ 1,526.5	$ 1,411.0
Cost of Goods Sold.................	(1,235.5)	(1,193.0)
Interest Expense	(32.0)	(42.5)
Other Expenses, including Taxes	(219.0)	(228.5)
Net Income (loss)	$ 40.0	$ (53.0)

EXHIBIT 4

Condensed Financial Statement Data for
Clark Equipment Company with VME Group
Accounted for Using the Full Consolidation Method
(amounts in millions)
(Case 7.2)

	December 31		
	Year 9	Year 10	Year 11
Balance Sheet			
Current Assets................	$1,145	$1,133	$1,321
Noncurrent Assets.............	496	697	857
Goodwill......................	13	11	9
Total Assets	$1,654	$1,841	$2,187
Current Liabilities.............	$ 591	$ 636	$ 970
Noncurrent Liabilities...........	442	470	853
Joint Owners' Interest...........	129	155	126
Shareholders' Equity............	492	580	238
Total Equities................	$1,654	$1,841	$2,187

	For the Year	
	Year 10	Year 11
Income Statement		
Sales	$ 2,189	$ 2,095
Cost of Goods Sold...................	(1,754)	(1,748)
Interest Expense	(42)	(59)
Other Expenses, including Taxes	(327)	(370)
Joint Owners' Interest.................	(26)	29
Net Income (loss)	$ 40	$ (53)

EXHIBIT 5

Clark Equipment Company
Profitability and Risk Ratios
(Case 7.2)

	Equity Method		Proportionate Consolidation		Full Consolidation	
	Year 10	Year 11	Year 10	Year 11	Year 10	Year 11
Profit Margin for ROA................	6.31%	(4.93%)	4.00%	(1.77%)	4.28%	(2.06%)
Assets Turnover......................	0.82	0.65	1.15	0.95	1.25	1.04
Return on Assets.....................	5.16%	(3.23%)	4.59%	(1.67%)	5.36%	(2.14%)
Common Earnings Leverage	0.73	1.48	0.65	2.12	0.43	1.23
Capital Structure Leverage.............	1.97	2.71	2.48	3.65	3.26	4.92
Return on Common Equity............	7.46%	(12.96%)	7.46%	(12.96%)	7.46%	(12.96%)
Current Ratios (December 31)..........	1.66	1.59	1.74	1.42	1.78	1.36
Fixed Asset Turnover[a]................	2.20	1.56	3.09	2.27	3.67	2.70
Long-Term Debt Ratio (December 31)[b] ..	29.10%	69.95%	37.90%	74.72%	39.00%	70.09%
Cost of Goods Sold/Sales..............	82.99%	87.76%	80.94%	84.55%	80.13%	83.44%

Exh. 5—Continued	Clark—Separate Company		VME—Separate Company	
	Year 10	Year 11	Year 10	Year 11
Profit Margin for ROA......................	3.30%	.88%	4.92%	(2.65%)
Assets Turnover............................	0.96	0.76	1.59	1.31
Return on Assets...........................	3.16%	.66%	7.82%	(3.47%)
Common Earnings Leverage	0.49	(1.70)	0.80	1.60
Capital Structure Leverage...................	1.68	2.35	2.94	3.72
Return on Common Equity..................	2.61%	(2.64%)	18.3%	(20.64%)
Current Ratios (December 31)................	1.66	1.59	1.88	1.25
Fixed Asset Turnover[a]......................	2.20	1.56	6.50	4.39
Long-Term Debt Ratio (December 31)[b]	29.10%	69.95%	42.80%	54.27%
Cost of Goods Sold/Sales....................	82.99%	87.76%	78.26%	81.14%

[a]Assuming that noncurrent assets represent property, plant and equipment.
[b]Assuming that noncurrent liabilities represent long-term debt.

CASE 7.3

LOUCKS CORPORATION: OBTAINING SECURITY IN TRANSLATION

Loucks Corporation, a U.S. company, manufactures and markets security alarm systems. Based on predictions of rapid economic growth in South America during the next decade, Loucks plans to establish a wholly owned subsidiary in Colombia as of January 1, Year 8, to manufacture and market security alarm systems in that country. The Colombian subsidiary will use technology developed by Loucks for the alarm systems. It will import from Loucks a portion of the electronic software needed for the systems. Assembly will take place in Colombia.

Loucks plans to contribute $100,000 to establish the subsidiary on January 1, Year 8. The exchange rate between the Colombian peso and the U.S. dollar is expected to be $.02:P1 on this date. Exhibit 1 presents pro forma financial statements for Year 8 for the Colombian subsidiary during its first year of operations. Exhibit 2 presents a partial pro forma consolidation worksheet for Loucks and its Colombian subsidiary for Year 8. The following additional information pertains to these companies during Year 8.

1. Loucks expects to sell electronic software to its Colombian subsidiary during Year 8 at a transfer (selling) price of P3,000,000. The Colombian subsidiary expects to sell all alarm systems in which this software is a component by the end of Year 8. The firms will denominate the transfers in Colombian pesos. Loucks plans to hedge its exchange exposure, including any transaction gain or loss and related loss or gain on the hedging instrument in other expenses.

2. The subsidiary expects to declare and pay a dividend to Loucks on December 31, Year 8.

REQUIRED

a. Discuss whether Loucks should use the U.S. dollar or the Colombian peso as the functional currency for its Colombian subsidiary.

b. Loucks expects the exchange rate between the U.S. dollar and the Colombian peso to change as follows during Year 8:

EXHIBIT 1

Colombian Subsidiary
Translation of Financial Statements—Year 8
(Case 7.3)

	Colombian Pesos	Exchange Rate	U.S. Dollars
Balance Sheet			
Assets			
Cash	P 700,000		
Accounts Receivable	2,000,000		
Inventories	3,500,000		
Fixed Assets (net)	5,700,000		
	P 11,900,000		
Liabilities and Equity			
Accounts Payable................	P 2,400,000		
Bonds Payable	4,000,000		
Common Stock	5,000,000		
Translation Adjustment...........	—		
Retained Earnings...............	500,000		
	P 11,900,000		
Income Statement			
Revenues.......................	P 15,000,000		
Cost of Goods Sold..............	(10,000,000)		
Depreciation Expense............	(300,000)		
Other Expenses..................	(2,500,000)		
Net Income	P 2,200,000		
Retained Earnings Statement			
Balance, January 1, Year 1........	—		
Plus Net Income	P 2,200,000		
Less Dividends...................	(1,700,000)		
Balance, December 31, Year 1......	P 500,000		

January 1, Year 8	$.020:P1
Average, Year 8	$.018:P1
December 31, Year 8	$.015:P1

Complete Exhibit 1, showing the translation of the subsidiary's accounts into U.S. dollars, assuming that the Colombian peso is the functional currency. Include a separate calculation of the translation adjustment. Using the translated amounts from part (*b*), complete the consolidation worksheet in Exhibit 2.

c. Repeat part (*b*), assuming that the U.S. dollar is the functional currency. Include a separate calculation of the translation gain or loss. The Colombian subsidiary expects to issue bonds denominated in Colombian pesos and acquire fixed assets on January 1, Year 8.

d. Why does the sign of the translation adjustment in part (*b*) differ from the sign of the translation gain or loss in part (*c*)?

EXHIBIT 2

Loucks Corporation and Colombian Subsidiary
Consolidation Worksheet
(Case 7.3)

	Loucks Corporation	Colombian Subsidiary	Adjustments and Eliminations	Consolidated
Balance Sheet				
Cash	$ 48,000			
Accounts Receivable	125,000			
Inventories	260,000			
Investment in Colombian Subsidiary	?			
Fixed Assets (net)	120,000			
Total Assets	$?			
Accounts Payable.........................	$ 280,000			
Bonds Payable	50,000			
Common Stock	100,000			
Translation Adjustment....................	—			
Retained Earnings........................	?			
Total Equities.........................	$?			
Income Statement				
Sales Revenue	$ 500,000			
Equity in Earnings of Colombian Subsidiary...	?			
Cost of Goods Sold.......................	(400,000)			
Depreciation Expense.....................	(20,000)			
Other Expenses..........................	(30,000)			
Net Income	$ 89,600			
Dividends...............................	(20,000)			
Increase in Retained Earnings...............	$?			
Retained Earnings, January 1	167,500			
Retained Earnings, December 31	$?			

---

e. Assume that actual financial statement amounts for Year 8 turn out to be exactly as projected in Exhibits 1 and 2, but that the exchange rate changes as follows:

January 1, Year 8	$.020:P1
Average, Year 8	$.022:P1
December 31, Year 8	$.025:P1

Calculate the amount of the translation adjustment under the all-current method and under the monetary/nonmonetary method for Year 8. Why do the signs of the translation adjustments in part (*e*) differ from those in parts (*b*) and (*c*)?

f. Compute the net income to revenues ratio based on (1) amounts originally measured in Colombian pesos, (2) amounts measured in U.S. dollars from part (*b*), and (3) amounts measured in U.S. dollars from part (*c*). Why is the net income to revenues percentage the same under (1) and (2) but different under (3)?

CHAPTER 8

PROFITABILITY ANALYSIS: AN EXTENDED LOOK

Learning Objectives

1. Understand the conditions when the analyst can meaningfully use ROA as a surrogate for the economic rate of return that a firm generates on its assets.
2. Use differences in the operating risk characteristics of firms (for example, operating leverage, sales cyclicality, stage and length of product life cycle) to explain differences in their ROAs.
3. Use differences in the extent of capital intensity and the presence or absence of entry barriers to explain differences in the mix of profit margin versus assets turnover.
4. Understand the role of ROA and financial leverage in explaining differences in ROCE.

Chapter 3 introduced two commonly used financial statement ratios for analyzing the overall profitability of a firm: the rate of return on assets (ROA) and the rate of return on common shareholders' equity (ROCE). This chapter explores these financial ratios more fully.

RATE OF RETURN ON ASSETS

ROA measures the return from using assets to generate earnings independent of the financing of those assets. The analyst uses ROA to assess a firm's operating performance relative to investments made without regard to whether the firm used debt or equity capital to finance the investments. ROA is computed as follows (level 1 analysis):

$$ROA = \frac{Net\ Income + (1 - Tax\ Rate)(Interest\ Expense)}{Average\ Total\ Assets}$$

The analyst obtains enhanced understanding of the behavior of ROA by disaggregating it into profit margin and total assets turnover components as follows (level 2 analysis):[1]

| **ROA** | = | **Profit Margin** | × **Total Assets Turnover** |

$$\frac{Net\ Income + (1 - Tax\ Rate)(Interest\ Expense)}{Average\ Total\ Assets} = \frac{Net\ Income + (1 - Tax\ Rate)(Interest\ Expense)}{Sales} \times \frac{Sales}{Average\ Total\ Assets}$$

This section examines more fully the economic and strategic significance of ROA, profit margin, and total assets turnover.

RELATING ROA TO ECONOMIC RATES OF RETURN

The economic value of any resource equals the present value of cash flows expected from that resource discounted at a rate that reflects the risk inherent in the cash flows. Thus

$$Value_t = \sum_{t=1}^{n} \frac{Expected\ Cash\ Flow_t\ ^2}{(1 + Discount\ Rate)^t}$$

The discount rate that equates the expected cash flows from a resource to its market price is referred to as the *economic*, or *internal, rate of return* (IRR).[3]

To illustrate, assume that a firm expects a new machine to save $1,000 a year in cash operating costs for five years and that the machine costs $3,791. The IRR is 10 percent, as Exhibit 8.1 shows. The amounts in column (4) represent the portion of each cash flow that is a return *of* capital (that is, a return of the amount originally invested in the machine). The amounts in column (3) represent the portion of each cash flow that is a return *on* the capital invested (that is, the IRR).

---

[1]Chapter 3 demonstrates that various expense to sales percentages enhance understanding of differences in profit margins and various asset turnovers (for example, accounts receivable turnover, inventory turnover) enhance understanding of differences in total assets turnovers (level 3 analysis). The analyst gains additional insight by studying ROA, profit margins, and total assets turnovers for the product and geographical segments of a firm (level 4 analysis).

[2]This general formulation permits inclusion of a residual value, or cash flow at the end of period *n*.

[3]An equilibrium position occurs for a firm when the IRR of the next best alternative investment equals the firm's cost of capital. This investment adds no present value in excess of the cost of the investment.

EXHIBIT 8.1

Amortization Schedule for Machine with Expected Annual
Cash Flows of $1,000 for 5 Years and Acquisition Cost of $3,791

Year	Present Value of Remaining Cash Flows at Beginning of Year (1)	Cash Flow (2)	Return at 10 Percent (3)	Economic Depreciation (4)	Present Value of Remaining Cash Flows at End of Year (5)
1	$3,791	$1,000	$ 379	$ 621	$3,170
2	3,170	1,000	317	683	2,487
3	2,487	1,000	249	751	1,736
4	1,736	1,000	174	826	910
5	910	1,000	90[a]	910	—
		$5,000	$1,209	$3,791	

$(3) = .10 \times (1)$

$(4) = (2) - (3)$

$(5) = (1) - (4)$

[a]Difference from $.10 \times \$910$ due to rounding.

We can express the equation for the value of any resource in terms of the IRR:

$$\text{Internal Rate of Return}_t = \sum_{t=1}^{n} \frac{\text{Cash Flow}_t - \text{Economic Depreciation}_t}{\text{Present Value of Remaining Cash Flows at Beginning of Year}_t}$$

This formulation expresses the IRR in parallel with ROA:

$$\text{ROA} = \frac{\text{Net Income Excluding Financing Costs}}{\text{Average Total Assets}}$$

This section addresses the question. How well, or under what conditions, does ROA reflect the average IRR of a firm's assets? Can the analyst meaningfully use ROA as a surrogate for the economic return? The response to this question has relevance to capital market participants in pricing firms' common shares, to credit analysts in pricing loans, to government regulators in monitoring firms' activities, and to others interested in using financial statement data in economic decisions.

At first glance, ROA appears to be a poor surrogate for the IRR for the following reasons:[4]

---

[4]For an elaboration of these points, see F. Fisher and J.J. McGowan, "On the Misuse of Accounting Rates of Return to Infer Monopoly Profits," *American Economic Review* 73, March, 1983, pp. 82–97.

1. The IRR uses cash flows in measuring returns, whereas ROA uses net income based on the principles of accrual accounting.
2. The IRR uses economic depreciation, reflecting a decelerated depreciation pattern, in measuring returns, whereas ROA generally uses the straight-line depreciation method in measuring net income.
3. The IRR uses the economic value of assets in the denominator, whereas ROA uses the depreciated acquisition cost of assets.

The issue for the analyst is how seriously these differences bias ROA as a useful surrogate for the IRR.

Addressing this question using data for actual firms is difficult because IRRs are not generally observable *ex post*. Researchers cannot trace a firm's total cash inflows during a period to each of the assets (for example, buildings, equipment, employee services) that gave rise to the cash flows. In addition, firms continually add and delete assets. The investment base against which cash flows are compared to compute IRRs is constantly changing.[5] Researchers can, however, address this question analytically and through simulation. Understanding the conditions when IRR and ROA are likely to be similar and the direction of any bias when such conditions are not present enhance the interpretability of ROA.

Cash Flows versus Income Flows.   Chapter 2 emphasizes that cash flows for discrete accounting periods do not necessarily equal income flows (that is, revenues and expenses). A growing firm will generally experience smaller cash flows than income flows (both flows excluding financing costs and depreciation) because increases in accounts receivable and inventories exceed increases in accounts payable and other current liabilities. A declining firm will often find that cash flows exceed income flows because decreases in accounts receivable and inventories exceed decreases in accounts payable and other current liabilities. A relatively mature firm, on the other hand, will find that income flows approximately equal cash flows. Changes in noncash working capital accounts should be small and capital expenditures should equal depreciation expense. Cash flow from operations (excluding financing costs) minus cash flows for investments (this net amount is sometimes referred to as *unleveraged free cash flow*) should equal net income excluding financing costs. Thus, income flows should serve as a useful surrogate for cash flows when the firm is relatively mature (that is, not growing or declining significantly).

Accounting's conservative bias in recognizing estimated holding losses as soon as they become evident but delaying the recognition of estimated holding gains until realized in a market transaction is another source of difference between cash flows and income flows. A firm holding an asset whose economic value has declined (for example, because of the development of a technologically superior product, machine, or process) will immediately write down the asset for accounting purposes and recognize the estimated loss. The cash flow effects of the decline in value occur in later

---

[5]Ijiri has suggested a measure, labeled the *cash recovery rate,* which analysts and researchers might use as an approximation to the IRR. See Yuji Ijiri, "Recovery Rate and Cash Flow Accounting," *Financial Executive,* March, 1980, pp. 54–60.

years when the firm generates smaller cash flows from using the asset than originally anticipated or realizes a smaller residual value when it sells the asset. Likewise, a firm that plans to discontinue an operation will immediately recognize any loss anticipated from such discontinuance in measuring net income. The cash flow effects of the loss will not usually occur immediately.

Chapters 2 and 5 emphasize that over sufficiently long periods, income flows equal cash flows. The effect of year-end accrual accounting adjustments lessens as the time period increases in length. One approach that the analyst might follow to deal with differences between cash flows and income flows is to calculate average ROA for several years. The average ROA for, say, three years will more closely approximate the IRR than the ROA for any single year. In settings where the analyst wishes to study realized IRRs in the past, the numerator of ROA should include income from continuing operations, discontinued operations, and extraordinary items. Each of these items affects the realized IRR. In settings in which the analyst wishes to use realized ROAs to project future IRRs (most valuation settings), the numerator of ROA should exclude nonrecurring sources of earnings.

Economic Depreciation versus Accounting Depreciation. Economic and straight-line depreciation for the machine illustrated in Exhibit 8.1 appears below:

Year	Economic Depreciation (IRR)	Straight-Line Depreciation (ROA)
1	$ 621	$ 758
2	683	758
3	751	758
4	826	758
5	910	759
	$3,791	$3,791

For firms that are not growing or declining significantly, the straight-line depreciation methods used in calculating net income and ROA should approximately equal economic depreciation (note that economic depreciation in the third year of $751 approximately equals straight-line depreciation of $758). For rapidly growing firms, the straight-line depreciation method overstates periodic economic depreciation. For a rapidly declining firm, the straight-line depreciation method understates periodic economic depreciation. Total depreciation over the life of an investment equals acquisition cost under all depreciation methods.

Economic Values versus Acquisition Cost Valuations of Assets. The valuation of the machine in Exhibit 8.1 using economic and straight-line depreciation appears below.

Beginning of Year	Economic Depreciation (IRR)	Straight-Line Depreciation (ROA)
1	$3,791	$3,791
2	3,170	3,033
3	2,487	2,275
4	1,736	1,517
5	910	759

Thus, the book value of the machine will be less than its economic value in all years.

Summarizing, the biases in the calculation of the numerator and denominator of ROA relative to corresponding amounts for the IRR are as follows:

	Income Flows Relative to Cash Flows	Straight-Line Depreciation Relative to Economic Depreciation	Acquisition Cost Valuation Relative to Economic Valuation
Stable (no growth) Firm	No difference	No Difference	Understatement
Growing Firm	Overstatement	Overstatement	Understatement
Declining Firm	Understatement	Understatement	Understatement

For a mature firm, ROA tends to overstate the IRR. The degree of overstatement is not particularly severe, however, when firms use the straight-line depreciation method, as is common in the United States.

For a growing firm, the misstatements in the numerator are offsetting (that is, overstated income flows minus overstated depreciation). The offsetting may not be precise, however. The net effect on ROA depends on the growth rate of assets. When the growth rate in assets is less than the IRR, which is the usual case, the net effect is that ROA overstates the internal rate of return. When the growth rate in assets exceeds the IRR, the net effect is that ROA understates the IRR.[6] The analyst can minimize the effect of any bias by computing weighted average ROAs for several years when using ROA to assess economic rates of return.

INTERPRETING THE RATE OF RETURN ON ASSETS[7]

Figure 8.1 depicts graphically the 10-year average of the median annual ROAs, profit margins, and assets turnovers of 24 industries for each of the years 1983 to 1992.

---

[6] If the accountant reported assets at current market values and included unrealized holding gains and losses in net income, then ROA would equal the IRR. This equality occurs because current market values and holding gains and losses reflect the present value of remaining (revised) cash flows.

[7] The material in this section draws heavily from Thomas I. Selling and Clyde P. Stickney, "The Effects of Business Environments and Strategy on a Firm's Rate of Return on Assets," *Financial Analysts Journal,* January/February 1989, pp. 43–52.

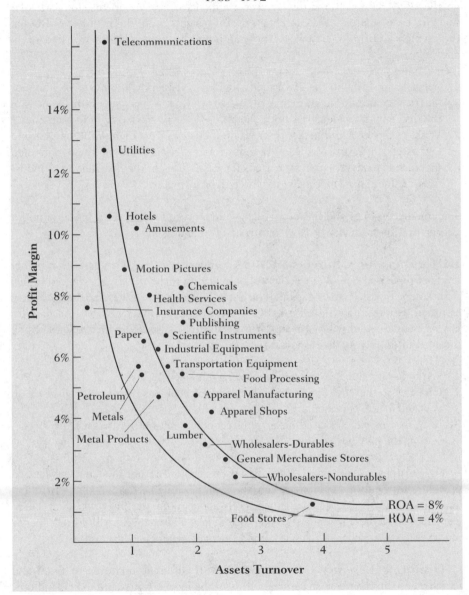

FIGURE 8.1

Average Median ROAs, Profit Margins, and Assets Turnovers for 24 Industries
1983–1992

The two isoquants reflect ROAs of 4 percent and 8 percent. The isoquants show the various combinations of profit margin and assets turnover that yield an ROA of 4 percent and 8 percent. For instance, an ROA of 8 percent results from any of the following profit margin/assets turnover combinations: 8 percent/1.0, 4 percent/2.0, 2 percent/4.0, 1 percent/8.0.

The data for ROA, profit margin, and assets turnover underlying the plots in Figure 8.1 reflect aggregated amounts across firms and across years (and should, therefore, approximate industry-level IRRs). The focus of financial statement analysis is on the ROAs of specific firms, or even segments of specific firms, for particular years (or even quarters). We can obtain useful insights about the behavior of ROA at the segment or firm level, however, by examining the average industry-level data. In particular,

1. What factors explain the consistently high or consistently low ROAs of some industries relative to the average of all industries (that is, reasons for differences in the distribution of industries in the bottom left versus the top right in Figure 8.1)?
2. What factors explain the fact that certain industries have high profit margins and low assets turnovers, while other industries experience low profit margins and high assets turnovers (that is, reasons for differences in the distribution of industries in the upper left versus the lower right in Figure 8.1)?

The microeconomics and business strategy literatures provide useful background for interpreting the behavior of ROA, profit margin, and assets turnover.

Differences or Changes in ROA.   Economic theory suggests that higher levels of perceived risk in any activity should lead to higher levels of expected return if that activity is to attract capital. The extra return compensates for the extra risk assumed. Realized rates of return (ROAs) derived from financial statement data for any particular period will not necessarily correlate as predicted with the level of risk involved in an activity as economic theory suggests because:

1. Faulty assumptions were used in deriving expected ROAs.
2. Changes in the environment after forming expectations cause realized ROAs to deviate from expectations.
3. ROA may provide a biased measure of economic rates of return (see the discussion in the previous section).

Despite these weaknesses, ROAs based on reported financial statement data do provide useful information for tracking the past, periodic performance of a firm and its segments and for developing expectations about future earnings potential. Three elements of risk help in understanding differences and changes in ROA: (1) operating leverage, (2) cyclicality of sales, and (3) length of product life cycles.

Operating Leverage.   Firms operate with different mixtures of fixed and variable costs in their cost structures. Firms in the metals, petroleum, hotel, and utilities industries are capital intensive. Depreciation and many operating costs are more or less fixed for any given period. Most retailers and wholesalers, on the other hand, have high proportions of variable costs in their cost structures. Firms with high proportions of fixed costs will experience significant increases in operating income as sales increase. The increased income occurs because the firm spreads fixed costs over a larger number of units sold, resulting in a decrease in average unit cost. Likewise, when sales decrease, these firms experience sharp decreases in operating income. Economists refer to this process of operating with high proportions of fixed costs as *operating leverage*. Firms with high levels of operating leverage experience greater variability in their ROAs than firms with low levels of operating leverage. All else being equal (see the discussion of cyclicality of sales in the next section), firms with high levels of operating leverage incur more risk in their operations and should earn higher rates of return.

Measuring the degree of operating leverage of a firm or its segments requires information about the fixed and variable cost structure. In Figure 8.2, the top panel shows the total revenue and total cost functions of two firms, A and B. The graphs assume that the two firms are the same size and have the same total revenue functions and the same breakeven points. These assumptions simplify the discussion of operating leverage but are not necessary when comparing actual companies.

Firm B has a higher level of fixed costs than Firm A, as measured by the intersection of the vertical axis at zero sales in the top panel of Figure 8.2. Firm A has a higher level of variable costs than Firm B, as measured by the slope of its total cost function as revenues increase above zero. The lower panel nets the total revenue and total cost functions to derive the operating income function. Operating income is negative in an amount equal to fixed costs when revenues are zero and operating income is zero at breakeven revenues. We use the slope of the operating income line as a measure of the extent of operating leverage. Firm B, with its higher fixed cost and lower variable cost mix, has more operating leverage. As revenues increase, its operating income increases more than that for Firm A. On the downside, however, income decreases more sharply as revenues decrease.

Another useful concept when studying operating leverage is contribution margin. Contribution margin equals revenues minus variable costs. The contribution margin percentage equals contribution margin divided by revenues. For every one dollar

FIGURE 8.2

Cost Structure and Operating Leverage

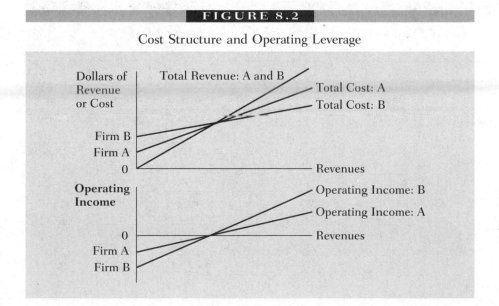

increase in sales, contribution margin increases by the contribution margin percentage. Because fixed costs do not change as revenues increase, operating income also increases by the contribution margin percentage as sales increase. *Thus, the slopes of the contribution margin function and the operating income function are the same.* This relationship is important when the analyst attempts to measure operating leverage for actual firms.

Unfortunately, firms do not publicly disclose information about their fixed and variable cost structures. To examine the influence of operating leverage on the behavior of ROA for a particular firm or its segments, the analyst must estimate the fixed/variable cost structure. One approach to such estimation is to study the various cost items of a firm and attempt to identify those items that are likely to behave as fixed costs. Firms incur some costs in particular amounts, referred to as *committed fixed costs,* regardless of the actual level of activity during the period. Examples include depreciation, amortization, and rent, all net of their tax effects. Firms can alter the amount of other costs, referred to as *discretionary fixed costs,* in the short run in response to operating conditions, but, in general, these costs do not vary directly with the level of activity. Examples include research and development, maintenance, advertising, and central corporate staff expenses. Whether the analyst should classify these latter costs as fixed costs or as variable costs in measuring operating leverage depends on their behavior in a particular firm.

Assuming that depreciation, amortization, and rent are the only fixed costs for Coke and Pepsi, Exhibit 8.2 illustrates the calculation of operating leverage. We net these costs of their tax savings at the statutory tax rate. We then add the net fixed operating costs to operating income to derive the contribution margin (thus, the calculations move from bottom to top in Exhibit 8.2). The contribution margin percent-

---

EXHIBIT 8.2

Estimation of Fixed and Variable Cost Structure of Coke and Pepsi
(amounts in millions)

	Coke			Pepsi		
	Year 6	Year 7	Year 8	Year 6	Year 7	Year 8
Depreciation & Amortization.....	$ 261	$ 322	$ 360	$ 1,035	$ 1,215	$ 1,444
Rent..........................	—	—	—	323	379	420
	$ 261	$ 322	$ 360	$ 1,358	$ 1,594	$ 1,864
Tax Effect.....................	(89)	(109)	(126)	(462)	(542)	(652)
Fixed Costs—Net	$ 172	$ 213	$ 234	$ 896	$ 1,052	$ 1,212
Revenues......................	$11,572	$ 13,074	$ 13,957	$ 19,292	$ 21,970	$ 25,021
Variable Costs	(9,081)	(10,091)	(10,621)	(16,284)	(18,547)	(20,902)
Contribution Margin............	$ 2,491	$ 2,983	$ 3,336	$ 3,008	$ 3,423	$ 4,119
Fixed Cost	(172)	(213)	(234)	(896)	(1,052)	(1,212)
Operating Income	$ 2,319	$ 2,770	$ 3,102	$ 2,112	$ 2,371	$ 2,907
Contribution Margin Percentage..	21.5%	22.8%	23.9%	15.6%	15.6%	16.5%

age equals contribution margin divided by revenues. The contribution margin percentage represents the slope of the operating income line in the lower panel of Figure 8.2 and indicates the degree of operating leverage. There is some imprecision in this approach to measuring operating leverage, so the analyst should interpret the resulting measurements cautiously.

These calculations indicate that Coke carries the greater amount of operating leverage. This result is surprising since Pepsi has a major involvement in restaurants, a more capital-intensive activity than soft drinks or consumer foods. Pepsi also has a higher percentage of its assets invested in fixed and intangible assets. The explanation may relate to the omission of certain fixed costs for Pepsi. Note that both Coke and Pepsi carry relatively low levels of operating leverage compared to many other industries.

Cyclicality of Sales. The sales of certain goods and services are sensitive to conditions in the economy. Examples include construction services, industrial equipment, computers, automobiles, and other durable goods. When the economy is in an upswing (healthy GNP growth, low unemployment, low interest rates), customers purchase these relatively high-priced items, and sales of these firms grow accordingly. When the economy enters a recession, customers curtail their purchases, and the sales of these firms decrease significantly. Contrast these cyclical sales patterns with those of grocery stores, food processors, nonfashion clothing, and similar nondurables. These latter industries sell products that most consumers consider necessities. Their products also tend to carry lower per unit costs, reducing the benefits of delaying purchases in order to realize cost savings. Firms with cyclical sales patterns incur more risk than firms with noncyclical sales.

One means of reducing the risk inherent in cyclical sales is to strive for a high proportion of variable cost in the cost structure. Pay employees an hourly wage instead of a fixed salary and rent building and equipment under short-term cancelable leases instead of purchasing these facilities. Cost levels should change proportionally with sales, thereby maintaining profit margin percentages and reducing risk.

The nature of the activities of some firms is such that they must carry high levels of fixed costs (that is, operating leverage). Examples include capital-intensive service firms such as airlines and railroads. Firms in these industries may attempt to transform the cost of their physical capacity from a fixed cost to a variable cost by engaging in short-term leases. However, lessors will then bear the risk of cyclical sales and demand higher returns (that is, rental fees). Thus, some firms bear a combination of operating leverage and cyclical sales risks.

A noncyclical sales pattern can compensate for high operating leverage and effectively neutralize this latter element of risk. Electric utilities, for example, carry high levels of fixed costs. Their monopoly positions in most service areas and guaranteed returns through regulation, however, permit them to achieve stable profitability.

Product Life Cycle. A third element of risk that affects ROA relates to the stage and length of a firm's product life cycle. Products move through four identifiable phases: introduction, growth, maturity, and decline. During the introduction and growth phases, a firm focuses on product development (product R&D spending) and capacity enlargement (capital spending). The objective is to gain market acceptance and market share. Considerable uncertainty may exist during these phases regarding the market viability of a firm's products. Products that have survived into the maturity phase have gained market acceptance. Also, firms have probably been able to cut back capital expenditures on new operating capacity. During the maturity phase, however, competition becomes more intense, and the emphasis shifts to reducing costs through improved capacity utilization (economies of scale) and more efficient production (process R&D spending). During the decline phase, firms exit the industry as sales decline and profit opportunities diminish.

Figure 8.3 depicts the behavior of revenues, operating income, investment, and ROA that corresponds to these four product life cycles. During the introduction and early growth phases, expenditures on product development and marketing, coupled with relatively low sales levels, lead to operating losses and negative ROAs. As sales accelerate during the high growth phase, operating income and ROAs turn positive. Extensive product development, marketing, and depreciation expenses during this phase moderate operating income, while heavy capital expenditures to build capacity for expected higher future sales increase the denominator of ROA. Thus, ROA does not grow as rapidly as sales. ROA increases significantly during the maturity phase due to benefits of economies of scale and learning curve phenomena and to curtail-

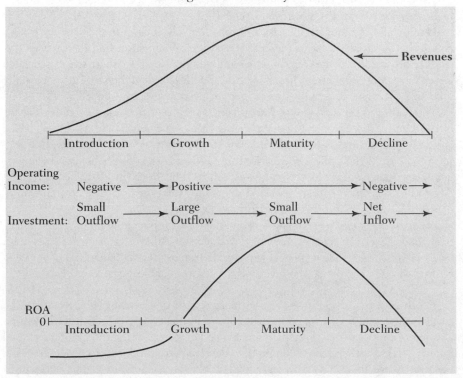

FIGURE 8.3

Relation between Sales, Operating Income, Investment, and ROA during Product Life Cycle

ments of capital expenditures. ROA deteriorates during the decline phase as operating income decreases but may remain positive or even increase for some time into this phase. Thus, as products move through their life cycles, their ROAs should move to the upper right area in Figure 8.1, peak during the maturity stage, and then move to the lower left area as the decline phase sets in. This movement in ROA appears negatively correlated with the level of risk. Risks are probably highest in the introduction and growth stages, when ROA is low or negative, and lowest in the maturity phase, when ROA is high. Taking a weighted average of ROAs over several years will reflect more accurately the economic returns generated by high growth firms.

Note that the product life cycle theory focuses on individual products. We can extend the theory to an industry level by examining the average stage in the product life cycle of all products within that industry. For instance, the products in the computer industry range from the introduction to the decline phases, but the overall industry is probably in the latter part of the high growth phase. The soft drink and food-processing industries, the primary involvements of Coke and Pepsi, are mature, although these firms and their competitors continually introduce new products. We might view the steel industry, at least in the United States, as in the early decline phase, although some companies have modernized production sufficiently to stave off the decline.[8]

In addition to the stage in the product life cycle, the length of the product life cycle is also an element of risk. Products with short product life cycles require more frequent expenditures to develop replacement or new products and thereby increase risks. The product life cycles of most computer products run one to two years. Most pharmaceutical products experience product life cycles of approximately seven years. In contrast, the life cycles of Coke's and Pepsi's soft drinks, branded food products, and some toys (for example, Barbie dolls) are much longer.

Refer now to the average industry ROAs in Figure 8.1. The positioning of several industries is consistent with their incurring one or more of these elements of risk. The relatively high ROAs of the amusements industry reflect its high operating leverage, growth, and dominant market positions in particular geographical locations. The chemicals industry, which includes pharmaceuticals, has high operating leverage, technological risks related to pharmaceutical life cycles, and product and environmental liability risks. Chemical companies other than pharmaceuticals are capital intensive and experience cyclical sales patterns. Apparel manufacturers and retailers face the risk of fashion obsolescence of their products. Insurance companies bear little risk from operating leverage, sales cyclicality, or life cycle phenomena and have relatively low ROAs.

Some of the industry positionings in Figure 8.1 appear inconsistent with these elements of risk. The petroleum, metals, and hotel industries are capital intensive and experience a degree of sales cyclicality. Their ROAs are lower than risk theory would suggest. Excess capacity and obsolete plant assets characterize all three

---

[8]Empirical support for a link between life cycle stage, sales growth, capital expenditure growth, and stock market reaction appears in Joseph H. Anthony and K. Ramesh, "Association between Accounting Performance Measures and Stock Prices: A Test of the Life Cycle Hypothesis," *Journal of Accounting and Economics* 15, 1992, pp. 203–227.

industries. Thus, the low ROAs may reflect the need for restructuring in these industries (that is, the lower ROAs represent disequilibrium positions).

The ROA positioning of several industries appears to be affected by generally accepted accounting principles (GAAP). A principal resource of food processors is the value of their brand names. Yet GAAP requires these firms to expense immediately advertising and other costs incurred to develop these brand names. Thus, their asset bases are understated and their ROAs tend to be overstated. Likewise, the publishing industry does not recognize the value of copyrights or authors' contracts as assets. In addition, most publishers subcontract out the production phases of publishing. These factors cause overstatement of ROAs. Pharmaceutical companies, included in the chemicals industry, expense research and development costs when incurred. Although such expensing reduces both the numerator and denominator of ROA, their net effect tends to be an overstatement of ROAs. A similar overstatement problem occurs for service firms, where the value of their employees does not appear as an asset.

One approach to dealing with these "off-balance-sheet assets" is to reverse the immediate expensing of a portion of advertising, research and development (R&D), and similar costs for some period of prior years and recognize that amount as an asset. For example, assume that the experience of a pharmaceutical firm is that 40 percent of expenditures on R&D eventually results in marketable drugs, that the drug approval process takes three years, and that the economic life of approved drugs is seven years. The analyst might recognize an asset equal to one-half (assuming straight-line amortization) of 40 percent of total R&D expenditures during the last 10 years. The analyst should add back to net income for the current year 40 percent of R&D expense and subtract amortization of the capitalized R&D amount (along with related tax effects).

Differences in the Profit Margin/Assets Turnover Mix.   The second relationship examined is the relative mix of profit margin and assets turnover at which a firm or industry operates. Explanations come from both the microeconomics and business strategy literatures.

Microeconomic Theory.   Figure 8.4 sets out some important economic factors that constrain certain firms and industries to operate in particular combinations of profit margins and assets turnover. Firms and industries characterized by heavy fixed capacity costs and lengthy periods required to add new capacity operate under a capacity constraint. There is an upper limit on the size of assets turnover achievable. In order to attract sufficient capital, these firms must generate a relatively high profit margin. Such firms will therefore operate in the area of Figure 8.4 marked *A*. The firms usually achieve the high profit margin through some form of entry barrier. The entry barrier may take the form of large required capital outlays, high risks, or regulation. Such factors help explain the profit margin/assets turnover mix of telecommunications, utilities, hotels, and amusements in Figure 8.1. The lack of such barriers coupled with excess capacity and high fixed costs helps explain the low ROAs in recent years of firms in the metals and petroleum industries.

Firms whose products are commodity-like in nature, that have few entry barriers, and that have intense competition operate under a competitive constraint. There is

FIGURE 8.4

Economic Factors Affecting the Profit Margin/Assets Turnover Mix

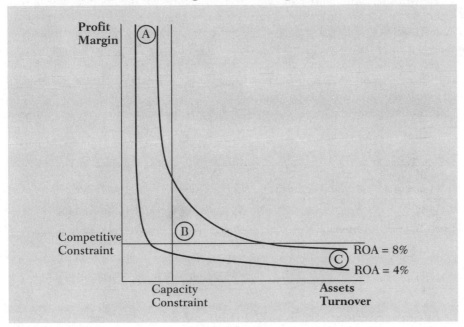

an upper limit on the level of profit margin achievable. In order to attract sufficient capital, these firms must strive for high assets turnovers. Such firms will therefore operate in the area of Figure 8.4 marked C. Firms achieve the high assets turnover by keeping costs as low as possible (for example, minimizing fixed overhead costs, purchasing in sufficient quantities to realize discounts, integrating vertically or horizontally to obtain cost savings, and similar moves). These firms match such actions to control costs with aggressively low prices to gain market share and drive out marginal firms. Most retailers and wholesalers operate in the C area of Figure 8.4.

Firms that operate in the area of Figure 8.4 marked B are not as subject to either capacity or competitive constraints as those that operate in the tails of the ROA curves. They thus have more flexibility to take actions that will increase profit margin, assets turnover, or both to achieve a higher ROA.

The notion of flexibility in trading off profit margin for assets turnover (or vice versa) is important when a firm considers strategic alternatives. The underlying economic concept is the marginal rate of substitution. Consider first a firm with a profit margin/assets turnover combination that puts it in the area A of Figure 8.4. Such a firm will have to give up a significant amount of profit margin to obtain a meaningful increase in assets turnover. To increase ROA, such a firm should therefore emphasize actions that increase profit margin. Likewise, a firm in area C of Figure 8.4 will have to give up considerable assets turnover to achieve a higher profit margin. To increase ROA, such a firm should emphasize actions that increase assets turnover. For firms operating in the tails of the ROA curves, the poor marginal rates of substitution do not favor trading off one variable for the other. Such firms must generally emphasize only one of these factors.

For firms operating in the area marked *B* in Figure 8.4, the marginal rate of substitution of profit margin for assets turnover is more equal. Such firms therefore have more flexibility to design strategies that promote profit margin, assets turnover, or some combination when striving to increase ROA. Unless the economic characteristics of a business constrain it to operate in area *A* or *C*, firms should strive to position themselves in area *B*. Such positioning provides greater potential to adapt to changing economic and business conditions.

In summary, the economic concepts underlying the profit margin/assets turnover mix are the following:

Area of Firm In Figure 8.4	Capital Intensity	Competition	Likely Strategic Focus
A	High	Monopoly	Profit Margin
B	Medium	Oligopolistic or Monopolistic Competition	Profit Margin, Assets Turnover, or Some Combination
C	Low	Pure Competition	Assets Turnover

Business Strategy. Both Hall[9] and Porter[10] suggest that firms have two generic, alternative strategies for any particular product: product differentiation and low-cost leadership. The thrust of the product-differentiation strategy is to differentiate a product in such a way as to obtain market power over revenues and therefore profit margins. The differentiation could relate to product capabilities, product quality, service, channels of distribution, or some other factor. The thrust of the low-cost leadership strategy is to become the lowest-cost producer, thereby enabling the firm to charge lower prices and achieve higher volumes. Such firms can achieve the low-cost position through economies of scale, production efficiencies, outsourcing, or similar factors or by asset parsimony (maintain strict controls on investments in receivables, inventories, and capital expenditures).[11]

In terms of Figure 8.4, movements in the direction of area *A from any point along the ROA curves* focus on product differentiation. Likewise, movements in the direction of area *C from any point along the ROA curves* focus on low-cost leadership. To illustrate, let us look at the average profit margins and assets turnovers for three types of retailers during the period 1983 to 1992:

---

[9]W. K. Hall, "Survival Strategies in a Hostile Environment," *Harvard Business Review,* September–October 1980, pp. 78–85.

[10]M. E. Porter, *Competitive Strategy* (New York: Free Press, 1980). Porter suggests that firms might also pursue a niche strategy. Because a niche strategy essentially represents differentiation within a market segment, we include it here under product differentiation strategy.

[11]Recent research in business strategy suggests that firms can simultaneously pursue product differentiation and low-cost leadership since product differentiation is revenue (output) oriented and low-cost leadership is more expense (input) oriented.

	Profit Margin	Assets Turnover
Specialty Retailers	4.45%	2.31
General Merchandise Stores	3.51%	2.02
Grocery Stores	2.03%	3.64

Within the retailing industry, specialty retailers have differentiated themselves by following a niche strategy and achieved a higher profit margin than the other two segments. Competition severely constrains the profit margin of grocery stores, and they must pursue more low-cost leadership strategies. Thus, a firm does not have to be in the tails of the ROA curves to be described as a product differentiator or low-cost leader. The appropriate basis of comparison is not other industries but other firms in the same industry. Remember, however, that the relative location along the ROA curve affects a firm's flexibility to trade off profit margin (product differentiation) for assets turnover (low-cost leadership).

Figure 8.5 shows the ROA, profit margin, and assets turnover of Coke and Pepsi for Year 8. These two firms dominate the soft drink industry. An average of their ratios essentially represents the soft drink industry's averages. Figure 8.5 also shows

FIGURE 8.5

ROA, Profit Margin, and Assets Turnover for Consumer Foods, Coke, and Pepsi for Year 8

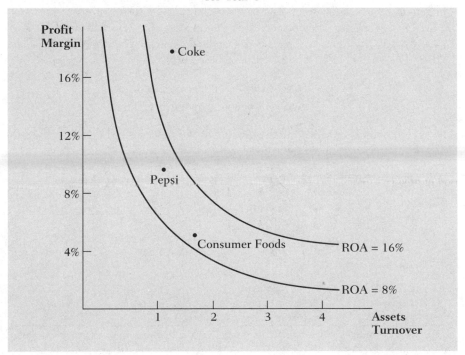

the average ROA, profit margin, and assets turnover for the consumer foods industry, which includes soft drinks as well as other food products. Note the following:

1. Pepsi's ROA is slightly higher than the consumer foods industry average for
   Year 8, while Coke's is significantly higher.
2. Both Coke and Pepsi experienced higher profit margins than the consumer foods
   industry average. This performance reflects brand recognition and brand loyalty
   as well as the lack of major competitors.
3. Both Coke and Pepsi had slower assets turnovers than the consumer foods industry average. Possible explanations include greater capital intensity of bottling
   and restaurant operations and more extensive foreign involvements.

Generalization such as these provide a useful first pass but require more in-depth
analysis before drawing conclusions.

Summarizing, differences in the profit margin/assets turnover mix relate to factors external to a firm, such as degree of competition, extent of regulation, entry
barriers, and similar factors, and to internal strategic choices, such as product differentiation and low-cost leadership. The external and internal factors are, of course,
interdependent and in a continual state of change.

RATE OF RETURN ON COMMON SHAREHOLDERS' EQUITY

The rate of return on common shareholders' equity (ROCE) measures the accounting return to common shareholders after subtracting all payments to providers of
capital (that is, creditors and preferred shareholders) senior to the common shareholders. The analyst calculates ROCE as follows:

$$\text{ROCE} = \frac{\text{Net Income} - \text{Preferred Dividends}}{\text{Average Common Shareholders' Equity}}$$

The analyst obtains enhanced understanding of the behavior of ROCE by disaggregating it into three components as follows:

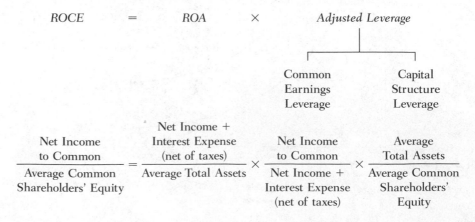

ROA indicates the return from operations independent of financing. Adjusted leverage indicates the multiplier effect of using debt and preferred stock financing to increase the return to common shareholders. Adjusted leverage is the product of two components: common earnings leverage and capital structure leverage. The common earnings leverage (CEL) ratio indicates the proportion of operating income (that is, net income before financing costs and related tax effects) allocable to the common shareholders. The capital structure leverage (CSL) ratio measures the degree to which firms use common shareholders to finance assets.

This section discusses the behavior of ROCE and the role of the three disaggregated components in explaining changes in ROCE. The emphasis in this chapter is on using ROCE to measure the profitability of a firm. Chapter 9 considers its use as a measure of risk and Chapter 12 discusses its use in the valuation of firms.

BEHAVIOR OF ROCE

Relation to Market Rates of Return. To the extent that accounting earnings serve as surrogates for economic earnings, one might expect a correlation between ROCE and market rates of return (that is, dividends plus changes in the market prices of common stock divided by the market price of the stock at the beginning of the period). Penman[12] regressed market rates of return on ROCE for each of the years 1969 to 1986 for all firms in the Compustat data file (includes all firms listed on the New York and American stock exchanges). The regression took the following form:

$$\text{Market Rate of Return}_t = \alpha + \beta(\text{ROCE}_t)$$

Values of 0 for the alpha coefficient and 1 for the beta coefficient are consistent with market rates of return and ROCE being the same, on average. Penman found a mean of the alpha coefficients across the 18 annual regressions of .049. The t statistic of .95 suggests that the alpha coefficient is not significantly different from zero. The mean of the beta coefficients across years was .879. The t statistic when assessed against zero was 10.98 and when assessed against unity was −1.92. These results suggest a relation between ROCE and market rates of return. However, the mean R^2 for the 18 years is only .09, indicating that ROCE explains only a small portion of the cross-section variation in market returns. We explore these relations more fully in Chapter 12.

Time-Series Behavior of ROCE. Two hypotheses regarding the time-series behavior of ROCE have been advanced in the literature. One hypothesis draws on the economic theory that different rates of return reflect different levels of risk. Firms engaged in more risky activities must generate higher returns to compensate for the higher risk incurred. As long as firms maintain their risk levels over time, their ROCEs should fluctuate randomly around the level of return commensurate

---

[12]Stephen H. Penman, "An Evaluation of Accounting Rates-of-Return," *Journal of Accounting, Auditing and Finance*, Spring 1991, pp. 233–255.

with their level of risk. (This view of the behavior of ROCE has been labeled the *random walk hypothesis,* similar in concept with the random walk hypothesis of stock prices.) Thus, firms generating ROCEs higher (lower) than the average of all firms in the economy should, because of their risk level, continue to earn higher (lower) ROCEs in the future.

An alternative hypothesis is that the ROCEs of individual firms revert over time to the average ROCE of all firms in the economy. The underlying rationale is that generating high or low ROCEs, relative to the economywide average, is a disequilibrium position. Competition will enter markets generating returns higher than the economywide average and force ROCEs down. Firms will exit industries generating lower than the economywide average ROCE until the surviving firms generate returns consistent with the economywide average. Firms earning the economywide average ROCE will continue to earn at this rate. Thus, firms with ROCEs higher (lower) than the average of all firms should experience lower (higher) ROCEs in the future. Firms with ROCEs close to the economywide average should experience little change in their ROCEs over time.

Penman[13] studied the time-series behavior of ROCE for the period 1969 to 1985 for all firms in the Compustat database. *For each year,* Penman grouped companies into twenty equal-sized portfolios based on the level of their ROCE for the year. ROCE was based on income from continuing operations. Penman then computed the median ROCE for these twenty portfolios of firms during each of the fifteen years following the base year. He repeated this process for each year between 1969 and 1985.[14] He then computed the mean of these portfolio medians for the base year and each subsequent year. Exhibit 8.3 presents the results.

The column labeled Year 0 shows the mean of portfolio median ROCEs in the base year. Note that portfolio 1 represents firms with the highest ROCE and portfolio 20 represents firms with the lowest ROCE. The mean of the portfolio median ROCEs one year after the base year appears in the second column, two years after the base year in the third column, and so forth. The mean ROCE in the base year for all firms is approximately 13 percent. Penman's results are supportive of the second hypothesis, reversion to economywide ROCEs, but the mean reversion process is slow. Firms with high ROCEs in the base year experience declines in their ROCEs over time to levels in the mid-teens. Firms with low ROCEs in the base year experience increases in their ROCEs over time, but the levels remain around 10 percent. Firms in the middle portfolios (portfolios 10 and 11) continue to generate ROCEs near the average for all firms throughout the years studied.

The mean rank order correlations at the bottom of Exhibit 8.3 represent the mean of the rank order correlations for each year subsequent to the base year with the rank orders in the base year. The rank order correlations remain relatively high until sometime after the sixth year, evidence that supports the first hypothesis of the behavior of ROCE over time. That is, differences in ROCE tend to persist for at least six years on average and revert to the economywide average only over an extended period of years. The implication of these results for the analyst is that ROCE of the current period should *on average* serve as a useful predictor of ROCE for the next

---

[13]Ibid.

[14]Portfolios formed after 1971 did not have a full 15 years of subsequent ROCEs.

EXHIBIT 8.3

Median Accounting Rates of Return (ROE) for Portfolios Formed on ROE, for Portfolio Formation Year and Subsequent Years 1969–1985

| ROE Portfolio | Year Ahead of Formation Year (Year 0) | | | | | | | | | | |
	0	1	2	3	4	5	6	9	12	15	N_0
1	0.433	0.313	0.239	0.205	0.183	0.171	0.171	0.153	0.136	0.130	2330
2	0.287	0.247	0.208	0.190	0.180	0.177	0.168	0.164	0.152	0.146	2330
3	0.238	0.217	0.193	0.182	0.173	0.162	0.165	0.157	0.156	0.148	2330
4	0.210	0.200	0.182	0.170	0.166	0.168	0.167	0.159	0.157	0.151	2330
5	0.191	0.183	0.169	0.162	0.157	0.155	0.155	0.150	0.144	0.140	2330
6	0.177	0.172	0.163	0.156	0.153	0.152	0.144	0.146	0.141	0.133	2330
7	0.165	0.161	0.153	0.151	0.145	0.144	0.143	0.142	0.142	0.142	2330
8	0.154	0.151	0.147	0.143	0.143	0.142	0.139	0.138	0.135	0.143	2330
9	0.144	0.144	0.141	0.138	0.138	0.136	0.138	0.136	0.137	0.131	2330
10	0.135	0.135	0.131	0.132	0.130	0.132	0.133	0.136	0.137	0.135	2330
11	0.126	0.127	0.129	0.129	0.131	0.132	0.130	0.133	0.128	0.134	2335
12	0.117	0.120	0.122	0.124	0.128	0.128	0.129	0.135	0.137	0.125	2330
13	0.106	0.112	0.117	0.122	0.124	0.126	0.127	0.133	0.128	0.127	2330
14	0.095	0.100	0.108	0.115	0.120	0.117	0.121	0.129	0.111	0.100	2330
15	0.083	0.088	0.097	0.105	0.111	0.115	0.112	0.113	0.099	0.096	2330
16	0.068	0.073	0.085	0.093	0.101	0.106	0.109	0.116	0.099	0.097	2330
17	0.049	0.061	0.074	0.087	0.094	0.099	0.104	0.116	0.097	0.087	2330
18	0.022	0.041	0.059	0.072	0.082	0.087	0.092	0.106	0.093	0.076	2330
19	−0.032	0.011	0.045	0.061	0.080	0.082	0.085	0.102	0.094	0.075	2330
20	−0.225	−0.060	0.030	0.064	0.088	0.096	0.100	0.115	0.105	0.056	2330
Mean Rank Correlation	1.000	0.999	0.989	0.968	0.907	0.871	0.857	0.698	0.821	0.764	

NOTES: Accounting rate of return is annual earnings before extraordinary times divided by beginning-of-year book values. Each calendar year, 1969–1985, is a base year (year 0). Reported ROE values are means of portfolio medians over years for the base year and subsequent years indicated at the head of the columns. N_0 is the number of firms in the portfolio for all base years.

SOURCE: Stephen H. Penman, "An Evaluation of Accounting Rates-of-Return," *Journal of Accounting, Auditing and Finance,* Spring 1991, vol. 6, no. 2 pp. 233–255. (Greenwood Subscription Publications, Westport, CT). Reprinted with permission. All rights reserved.

several periods. Any long-term reversion toward the economywide average ROCE should take many years and is not likely to have a major influence on the market valuation of the firm. These results, though, reflect amounts for the large group of firms studied. Such findings are not necessarily inconsistent with an analyst identifying a particular firm whose future ROCE will remain significantly higher or lower than the economywide average or that will revert to the mean more quickly than the average results in Exhibit 8.3 indicate.

BEHAVIOR OF THE DISAGGREGATED COMPONENTS OF ROCE

The disaggregated components of ROCE suggests that ROCE relates to (1) an ability to generate a return from using assets in operations (that is, ROA) and (2) an ability to leverage this return successfully for the benefit of shareholders. This section explores more fully the association of ROA and financial leverage to ROCE.

Exhibit 8.4 classifies the 24 industries studied earlier in this chapter into a three-by-three matrix based on the level of the average of their median annual ROAs and capital structure leverage ratios for each of the years 1983 to 1992. The cells represent the lower, middle, and upper thirds in the rank orderings on each of these ratios. The average of the median ROCEs for each industry over the same time period appears in parentheses.

Observe the high degree of association between the level of ROA and the level of ROCE. The Spearman rank order correlation coefficient is .73. If we remove insurance companies, which have very low ROAs and very high capital structure leverage ratios, the Spearman rank order correlation is .78. Although we would expect firms with high ROAs to have high ROCEs, and vice versa, the important insight from Exhibit 8.4 is that the extent of financial leverage does not seem to make much difference in the rank ordering of ROA and ROCE (that is, the industries do not line up on an upward-sloping diagonal suggestive of a positive relation between ROA and capital structure leverage). The Spearman rank order correlation coefficient between the capital structure leverage ratio and ROCE is zero. The lack of association between ROCE and the capital structure leverage ratio suggests that enhancing ROCE does not appear to drive firms' capital structure decisions.

A research study of firms in 22 industries for the years 1977 to 1986 found that the major portion of the annual changes in ROCE resulted from changes in ROA, not from financial leveraging activities.[15] Firms did not appear to make significant changes in their capital structure, at least during the annual reporting periods stud-

---

EXHIBIT 8.4

Relation to ROCE to ROA and Capital Structure Leverage Ratio
1983–1992
(ROCE in parentheses)

	Lower Third	Middle Third	Upper Third	
Upper Third	Apparel Products (14.8%) Publishing (15.2%) Chemicals (15.5%) Scientific Instru. (11.8%) Apparel Retailing (17.2%)	Food Processing (15.1%) Amusements (13.9%) Health Services (13.7%)		Mean ROCE = 14.7%
Middle Third ~~ROA~~	Paper (12.7%) Metal Products (9.0%) Ind. Equip. (12.2%)	Transportation Eq. (13.6%) Motion Pictures (12.8%)	Telecommunications (13.6%) Gen. Merch. Stores (13.9%) Food Stores (15.0%)	13.4%
Lower Third		Lumber (11.5%) Metals (10.5%) Wholesalers–Durables (10.9%)	Utilities (13.0%) Hotels (9.8%) Insurance (13.3%) Petroleum (11.0%) Wholesalers–Nondur. (11.3%)	11.4%

Capital Structure Leverage Ratio

Mean ROCE = 13.9%	12.8%	12.8%

ied, to compensate for changes in ROA. This result makes intuitive sense since major changes in capital structure take time and are costly to execute. The results are also consistent with the philosophy of identifying and maintaining an optimal or desired capital structure over time, independent of short-term changes in operating profitability. Chapter 9 explores more fully the factors that explain differences in debt levels.

SUMMARY

The objective of this chapter was to enhance understanding of the behavior of ROA and ROCE so that the analyst can make more meaningful interpretations of a firm's profitability. The principal insights of the chapter are summarized below:

1. A firm's ROA for any single year is usually a reasonable surrogate for its economic rate of return if the firm is not growing or declining. For companies experiencing growth or decline, an average of the ROAs for several years is a better surrogate of the economic rate of return than the ROA of any single year.
2. Differences in ROA appear related to differences in risk, including degree of operating leverage, sales cyclicality, and stage and length of product life cycles.
3. Differences in the mix of profit margin and assets turnover relate to the extent of capital intensity and the presence or absence of entry barriers (brand name recognition, patents, regulated monopoly positions, and differentiated versus commodity products).
4. Differences in ROCE correlate highly with differences in ROA. Differences in the use of financial leverage do not seem to explain much about differences in ROCE.

CASE 8.1

INTERPRETING INDUSTRY-LEVEL ROAs AND ROCEs*

The rate of return on assets (ROA) measures the earnings generated by a firm from using assets in its principal operating activities. ROA disregards the manner in which the firm financed its assets (that is, its use of debt versus equity). The rate of return on common shareholders' equity (ROCE) measures the earnings generated by a firm on resources provided by the common shareholders. ROCE considers both the firm's ability to generate earnings from operations and to use financial leverage (debt financing) successfully. This case uses the framework on page 470 to enhance understanding of ROA and ROCE.

This case uses amounts for these financial statement ratios for various related industries to gain insights into the operating and financing characteristics of these industries. The financial statement ratios use data provided by Compustat for each of the years 1983 to 1992. The six ratios are computed for each firm for each year. The median value for each year for each ratio for each two-digit SIC industry code is then determined. Using the median value instead of the mean value reduces the impact of outliers. The mean of the ten annual median

[15]Thomas I. Selling and Clyde P. Stickney, "Disaggregating the Rate of Return on Common Shareholders' Equity: A New Approach," *Accounting Horizons*, December 1990, pp. 9–17.

*The author gratefully acknowledges the assistance of Victor McGee in the preparation of this case.

Financial Statement Ratio	Numerator	Denominator
Profit Margin	Net Income Excluding Financing Costs	Sales
×		
Assets Turnover	Sales	Average Total Assets
=		
Return on Assets	Net Income Excluding Financing Costs	Average Total Assets
×		
Common Earnings Leverage	Net Income to Common Shareholders	Net Income Excluding Financing Costs
×		
Capital Structure Leverage	Average Total Assets	Average Common Shareholders' Equity
=		
Return on Common Shareholders' Equity	Net Income to Common Shareholders	Average Common Shareholders' Equity

EXHIBIT 1

Average Median Financial Statement Ratios
for Selected Industries—1983 to 1992
(Case 8.1)

Industry	Profit Margin	Assets Turnover	ROA	Common Earnings Leverage	Capital Structure Leverage	ROCE
Group 1						
Food Processors....................	5.1%	1.60	8.4%	.79	2.28	15.2%
Food Stores	2.0%	3.64	7.3%	.71	2.95	15.0%
Restaurants.......................	5.2%	1.60	8.3%	.75	2.18	13.1%
Group 2						
Wholesalers—Durables	3.4%	1.83	6.6%	.73	2.44	10.9%
Wholesalers—Nondurables	2.0%	2.55	5.8%	.68	2.75	11.3%
Group 3						
Oil and Gas Exploration and Drilling ..	16.6%	.30	5.8%	.78	1.75	7.2%
Petroleum Refining and Related	5.7%	1.09	6.4%	.72	2.56	11.0%
Group 4						
Lumber and Wood Products	3.8%	1.65	6.9%	.81	2.29	11.5%
Paper and Allied Products	6.5%	1.16	7.7%	.77	2.14	12.7%
Printing and Publishing	6.9%	1.27	9.2%	.85	2.07	15.1%
Group 5						
Textile Mill Products	4.8%	1.55	7.4%	.68	2.33	11.2%
Apparel Manufacturing	5.1%	1.80	9.3%	.75	2.03	14.8%
Apparel Retailing..................	4.5%	2.30	10.2%	.86	1.93	17.2%

Exh. 1—Continued

Industry	Profit Margin	Assets Turnover	ROA	Common Earnings Leverage	Capital Structure Leverage	ROCE
Group 6						
Metal Mining.....................	18.1%	.35	7.0%	.84	1.42	8.6%
Primary Metals (Steel)	5.5%	1.20	6.6%	.73	2.33	10.5%
Metal Products	5.2%	1.34	7.5%	.76	2.27	11.8%
Industrial Machinery	6.1%	1.21	8.0%	.86	1.90	12.2%
Transportation Equipment	5.2%	1.43	7.9%	.76	2.45	13.6%
Group 7						
Air Transportation..................	5.6%	1.20	7.3%	.68	3.22	14.1%
Motor Freight Transportation..........	4.7%	1.77	7.5%	.77	2.55	13.9%
Railroad Transportation	11.0%	.51	5.7%	.65	2.59	9.3%
Water Transportation.................	14.0%	.50	6.1%	.61	2.27	10.6%
Group 8						
Depository Financial Institutions.......	37.1%	.10	3.9%	.23	16.65	13.7%
Security Brokerage Firms.............	13.7%	.46	5.7%	.67	3.90	16.7%
Insurance Companies................	7.8%	.42	3.7%	.90	4.37	13.3%

values for each ratio for each two-digit SIC industry code is then computed. The mean of the medians serves as a long-term (10-year) measure for each financial statement ratio by industry. At the level of the individual firm, the six financial statement ratios are mathematically related as summarized above. Because the firm that represents the median value differs across the six ratios in any single year and across years, the means of the medians of the six ratios will not precisely net mathematically at the aggregate industry level as summarized above. However, the average median ratios for various related industries provide useful information about the operating profitability and financial risk of these industries.

Exhibit 1 presents the average median ratios for eight industry groupings.

REQUIRED

For each group:
a. Suggest reasons for the differences in the mix of profit margin and assets turnover.
b. Suggest reasons for the differences in ROA, giving particular consideration to differences in operating risk characteristics.
c. Suggest reasons for differences in the use of financial leverage and its effectiveness in enhancing the return to common shareholders.

CASE 8.2

COMPUTER INDUSTRY ANALYSIS: HEWLETT-PACKARD AND SUN MICROSYSTEMS*

The high growth rates and superior profitability enjoyed by the computer industry during the last four decades is now history. The computer industry as a whole is rapidly approaching ma-

*The author gratefully acknowledges the assistance of David Crowley in the preparation of this case.

turity, with most products displaying commodity-like characteristics. New technological breakthroughs are quickly copied by competitors. Consolidation (through strategic alliances) and downsizing (through employee layoffs) appear the order of the day.

The workstation segment of the computer industry is one bright spot in an otherwise pessimistic picture. Workstations were originally developed in the early 1980s to serve the design and graphic needs of engineers and scientists and enjoyed growth rates 40 percent per year throughout the 1980s. Industry analysts project annual growth rates in the mid-teens in the 1990s as workstation manufacturers begin targeting business users desiring to establish networked systems.

This case analyzes the two leading firms in the workstation segment of the computer industry: Hewlett-Packard Corporation (HP) and Sun Microsystems (Sun). These two firms commanded a 59.8 percent combined market share in 1993.

OVERVIEW OF THE COMPUTER INDUSTRY

The computer industry during the last four decades has shifted its emphasis from the question: What can the machines do? (a technology-oriented question) to the question: What can the machines do for particular customers? (a user-oriented question).

The technology-driven phase witnessed the development of various computer types.

1. *Mainframe computers:* Designed to satisfy data processing needs of large business and governmental entities.
2. *Minicomputers:* Designed to provide more cost-effective computer power than the mainframes for medium-sized businesses and technical applications.
3. *Microcomputers:* Designed to provide more cost-effective computer power than mainframes and minicomputers for individuals.

Technological innovations in all three computer types increased computing power at an improving value/cost ratio, ushering in supercomputers, superminicomputers, and supermicrocomputers.

The distinctions between computer types began losing significance in the 1980s as the technological differences between them dissipated and increased competition forced the industry to turn its attention to satisfying particular users' needs. Certain companies, for example, targeted the engineering/scientific market (Apollo Computer, Sun Microsystems), while others focused on the education market (Apple Computer) or the large-scale data processing market (Amdahl Computer, Cray Computer). Other companies maintained a presence in multiple markets (for example, IBM, Digital Equipment). Each company attempted to develop proprietary systems (hardware and software) to lock in customers and build monopoly power.

The rate of technological change and commodity nature of most computer hardware led customers, particularly business firms, to switch to competitors' products when they added to or replaced existing computers. These customers quickly learned that their old software would not run on their new hardware and that their old hardware would not interact with their new hardware. Efforts by the computer companies to offer proprietary products began backfiring on the industry. Customers clamored for standardized operating systems and software. Resistance to purchasing new computer hardware and software until the industry tackled the standardization problem, coupled with U.S., and increasingly worldwide, recessions in the early 1990s, dampened computer industry sales. The industry is currently engaged in a restructuring that will likely change significantly the players, their products, and their ways of serving customers' needs in the years ahead.

ECONOMICS OF THE COMPUTER INDUSTRY

The following discussion summarizes the more important economic characteristics of the computer industry.

1. *Large Fixed Costs:* High front-end research and development costs plus fixed costs from capital-intensive manufacturing processes provide for significant amounts of operating leverage.
2. *High Rate of Technological Change:* Products often move from the growth to the maturity stages in one to two years, increasing the risk that firms will not realize the benefits of economies of scale possible with their operating leverage.
3. *Relatively Little Product Differentiation:* The increased number of competitors in most industry segments coupled with blurred distinctions between hardware have caused customers to view hardware as a commodity, with relatively elastic demand. Suppliers are attempting to differentiate themselves on software, networking capabilities, service, installed base, and other dimensions.
4. *Growth Rates:* The historical annual growth rate for the overall computer industry of over 20 percent has decreased to less than 10 percent during the last few years, with much of the increase coming from abroad.
5. *Cyclical Sales:* General business profitability, interest rates, anticipated tax law changes, and similar factors affect computer sales. With 24 percent of capital expenditures by business firms going into computers, discretionary changes that companies make in their capital budgets in response to economic conditions impact the revenue of computer firms.
6. *Low Financial Leverage:* Firms in the industry carry high operating leverage and product obsolescence risks and tend not to add financial risk as well.
7. *Exchange Rate Changes:* U.S. computer firms derive approximately 50 percent of their revenues from abroad. They source computer system components from various countries. Thus, exchange rate changes can significantly impact profitability.

COMPUTER WORKSTATION MARKET

Industry historians credit Digital Equipment Corporation for beginning the evolution of what popular parlance now calls the "workstation market." In 1965 Digital introduced the first minicomputer that, when coupled with appropriate software, satisfied the computation, design, and graphics needs of technical users (scientists, architects, engineers). Data General entered the market in 1971, Prime Computer in 1975, Apollo Computer in 1981, and Sun Microsystems in 1982.

Apollo Computer receives credit for creating the high performance engineering workstation segment of this technical market in 1981. This segment caters to the design flexibility and high-quality graphics capabilities needed by engineers in computer-aided design (CAD), computer-aided manufacturing (CAM), and computer-aided engineering (CAE). The initial workstations used minicomputers, were single user, and relied on proprietary hardware and software. Apollo commanded a 50 percent market share in the mid-1980s, a period when engineering workstation sales doubled and sometimes tripled each year. Sun Microsystems targeted the low end of the engineering workstation market at the time of its entry in 1982 and commanded a market share of approximately 15 percent in the mid-1980s. Competition in this high growth market intensified in the mid-1980s when DEC introduced its Micro VAXII computer and IBM packaged a workstation around its PC-RT.

Two developments dramatically affected the proprietary strategies of these industry competitors in the second half of the 1980s. First, rapid technological change in the areas of processing speed and storage capability resulted in decreasing product life cycles of most products (less than two years). Customers often delayed purchasing workstations when they anticipated that new, innovative products would arrive on the market. Desiring to maintain an edge over their competitors, these customers often satisfied a portion of their workstation needs with the most technologically advanced products. As a consequence, business firms often found that they had workstations manufactured by Apollo, Sun, DEC, and other firms scattered among their engineers. The proprietary strategies of these firms meant that operating systems and applications software designed for one supplier's computer would not work on competitors' offerings. Customers demanded greater standardization. Sun Microsystems played an initial leadership role in striving toward standardization and, as a consequence, achieved the highest market share in the workstation market by the late 1980s. The UNIX operating system is now the accepted industry standard.

A second development in the late 1980s was the movement from single use/single user systems to multiple use/multiple user networked systems. The ability to access databases, integrate design activities of several engineers or scientists, and communicate effectively became a priority. The lack of industry standards discussed above served as an impediment as networking developed.

Although competitors in the workstation market have not yet achieved full standardization, they have made considerable progress in a few short years. Four firms dominate the market in 1993: Sun Microsystems, Hewlett-Packard (which acquired Apollo Computer in 1989), Digital Equipment, and IBM. These four firms commanded a 78.9 percent market share in that year.

Although the technical user market continues to grow, these firms are now targeting a wide range of business users. Many business firms find themselves with personal computers (PCs) sitting on office desks with little or no ability to interact with each other or to deal with large databases. In a word, networking has come of age in the office. Firms in the workstation market have recently tackled networking problems in the technical market and appear well positioned to move into the office market. The more advanced workstations have the capabilities of low-end mainframe computers and can serve as a central storage and processing center in such networks. Industry analysts expect the office networking market to grow at a rate greater than 20 percent a year in the 1990s and the competition to be fierce. Some of the factors affecting this new market are as follows.

1. Microsoft's DOS and Windows NT operating systems dominate the PC market, whereas the UNIX operating system developed by AT&T is the standard in the workstation market. The vast inventory of applications software written for the PC runs for the most part on DOS or Windows NT. A version of UNIX has recently been developed for the PC, which permits PC owners to run applications software written for workstations.

2. The full benefits of networking occur when PCs, workstations, and mainframes link together. The four major workstation competitors enter this rapidly evolving market with different positionings. Sun and HP maintain positions in the market for mid-sized systems, with only a minor presence in PCs or mainframes. DEC's emphasis ranges from mid-sized systems to the lower end of mainframes, with little presence in the PC market. IBM is the dominant player in the PC and mainframe market and achieved a close fourth position in the workstation market as of 1993. Given IBM's installed base in the two ends of the computer continuum, it should generate a greater presence in the mid-range as well as networking evolves.

3. Computer companies have traditionally marketed workstations through direct sales forces or value-added resellers, whereas computer dealers and retailers dominate the marketing of PCs. Competition has squeezed margins throughout the industry, reducing the economic feasibility of maintaining direct sales forces and opening multiple new distribution channels.

4. Business firms have increasingly used network systems specialists instead of hardware manufacturers (for example, HP, Sun) to design, implement, and manage their network systems. This move reflects in part the in-place hardware from several manufacturers as well as a desire on the part of business firms to disentangle the design of network systems from the particular hardware offered by any one manufacturer.
5. Recent technological advances in the PC market provide PCs with the computing power of low-end workstations. Microsoft's Windows provides much of the graphic capabilities of the graphical software written in UNIX for workstations.

COMPANIES STUDIED

Hewlett-Packard.   HP has traditionally maintained its primary presence in the market for mid-sized computers for business. Its acquisition of Apollo Computer in 1989 provided it with a major presence in the high end of the workstation market. Sales of its LaserJet and DeskJet printers have become an increasing proportion of its sales mix in recent years. HP has recently shifted more of its distribution function from its own sales staff to distributors and retailers. Exhibits 1 to 4 present financial statement and other information for HP. The notes to the financial statements reveal the following:

1. HP adopted the provisions of *Statement of Financial Accounting Standards No. 106* as of the beginning of its 1992 fiscal year.
2. HP made a $137 million pretax provision for employee severance and facilities consolidation in fiscal 1992 (after making a similar provision of $150 million pretax in fiscal 1991). The provision is included in selling and administrative expenses in Exhibit 2.
3. HP uses a first-in, first-out cost-flow assumption for inventories, an accelerated depreciation method, and the U.S. dollar as the functional currency for foreign operations.

EXHIBIT 1

Hewlett-Packard—Balance Sheets
(amounts in millions)
(Case 8.2)

	October 31			
	1991	1992	1993	1994
Assets				
Cash	$ 625	$ 641	$ 889	$ 1,357
Marketable Securities	495	394	755	1,121
Accounts Receivable	2,976	3,497	4,208	5,028
Inventories	2,273	2,605	3,691	4,273
Prepayments	347	542	693	730
Total Current Assets	$ 6,716	$ 7,679	$10,236	$12,509
Property, Plant, and Equipment (cost)	$ 5,961	$ 6,592	$ 7,527	$ 7,938
Accumulated Depreciation	(2,616)	(2,943)	(3,347)	(3,610)
Property, Plant, and Equipment (net)	$ 3,345	$ 3,649	$ 4,180	$ 4,328
Other Assets	$ 1,912	$ 2,372	$ 2,320	$ 2,730
Total Assets	$11,973	$13,700	$16,736	$19,567

Exh. 1—Continued	October 31			
	1991	**1992**	**1993**	**1994**
Liabilities and Shareholders' Equity				
Accounts Payable............................	$ 686	$ 925	$ 1,223	$ 1,466
Notes Payable...............................	1,201	1,384	2,190	2,469
Other Current Liabilities	2,176	2,785	3,455	4,295
Total Current Liabilities....................	$ 4,063	$ 5,094	$ 6,868	$ 8,230
Long-Term Debt	188	425	667	547
Deferred Income Taxes.......................	243	49	31	—
Other Noncurrent Liabilities	210	633	659	864
Total Liabilities	$ 4,704	$ 6,201	$ 8,225	$ 9,641
Common Stock	$ 1,010	$ 874	$ 937	$ 1,033
Retained Earnings...........................	6,259	6,625	7,574	8,893
Total Shareholders' Equity	$ 7,269	$ 7,499	$ 8,511	$ 9,926
Total Liabilities and Shareholders' Equity	$11,973	$13,700	$16,736	$19,567

EXHIBIT 2

Hewlett-Packard—Income Statements
(amounts in millions)
(Case 8.2)

	Fiscal Year Ended October 31		
	1992	**1993**	**1994**
Sales	$16,410	$ 20,317	$ 24,991
Other Revenues	17	25	29
Cost of Goods Sold....................	(9,158)	(12,123)	(15,490)
Selling and Administrative..............	(4,228)	(4,554)	(4,925)
Research and Development	(1,620)	(1,761)	(2,027)
Interest	(96)	(121)	(155)
Income Taxes.........................	(444)	(606)	(824)
Income from Continuing Operations	$ 881	$ 1,177	$ 1,599
Adjustment for Change in Accounting Principles: Adoption of *SFAS No. 106* ..	(332)	—	—
Net Income	$ 549	$ 1,177	$ 1,599

4. The present values of operating lease commitments at a discount rate of 10 percent at the end of each fiscal year are as follows (in millions): 1991, $452; 1992, $535; 1993, $618; 1994, $496.

5. The statutory federal income tax rate was 34 percent for the year ended October 31, 1992, 34.8 percent for the year ended October 31, 1993, and 35 percent for the year ended October 31, 1994.

| EXHIBIT 3 |

Hewlett-Packard
Statements of Cash Flows
(amounts in millions)
(Case 8.2)

	Fiscal Year Ended October 31		
	1992	1993	1994
Operations			
Net Income	$ 549	$ 1,177	$ 1,599
Depreciation and Amortization	673	846	1,006
Other Addbacks	332	9	57
Other Subtractions	(35)	(137)	(156)
(Increase) Decrease in Accounts Receivable	(480)	(709)	(848)
(Increase) Decrease in Inventories	(267)	(1,056)	(582)
(Increase) Decrease in Prepayments	(195)	(151)	(27)
Increase (Decrease) in Accounts Payable	226	283	243
Increase (Decrease) in Other Current Liabilities	485	880	932
Cash Flow from Operations	$ 1,288	$ 1,142	$ 2,224
Investing			
Sale of Marketable Securities	$ 887	$ 1,305	$ 2,439
Acquisition of Marketable Securities	(835)	(1,656)	(3,090)
Sale of Property, Plant, and Equipment	183	215	291
Acquisition of Property, Plant, and Equipment	(1,032)	(1,405)	(1,257)
Other Investing Transactions	(469)	(63)	7
Cash Flow from Investing	$(1,266)	$(1,604)	$(1,610)
Financing			
Increase (Decrease) in Short-Term Borrowing	$ 186	$ 807	$ 250
Increase in Long-Term Borrowing	309	387	64
Issue of Common Stock	293	308	300
Decrease in Long-Term Borrowing	(79)	(228)	(159)
Acquisition of Common Stock	(530)	(314)	(325)
Dividends	(183)	(228)	(280)
Other Financing Transactions	(2)	(22)	4
Cash Flow from Financing	$ (6)	$ 710	$ (146)
Change in Cash	$ 16	$ 248	$ 468
Cash—Beginning of Year	625	641	889
Cash—End of Year	$ 641	$ 889	$ 1,357

Sun Microsystems. Sun operates primarily in the workstation market. Its traditional presence has been in the low end of this market. It introduced a new high-end workstation mid-way through 1993. Exhibits 5 to 8 present financial statements and other information for Sun. The notes to the financial statements reveal the following:

EXHIBIT 4

Hewlett-Packard
Selected Data
(Case 8.2)

	Sales Mix			Asset Mix		
	1992	1993	1994	1992	1993	1994
United States	43.9%	46.0%	48.2%	55.4%	54.5%	52.1%
Europe	37.1	35.3	28.3	29.3	27.0	26.4
Other............	19.0	18.7	23.5	15.3	18.5	21.5
	100.0%	100.0%	100.0%	100.0%	100.0%	100.0%

	ROA			Profit Margin			Assets Turnover		
	1992	1993	1994	1992	1993	1994	1992	1993	1994
United States ...	15.8%	16.5%	14.9%	16.0%	15.9%	12.8%	0.99	1.04	1.16
Europe	8.0%	10.0%	13.2%	5.1%	6.2%	7.8%	1.57	1.61	1.69
Other..........	18.4%	20.6%	20.3%	11.9%	16.6%	16.2%	1.54	1.24	1.26

EXHIBIT 5

Sun Microsystems
Balance Sheets
(amounts in millions)
(Case 8.2)

	June 30			
	1991	1992	1993	1994
Assets				
Cash	$ 621	$ 847	$ 829	$ 434
Marketable Securities	213	373	310	449
Accounts Receivable	515	504	627	853
Inventories	224	179	256	295
Prepayments..................................	228	245	250	274
Total Current Assets	$1,801	$2,148	$2,272	$2,305
Property, Plant, and Equipment (cost)	$ 701	$ 789	$ 775	$ 877
Accumulated Depreciation	(350)	(428)	(426)	(517)
Property, Plant, and Equipment (net).............	$ 351	$ 361	$ 349	$ 360
Other Assets..................................	$ 174	$ 163	$ 147	$ 233
Total Assets	$2,326	$2,672	$2,768	$2,898

Exh. 5—Continued	June 30			
	1991	**1992**	**1993**	**1994**
Liabilities and Shareholders' Equity				
Accounts Payable............................	$ 212	$ 236	$ 271	$ 364
Notes Payable.............................	73	91	91	79
Current Portion of Long-Term Debt.............	7	42	38	38
Other Current Liabilities	421	470	547	667
Total Current Liabilities......................	$ 713	$ 839	$ 947	$1,148
Long-Term Debt	401	348	178	122
Total Liabilities	$1,114	$1,187	$1,125	$1,270
Common Stock	$ 905	$ 929	$1,054	$1,066
Retained Earnings...........................	486	591	706	879
Cumulative Translation Adjustment	2	8	2	12
Treasury Stock.............................	(181)	(43)	(119)	(329)
Total Shareholders' Equity....................	$1,212	$1,485	$1,643	$1,628
Total Liabilities and Shareholders' Equity	$2,326	$2,672	$2,768	$2,898

EXHIBIT 6

Sun Microsystems
Income Statements
(amounts in millions)
(Case 8.2)

	Fiscal Year Ended June 30		
	1992	**1993**	**1994**
Sales	$ 3,589	$ 4,309	$ 4,690
Other Revenues	39	33	28
Cost of Goods Sold...............	(1,963)	(2,518)	(2,753)
Selling and Administrative.........	(984)	(1,120)	(1,205)
Research and Development	(382)	(445)	(455)
Interest	(45)	(35)	(22)
Income Taxes....................	(81)	(67)	(87)
Net Income	$ 173	$ 157	$ 196

1. Sun made a $15 million pretax provision to settle a lawsuit with shareholders in its fiscal year ended June 30, 1993. This provision is included in selling and administrative expenses in Exhibit 6.
2. Sun uses a first-in, first-out cost-flow assumption for inventories, straight-line depreciation, and foreign currencies as the functional currency for foreign operations.
3. Sun entered into an agreement in June 1991 to sell on a revolving basis up to $100 million of its accounts receivable. The purchaser has limited recourse against Sun. As of June 1994, Sun has sold receivables up to the $100 million limit.

EXHIBIT 7

Sun Microsystems
Statements of Cash Flows
(amounts in millions)
(Case 8.2)

	Fiscal Year Ended June 30		
	1992	1993	1994
Operations			
Net Income	$ 173	$ 157	$ 196
Depreciation and Amortization	215	232	248
Other Addbacks.....................................	29	27	14
(Increase) Decrease in Accounts Receivable	10	(103)	(226)
(Increase) Decrease in Inventories	44	(76)	(39)
(Increase) Decrease in Prepayments	(17)	(4)	(35)
Increase (Decrease) in Accounts Payable	24	35	94
Increase (Decrease) in Other Current Liabilities	30	68	103
Cash Flow from Operations........................	$ 508	$ 336	$ 355
Investing			
Sale of Marketable Securities	$ 2,152	$ 2,120	$ 2,660
Acquisition of Marketable Securities	(2,312)	(2,057)	(2,799)
Acquisition of Property, Plant, and Equipment	(185)	(197)	(213)
Other Investing Transactions	(24)	(46)	(115)
Cash Flow from Investing	$ (369)	$ (180)	$ (467)
Financing			
Increase (Decrease) in Short-Term Borrowing	$ 18	—	$ (12)
Issue of Common Stock	70	$ 81	61
Decrease in Long-Term Borrowing......................	(1)	(40)	(38)
Acquisition of Common Stock.........................	—	(215)	(294)
Cash Flow from Financing	$ 87	$ (174)	$ (283)
Change in Cash.....................................	$ 226	$ (18)	$ (395)
Cash—Beginning of Year.............................	621	847	829
Cash—End of Year..................................	$ 847	$ 829	$ 434

4. The present values of operating lease commitments at a discount rate of 10 percent at the end of each fiscal year are as follows (in millions): 1991, $255; 1992, $260; 1993, $264; 1994, $265.

5. The statutory federal income tax rate was 34 percent for the years ended June 30, 1992 and 1993, and 35 percent for the year ended June 30, 1993.

REQUIRED

Assess the relative profitability and risk of HP and Sun, identifying the likely reasons for changes over time and differences between these firms.

EXHIBIT 8

Sun Microsystems—Selected Data
(Case 8.2)

	Sales Mix			Asset Mix		
	1992	1993	1994	1992	1993	1994
United States	49.7%	53.9%	52.9%	77.4%	69.7%	65.6%
Europe	28.1	25.5	25.0	12.5	19.8	22.3
Other.............	22.2	20.6	22.1	10.1	10.5	12.1
	100.0%	100.0%	100.0%	100.0%	100.0%	100.0%

	ROA			Profit Margin			Assets Turnover		
	1992	1993	1994	1992	1993	1994	1992	1993	1994
United States ...	7.6%	4.2%	1.6%	10.9%	4.9%	1.8%	0.70	0.85	0.88
Europe	3.4%	5.3%	16.3%	1.4%	3.7%	13.4%	2.44	1.42	1.21
Other.........	3.2%	10.6%	12.3%	1.3%	4.9%	6.2%	2.40	2.16	1.98

CASE 8.3

PHARMACEUTICAL INDUSTRY ANALYSIS: BRISTOL-MYERS SQUIBB, MERCK, MYLAN LABORATORIES

Health-care expenditures in the United States totaled $940 billion in 1993, making up approximately 14.9 percent of GNP. Annual health-care expenditures increased at an average annual rate of 11.2 percent during the last decade, two to three times larger than consumer prices in general. The increases in health-care expenditures resulted from the insulation of most health-care consumers from cost increases by Medicare and third-party reimbursement systems, the overuse of expensive medical procedures by physicians to avert costly medical malpractice lawsuits, the aging of the population, and the expanded use of technologically more sophisticated equipment. Control of the health-care business during this period rested primarily with health-care providers (hospitals and physicians). The consumers of health-care and those providing financing (governments, businesses, and private insurers) acted essentially as price takers in this environment.

In response to the rapid rate of price increases and the sense that the system was escalating out of control, the Clinton administration and Congress launched major efforts to restructure the health care industry in 1993. The aim of the proposed restructuring was to balance market power between those providing health care and those financing it, with the hope that competitive forces could serve as an effective control mechanism on the quality and price of health care. The proposals envisioned a managed care system in which providers were paid a fixed fee each year to provide medical services to a particular group of people. Even though Congress passed none of these proposals, the possibility of significant reform had a major impact on the health-care industry. Responding in part to the threat of government price controls, health-care providers limited increases in health-care expenditures to 5.4 percent in 1993, the lowest annual rate of increase in over a decade.

The pharmaceutical segment of the health-care business, which comprises approximately 8 percent of health-care expenditures, has experienced particularly heavy criticism because of the perceived high rates of return earned. Debates continue as to whether the risks incurred by pharmaceutical firms to develop and market new drugs justify the returns generated. Nonetheless, pharmaceutical firms have commenced actions of their own to maintain their competitive position in this rapidly changing environment. This case examines the strategies of three pharmaceutical firms, Bristol-Myers Squibb, Merck, and Mylan Laboratories, and the financial success of these strategies during the last several years.

OVERVIEW OF THE PHARMACEUTICAL INDUSTRY

Three main segments compose the pharmaceutical industry: (1) ethical drugs, (2) generic drugs, and (3) proprietary drugs.

Ethical Drugs.   The ethical drug segment includes products that customers can obtain only by a physician's prescription. Ethical drugs represent approximately 70 percent of pharmaceutical sales. The ethical drug segment tends to have the highest margins and rates of return of all segments of the industry because

1. High levels of front-end research and development cost (approximately $230 million and 12 years to develop and obtain approval for a new product) create barriers to entry. R&D expenditures have historically averaged 11 percent of sales in this segment of the industry, with the percentage closer to 16 percent in recent years. Domestic pharmaceutical firms spend approximately one-fifth of their R&D budgets abroad.
2. Patent protection creates near monopoly positions. The lengthy approval process by the Food and Drug Administration and increasing competition have effectively reduced patent life for new drugs from 17 to 7 years.
3. Relatively inelastic demand permits almost unbridled price increases, although competition from generic drugs, constraints imposed by the Medicare reimbursement system, and the threat of government price controls have dampened margins in recent years.

The high levels of fixed cost in the ethical drug segment (from both R&D and capital-intensive manufacturing facilities) create both large risks and opportunities for economies of scale. To capitalize on these economies, most pharmaceutical firms have extensive foreign operations (composing 40 percent to 50 percent of sales). U.S. pharmaceutical companies are responsible for more than one-half of total worldwide pharmaceutical shipments. Of the world's top 20 drug producers, 11 are U.S. firms. Changes in exchange rates therefore significantly impact sales and margins. The degree of operating leverage in the industry creates healthy cash flow from operations, resulting in relatively little need for financial leverage.

Positive factors currently affecting the ethical drug segment include (1) the aging of the population (persons over 65 years of age average 11 prescriptions per year versus 7 for the general population) and (2) a streamlining of the drug approval process for new breakthrough drugs and drugs that treat life-threatening ailments. Negative factors include (1) threats of government price controls, (2) phased elimination of favorable U.S. tax credits that pharmaceutical firms currently earn from conducting manufacturing operations in Puerto Rico, (3) increased worldwide competition from pharmaceutical firms in Germany, Switzerland, and Japan, (4) increased competition from generic drug companies on the product side and from wholesale and mail order firms on the distribution side, and (5) uncertainty regarding the nature of health-care reforms that might ultimately pass Congress.

Ethical drug firms have responded to these factors in various ways. Some firms have exerted leadership in curtailing price increases and offering price discounting arrangements to major purchasers. Mergers and acquisitions occur frequently as firms attempt to position themselves for the uncertain environment ahead. Firms form joint ventures and strategic alliances to develop new drugs, thereby sharing risk and technical expertise. Firms also use these vehicles to broaden product lines and obtain distribution economies.

Generic Drugs. The generic drug segment includes products that have chemical compositions similar to established ethical drugs but sell at prices that are approximately 50 percent less. The ability to charge the lower price reflects the absence of the large front-end R&D and governmental approval costs that ethical drug companies must cover. Nine of 10 of the most widely used prescription drugs are available generically. Generic drugs account of approximately 40 percent of all prescriptions filled. Drug product selection laws enacted in many states that permit or compel pharmacists to substitute generic drugs for ethical drugs have enhanced growth in the generic business. Also enhancing growth in this segment are efforts by hospitals operating under the fixed fee reimbursement system of Medicare to control their expenditures on drugs. Similar that for ethical drugs, the manufacturing process for generic drugs is capital intensive. With lower barriers to entry than for ethical drugs, many firms are now entering this market. Most established ethical drug companies maintain a generic drug segment and account for approximately 55 percent of generic drug industry sales. Ethical drugs with a combined sales value of $10 billion are expected to come off of patents in the next five years, providing the stimulus for continued growth in the generic segment.

Proprietary Drugs. The proprietary drug segment includes health-care products that consumers can purchase without a prescription. Proprietary drugs represent approximately 25 percent of pharmaceutical sales, growing at a rate almost as fast as ethical drugs in recent years. The aging of the population, introduction of new proprietary drugs, switching of ethical drugs to proprietary status (ethical drugs cleared for nonprescription status receive two years of marketing exclusivity), and increased self-treatment to avoid the high cost of medical advice have aided this segment. The Commerce Department suggests that every dollar spent on nonprescription drugs saves an estimated $2 in health-care cost. Unlike ethical drugs prescribed by physicians, proprietary drug companies market their products directly to consumers. Advertising therefore plays a critical role. Branded proprietary drugs can maintain their market positions for many more years than patent protection provides for ethical drugs. Advertising expenditures represent approximately 12 percent of sales for proprietary drugs.

Some pharmaceutical firms participate in the medical supplies and equipment segment of the health-care business or offer personal care products.

Medical Supplies and Equipment. The products of this segment vary from gauze pads costing a few cents to technologically sophisticated imaging equipment costing millions of dollars. Demands for price concessions by health-care providers for frequently purchased supplies have dampened margins for commodity products. Concerns about future health cost reimbursement policies have led health-care providers to delay investments in costly equipment, dampening margins in this end of the market.

Personal Care Products. Firms in the proprietary segment of the pharmaceutical market often leverage their consumer marketing expertise by offering personal care products such as hair colorings, cosmetics, skin preparations, and similar products. Brand name recognition for these products can provide ongoing sources of profitability and cash flows to finance R&D efforts in ethical drugs.

OVERVIEW OF COMPANIES STUDIED

Bristol-Myers Squibb. Incorporated in 1933, Bristol's traditional niche was proprietary drugs. Its corporate strategy now has it moving more heavily into ethical drugs. It merged with Squibb Corporation in 1989 in an effort to boost its involvement in ethical drugs and medical supplies and equipment. Bristol is the most diversified of the three companies studied; 10 percent of its sales come from personal care products. Exhibits 1 to 6

EXHIBIT 1

Balance Sheets for Bristol-Myers and Squibb
(amounts in millions)
(Case 8.3)

	December 31			
	1990	1991	1992	1993
Assets				
Cash	$ 596	$ 1,435	$ 2,137	$ 2,421
Marketable Securities	1,362	148	248	308
Accounts Receivable	1,776	1,971	1,984	1,859
Inventories	1,366	1,451	1,490	1,322
Prepayments	570	562	762	660
Total Current Assets	$ 5,670	$ 5,567	$ 6,621	$ 6,570
Property, Plant, and Equipment (cost)	$ 4,271	$ 4,718	$ 5,032	$ 5,236
Accumulated Depreciation	(1,640)	(1,782)	(1,891)	(1,862)
Property, Plant, and Equipment (net)	$ 2,631	$ 2,936	$ 3,141	$ 3,374
Other Assets	$ 914	$ 913	$ 1,042	$ 2,157
Total Assets	$ 9,215	$ 9,416	$10,804	$12,101
Liabilities and Shareholders' Equity				
Accounts Payable	$ 530	$ 537	$ 562	$ 649
Notes Payable	397	553	375	177
Other Current Liabilities	1,894	1,662	2,363	2,239
Total Current Liabilities	$ 2,821	$ 2,752	$ 3,300	$ 3,065
Long-Term Debt	231	135	176	588
Deferred Income Taxes	150	112	0	0
Other Noncurrent Liabilities	595	622	1,308	2,508
Total Liabilities	$ 3,797	$ 3,621	$ 4,784	$ 6,161
Common Stock	$ 53	$ 53	$ 53	$ 53
Additional Paid-in Capital	504	485	435	353
Retained Earnings	5,428	6,235	6,769	7,243
Cumulative Translation Adjustment	(61)	(90)	(208)	(332)
Treasury Stock	(506)	(888)	(1,029)	(1,377)
Total Shareholders' Equity	$ 5,418	$ 5,795	$ 6,020	$ 5,940
Total Liabilities and Shareholders' Equity	$ 9,215	$ 9,416	$10,804	$12,101

EXHIBIT 2

Bristol-Myers Squibb—Income Statements
(amounts in millions)
(Case 8.3)

	Year Ended December 31		
	1991	1992	1993
Sales	$10,571	$11,156	$11,413
Other Revenues	177	76	225
Cost of Goods Sold	(2,717)	(2,857)	(3,029)
Selling and Administrative	(4,209)	(4,366)	(4,353)
Research and Development	(983)	(1,083)	(1,128)
Restructuring and Special Charge	—	(890)	(500)
Interest	(55)	(49)	(57)
Income Taxes	(793)	(449)	(612)
Income from Continuing Operations	$ 1,991	$ 1,538	$ 1,959
Income from Discontinued Operations	65	670	—
Cumulative Effect of Change in Accounting Principles	—	(246)	—
Net Income	$ 2,056	$ 1,962	$ 1,959

EXHIBIT 3

Bristol-Myers Squibb—Statements of Cash Flows
(amounts in millions)
(Case 8.3)

	Year Ended December 31		
	1991	1992	1993
Operations			
Income from Continuing Operations	$ 1,991	$ 1,538	$ 1,959
Depreciation and Amortization	246	295	308
Restructuring and Special Charges	—	890	500
Other Addbacks	103	50	49
(Increase) Decrease In Accounts Receivable	(269)	(125)	41
(Increase) Decrease in Inventories	(114)	(163)	129
(Increase) Decrease in Prepayments	4	(121)	92
Increase (Decrease) in Accounts Payable	40	75	134
Increase (Decrease) in Other Current Liabilities	(166)	(411)	(632)
Cash Flow from Operations	$ 1,835	$ 2,028	$ 2,580
Investing			
Sale of Marketable Securities	$ 4,090	$ 169	$ 993
Purchase of Marketable Securities	(2,865)	(269)	(1,049)
Purchase of Property, Plant, and Equipment	(628)	(647)	(570)
Sale of Businesses	—	1,150	98
Other Investing Transactions	(26)	27	(69)
Cash Flow from Investing	$ 571	$ 430	$ (597)

Exh. 3—Continued	Year Ended December 31		
	1991	1992	1993
Financing			
Increase (Decrease) in Short-Term Borrowing	$ 169	$ (169)	$ (228)
Increase in Long-Term Borrowing	—	40	394
Issue of Common Stock	46	37	38
Decrease in Long-Term Borrowing.	(96)	—	—
Acquisition of Treasury Stock	(447)	(228)	(419)
Dividends	(1,249)	(1,428)	(1,485)
Other Financing Transactions	10	(8)	1
Cash Flow from Financing	$(1,567)	$(1,756)	$(1,699)
Change in Cash.	$ 839	$ 702	$ 284
Cash—Beginning of Year.	596	1,435	2,137
Cash—End of Year	$ 1,435	$ 2,137	$ 2,421

present financial statements and other information for Bristol. The notes to the financial statements reveal the following:

1. Bristol made a $890 million ($570 million after taxes) provision in 1992 to restructure operations of its four core businesses in recognition of changing worldwide health-care trends.
2. Bristol sold its household products business in 1992 at an after-tax gain of $605 million. This business generated earnings of $65 million in both 1991 and 1992.
3. Bristol adopted the provisions of *Statement of Financial Accounting Standards No. 106* on January 1, 1992, and included a $246 million charge ($390 million pretax) in earnings.
4. Bristol made a special charge of $500 million ($310 million after taxes) in connection with pending and future breast implant product liability. It includes $1,000 million in an Insurance Recoverable account on its balance sheet (included in Other Assets in Exhibit 1) and $1,310 million in Other Noncurrent Liabilities.
5. The present values of operating lease commitments at a discount rate of 10 percent are (in millions): 1990, $428; 1991, $466; 1992, $407; $1993, $385.
6. The underfunded pension and postretirement benefit obligations and the amounts reported by Bristol are as follows (in millions):

	1990	1991	1992	1993
Pensions				
Underfunded Projected Benefit Obligation.	$72	$ 36	$211	$637
Prepaid Pension Asset on Balance Sheet	35	68	78	—
Accrued Pension Liability on Balance Sheet	—	—	—	305
Postretirement Benefits				
Underfunded Benefit Obligation	*	$390	$402	$493
Accrued Postretirement Benefits Obligation on Balance Sheet	*	0	402	452

*Amounts not disclosed for 1990.

EXHIBIT 4

Bristol-Myers Squibb
Financial Data
(Case 8.3)

	1991	1992	1993
R&D/Sales	9.3%	9.7%	9.9%
Advertising/Sales	11.9%	11.6%	11.0%
Sales Mix			
Pharmaceutical Products	55.9%	56.6%	57.2%
Medical Devices	14.7	14.9	14.8
Nonprescription Health Products	18.0	17.6	17.2
Personal Products	11.4	10.9	10.8
	100.0%	100.0%	100.0%
United States	60.4%	58.8%	59.2%
Europe, Mid-East, & Africa...........	24.4	25.3	23.7
Other Western Hemisphere	7.3	7.5	7.6
Pacific..............................	7.9	8.4	9.5
	100.0%	100.0%	100.0%
Pretax Operating Income Mix			
Pharmaceutical Products	65.0%	73.1%	78.0%
Medical Devices	12.5	14.1	(0.9)
Nonprescription Health Products	15.3	12.4	16.9
Personal Products	7.2	0.4	6.0
	100.0%	100.0%	100.0%
United States	68.9%	65.9%	64.4%
Europe, Mid-East, & Africa...........	21.9	24.0	21.4
Other Western Hemisphere	5.9	6.2	7.1
Pacific..............................	3.3	3.9	7.1
	100.0%	100.0%	100.0%
Asset Mix			
Pharmaceutical Products	61.9%	65.4%	57.3%
Medical Devices	15.1	15.0	25.1
Nonprescription Health Products	12.1	11.9	10.8
Personal Products	10.9	7.7	6.8
	100.0%	100.0%	100.0%
United States	59.9%	60.8%	65.2%
Europe, Mid-East, & Africa...........	25.1	24.0	19.9
Other Western Hemisphere	5.7	5.7	5.2
Pacific..............................	9.3	9.5	9.7
	100.0%	100.0%	100.0%

7. Bristol uses a weighted average cost-flow assumption for inventories, the straight-line depreciation method, and foreign currencies as the functional currency for foreign operations.

8. The income tax note reveals the following (see bottom of page 490):

EXHIBIT 5

Bristol-Myers Squibb—Segment Profitability Analysis
(Case 8.3)

ROA Analysis	Pharmaceutical Products	Medical Devices	Nonprescription	Personal Products
1991 *(as reported)*				
Profit Margin.....	31.2%	16.3%	22.9%	16.9%
Assets Turnover...	1.4	1.5	2.3	1.6
Return on Assets..	43.7%	24.6%	52.6%	27.2%
1992 *(as reported)*				
Profit Margin.....	25.1%	18.3%	13.7%	.8%
Assets Turnover...	1.4	1.6	2.3	2.2
Return on Assets..	34.3%	28.7%	31.9%	1.8%
1992 *(as restated[a])*				
Profit Margin.....	31.0%	27.6%	21.3%	13.1%
Assets Turnover...	1.4	1.6	2.3	2.2
Return on Assets..	42.3%	43.3%	49.8%	29.3%
1993 *(as reported)*				
Profit Margin.....	32.7%	(1.4%)	23.6%	13.2%
Assets Turnover...	1.4	0.8	2.3	2.2
Return on Assets..	46.1%	(1.2%)	53.1%	29.7%
1993 *(as restated[a])*				
Profit Margin.....	32.7%	28.1%	23.6%	13.2%
Assets Turnover...	1.4	1.6	2.3	2.2
Return on Assets..	46.1%	46.2%	53.1%	29.7%

	U.S.	Europe, Etc.	W. Hemisphere	Pacific
1991 *(as reported)*				
Profit Margin.....	28.1%	22.1%	19.8%	10.3%
Assets Turnover...	1.6	1.6	2.0	1.4
Return on Assets..	45.5%	34.5%	40.3%	14.1%
1992 *(as reported)*				
Profit Margin.....	19.9%	16.9%	14.7%	8.2%
Asset Turnover....	1.6	1.7	2.2	1.5
Return on Assets..	32.0%	29.5%	32.4%	12.5%
1992 *(as restated[a])*				
Profit Margin.....	28.0%	21.1%	20.1%	12.6%
Assets Turnover...	1.6	1.7	2.2	1.5
Return on Assets..	45.0%	36.8%	44.4%	18.4%
1993 *(as reported)*				
Profit Margin.....	23.2%	19.3%	20.0%	15.8%
Assets Turnover...	1.4	1.8	2.2	1.5
Return on Assets..	31.8%	34.6%	44.5%	23.4%
1993 *(as restated[a])*				
Profit Margin.....	35.1%	19.3%	20.0%	15.8%
Assets Turnover...	1.4	1.8	2.2	1.5
Return on Assets..	48.0%	34.6%	44.5%	23.4%

[a]Restated amounts for 1992 exclude the restructuring provision, discontinued operations, and change in accounting principles. Restated amounts for 1993 exclude the special charge related to the breast implant liability.

EXHIBIT 6

Analysis of Changes in Sales for Bristol-Myers Squibb
(Case 8.3)

| | 1990–1991 | | | | 1991–1992 | | | | 1992–1993 | | | |
	Volume	Price	Exchange Rates	Total	Volume	Price	Exchange Rates	Total	Volume	Price	Exchange Rates	Total
Pharmaceutical . . .	9%	4%	(1%)	12%	2%	4%	1%	7%	5%	1%	(3%)	3%
Medical Devices . .	3%	6%	—	9%	1%	5%	1%	7%	1%	3%	(2%)	2%
Nonprescription Health.	3%	5%	(1%)	7%	(2%)	5%	—	3%	(5%)	5%	—	—
Personal and Household	(6%)	4%	—	(2%)	(2%)	3%	—	1%	1%	2%	(2%)	1%
Total	5%	4%	(1%)	8%	1%	4%	1%	6%	3%	2%	(3%)	2%

EXHIBIT 7

Merck—Balance Sheets
(amounts in millions)
(Case 8.3)

	December 31			
	1990	1991	1992	1993
Assets				
Cash	$ 806	$ 798	$ 575	$ 829
Marketable Securities	391	614	518	713
Accounts Receivable	1,346	1,546	1,737	2,094
Inventories	893	991	1,182	1,642
Prepayments	331	362	388	456
Total Current Assets	$ 3,767	$ 4,311	$ 4,400	$ 5,734
Investments in Securities	$ 1,012	$ 1,044	$ 1,416	$ 1,780
Property, Plant, and Equipment (cost)	$ 4,631	$ 5,607	$ 6,531	$ 7,173
Accumulated Depreciation	(1,909)	(2,102)	(2,260)	(2,278)
Property, Plant, and Equipment (net)	$ 2,722	$ 3,505	$ 4,271	$ 4,895
Other Assets	$ 529	$ 639	$ 999	$ 7,519
Total Assets	$ 8,030	$ 9,499	$11,086	$19,928
Liabilities and Shareholders' Equity				
Accounts Payable and Accrued Liabilities	$ 1,138	$ 1,400	$ 1,462	$ 2,378
Notes Payable	793	338	825	1,736
Other Current Liabilities	896	1,076	1,330	1,782
Total Current Liabilities	$ 2,827	$ 2,814	$ 3,617	$ 5,896
Long-Term Debt	124	494	496	1,121
Deferred Income Taxes	256	291	89	363
Other Noncurrent Liabilities	439	389	1,254	1,382
Total Liabilities	$ 3,646	$ 3,988	$ 5,456	$ 8,762
Minority Interest in Subsidiaries	$ 549	$ 595	$ 627	$ 1,144
Common Stock	$ 167	$ 185	$ 205	$ 4,577
Retained Earnings	6,387	7,589	8,466	9,393
Treasury Stock	(2,719)	(2,858)	(3,668)	(3,948)
Total Shareholders' Equity	$ 3,835	$ 4,916	$ 5,003	$10,022
Total Liabilities and Shareholders' Equity	$ 8,030	$ 9,499	$11,086	$19,928

	1991	1992	1993
Statutory Tax Rate	34.0%	34.0%	35.0%
Tax Exemption from Operations in Puerto Rico	(7.9)	(8.7)	(10.1)
State and Local Taxes	1.6	0.2	1.1
Non-U.S. Operations	1.3	(1.8)	(0.2)
Other	(0.5)	(1.1)	(2.0)
Effective Tax Rate	28.5%	22.6%	23.8%

Merck.   Incorporated in 1934, Merck focuses almost entirely on ethical drugs. It derives almost one-half of its sales from outside the United States. Merck has actively used joint ventures and strategic alliances (du Pont and Johnson & Johnson) to develop new drugs and enter new product and/or geographical territories. It acquired Medco Containment Services in 1993, a leading firm in managed drug prescription programs. Exhibits 7 to 10 present financial statements and other data for Merck. The notes to the financial statements reveal the following:

1. Merck adopted the provisions of three financial reporting standards as of January 1, 1992, as follows (in millions):

	Pretax Effect	Tax Effect	After-Tax Effect
Standard			
SFAS No. 106 (Health-Care Benefits).	$625	$255	$370
SFAS No. 109 (Income Taxes)	62	—	62
SFAS No. 112 (Other Post-Employment Benefits) .	50	20	30

2. Merck made a $775 million pretax provision ($504 million after taxes) to streamline and restructure operations in 1993.
3. Merck's other income (net) for 1993 includes a gain on the sale of Calgon Water Management of $149 million, a provision for environmental cost of $79 million, and a contribution to the Merck Foundation of $60 million.

EXHIBIT 8

Merck—Income Statements
(amounts in millions)
(Case 8.3)

	Year Ended December 31		
	1991	1992	1993
Sales	$ 8,603	$ 9,662	$10,498
Other Revenues	151	177	99
Cost of Goods Sold.	(1,935)	(2,096)	(2,497)
Selling and Administrative.	(2,570)	(2,963)	(2,914)
Research and Development	(988)	(1,112)	(1,173)
Restructuring Charge.	—	—	(775)
Interest	(69)	(73)	(85)
Income Taxes	(1,045)	(1,117)	(937)
Minority Interest in Earnings	(25)	(32)	(50)
Income from Continuing Operations	$ 2,122	$ 2,446	$ 2,166
Cumulative Effect of Changes in Accounting Principles	—	(462)	—
Net Income	$ 2,122	$ 1,984	$ 2,166

EXHIBIT 9

Merck
Statements of Cash Flows
(amounts in millions)
(Case 8.3)

	Year Ended December 31		
	1991	**1992**	**1993**
Operations			
Net Income	$ 2,122	$ 1,984	$ 2,166
Depreciation and Amortization	264	321	386
Effect of Changes in Accounting Principles	—	462	—
Restructuring Charge	—	—	775
Other Subtractions	(12)	(92)	(230)
(Increase) Decrease in Accounts Receivable	(195)	(298)	(263)
(Increase) Decrease in Inventories	(99)	(177)	(47)
Increase (Decrease) in Accounts Payable and Accrued Liabilities	226	101	(123)
Increase (Decrease) in Other Current Liabilities	128	203	384
Cash Flow from Operations	$ 2,434	$ 2,504	$ 3,048
Investing			
Sale of Marketable Securities	$ 8,519	$ 4,983	$ 9,863
Acquisition of Marketable Securities	(8,801)	(5,256)	(9,521)
Acquisition of Property, Plant, and Equipment	(1,041)	(1,067)	(1,013)
Other Investing Transactions	23	(12)	(1,917)
Cash Flow from Investing	$(1,300)	$(1,352)	$(2,588)
Financing			
Increase (Decrease) in Short-Term Borrowing	$ (591)	$ 480	$ 911
Increase in Long-Term Borrowing	560	141	354
Issue of Common Stock	48	52	83
Decrease in Long-Term Borrowing	(94)	(121)	(39)
Acquisition of Common Stock	(184)	(863)	(371)
Dividends	(893)	(1,064)	(1,174)
Other Financing Transactions	11	—	30
Cash Flow from Financing	$(1,143)	$(1,375)	$ (206)
Change in Cash	$ (9)	$ (223)	$ 254
Cash—Beginning of Year	806	798	575
Cash—End of Year	$ 797	$ 575	$ 829

4. Merck acquired Medco on November 18, 1983. Merck gave $2,400 million in cash, $4,200 million in common stock and options, and assumed $1,500 million of Medco's liabilities in acquiring $8,100 million in assets. Merck used the purchase method to account for the acquisition.

EXHIBIT 10

Merck
Financial Data
(Case 8.3)

	1991	1992	1993
R&D/Sales	11.5%	11.5%	11.2%
Advertising/Sales	2.9%	2.9%	2.2%

Sales Mix

	1991	1992	1993
Human/Animal Care	93.2%	93.8%	95.1%
Spec. Chem./Environmental	6.8	6.2	4.9
	100.0%	100.0%	100.0%
U.S.	53.7%	53.6%	56.3%
OECD	44.3	44.1	40.0
Other	2.0	2.3	3.7
	100.0%	100.0%	100.0%

Pretax Operating Income Mix

	1991	1992	1993
Human/Animal Care	97.4%	97.7%	94.0%
Spec. Chem./Environmental	2.6	2.3	6.0
	100.0%	100.0%	100.0%
U.S.	73.1%	73.3%	77.1%
OECD	27.0	26.5	21.7
Other	(0.1)	0.2	1.2
	100.0%	100.0%	100.0%

Identifiable Assets Mix

	1991	1992	1993
Human/Animal Care	91.4%	92.4%	97.1%
Spec. Chem./Environmental	8.6	7.6	2.9
	100.0%	100.0%	100.0%
U.S.	59.0%	59.9%	78.4%
OECD	39.1	37.6	19.7
Other	1.9	2.5	1.9
	100.0%	100.0%	100.0%

Segment Profitability

	1991		1992		1993		1993[a]	
	U.S.	OECD	U.S.	OECD	U.S.	OECD	U.S.	OECD
Profit Margin	48.8%	21.8%	49.3%	21.6%	40.2%	15.9%	49.3%	21.7%
Asset Turnover	1.1	1.4	1.0	1.4	0.5	1.3	1.2	1.3
Return on Assets	53.8%	30.0%	51.3%	29.5%	18.5%	20.7%	60.9%	28.1%

[a]Restated to eliminate the restructuring charge and recompute assets related to the Medco acquisition.

5. The underfunded pension and postretirements benefits obligations and the amounts reported by Merck are as follows (in millions):

	1990	1991	1992	1993
Pensions				
Underfunded Projected Benefit Obligation.......	$109	$ 53	$161	$505
Prepaid Pension Asset on Balance Sheet			2	27
Accrued Pension Liability on Balance Sheet	42	19		238
Postretirement Benefits				
Underfunded Benefit Obligation	*	$625	$728	$670
Accrued Postretirement Benefits Obligation on Balance Sheet	*	0	762	596

*Amounts not disclosed for 1990.

6. Merck uses a combination of first-in, first-out and last-in, first-out cost-flow assumptions for inventories. The excess of current cost over LIFO inventories was (in millions): 1990, $98; 1991, $110; 1992, $21; 1993, $19. Merck uses the straight-line depreciation method and the U.S. dollar as its functional currency for foreign operations.

7. The income tax note reveals the following:

	1991	1992	1993
Federal Statutory Tax Rate	34.0%	34.0%	35.0%
Tax Exemption from Puerto Rico Operations	(5.1)	(5.1)	(5.1)
Foreign Operations	2.6	0.9	(1.5)
State Taxes	2.2	1.7	2.8
Other.......................................	(0.7)	(0.2)	(1.0)
Effective Tax Rate	33.0%	31.3%	30.2%

8. The contributing factors to the changes in sales each year appear below.

	1990–1991	1991–1992	1992–1993
Volume	10%	10%	9%
Price	2	1	—
Exchange Rate	—	1	(2)
Total	12%	12%	7%

Mylan. Incorporated in 1970, Mylan is a leading manufacturer of generic drugs. Mylan markets its 50-plus generic drugs through other drug manufacturers, distributors, and directly to hospitals and pharmacies. It markets its proprietary drug, Maxzide, through American Cyanamid. Its ethical drug, Eldepryl, is the principal drug of its joint venture, Somerset Pharmaceuticals. Mylan merged with Dow B. Hickam Company in 1991 and thereby ac-

EXHIBIT 11

Mylan Laboratories—Balance Sheets
(amounts in thousands)
(Case 8.3)

	March 31			
	1991	1992	1993	1994
Assets				
Cash	$ 37,475	$ 60,324	$ 98,246	$ 75,526
Marketable Securities	—	—	—	12,925
Accounts Receivable	16,067	22,383	32,396	55,430
Inventories	29,098	35,127	45,949	57,996
Prepayments................................	740	2,180	3,891	7,696
Total Current Assets......................	$ 83,380	$120,014	$180,482	$209,573
Investments in and Advances to Somerset	$ 18,045	$ 13,674	$ 14,844	$ 17,763
Property, Plant, and Equipment (cost)	$ 49,305	$ 65,034	$ 94,950	$115,114
Accumulated Depreciation	(15,847)	(22,798)	(26,431)	(32,600)
Property, Plant, and Equipment (net)..........	$ 33,458	$ 42,236	$ 68,519	$ 82,514
Other Assets................................	$ 34,670	$ 50,796	$ 87,260	$ 93,475
Total Assets	$169,553	$226,720	$351,105	$403,325
Liabilities and Shareholders' Equity				
Accounts Payable...........................	$ 2,252	$ 3,469	$ 6,492	$ 6,699
Other Current Liabilities	9,682	14,440	19,990	11,227
Total Current Liabilities...................	$ 11,934	$ 17,909	$ 26,482	$ 17,926
Long-Term Debt	2,057	3,600	5,125	4,609
Deferred Income Taxes......................	2,288	1,759	2,223	821
Acquisition Obligation.......................	—	—	21,303	—
Total Liabilities	$ 16,279	$ 23,268	$ 55,133	$ 23,356
Common Stock	$ 18,257	$ 19,317	$ 39,309	$ 39,849
Additional Paid-in Capital	1,115	7,699	29,866	54,272
Retained Earnings..........................	134,274	176,789	227,139	288,357
Treasury Stock.............................	(372)	(353)	(342)	(2,509)
Total Shareholders' Equity	$153,274	$203,452	$295,972	$379,969
Total Liabilities and Shareholders' Equity	$169,553	$226,720	$351,105	$403,325

quired Hickam's wound care business and its national sales force. In 1993, Mylan acquired Bertek, Inc., a manufacturer of transdermal drug delivery systems. Exhibits 11 to 13 present financial statement data for Mylan. The notes to the financial statements reveal the following information (amounts in thousands).

1. The acquisition of Bertek occurred on February 25, 1993. Mylan issued common stock with a market value of $17,701 and incurred an acquisition obligation of $21,411 as consideration for the net assets of Bertek (assets of $49,202 and liabilities of $10,090). As of

March 31, 1993, $21,303 of the acquisition obligation remains unpaid. Mylan satisfied this obligation during the fiscal year ended March 31, 1994, by paying cash of $977 and issuing shares of its common stock valued at $20,326. Mylan accounted for this acquisition using the purchase method.

2. Selling and administrative expenses for the 1994 fiscal year include a $2,861 pretax payment ($1,900 after taxes) in connection with the death of its former chairman.

3. Mylan adopted the provisions of *Statement No. 109* during the 1994 fiscal year. The cumulative effect of adopting this reporting standard increased earnings by $1,124 for the year. Mylan included this effect in income tax expense.

4. Mylan uses a first-in, first-out cost-flow assumption for inventories and straight-line depreciation. Mylan does not engage in foreign operations.

5. The income tax note reveals the following:

	Fiscal Year Ended March 31		
	1992	1993	1994
Statutory Federal Tax Rate	34.0%	34.0%	35.0%
State Taxes	0.6	1.5	1.7
Dividend Exclusion	(10.1)	(5.9)	(7.7)
Tax Credits	(4.7)	(2.2)	(7.6)
SFAS No. 109	—	—	(1.3)
Changes in Tax Code	—	—	(3.7)
Other	0.2	—	(0.3)
Effective Tax Rate	20.0%	27.4%	16.1%

REQUIRED

Assess the relative profitability and risk of these three companies, evaluating the success of their corporate strategies and their current position. Your assessment should begin by addressing data issues that might impact your time-series or cross-sectional comparisons of these companies.

EXHIBIT 12

Mylan Laboratories
Income Statements
(amounts in thousands)
(Case 8.3)

	Fiscal Year Ended March 31		
	1992	1993	1994
Sales	$131,936	$211,964	$ 251,773
Equity in Earnings of Somerset	18,664	21,136	23,596
Other Revenues	5,490	3,879	8,148
Cost of Goods Sold	(69,877)	(89,400)	(125,631)
Selling and Administrative	(27,832)	(36,650)	(49,143)
Research and Development	(7,885)	(13,524)	(21,648)
Interest	(354)	(64)	(30)
Income Taxes	(10,028)	(26,720)	(13,998)
Net Income	$ 40,114	$ 70,621	$ 73,067

EXHIBIT 13

Mylan Laboratories—Statements of Cash Flows
(amounts in thousands)
(Case 8.3)

	Fiscal Year Ended March 31		
	1992	1993	1994
Operations			
Net Income	$ 40,114	$ 70,621	$ 73,067
Depreciation and Amortization	5,060	5,089	11,154
Equity of Earnings in Somerset......................	(18,664)	(21,136)	(23,596)
Dividends Received from Somerset....................	22,461	19,966	20,676
Other Addbacks......................................	902	2,870	3,536
(Increase) Decrease in Accounts Receivable	(5,622)	(9,073)	(23,485)
(Increase) Decrease in Inventories	(3,571)	(9,825)	(12,002)
(Increase) Decrease in Prepayments	(797)	(1,711)	(3,805)
Increase (Decrease) in Accounts Payable	876	1,911	207
Increase (Decrease) in Other Current Liabilities	4,595	9,625	(10,119)
Cash Flow from Operations.........................	$ 45,354	$ 68,337	$ 35,633
Investing			
Acquisition of Marketable Securities	—	—	$(12,925)
Acquisition of Property, Plant, and Equipment..........	$(10,041)	$(12,294)	(20,164)
Other Investing Transactions.........................	(12,825)	(10,833)	(10,347)
Cash Flow from Investing	$(22,866)	$(23,127)	$(43,436)
Financing			
Increase in Long-Term Borrowing	$ 6,000	—	—
Issue of Common Stock	2,650	9,561	$ 1,406
Decrease in Long-Term Borrowing....................	(7,081)	(8,373)	(4,320)
Dividends	(7,355)	(8,476)	(11,026)
Other Financing Transactions	—	—	(977)
Cash Flow from Financing	$ (5,786)	$ (7,288)	$(14,917)
Change in Cash.....................................	$ 16,702	$ 37,922	$(22,720)
Cash—Beginning of Year.............................	43,622	60,324	98,246
Cash—End of Year..................................	$ 60,324	$ 98,246	$ 75,526

CASE 8.4

TEMPORARY PERSONNEL SUPPLY SERVICES: KELLY SERVICES AND ADIA SERVICES*

The temporary personnel supply business is a classic service business. It places employees at clients' businesses on a temporary basis. The personnel supply firm charges the client a fee

*The author gratefully acknowledges the assistance of Tristam Collins and Mark Mandel in the preparation of this case.

intended to cover the payroll cost of the temporary employee plus administrative costs of operating the personnel supply offices. The latter includes the payroll cost of permanent employees running the offices, data processing costs relating primarily to payroll of all employees, and rent, taxes, and insurance on office space. Amounts receivable from clients appear in accounts receivable and amounts payable to temporary and permanent employees appear in accounts payable and accrued expenses. This case examines the appropriateness of using the rate of return on assets (ROA) as a measure of operating profitability. The principal issues are (1) the omission of the value of employees and of client contacts from the balance sheet (unless capitalized as part of goodwill in a corporate acquisition), (2) the omission of the value of office space rented under operating leases, (3) the reporting of accounts receivable from clients gross of amounts payable to employees, and (4) the practice of using company-owned offices, franchised offices, or a combination of the two.

ECONOMIC CHARACTERISTICS

The temporary personnel supply business offers clients flexibility in adjusting their number of workers to meet changing capacity needs. Clients can observe the quality of work of temporary employees before hiring them permanently. Temporary workers are typically less costly than permanent workers because they have fewer fringe benefits. Personnel supply firms provide payroll recordkeeping and data processing services.

One negative factor in this industry is that temporary employees usually require more training, are less efficient initially, and likely carry less loyalty to client firms than permanent employees in these firms. Some client firms find that paying permanent workers overtime is more cost effective than hiring temporary employees. A second factor is the low barriers to entry in the personnel supply business. This business does not require capital for physical facilities (most office space is rented), there are no specialized assets (most temporary employees do not possess unique skills, needed data processing technology is readily available), and regulation is relatively low. Thus, competition is strong and margins tend to be thin.

CURRENT CONDITIONS

The downsizing that occurred in the United States in the early 1990s in response to both competition from abroad and recessionary economic conditions in the United States helped the personnel supply market to grow by 20 percent annually. Firms laying off permanent employees hired temporary employees to meet capacity needs. The increasing cost of fringe benefits for pensions, health, and life insurance led employers to satisfy part of their employment needs with temporary workers. Previously employed workers became a valuable source of talent for the personnel supply firms. Such individuals often accepted lower compensation levels just to have a job.

The increasing demand for temporary employees caused revenues to increase, but the increasing supply of available workers led new entrants into the industry, increasing competition, and decreasing profit margins.

STRATEGIC POSITIONING

Personnel supply firms are currently attempting to differentiate themselves along several dimensions:

1. *Geographical Reach:* Firms provide temporary employees anywhere in the United States and in some foreign countries, attempting to meet the needs of large, geographically diversified clients.
2. *Product Diversification:* Firms offer outplacement counseling services to clients laying off workers, permanent job recruiting services, and executive searches, in addition to placing temporary workers with clients.
3. *Specialized Services:* Firms might specialize in providing temporary workers with particular skills, such as accounting, data processing, nursing, or physical therapy.
4. *Size:* Growth may provide benefits of economies of scale in data processing and brand name recognition.

COMPANIES STUDIED

Kelly Services focuses on providing temporary employees for clerical and light manufacturing needs. It maintains 900 offices in the United States and 12 foreign countries. Kelly owns 99 percent of its offices. Selected data for Kelly follow:

	1991	1992	1993
Number of Offices	950	920	900
Permanent Employees.	3,900	4,000	4,300
Temporary Employees.	550,000	580,000	630,000

Adia Services is 81.4 percent owned by Adia S.A., a Swiss corporation. Adia offers a diversified line of services through its 523 offices, including 320 offices offering temporary clerical and manufacturing personnel, 99 offices offering health-care personnel, 57 offices offering accounting personnel, 20 offices offering data processing personnel, and 28 offices offering outplacement services. Adia owns its data processing and outplacement offices, franchises its health-care offices, and uses a combination of ownership and franchises for its clerical/manufacturing and accounting personnel supply offices. Adia has grown its office network by internal growth, franchising, and corporate acquisitions. Selected data for Adia follow:

	1991	1992	1993
Number of Offices	553	533	523
Permanent Employees.	1,950	1,900	2,050
Temporary Employees.	200,000	225,000	250,000

FINANCIAL STATEMENT DATA

Exhibits 1 through 3 present financial statement data for Kelly. Exhibits 4 through 6 present similar data for Adia. Additional data regarding these companies follow.

1. The present values of operating lease commitments at a discount rate of 10 percent are (amounts in millions):

	1990	1991	1992	1993
Kelly	52	58	56	55
Adia............	31	29	26	39

2. These firms use an accounting period ending on the Friday nearest December 31 each year. The annual accounting period includes 52 weeks in some years and 53 weeks in other years. The year end for these firms will not necessarily coincide precisely with the periodic pay periods of their clients, resulting in variations each year in the year-end amounts of accounts receivable.

3. Adia entered into a tax-sharing agreement with its parent company during 1991. The tax-sharing agreement allocates income taxes between Adia and its parent based on the entity most responsible for generating taxable incomes.

EXHIBIT 1

Kelly Services
Balance Sheets
(amounts in millions)
(Case 8.4)

	December 28, 1990	January 3, 1991	January 1, 1992	December 31, 1993
Assets				
Cash	$ 96	$ 41	$ 30	$ 36
Short-Term Investments	122	186	155	145
Accounts Receivable	163	171	209	248
Prepayments............................	12	13	15	18
Total Current Assets....................	$393	$411	$409	$447
Property, Plant, and Equipment (net)........	38	52	69	68
Goodwill and Other Assets	13	16	18	27
Total Assets	$444	$479	$496	$542
Liabilities and Shareholders' Equity				
Accounts Payable and Accrued Expenses.....	$ 87	$115	$116	$145
Income Taxes Payable	19	9	13	11
Total Current Liabilities.................	$106	$124	$129	$156
Common Stock	$ 32	$ 32	$ 32	$ 40
Additional Paid-in Capital	1	2	4	1
Retained Earnings.......................	311	327	338	352
Treasury Stock..........................	(6)	(6)	(7)	(7)
Total Shareholders' Equity	$338	$355	$367	$386
Total Liabilities and Shareholders' Equity ..	$444	$479	$496	$542

EXHIBIT 2

Kelly Services—Income Statements
(amounts in millions)
(Case 8.4)

	For the Year Ended		
	January 3, 1991	**January 1, 1992**	**December 31, 1993**
Sales	$ 1,424	$ 1,713	$ 1,955
Other Revenues	14	9	7
Cost of Services of Temporary Employees	(1,116)	(1,372)	(1,574)
Selling and Administrative Expenses	(262)	(289)	(317)
Income Tax Expense	(21)	(22)	(26)
Net Income	$ 39	$ 39	$ 45

EXHIBIT 3

Kelly Services—Statements of Cash Flows
(amounts in millions)
(Case 8.4)

	For the Year Ended		
	January 3, 1991	**January 1, 1992**	**December 31, 1993**
Operating			
Net Income	$ 39	$ 39	$ 45
Depreciation and Amortization	10	14	17
(Increase) Decrease in Accounts Receivable . . .	(7)	(38)	(39)
(Increase) Decrease in Prepayments	(1)	(2)	(3)
Increase (Decrease) in Current Liabilities	17	(1)	25
Cash Flow from Operations	$ 58	$ 12	$ 45
Investing			
Short-Term Investments Sold (Acquired)	$(65)	$ 31	$ 9
Fixed Assets Acquired	(23)	(32)	(16)
Other Investing Transactions	(4)	(2)	(9)
Cash Flow from Investing	$(92)	$ (3)	$(16)
Financing			
Common Stock Issued	$ 1	$ 2	$ 1
Dividends	(22)	(22)	(24)
Cash Flow from Financing	$(21)	$(20)	$(23)
Change in Cash	$(55)	$(11)	$ 6
Cash—Beginning of Year	96	41	30
Cash—End of Year	$ 41	$ 30	$ 36

EXHIBIT 4

Adia Services
Balance Sheets
(amounts in millions)
(Case 8.4)

	December 28, 1990	January 3, 1991	January 1, 1992	December 31, 1993
Assets				
Cash and Short-Term Investments	$ 44	$ 52	$ 21	$ 68
Accounts Receivable	79	78	133	123
Prepayments.............................	9	9	16	21
Total Current Assets....................	$132	$139	$170	$212
Property, Plant, and Equipment (net)........	11	13	13	14
Goodwill and Other Assets	100	89	81	77
Total Assets	$243	$241	$264	$303
Liabilities and Shareholders' Equity				
Accounts Payable and Accrued Expenses.....	$ 45	$ 43	$ 57	$ 77
Notes Payable............................	0	1	0	0
Current Portion of Long-Term Debt.........	6	5	1	0
Income Taxes Payable.....................	3	1	4	5
Total Current Liabilities.................	$ 54	$ 50	$ 62	$ 82
Long-Term Debt	7	1	1	1
Total Liabilities	$ 61	$ 51	$ 63	$ 83
Common Stock	$ 3	$ 3	$ 3	$ 3
Additional Paid-in Capital	100	101	101	102
Retained Earnings........................	79	86	97	115
Total Shareholders' Equity...............	$182	$190	$201	$220
Total Liabilities and Shareholders' Equity ..	$243	$241	$264	$303

EXHIBIT 5

Adia Services
Income Statements
(amounts in millions)
(Case 8.4)

	For the Year Ended		
	January 3, 1991	January 1, 1992	December 31, 1993
Sales	$ 644	$ 743	$ 918
Other Revenues..........................	3	3	3
Cost of Services of Temporary Employees....	(447)	(531)	(667)
Selling and Administrative Expenses	(185)	(196)	(221)
Income Tax Expense......................	(7)	(7)	(12)
Net Income	$ 8	$ 12	$ 21

EXHIBIT 6

Adia Services
Statements of Cash Flows
(amounts in millions)
(Case 8.4)

	For the Year Ended		
	January 3, 1991	January 1, 1992	December 31, 1993
Operating			
Net Income	$ 8	$ 12	$ 21
Depreciation and Amortization	12	11	11
Other Addbacks (Subtractions)	1	(1)	(5)
(Increase) Decrease in Accounts Receivable	3	(19)	(28)
Increase (Decrease) in Current Liabilities	(5)	15	20
Cash Flow from Operations	$ 19	$ 18	$ 19
Investing			
Short-Term Investments Sold (Acquired)	$ 0	$(38)	$ 38
Fixed Assets Acquired	(11)	(6)	(7)
Cash Flow from Investing	$(11)	$(44)	$ 31
Financing			
Increase in Short-Term Borrowing	$ 1	$ 0	$ 0
Increase in Long-Term Borrowing	1	0	0
Decrease in Long-Term Borrowing	(5)	(3)	(1)
Dividends	(2)	(2)	(2)
Other Financing Transactions	5	—	—
Cash Flow from Financing	$ 0	$ (5)	$ (3)
Change in Cash	$ 8	$(31)	$ 47
Cash—Beginning of Year	44	52	21
Cash—End of Year	$ 52	$ 21	$ 68

4. Adia nets a minor amount of interest expense on short- and long-term borrowing against interest revenue on short-term investments.

REQUIRED

Assess the time-series and cross-section profitability and risk of Kelly and Adia. Consider the appropriateness of using ROA and ROCE as measures of profitability, including adjustments you would make to these financial ratios and other measures of profitability that use the number of offices and the number of temporary/permanent employees.

CHAPTER 9

RISK ANALYSIS: AN EXTENDED LOOK

Learning Objectives

1. Explore the strengths and weaknesses of various univariate and multivariate statistical models for predicting financial distress.
2. Apply multivariate statistical models for predicting financial distress to the financial statements of actual companies.
3. Explore the relation between financial statement measures of risk and market beta.

Chapter 8 extended the discussion of profitability analysis in Chapter 3 by examining the relation between *accounting* measures of profitability (ROA, ROCE) and *economic* or *market* measures of return (IRR, dividends plus (minus) capital gains (losses)). This chapter extends the discussion of risk analysis in Chapter 3 by examining the relation between *accounting* measures of risk (short-term liquidity ratios, long-term solvency ratios) and *economic* or *market* measures of risk (financial distress, market beta).

Research on the risk of a firm has not evolved to the point to which there is a well-structured and well-accepted theory of risk. Multiple research streams have studied various dimensions of risk using a variety of research methodologies. This chapter attempts to synthesize the findings of these multiple research streams into a framework for analyzing risk using financial statement data.

DEFINITION OF RISK

Several research streams have defined *risk* in terms of *financial distress*. The analyst might view financial distress along a continuum from (1) failing to make a required interest payment on time, to (2) defaulting on a principal payment on debt, to (3) filing for bankruptcy, to (4) liquidating a firm. Analysts concerned with the economic loss of a portion or all of the amount lent to or invested in a firm would examine financial distress risk.

Less than 5 percent of publicly traded firms experience financial distress according to one of these definitions. We therefore need a broader definition that encompasses elements of risk common to all firms. A research stream that strives for a broader definition of risk is one that attempts to explain differences in market rates of return of common stocks. Economic theory teaches that differences in market returns must relate to differences in perceived risk. Studies of this returns/risk relation use market beta as the measure of risk. Market beta measures the covariability of a firm's returns with the returns of all securities in the market. Because only a small percentage of publicly traded firms experience significant risk from financial distress, additional factors besides financial distress must explain market beta.

We discuss more fully the research that examines financial distress risk and market beta risk in the following sections.

FINANCIAL DISTRESS RISK

Studies of financial distress attempt to distinguish between firms that experience financial distress and those that do not, a dichotomous outcome state. Thus, this research develops models to distinguish firms that file for bankruptcy versus those that do not or those firms in bankruptcy that successfully reorganize versus those that liquidate.

UNIVARIATE ANALYSIS

Research in the mid-1960s used univariate analysis, examining the relation between particular financial statement ratios of distressed and nondistressed firms. Beaver studied 29 financial statement ratios for the five years preceding bankruptcy for a sample of bankrupt and nonbankrupt firms.[1] The objective was to identify the ratios that distinguished best between these two groups of firms and to determine how many years prior to bankruptcy the differences in the ratios emerged. The six ratios with the best discriminating power (and the nature of the risk each ratio measures) were

1. Net income plus depreciation, depletion, and amortization/total liabilities (long-term solvency risk[2]).
2. Net income/total assets (profitability).

---

[1]William Beaver, "Financial Ratios as Predictors of Failure," *Empirical Research in Accounting: Selected Studies, 1966,* supplement to Journal of Accounting Research, 1966, pp. 71–102.

[2]This ratio is similar to the cash flow from operations to total liabilities ratio discussed in Chapter 3 except that the numerator of Beaver's ratio does not include changes in working capital accounts. Published "funds flow" statements at the time of Beaver's study defined funds as working capital (instead of cash).

3. Total debt/total assets (long-term solvency risk).
4. Net working capital/total assets (short-term liquidity risk).
5. Current assets/current liabilities (short-term liquidity risk).
6. Cash, marketable securities, accounts receivable/operating expenses excluding depreciation, depletion, and amortization (short-term liquidity risk[3]).

Note that this list includes profitability, short-term liquidity, and long-term solvency ratios. Beaver's best predictor was net income before depreciation, depletion, and amortization divided by total liabilities. Exhibit 9.1 summarizes the success of this ratio in correctly classifying sample firms as bankrupt or not for each of the five years preceding bankruptcy. The classification accuracy increased as bankruptcy approached but was close to 80 percent for as early as five years preceding bankruptcy.

The error rates deserve particular attention however. A Type I error is classifying a firm as nonbankrupt when it ultimately goes bankrupt. A Type II error occurs when a firm is classified as bankrupt and ultimately survives. A Type I error is more costly to an investor because of the likelihood of losing the full amount invested. A Type II error costs the investor the opportunity cost of funds invested. Note that the Type I error rates are much higher than the Type II error rates in Beaver's sample. Four years prior to bankruptcy, this particular financial ratio does only slightly better in predicting which firms will enter bankruptcy than flipping a coin.

Univariate analysis helps to identify factors related to financial distress and is therefore a necessary step in the initial development of a theory of risk. However, univariate analysis does not provide a means of measuring the relative importance of individual financial statement ratios or of combining them when assessing risk. For example, does a firm with a high current ratio and a high debt to assets ratio have more financial distress risk than a firm with a low current ratio and a low debt to assets ratio?

EXHIBIT 9.1

Classification Accuracy and Error Rates for Net Income before Depreciation, Depletion, and Amortization/Total Liabilities

		Error Rate	
Years Prior to Bankruptcy	**Proportion Correctly Classified**	**Type I**	**Type II**
5	78%	42%	4%
4	76%	47%	3%
3	77%	37%	8%
2	79%	34%	8%
1	87%	22%	5%

Source: William Beaver, "Financial Ratios as Predictors of Failure," *Empirical Research in Accounting: Selected Studies, 1966,* supplement to *Journal of Accounting Research,* 1966, p. 90.

---

[3]This ratio, referred to as the *defensive interval,* indicates the proportion of a year that a firm could continue to operate by paying cash operating expenses with cash and near-cash assets.

MULTIPLE DISCRIMINANT ANALYSIS

Deficiencies of univariate analysis led researchers during the late 1960s and throughout the 1970s to use multiple discriminant analysis (MDA), a multivariate statistical technique. Researchers typically selected a sample of distressed firms and matched these firms with healthy firms of approximately the same size and in the same industry. This matching attempts to control for size and industry factors so the researcher can examine the impact of other factors that might explain financial distress. The researcher then calculates a large number of financial statement ratios expected *a priori* to help explain the financial distress. Using these financial ratios as inputs, the MDA model selects the subset (usually four to six ratios) that best discriminates between distressed and nondistressed firms. The resulting MDA model includes a set of coefficients that, when multiplied times the particular financial statement ratios and then summed, yields a multivariate score. Scores below a critical cutoff point suggest a high probability of financial distress, and scores above that point suggest a low probability. Researchers usually develop the MDA model on an estimation sample and then apply the resulting model to a separate holdout or prediction sample to check on the generalizability and predictability of the model.

Perhaps the best-known MDA bankruptcy prediction model is Altman's Z-score.[4] Altman used manufacturing firms in developing the model. The calculation of the Z-score appears below:

$$\text{Z-score} = 1.2\left[\frac{\text{Net Working Capital}}{\text{Total Assets}}\right] + 1.4\left[\frac{\text{Retained Earnings}}{\text{Total Assets}}\right]$$

$$+ 3.3\left[\frac{\text{Earnings before Interest and Taxes}}{\text{Total Assets}}\right]$$

$$+ .6\left[\frac{\text{Market Value of Equity}}{\text{Book Value of Liabilities}}\right] + 1.0\left[\frac{\text{Sales}}{\text{Total Assets}}\right]$$

Each of the ratios measures a different dimension of profitability or risk:

1. *Net Working Capital/Total Assets:* The proportion of total assets comprising relatively liquid net current assets (current assets minus current liabilities). This ratio measures short-term liquidity risk.
2. *Retained Earnings/Total Assets:* Accumulated profitability and relative age of a firm.
3. *Earnings before Interest and Taxes/Total Assets:* A version of ROA. This ratio measures current profitability.
4. *Market Value of Equity/Book Value of Liabilities:* This is a form of the debt/equity ratio, but it incorporates the market's assessment of the value of the firm's shareholders' equity. This ratio therefore measures long-term solvency risk and the market's overall view about the profitability and risk of the firm.

---

[4]Edward Altman, "Financial Ratios, Discriminant Analysis, and the Prediction of Corporate Bankruptcy," *Journal of Finance,* September 1968, pp. 589–609.

5. *Sales/Total Assets:* This ratio is similar to the total assets turnover ratio and indicates the ability of a firm to use assets to generate sales.

The coefficients on each of the ratios do not necessarily indicate relative importance. They represent in part scaling devices for each ratio. For example, the 3.3 coefficient for earnings before interest and taxes divided by total assets reflects the fact that this ratio usually falls in the range of 0.04 to 0.10. The 1.0 coefficient for sales divided by total assets reflects the fact that this ratio usually falls in the range of 0.8 to 2.5 or more. In applying this model, Altman found that Z-scores of less than 1.81 indicated a high probability of bankruptcy, while Z-scores higher than 3.00 indicated a low probability of bankruptcy. Scores between 1.81 and 3.00 were in the gray area.

Altman obtained a 95 percent correct classification accuracy rate one year prior to bankruptcy, with a Type I error rate of 6 percent and a Type II error rate of 3 percent. The correct classification rate two years before bankruptcy was 83 percent, with a Type I error rate of 28 percent and a Type II error rate of 6 percent. As with Beaver's study, the more costly Type I error rate is larger than the Type II error rate.

Exhibit 9.2 shows the calculation of Altman's Z-score for Coke and Pepsi for their most recent year reported in Appendices A and B, respectively. Coke's Z-score clearly indicates a low probability of bankruptcy, whereas Pepsi's Z-score is at the high end of the gray area. Coke's policy of not consolidating its bottlers, however, significantly affects its Z-score. Exhibit 7.5 in Chapter 7 presents the worksheet to consolidate Coke with its bottlers. The revised Z-score for Coke based on these consolidated amounts is 3.3239, still clearly indicating a low probability of bankruptcy. However,

---

EXHIBIT 9.2

Altman's Z-Score for Coke and Pepsi

	Coke	Pepsi
Net Working Capital/Total Assets		
Coke: 1.2[($4,434 − $5,171)/$12,021]	−.0736	
Pepsi: 1.2[($5,164.1 − $6,574.9/$23,705.8]		−.0714
Retained Earnings/Total Assets		
Coke: 1.4[$9,458/$12,021]	1.1015	
Pepsi: 1.4[$6,541.9/$23,705.8]		.3863
Earnings before Interest and Taxes/Total Assets		
Coke: 3.3[($3,185 + $168)/$12,021]	.9205	
Pepsi: 3.3[($2,422.5 + $572.7)/$23,705.8]		.4170
Market Value of Equity/Book Value of Liabilities		
Coke: 0.6[($44.63 × 1,297.5)/$7,437]	4.6718	
Pepsi: 0.6[($40.88 × 798.8)/$17,367.1]		1.1282
Sales/Total Assets		
Coke: 1.0[$13,957/$12,021]	1.1611	
Pepsi: 1.0[$25,020.7/$23,705.8]		1.0555
Z-Score	7.7813	2.9156

this Z-score is closer to that of Pepsi. Pepsi's recent acquisitions decreased the accumulated and current profitability components of its Z-score relative to that for Coke.

The principal strengths of MDA are

1. Its incorporation of multiple financial ratios simultaneously.
2. Its provision of appropriate coefficients for combining the independent variables.
3. Its ease of application once the initial model has been developed.

The principal criticisms of MDA are

1. As in univariate applications, the researcher cannot be sure that the MDA model includes all relevant discriminating financial ratios. Most early studies, for example, used accrual basis income statement and balance sheet data instead of cash-flow data. MDA selects the best ratios from those provided to it, but that set does not necessarily provide the best explanatory power.
2. The researcher must judge subjectively the value of the cutoff score that best distinguishes distressed from nondistressed firms.
3. The development and application of the MDA model requires firms to disclose the necessary information to compute each financial ratio. Firms excluded because they do not provide the necessary data may bias the MDA model.
4. MDA assumes that each of the financial ratios for distressed and nondistressed firms is normally distributed. Firms experiencing financial distress often display unusually large or small ratios that can skew the distribution away from normalcy. In addition, the researcher cannot include dummy variables (for example, 0 if financial statements are audited, 1 if they are not audited). Dummy variables are not normally distributed.
5. MDA requires that the variance-covariance matrix of the explanatory variables be the same for distressed and nondistressed firms.[5]

LOGIT ANALYSIS

A third stage in the methodological development of distress prediction research was the move during the 1980s and early 1990s to using logit analysis instead of MDA. Logit does not require that the data display the underlying statistical properties described above for MDA. In addition, logit provides a probability of bankruptcy instead of the numerical score obtained from MDA. The development of the logit model follows a similar procedure to MDA: (1) initial calculation of a large set of financial ratios, (2) reduction of the set of financial ratios to a subset that best discriminates distressed and nondistressed firms, and (3) specification of coefficients for each included variable.

---

[5]For an elaboration of these criticisms, see James A. Ohlson, "Financial Ratios and the Probabalistic Prediction of Bankruptcy," *Journal of Accounting Research,* Spring 1980, pp. 109–131; and Mark E. Zmijewski, "Methodological Issues Related to the Estimation of Financial Distress Prediction Models," *Journal of Accounting Research—Supplement 1984,* pp. 59–82.

The logit model defines the probability of bankruptcy as follows:

$$\text{Probability of Bankruptcy for a Firm} = \frac{1}{1 + e^y}$$

where e equals approximately 2.718282. The exponent y is a multivariate function that includes a constant and coefficients for a set of explanatory variables (that is, financial statement ratios).

Zavgren used logit to discriminate bankrupt from nonbankrupt firms. Zavgren's model for one year prior to bankruptcy, somewhat adapted for presentation here, defined y as follows:[6]

$$y = 0.23883 - 0.108(\text{INV}) - 1.583(\text{REC}) - 10.78(\text{CASH}) + 3.074(\text{QUICK})$$
$$+ 0.486(\text{ROI}) - 4.35\,(\text{DEBT}) + 0.11\,(\text{TURNOVER}).$$

The definition of the independent variables is as follows:

INV   = Average inventories/sales

REC   = Average receivables/average inventories

CASH   = (Cash + marketable securities)/total assets

QUICK   = Quick assets/current liabilities

ROI   = Income from continuing operations/(total assets − current liabilities)

DEBT   = Long-term debt/(total assets − current liabilities)

TURNOVER = Sales/(net working capital + fixed assets)

Explanatory variables with a negative coefficient increase the probability of bankruptcy because they reduce e^y toward zero, with the result that the bankruptcy probability function approaches 1/1, or 100 percent. Likewise, independent variables with a positive coefficient decrease the probability of bankruptcy. The analyst must interpret the sign of the coefficient for a particular financial statement ratio cautiously because the coefficients of the various ratios in a multivariate model are not independent of each other. With this caveat in mind, consider each of the seven independent variables in Zavgren's logit model.

1. *INV:* Firms with a high INV ratio turn over inventory slowly, thereby increasing short-term liquidity risk and the probability of bankruptcy.

---

[6]Christine V. Zavgren, "Assessing the Vulnerability to Failure of American Industrial Firms: A Logistic Analysis," *Journal of Business Finance and Accounting,* Spring 1985, pp. 19–45. Two adaptations were made: (1) the sign of the exponent y in the logit probability function and the signs of all coefficients in the y function were reversed to ease interpretation and (2) the decimal point for each of the coefficients in the y function in the original Zavgren paper was moved two places to the left to attain consistency with the measurement of the financial ratios as decimal amounts (that is, .32) instead of percentages (that is, 32 percent).

2. *REC:* Firms with a high REC ratio generally turn over receivables slowly relative to inventories, thereby increasing short-term liquidity risk and the probability of bankruptcy. An alternative explanation for a high REC ratio, however, is that a firm's selling prices reflect a high markup on manufacturing costs (for example, because of brand recognition or patent protection). Bankruptcy risk would likely be lower in these cases, but Zavgren's model would show a higher probability of bankruptcy for such firms.

3. *CASH:* The negative coefficient for the CASH ratio seems counterintuitive. Firms with a high proportion of cash and marketable securities among their assets have a greater capacity to service their debt and cope with short-term operating problems. Thus, it seems that the CASH ratio should have a positive coefficient. Its negative sign illustrates the difficulty interpreting the signs of individual coefficients in a multivariate model. The QUICK ratio, discussed next, reflects the relative liquidity of a firm's short-term assets to satisfy short-term obligations. The coefficient for the QUICK ratio carries a positive sign as expected. The negative sign for the CASH coefficient combined with the positive sign for the QUICK coefficient suggests that having quick assets in the form of cash and marketable securities instead of accounts receivable increases bankruptcy risk. Zavgren offered the interpretation that firms with high proportions of cash and marketable securities among their assets may have limited operating investment alternatives. As a result, their ability to sustain and grow their operations in the future may be questionable.

4. *QUICK:* A high quick ratio indicates a capacity to pay liabilities coming due soon with highly liquid assets. Thus, as the QUICK ratio increases, the probability of bankruptcy decreases.

5. *ROI:* The higher is the rate of profitability, the less likely a firm will experience difficulty servicing debt and therefore the lower the probability of bankruptcy.

6. *DEBT:* A high proportion of debt in the capital structure increases the probability of bankruptcy.

7. *TURNOVER:* A high TURNOVER ratio indicates that a firm turns its assets into sales quickly (and into cash soon thereafter; the REC explanatory variable picks up this factor). Thus, the probability of bankruptcy decreases as the TURNOVER ratio increases.

Zavgren developed this logit model on 45 bankrupt and 45 nonbankrupt firms, paired on industry and asset size. Using a probability cutoff of 50 percent, the model correctly classified 82.2 percent of the firms.

Exhibit 9.3 shows the calculation of the value of y in Zavgren's logit model for Coke and Pepsi for Year 8. The calculation of the probability of bankruptcy appears below:

Coke: $1/1 + e^{-1.37737} = 1/1 + 0.25224 = 79.9\%$

Pepsi: $1/1 + e^{-3.58019} = 1/1 + 0.02787 = 97.3\%$

The bankruptcy risk of these two firms is obviously not as high as these percentages suggest. The relatively high value for the REC ratio is part of the explanation.

EXHIBIT 9.3		
Zavgren's Probability of Bankruptcy for Coke and Pepsi		
	Coke	**Pepsi**
Constant.....................................	.23883	.23883
INV		
Coke: −0.108[$1,034/$13,957].............	−.00800	
Pepsi: −0.108[$846.8/$25,020.7]...........		−.00366
REC		
Coke: −1.583[$1,164.5/$1,034.0]...........	−1.78279	
Pepsi: −1.583[$1,736.0/$846.8]		−3.24526
CASH		
Coke: −10.78[$1,078/$12,021].............	−.96671	
Pepsi: −10.78[$1,856.2/$23,705.8].........		−.84409
QUICK		
Coke: 3.074[$2,321/$5,171]...............	1.37976	
Pepsi: 3.074[$3,739.6/$6,574.9]		1.74840
ROI		
Coke: 0.486[$2,188/$6,850]...............	.15524	
Pepsi: 0.486[$1,587.9/$17,130.9]		.04505
DEBT		
Coke: −4.35[$1,428/$6,850]	−.90683	
Pepsi: −4.35[$7,442.6/$17,130.9]..........		−1.88988
TURNOVER		
Coke: 0.11[$13,957/$2,992]...............	.51313	
Pepsi: 0.11[$25,070.7/$7,444.8]		.37043
Value of y.................................	−1.37737	−3.58018

The brand names of these firms permit them to include a substantial markup on manufacturing cost in setting selling prices. In addition, Coke and Pepsi carry receivables from their bottlers (Coke) and restaurant franchisees (Pepsi) but carry none of the inventories of these independent entities. Another part of the explanation for the high bankruptcy probability is the amount for the CASH ratio. Both firms experience healthy profit margins and cash flows from operations. The cash flow is more than sufficient to finance capital expenditures resulting in a buildup of cash and marketable securities on the balance sheet. Thus, Zavgren's model would misclassify Coke and Pepsi as firms with high bankruptcy potential.

APPLICATION OF BANKRUPTCY PREDICTION MODELS TO W.T. GRANT COMPANY

W.T. Grant Company (Grant), one of the largest retailers in the United States, filed for bankruptcy in October 1975. Case 2.1 at the end of Chapter 2 includes financial statement data for Grant for its fiscal years ended January 31, 1967, through 1975. Exhibit 9.4 shows the calculation of Altman's Z-score and Zavgren's probability of

EXHIBIT 9.4

Application of Altman's and Zavgren's Bankruptcy Prediction Models to W.T. Grant

	Fiscal Year								
	1967	1968	1969	1970	1971	1972	1973	1974	1975
Altman's Z-Score Model									
Net Wk. Cap./Assets....	.53827	.54353	.51341	.44430	.37791	.44814	.36508	.38524	.19390
Ret. Earn./Assets.....	.41970	.43738	.42669	.41929	.38511	.34513	.31023	.25712	.04873
EBIT/Assets	.41656	.41358	.44611	.44228	.38848	.27820	.26029	.25470	−.63644
Mkt. Value Equity/									
Bk. Value Liabilities	.53092	.86643	1.01740	.95543	.89539	.69788	.50578	.10211	.01730
Sales/Assets	1.79595	1.77564	1.76199	1.71325	1.67974	1.57005	1.58678	1.54797	1.62802
Score.............	3.70140	4.03656	4.16560	3.97455	3.72663	3.33940	3.02816	2.54714	1.25151
Probability of Bankruptcy									
Range	Low	Low	Low	Low	Low	Low	Gray	Gray	High
Zavgren's Logit Model									
Constant	.23883	.23883	.23883	.23883	.23883	.23883	.23883	.23883	.23883
INV..............	−.01912	−.01976	−.01933	−.01921	−.02078	−.02196	−.02292	−.02482	−.02630
REC..............	−1.95757	−2.22142	−2.36121	−2.50281	−2.38357	−2.17060	−1.98809	−1.87945	−1.79335
CASH.............	−.82084	−.49133	−.44428	−.50296	−.49104	−.61371	−.32181	−.41452	−.79328
QUICK............	3.79627	3.88534	3.64658	3.36340	2.85158	3.23616	2.60102	2.72847	2.09404
ROI..............	.05209	.05072	.05509	.05980	.05469	.03490	.03809	.00992	−.25932
DEBT	−1.03392	−.86161	−.53856	−.45283	−.43424	−1.26842	−1.23501	−1.79511	−2.83151
TURNOVER	.36424	.36224	.38146	.42019	.46456	.37116	.44478	.41988	.70018
Total	.61998	.94301	.95858	.60441	.28003	−.19364	−.24511	−.71680	−2.67071
Probability of Bankruptcy..	35.0%	28.0%	27.7%	35.3%	43.0%	54.8%	56.1%	67.2%	93.5%

bankruptcy for each of these fiscal years using amounts from Exhibits 3 and 4 of Case 2.1.

Altman's model shows a low probability of bankruptcy prior to 1973, a move into the gray area in 1973 and 1974, and a high probability of bankruptcy in 1975. The absolute levels of these Z scores are inflated because Grant is a retailer, whereas Altman developed the model using manufacturing firms. Retailing firms typically have a faster assets turnover than manufacturing firms. In this case, the trend of the Z-score is more meaningful than its absolute level. Note that the Z-score declined steadily beginning in 1970. With a few exceptions in individual years, each of the five components also declined steadily.[7]

The lower panel of Exhibit 9.4 shows the probability of bankruptcy using Zavgren's model. The model indicates a steady increase in the probability of bankruptcy beginning with the 1970 fiscal year. The QUICK ratio declined between 1969 and 1970 as a result of increased short-term borrowing to carry increased accounts receivable. The QUICK ratio deteriorated still further in 1971 with additional short-term borrowing. The DEBT ratio increased in 1972 and 1974 when Grant increased its long term borrowing. Grant's profitability continually declined.

OTHER METHODOLOGICAL ISSUES IN FINANCIAL DISTRESS RESEARCH

Financial distress prediction research has addressed several other methodological issues.

1. *Equal Sample Sizes of Distress and Nondistressed Firms:* The proportion of distressed firms in the economy is substantially smaller than the proportion of nondistressed firms. The matched pairs research design results in overfitting the MDA and logit models toward the characteristics of distressed firms. This overfitting is not necessarily a problem if the objective is to identify characteristics of distressed firms. However, it will likely result in classifying too many nondistressed firms as distressed when the model is applied to the broader population of firms. Researchers have addressed this criticism by using a larger proportion of nondistressed firms.

2. *Matching Distressed and Nondistressed Firms on Size and Industry Characteristics:* This matching precludes consideration of either of these factors as possible explanatory variables for financial distress. Yet small firms may experience greater difficulty obtaining funds when needed than larger firms. Industry membership, particularly for cyclical industries, may be an important factor explaining financial distress. Some researchers select a random sample of nondistressed firms. Another approach is to develop the MDA or logit models for each industry. Platt, for example, developed models for 16 two-digit SIC industries.[8] The

---

[7]The teaching note to the Grant case indicates that prior to its 1975 fiscal year, Grant failed to provide adequately for uncollectible accounts. The effect of this action was to overstate the Net Working Capital/Assets, Retained Earnings/Assets, and EBIT/Assets components of the Z-score, understate the Sales/Assets component, and probably overstate the overall Z-score.

[8]Harlan D. Platt, "The Determinants of Interindustry Failure," *Journal of Economics and Business,* 1989, pp. 107–126.

explanatory variables and their coefficients varied across the various industries. Platt and Platt normalized the financial ratios of each firm by relating them to the corresponding average industry ratio of the firm's industry.[9] They found that normalized financial ratios increased the classification accuracy of their sample to 90 percent, versus 78 percent based on a model of nonnormalized ratios.

3. *Use of Accrual versus Cash Flow Variables:* Until the mid 1980s, most financial distress research used accrual basis balance sheet and income statement ratios or ratios from the "funds flow" statement, which defined funds as working capital. The transition to a cash definition of funds in the statement of cash flows led researchers to add cash flow variables to bankruptcy prediction models. Casey and Bartczak, among others, found that adding cash flow from operations/current liabilities and cash flow from operations/total liabilities did not significantly add explanatory power to models based on accrual basis amounts.[10] Other researchers have found contrary results.[11]

4. *Stability in Financial Distress Prediction Models Over Time:* A final methodological issue in distress prediction research concerns the stability of the distress prediction models over time, both with regard to the explanatory variables included and their coefficients. Bankruptcy laws and their judicial interpretation change over time. The frequency of bankruptcy filings changes as economic conditions change. New financing vehicles emerge (for example, redeemable preferred stock, debt and equity securities with various option rights) that previous MDA or logit models did not consider in their formulation. To apply these models in practical settings, the analyst should periodically update them. A promising area for research is the use of neural networks to carry out the updating process.[12]

SYNTHESIS OF FINANCIAL DISTRESS RESEARCH

Preceding sections of this chapter discussed distress prediction models in bankruptcy settings. Similar streams of research relate to commercial bank lending,[13] bond ratings,[14] corporate restructurings,[15] and corporate liquidations.[16] Although the

---

[9]Harlan D. Platt and Marjorie B. Platt, "Development of a Class of Stable Predictive Variables: The Case of Bankruptcy Prediction," *Journal of Business, Finance, and Accounting,* Spring 1990, pp. 31–51.

[10]Cornelius J. Casey and Norman J. Bartczak, "Cash Flow—It's Not the Bottom Line," *Harvard Business Review,* June 1984, pp. 61–67.

[11]For a summary of this research, see M. F. Gombola, M.E. Haskins, J. E. Ketz, and D. D. Williams, "Cash Flow in Bankruptcy Predition," *Financial Management,* Winter 1987, pp. 55–65.

[12]See Delvin D. Hawlay, John D. Johnson and Dijjotam Raina, "Artificial Neural Systems: A New Tool for Financial Decision Making," *Financial Analysts Journal,* November–December 1990, pp. 63–72.

[13]Edward Altman, *Corporate Financial Distress and Bankruptcy,* 2nd ed. (New York: John Wiley, 1993), pp. 245–266.

[14]G. E. Pinches and K.A. Mingo, "A Multivariate Analysis of Industrial Bond Ratings," *Journal of Finance,* March 1973, pp. 1–18.

[15]James E. Seward, "Corporate Restructuring and Reorganization," in *Handbook of Modern Finance,* ed. Dennis Logue (New York: Warren, Gorham & Lamont, 1993), pp. E8-1 to E8-36.

[16]Cornelius J. Casey, Victor McGee, and Clyde P. Stickney, "Discriminating between Reorganized and Liquidated Firms in Bankruptcy," *Accounting Review,* April 1986, pp. 249–262.

statistical models used and the relevant financial statement ratios vary across the numerous studies, certain commonalities appear as well. This section attempts to summarize the factors that seem to explain financial distress most consistently across various studies.

Investment Factors. Two factors relate to the asset side of the balance sheet.

1. *Relative Liquidity of a Firm's Assets:* The probability of financial distress decreases as the relative liquidity of a firm's assets increases. Firms with relatively large proportions of current assets tend to experience less financial distress than firms with fixed assets or intangible assets as the dominate assets. Greater asset liquidity means that the firm will either have or will generate soon the necessary cash to meet creditors' claims. It is of interest to note that the expected return from more liquid assets, such as cash, marketable securities, and accounts receivable, is usually less (reflecting lower risk) than the expected return from fixed and intangible assets. Thus, firms must balance its mix of assets to obtain the desired return/risk profile. Researchers typically use the following ratios to measure relative liquidity: cash/total assets, current assets/total assets; or relative illiquidity: fixed assets/total assets.

2. *Rate of Asset Turnover:* The investment of funds in any asset eventually ends up in cash. Firms acquire fixed assets or create intangibles to produce a salable product (inventory) or create a desired service. Goods or services are often sold on account (accounts receivable) and later collected in cash. The faster assets turn over, the more quickly funds work their way toward cash on the balance sheet. Thus, a retailer may have the same proportion of fixed assets to total assets as a manufacturing firm. The other assets of the retailer (that is, accounts receivable, inventories) are likely to turn over more quickly and are thus more liquid. Commonly used financial ratios for this factor are total assets turnover, accounts receivable turnover, and inventory turnover. The working capital turnover ratio [sales/(current assets − current liabilities)] and fixed asset turnover ratios have not generally showed statistical significance in studies of financial distress.

Financing Factors. Two factors relate to the liability side of the balance sheet.

1. *Relative Proportion of Debt in Capital Structure:* Firms experience financial distress because they are unable to pay liabilities as they come due. The higher the proportion of liabilities in the capital structure, the higher the probability that firms will experience financial distress. Firms with lower proportions of debt tend to have unused borrowing capacity that they can use in times of financial distress. Some measure of debt in the capital structure appears in virtually all financial distress models. Commonly used ratios include total liabilities/total assets and total liabilities/shareholders' equity.

2. *Relative Proportion of Short-Term Debt in the Capital Structure:* This factor has a similar rationale to the preceding one except that the nearer due date of

short-term debt increases the risk of financial distress. Thus, considering only the financing side of the balance sheet, a retailer using extensive bank and creditor financing will likely have greater risk from financial distress than a manufacturer with a similar proportion of total liabilities but whose liabilities are primarily long-term debt. A commonly used ratio for this factor is current liabilities/total assets.

Operating Factors.   Two factors relate to the operating activities of a firm.

1. *Relative Level of Profitability:* Profitable firms ultimately turn their profits into cash. Profitable firms are also usually able to borrow funds more easily than unprofitable firms. Firms with low or negative profitability must often rely on available cash or additional borrowing to meet financial commitments as they come due. Research has demonstrated that most financial distress initiates with one or more years of poor operating performance. Firms with unused debt capacity can often borrow for a year or so until the operating difficulties reverse. A combination of weak profitability and high debt ratios usually spells "financial distress." Commonly used financial ratios for profitability are net income/assets, income before interest and taxes/assets, net income/sales, and cash flow from operations/assets. The second profitability measure above identifies profitability problems in the core input/output markets of a firm before considering debt service costs and income taxes. The third measure appears in financial distress prediction models because profit margin, rather than assets turnover, is usually the driving force behind return on assets. The fourth measure substitutes cash flow from operations for net income in measuring profitability on the premise that cash pays the bills, not earnings.

2. *Variability of Operations:* Firms that experience variability in their operations, such as from cyclical sales patterns, exhibit a greater likelihood of financial distress than firms with low variability. During the down times in the cycle, such firms must obtain financing to meet financial commitments and maintain operating levels. The risk of financial distress in these cases relates to the unknown length of the down portion of the cycle. For how many years can a firm hold on until the cycle reverses? Researchers typically use the change in sales or the change in net income from the previous year to measure variability, although a longer period would seem more reasonable.

Two other factors examined in financial distress research warrant discussion.

1. *Size:* Studies of financial distress, particularly since the early 1980s, have increasingly identified size as an important explanatory variable. Larger firms generally have access to a wider range of financing sources and more flexibility to redeploy assets than smaller firms. Larger firms therefore experience a lower probability of financial distress than smaller firms. Most studies use total assets as the measure of size.

2. *Growth:* Studies of financial distress often include some measure of growth (for example, growth in sales, assets, or net income) as a possible explanatory variable. The statistical significance of growth as an independent variable has varied considerably across studies. It is therefore difficult to conclude much about its

relative importance. The mixed results may relate in part to ambiguity as to how growth relates to financial distress. Rapidly growing firms often need external financing to cover cash shortfalls from operations and permit acquisitions of fixed assets. These firms often display financial ratios typical of a firm in financial distress (that is, high debt ratios, weak profitability). Yet their growth potential provides access to capital that permits them to survive. Firms in the late maturity or early decline phase of their life cycles may display healthy financial ratios, but prospects are sufficiently poor that the probability of future financial distress is high.

Exhibit 9.5 relates these financial distress factors to the profitability and risk ratios discussed in Chapter 3.

EXHIBIT 9.5

Relation between Profitability and Risk Ratios and Financial Distress Factors

	Financial Statement Ratio	**Financial Distress Factor**
Profitability Ratios	Profit Margin for ROA	Operating Profitability
	Total Assets Turnover	Liquidity of Assets
	Rate of Return on Assets	Operating Profitability
	Common Earnings Leverage	Operating Profitability; Proportion of Debt in Capital Structure
	Capital Structure Leverage	Proportion of Debt in Capital Structure
	Rate of Return on Common Shareholders' Equity	Operating Profitability
Short-Term Liquidity Ratios	Current Ratio	Liquidity of Assets; Proportion of Short-Term Debt in Capital Structure
	Quick Ratio	Liquidity of Assets; Proportion of Short-Term Debt in Capital Structure
	Cash Flow from Operations to Current Liabilities	Liquidity of Operations; Proportion of Short-Term Debt in Capital Structure
	Days Accounts Receivable	Liquidity of Assets; Assets Turnover
	Days Inventory	Liquidity of Assets; Assets Turnover
	Days Payable	Proportion of Short-Term Debt in Capital Structure
Long-Term Solvency Ratios	Total Liabilities/Total Assets	Proportion of Debt in Capital Structure
	Long-Term Debt/Total Assets	Proportion of Debt in Capital Structure
	Long-Term Debt/Shareholders' Equity	Proportion of Debt in Capital Structure
	Cash Flow from Operations to Total Liabilities	Liquidity of Operations; Proportion of Debt in Capital Structure
	Interest Coverage	Operating Profitability; Proportion of Debt in Capital Structure
	Cash Flow from Operations to Capital Expenditures	Liquidity of Operations; Liquidity of Assets

MARKET RISK

Firms face additional risks besides the risk of financial distress. Firms operating in certain countries experience political risks related to changes in governments and the possibility of expropriation of assets. Firms that are unionized face the risk of labor strikes. Firms in high technology industries encounter product obsolescence risks. These and similar sources of risk lead firms only infrequently into financial distress, yet the investor in a firm's common stock must consider these dimensions of risk when making investment decisions. Economic theory teaches that differences in expected rates of return between investment alternatives must relate to differences in risk. Thus, we can turn to equity markets to obtain a broader measure of risk. We will then relate this market measure of risk to financial statement information.

Studies of market rates of return have traditionally used the capital asset pricing model (CAPM). The research typically regresses the returns on a particular firm's common shares (dividends plus (minus) capital gains (losses)) over some period of time on the excess of the returns of all common stocks over the risk-free rate. The regression takes the following form:

$$\begin{array}{l} \text{Returns on Common Stock} \\ \text{of a Particular Firm} \end{array} = \begin{array}{l} \text{Risk-Free} \\ \text{Interest Rate} \end{array} + \begin{array}{l} \text{Market Beta} \\ \text{of a Parti-} \\ \text{cular Firm} \end{array} \left[\begin{array}{l} \text{Market} \\ \text{Return} \end{array} - \begin{array}{l} \text{Risk-Free} \\ \text{Interest Rate} \end{array} \right]$$

The beta coefficient measures the covariability of a firm's returns with those of all shares traded on the market (in excess of the risk-free interest rate). Beta captures the *systematic* risk of the firm. The market, through the pricing of a firm's shares, rewards shareholders for the systematic risk assumed. Elements of risk that do not contribute to systematic risk are referred to as *nonsystematic risk*. By constructing a diversified portfolio of securities, the investor can eliminate nonsystematic risk. Thus, market pricing should provide no returns for the assumption of nonsystematic risk.

Studies of the determinants of market beta have identified three principal explanatory variables:[17]

1. Degree of operating leverage.
2. Degree of financial leverage.
3. Variability of sales.

Each of these factors causes the earnings of a particular firm to vary over time.

Operating leverage refers to the extent of fixed operating costs in the cost structure. Costs such as depreciation and amortization do not vary with the level of sales.

---

[17]Robert S. Hamada, "The Effect of a Firm's Capital Structure on the Systematic Risk of Common Stocks," *Journal of Finance*, May 1972, pp. 435–452; Barr Rosenberg and Walt McKibben, "The Prediction of Systematic and Specific Risk in Common Stocks," *Journal of Financial and Quantitative Analysis*, March 1973, pp. 317–333; James M. Gahlon and James A. Gentry, "On the Relationship between Systematic Risk and Degrees of Operating and Financial Leverage," *Financial Management*, Summer 1982, pp. 15–23.

Other costs, such as research and development and advertising, may vary somewhat with the level of sales but remain relatively fixed for any particular period. The presence of fixed operating costs leads to variations in operating earnings as sales increase and decrease. Likewise, the presence of debt in the capital structure adds a fixed cost for interest and creates the potential for causing earnings to increase or decrease as sales varies.

The presence of these fixed costs does not necessarily lead to earnings fluctuations over time. A firm with stable or growing sales may be able to adjust the level of fixed assets and related financing (for example, through leasing) to the level of sales, in effect converting fixed costs into variable costs. Firms such as electric utilities with high fixed costs from operating and financial leverage have monopoly power to price their services to cover costs regardless of demand. Such firms likewise do not experience wide variations in earnings. Operating and financial leverage create variations in earnings when sales vary and firms cannot alter their level of fixed costs. Thus, we would expect capital-intensive firms in cyclical industries to experience wide variations in earnings over the business cycle.

Research has shown a link between changes in earnings and changes in stock prices.[18] Thus, operating leverage, financial leverage, and variability of sales should result in fluctuations in the market returns for a particular firm's common shares. The average returns for all firms in the market should reflect the average level of operating leverage, financial leverage, and sales variability of these firms. Thus, the market beta for a particular firm reflects its degree of variability relative to the average firm. Firms with a market beta of 1.0 experience variability equal to the average. Firms with a beta greater than 1.0 experience greater variability than the average. Firms with a beta less than 1.0 experience less variability than the average firm. A beta of 1.20 suggests 20 percent greater variability. A beta of .80 suggests 20 percent less variability.

It is important to note that financial distress risk and market beta risk share several similar explanatory factors. High proportions of fixed assets in the asset structure provide relatively illiquid assets (increasing financial distress risk) and high fixed costs (increasing market beta risk). High proportions of debt in the capital structure require regular debt servicing (increasing financial distress risk) and high fixed costs for interest (increasing market beta risk). Variability of sales creates the possibility of not having sufficient liquid assets to service debt (increasing financial distress risk) and causing fluctuations in earnings (increasing market beta risk). Financial distress risk relates primarily to an illiquidity problem, whereas market beta risk relates more to an earnings problem. Financial distress risk, when it becomes important for a particular firm, intensifies the preexisting market beta risk. Research has shown that the market betas for a sample of firms filing for bankruptcy increased from week 25 prior to filing up to week 9 prior to filing, whereas the beta

---

[18]Ray Ball and Philip Brown, "An Empirical Evaluation of Accounting Income Numbers," *Journal of Accounting Research,* Autumn, 1968, pp. 159–178.

[19]Byung T. Ro, Christine V. Zavgren and Su-Jane Hsieh, "The Effect of Bankruptcy on Systematic Risk of Common Stock: An Empirical Assessment," *Journal of Business, Finance and Accounting,* April 1992, pp. 309–328.

of a matched pair of nonbankrupt firms decreased slightly.[19] The market beta of the bankrupt firms remained relatively stable for the nine weeks preceding the bankruptcy, suggesting that the market had fully reflected the effects of the filing by that time.

The use of market beta as a measure of risk continues to be controversial. Finance texts discuss the issues more fully, but the questions below identify some of the concerns.

1. Should the risk-free rate be the rate on short-term U.S. Treasury bills (for example, three- to six-month maturities) or the rate on U.S. Treasury bonds that have maturities similar to the average holding period for common stock investments?

2. Should the measure of market return represent the return on publicly traded common stocks only or on other investments (for example, bonds, preferred stock, real estate) as well?

3. What index of market returns should be used (Dow Jones 30 industrials, S&P 500 industrials, all exchange-listed stocks, all publicly traded stocks, all domestic and foreign stocks)?

4. Does a single factor (excess of market return over the risk-free rate) adequately capture firm-specific returns, or should the set of independent variables be expanded (as in the arbitrage pricing model) or replaced with other independent variables (for example, size, market value to book value ratios)?

5. Are market betas sufficiently stable over time to serve as a measure of risk?

CASE 9.1

FLY-BY-NIGHT INTERNATIONAL GROUP: CAN THIS COMPANY BE SAVED?*

Douglas C. Mather, founder, chairman, and chief executive of Fly-By-Night International Group (FBN), lived the fast-paced, risk-seeking life that he tried to inject into his company. Flying the company's Learjets, he logged 28 world speed records. Once he throttled a company plane to the top of Mount Everest in 3 1/2 minutes.

These activities seemed perfectly appropriate at the time. Mather was a Navy fighter pilot in Vietnam and then flew commercial airlines. In the mid-1970s, he started FBN as a pilot training school. With the defense buildup beginning in the early 1980s, Mather branched out into government contracting. He equipped the company's Learjets with radar jammers and other sophisticated electronic devices to mimic enemy aircraft. He then contracted his "rent-an-enemy" fleet to the Navy and Air Force for use in fighter-pilot training. The Pentagon liked the idea, and FBN's revenues grew to $55 million in the fiscal year ending April 30, 1994. Its common stock, issued to the public in 1989 at $8.50 a share, reached a high of $16.50 in mid-1993. Mather and FBN received glowing write-ups in *Business Week* and *Fortune*.

---

*The author gratefully acknowledges the assistance of Lawrence C. Calcano in the preparation of this case.

In mid-1994, however, FBN began a rapid descent. Although still growing rapidly, its cash flow was inadequate to service its debt. According to Mather, he was "just dumbfounded. There was never an inkling of a problem with cash."

In the fall of 1994, the Board of Directors withdrew the company's financial statements for the year ending April 30, 1994, stating that there appeared to be material misstatements that needed investigation. In December 1994, Mather was asked to step aside as manager and director of the Company pending completion of an investigation of certain transactions between Mather and the company. On December 29, 1994, NASDAQ (over-the-counter stock market) discontinued quoting the company's common shares. In February 1995, the Board of Directors, following its investigation, terminated Mather's employment and membership on the Board.

Exhibits 1 to 3 present the financial statements and related notes of FBN for the five years ending April 1990 through April 1994. The financial statements for 1990 to 1992 use the amounts as originally reported for each year. The amounts reported on the statement of cash flows for 1990 (for example, the change in accounts receivable) do not precisely reconcile to the amounts on the balance sheet at the beginning and end of the year because certain items classified as relating to continuing operations on the balance sheet at the beginning of 1990 were reclassified as relating to discontinued operations on the balance sheet at the end of 1990. The financial statements for 1993 and 1994 represent the restated financial statements for those years after the Board of Directors completed its investigation of suspected material misstatements that caused it to withdraw the originally issued financial statements for fiscal 1994.

REQUIRED

You are asked to study these financial statements and notes and respond to the following questions.

a. What evidence can you observe from analyzing the financial statements that might signal the cash-flow problems experienced in mid-1994?

b. Can FBN avoid bankruptcy during 1995? What changes in either the design or implementation of FBN's strategy would you recommend?

NOTES TO FINANCIAL STATEMENTS

Note A: *Summary of Significant Accounting Policies*

Consolidation. The consolidated financial statements include the accounts of the company and its wholly owned subsidiaries. The company uses the equity method for subsidiaries not majority owned (50 percent or less) and eliminates significant intercompany transactions and balances.

Inventories. Inventories, which consist of aircraft fuel, spare parts and supplies, appear at lower of FIFO cost or market.

Property and Equipment. Property and equipment appear at acquisition cost. The company capitalizes major inspections, renewals, and improvements, while it expenses replacements, maintenance, and repairs which do not improve or extend the life of the respective assets. The company computes depreciation of property and equipment using the straight-line method.

Contract Income Recognition. Contractual specifications (that is, revenue rates, reimbursement terms, functional considerations) vary among contracts; accordingly, the company recognizes guaranteed contract income (guaranteed revenue less related

EXHIBIT 1

Fly-By-Night International Group
Comparative Balance Sheet
(amounts in thousands)
(Case 9.1)

	April 30					
	1989	1990	1991	1992	1993	1994
Current Assets						
Cash	$ 192	$ 753	$ 142	$ 313	$ 583	$ 159
Notes Receivable	—	—	1,000	—	—	—
Accounts Receivable	2,036	1,083	1,490	2,675	4,874	6,545
Inventories	686	642	602	1,552	2,514	5,106
Prepayments.....................	387	303	57	469	829	665
Net Assets of Discontinued Businesses.....................	—	1,926	—	—	—	—
Total Current Assets	$ 3,301	$ 4,707	$ 3,291	$ 5,009	$ 8,800	$ 12,475
Property, Plant, and Equipment	$17,471	$37,250	$17,809	$24,039	$76,975	$106,529
Less Accumulated Depreciation.....	(2,593)	(4,462)	(4,288)	(5,713)	(8,843)	(17,231)
Net	$14,878	$32,788	$13,521	$18,326	$68,132	$ 89,298
Other Assets.....................	$ 1,278	$ 1,566	$ 1,112	$ 641	$ 665	$ 470
Total Assets	$19,457	$39,061	$17,924	$23,976	$77,597	$102,243
Current Liabilities						
Accounts Payable.................	$ 1,436	$ 2,285	$ 939	$ 993	$ 6,279	$ 12,428
Notes Payable....................	—	4,766	1,021	140	945	—
Current Portion of Long-Term Debt.	1,239	2,774	1,104	1,789	7,018	60,590
Other Current Liabilities	435	1,845	1,310	2,423	12,124	12,903
Total Current Liabilities	$ 3,110	$11,670	$ 4,374	$ 5,345	$26,366	$ 85,921
Noncurrent Liabilities						
Long-Term Debt	9,060	20,041	6,738	9,804	41,021	—
Deferred Income Taxes...........	1,412	1,322	—	803	900	—
Other Noncurrent Liabilities	—	248	—	226	—	—
Total Liabilities	$13,582	$33,281	$11,112	$16,178	$68,287	$ 85,921
Shareholders' Equity						
Common Stock	$ 20	$ 20	$ 20	$ 21	$ 22	$ 34
Additional Paid-in Capital	3,611	3,611	4,323	4,569	5,685	16,516
Retained Earnings................	2,244	2,149	2,469	3,208	3,802	(29)
Treasury Stock...................	—	—	—	—	(199)	(199)
Total Shareholders' Equity	$ 5,875	$ 5,780	$ 6,812	$ 7,798	$ 9,310	$ 16,322
Total Liabilities and Shareholders' Equity........................	$19,457	$39,061	$17,924	$23,976	$77,597	$102,243

direct costs) either as it logs flight hours or on a straight-line monthly basis over the contract year, whichever method better reflects the economics of the contract. The

EXHIBIT 2

Fly-By-Night International Group
Comparative Income Statement for the Year Ended April 30
(amounts in thousands)
(Case 9.1)

	1990	1991	1992	1993	1994
Continuing Operations					
Sales	$31,992	$19,266	$20,758	$36,597	$54,988
Expenses					
Cost of Services....................	22,003	9,087	12,544	26,444	38,187
Selling and Administrative...........	4,236	2,989	3,467	3,020	5,880
Depreciation......................	3,003	2,798	1,703	3,150	9,810
Interest	2,600	2,743	1,101	3,058	5,841
Income Taxes.....................	74	671	803	379	(900)
Total Expenses....................	$31,916	$18,288	$19,618	$36,051	$58,818
Income—Continuing Operations	$ 76	$ 978	$ 1,140	$ 546	$ (3,830)
Income—Discontinued Operations.....	(171)	(659)	(400)	47	—
Net Income	$ (95)	$ 319	$ 740	$ 593	$ (3,830)

company recognizes income from discretionary hours flown in excess of the minimum guaranteed amount each month as it logs such discretionary hours.

Income Taxes. The company recognizes deferred income taxes for timing differences between financial and tax reporting amounts.

Note B: *Transactions with Major Customers.* The company provides contract flight services to three major customers: the U.S. Air Force, the U.S. Navy, and the Federal Reserve Bank System. These contracts have termination dates in 1996 or 1997. Revenues from all government contracts as a percentage of total revenues were as follows: 1990, 31 percent; 1991, 68 percent; 1992, 73 percent; 1993 72 percent; 1994, 62 percent.

Note C: *Segment Data.* During 1990, the company operated in five business segments as follows:

Flight Operations—Business. Provides combat readiness training to the military and nightly transfer of negotiable instruments for the Federal Reserve Bank System, both under multiyear contracts.

Flight Operations—Transport. Provides charter transport services to a variety of customers.

Fixed Base Operations. Provides ground support operations (fuel, maintenance) to commercial airlines at several major airports.

Education and Training. Provides training for nonmilitary pilots.

Aircraft Sales and Leasing. Acquires aircraft that the company then either resells or leases to various firms.

EXHIBIT 3

Fly-By-Night International Group
Comparative Statements of Cash Flows for the Year Ended April 30
(amounts in thousands)
(Case 9.1)

	1990	1991	1992	1993	1994
Operations					
Income—Continuing Operations	$ 76	$ 978	$ 1,140	$ 546	$ (3,830)
Depreciation	3,003	2,798	1,703	3,150	9,810
Other Adjustments	74	671	1,119	1,817	1,074
Working Capital from Operations	$ 3,153	$ 4,447	$ 3,962	$ 5,513	$ 7,054
Changes in Working Capital					
(Increase) Decrease in Receivables	403	(407)	(1,185)	(2,199)	(1,671)
(Increase) Decrease in Inventories	19	40	(950)	(962)	(2,592)
(Increase) Decrease in Prepayments	36	246	(412)	(360)	164
Increase (Decrease) in Accounts Payable	359	(1,346)	54	5,286	6,149
Increase (Decrease) in Other Current					
Liabilities	596	(535)	1,113	9,701	779
Cash Flow from Continuing Operations	$ 4,566	$ 2,445	$ 2,582	$ 16,979	$ 9,883
Cash Flow from Discontinued Operations	(335)	(752)	(472)	(77)	—
Net Cash Flow from Operations	$ 4,231	$ 1,693	$ 2,110	$ 16,902	$ 9,883
Investing					
Sale of Property, Plant, and Equipment	$ 12	$ 18,387	$ 119	$ 3	$ 259
Acquisition of Property, Plant, and Equipment . .	(20,953)	(2,424)	(6,573)	(52,960)	(33,035)
Other	30	(679)	1,017	78	(1,484)
Net Cash Flow from Investing	$(20,911)	$ 15,284	$(5,437)	$(52,879)	$(34,260)
Financing					
Increase in Short-Term Borrowing	$ 4,766	$ —	$ —	$ 805	$ —
Increase in Long-Term Borrowing	14,739	5,869	5,397	42,152	43,279
Issue of Common Stock	—	—	428	191	12,266
Decrease in Short-Term Borrowing	—	(3,745)	(881)	—	(945)
Decrease in Long-Term Borrowing	(2,264)	(19,712)	(1,647)	(7,024)	(30,522)
Acquisition of Common Stock	—	—	—	(198)	—
Other	—	—	201	321	(125)
Net Cash Flow from Financing	$ 17,241	$(17,588)	$ 3,498	$ 36,247	$ 23,953
Change in Cash	$ 561	$ (611)	$ 171	$ 270	$ (424)

The company discontinued the Flight Operations—Transport and Education and Training segments in 1991. It sold most of the assets of the Aircraft Sales and Leasing segment in 1991. Segment revenue, operating profit, and asset data for the various segments appear in Exhibit 4.

Note D: *Discontinued Operations.* Income from discontinued operations consists of the following (amounts in thousands):

EXHIBIT 4

Fly-By-Night International Group
Revenue, Profit, and Assets for Various Segments
(amounts in thousands)
(Case 9.1)

			April 30		
	1990	1991	1992	1993	1994
Revenues					
Flight Operations—Business......	$10,803	$11,236	$16,026	$31,297	$ 44,062
Flight Operations—Transport.....	13,805	—	—	—	—
Fixed Base Operations	3,647	3,911	4,651	4,832	9,597
Education and Training	542	—	—	—	—
Aircraft Sales and Leasing........	3,195	4,119	81	468	1,329
Total	$31,992	$19,266	$20,758	$36,597	$ 54,988
Operating Profit					
Flight Operations—Business......	$ 849	$ 2,463	$ 3,455	$ 4,863	$ 5,707
Flight Operations—Transport.....	(994)	—	—	—	—
Fixed Base Operations	332	174	1,038	1,362	(2,041)
Education and Training	12	—	—	—	—
Aircraft Sales and Leasing........	2,726[a]	1,217[b]	(15)	378	1,175
Total	$ 2,925	$ 3,854	$ 4,478	$ 6,603	$ 4,841
Assets					
Flight Operations—Business......	$13,684	$11,130	$17,738	$64,162	$ 85,263
Flight Operations—Transport.....	1,771	—	—	—	—
Fixed Base Operations	4,784	5,011	5,754	13,209	16,544
Education and Training	1,789	—	—	—	—
Aircraft Sales and Leasing........	18,524	1,262	438	226	436
Total	$40,552	$17,403	$23,930	$77,597	$102,243

[a]Includes a gain of $2.6 million on the sale of aircraft.

[b]Includes a gain of $1.2 million on the sale of aircraft.

1990

Loss from Operations of Charter Tour Business (net of income tax
benefits of $164) .... $(171)

1991

Loss from Operations of Flight Operations—Transport ($1,261) and
Education and Training ($172) Segments (net of income tax benefits
of $685) .... $(748)
Gain on Disposal of Education and Training Business (net of income taxes
of $85)   89

Total .... $(659)

1992

Loss from Write-Off of Airline Operations Certificates in Flight
Operations—Transport Business . . . . $(400)

1993

Income from Operations of Flight Operations—Transport ($78), net of
income taxes of $31 . . . . $ 47

Note E: *Related Party Transactions.* On April 30, 1991, the company sold most of the net assets of the Aircraft Sales and Leasing segment to Interlease, Inc., a Georgia corporation wholly owned by the company's majority stockholder, whose personal holdings represented at that time approximately 75 percent of the company.

Under the terms of the sale, the sale price was $1,368,000, of which the buyer paid $368,000 in cash and gave a promissory note for the remaining $1,000,000. The company treated the proceeds received in excess of the book value of the net assets sold of $712,367 as a capital contribution due to the related-party nature of the transaction. FBN originally acquired the assets of the Aircraft Sales and Leasing segment during 1990.

On September 29, 1994, the company's Board of Directors established a Transaction Committee to examine certain transactions between the company and Douglas Mather, its chairman, president, and majority stockholder. These transactions appear below:

Eastwind Transaction. On April 27, 1994, the company acquired four Eastwind aircraft from a German company. FBN subsequently sold these aircraft to Transreco, a corporation owned by Douglas Mather, for a profit of $1,600,000. In late September and early October, Transreco sold these four aircraft at a profit of $780,000 to unaffiliated third parties. The Transactions Committee determined that none of the officers or directors of the company were aware of the Eastwind transaction until late September 1994.

ESOP Transaction. On February 28, 1994, the company's Employee Stock Ownership Plan (ESOP) acquired 100,000 shares of the company's common stock from Mr. Mather at $14.25 per share. FBN financed the purchase. The ESOP gave the company a $1,425,000 unsecured demand note. To complete the transaction, the company cancelled a $1,000,000 promissory note from Mr. Mather and paid the remaining $425,000 in cash. The Transaction Committee determined that the Board of Directors did not authorize the $1,425,000 loan to the ESOP, the cancellation of Mather's $1,000,000 note or the payment of $425,000 in cash.

Certain Loans to Mr. Mather. In early September 1993, the Board of Directors authorized a $1,000,000 loan to Mr. Mather at the company's cost of borrowing plus 1/8 percent. On September 19, 1993, Mr. Mather tendered a $1,000,000 check to the company in repayment of the loan. On September 22, 1993, at Mr. Mather's direction, the company made an additional $1,000,000 loan to him, the proceeds of which Mather apparently used to cover his check in repayment of the first $1,000,000 loan. The Transaction Committee concluded that the Board of Directors did not authorize the September 22, 1993, loan to Mr. Mather, nor was any director aware of the loan at the time other than Mr. Mather. The company's 1993 Proxy Statement, dated September 27, 1993, incorrectly stated that "as of September 19, 1993, Mr. Mather had repaid the principal amount of his indebtedness to the company." Mr. Mather's $1,000,000 loan remained outstanding until it was cancelled in connection with the ESOP Transaction discussed above.

On December 12, 1994, the company announced that Mr. Mather had agreed to step aside as Chairman and a Director and take no part in the management of the company pending resolution of the matters presented to the Board by the Transactions Committee. On February 13, 1995, the company announced that it had entered into a settlement agreement with Mr. Mather and Transreco resolving certain of the issues addressed by the Transactions Committee. Pursuant to the agreement, the company will receive $211,000, the bonus paid to Mr. Mather for fiscal 1994, and $780,000, the gain recognized by Transreco on the sale of the Eastwind aircraft. Also pursuant to the settlement, Mr. Mather will resign all positions with the company and waive his rights under his employment agreement to any future compensation or benefits to which he might otherwise have a claim.

Note F: *Long-Term Debt.* Long-term debt appears in Exhibit 5. Substantially all of the company's property, plant, and equipment serves as collateral for this debt. The borrowings from bank and finance companies contain restrictive covenants, the most restrictive of which appear in the following table:

	1990	1991	1992	1993	1994
Liabilities/Tangible Net Worth ...	≤ 6.7	≤ 5.5	≤ 4.2	≤ 3.0	≤ 2.5
Tangible Net Worth	≥ 5,100	≥ 5,300	≥ 5,400	≥ 5,800	≥ 20,000
Working Capital................	—	—	—	—	≥ 5,000
Interest Coverage Ratio.........	—	—	—	—	≥ 1.15

EXHIBIT 5

Fly-By-Night International Group
Long-Term Debt
(amounts in thousands)
(Case 9.1)

	1990	1991	1992	1993	1994
April 30					
Notes Payable to Banks					
Variable Rate	$ 3,497	$ 2,504	$ 2,086	$30,495	$ 44,702
Fixed Rate	1,228	3,562	6,292	14,679	13,555
Notes Payable to Finance Companies					
Variable Rate	10,808	1,667	1,320	—	—
Fixed Rate	325	—	—	—	—
Capitalized Lease					
Obligations	5,297	70	1,295	2,865	2,333
Other................	1,660	39	600	—	—
Total	$22,815	$ 7,842	$11,593	$48,039	$ 60,590
Less Current Portion ...	(2,774)	(1,104)	(1,789)	(7,018)	(60,590)
Net	$20,041	$ 6,738	$ 9,804	$41,021	$ —

EXHIBIT 6

Fly-By-Night International Group
Income Tax Expense
(amounts in thousands)
(Case 9.1)

	Year Ended April 30				
	1990	**1991**	**1992**	**1993**	**1994**
Current					
Federal	$ —	$—	$ —	$ —	$ —
State	—	—	—	—	—
Deferred					
Federal	$(85)	$67	$685	$380	$(845)
State	(5)	4	118	30	(55)
Total	$(90)	$71	$803	$410	$(900)

As of April 30, 1994, the company is in default of its debt covenants. It is also in default with respect to covenants underlying its capitalized lease obligations. As a result, lenders have the right to accelerate repayment of their loans. Accordingly, the company has classified all of its long-term debt as a current liability.

The company has entered into operating leases for aircraft and other equipment. The estimated present value of the minimum lease payments under these operating leases as of April 30 of each year is

1990	$4,083
1991	3,971
1992	3,594
1993	3,142
1994	2,706

Note G: *Income Taxes.* Income tax expense appears in Exhibit 6. The cumulative tax loss and tax credit carryovers as of April 30 of each year are as follows:

April 30	Tax Loss	Tax Credit
1990	$ 4,500	$750
1991	2,100	450
1992	1,400	300
1993	5,200	280
1994	10,300	250

The deferred tax provision results from timing differences in the recognition of revenues and expenses for income tax and financial reporting. The sources and amounts of these differences for each year are as follows:

	1990	1991	1992	1993	1994
Depreciation..............	$ 778	$(770)	$ 336	$ 503	$ —
Aircraft Modification Costs...	703	982	382	1,218	—
Net Operating Losses........	(1,729)	—	290	(1,384)	(900)
Other.....................	158	(141)	(205)	73	—
	$ (90)	$ 71	$ 803	$ 410	$(900)

A reconciliation of the effective tax rate with the statutory tax rate is as follows:

	1990	1991	1992	1993	1994
Federal Taxes at Statutory Rate...	(34.0%)	34.0%	34.0%	35.0%	(35.0%)
State Income Taxes.............	(3.0)	3.0	3.0	3.0	(2.5)
Effect of Net Operating Loss and Investment Credits........	—	(29.9)	(7.2)	—	16.5
Other.......................	(12.0)	11.1	22.2	2.9	2.0
	(49.0%)	18.2%	52.0%	40.9%	(19.0%)

Note H: *Market Price Information.* The company's common stock trades on the NASDAQ National Market System under the symbol FBN. Trading in the company's common stock commenced on January 10, 1990. High and low bid prices during each fiscal year are as follows:

Fiscal Year	High Bid	Low Bid
1990	$ 5.25	$3.25
1991	$ 4.63	$3.00
1992	$11.25	$3.25
1993	$14.63	$6.25
1994	$16.50	$9.50

On December 29, 1994, the company announced that the NASDAQ decided to discontinue quoting the company's common stock because of the company's failure to comply with NASDAQ's filing requirements.

Ownership of the company's stock at various dates appears in the following table:

	April 30				
	1990	1991	1992	1993	1994
Douglas Mather.............	75%	75%	72%	68%	42%
Public	25	25	24	23	48
Company ESOP.............	—	—	4	9	10
	100%	100%	100%	100%	100%
Common Shares Outstanding (000s)	2,000.0	2,000.0	2,095.0	2,222.8	3,357.5

MASSACHUSETTS STOVE COMPANY: BANK LENDING DECISION

Massachusetts Stove Company manufactures wood-burning stoves for the heating of homes and businesses. The company has approached you as chief lending officer for the Massachusetts Regional Bank, seeking to increase its loan from the current level of $93,091 as of September 15, 1991, to $125,000. Jane O'Neil, Chief Executive Officer and majority stockholder of the company, indicates that the company needs the loan to finance the working capital required for an expected 25 percent annual increase in sales during the next two years, to repay suppliers, and to provide funds for expected nonrecurring legal and retooling costs.

The company's wood stoves have two distinguishing characteristics: (1) the metal frame of the stoves includes inlaid ceramic tile, which increases the intensity and duration of the heat provided by the stoves and enhances their appearance as an attractive piece of furniture, and (2) a catalytic combuster, which adds heating potential to the stoves and reduces air pollution.

The company manufactures wood-burning stoves in a single plant located in Greenfield, Massachusetts. It purchases metal castings for the stoves from foundries located in Germany and Belgium. The ceramic tile comes from a supplier in Canada. These purchases are denominated in U.S. dollars. The catalytic combuster is purchased from a supplier in the United States. The manufacturing process is essentially an assembly operation. The plant employs an average of eight workers. The two keys to quality control are structural air tightness and effective operation of the catalytic combuster.

The company rents approximately 60 percent of the 25,000 square foot building that it uses for manufacturing and administrative activities. This building also houses the company's factory showroom. The remaining 40 percent of the building is not currently rented.

The company's marketing of wood stoves follows three channels:

1. *Wholesaling of Stoves to Retail Hardware Stores:* This channel represents approximately 20 percent of the company's sales in units.
2. *Retail Direct Marketing to Individuals in All 50 States:* This channel utilizes (a) national advertising in construction and design magazines and (b) the sending of brochures to potential customers identified from personal inquiries. This channel represents approximately 70 percent of the company's sales in units. The company is the only firm in the industry with a strategic emphasis on retail direct marketing.
3. *Retailing from the Company's Showroom:* This channel represents approximately 10 percent of the company's sales in units.

The company offers three payment options to retail purchasers of its stoves:

1. *Full Payment:* Check, money order, or charge to a third-party credit card.
2. *Lay-Away Plan:* Monthly payments over a period not exceeding one year. The company ships the stove after receiving the final payment.
3. *Installment Financing Plan:* The company has a financing arrangement with a local bank to finance the purchase of stoves by credit-approved customers. The company is not liable if customers fail to repay their installment bank loans.

The imposition of strict, new air emission standards by the Environmental Protection Agency (EPA) has resulted in a major change in the wood stove industry. By 1990, firms were required by EPA regulations to demonstrate that their wood stoves met or surpassed specified air emission standards. Not only were these standards more strict than industry practices at the time, but also firms had to engage in numerous company-sponsored and independent testing of their stoves to satisfy EPA regulators. As a consequence, the number of firms in the wood stove industry decreased from over 200 in the late 1980s to approximately 35 by 1991.

The company received approval for its Tile Stove I in 1990, after incurring retooling and testing costs of $63,001. It capitalized these costs in the Property, Plant, and Equipment account. It depreciates these costs over the five-year EPA approval period. A second stove, Tile Stove II, is currently undergoing retooling and testing. The company incurred costs of $19,311 in the 1990 fiscal year and $8,548 in the 1991 fiscal year on this stove and has received preliminary EPA approval. It anticipates additional design, tooling, and testing costs of approximately $55,000 in the 1992 fiscal year and $33,000 in the 1993 fiscal year in order to obtain final EPA approval.

The company holds an option to purchase the building in which it is located for $608,400. The option also permits the company to assume the unpaid balance on a low interest rate loan on the building from the New England Regional Industrial Development Authority. The interest rate on this loan is adjusted annually and equals 80 percent of the bank prime interest rate. The unpaid balance on the loan exceeds the option price and will result in a cash transfer to the company from the owner of the building at the time of transfer. The company exercised its option in 1989, but the owner of the building refused to comply with the option provisions. The company sued the owner. The case has gone through the lower court system in Massachusetts and is currently under review at the Massachusetts Supreme Court. The company incurred legal costs totaling $68,465 through the 1991 fiscal year and anticipates additional costs of approximately $45,000 in the 1992 fiscal year. The lower courts have ruled in favor of the company's position on all of the major issues in the case. The company expects the Massachusetts Supreme Court to concur with the decisions of the lower courts when it renders its final decision in the spring of 1992. The company has held discussions with two prospective tenants for the 10,000 square feet of the building that it does not use in its operations.

Jane O'Neil owns 51 percent of the company's common stock. The remaining stockholders include John O'Neil (chief financial officer and father of Jane O'Neil), Mark Forest (vice president for manufacturing), and four independent local investors.

To assist in the loan decision, the company provides you with financial statements, notes, and selected financial ratios for the three fiscal years ending August 31, 1989, 1990, and 1991 (see Exhibits 1 through 4). These financial statements were prepared by John O'Neil, chief financial officer, and are not audited. The company also provides you with pro forma financial statements for the 1992 and 1993 fiscal years to demonstrate both its need for the loan and its ability to repay. The loan requested involves an increase in the current loan amount from $93,091 to $125,000. The company will pay interest monthly and repay the $31,909 additional amount borrowed by August 31, 1993.

The assumptions underlying the pro forma financial statements are as follows:

Sales: Projected to increase 25 percent annually during the next two years, after increasing 17.7 percent in the 1990 fiscal year and 21.9 percent in the 1991 fiscal year. The increase reflects continuing market opportunities related to the company's strategic emphasis on retail direct marketing and to the expected continuing contraction in the number of competitors in the industry.

EXHIBIT 1

Massachusetts Stove Company—Income Statements
(Case 9.2)

	Year Ended August 31				
	Actual			**Pro Forma**	
	1989	**1990**	**1991**	**1992**	**1993**
Sales	$ 665,771	$ 783,754	$ 955,629	$1,194,537	$1,493,171
Cost of Goods Sold.........	(460,797)	(474,156)	(514,907)	(597,268)	(746,585)
Selling and Administrative....	(165,470)	(278,658)	(378,532)	(477,815)	(597,268)
Legal (Note 1)	(28,577)	(30,092)	(9,796)	(45,000)	—
Interest	(38,109)	(36,183)	(35,945)	(38,138)	(38,562)
Income Tax (Note 2)........	—	—	—	—	—
Net Income (Loss)..........	$ (27,182)	$ (35,335)	$ 16,449	$ 36,316	$ 110,756

Cost of Goods Sold: Most manufacturing costs vary with sales. The company projects cost of goods sold to equal 50 percent of sales, having declined from 60.2 percent of sales in the 1989 fiscal year to 53.9 percent of sales in the 1991 fiscal year. The reductions resulted from a higher proportion of retail sales in the sales mix (which have a higher gross margin than wholesale sales), a more favorable pricing environment in the industry (fewer competitors), switching to lower-cost suppliers, and more efficient production.

Selling and Administrative Expenses: The company projects these costs to equal 40 percent of sales, having increased from 25.2 percent of sales in the 1989 fiscal year to 38.3 percent of sales in the 1991 fiscal year. The increases resulted from a heavier emphasis on retail sales, which require more aggressive marketing than wholesale sales.

Legal Expenses: The additional $45,000 of legal costs represent the best estimate by the company's attorneys.

Interest Expense: Interest expense has averaged approximately 9 percent of short- and long-term borrowing during the last three years. The pro formas assume a continuation of the 9 percent average rate.

Income Tax Expense: The company has a tax loss carryforward of $617,285 as of August 31, 1991. This tax loss carryforward comes almost entirely from the acquisition of a lawn products company in 1985. The company discontinued the lawn products business in 1989. It does not anticipate having to pay income taxes during the next two years.

Cash: The pro forma amounts for cash represent a plug to equate projected assets with projected liabilities and shareholders' equity. Projected liabilities include the requested loan during the 1992 fiscal year and its repayment during the 1993 fiscal year.

Accounts Receivable and Inventories: Projected to grow at the growth rate in sales.

Property, Plant, and Equipment: Capital expenditures for fiscal year 1992 include $55,000 cost for retooling the Tile Stove II and $7,500 for other equipment, and for fiscal year 1993 include $33,000 for retooling the Tile Stove II and $14,500 for other equipment. The pro formas exclude the cost of acquiring the building, its related debt, the cash to be received at the time of transfer, and rental revenues from leasing the unused 40 percent of the building to other businesses.

EXHIBIT 2

Massachusetts Stove Company
Balance Sheets
(Case 9.2)

	Year Ended August 31					
	Actual				Pro Forma	
	1988	1989	1990	1991	1992	1993
Assets						
Cash	$ 3,925	$ 11,707	$ 8,344	$ 37,726	$ 5,094	$ 27,053
Accounts Receivable	94,606	54,772	44,397	31,964	39,955	49,944
Inventories	239,458	208,260	209,004	225,490	281,863	352,328
Total Current Assets	$ 337,989	$ 274,739	$ 261,745	$ 295,180	$ 326,912	$ 429,325
Property, Plant, and Equipment (at Cost)	$ 258,870	$ 316,854	$ 362,399	$ 377,784	$ 440,284	$ 487,784
Accumulated Depreciation	(205,338)	(228,985)	(250,189)	(274,347)	(304,570)	(339,792)
Property, Plant, and Equipment (Net)	$ 53,532	$ 87,869	$ 112,210	$ 103,437	$ 135,714	$ 147,992
Other Assets	$ 17,888	$ 17,888	$ 17,594	$ 17,006	$ 16,418	$ 15,830
Total Assets	$ 409,409	$ 380,496	$ 391,549	$ 415,623	$ 479,044	$ 593,147
Liabilities and Shareholders' Equity						
Accounts Payable	$ 148,579	$ 139,879	$ 189,889	$ 160,905	$ 185,041	$ 212,797
Notes Payable—Banks (Note 3)	152,985	140,854	125,256	93,091	125,000	93,091
Other Current Liabilities (Note 4)	13,340	11,440	23,466	62,440	33,500	41,000
Total Current Liabilities	$ 314,904	$ 292,173	$ 338,611	$ 316,436	$ 343,541	$ 346,888
Long-Term Debt (Note 3)	248,000	269,000	268,950	298,750	298,750	298,750
Total Liabilities	$ 562,904	$ 561,173	$ 607,561	$ 615,186	$ 642,291	$ 645,638
Common Stock	$ 2,000	$ 2,000	$ 2,000	$ 2,000	$ 2,000	$ 2,000
Additional Paid-in Capital	435,630	435,630	435,630	435,630	435,630	435,630
Accumulated Deficit	(591,125)	(618,307)	(653,642)	(637,193)	(600,877)	(490,121)
Total Shareholders' Equity	$(153,495)	$(180,677)	$(216,012)	$(199,563)	$(163,247)	$ (52,491)
Total Liabilities and Shareholders' Equity	$ 409,409	$ 380,496	$ 391,549	$ 415,623	$ 479,044	$ 593,147

EXHIBIT 3

Massachusetts Stove Company
Statements of Cash Flows
(Case 9.2)

| | Year Ended August 31 | | | | |
| | Actual | | | Pro Forma | |
	1989	1990	1991	1992	1993
Operations					
Net Income (Loss)..........................	$(27,182)	$(35,335)	$ 16,449	$ 36,316	$110,756
Depreciation and Amortization	23,647	21,498	24,746	30,811	35,810
(Increase) Decrease in Accounts Receivable ...	39,834	10,375	12,433	(7,991)	(9,989)
(Increase) Decrease in Inventories	31,198	(744)	(16,486)	(56,373)	(70,465)
Increase (Decrease) in Accounts Payable	(8,700)	50,010	(28,984)	24,136	27,756
Increase (Decrease) in Other Current Liabilities	(1,900)	12,026	38,974	(28,940)	7,500
Cash Flow from Operations.................	$ 56,897	$ 57,830	$ 47,132	$ (2,041)	$101,368
Investing					
Fixed Assets Acquired.....................	$(57,984)	$(45,545)	$(15,385)	$(62,500)	$ (47,500)
Financing					
Increase (Decrease) in Short-Term Borrowing .	$(12,131)	$(15,598)	$(32,165)	$ 31,909	$ (31,909)
Increase (Decrease) in Long-Term Borrowing..	21,000	(50)	29,800	—	—
Cash Flow from Financing	$ 8,869	$(15,648)	$ (2,365)	$ 31,909	$ (31,909)
Change in Cash...........................	$ 7,782	$ (3,363)	$ 29,382	$(32,632)	$ 21,959
Cash—Beginning of Year..................	3,925	11,707	8,344	37,726	5,094
Cash—End of Year	$ 11,707	$ 8,344	$ 37,726	$ 5,094	$ 27,053

Accumulated Depreciation: Continuation of the historical relation between depreciation expense and the cost of property, plant and equipment.

Other Assets: Continuation of the historical amortization rate for intangibles.

Accounts Payable: Projected to increase each year by the 25 percent growth rate in sales but to decrease by 10 percent each year due to the ability to repay suppliers more quickly with proceeds of the increased bank loan.

Notes Payable: Projected to increase in the amount of the bank loan in the 1992 fiscal year and to decrease by the loan repayment in the 1993 fiscal year.

Other Current Liabilities: The large increase at the end of the 1991 fiscal year resulted from a major promotional offer in the summer of 1991, which increased the amount of deposits by customers. The projected amounts for the 1992 and 1993 fiscal years represent more normal expected levels of deposits.

Long-Term Debt: Long-term borrowing represents loans from shareholders to the company. The company does not plan to repay any of these loans in the near future.

EXHIBIT 4

Massachusetts Stove Company
Financial Ratios
(Case 9.2)

	Actual			Pro Forma	
	1989	1990	1991	1992	1993
Profit Margin for Return on Assets	(1.6%)	(0.1%)	5.5%	6.2%	10.0%
Assets Turnover	1.7	2.0	2.4	2.7	2.8
Return on Assets	(2.8%)	(0.2%)	13.0%	16.6%	27.9%
Cost of Goods Sold ÷ Sales	69.2%	60.5%	53.9%	50.0%	50.0%
Selling and Administrative ÷ Sales	24.9%	35.6%	39.6%	40.0%	40.0%
Days Accounts Receivable	41	23	15	11	11
Days Inventory	177	161	154	155	155
Days Accounts Payable	123	127	120	97	89
Current Ratio	0.9	0.8	0.9	1.0	1.2
Quick Ratio	0.2	0.2	0.2	0.1	0.2
Cash Flow from Operations ÷ Average Current					
Liabilities	18.7%	18.3%	14.4%	(0.6%)	29.4%
Total Liabilities ÷ Total Assets	147.5%	155.2%	148.0%	134.1%	108.8%
Long-Term Debt ÷ Total Assets	70.7%	68.7%	71.9%	62.4%	50.4%
Cash Flow from Operations ÷ Average Total					
Liabilities	10.1%	9.9%	7.7%	(0.3%)	15.7%
Interest Coverage Ratio	0.3	—	1.5	2.0	3.9
Cash Flow from Operations ÷ Capital Expenditures ...	1.0	1.3	3.1	—	2.1

Retained Earnings: The change each year represents net income or net loss from operations. The company does not pay dividends.

Statement of Cash Flows: Amounts are taken from the change in various accounts on the actual and pro forma balance sheets.

REQUIRED

Would you make the loan to the company in accordance with the stated terms? In responding, consider the reasonableness of the company's projections, positive and negative factors affecting the industry and the company, and the likely ability of the company to repay the loan.

NOTES TO FINANCIAL STATEMENTS

Note 1: The company has incurred legal costs to enforce its option to purchase the building used in its manufacturing and administrative activities. The case is under review at the Massachusetts Supreme Court, with a decision expected in the spring of 1992.

Note 2: The company has a tax loss carryforward of $617,285 as of August 31, 1991.

Note 3: The notes payable to banks are secured by machinery and equipment, shares of common stock of companies traded on The New York Stock Exchange owned by two shareholders, and by personal guarantees of three of the shareholders. The long-term debt consists of unsecured loans from three shareholders.

Note 4: Other current liabilities includes the following:

	August 31			
	1988	1989	1990	1991
Customer Deposits	$11,278	$ 9,132	$20,236	$59,072
Employee Taxes Withheld	2,062	2,308	3,230	3,368
	$13,340	$11,440	$23,466	$62,440

CASE 9.3

KROGER COMPANY: RISKY TIMES*

The Kroger Company operates one of the largest supermarket chains in the United States. During the fall of 1988, Kroger became the target of unfriendly takeover bids by the Haft family and Kohlberg, Kravis, Roberts and Company. Prior to these bids, Kroger's common shares traded for $34 per share. The bidding was started at a price of $55 per share and increased to $64 per share. To defend itself against a takeover, Kroger issued a package of senior and subordinated debt totaling $3.6 billion and used the proceeds to partially fund a special dividend $3.9 billion. The special dividend included cash of $40 per share (total of $3.2 billion) and a senior subordinated, increasing rate debenture with a face value of $12.50 and a market value of $8.69 per share (total of $695 million).

This case analyzes the factors that made Kroger an attractive buyout candidate in 1988 and the subsequent effect of the special dividend on its profitability and risk. Exhibits 1, 2, and 3 present Kroger's financial statements for its fiscal years ending December 1986 to December 1990. Several unusual items affect these financial statements.

1. *Disposal of Drug Store Operations:* Kroger sold its drug store operations in 1986 and included a loss in discontinued operations for that year.
2. *Restructuring Provisions:* Kroger made two major provisions for restructuring of its business. It made a pretax provision of $164 million in 1986 to downside corporate headquarters staff and close 100 stores and related manufacturing operations. Kroger made a pretax provision of $195 million in 1988 to cover a portion of the cost of its financial restructuring and special dividend.
3. *Change in Accounting for Income Taxes:* Kroger adopted the liability method of accounting for deferred income taxes in 1987. Because income tax rates declined as a result of the Tax Reform Act of 1986, Kroger's deferred tax liability overstated the amount of taxes it expected to pay when timing differences reversed. Kroger reduced its deferred tax liability and included a special credit in earnings of $63 million in 1987.
4. *Write-Off of Deferred Restructuring Costs:* Kroger originally capitalized as assets certain debt issue costs incurred in connection with its corporate restructuring in 1988. Kroger

---

*The author gratefully acknowledges the assistance of Yannis Vasatis in the preparation of this case.

EXHIBIT 1

Kroger Company
Comparative Income Statements
(in millions)
(Case 9.3)

	1986	1987	1988	1989	1990
Sales	$ 17,123	$ 17,660	$ 19,053	$ 19,104	$ 20,261
Other Revenues & Gains	13	11	10	16	6
Cost of Goods Sold....................	(13,163)	(13,696)	(14,824)	(14,846)	(15,670)
Sell. & Admin. Expense...............	(3,609)	(3,553)	(3,784)	(3,652)	(3,918)
Restructuring (Charges) Credits[a]	(164)	8	(195)	18	27
Interest Expense	(104)	(107)	(208)	(649)	(564)
Income Tax Expense[a]	(40)	(140)	(17)	(7)	(59)
Income from Continued Operations......	$ 56	$ 183	$ 35	$ (16)	$ 83
Income from Discontinued Operations....	(4)[b]	0	0	0	0
Extraordinary Gains (Losses)...........	0	0	0	(56)[d]	(1)[d]
Changes in Accounting Principles	0	63[c]	0	0	0
Preferred Stock Dividend..............	(3)	(6)	(16)	(2)	0
Net Income to Common..............	$ 49	$ 240	$ 19	$ (74)	$ 82
Average Number of Shares Outstanding ..	86.9	80.4	79.3	81.6	86.6

[a]Includes restructuring changes and credits (and related tax effects) as follows:

   1986: Provision for downsizing corporate overhead staff and closing of 100 stores, $164 million charge; tax effect, $82 million.

   1987: Reversal of provision in 1986 when actual charges and costs were less than expected, $8 million credit; tax effect, $4 million.

   1988: Provision for corporate restructuring relating to issue of debt and distribution of special dividend, $195 million charge; tax effect, $67 million.

   1989, 1990: Reversal of provision for corporate restructuring when actual charges were less than anticipated, $18 million credit in 1989 (tax effect 6 million); $27 million credit in 1990 (tax effect, $9 million).

[b]Loss from operations of drug store segment sold during 1986.

[c]Change to the liability method of accounting for deferred income taxes.

[d]Write-off of deferred costs incurred in corporate restructuring in 1988 (net of tax effects).

later refinanced some of the debt in 1989 and wrote off deferred costs totaling $56 million in 1989 and $1 million in 1990.

5. *Operating Lease Commitments:* Kroger leases a substantial portion of its stores under operating lease arrangements. The present value of these operating lease commitments when discounted at 10 percent appear below (in millions):

1985	$1,785	1987	$1,823	1989	$1,692
1986	$1,693	1988	$1,732	1990	$1,632

Exhibit 4 presents selected financial statement and market price data for Kroger and three leading competitors for fiscal years 1985, 1986, and 1987, the three years prior to Kroger's

EXHIBIT 2

Kroger Company
Comparative Balance Sheets
(in millions)
(Case 9.3)

	1985	1986	1987	1988	1989	1990
Cash	$ 106	$ 212	$ 113	$ 211	$ 115	$ 55
Accounts Receivable	215	262	253	258	280	277
Inventories	1,473	1,197	1,448	1,275	1,395	1,448
Other Current Assets[a]	208	277	341	726	258	170
Current Assets	$2,002	$1,948	$2,155	$ 2,470	$ 2,048	$ 1,950
Investments	0	0	0	0	0	0
Property, Plant, & Equip. (net) . . .	1,991	1,968	2,137	1,910	1,912	1,874
Other Assets	185	170	168	234	282	295
Total Assets	$4,178	$4,086	$4,460	$ 4,614	$ 4,242	$ 4,119
Accounts Payable—Trade	$ 986	$ 912	$1,005	$ 1,095	$ 1,132	$ 1,198
Notes Payable—Nontrade	122	10	315	6	13	0
Current Part Long-Term Debt	42	50	29	341	171	96
Other Current Liabilities	577	738	614	723	753	768
Current Liabilities	$1,727	$1,710	$1,963	$ 2,165	$ 2,069	$ 2,062
Long-Term Debt	925	830	987	4,724	4,724	4,558
Deferred Tax	314	292	292	302	294	273
Other Noncurrent Liabilities	23	99	84	102	120	86
Total Liabilities	$2,989	$2,931	$3,326	$ 7,293	$ 7,207	$ 6,979
Preferred Stock	$ 0	$ 125	$ 125	$ 250	$ 0	$ 0
Common Stock	396	410	424	101	102	104
Retained Earnings	980	939	1,095	(2,517)	(2,609)	(2,541)
Treasury Stock	(187)	(319)	(510)	(513)	(458)	(423)
Shareholders' Equity	$1,189	$1,155	$1,134	$(2,679)	$(2,965)	$(2,860)
Total Equities	$4,178	$4,086	$4,460	$ 4,614	$ 4,242	$ 4,119

[a]Includes assets that Kroger expects to sell at a net realizable value of $88 million in 1985, $101 million in 1986, $115 million in 1987, $483 million in 1988, $37 million in 1989, and $23 million in 1990.

special dividend. These data use the originally reported amounts for each company (except for the elimination of Kroger restructuring charge for 1986). The rates of return ratios use end-of-the-period values for assets and common shareholders' equity instead of the average values for these items.

REQUIRED

a. An analyst desires to study the changes in the profitability and risk of Kroger prior to and subsequent to the special dividend to assess why Kroger needed to pay the special dividend and how well it performed with its heavier debt load after the special dividend. Discuss the adjustments that the analyst should make to the financial statement data in Exhibits 1 to 3 before performing the profitability and risk analysis.

EXHIBIT 3

Kroger Company
Comparative Statement of Cash Flows (in millions)
(Case 9.3)

	1986	1987	1988	1989	1990
Operations					
Income from Continuing Operations .	$ 56	$ 183	$ 35	$ (16)	$ 83
Depreciation and Amortization	231	223	254	241	245
Other Addbacks...................	52	0	8	104	113
Other Subtractions	0	(20)	0	0	0
WC Provided by Operations.......	$ 339	$ 386	$ 297	$ 329	$ 441
(Increase) Decrease in Receivables ...	(45)	8	(6)	(1)	4
(Increase) Decrease in Inventories ...	83	(261)	15	(84)	(53)
(Increase) Decrease in Other CA	(50)	(39)	(24)	42	75
Increase (Decrease) in Accounts Pay-Trade.........................	(74)	93	90	37	66
Increase (Decrease) in Other CL	120	(7)	157	85	(35)
Cash from Continued Operations..	$ 373	$ 180	$ 529	$ 408	$ 498
Cash from Discontinued Operations..	(4)	0	0	0	0
Cash from Extreme Gain/Loss	0	0	0	0	0
Net Cash Flow from Operations	$ 369	$ 180	$ 529	$ 408	$ 498
Investing					
Fixed Assets Sold.................	$ 129	$ 62	$ 93	$ 13	$ 25
Investments Sold	406[a]	21	0	0	30
Fixed Assets Acquired.............	(475)	(416)	(324)	(131)	(219)
Investments Acquired	(26)	0	(86)	(15)	(14)
Other Investment Transactions	(22)	(76)	7	299[b]	(13)
Net Cash Flow from Investing	$ 12	$(409)	$ (310)	$ 166	$(191)
Financing					
Increase Short-Term Borrowing	$ 0	$ 305	$ 0	$ 0	$ 0
Increase Long-Term Borrowing......	164	141	4,191[c]	2,706[f]	306
Issue of Capital Stock..............	146	12	181	16	22
Decrease Short-Term Borrowing.....	(112)	0	(309)	0	0
Decrease Long-Term Borrowing	(241)	(48)	(861)[d]	(3,141)[f]	(697)
Acquisition of Capital Stock.........	(140)	(191)	(3)	(251)	0
Dividends	(93)	(91)	(3,347)[e]	(2)	0
Other Financing Transactions	2	2	26	2	1
Net Cash Flow from Financing......	$(274)	$ 130	$ (122)	$ (670)	$(368)
Net Change in Cash.............	$ 107	$ (99)	$ 97	$ (96)	$ (61)

[a]Represents proceeds from the sale of drug store operations.

[b]Includes $224 million from the sale of assets; see Note a to Exhibit 2.

[c]Includes $3.6 billion of financing for payment of special dividend.

[d]Includes $360 million of existing debt obligations refinanced as part of restructuring.

[e]Includes approximately $3.2 billion in the cash portion of the special dividend.

[f]Includes $625 million of senior debentures and $625 million of subordinated debentures, the proceeds of which refinanced $1,000 million of senior, increasing rate subordinated debentures issued in 1988 to finance the special dividend.

EXHIBIT 4

Comparative Data for Supermarket Competitors
(Case 9.3)

Fiscal Year	Total Assets	Return on Assets	Long-Term Debt ÷ Long-Term Capital	Return on Common Equity	Current Ratio	Price-Earnings Ratio
Kroger						
1985	$4,178	4.7%	38.1%	15.7%	1.2	12
1986	$4,076	3.4%[a]	34.4%[a]	11.8%[a]	1.1	11[a]
1987	$4,460	4.4%	40.9%	18.0%	1.1	11
A&P						
1985	$1,664	3.7%	33.6%	8.9%	1.3	15
1986	$2,080	3.7%	35.3%	9.7%	1.1	14
1987	$2,243	4.8%	30.4%	12.9%	1.1	14
American Stores						
1985	$3,463	4.4%	50.5%	18.0%	1.2	15
1986	$3,590	4.1%	47.0%	14.9%	1.2	15
1987	$3,650	4.3%	46.6%	15.2%	1.2	15
Winn Dixie Stores						
1985	$705	9.0%	12.8%	17.7%	1.6	14
1986	$830	8.9%	12.3%	17.1%	1.7	16
1987	$851	8.1%	12.2%	15.6%	1.6	17

[a]The amounts for Kroger for 1986 exclude a $164 million ($82 million net of taxes) restructuring charge.

SOURCE: Standard & Poor, *Stock Reports*.

b. Prepare a profitability and risk analysis of Kroger for 1986 and 1987. Using this analysis and the data in Exhibit 4, indicate the apparent reasons that Kroger became a takeover target in the fall of 1988.

c. Prepare a profitability and risk analysis of Kroger for 1988 to 1990. Evaluate the changes in Kroger's profitability and risk since the special dividend.

CHAPTER 10

PRO FORMA
FINANCIAL STATEMENTS

Learning Objectives

1. Observe the flow of preparing pro forma financial statements that includes projecting amounts in the following order: (a) sales, (b) operating expenses excluding the cost of debt financing, (c) assets, (d) liabilities and shareholders' equity excluding retained earnings, (e) interest expense on debt financing, (f) net income, dividends, and the change in retained earnings, and (g) the statement of cash flows.
2. Observe the critical role of sales projections in preparing pro forma financial statements.
3. Understand the conditions when common size percentages, growth rates, and turnovers provide the best projections of financial statement amounts.
4. Prepare comprehensive pro forma financial statements.

The economic value of any resource is a function of the returns expected from that resource relative to the risk involved. Previous chapters discussed tools for analyzing the profitability (returns) and risks of a firm using published financial statement data. This analytical task is a backward-looking exercise. Valuing any economic resource, however, is a forward-looking exercise. The task is to project future returns and risks. The analytical tool used in making these projections is *pro forma financial statements*. The analyst makes predictions about likely future general economic conditions, specific industry conditions, and firm-specific abilities and strategies. The analyst then incorporates these predictions into a set of pro forma, or projected, financial statements. A study of the past profitability and risks of a firm often assists in making these projections. This chapter describes and illustrates the techniques for preparing pro forma financial statements. Chapters 11 and 12 explore the use of pro forma financial statements in valuation. Chapter 11 presumes that *projected cash flows* is the appropriate measure of returns for valuing a firm. Chapter 12 presumes that *projected earnings* is the appropriate measure of returns.

PREPARING PRO FORMA FINANCIAL STATEMENTS

The preparation of pro forma financial statements involves the following steps:

1. Project sales revenue for the desired number of future periods.
2. Project operating expenses (cost of goods sold, selling and administrative, income taxes) and derive projected operating income. Operating income is the numerator of ROA. It excludes all financing costs and related tax effects.
3. Project the assets, liabilities, and shareholders' equity (except retained earnings) needed to support the level of operations projected in steps 1 and 2.
4. Determine the cost of financing the capital structure derived in step 3. Subtract the after-tax cost of this financing from operating income to obtain projected net income and retained earnings.
5. Derive the statement of cash flows from the projected income statements and comparative balance sheets.

We illustrate this five-step procedure for Pepsi for Year 9 through Year 12. Appendix B presents the financial statements and notes for Pepsi for Year 8. Appendix C presents printouts of FSAP for Pepsi. We use selected data from these printouts in making the projections for Pepsi.

PROJECTING SALES

The key starting point is projected sales. The expected level of sales serves as a basis for deriving most of the other amounts in the pro forma financial statements.

Sales has both a volume component and a price component. Although firms typically do not report separately these two elements of total sales, the analyst might use them as a framework for thinking about likely future sales. A firm in a mature industry (for example, consumer foods) with little change expected in its market share might anticipate volume increases equal to the growth rate in the general population. A firm that has increased its operating capacity consistent with the high growth rate anticipated in a particular industry (for example, biotechnology) might use this growth rate in projecting volume increases. Projecting price increases involves consideration of the expected rate of general price inflation in the economy as well as specific industry factors that might affect demand, such as excess capacity, shortages of raw materials, prices of substitute products, and similar factors. A capital-intensive industry, such as paper manufacturing, often takes several years to add new capacity. If firms in this industry anticipate operating near capacity for the next few years, then price increases are likely to occur. On the other hand, if excess capacity already exists or new capacity is expected to become available soon, then price increases are less likely. A firm operating in an industry that is expected to transition from the high growth to the maturity phase of its life cycle (for example, some portions of the computer industry) might expect decreases from the historical rate of volume and price increases.

If sales have grown at a reasonably steady rate in prior periods and there is no indication that economic, industry, or firm-specific factors will change significantly, then the analyst can project this growth rate into the future. If a major acquisition or sale affected the historical growth rate, then the analyst should filter out the effect of this event when making projections (unless the firm's strategy is to make additional acquisitions). The most difficult sales projections occur for firms with cyclical sales patterns (for example, heavy machinery, computers). Their historical growth rates for sales might reflect wide variations in both direction and amount from year to year. The analyst should project a varying growth rate that maintains this cyclical sales pattern in these cases.

The historical growth rates in sales for Pepsi appear below:

Year 5	16.8%
Year 6	8.4%
Year 7	13.9%
Year 8	13.9%
Four-Year Compound Average	13.2%

Earlier chapters indicated that the consumer foods industry in the United States is in its maturity phase. Industry sales have grown recently at the growth rate for the general population, approximately 2 percent per year. The primary vehicles for growth by consumer foods companies are acquisitions and international sales. Pepsi made acquisitions in each of the last four years. Assuming that Pepsi continues to grow through acquisitions and international expansion, we use a compound annual growth rate of 13.9 percent in projecting sales, the growth rate in sales during Year 7 and Year 8. This growth rate is just slightly more than the 13.2 percent compound annual growth rate over the last four years. Projected sales appear below (in millions):

	Amount[a]	Percentage Change
Year 8 Actual Sales	$25,021	—
Year 9 Projected Sales	$28,499	13.9%
Year 10 Projected Sales	$32,460	13.9%
Year 11 Projected Sales	$36,972	13.9%
Year 12 Projected Sales	$42,111	13.9%

[a]Amounts rounded.

PROJECTING OPERATING EXPENSES

The procedure for projecting operating expenses depends on the behavior of various cost items. If all costs behave as variable costs and the analyst anticipates no changes in their behavior relative to sales, then the common size income statement percentages can serve as the basis for projecting future operating expenses. We would multiply projected sales by the cost of goods sold percentage, selling and administrative expense percentage, and so on to derive the amounts for operating expenses. Alternatively, we can project each operating expense to grow at the same rate as sales (13.9 percent for Pepsi).

On the other hand, if the cost structure reflects a high proportion of fixed cost that will not change as sales increase, then using the common size income statement approach described above can result in poor projections. In this case, the analyst should attempt to estimate the variable and fixed cost structure of the firm. Alternatively, the analyst can use the historical growth rates for individual cost items. Capital-intensive manufacturing firms often have high proportions of fixed costs in their cost structures. One clue suggesting the presence of fixed costs is that the percentage change in cost of goods sold or selling, and administrative expenses in prior years differs significantly from the percentage change in sales. Using the historical growth rates for individual cost items is one way of reflecting the effects of different mixes of variable and fixed costs.

Pepsi has a relatively low level of fixed costs. Thus, we project Pepsi's operating expenses using the common size income statement approach. Pepsi's cost of goods sold percentage declined between Year 6 (48.5 percent) and Year 7 (47.8 percent) but was relatively stable between Year 7 and Year 8 (47.7 percent). We use 47.7 percent to project cost of goods sold. The selling and administrative expense percentage varied between 40.4 percent and 40.6 percent during Year 5, Year 6, and Year 8 (showing an apparent one-time increase to 41.4 percent in Year 7). We use 40.6 percent to project selling and administrative expenses.

Pepsi's other revenue represents interest income from investments in marketable securities. Pepsi's investments in marketable securities have varied between $1,629 million and $1,889 million during the last four years. It appears that Pepsi maintains a portfolio of such investments, either as a temporary cushion for cash shortages or more likely for trading purposes. We assume that Pepsi will maintain a portfolio of $1,753 million of marketable securities during the next four years, the average investment during the last four years. Pepsi generated a return of 5.1 percent [$= \$89 \div .5(\$1,889 + \$1,629)$] during Year 8 on its investments in marketable securities. Interest rates started increasing during Year 8. We assume a period of continuing interest rate increases in the near future and therefore assume yields of 5.5 percent in Year 9, 6.0 percent in Year 10, 6.5 percent in Year 11, and 7.0 percent in Year 12.

Pepsi's income note (Note 13) shows the reconciliation between the statutory tax rate and the average, or effective, tax rate. The statutory tax rate increased from 34 percent to 35 percent during Year 8. Pepsi experienced increases in its effective tax rate from state income taxes of 2.4 percent to 2.9 percent and from nondeductible amortization of goodwill of 0.8 percent to 0.9 percent. Pepsi experienced decreases in its effective tax rate for lower foreign tax rates of 2.7 percent to 5.0 percent and from other reconciling items of zero to 0.8 percent between Year 6 and Year 8. These four reconciling items approximately offset each other. The remaining two reconciling items occur only in Year 8. Thus, we assume that the effective tax rate in the future will equal the statutory tax rate of 35 percent.

Exhibit 10.1 presents the pro forma income statement for Pepsi for Year 9 to Year 12. We consider the projection of interest expense after projecting the firm's financing.

PROJECTING THE BALANCE SHEET

We prepare the pro forma balance sheet next. The analyst most easily accomplishes this step by projecting the asset side of the balance sheet first and then determining the appropriate mix of financing for the projected level of assets.

PROJECTING TOTAL ASSETS

Two general approaches to projecting assets are:

1. Project total assets and then use the common size balance sheet percentages to allocate this total among individual asset items.
2. Project individual assets and then sum individual asset amounts to obtain total assets.

Projected Total Assets Approach. We can project total assets using the historical growth rate in assets. Pepsi's assets grew at a 16.3 percent compound annual

EXHIBIT 10.1

Pepsi
Pro Forma Income Statements
(amounts in millions)

	Year 8 Actual	Year 9 Projected	Year 10 Projected	Year 11 Projected	Year 12 Projected
Sales[a]	$ 25,021	$ 28,499	$ 32,460	$ 36,972	$ 42,111
Cost of Goods Sold[b]	(11,946)	(13,594)	(15,483)	(17,636)	(20,087)
Selling and Administrative[c]	(10,168)	(11,571)	(13,170)	(15,011)	(17,097)
Other Revenues and Expenses[d]	89	93	105	114	123
Income Taxes[e]	(1,036)	(1,199)	(1,366)	(1,554)	(1,768)
Operating Income	$ 1,960	$ 2,228	$ 2,537	$ 2,885	$ 3,282
Interest Expense (net of taxes)[f]	(372)	(455)	(534)	(637)	(757)
Net Income	$ 1,588	$ 1,773	$ 2,003	$ 2,248	$ 2,525

[a]Projected using 13.9 percent growth rate.

[b]Projected assuming 47.7 percent of sales.

[c]Projected assuming 40.6 percent of sales.

[d]Projected assuming a portfolio of marketable securities of $1,753 million and a yield of 5.5 percent in Year 9, 6.0 percent in Year 10, 6.5 percent in Year 11, and 7.0 percent in Year 12.

[e]Projected assuming 35 percent of operating income before taxes.

[f]Projected assuming an interest rate of 7.0 percent in Year 9, 7.5 percent in Year 10, 8.0 percent in Year 11, and 8.5 percent in Year 12, and a 35 percent tax savings at the statutory marginal tax rate.

growth rate during the last five years. If this growth rate continues, total assets will increase as follows (in millions):

	Amount[a]	Percentage Change
Year 8 Actual Assets	$23,706	—
Year 9 Projected Assets	$27,570	16.3%
Year 10 Projected Assets	$32,064	16.3%
Year 11 Projected Assets	$37,290	16.3%
Year 12 Projected Assets	$43,369	16.3%

[a]Amounts rounded.

Using historical growth rates to project total assets can result in erroneous projections if the analyst fails to consider the link between sales growth and asset growth. We assumed a sales growth rate for Pepsi of 13.9 percent in Exhibit 10.1. Pepsi would not likely increase assets by 16.3 percent each year if sales continue to grow by only 13.9 percent. Pepsi made major acquisitions in recent years that inflated its historical growth rate in assets. Because sales usually lag increases in assets, the analyst should probably use a lower growth rate for assets than the historical rate.

An alternative approach to projecting total assets uses the total assets turnover ratio. Pepsi's total assets turnover was 1.1 in Year 5 through Year 8. Assume that Pepsi's total assets turnover will remain at 1.1 over the next four years. The calculation of projected total assets using the assets turnover follows:

	Sales	Total Assets Turnover	Average Total Assets	Total Assets Beginning of Year	Total Assets End of Year
Year 9 Projected. . . .	$28,499	1.1	$25,908	$23,706	$28,110
Year 10 Projected. . .	$32,460	1.1	$29,509	$28,110	$30,908
Year 11 Projected. . .	$36,972	1.1	$33,611	$30,908	$36,314
Year 12 Projected. . .	$42,111	1.1	$38,283	$36,314	$40,251

This approach ties the projection of total assets to the level of projected sales. One difficulty sometimes encountered with using total assets turnover to project total assets is that it can result in unusual patterns for projected total assets. The total assets turnover uses *average* total assets in the denominator. If total assets changed by an unusually large (small) percentage in the most recent year before making the projections, then the next year's assets must change by an unusually small (large) proportion to compensate. Refer to Figure 10.1. Assume that a firm has historically experienced a total assets turnover of 2.0. An acquisition late in Year 3 caused its total assets to increase, but the firm expects the assets turnover to remain at 2.0 longer term (dotted line). Projecting Year 4 assets using an assets turnover of 2.0 means that projected assets must decrease to maintain the *average* total assets commensurate with an assets turnover of 2.0. This "sawtooth" pattern makes little intuitive sense, given the growth rate in sales.

We encounter this problem in projecting total assets for Pepsi using its total assets turnover. Note that Pepsi's total assets increased 13.1 percent during Year 8, which is

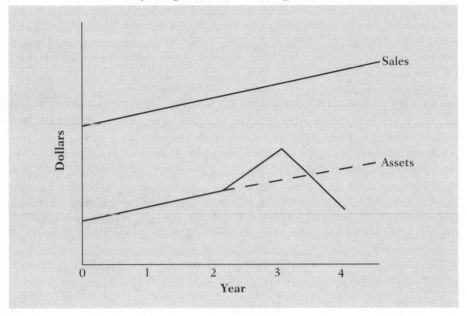

FIGURE 10.1

Illustration of Difficulty Sometimes Encountered
When Projecting Total Assets Using Assets Turnover

less than its average rate of increase in recent years. Using an assets turnover of 1.1 to project total assets, we determined above that total assets would increase as shown in the first two columns below:

	Year-End Assets[a]	Percentage Increase	Year-End Assets[a]	Percentage Increase
Year 8	$23,706	13.1%	$23,706	
Year 9	$20,110	10.6%	$27,060	11.15%
Year 10	$30,908	10.0%	$30,889	14.15%
Year 11	$36,314	17.5%	$35,260	14.15%
Year 12	$40,251	10.8%	$40,251	14.15%

[a]Amounts rounded.

Note that the growth rate in total assets fluctuates in a systematic pattern each year. The analyst can deal with that "sawtooth problem" by smoothing the rate of increase in assets. An increase in assets from $23,706 million to $40,251 million over four years grows at a compound average annual rate of 14.15 percent. The last two columns above show the revised projected assets following this smoothed approach. Note that total assets equal $40,251 million at the end of Year 12 in both cases. The amounts in the last two columns smooth this growth in assets to obtain this asset level. We could use these revised total assets amounts in preparing the pro forma balance sheet for Pepsi.

Once the analyst projects total assets, common size balance sheet percentages provide the basis for allocating this total to individual assets. The assumption made in using these common size percentages is that the firm maintains a constant mix of assets regardless of the level of total assets. The common size balance sheet for Pepsi in Appendix C indicates that the composition of its assets has displayed a relatively stable pattern during the last three years. We might use an average of the common size percentages during this period to allocate projected total assets to individual asset components.

Using common size balance sheet percentages to project individual assets encounters two shortcomings, however. First, the common size percentages for individual assets are not independent of each other. For example, a firm such as Pepsi that makes corporate acquisitions on an ongoing basis may experience an increasing proportion of goodwill among its assets. Other asset categories will therefore show decreasing percentages even though their dollar amounts are increasing. The analyst must interpret these decreasing percentages carefully. Second, using the common size percentages does not permit the analyst to change the assumptions about the future behavior of an individual asset easily. For example, assume that Pepsi intended to implement inventory control systems that should increase its inventory turnover in the future. Inventory will likely represent a smaller percentage of total assets in the future than it has in the past. The analyst encounters difficulties adjusting the common size balance sheet percentages to reflect the changes in inventory policies.

Projected Individual Asset Approach.   The second general approach to projecting total assets focuses on each asset individually. We can again use either historical growth rates or asset turnovers.

As with using historical growth rates to project total assets, the analyst must link historical growth rates for individual assets to the assumption made regarding the growth in sales, particularly for assets integrally related to operations (accounts receivable, inventories, fixed assets). For example, Pepsi's inventories grew at a 15.9 percent rate during the last five years. It is unlikely that inventories will continue to grow at such a rate if sales grow at 13.9 percent. Asset turnovers probably provide better projections for individual assets because they incorporate the projected level of operating activity and permit changes in the expected behavior of individual assets. Our projections of individual assets for Pepsi use a combination of common size percentages, growth rates, and asset turnovers. Exhibit 10.2 presents the projected balance sheet. The sections below discuss the projection of individual assets.

Cash.   Cash has composed approximately 1 percent of total assets during the last three years. We assume a continuation of this common size percentage in the future. We project the dollar amount for cash after projecting the amounts for all other assets.

Marketable Securities.   As discussed earlier, Pepsi has maintained an investment in marketable securities between $1,629 million and $1,889 million during the last three years. We assume that Pepsi will continue to hold a portfolio of marketable securities equal to the average amounts on its last four balance sheets of $1,753 million [= .25($1,645 + $1,849 + $1,889 + $1,629)].

EXHIBIT 10.2

Pepsi
Pro Forma Balance Sheet

	Year 8 Actual	Year 9 Projected	Year 10 Projected	Year 11 Projected	Year 12 Projected
Assets					
Cash	$ 227	$ 266	$ 297	$ 332	$ 371
Marketable Securities	1,629	1,753	1,753	1,753	1,753
Accounts Receivable	1,883	2,141	2,435	2,767	3,146
Inventories	925	1,048	1,189	1,348	1,528
Prepayments	500	570	649	739	842
Total Current Assets	$ 5,164	$ 5,778	$ 6,323	$ 6,939	$ 7,640
Investments	1,757	1,792	1,828	1,865	1,902
Property, Plant, and Equipment (cost)	14,250	16,182	18,376	20,868	23,698
Accumulated Depreciation	(5,394)	(6,125)	(6,955)	(7,899)	(8,970)
Other Assets	7,929	8,944	10,089	11,380	12,837
Total Assets	$23,706	$26,571	$29,661	$33,153	$37,107
Liabilities and Shareholders' Equity					
Accounts Payable	$ 1,390	$ 1,585	$ 1,807	$ 2,061	$ 2,350
Notes Payable	2,191	1,222	1,364	1,525	1,707
Other Current Liabilities	2,994	3,410	3,884	4,424	5,039
Total Current Liabilities	$ 6,575	$ 6,217	$ 7,055	$ 8,010	$ 9,096
Long-Term Debt	7,443	9,140	10,203	11,405	12,765
Deferred Income Taxes	2,008	2,273	2,573	2,913	3,297
Other Noncurrent Liabilities	1,342	1,529	1,741	1,983	2,259
Total Liabilities	$17,368	$19,159	$21,572	$24,311	$27,417
Common Stock	$ 14	$ 17	$ 21	$ 26	$ 32
Additional Paid-in Capital	879	1,081	1,330	1,636	2,012
Retained Earnings	6,542	7,772	9,137	10,635	12,278
Cumulative Translation Adjustment	(184)	(266)	(297)	(332)	(371)
Treasury Stock	(913)	(1,192)	(2,102)	(3,123)	(4,261)
Total Shareholders' Equity	$ 6,338	$ 7,412	$ 8,089	$ 8,842	$ 9,690
Total Liabilities and Shareholders' Equity	$23,706	$26,571	$29,661	$33,153	$37,107

Accounts Receivable. Pepsi's accounts receivable turnover was 14.3 in Year 7 and 14.4 in Year 8. We project accounts receivable assuming a turnover of 14.4 for Year 9 to Year 12. The projected amounts appear below:

	Sales	Accounts Receivable Turnover	Average Accounts Receivable	Accounts Receivable Beginning of Year	Accounts Receivable End of Year
Year 9 Projected	$28,499	14.4	$1,979	$1,883	$2,075
Year 10 Projected	$32,460	14.4	$2,254	$2,075	$2,433
Year 11 Projected	$36,972	14.4	$2,568	$2,433	$2,702
Year 12 Projected	$42,111	14.4	$2,924	$2,702	$3,146

The increase in accounts receivable portrays the sawtooth pattern depicted in Figure 10.1. We smooth this increase over time using the same procedure illustrated earlier for total assets. An increase in accounts receivable from $1,883 million to $3,146 million over four years represents a compound annual rate of increase of 13.69 percent. Thus, projected accounts receivable are:

	Year-End Accounts Receivable[a]	Percentage Increase
Year 8 Actual.....................	$1,883	—
Year 9 Projected..................	$2,141	13.69%
Year 10 Projected.................	$2,435	13.69%
Year 11 Projected.................	$2,767	13.69%
Year 12 Projected.................	$3,146	13.69%

[a]Amounts rounded.

Inventories.   Pepsi experienced a decreasing inventory turnover during the last four years, with most of the decrease occurring during Year 7 and Year 8. It is likely that Pepsi acquired companies with slower inventory turnovers than Pepsi's existing businesses. We project inventories using an inventory turnover of 14.4, the average of the last two years. The projected amounts follow:

	Cost of Goods Sold	Inventory Turnover	Average Inventories	Inventories Beginning of Year	End of Year
Year 9 Projected...	$13,594	14.4	$ 944	$ 925	$ 963
Year 10 Projected..	$15,483	14.4	$1,075	$ 963	$1,187
Year 11 Projected..	$17,636	14.4	$1,225	$1,187	$1,262
Year 12 Projected..	$20,087	14.4	$1,395	$1,262	$1,528

The increases in inventories also display a sawtooth pattern. We smooth the increases using a compound annual rate of increase of 13.37 percent as follows:

	Year-End Inventories[a]	Percentage Increase
Year 8 Actual.....................	$ 925	—
Year 9 Projected..................	$1,048	13.37%
Year 10 Projected.................	$1,189	13.37%
Year 11 Projected.................	$1,348	13.37%
Year 12 Projected.................	$1,528	13.37%

[a]Amounts rounded.

Prepayments.   Prepayments usually vary in relation to the level of operating activity. We assume that prepayments will increase at the growth rate of sales.

	Year-End Prepayments[a]	Percentage Increase
Year 8 Actual....................	$500	—
Year 9 Projected..................	$570	13.9%
Year 10 Projected.................	$649	13.9%
Year 11 Projected.................	$739	13.9%
Year 12 Projected.................	$842	13.9%

[a]Amounts rounded.

Property, Plant, and Equipment.   Pepsi experienced a fixed assets turn-over of 3.1 for each of the last three years. We assume a continuation of this fixed turnover rate.

	Sales	Fixed Asset Turnover	Average Net Fixed Assets	Net Fixed Assets	
				Beginning of Year	End of Year
Year 9 Projected....	$28,499	3.1	$ 9,193	$ 8,856	$ 9,530
Year 10 Projected...	$32,460	3.1	$10,471	$ 9,530	$11,412
Year 11 Projected...	$36,972	3.1	$11,926	$11,412	$12,440
Year 12 Projected...	$42,111	3.1	$13,584	$12,440	$14,728

Smoothing the sawtooth rate of increase in net fixed assets yields a compound an-nual rate of increase of 13.56 percent. We use this rate to project both gross property, plant, and equipment and accumulated depreciation.

	Year-End Gross Fixed Assets[a]	Year-End Accumulated Depreciation[a]	Percentage Increases
Year 8 Actual...........	$14,250	$5,394	—
Year 9 Projected........	$16,182	$6,125	13,56%
Year 10 Projected.......	$18,376	$6,955	13.56%
Year 11 Projected.......	$20,868	$7,899	13.56%
Year 12 Projected.......	$23,698	$8,970	13.56%

[a]Amounts rounded.

Other Assets.   Other assets for Pepsi primarily include goodwill and other in-tangibles from acquisitions. These assets increased at an average rate of 9.9 percent during the last four years and 15.6 percent during the last two years. The variation in these growth rates results from the amount and nature of the acquisitions each year. We project other assets using a 12.8 percent compound annual growth rate [= .5(9.9 percent + 15.6 percent)], in effect weighting the growth rate in Year 7 and Year 8 more heavily than that in Year 5 and Year 6 but giving consideration to the growth rate in all years. The projected amounts for other assets are:

	Year-End Other Assets[a]	Percentage Increase
Year 8 Actual....................	$ 7,929	—
Year 9 Projected.................	$ 8,944	12.8%
Year 10 Projected................	$10,089	12.8%
Year 11 Projected................	$11,380	12.8%
Year 12 Projected................	$12,837	12.8%

[a]Amounts rounded.

The following diagram summarizes the approaches to projecting assets:

	Project Total Assets	Project Individual Assets
Use Historical Growth Rates for Projections		
Use Asset Turnovers for Projections		

These four possible combinations yield similar projections for assets when a firm has experienced relatively stable historical growth rates for total assets and individual asset items and relatively stable asset turnovers. If historical growth rates have varied significantly from year to year, then using *average* historical growth rates provide more reasonable projections than asset turnovers. One desirable feature of using asset turnovers, however, is that projected asset amounts incorporate projections of the level of sales. Also, management's actions to improve profitability often focus on improving asset turnovers. The analyst can incorporate the effects of these actions into the projections more easily by using the asset turnovers approach than by adjusting the compound annual growth rates or common size balance sheet percentages.

PROJECTING LIABILITIES AND SHAREHOLDERS' EQUITY

Once the analyst completes the asset side of the pro forma balance sheet, projections of liabilities and shareholders' equity come next. For firms that target and maintain a particular capital structure over time, the analyst can use the common size balance sheet percentages to project amounts of individual liabilities and shareholders' equities. The common size balance sheet for Pepsi in Appendix C shows that, except for a shift in the notes payable and long-term debt percentages, the common size balance sheet percentages for liabilities and shareholders' equity remained relatively stable between Year 7 and Year 8. Thus, using the common size percentages appears reasonable in this case. Alternatively, the analyst can project individual liabilities and shareholders' equity accounts using historical growth rates or turnover ratios.

We use a combination of common size percentages, growth rates, and turnover ratios to project the liabilities and shareholders' equities for Pepsi. We consider each account next.

Accounts Payable. Pepsi experienced an average days payable during Year 7 and Year 8 of 40 days, translating into an accounts payable turnover of 9.13 times (365 ÷ 40). We assume a continuation of this turnover rate in projecting accounts payable. We begin by calculating purchases on account.

	Year 9	Year 10	Year 11	Year 12
Cost of Goods Sold..........	$13,594	$15,483	$17,636	$20,087
Plus Ending Inventory	1,048	1,189	1,348	1,528
Less Beginning Inventory.....	(925)	(1,048)	(1,189)	(1,348)
	$13,717	$15,624	$17,795	$20,267

The projection of accounts payable is as follows:

	Purchases	Accounts Payable Turnover	Average Accounts Payable	Accounts Payable Beginning of Year	Accounts Payable End of Year
Year 9 Projected....	$13,717	9.13	$1,502	$1,390	$1,614
Year 10 Projected...	$15,624	9.13	$1,711	$1,614	$1,808
Year 11 Projected...	$17,795	9.13	$1,949	$1,808	$2,090
Year 12 Projected...	$20,267	9.13	$2,220	$2,090	$2,350

Projected accounts payable display a sawtooth pattern over time. We smooth the variations in growth rates using a 14.03 compound annual growth rate as follows:

	Year-End Accounts Payable[a]	Percentage Increase
Year 8 Actual..................	$1,390	—
Year 9 Projected...............	$1,585	14.03%
Year 10 Projected..............	$1,807	14.03%
Year 11 Projected..............	$2,061	14.03%
Year 12 Projected..............	$2,350	14.03%

[a]Amounts rounded

Notes Payable. Given that Pepsi maintains a portfolio of marketable securities of $1.6 billion to $1.8 billion, it is unlikely that Pepsi borrows short-term for temporary operating needs. The wide fluctuations in the common size balance sheet percentages for notes payable suggest that Pepsi periodically borrows either to take advantage of relatively low interest rates or to finance an acquisition. It appears to repay this debt soon afterwards. We use the average common size percentage for notes payable during the last three years of 4.6 percent to project notes payable as follows:

	Year-End Notes Payable[a]	Common Size Balance Sheet Percentage
Year 9 Projected................	$1,222	4.6%
Year 10 Projected...............	$1,364	4.6%
Year 11 Projected...............	$1,525	4.6%
Year 12 Projected...............	$1,707	4.6%

[a]Amounts rounded.

Other Current Liabilities.   Other current liabilities relate primarily to operating activities (for example, salaries payable, utilities payable, taxes payable). We project this account to grow at the growth rate in sales of 13.9 percent.

	Year-End Other Current Liabilities[a]	Percentage Increase
Year 8 Actual....................	$2,994	
Year 9 Projected.................	$3,410	13.9%
Year 10 Projected................	$3,884	13.9%
Year 11 Projected................	$4,424	13.9%
Year 12 Projected................	$5,039	13.9%

[a]Amounts rounded.

Long-Term Debt.   Similar to notes payable, long-term debt as a percentage of total assets fluctuated significantly during the last five years. The fluctuations probably relate to the need to finance corporate acquisitions. This debt is sometimes repaid with proceeds from the sale of a portion of the assets acquired. Notes payable plus long-term debt as a percentage of total assets was 42.8 percent in Year 6, 41.4 percent in Year 7, and 40.6 percent in Year 8. Thus, it appears that Pepsi has attempted to reduce the proportion of interest-bearing debt in its capital structure. We assume that Pepsi will reduce this percentage to 39 percent for Year 9 through Year 12. We assumed earlier a notes payable to total assets percentage of 4.6 percent. Thus, we use a long-term debt to assets percentage of 34.4 percent (= 39.0 percent − 4.6 percent) for projecting the balance sheet.

	Year-End Long-Term Debt[a]	Common Size Balance Sheet Percentage
Year 9 Projected................	$ 9,140	34.4%
Year 10 Projected..............	$10,203	34.4%
Year 11 Projected..............	$11,405	34.4%
Year 12 Projected..............	$12,765	34.4%

[a]Amounts rounded.

We can now project interest expense. As the analysis below shows, interest expense equaled 6.3 percent of average interest-bearing debt (notes payable and long-term debt) in Year 8. Interest rates are expected to increase in the near future. We assume interest rates of 7.0 percent for Year 9, 7.5 percent for Year 10, 8.0 percent for Year 11, and 8.5 percent for Year 12.

	Year 8	Year 9	Year 10	Year 11	Year 12
Average Notes Payable	$1,449	$1,707	$ 1,293	$ 1,445	$ 1,616
Average Long-Term Debt ...	7,704	8,291	9,672	10,804	12,085
Total	$9,153	$9,998	$10,965	$12,249	$13,701
Interest Expense	$ 573	$ 700	$ 822	$ 980	$ 1,165
Interest Rate.............	6.3%	7.0%	7.5%	8.0%	8.5%

We can now enter these interest expense amounts (net of their income tax savings of 35 percent) in the projected income statement in Exhibit 10.1.

Deferred Income Taxes.   The income tax note for Pepsi indicates that most deferred tax liabilities relate to depreciable and intangible assets. We assumed earlier that property, plant, and equipment would grow 13.56 percent and that other assets (intangibles) would grow 12.8 percent. We project deferred tax liabilities to grow at the 13.2 percent average [= .5(13.56 percent + 12.8 percent)] of these two growth rates.

	Year-End Deferred Income Taxes[a]	Percentage Increase
Year 8 Actual....................	$2,008	—
Year 9 Projected.................	$2,273	13.2%
Year 10 Projected................	$2,573	13.2%
Year 11 Projected................	$2,913	13.2%
Year 12 Projected................	$3,297	13.2%

[a]Amounts rounded.

Other Noncurrent Liabilities.   Other noncurrent liabilities relate to pension obligations, health-care obligations, and other operating related items. We therefore project other noncurrent liabilities to grow at the growth rate in sales of 13.9 percent.

	Year-End Other Noncurrent Liabilities[a]	Percentage Increase
Year 8 Actual....................	$1,342	—
Year 9 Projected.................	$1,529	13.9%
Year 10 Projected................	$1,741	13.9%
Year 11 Projected................	$1,983	13.9%
Year 12 Projected................	$2,259	13.9%

[a]Amounts rounded.

Common Stock and Additional Paid-in Capital.   Common stock and additional paid-in capital have increased from the reissuance of treasury stock in connection with corporate acquisitions and employee stock option plans. These accounts increased at a compound annual rate of 23 percent between Year 4 and Year 8. We assume this same rate of increase for Year 9 through Year 12.

	Year-End Common Stock[a]	Year-End Additional Paid-in Capital	Percentage Increases
Year 8 Actual.........	$14	$ 879	—
Year 9 Projected.......	$17	$1,081	23.0%
Year 10 Projected......	$21	$1,330	23.0%
Year 11 Projected......	$26	$1,636	23.0%
Year 12 Projected......	$32	$2,012	23.0%

[a]Amounts rounded.

Retained Earnings.   Retained earnings increase by the amount of projected net income and decrease for dividends. Dividends grew at a compound annual rate of 17.55 percent rate during the last five years. We project dividends to grow at this same rate between Year 8 and Year 12 as follows:

	Dividend for Year[a]	Percentage Increase
Year 8 Actual........................	$462	—
Year 9 Projected.....................	$543	17.55%
Year 10 Projected....................	$638	17.55%
Year 11 Projected....................	$750	17.55%
Year 12 Projected....................	$882	17.55%

[a]Amounts rounded.

Thus, the change in retained earnings is as follows:

	Year 9	Year 10	Year 11	Year 12
Beginning of Year	$6,542	$7,772	$ 9,137	$10,635
Plus Net Income	1,773	2,003	2,248	2,525
Less Dividends.........	(543)	(638)	(750)	(882)
End of Year	$7,772	$9,137	$10,635	$12,278

Cumulative Translation Adjustment.   The cumulative translation adjustment account has varied from a positive to a negative amount during the last five years in amounts equal to 1 to 2 percent of total assets. Pepsi will likely continue to expand its international operations, particularly in developing countries. These countries often experience decreases in the value of their currencies relative to the U.S.

dollar as the development process proceeds. Thus, we project a continuing negative translation adjustment equal to 1 percent of total assets.

	Year-End Cumulative Translation Adjustment[a]	Common Size Balance Sheet Percentage
Year 9 Projected............	$-266	1.0%
Year 10 Projected...........	$-297	1.0%
Year 11 Projected...........	$-332	1.0%
Year 12 Projected...........	$-371	1.0%

[a]Amounts rounded.

Treasury Stock. Pepsi has repurchased significant amounts of its common stock to use in corporate acquisitions and for employee stock options and is likely to continue doing so. The projected amounts for treasury stock are the amounts necessary to equate projected assets with projected liabilities and shareholders' equity. The projected amounts for treasury stock appear unreasonably large relative to their historical amounts. Note though that projected *total* common shareholders' equity as a percentage of total assets is in the range of 26 percent to 28 percent, similar to its historical relationship. The large dollar amounts for treasury stock reflect in part the 23 percent growth rate in the issuance of common stock and 17.7 percent growth rate in the retention of earnings. For projection purposes, total common shareholders' equity is of greater significance than its components.

PROJECTING THE STATEMENT OF CASH FLOWS

The final step involves preparing a projected statement of cash flows. We prepare the statement of cash flows directly from the projected income statement and projected balance sheet. We follow the usual procedure for preparing this statement described in Chapter 2. Exhibit 10.3 presents the pro forma statement of cash flows for Pepsi. The derivation of each of the line items follows.

(1) *Net Income:* We use the amounts in the pro forma income statement (Exhibit 10.1).

(2) *Depreciation and Amortization:* We assume that these items will increase at the average rate of increase of the respective assets. We assumed earlier that property, plant, and equipment would grow at a 13.56 percent rate and intangible assets at a 12.8 percent rate. We use an average of these two growth rates, 13.18 percent (= .5(13.56 percent + 12.8 percent)], to project depreciation and amortization expense.

(3) *Other Addbacks:* This item includes the increase in Deferred Income Taxes and Other Noncurrent Liabilities on the projected balance sheet. The inclusion of the change in Other Current Liabilities in the operations section assumes that this account primarily includes pension, health-care, and other retirement obligations, as well as noncurrent expense provisions.

EXHIBIT 10.3

Pepsi
Pro Forma Statement of Cash Flows

	Year 8 Actual	Year 9 Projected	Year 10 Projected	Year 11 Projected	Year 12 Projected
Operations					
(1) Net Income.........................	$ 1,588	$ 1,773	$ 2,003	$ 2,248	$ 2,525
(2) Depreciation and Amortization.............	1,444	1,634	1,850	2,094	2,369
(3) Other Addbacks	428	452	512	582	660
(4) (Increase) Decrease in Accounts Receivable..	(161)	(258)	(294)	(332)	(379)
(5) (Increase) Decrease in Inventories..........	(89)	(123)	(141)	(159)	(180)
(6) (Increase) Decrease in Prepayments	3	(70)	(79)	(90)	(103)
(7) Increase (Decrease) in Accounts Payable	143	195	222	254	289
(8) Increase (Decrease) in Other Current Liabilities...............................	(222)	416	474	540	615
Cash Flow from Operations	$ 3,134	$ 4,019	$ 4,547	$ 5,137	$ 5,796
Investing					
(9) Acquisition of Marketable Securities and Investments (net)	$ (752)	$ (159)	$ (36)	$ (37)	$ (37)
(10) Acquisition of Property, Plant, and Equipment (net)	(1,910)	(1,932)	(2,194)	(2,492)	(2,830)
(11) Other Investing Transactions	(109)	(1,918)	(2,165)	(2,441)	(2,755)
Cash Flow from Investing................	$(2,771)	$ (4,009)	$ (4,395)	$(4,970)	$(5,622)
Financing					
(12) Increase (Decrease) in Short-Term Borrowing..............................	$ 1,081	$ (969)	$ 142	$ 161	$ 182
(13) Increase in Long-Term Debt	(491)	1,697	1,063	1,202	1,360
(14) Increase in Common Stock................	69	205	253	311	382
(15) Dividends	(462)	(543)	(638)	(750)	(882)
(16) Acquisition of Common Stock	(463)	(279)	(910)	$(1,021)	(1,138)
(17) Other Financing Transactions	(40)	(82)	(31)	(35)	(39)
Cash Flow from Financing................	$ (306)	$ 29	$ (121)	$ (132)	$ (135)
(18) Change in Cash........................	$ 57	$ 39	$ 31	$ 35	$ 39
Cash—Beginning of Year.................	170	227	266	297	332
Cash—End of Year	$ 227	$ 266	$ 297	$ 332	$ 371

(4),(5),(6),(7),(8) Changes in operating current asset and current liability accounts other than cash appearing on the pro forma balance sheet.

(9) *Acquisition of Marketable Securities and Investments (net):* The statement of cash flows classifies purchases and sales of marketable securities (current asset) and investments in securities (noncurrent asset) as "investing" transactions. We use the changes in these accounts on the pro forma balance sheet to derive the amounts for these items on the statement of cash flows. If part of the change relates to an income item (for example, equity in earnings of an affiliate), then the analyst should include the associated amount in the "operations" section instead of the "investing" section.

(10) *Acquisition of Property, Plant, and Equipment (net):* The amount on this line equals the change in property, plant, and equipment (at cost) on the pro forma balance sheet in Exhibit 10.2.

(11) *Other Investing Transactions:* We enter the acquisition of Other Assets (intangibles and goodwill) on this line. The change in Other Assets on the pro forma balance sheet is the net of acquisitions and amortization. We derive the amortization amount by subtracting from depreciation and amortization (line 2 above) the change in the Accumulated Depreciation account. For example, Other Assets increased by \$1,015 million (= \$8,944 − \$7,929) between Year 8 and Year 9. Total depreciation and amortization for Year 9 is \$1,634 million. The Accumulated Depreciation account increased by \$731 million (= \$6,125 − \$5,394). Thus, amortization of intangibles totaled \$903 million (= \$1,634 − \$731). The acquisition of intangibles (other assets) equals \$1,918 million (= \$1,015 + \$903).

(12),(13) Increases in borrowings (notes payable and long-term debt) are financing activities.

(14,16) *Changes in Common Stock:* The amount entered on lines (14) and (16) represent the changes in the Common Stock, Additional Paid-in Capital, and Treasury Stock accounts on the pro forma balance sheet.

(15) *Dividends:* The amount for dividends equals the projected amount each year (discussed earlier in the section on Retained Earnings in the pro forma balance sheet).

(17) *Other Financing Transactions:* The amount on this line reflects the change in the Cumulative Translation Adjustment account on the pro forma balance sheet. In published statements of cash flow, the amount on this line represents the effects of exchange rate changes on cash only. The effect of exchange rate changes on other accounts appears in one of the three main sections of the statement of cash flows. Because the amounts involved are immaterial, we do not employ this refinement in Exhibit 10.3.

(18) *Change in Cash:* The amounts on lines (1) to (17) net to the change in cash on the comparative balance sheet.

ANALYZING PRO FORMA FINANCIAL STATEMENTS

We can analyze the pro forma financial statements using the same ratios and other analytical tools discussed in previous chapters. Exhibit 10.4 presents a ratio analysis for Pepsi based on actual results for Year 8 and pro forma results for Year 9, Year 10, Year 11, and Year 12.

Note that the projected financial statement ratios for Pepsi remain essentially the same as the amounts for Year 8. This occurs because all income statement, balance sheet, and statement of cash flows amounts tie directly or indirectly to the increases in sales revenue. These pro forma financial statements might serve as the base case from which the analyst can assess the impact of various changes for Pepsi.

EXHIBIT 10.4

Pepsi
Ratio Analysis
Based on Pro Forma Financial Statements

	Year 8 Actual	Year 9 Projected	Year 10 Projected	Year 11 Projected	Year 12 Projected
Profitability					
Profit Margin for ROA........................	7.8%	7.8%	7.8%	7.8%	7.8%
Asset Turnover...............................	1.1	1.1	1.2	1.2	1.2
Rate of Return on Assets.....................	8.8%	8.9%	9.0%	9.2%	9.3%
Common Earnings Leverage	81.0%	79.6%	78.9%	77.9%	76.9%
Capital Structure Leverage....................	3.8	3.7	3.6	3.7	3.8
Rate of Return on Common Shareholders' Equity .	27.2%	25.8%	25.8%	26.6%	27.3%
Cost of Goods Sold/Sales......................	47.7%	47.7%	47.7%	47.7%	47.7%
Selling and Administrative Expense/Sales	40.6%	40.6%	40.6%	40.6%	40.6%
Interest Expense/Sales	2.3%	2.5%	2.5%	2.7%	2.8%
Income Tax Expense/Sales......................	3.3%	3.3%	3.3%	3.3%	3.2%
Accounts Receivable Turnover..................	14.4	14.2	14.2	14.2	14.2
Inventory Turnover	14.1	13.8	13.8	13.9	14.0
Fixed Asset Turnover	3.1	3.0	3.0	3.0	3.0
Short-Term Liquidity					
Current Ratio.................................	0.8	0.9	0.9	0.9	0.8
Quick Ratio	0.6	0.7	0.6	0.6	0.6
Operating Cash Flow to Current Liabilities.......	56.3%	62.8%	68.5%	68.2%	67.8%
Long-Term Solvency					
Total Liabilities to Total Assets	73.3%	72.1%	72.7%	73.3%	73.9%
Long-Term Debt to Total Assets	31.4%	34.4%	34.4%	34.4%	34.4%
Long-Term Debt to Shareholders' Equity.........	117.4%	123.3%	126.1%	129.0%	131.7%
Times Interest Earned.........................	5.2	4.9	4.8	4.5	4.3
Operating Cash Flow to Total Liabilities	19.0%	22.0%	22.3%	22.4%	22.4%
Operating Cash Flow to Capital Expenditures	1.6	2.1	2.1	2.1	2.1

For example, assume that Pepsi anticipates an economic recession during Year 9. To maintain the same volume of units sold, Pepsi will need to lower prices by 3.5 percent. Assuming no changes in inventory holding policies, Pepsi's revised profitability ratios follow:

	Originally Projected	Revised Projected
Profit Margin.....................................	7.8%	5.7%
Assets Turnover...................................	1.1	1.1
Rate of Return on Assets	8.9%	6.3%
Common Earnings Leverage	79.6%	71.2%
Capital Structure Leverage..........................	3.7	3.7
Rate of Return on Common Shareholders' Equity	25.8%	16.3%

Various other changes in assumptions are possible. For example, the analyst might question Pepsi's ability to continue making major acquisitions each year. Slowing the rate of growth in sales and assets provides an alternative scenario for Pepsi's future.

SUMMARY

The preparation of pro forma financial statements requires numerous assumptions (growth rate in sales, cost behavior of various expenses, levels of investment in working capital and fixed assets, mix of financing). The analyst should study the sensitivity of the pro forma financial statements to the assumptions made and to the impact of different assumptions. Spreadsheet computer programs assist in this sensitivity analysis. The analyst can study alternative assumptions quickly and trace through their effects on the financial statements. Two comments should be kept in mind, however, when preparing pro forma financial statements.

1. The preparation of pro forma financial statements can easily deteriorate into a mechanical exercise. Spreadsheet computer programs permit the analyst to input a handful of assumptions and the program outputs financial statements for many years into the future. The old adage of "garbage-in, garbage-out" applies with particular force to the preparation of pro forma financial statements. The analyst should (a) carefully study past financial statement relations to gain an understanding of the economic characteristics of the business and (b) consider changes in economic conditions, business strategy, and other factors that affect the projections. Projecting more than four or five years into the future probably results in projections of questionable reliability.
2. The analyst should ensure that the pro forma financial statements are internally consistent. Assumptions about sales and various expenses should articulate with the levels of accounts receivable, inventories, and other assets. Amounts on the statement of cash flows should articulate with changes in balance sheet accounts and with related income statement amounts.

CASE 10.1

WAL-MART STORES: WHAT WILL THE FUTURE HOLD?

Wal-Mart Stores (Wal-Mart) is the largest retailing firm in the world. Building on a base of discount stores, Wal-Mart has expanded into warehouse clubs and more recently into superstores. Its superstores combine traditional discount store items with grocery products.

Exhibits 1 to 3 present the financial statements of Wal-Mart for Year 2, Year 3, and Year 4. Exhibit 4 presents selected financial statement ratios.

REQUIRED

a. Prepare a set of pro forma financial statements for Wal-Mart for Year 5 and Year 6, following the assumptions set forth below. Perform the projections in the order presented (unless indicated otherwise), beginning with the income statement, then the balance sheet, and then the statement of cash flows.

EXHIBIT 1

Wal-Mart Stores—Income Statements
(amounts in millions)
(Case 10.1)

	Year Ended January 31		
	Year 2	Year 3	Year 4
Sales	$ 43,915	$ 55,520	$ 67,392
Other Revenues......................	374	465	593
Cost of Goods Sold...................	(34,786)	(44,175)	(53,444)
Selling and Administrative Expenses	(6,684)	(8,320)	(10,333)
Interest Expenses....................	(266)	(323)	(517)
Income Tax Expense..................	(945)	(1,172)	(1,358)
Net Income	$ 1,608	$ 1,995	$ 2,333

EXHIBIT 2

Wal-Mart Stores—Balance Sheets
(amounts in millions)
(Case 10.1)

	January 31			
	Year 1	Year 2	Year 3	Year 4
Assets				
Cash	$ 13	$ 31	$ 12	$ 20
Accounts Receivable	305	419	525	690
Inventories	5,809	7,384	9,268	11,014
Prepayments................................	288	741	393	391
Total Current Assets	$ 6,415	$ 8,575	$10,198	$12,115
Property, Plant, and Equipment (at cost)........	$ 5,996	$ 8,141	$11,847	$15,858
Accumulated Depreciation	(1,285)	(1,707)	(2,055)	(2,683)
Property, Plant, and Equipment (net)...........	$ 4,711	$ 6,434	$ 9,792	$13,175
Other Assets................................	$ 262	$ 434	$ 575	$ 1,151
Total Assets	$11,388	$15,443	$20,565	$26,441
Liabilities and Shareholders' Equity				
Accounts Payable............................	$ 2,651	$ 3,454	$ 3,873	$ 4,104
Notes Payable...............................	425	494	1,598	1,646
Other Current Liabilities	913	1,056	1,283	1,656
Total Current Liabilities....................	$ 3,989	$ 5,004	$ 6,754	$ 7,406
Long-Term Debt	1,899	3,278	4,845	7,960
Deferred Income Taxes.......................	134	172	207	322
Total Liabilities	$ 6,022	$ 8,454	$11,806	$15,688
Common Stock	$ 530	$ 740	$ 757	$ 766
Retained Earnings...........................	4,836	6,249	8,002	9,987
Total Shareholders' Equity..................	$ 5,366	$ 6,989	$ 8,759	$10,753
Total Liabilities and Shareholders' Equity	$11,388	$15,443	$20,565	$26,441

EXHIBIT 3

Wal-Mart Stores
Statements of Cash Flows
(amounts in millions)
(Case 10.1)

	Year Ended January 31		
	Year 2	Year 3	Year 4
Operations			
Net Income	$ 1,608	$ 1,995	$ 2,333
Depreciation	475	649	849
Other Addbacks (Subtractions)	(8)	13	(75)
(Increase) Decrease in Accounts Receivable	(114)	(106)	(165)
(Increase) Decrease in Inventories	(1,460)	(1,884)	(1,324)
(Increase) Decrease in Prepayments	(10)	(20)	(1)
Increase (Decrease) in Accounts Payable	710	420	230
Increase (Decrease) in Other Current Liabilities	156	211	349
Cash Flow from Operations	$ 1,357	$ 1,278	$ 2,196
Investing			
Fixed Assets Acquired	$(2,142)	$(3,366)	$(3,644)
Other Investing Transactions	(8)	(140)	(842)
Cash Flow from Investing	$(2,150)	$(3,506)	$(4,486)
Financing			
Increase (Decrease) in Short-Term Borrowing	$ 58	$ 1,134	$ (14)
Increase (Decrease) in Long-Term Borrowing	935	1,300	2,652
Increase in Common Stock	13	16	10
Dividends	(195)	(241)	(299)
Other Financing Transactions	—	—	(51)
Cash Flow from financing	$ 811	$ 2,209	$ 2,298
Change in Cash	$ 18	$ (19)	$ 8
Cash—Beginning of Year	13	31	12
Cash—End of Year	$ 31	$ 12	$ 20

INCOME STATEMENT

Sales: The growth rate in sales was 34.6 percent in Year 2, 26.4 percent in Year 3, and 21.4 percent in Year 4. The decreasing growth reflects increasing market saturation of discount stores. Assume that sales will increase 20 percent in Year 5 and 18 percent in Year 6. This growth rate reflects the offsetting effects of increased market saturation of discount stores but the growth of warehouse clubs and superstores.

Other Revenues: Other revenues averaged 0.9 percent of sales during the last three years. Assume a continuation of this percentage.

Cost of Goods Sold: The increasing proportion of warehouse clubs and food products in the sales mix should result in an increase in the cost of goods sold percentage. Assume

EXHIBIT 4

Wal-Mart Stores
Financial Ratio Analysis
(Case 10.1)

	Year 2	Year 3	Year 4
Profit Margin	4.0%	4.0%	3.9%
Assets Turnover	3.3	3.1	2.9
Rate of Return on Assets	13.2%	12.2%	11.3%
Common Earnings Leverage	90.6%	90.7%	87.7%
Capital Structure Leverage	2.2	2.3	2.4
Rate of Return on Common Shareholders' Equity	26.0%	25.3%	23.9%
Cost of Goods Sold ÷ Sales	79.2%	79.6%	79.3%
Selling & Administrative Expense ÷ Sales	15.2%	15.0%	15.3%
Interest Expense ÷ Sales	.6%	.6%	.8%
Income Tax Expense ÷ Sales	2.6%	2.5%	2.6%
Accounts Receivable Turnover	121.3	117.6	110.9
Inventory Turnover	5.3	5.3	5.3
Fixed Asset Turnover	7.9	6.8	5.9
Current Ratio	1.7	1.5	1.6
Quick Ratio	.1	.1	.1
Days Accounts Payable	31.0	29.0	26.0
Cash Flow from Operations ÷ Current Liabilities	30.2%	21.7%	31.0%
Total Liabilities ÷ Total Assets	54.7%	57.4%	59.3%
Long-Term Debt ÷ Total Assets	21.2%	23.6%	30.1%
Long-Term Debt ÷ Shareholders' Equity	46.9%	55.3%	74.0%
Cash Flow from Operations ÷ Total Liabilities	18.7%	12.6%	16.0%
Interest Coverage Ratio	10.6	10.8	8.1
Cash Flow from Operations ÷ Capital Expenditures	.6	.4	.6

a cost of goods sold to sales percentage of 79.5 percent for Year 5 and 79.7 percent for Year 6.

Selling and Administrative Expenses: The increasing proportion of warehouse clubs and superstores in the sales mix should reduce the selling and administrative expense percentage. Assume a selling and administrative expense to sales percentage of 15.1 percent for Year 5 and 15.0 percent for Year 6.

Interest Expense: Interest expense as a percentage of average interest-bearing debt (notes payable and long-term debt) was 6.4 percent in Year 3 and 6.5 percent in Year 4. Assume that interest rates will continue to increase and will equal 7.0 percent in Year 5 and 7.5 percent in Year 6. Delay projecting interest expense until after projecting the amount of interest-bearing debt in the capital structure.

Income Tax Expense: Income tax expense averaged 37 percent of income before income taxes during the last three years. Assume a continuation of this average tax rate during the next two years. Wal-Mart's income tax note indicates that state and local taxes are the only significant reconciling item, so assume that 37 percent is both the statutory tax rate and the average tax rate. Delay projecting income tax expense until after projecting interest expense.

BALANCE SHEET

Cash: Cash has averaged 0.1 percent of total assets during the last three years. Assume a continuation of this percentage. Delay projecting cash until after projecting all other assets.

Accounts Receivable: Wal-Mart's accounts receivable turnover declined from 121.3 to 110.9 during the last three years. This rapid turnover represents a holding period of only three days. Assume an accounts receivable turnover of 110 for Year 5 and Year 6. The projected amounts for accounts receivable following this assumption results in a "sawtooth" pattern of growth. Smooth the rate of increase in accounts receivable between Year 4 and Year 6.

Inventories: The inventory turnover ratio was 5.3 during the last three years. Assume a continuation of this turnover rate during Year 5 and Year 6.

Prepayments: Assume that prepayments relate to operating costs and will increase at the growth rate in sales.

Property, Plant, and Equipment: Property, plant, and equipment have grown faster than sales during each of the last three years as Wal-Mart has built new warehouse clubs and supercenters. Assume that fixed assets at cost will increase 30 percent in Year 5 and 28 percent in Year 6.

Accumulated Depreciation: Accumulated depreciation has increased more slowly than property, plant, and equipment because of the relatively long lives of buildings. Assume that accumulated depreciation as a percentage of the property, plant, and equipment (as cost) will equal 18 percent in Year 5 and 19 percent in Year 6.

Other Assets: Assume that other assets relate to operating activities (for example, deposits on facilities) and will increase at the growth rate in sales.

NOTE: Project the amount of cash at this point.

Accounts Payable: Except for a decrease in Year 4, the days accounts payable have averaged 30 days in recent years. Assume a continuation of this holding period. The projected amounts following this assumption result in a "sawtooth" pattern of growth. Smooth the rate of increase in accounts payable between Year 4 and Year 6.

Notes Payable: Wal-Mart uses short-term borrowing to finance working capital. The current ratio has averaged 1.62 during the last three years. Assume that Wal-Mart will adjust short-term borrowing to maintain a current ratio of 1.62. Delay projecting notes payable until projecting other current liabilities.

Other Current Liabilities: Other current liabilities relate to various operating costs. Assume that this account will increase with the growth rate in sales.

NOTE: Project the amount of notes payable at this point.

Long-Term Debt: Wal-Mart's long-term debt to shareholders' equity ratio increased from 35.4 percent to 74.0 percent during the last three years to finance its growth in stores. Assume that this percentage will stabilize at 75 percent at the end of Year 5 and Year 6. Delay projecting long-term debt until projecting the deferred tax liability.

Deferred Tax Liability: Assume that deferred taxes will increase with the growth rate in sales.

NOTE: Project the amount of long-term debt, interest expense on average notes payable and long-term debt, income tax expense, and net income at this point.

Common Stock: Increase (common stock issued) or decrease (common stock repurchased) common stock to achieve the desired ratio of long-term debt to shareholders' equity of 0.75. Delay projecting common stock until after projecting retained earnings.

Retained Earnings: The increase in retained earnings equals net income minus dividends. Dividends increased by 23.6 percent in Year 3 and 24.1 percent in Year 4. Assume that dividends will increase 24.6 percent in Year 5 and 25.1 percent in Year 6.

NOTE: Project the amount of common stock at this time.

STATEMENT OF CASH FLOWS

Depreciation Addback: Set equal to the change in accumulated depreciation.

Other Addbacks: Set equal to the increase in the Deferred Tax Liability account.

Fixed Assets Acquired: Set equal to increase in property, plant, and equipment (at cost).

Other Investing Transactions: Set equal to increase in other assets.

REQUIRED

a. Assess the projected changes in the profitability and risk of Wal-Mart during Year 5 and Year 6.

b. Wal-Mart is concerned about the projected profitability in parts (*a*) and (*b*). The firm wonders about the impact on profitability and risk if it increases the ratio of long-term debt to common shareholders' equity from 0.75 to 1.00 (that is, equal amounts of long-term debt and common shareholders' equity). The increased proportion of debt in the capital structure will increase the interest rate on borrowing to 8.0 percent for Year 5 and 8.5 percent for Year 6. Recast the pro forma financial statements for Year 5 and Year 6 to incorporate these changes.

c. Evaluate the effect of increasing the proportion of debt in the capital structure of Wal-Mart.

CASE 10.2

McDONALD'S CORPORATION: A FRANCHISING EXPERIENCE

McDonald's Corporation maintains a leading market share in the fast-food industry. It both owns its own restaurants and franchises them to others. McDonald's charges franchisees an initial franchise fee at the time of awarding a franchise and an ongoing franchise fee based on sales and other performance measures. McDonald's includes franchise fees in its revenues. Neither the sales, expenses, assets, or liabilities of franchisees generally appear in the financial statements of McDonald's. McDonald's has increased the proportion of restaurants operated through franchising arrangements in recent years.

Exhibits 1 to 3 present the financial statements for McDonald's for Year 2, Year 3, and Year 4. Exhibit 4 presents selected financial statement ratios.

EXHIBIT 1

McDonald's Corporation
Income Statements
(amounts in millions)
(Case 10.2)

	Year Ended January 31		
	Year 2	Year 3	Year 4
Revenues............................	$ 6,695	$ 7,133	$ 7,408
Cost of Goods Sold...................	(4,336)	(4,475)	(4,545)
Selling and Administrative Expenses	(669)	(837)	(872)
Interest Expenses.....................	(391)	(374)	(316)
Income Tax Expense..................	(440)	(489)	(593)
Net Income	$ 859	$ 958	$ 1,082

REQUIRED

a. What evidence do you see in Exhibit 4 of the increasing proportion of franchise-owned McDonald's restaurants?

b. Prepare a set of pro forma financial statements for Year 5 and Year 6 under two strategic scenarios:

Scenario 1: An increasing proportion of franchised restaurants in the sales mix

Scenario 2: A decreasing proportion of franchised restaurants in the sales mix.

Follow the assumptions set forth below to implement each of these strategies.

INCOME STATEMENT

Sales:

Scenario 1: Increase 3 percent in Year 5 and 2 percent in Year 6.

Scenario 2: Increase 5 percent in Year 5 and 6 percent in Year 6.

Cost of Goods Sold:

Scenario 1: 60.0 percent of sales in Year 5 and 58.6 percent of sales in Year 6.

Scenario 2: 62.8 percent of sales in Year 5 and 64.2 percent of sales in Year 6.

Selling and Administrative Expenses:

Scenario 1: 12.0 percent of sales in Year 5 and 12.3 percent in Year 6.

Scenario 2: 11.6 percent of sales in Year 5 and 11.3 percent in Year 6.

EXHIBIT 2

McDonald's Corporation
Balance Sheets
(amounts in millions)
(Case 10.2)

	January 31			
	Year 1	Year 2	Year 3	Year 4
Assets				
Cash	$ 143	$ 226	$ 436	$ 186
Accounts Receivable	255	274	280	315
Inventories	43	43	44	43
Prepayments	108	104	105	119
Total Current Assets	$ 549	$ 647	$ 865	$ 663
Investments	335	374	400	447
Property, Plant, and Equipment (at cost)	11,535	12,368	12,658	13,459
Accumulated Depreciation	(2,488)	(2,801)	(3,061)	(3,378)
Other Assets	736	761	819	844
Total Assets	$10,667	$11,349	$11,681	$12,035
Liabilities and Shareholders' Equity				
Accounts Payable	$ 356	$ 314	$ 343	$ 396
Notes Payable	299	278	411	193
Current Portion of Long-Term Debt	65	69	269	30
Other Current Liabilities	477	627	522	483
Total Current Liabilities	$ 1,197	$ 1,288	$ 1,545	$ 1,102
Long-Term Debt	4,429	4,267	3,176	3,489
Deferred Income Taxes	695	734	749	835
Other Noncurrent Liabilities	163	225	319	335
Total Liabilities	$ 6,484	$ 6,514	$ 5,789	$ 5,761
Preferred Stock	$ 3	$ 10	$ 409	$ 423
Common Stock	220	249	306	349
Retained Earnings	5,215	5,925	6,727	7,613
Cumulative Translation Adjustment	47	33	(127)	(192)
Treasury Stock	(1,302)	(1,382)	(1,423)	(1,919)
Total Shareholders' Equity	$ 4,183	$ 4,835	$ 5,892	$ 6,274
Total Liabilities and Shareholders' Equity	$10,667	$11,349	$11,681	$12,035

Interest Expense:

Scenario 1: 8.2 percent of interest-bearing debt in Year 5 and 8.1 percent of interest-bearing debt in Year 6.

Scenario 2: 8.5 percent of interest-bearing debt in Year 5 and 8.6 percent of interest-bearing debt in Year 6.

EXHIBIT 3

McDonald's Corporation
Statements of Cash Flows
(amounts in millions)
(Case 10.2)

	Year Ended January 31		
	Year 2	Year 3	Year 4
Operations			
Net Income	$ 859	$ 958	$1,082
Depreciation.	514	555	569
Other Addbacks (Subtractions)	65	22	52
(Increase) Decrease in Accounts Receivable	(41)	(29)	(48)
(Increase) Decrease in Inventories	—	1	—
(Increase) Decrease in Prepayments	—	1	(9)
Increase (Decrease) in Accounts Payable	(23)	1	45
Increase (Decrease) in Other Current Liabilities . . .	49	(83)	(11)
Cash Flow from Operations.	$1,423	$1,426	$1,680
Investing			
Fixed Assets Acquired (net)	$ (941)	$ (974)	$(1,205)
Other Investing Transactions	1	(25)	(13)
Cash Flow from Investing	$ (940)	$ (999)	$(1,218)
Financing			
Increase (Decrease) in Short-Term Borrowing	$ (677)	$ 17	$ (9)
Increase (Decrease) in Long-Term Borrowing.	397	(532)	55
Issue of Common Stock	100	485	—
Acquisition of Treasury Stock	(109)	(80)	(620)
Dividends on Preferred Stock	(19)	(15)	(47)
Dividends on Common Stock	(129)	(146)	(154)
Other Financing Transactions	37	54	63
Cash Flow from Financing	$ (400)	$ (217)	$ (712)
Change in Cash.	$ 83	$ 210	$ (250)
Cash—Beginning of Year.	143	226	436
Cash—End of Year.	$ 226	$ 436	$ 186

NOTE: Delay calculating interest expense until after computing interest-bearing debt on the balance sheet.

Income Tax Expense:

Scenarios 1 and 2: 35 percent of net income before income taxes.

NOTE: Delay computing income tax expense until after computing interest expense and net income before taxes.

EXHIBIT 4

McDonald's Corporation
Financial Statement Ratios
(Case 10.2)

	Year 2	Year 3	Year 4
Profit Margin....................................	16.6%	16.8%	17.4%
Total Assets Turnover...........................	0.6	0.6	0.6
Rate of Return on Assets........................	10.1%	10.4%	10.9%
Common Earnings Leverage......................	75.5%	78.5%	80.4%
Capital Structure Leverage......................	2.4	2.2	2.1
Rate of Return on Common Shareholders' Equity	18.7%	18.3%	18.3%
Cost of Goods Sold ÷ Revenues...................	64.8%	62.7%	61.4%
Selling and Administrative Expenses ÷ Revenues	10.0%	11.7%	11.8%
Interest Expense ÷ Revenues.....................	5.8%	5.2%	4.3%
Income Tax Expense ÷ Revenues..................	10.6%	10.5%	11.0%
Accounts Receivable Turnover....................	25.3	25.8	24.9
Inventory Turnover	100.8	102.9	104.5
Fixed Asset Turnover	0.7	0.7	0.8
Current Ratio..................................	0.5	0.6	0.6
Quick Ratio	0.4	0.5	0.5
Days Accounts Payable..........................	28	27	30
Cash Flow from Operations ÷ Current Liabilities	114.5%	100.7%	126.9%
Total Liabilities to Total Assets	57.4%	49.6%	47.9%
Long-Term Debt to Total Assets	37.6%	27.2%	29.0%
Long-Term Debt to Shareholders' Equity............	88.3%	53.9%	55.6%
Cash Flow from Operations to Total Liabilities	21.9%	23.2%	29.1%
Interest Coverage Ratio..........................	4.3	4.9	6.3
Cash Flow from Operations to Capital Expenditures..	1.3	1.3	1.3

BALANCE SHEET

Scenarios 1 and 2: Total assets will grow at the growth rates in sales. Use the common size balance sheet percentages in Exhibit 5 to allocate the total assets amounts to individual assets, liabilities, and shareholders' equity accounts. Leave the amounts for retained earnings and treasury stock blank at this point.

NOTE: You can now compute interest expense on interest-bearing debt, income tax expense, and net income.

Retained Earnings: The change in retained earnings equals net income minus preferred and common dividends. Assume that preferred dividends each year will increase at the growth rate in preferred stock. Assume that common dividends will increase at the growth rate in net income available to common.

Treasury Stock: The amount for treasury stock is the amount necessary to equate total assets with total liabilities plus shareholders' equity.

EXHIBIT 5

McDonald's Corporation
Pro Forma Common Size Balance Sheet Percentages
(Case 10.2)

	Scenario 1		Scenario 2	
	Year 5	Year 6	Year 5	Year 6
Assets				
Cash	1.5%	1.8%	1.5%	1.8%
Accounts Receivable	2.7	2.8	2.5	2.4
Inventories	0.4	0.4	0.4	0.4
Prepayments.........................	1.0	1.0	1.0	1.0
Total Current Assets.................	5.6%	6.0%	5.4%	5.6%
Investments	3.9	4.1	3.6	3.4
Property, Plant, and Equipment (at cost)...	114.5	117.7	115.3	118.0
Accumulated Depreciation	(31.8)	(35.6)	(31.3)	(34.0)
Other Assets..........................	7.8	7.8	7.0	7.0
Total Assets	100.0%	100.0%	100.0%	100.0%
Liabilities and Shareholders' Equity				
Accounts Payable......................	3.3%	3.3%	3.4%	3.4%
Notes Payable........................	1.9	2.8	1.3	1.4
Current Portion of Long-Term Debt.......	0.3	0.3	0.3	0.3
Other Current Liabilities	3.8	3.6	4.2	4.4
Total Current Liabilities...............	9.3%	10.0%	9.2%	9.5%
Long-Term Debt	28.0	27.0	30.0	31.0
Deferred Income Taxes..................	6.9	6.9	6.9	6.9
Other Noncurrent Liabilities	2.9	3.0	2.9	3.0
Total Liabilities	47.1%	46.9%	49.0%	50.4%
Preferred Stock	3.5%	3.5%	3.5%	3.5%
Common Stock	2.9	2.9	2.9	2.9
Retained Earnings.....................	?	?	?	?
Cumulative Translation Adjustment	(1.1)	0.3	(1.1)	0.3
Treasury Stock........................	?	?	?	?
Total Shareholders' Equity.............	52.9%	53.1%	51.0%	49.6%
Total Liabilities and Shareholders' Equity	100.0%	100.0%	100.0%	100.0%

STATEMENT OF CASH FLOWS

The amounts for the statement of cash flows reflect the changes in various balance sheet accounts. Assume that changes in deferred income taxes and other noncurrent liabilities are operating items, the changes in other assets are investing transactions, and the changes in the cumulative translation adjustment account are financing transactions.

REQUIRED (continued from page 569)

c. Assess the changes in the profitability and risk of McDonald's under the two strategic scenarios.

Learning Objectives

1. Consider the following issues in applying the present value of expected cash flows valuation method: use of cash flows versus earnings, cash flows to the investor versus cash flows to the firm, relevant cash flows for the firm (unleveraged- versus leveraged-free cash flows), nominal versus real cash flows, pretax versus after-tax cash flows, the forecast horizon, the terminal value, and the cost of capital.
2. Apply the present value of future cash flows valuation method.

Much of the work of security analysts and investment bankers involves valuation. Questions typically addressed include: Should I make a buy, sell, or hold recommendation on a particular firm's common shares? At what price should we price the initial public offering of a firm's common shares? What is a reasonable price to accept (seller) or pay (buyer) for a firm involved in a corporate acquisition?

Economic theory teaches that the value of any resource equals the present value of the returns expected from the resource discounted at a rate that reflects the risk inherent in those expected returns. Thus,

$$\text{Value}_t = \sum_{t=1}^{n} \frac{\text{Returns}_t}{(1 + \text{Discount Rate})^t}$$

This chapter discusses valuation approaches that use expected *cash flows* as the measure of returns. Chapter 12 discusses valuation methods that use accrual accounting *earnings* as the measure of returns.

RATIONALE FOR CASH FLOW—BASED VALUATION

The rationale for using expected cash flows in valuation is twofold:

1. Cash is the ultimate source of value. When individuals and firms invest in any resource, they delay current consumption in favor of future consumption. Cash is the medium of exchange that will permit them to consume various goods and services in the future. A resource has value because of its ability to provide future cash flows.
2. Cash serves as a measurable common denominator for comparing the future benefits of alternative investment opportunities. A machine used in a factory provides benefits in the form of production services. An office building leased to others provides benefits in the form of rental services. An airplane or automobile provides transportation services. Comparing these investment alternatives requires a common measuring unit of their future benefits. The future cash flows derived from their future services serve such a function. The factory machine produces a product that the firm can sell for cash. The office building provides monthly rental fees. The airplane provides cash from ticket sales. The automobile saves cash that the individual or firm would otherwise have to pay to lease transportation services from others.

Chapter 12 considers earnings as an alternative to cash flows as a measure of future benefits. Economists argue that (1) the investor cannot spend earnings for future consumption, (2) accrual earnings are subject to numerous questionable accounting methods (for example, acquisition cost valuations of assets, immediate expensing of research and development costs), as well as manipulation by management. Thus, earnings is not as reliable or meaningful as a common denominator for comparing investment alternatives as cash. A dollar of cash is a dollar of cash. A dollar of earnings by one firm is not necessarily equal to a dollar of earnings by another firm.[1]

OVERVIEW OF CASH FLOW—BASED VALUATION

The valuation of any resource using cash flows involves identifying three elements:

1. The expected periodic cash flows.
2. The expected cash flow at the end of the forecast horizon, referred to as the *terminal value.*
3. The discount rate used to compute the present value of the future cash flows.

The sections following discuss each of these elements more fully.

---

[1] Chapter 12 addresses these concerns and raises questions about the meaningfulness of cash flows as a measure of benefits received.

PERIODIC CASH FLOWS

Cash Flows to the Investor versus Cash Flows to the Firm.   Most of the valuation settings considered in this chapter involve valuing the common stock equity of a firm. Should the analyst use as the measure of periodic cash flows the dividends expected to be paid to the investor or the cash flows expected to be generated by the firm from using assets? Cash flows to the investor and cash flows generated by a firm each period will differ to the extent that the firm reinvests a portion (or all) of the cash flows generated during the period.

If the firm generates a rate of return on retained cash flow equal to the discount rate used by the investor (that is, the cost of equity capital), then either set of cash flows will yield the same valuation of a firm's shares at a point in time. Consider the following scenarios.

Example 1.   A firm expects to generate cash flows of 15 percent annually on invested equity capital. Equity investors in this firm desire a return of 15 percent each year. Assume that the firm pays out 100 percent of these operating cash flows each year as a dividend. Thus, the cash flows generated by the firm equal the cash received by the investor. Each dollar of capital committed by the investor has a present value of future cash flows equal to one dollar. That is,

$$\$1 = \sum_{t=1}^{n} \frac{\$.15}{(1.15)^t}$$

Example 2.   Assume the same facts as in Example 1, except that the firm pays out none of the cash flows from operations as a dividend. The firm retains the $.15 cash inflow on each dollar of capital committed and reinvests it at 15 percent. In this case, the investor receives cash only when the common stock is sold or the firm liquidates. Define this terminal date as n. In this case also, each dollar of capital committed by the investor has a present value of future cash flows equal to one dollar. That is,

$$\$1 = \frac{(1.15)^n}{(1.15)^n}$$

Example 3.   Assume the same facts as in Example 1, except that the firm pays out 25 percent of the cash flow from operations as a dividend and retains the other 75 percent. The retained cash flows generate a return of 15 percent. In this case also, each dollar of capital committed by the investor has a present value of future cash flows equal to one dollar. Thus,

$$\$1 = \sum_{t=1}^{n} \frac{(.25)(.15)}{(1.15)^t} + \frac{(.75)(1.15)^n}{(1.15)^n}$$

These three examples simply illustrate the irrelevance of dividend policy in the valuation of a firm. The same valuation should arise whether the analyst discounts

(1) the expected periodic and liquidating dividend to the investor or (2) the expected cash flows to the firm. Because liquidating dividends are seldom observable, most empirical research involving valuation discounts the firm's expected cash flows. We follow this approach as well in this chapter.

Relevant Firm-Level Cash Flows.   Which cash-flow amounts from the projected statement of cash flows should the analyst discount to a present value when valuing a firm? Consider the following possibilities:

1. Cash flow from operations.
2. Cash flow from operations before subtracting cash required to service debt, net of tax effects, minus the net cash outflow for investing, commonly referred to as *unleveraged-free cash flow*.
3. Cash flow from operations after subtracting debt service costs net of taxes minus the net cash outflow for investing plus or minus the increase or decrease in debt financing, commonly referred to as *leveraged-free cash flow* or *cash flow available to shareholders*.[2]

The appropriate cash-flow measure depends on the resource to be valued.

1. If the objective is to value the *assets* of a firm, then the unleveraged-free cash flow (measure 2 above) is the appropriate cash flow. A subsequent section of this chapter indicates that the appropriate discount rate is the weighted average cost of capital.
2. If the objective is to value the *common shareholders' equity* of a firm, then the leveraged-free cash flow (measure 3 above) is the appropriate cash flow. A later section indicates that the appropriate discount rate is the cost of equity capital.

The difference between these two valuations is, of course, the value of total liabilities. One could always value total liabilities by discounting the debt service costs (including repayments of principal) at the after-tax cost of debt capital. Subtracting the value of total liabilities from the value of total assets will yield the value of common equity. The approach followed depends on the valuation setting.

Example 4.   One firm desires to acquire the operating assets of a division of another firm. The acquiring firm will replace the current financing structure of the division with a financing structure of its own. The relevant cash flows for deciding on the price to pay for the division's assets are the operating cash flows that those assets are expected to generate (before subtracting financing costs) minus the net cash outflow for investing. Subtracting the net cash outflow for investing provides for

---

[2]It might appear inappropriate to include changes in debt financing, which appear in the financing section of the statement of cash flows, in the valuation of a firm. Theory suggests that the capital structure (that is, the proportion of debt versus equity) should not affect the value. Changes in debt, however, affect the amount of cash available to the common shareholders. The analyst includes cash flows related to debt but adjusts the cost of equity capital to reflect the amount of debt in the capital structure.

the needed replacement or enhancement of fixed assets to sustain or increase future operating cash flows. The acquiring firm would then discount these projected cash flows at the weighted average cost of capital of the new division (which, in theory, should be the weighted average cost of capital of the acquiring firm because all financing finances all investments).

Example 5.   An investor desires to value a potential common stock equity investment in a firm. The relevant cash flows are the leveraged-free cash flows. Cash flow from operations includes the returns generated from using debt capital as well as the cash required to service the debt. Thus, cash flow from operations (plus or minus changes in debt in the financing section of the statement of cash flows) captures the beneficial (or detrimental) effects of financial leverage on the value of the common equity. The investor should discount projected leveraged-free cash flows at the desired return on equity capital.

Example 6.   The managers of a firm intend to engage in a leveraged buyout (LBO) of a firm. The structure of a typical LBO is as follows:

1. The managers offer to purchase the outstanding common shares of the target firm at a particular price if current shareholders will tender them.
2. The managers invest their own funds for a portion of the purchase price (usually 20 to 25 percent) and borrow the remainder from various lenders. The borrowing is generally contingent on having a certain proportion of the outstanding shares tendered (at least 51 percent but usually a higher percentage). The tendered shares serve as collateral for the loan (called a *bridge loan* for the reason explained below).
3. The managers use the equity and debt capital raised to purchase the tendered shares.
4. After gaining voting control of the firm, the managers have the firm engage in sufficient new borrowing to repay the bridge loan obtained to execute the LBO. In this way, the lenders have a direct claim on the assets of the firm. Also, the managers shift any personal guarantees they may have made on the bridge loan to the firm itself on the new borrowing.

Deciding on the price to pay for the tendered common shares can follow the usual procedure for an equity investment (see Example 5 above). This price should equal the present value of leveraged-free cash flows discounted at the cost of common equity capital. The projected debt service costs after the LBO will differ significantly from their historical levels. The valuation of the equity must reflect the new capital structure and the related debt service costs. Also, the cost of equity capital will likely increase as a result of the higher level of debt in the capital structure (that is, the common shareholders bear more risk as residual claimants on the assets of the firm). The valuation must likewise reflect the new cost of equity capital.

An alternative approach that produces the same value for the common equity is to treat an LBO as a purchase of assets (similar to Example 4 above). That is, compute the present value of the unleveraged-free cash flows using the weighted average cost of debt and equity capital. This amount represents the value of total assets. Subtract from total assets the market value of debt raised to execute the LBO (the debt to assets percentage used here should be the same as the weight for debt in the weighted average cost of capital).[3] The result is the market value of the common equity.

Nominal versus Real Cash Flows.   Changes in general price levels (that is, inflation or deflation) cause the purchasing power of the monetary unit to vary over time. Even after adjusting for the time value of money, a dollar expected to be received one year from today does not necessarily have the same purchasing power as a dollar on hand. Should the projected cash flows used in valuing a resource reflect *nominal amounts,* which include inflationary or deflationary components, or *real amounts,* which filter out the effect of changes in general purchasing power?[4]

The valuation of a resource should be the same whether one uses nominal cash-flow amounts or real cash-flow amounts as long as the discount rate used is consistent with the cash flows. That is, if projected cash flows ignore changes in the general purchasing power of the monetary unit, then the discount rate should incorporate an inflation component. If projected cash flows filter out the effects of general price changes, then the discount rate should exclude the inflation component.

Example 7.   A firm owns a tract of land that it expects to sell one year from today for $115 million. This selling price reflects a 15 percent increase in the selling price of the land during the coming year. The general price level is expected to increase 10 percent during this period. The real interest rate is 2 percent.

The value of the land today to the firm is $102.5 million, as shown below:[5]

Nominal Cash Flow ×	Discount Rate Including Expected Inflation	=	Value
$115 million ×	$1/(1.02)(1.10)$	=	$102.5 million
Real Cash Flow ×	**Discount Rate Excluding Expected Inflation**	=	**Value**
$115 million/1.10 ×	$1/(1.02)$	=	$102.5 million

---

[3]It is irrelevant whether any debt on the books of the target firm carries over after the LBO or whether the firm engages in additional borrowing to repay existing debt, as long as the weighted average cost of capital properly reflects the costs of each financing arrangement.

[4]Note that the issue here is not with specific price changes of a firm's particular assets, liabilities, revenues, and expenses. These specific price changes affect cash flows and should enter into the valuation of the firm. The issue is whether some portion, all, or more than all of the specific price changes represents simply a change in the purchasing power of the monetary unit, which should not affect the value of a firm.

[5]A 15 percent specific price increase for the land suggests that the market value today is $100 million, not $102.5 million. Perhaps the firm expects a higher rate of specific price change (15 percent) than the market in general anticipates.

The discounting of nominal cash flows using nominal discount rates is usually easier in practical settings than discounting real cash flows using real interest rates. The latter approach requires the identification of expected inflation rates for many future periods, a procedure likely to include considerable measurement error.

Pretax versus After-Tax Cash Flows.   Extending the discussion in the preceding section, will the same valuation arise if the analyst discounts pretax cash flows at a pretax cost of capital and after-tax cash flows at an after-tax cost of capital? The answer to this question is no.

Example 8.   Consider the following calculation of the cost of capital for a firm.

	Proportion in Capital Structure	Pretax Cost	Tax Effect	After-Tax Cost	Weighted Average Cost of Capital	
					Pretax	After-Tax
Debt	0.33	10%	0.4	6%	3.33%	2.00%
Equity	0.67	18%	—	18%	12.00	12.00
	1.00				15.33%	14.00%

Assume that this firm expects to generate $90 million of pretax unleveraged-free cash flows and $54 million of after-tax unleveraged-free cash flows [$= (1 - 0.4)(\$90$ million)] one year from today. The valuation of this firm using pretax and after-tax amounts (assuming a one-year horizon) is as follows:

Pretax	$90 million $\times$ 1/1.1533 = $78.04 million
After-tax	$54 million $\times$ 1/1.14 = $47.37 million

The lack of equivalence in valuation occurs because cash inflows from assets are taxed at 40 percent and cash outflows to service debt give rise to a tax savings of 40 percent. The cost of equity capital, however, does not provide a tax benefit. The appropriate valuation in this case is $47.37 million. Thus, the analyst should use after-tax cash flows and the after-tax cost of capital.

Selecting a Forecast Horizon.   For how many future years should the analyst project periodic cash flows? The correct answer theoretically is the expected life of the resource to be valued. This life is a finite number of years for a machine, building, or similar resource with limits to its physical existence. In many valuation contexts, however, the resource to be valued is an equity claim on the portfolio of net assets of a firm, a resource that has an infinite life (except in the event of bankruptcy). The analyst must project future periodic cash flows for some number of years and then estimate the likely residual, or terminal, value at the end of this forecast horizon. Chapter 10 demonstrated that the prediction of future periodic cash flows involves the making of assumptions regarding each item in the income statement and balance sheet and then deriving its related cash-flow effect. As the next section discusses, estimation of the residual value generally involves short-cut procedures that do not require the analyst to project individual financial statement items for too many years into the future.

Selecting a forecast horizon involves trade-offs. Using a relatively short forecast horizon, such as three to five years, increases the likely accuracy of the projected periodic cash flows, since the near term is often an extrapolation of the recent past. These near-term periodic cash flows also have the heaviest weight in the present value computations. Using a relatively short forecast horizon, however, results in a large portion of the total present value being related to the residual value. The valuation process is particularly difficult when the near-term cash flows are projected to be negative, as is common for a rapidly growing firm that finances its growth by issuing common stock. In this case, all of the firm's value relates to the less detailed estimation of the residual value.

Selecting a larger number of years in the forecast of periodic cash flows, such as ten to fifteen years, reduces the influence of the estimated residual value on the total present value. However, the predictive accuracy of detailed cash flow forecasts this far into the future is likely to be questionable.

It is desirable to select as a forecast horizon the point at which a firm's cash-flow pattern has settled into an equilibrium. This equilibrium position could be either no growth in future cash flows or growth at a stable rate. Security analysts typically select a forecast horizon in the range of four to seven years.

RESIDUAL VALUE

When a firm's cash-flow pattern has settled into an equilibrium at the end of the forecast horizon, the analyst can estimate the residual value at that time using the following valuation model.[6]

$$\text{Residual Value at End of Forecast Horizon}_n = \text{Periodic Cash Flow}_{n-1} \times \frac{1 + g}{r - g}$$

where

         g = annual growth rate in periodic cash flows after the forecast horizon
         r = discount rate
         n = forecast horizon

Example 9.   An analyst forecasts that the leveraged-free cash flow of a firm in Year 5 is $30 million. This firm is mature with zero growth expected in future cash flows (that is, the operating cash inflows from investments made in previous years exactly equal the cash outflow for investments each year). The residual value at the

---

[6]This formula is simply the algebraic simplification for the present value of a growing perpetuity.

end of the forecast period, assuming a 15 percent cost of equity capital, is computed as follows:

$$\text{Residual Value at End of Forecast period} = \$30 \text{ million} \times \frac{1 + .00}{.15 - .00} = \frac{\$30 \text{ million}}{.15}$$

$$= \$200 \text{ million}$$

The present value at the beginning of Year 1 of this estimated residual value is $99.4 million [= $200 million $\times 1/(1.15)^5$].

Example 10.   Assume the same facts as in Example 9 except that the analyst expects the cash flow after Year 5 to grow at 6 percent each year. The computation of the residual value is as follows:

$$\text{Residual Value at End of Forecast Period} = \$30 \text{ million} \times \frac{1 + .06}{.15 - .06}$$

$$= \$30 \text{ million} \times \frac{1.06}{.09} = \$353.3 \text{ million}$$

The present value of the residual value at the beginning of Year 1 is $175.7 million.

Example 11.   Assume the same facts as in Example 9 except that the analyst expects the cash flow after Year 5 to decline 6 percent each year. The computation of the residual value appears follows:

$$\text{Residual Value at End of Forecast Period} = \$30 \text{ million} \times \frac{1 - .06}{.15 - (-.06)}$$

$$= \$30 \text{ million} \times \frac{.94}{.21} = \$134.3 \text{ million}$$

The present value of the residual value at the beginning of Year 1 is $66.8 million. The cash flows of a firm in decline will eventually reach zero (or the firm will become bankrupt). As long as this point occurs many years in the future, it will not have much influence on the present value.

Analysts frequently estimate a residual value using multiples of six to eight times leveraged-free cash flow in the last year of the forecast horizon. The table below shows the cash-flow multiples using $(1 + g)/(r - g)$ for various costs of equity capital and growth rates.

Cash Flow Multiples

Cost of Equity Capital	Growth Rate		
	2%	4%	6%
15%	7.8	9.5	11.8
18%	6.4	7.4	8.8
20%	5.7	6.5	7.6

Thus, multiples of six to eight times free cash flow fall within the range of common levels for the cost of equity capital and growth rates.

An alternative approach for estimating the residual value is to use the free cash-flow multiples for comparable firms that currently trade in the market. This approach provides a degree of market validation for the theoretical model discussed above. The analyst identifies comparable companies by studying growth rates in free cash flows, profitability levels, risk characteristics, and similar factors. These same inputs are also needed to apply the theoretical model.

Analysts also frequently use earnings-based models, such as price-earnings ratios or market to book value ratios, to estimate a residual value. We discuss earnings-based valuation models in Chapter 12.

COST OF CAPITAL

A third valuation variable in the present value of cash-flows model is the discount rate. This discount rate equals to the rate of return that investors require the firm to generate to induce them to commit capital, given the level of risk involved.

For purposes of computing the weighted average cost of capital (used when valuing the assets of a firm), the cost of debt capital equals one minus the marginal tax rate appropriate to interest deductions times the yield to maturity of debt. The yield to maturity is the rate that discounts the contractual cash flows on the debt to the debt's current market value. The yield to maturity will equal the coupon rate on the debt only if the debt sells on the market at par, or face, value.

Capitalized lease obligations have a cost equal to the current interest rate on collateralized borrowing with equivalent risk. The analyst should include the present value of significant operating lease commitments in the calculation of the weighted average cost of capital. The lessor bears more risk in an operating lease than in a capital lease, so the cost of capital represented by operating leases is higher than for capital leases. If the analyst treats operating leases as part of debt financing, then the cash outflow for rent should be reclassified as interest and repayment of debt when computing leveraged- and unleveraged-free cash flows.

The common practice is to exclude accounts payable and other current operating liability accounts from the calculation of the weighted average cost of capital. Instead, analysts typically treat these items as negative working capital investments. The present value of unleveraged-free cash flows is the value of total assets net of current operating liabilities.

The cost of underfunded pension liabilities is the discount rate used to compute the accumulated and projected benefit obligations. This discount rate changes each period in response to market interest rates, similar to the yield to maturity on debt.

The treatment of deferred tax liabilities in the calculation of the weighted average cost of capital is controversial. Critics of deferred tax accounting argue that only shrinking firms ever pay deferred taxes. Thus, deferred taxes are not a liability for most firms. They merely represent an attempt by accountants to allocate income tax expense between periods. Such critics would transfer the balance in the deferred tax liability account back to retained earnings. This transfer increases the proportion of common equity in the capital structure and therefore the weight applied to the cost of common equity capital. Proponents of deferred tax accounting argue that the accounting for income taxes under FASB *Statement No. 109* gives deferred tax accounting many attributes of liabilities. For example, the accountant uses the income tax rate that applies to the period when timing differences reverse and deferred taxes are paid to measure the deferred tax liability. The deferred tax liability, however, does not incorporate a valuation allowance to reflect the probability of payment, as is required for deferred tax assets. Also, accountants report deferred tax liabilities at their undiscounted amount, which is inconsistent with other noncurrent liabilities. Using the reported amount of deferred tax liabilities to determine their weight in the cost of capital therefore overstates their relative importance. In the few cases where deferred taxes compose a large portion of a firm's capital structure, the analyst should assess the likelihood of payment (for example, whether the firm is growing, stable, or declining) and treat deferred taxes as either equity or debt accordingly. In most cases, treatment of deferred taxes as either equity or debt will not materially influence the weighted average cost of capital.

The cost of any preferred stock capital depends on the preference conditions. Preferred stock that has a preference as to dividends and ordering in liquidation, relative to common shares, generally sells near its par value. Its cost is therefore the dividend rate on the preferred stock. Because dividends on preferred stock are not tax deductible, its pretax and after-tax costs are the same. Preferred stock that is convertible into common stock has both preferred and common equity attributes. Its cost is a blending of the cost of nonconvertible preferred stock and common equity.

Several approaches appear in the literature for measuring the cost of common equity capital. The approach most commonly encountered uses the theory underlying the capital asset pricing model (CAPM). In equilibrium, the cost of common equity capital equals the market rate of return earned by common equity capital. The market rate of return is a function of level of systematic risk inherent in a particular firm's common stock.[7] Systematic risk relates to the covariability of a firm's stock price with stock prices of all firms in the market. As Chapter 9 discusses, CAPM measures systematic risk using the market beta for a firm's common stock. The cost of common equity capital is as follows:

$$
\begin{array}{c} \text{Cost of Common} \\ \text{Equity Capital} \end{array} = \begin{array}{c} \text{Interest Rate} \\ \text{on Risk-Free} \\ \text{Securities} \end{array} + \begin{array}{c} \text{Market} \\ \text{Beta} \end{array} \left[\begin{array}{c} \text{Average Return on} \\ \text{the Market Portfolio} \end{array} - \begin{array}{c} \text{Interest Rate} \\ \text{on Risk-Free} \\ \text{Securities} \end{array} \right]
$$

All common equity securities have a cost at least equal to the interest rate on risk-free securities. Equity securities are not risk free, of course. The term in brackets represents the *average* excess return over the risk-free rate that the market provides to investors for assuming more systematic risk as equity investors. An equity security with the average amount of systematic risk of all equity securities in the market

---

[7]Note that this model views nonsystematic risk as diversifiable by the investor. The market, according to CAPM, does not provide a return for a firm's nonsystematic risk.

has a market beta of 1.0. The cost of common equity capital for such a firm is the average return on the market portfolio. Firms with a market beta larger than 1.0 have higher systematic risk than average; their cost of capital is commensurately higher. Firms with market betas less than 1.0 have lower systematic risk than average and thereby have a lower cost of equity capital. Figure 11.1 sets out the relations graphically.

The objective in selecting a risk-free interest rate is to use securities that have zero systematic risk, or correlation with market rates of return, and zero default risk. It might seem appropriate to use the yield on long-term U.S. government securities. However, the longer the term to maturity, the greater is the sensitivity of the yields on U.S. government securities to changes in inflation and interest rates, and therefore the greater the systematic risk (although the systematic risk is still quite low). Common practice uses the yield on ether short- or intermediate-term U.S. government securities as the risk-free rate. This rate has historically averaged around 3 percent.

The average return on the market portfolio depends on the period studied and whether the analyst uses a geometric mean or arithmetic mean in measuring market returns. Historically, the market rate of return has varied between 9 and 13 percent.

Various financial reference sources regularly publish market betas for publicly traded firms, including Standard & Poor's *Stock Reports.* It is not uncommon to find considerable variation in the published amounts for market beta among the various sources. This occurs in part because of variations in the period used to calculate the betas.

FIGURE 11.1

Relation between Cost of Equity Capital and Systematic Risk

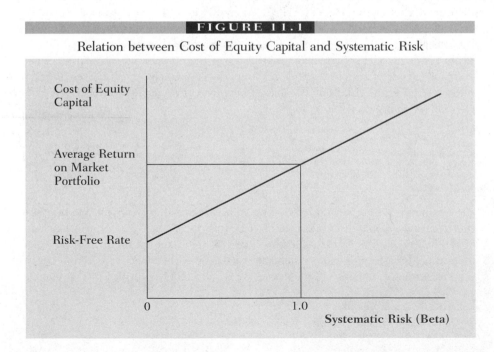

Using CAPM to calculate the cost of equity capital has been subject to various criticisms:

1. Market betas do not appear to be stable over time and are sensitive to the time period used in their computation.
2. The excess market rate of return is not stable over time and is likewise sensitive to the time period used in its calculation.
3. Recent research by Fama and French suggests that during the 1980s, size was a better proxy for risk than was market beta.[8]

An alternative approach to using CAPM to measure the cost of equity capital is to use arbitrage price theory models (APT). APT is similar to CAPM in that the cost of equity capital equals the risk-free rate plus an incremental amount for the systematic risk in an equity security. Unlike CAPM, which relies on a single measure of systematic risk (market beta), APT relies on multiple measures. Empirical research suggests five important components of systematic risk:

1. Industrial production.
2. Short-term real interest rate on U.S. government securities.
3. Unexpected changes in inflation in the short term.
4. Long-term inflation.
5. Default risk on long-term debt securities.

One might view APT as an extension of CAPM that attempts to identify more fully the factors that explain systematic risk.

ILLUSTRATION OF CASH FLOW—BASED VALUATION

To illustrate this valuation approach, refer to the pro forma statement of cash flows for Pepsi in Exhibit 10.3. Suppose the analyst concludes that the projected cash flows reliably reflect Pepsi's expected cash flows during Year 9 through Year 12. The net cash flows available to common shareholders' follow.

	Year 9	Year 10	Year 11	Year 12
Cash Flow from Operations.......	$ 4,019	$ 4,547	$ 5,137	$ 5,796
Cash Flow from Investing	(4,009)	(4,395)	(4,970)	(5,622)
Cash Flow from Debt Financing...	646	1,174	1,328	1,503
Leveraged-Free Cash Flow........	$ 656	$ 1,326	$ 1,495	$ 1,677
Growth Rate for the Year.........	(28.1%)	202.1%	12.7%	12.2%

---

[8]Eugene F. Fama and Kenneth R. French, "The Cross Section of Expected Stock Returns," *The Journal of Finance*, June 1992, pp. 427–465.

The analyst must make some assumption about net cash flows after Year 12. The growth rate in leveraged-free cash flows settled down in Year 11 and Year 12 after fluctuating widely in Year 9 and Year 10. The average compound annual growth rate between Year 10 and Year 12 is 12.46 percent. We assume that this growth rate will continue after Year 12.

The analyst must discount these cash flows to their present value. The discount rate should reflect the investor's desired rate of return, adjusted to reflect the risk inherent in investing in Pepsi. Pepsi's market beta at the end of Year 8 is 1.1. Assuming a 3 percent risk-free rate and an excess of market return over the risk-free rate of 12 percent, the cost of equity capital is 16.2 percent [= 3.0% + 1.1(12.0%)].[9] The valuation of Pepsi using the present value valuation model is $31,079 million, as shown:

Year	Cash Flow	Present Value Factor at 16.2 Percent	Present Value
9	$ 656	.86059	$ 565
10	$ 1,326	.74061	$ 982
11	$ 1,495	.63736	$ 953
12	$ 1,677	.54845	$ 920
After Year 12	$50,427[a]	.54845	$27,657
Total Present Value			$31,077

[a]$1,677 \times \dfrac{1.1246}{.1620 - .1246} = \$50,427.$

Based on the 798.8 million shares outstanding at the end of Year 8, the market price should be $38.91 (= $31,077/798.8) to yield a return of 16.2 percent. Pepsi's actual market price at the end of Year 8 was $40.88. The difference between these two prices might result from (1) inaccurate projections of future cash flows, (2) error in measuring the cost of equity capital, and (3) market inefficiencies in the pricing of Pepsi.

SUMMARY

This chapter illustrates valuation using the present value of future cash flows. As with the preparation of pro forma financial statements in Chapter 10, the reasonableness of the valuation depends on the reasonableness of the assumptions. The analyst should assess the sensitivity of the valuation to alternative assumptions regarding growth and discount rates.

---

[9]An excess of the market return over the risk-free rate of 12 percent is somewhat high. We assume this rate for illustrative purposes in order to use the terminal value valuation model of $(1 + g)/(r - g)$. This valuation model "explodes" when r and g are similar. The value of g for Pepsi is 12.46 percent. Assuming, say, a 10 percent excess of the market return over the risk-free rate results in a value for r of 14 percent, an amount close to the g for Pepsi of 12.46 percent.

Because we used only a four-year horizon for projecting Pepsi's cash flows, the terminal value dominates the valuation. This terminal value is heavily influenced by the assumed growth rate in cash flows. The analyst should also compute the value of firms by using other approaches, such as the earnings-based approaches discussed in Chapter 12, to validate the cash-based approach.

HOLMES CORPORATION: LBO VALUATION

Holmes Corporation is a leading designer and manufacturer of material handling and process equipment for heavy industry in the United States and abroad. Its sales have more than doubled and its earnings increased more than sixfold in the past five years. In material handling, Holmes is a major producer of electric overhead and gantry cranes, ranging from 5 tons in capacity to 600-ton giants, the latter used primarily in nuclear and conventional power generating plants. It also builds underhung cranes and monorail systems for general industrial use carrying loads up to 40 tons, railcar movers, railroad and mass transit shop maintenance equipment, and a broad line of advanced package conveyors. Holmes is a world leader in evaporation and crystallization systems and also furnishes dryers, heat exchangers, and filters to complete its line of chemical processing equipment sold internationally to the chemical, fertilizer, food, drug, and paper industries. For the metallurgical industry, it designs and manufactures electric arc and induction furnaces, cupolas, ladles, and hot metal distribution equipment.

The information on the following pages appears in the 1995 annual report of Holmes Corporation.

HIGHLIGHTS

	1995	1994
Net Sales	$102,698,836	$109,372,718
Net Earnings	6,601,908	6,583,360
Net Earnings per Share	3.62[a]	3.61[a]
Cash Dividends Paid	2,241,892	1,426,502
Cash Dividends per Share	1.22[a]	.78[a]
Shareholders' Equity	29,333,803	24,659,214
Shareholders' Equity per Share	16.07[a]	13.51[a]
Working Capital	23,100,863	19,029,626
Orders Received	95,436,103	80,707,576
Unfilled Orders at End of Period	77,455,900	84,718,633
Average Number of Common Shares Outstanding during Period	1,824,853[a]	1,824,754[a]

[a]Adjusted for June 1995 and June 1994 5-for-4 stock distributions.

Net Sales, Net Earnings, and Net Earnings per Share by Quarter. (adjusted for 5-for-4 stock distribution in June 1995 and June 1994)

	1995			1994		
	Net Sales	Net Earnings	Per Share	Net Sales	Net Earnings	Per Share
First Quarter	$ 25,931,457	$1,602,837	$ .88	$ 21,768,077	$1,126,470	$ .62
Second Quarter	24,390,079	1,727,112	.95	28,514,298	1,716,910	.94
Third Quarter	25,327,226	1,505,118	.82	28,798,564	1,510,958	.82
Fourth Quarter	27,050,074	1,766,841	.97	30,291,779	2,229,022	1.23
	$102,698,836	$6,601,908	$3.62	$109,372,718	$6,583,360	$3.61

Common Stock Prices and Cash Dividends Paid per Common Share by Quarter. (adjusted for 5-for-4 stock distribution in June 1995 and June 1994)

	1995			1994		
	Stock Prices		Cash Dividends per Share	Stock Prices		Cash Dividends per Share
	High	Low		High	Low	
First Quarter	22 1/2	18 1/2	$ .26	11 1/4	9 1/2	$.16
Second Quarter ..	25 1/4	19 1/2	.26	12 3/8	8 7/8	.16
Third Quarter ...	26 1/4	19 3/4	.325	15 7/8	11 5/8	.20
Fourth Quarter ..	28 1/8	23 1/4	.375	20 7/8	15 7/8	.26
			$1.22			$.78

MANAGEMENT'S REPORT TO SHAREHOLDERS

1995 was a pleasant surprise for all of us at Holmes Corporation. When the year started, it looked as though 1995 would be a good year but not up to the record performance of 1994. However, due to the excellent performance of our employees and the benefit of a favorable acquisition, 1995 produced both record earnings and the largest cash dividend outlay in the company's 93-year history.

There is no doubt that some of the attractive orders received in late 1992 and early 1993 contributed to 1995 profit. But of major significance was our organization's favorable response to several new management policies instituted to emphasize higher corporate profitability. 1995 showed a net profit on net sales of 6.4 percent, which not only exceeded the 6.0 percent of last year but also represents the highest net margin in several decades.

Net sales for the year were $102,698,836, down 6 percent from the $109,372,718 of a year ago but still were the second largest volume in our history. Net earnings, however, set a new record at $6,601,908, or $3.62 per common share, which slightly exceeded the $6,583,360, or $3.61 per common share earned last year.

Cash dividends paid in 1995 of $2,241,892 were 57 percent above the $1,426,502 paid a year ago. The record total resulted from your Board's approval of two increases during the year. When we implemented the 5-for-4 stock distribution in June 1995, we maintained the quarterly dividend rate of $.325 on the increased number of shares for the January payment. Then, in December 1995, we increased the quarterly rate to $.375 per share.

1995 certainly was not the most exuberant year in the capital equipment markets. Fortunately, our heavy involvement in ecology improvement, power generation, and international markets continued to serve us well, with the result that new orders of $95,436,103 were 18 percent over the $80,707,576 of 1994.

Economists have predicted a substantial capital spending upturn for well over a year, but so far our customers have displayed stubborn reluctance to place new orders amid the uncertainty concerning the economy. Confidence is the answer. As soon as potential buyers can see clearly the future direction of the economy, we expect the unleashing of a large latent demand for capital goods, producing a much-expanded market for Holmes' products.

Fortunately, the accelerating pace of international markets continues to yield new business. 1995 was an excellent year on the international front as our foreign customers continue to recognize our technological leadership in several product lines. Net sales of Holmes products shipped overseas and fees from foreign licensees amounted to $30,495,041, which represents a 31 percent increase over the $23,351,980 of a year ago.

Management fully recognizes and intends to take maximum advantage of our technological leadership in foreign lands. The latest manifestation of this policy was the acquisition of a controlling interest in Societé Francaise Holmes Fermont, our Swenson process equipment licensee located in Paris. Holmes and a partner started this firm 14 years ago as a sales and engineering organization to function in the Common Market. The company currently operates in the same mode. It owns no physical manufacturing assets, subcontracting all production. Its markets have expanded to include Spain and the East European countries.

Holmes Fermont is experiencing strong demand in Europe. For example, in early May, a $5.5 million order for a large potash crystallization system was received from a French engineering company representing a Russian client. Management estimates that Holmes Fermont will contribute approximately $6 to $8 million of net sales in 1996.

Holmes' other wholly owned subsidiaries—Holmes Equipment Limited in Canada, Ermanco Incorporated in Michigan, and Holmes International, Inc., our FSC (Foreign Sales Corporation)—again contributed substantially to the success of 1995. Holmes Equipment Limited registered its second best year. However, capital equipment markets in Canada have virtually come to a standstill in the past two quarters. Ermanco achieved the best year in its history, while Holmes International, Inc., had a truly exceptional year because of the very high level of activity in our international markets.

The financial condition of the company showed further improvement and is now unusually strong as a result of very stringent financial controls. Working capital increased to $23,100,863 from $19,029,626, a 21 percent improvement. Inventories decreased 6 percent from $18,559,231 to $17,491,741. The company currently has no long-term or short-term debt and has considerable cash in short-term instruments. Much of our cash position, however, results from customers' advance payments, which we will absorb as we make shipments on the contracts. Shareholders' equity increased 19 percent to $29,393,803 from $24,690,214 a year ago.

Plant equipment expenditures for the year were $1,172,057, down 18 percent from $1,426,347 of 1994. Several appropriations approved during the year did not require expenditures because of delayed deliveries beyond 1995. The major emphasis again was on our continuing program of improving capacity and efficiency through the purchase of numerically controlled machine tools. We expanded the Ermanco plant by 50 percent, but since this is a leasehold arrangement, we made only minor direct investment. We also improved the Canadian operation by adding more manufacturing space and installing energy-saving insulation.

Labor relations were excellent throughout the year. The Harvey plant continues to be nonunion. We negotiated a new labor contract at the Canadian plant that extends to March 1, 1997. The Pioneer Division in Alabama has a labor contract that does not expire until April 1996. While the union contract at Ermanco expired June 1, 1995, work continues while negotiation proceeds on a new contract. We anticipate no difficulty in reaching a new agreement.

We exerted considerable effort during the year to improve Holmes' image in the investment community. Management held several informative meetings with security analyst groups to enhance the awareness of our activities and corporate performance.

The outlook for 1996, while generally favorable, depends in part on the course of capital spending over the next several months. If the spending rate accelerates, the quickening pace of new orders, coupled with present backlogs, will provide the conditions for another fine year. On the other hand, if general industry continues the reluctant spending pattern of the last two years, 1996 could be a year of maintaining market positions while awaiting better market conditions. Management takes an optimistic view and thus looks for a successful 1996.

The achievement of record earnings and the highest profit margin in decades demonstrates the capability and the dedication of our employees. Management is most grateful for their efforts throughout the excellent year.

T. R. Varnum
President

T. L. Fuller
Chairman

March 15, 1996

REVIEW OF OPERATIONS

1995 was a very active year, although the pace was not at the hectic tempo of 1994. It was a year that showed continued strong demand in some product areas but a dampened rate in others. The product areas that had some special economic circumstances enhancing demand fared well. For example, the continuing effort toward ecological improvement fostered excellent activity in Swenson process equipment. Likewise, the energy concern and the need for more electrical power generation capacity boded well for large overhead cranes. On the other hand, Holmes' products that relate to general industry and depend on the overall capital spending rate for new equipment experienced lesser demand, resulting in lower new orders and reduced backlogs. The affected products were small cranes, underhung cranes, railcar movers, and metallurgical equipment.

1995 was the first full year of operations under some major policy changes instituted to improve Holmes' profitability. The two primary revisions were the restructuring of our marketing effort along product division lines and the conversion of the product division incentive plans to a profit-based formula. The corporate organization adapted extremely well to the new policies. The improved profit margin in 1995, in substantial part, was a result of the changes.

International activity increased markedly during the year. Surging foreign business and the expressed objective to capitalize on Holmes' technological leadership overseas resulted in the elevation of Mr. R. E. Foster to officer status as Vice President–International. The year involved heavy commitments of the product division staffs, engineering groups, and manufacturing organization to such important contracts as the $14 million Swenson order for Poland, the $8 million Swenson project for Mexico, $2 million crane order for Venezuela, and several millions of dollars of railcar movers for all areas of the world.

The acquisition of control and commencement of operating responsibility of Societé Francaise Holmes Fermont, the Swenson licensee in Paris, was a major milestone in our international strategy. This organization has the potential of becoming a very substantial contributor in the years immediately ahead. Its long-range market opportunities in Europe and Asia are excellent.

Material Handling Products.   Material handling equipment activities portrayed conflicting trends. During the year when total backlog decreased, the crane division backlog increased. This was a result of several multimillion dollar contracts for power plant cranes. The small crane market, on the other hand, experienced depressed conditions during most of the year as general industry withheld appropriations for new plant and equipment. The underhung crane market experienced similar conditions. However, as Congressional attitudes and policies on investment unfold, we expect capital spending to show a substantial upturn.

The Transportation Equipment Division secured the second order for orbital service bridges, a new product for the containment vessels of nuclear power plants. This design is unique and allows considerable cost savings in erecting and maintaining containment shells.

The Ermanco Conveyor Division completed its best year with the growing acceptance of the unique XenoROL® design. We expanded the Grand Haven plant by 50 percent to effect further cost reduction and new concepts of marketing.

The railcar moving line continued to produce more business from international markets. We installed the new 11TM unit in six domestic locations, a product showing signs of exceptional performance. We shipped the first foreign 11TM machine to Sweden.

Process Equipment Products.   Process equipment again accounted for slightly more than half of the year's business.

Swenson activity reached an all-time high level with much of the division's effort going into international projects. The large foreign orders required considerable additional work to cover the necessary documentation, metrification when required, and general liaison.

We engaged in considerably more subcontracting during the year to accommodate one-piece shipment of the huge vessels pioneered by Swenson to effect greater equipment economies. The division continued to expand the use of computerization for design work and contract administration. We developed more capability during the year to handle the many additional tasks associated with turnkey projects. Swenson research and development efforts accelerated in search of better technology and new products. We conducted pilot plant test work at our facilities and in the field to convert several sales prospects into new contracts.

The metallurgical business proceeded at a slower pace in 1995. However, with construction activity showing early signs of improvement and automotive and farm machinery manufacturers increasing their operating rates, we see intensified interest in metallurgical equipment.

FINANCIAL STATEMENTS

The financial statements of Holmes Corporation and related notes appear in Exhibits 1 through 3.

NOTES TO CONSOLIDATED FINANCIAL STATEMENTS, 1994 AND 1995

Note A: Summary of Significant Accounting Policies.   Significant accounting policies consistently applied appear below to assist the reader in reviewing the company's consolidated financial statements contained in this report.

> *Consolidation.*   The consolidated financial statements include the accounts of the company and its subsidiaries after eliminating all intercompany transactions and balances.

EXHIBIT 1

Holmes Corporation—Balance Sheet
(amounts in thousands)
(Case 11.1)

	1990	1991	1992	1993	1994	1995
Cash	$ 955	$ 962	$ 865	$ 1,247	$ 1,540	$ 3,857
Marketable Securities	0	0	0	0	0	2,990
Accounts/Notes Receivable..........	6,545	7,295	9,718	13,307	18,759	14,303
Inventories	7,298	8,685	12,797	20,426	18,559	17,492
Current Assets..................	$14,798	$16,942	$23,380	$34,980	$38,858	$38,642
Investments	0	0	0	0	0	422
Property, Plant, & Equipment	12,216	12,445	13,126	13,792	14,903	15,876
Less: Accumulative Depreciation.....	7,846	8,236	8,558	8,988	9,258	9,703
Other Assets......................	470	420	400	299	343	276
Total Assets	$19,638	$21,571	$28,348	$40,083	$44,846	$45,513
Accounts Payable—Trade...........	$ 2,894	$ 4,122	$ 6,496	$ 7,889	$ 6,779	$ 4,400
Notes Payable—Nontrade...........	0	0	700	3,500	0	0
Current Part Long-Term Debt.......	170	170	170	170	170	0
Other Current Liabilities	550	1,022	3,888	8,624	12,879	11,142
Current Liabilities...............	$ 3,614	$ 5,314	$11,254	$20,183	$19,828	$15,542
Long-Term Debt	680	510	340	170	0	0
Deferred Tax (NCL)	0	0	0	216	328	577
Other Noncurrent Liabilities	0	0	0	0	0	0
Total Liabilities	$ 4,294	$ 5,824	$11,594	$20,569	$20,156	$16,119
Common Stock	$ 2,927	$ 2,927	$ 2,927	$ 5,855	$ 7,303	$ 9,214
Additional Paid-in Capital	5,075	5,075	5,075	5,075	5,061	5,286
Retained Earnings.................	7,342	7,772	8,774	8,599	12,297	14,834
Cumulative Translation Adjustment ..	0	0	5	12	29	60
Treasury Stock....................	0	(27)	(27)	(27)	0	0
Shareholder's Equity.............	$15,344	$15,747	$16,754	$19,514	$24,690	$29,394
Total Equities...................	$19,638	$21,571	$28,348	$40,083	$44,846	$45,513

EXHIBIT 2

Holmes Corporation—Income Statement
(amounts in thousands)
(Case 11.1)

	1991	1992	1993	1994	1995
Sales	$ 41,428	$ 53,541	$ 76,328	$109,373	$102,699
Other Revenues & Gains	0	41	0	0	211
Cost of Goods Sold................	(33,269)	(43,142)	(60,000)	(85,364)	(80,260)
Selling & Administrative Expense ...	(6,175)	(7,215)	(9,325)	(13,416)	(12,090)
Other Expenses & Losses...........	(2)	0	(11)	(31)	(1)
EBIT.........................	$ 1,982	$ 3,225	$ 6,992	$ 10,562	$ 10,559
Interest Expense	(43)	(21)	(284)	(276)	(13)
Income Tax Expense...............	(894)	(1,471)	(2,992)	(3,703)	(3,944)
Net Income	$ 1,045	$ 1,733	$ 3,716	$ 6,583	$ 6,602

EXHIBIT 3

Holmes Corporation—Statement of Cash Flow
(amounts in thousands)
(Case 11.1)

	1991	1992	1993	1994	1995
Operations					
Net Income	$ 1,045	$ 1,733	$ 3,716	$ 6,583	$ 6,602
Depreciation and Amortization	491	490	513	586	643
Other Addbacks	20	25	243	151	299
Other Subtractions	0	0	0	0	(97)
WC Provided by Operations	$ 1,556	$ 2,248	$ 4,472	$ 7,320	$ 7,447
(Increase) Decrease in Receivables	(750)	(2,424)	(3,589)	(5,452)	4,456
(Increase) Decrease in Inventories	(1,387)	(4,111)	(7,629)	1,867	1,068
Increase (Decrease) Accounts Payable—Trade	1,228	2,374	1,393	1,496	(2,608)
Increase (Decrease) in Other Current Liabilities	473	2,865	4,737	1,649	(1,508)
Cash from Operations	$ 1,120	$ 952	$ (616)	$ 6,880	$ 8,855
Investing					
Fixed Assets Acquired (net)	$ (347)	$ (849)	$ (749)	$(1,426)	$(1,172)
Investments Acquired	0	0	0	0	(3,306)
Other Investment Transactions	45	0	81	(64)	39
Cash Flow from Investing	$ (302)	$ (849)	$ (668)	$(1,490)	$(4,439)
Financing					
Increase in Short-Term Borrowing	$ 0	$ 700	$ 2,800	$ 0	$ 0
Increase in Long-Term Borrowing	0	0	0	0	0
Issue of Capital Stock	0	0	0	0	315
Decrease in Short-Term Borrowing	0	0	0	(3,500)	0
Decrease in Long-Term Borrowing	(170)	(170)	(170)	(170)	(170)
Acquisition of Capital Stock	(27)	0	0	0	0
Dividends	(614)	(730)	(964)	(1,427)	(2,243)
Other Financing Transactions	0	0	0	0	0
Cash Flow from Financing	$ (811)	$ (200)	$ 1,666	$(5,097)	$(2,098)
Net Change in Cash	$ 7	$ (97)	$ 382	$ 293	$ 2,318

Inventories.   Inventories generally appear at the lower of cost or market, with cost determined principally on a first-in, first-out method.

Property, Plant, and Equipment.   Property, plant, and equipment appear at acquisition cost less accumulated depreciation. When the company retires or disposes of properties, it removes the related costs and accumulated depreciation from the respective accounts and credits or charges any gain or loss to earnings. The company expenses maintenance and repairs as incurred. It capitalizes major betterments and renewals. Depreciation results from applying the straight-line method over the estimated useful lives of the assets as follows:

Buildings	30 to 45 years
Machinery and Equipment	4 to 20 years
Furniture and Fixtures	10 years

Intangible Assets. The company amortizes the unallocated excess of cost of a subsidiary over net assets acquired over a 17-year period.

Research and Development Costs. The company charges research and development costs to operations as incurred ($479,410 in 1995 and $467,733 in 1994).

Pension Plans. The company and its subsidiaries have noncontributory pension plans covering substantially all of their employees. The company's policy is to fund accrued pension costs as determined by independent actuaries. Pension costs amounted to $471,826 in 1995 and $366,802 in 1994.

Revenue Recognition. The company generally recognizes income on a percentage-of-completion basis. It records advance payments as received and reports them as a deduction from billings when earned. The company recognizes royalties, included in net sales, as income when received. Royalties total $656,043 in 1995 and $723,930 in 1994.

Income Taxes. The company provides no income taxes on unremitted earnings of foreign subsidiaries since it anticipates no significant tax liabilities should foreign units remit such earnings. The company makes provision for deferred income taxes applicable to timing differences between financial statement and income tax accounting, principally on the earnings of a foreign sales subsidiary which existing statutes defer in part from current taxation.

Note B: Foreign Operations. The consolidated financial statements include net assets of $2,120,648 ($1,847,534 in 1994), undistributed earnings of $2,061,441 ($1,808,752 in 1994), sales of $7,287,566 ($8,603,225 in 1994), and net income of $454,999 ($641,454 in 1994) applicable to the Canadian subsidiary.

The company translates balance sheet accounts of the Canadian subsidiary into U.S. dollars at the exchange rates at the end of the year, and operating results at the average of exchange rates for the year.

Note C: Inventories. Inventories used in determining cost of sales follow:

	1995	1994	1993
Raw Materials and Supplies.....	$ 8,889,147	$ 9,720,581	$ 8,900,911
Work in Process	8,602,594	8,838,650	11,524,805
	$17,491,741	$18,559,231	$20,425,716

Note D: Short-Term Borrowing. The company has short-term credit agreements which principally provide for loans of 90-day periods at varying interest rates. There were no borrowings in 1995. In 1994, the maximum borrowing at the end of any calendar month was $4,500,000 and the approximate average loan balance and weighted average interest rate, computed by using the days outstanding method, was $3,435,000 and 7.6 percent. There were no restrictions upon the company during the period of the loans and no compensating bank balance arrangements required by the lending institutions.

Note E: Income Taxes.   Provision for income taxes consists of:

	1995	1994
Current		
Federal............	$2,931,152	$2,633,663
State..............	466,113	483,240
Canadian..........	260,306	472,450
	$3,657,571	$3,589,353
Deferred		
Federal............	263,797	91,524
Canadian..........	22,937	21,706
	286,734	113,230
	$3,944,305	$3,702,583

Reconciliation of the total provision for income taxes to the current federal statutory rate of 35 percent is as follows:

	1995		1994	
	Amount	%	Amount	%
Tax at Statutory Rate	$3,691,000	35.0%	$3,600,100	35.0%
State Taxes (net of U.S. tax credit) ..	302,973	2.9	314,106	3.1
All Other Items	(49,668)	(0.5)	(211,623)	(2.1)
	$3,944,305	37.4%	$3,702,583	36.0%

Note F: Pensions.   The components of pension expense follow:

	1995	1994
Service Cost.................................	$ 476,490	$ 429,700
Interest Cost.................................	567,159	446,605
Actual Return on Pension Investments............	(614,210)	(592,900)
Amount Deferred	55,837	98,817
Amortization of Actuarial Gains and Losses	(13,450)	(15,420)
Pension Expense	$ 471,826	$ 366,802

The funded status of the pension plan follows:

	December 31,	
	1995	1994
Accumulated Benefit Obligation	$5,763,450	$5,325,291
Effect of Salary Increases	1,031,970	976,480
Projected Benefit Obligation	6,795,420	6,301,771
Pension Fund Assets.....................	6,247,940	5,583,730
Excess Pension Obligation	$ 547,480	$ 718,041

Assumptions used in accounting for pensions follow:

	1995	1994
Expected Return on Pension Assets	10%	10%
Discount Rate for Projected Benefit Obligation............	9%	8%
Salary Increases	5%	5%

Note G: Common Stock.   As of March 20, 1995, the company increased the authorized number of shares of common stock from 1,800,000 shares to 5,000,000 shares.

On December 29, 1995, the company increased its equity interest (from 45 percent to 85 percent) in Societé Francaise Holmes Fermont, a French affiliate, in exchange for 18,040 of its common shares in a transaction accounted for as a purchase. The company credited the excess of the fair value ($224,373) of the company's shares issued over their par value ($90,200) to additional contributed capital. The excess of the purchase cost over the underlying value of the assets acquired was insignificant.

The company made a 25 percent common stock distribution on June 15, 1994, and on June 19, 1995, resulting in increases of 291,915 shares in 1994 and 364,433 shares in 1995, respectively. We capitalized the par value of these additional shares by a transfer of $1,457,575 in 1994 and $1,822,165 in 1995 from retained earnings to the common stock account. In 1994 and 1995, we paid cash of $2,611 and $15,340, respectively, in lieu of fractional share interests.

In addition, the company retired 2,570 shares of treasury stock in June 1994. The earnings and dividends per share for 1994 and 1995 in the accompanying consolidated financial statements reflect the 25 percent stock distributions.

Note H: Contingent Liabilities.   The company has certain contingent liabilities with respect to litigation and claims arising in the ordinary course of business. The company cannot determine the ultimate disposition of these contingent liabilities, but, in the opinion of management, they will not result in any material effect upon the company's consolidated financial position or results of operations.

Note I: Quarterly Data (unaudited).   Quarterly sales, gross profit, net earnings and earnings per share for 1995 follow:

	Net Sales	Gross Profit	Net Earnings	Earnings per Share
First	$ 25,931,457	$ 5,606,013	$1,602,837	$ .88
Second......	24,390,079	6,148,725	1,727,112	.95
Third.......	25,327,226	5,706,407	1,505,118	.82
Fourth	27,050,074	4,977,774	1,766,841	.97
Year	$102,698,836	$22,438,919	$6,601,908	$3.62

The first quarterly results are restated for the 25 percent stock distribution on June 19, 1995.

AUDITORS' REPORT

Board of Directors and Stockholders
Holmes Corporation

We have examined the consolidated balance sheets of Holmes Corporation and Subsidiaries as of December 31, 1995 and 1994, and the related consolidated statements of earnings and cash flows for the years then ended. Our examination was made in accordance with generally accepted auditing standards, and accordingly included such tests of the accounting records and such other auditing procedures as we considered necessary in the circumstances.

In our opinion, the financial statements referred to above present fairly the consolidated financial position of Holmes Corporation and Subsidiaries at December 31, 1995 and 1994, and the consolidated results of their operations and changes in cash flows for the years then ended, in conformity with generally accepted accounting principles applied on a consistent basis.

Chicago, Illinois
March 15, 1996

FIVE-YEAR SUMMARY OF OPERATIONS

	1995	1994	1993	1992	1991
Orders Received	$ 95,436,103	$ 80,707,576	$121,445,731	$89,466,793	$55,454,188
Net Sales	102,698,836	109,372,718	76,327,664	53,540,699	41,427,702
Backlog of Unfilled Orders	77,455,900	84,718,633	113,383,775	68,265,708	32,339,614
Earnings before Taxes on Income	10,546,213	10,285,943	6,708,072	3,203,835	1,939,414
Taxes on Income	3,944,305	3,702,583	2,991,947	1,470,489	894,257
Net Earnings	6,601,908	6,583,360	3,716,125	1,733,346	1,045,157
Net Property, Plant, and Equipment . . .	6,173,416	5,644,590	4,803,978	4,568,372	4,209,396
Net Additions to Property	1,172,057	1,426,347	748,791	848,685	346,549
Depreciation and Amortization	643,231	585,735	513,402	490,133	491,217
Cash Dividends Paid.	2,242,892	1,426,502	963,935	730,254	614,378
Working Capital	23,100,463	19,029,626	14,796,931	12,126,491	11,627,875
Shareholders' Equity.	29,393,803	24,690,214	19,514,358	15,754,166	15,747,116
Earnings per Share of Common (1)	3.62	3.61	2.03	.96	.57
Dividends per Share of Common (1) . . .	1.22	.78	.53	.40	.34
Book Value per Share of Common (1) . .	16.07	13.51	10.68	9.18	8.62
Number of Shareholders December 31 .	2,157	2,024	1,834	1,792	1,787
Number of Employees December 31 . . .	1,549	1,550	1,551	1,425	1,303
Shares of Common Outstanding December 31 (1)	1,824,853	1,824,754	1,824,754	1,824,941	1,827,515
Percentage Net Sales by Product Line Material Handling Equipment	46.1%	43.6%	51.3%	54.4%	63.0%
Processing Equipment	53.9%	56.4%	48.7%	45.6%	37.0%

Note: (1) Based on number of shares outstanding on December 31 adjusted for the 5-for-4 stock distributions in June 1993, 1994 and 1995.

REQUIRED

A group of Holmes' top management is interested in acquiring Holmes in a leveraged buyout.

a. Describe briefly the factors that make Holmes an attractive leveraged buyout candidate and the factors that make it an unattractive leveraged buyout candidate.

b. (This question requires coverage of Chapter 10.) Prepare pro forma financial statements for Holmes Corporation for 1996 through 2000 excluding all financing (that is, project the amount of operating income after taxes, assets, and cash flows from operating and investing activities). State the underlying assumptions made.

c. (This question requires coverage of Chapter 11.) Ascertain the value of Holmes' common shareholders' equity using the present value of its future cash flows valuation approach. Assume the following financing structure for the leveraged buyout:

Type	Proportion	Interest Rate	Term
Term Debt	50%	8%	7-Year Amortization[a]
Subordinated Debt	25	12%	10-Year Amortization[a]
Shareholders' Equity	25		
	100%		

[a]Holmes must repay principal and interest in equal annual payments.

d. (This question requires coverage of Chapter 12.) Ascertain the value of Holmes' common shareholders' equity using the price-earnings ratio and market value to book value valuation approaches. Selected data for similar companies for 1995 appear below (amounts in thousands):

Company	Agee Robotics	GI Handling Systems	LJG Industries	Gelas Corp.
Industry	Conveyor Systems	Conveyor Systems	Cranes	Industrial Furnaces
Sales.................	$4,214	$28,998	$123,034	$75,830
Net Income	$ 309	$ 2,020	$ 9,872	$ 5,117
Assets	$2,634	$15,197	$ 72,518	$41,665
Common Shareholders' Equity..............	$1,551	$ 7,473	$ 38,939	$26,884
Market Value of Common Equity	$6,915	$20,000	$102,667	$41,962
Market Beta...........	1.12	.88	.99	.85

e. Would you attempt to acquire Holmes Corporation after completing the analyses in parts (*a*) to (*d*)? If not, how would you change the analyses to make this an attractive leveraged buyout?

MASSACHUSETTS STOVE COMPANY: A VALUATION ANALYSIS

As a valuation analyst for New England Appraisal Company, you have been approached by Jane O'Neil, majority shareholder and chief executive officer of Massachusetts Stove Company, to conduct a valuation of the Company as of August 31, 1994. A copy of the Company's financial statements for the 1992, 1993, and 1994 fiscal years ending August 31 and interim financial statements for the six months ending February 28, 1995, are attached (Exhibits 1 through 3). The company also provides you with recent historical information (Case 9.2).

After reviewing the above information, you arrange to meet with Jane O'Neil at the company's headquarters to gather additional information relevant to the valuation. Upon arrival, Jane meets you in the factory showroom.

Valuation Analyst: Jane, these stoves are quite attractive. I had expected to see ugly, cast iron stoves. These stoves would blend well with nice furniture.

Jane O'Neil: Yes, that is one of our major selling points. We emphasize not only the attractiveness of the various ceramic tile colors inlaid into each stove but also the ability of the tile to retain heat longer than cast iron. In addition, the glass fronts permit the viewing of the fire inside the stove, giving the serenity of a fireplace.

Valuation Analyst: I see two different stove designs here. How do these stoves differ?

Jane O'Neil: The Tile Stove I is our original stove. It heats areas between 900 and 1,600 square feet and can burn 10 to 12 hours before reloading wood. The Tile Stove II heats areas between 800 and 1,300 square feet and can burn 8 to 10 hours between reloadings.

Valuation Analyst: I hear noise coming from behind this back wall. I assume the factory is on the other side.

Jane O'Neil: Yes, let's take a quick walk through the factory. You will note that we employ only ten workers in the factory. Stove making is essentially an assembly operation. We purchase metal castings from suppliers in Belgium and the Netherlands, ceramic tile from a supplier in Canada, and catalytic combusters from a supplier in the United States. Because structural air tightness is critical to the efficient operation of the stoves, the primary task of our workers is aligning and sealing the adjoining parts.

Valuation Analyst: Buying from foreign suppliers must subject you to considerable foreign exchange risk.

Jane O'Neil: All of our purchases except the metal castings from the Belgium supplier are priced in U.S. dollars. We purchase a three-month supply of castings at a time to obtain purchase discounts and minimize foreign exchange exposure. This purchasing strategy also saves on shipping costs. As you can see, we have plenty of room to store the castings in the factory.

Valuation Analyst: You mentioned the catalytic combuster. What function does it serve?

Jane O'Neil: This is a good point to go into my office to continue our discussions. The catalytic combuster reburns gases emitted from the burning of wood. This reburning not only provides additional heat but also reduces pollutants that would otherwise be emitted into the air.

EXHIBIT 1

Massachusetts Stove Company
Balance Sheets
(amounts in thousands)
(Case 11.2)

	August 31				February 28, 1995
	1991	1992	1993	1994	
Assets					
Cash	$ 37	$ 51	$ 19	$ 146	$ 278
Accounts Receivable	26	13	57	31	18
Inventories (Note 1).	244	252	328	348	300
Total Current Assets	$ 307	$ 316	$ 404	$ 525	$ 596
Property, Plant, and Equipment (Notes 2 and 3)					
Land	—	$ 120	$ 120	$ 120	$ 120
Building	—	493	493	493	493
Building Improvements.	—	—	46	46	46
Equipment, Furniture, & Fixtures	378	443	490	506	513
Less Accumulated Depreciation.	(274)	(297)	(353)	(427)	(460)
Property, Plant, and Equipment, (Net)	$ 104	$ 759	$ 796	$ 738	$ 712
Deferred Income					
Taxes (Note 7)	—	—	—	62	35
Total Assets	$ 411	$1,075	$1,200	$1,325	$1,343
Liabilities and Shareholders' Equity					
Accounts Payable.	$ 152	$ 137	$ 113	$ 43	$ 46
Bank Loans (Note 5)	25	25	12	—	—
Current Portion of Long-Term Debt (Note 4) . .	—	28	29	22	23
Customer Advance Payments.	59	35	83	166	138
Other Current Liabilities	2	4	17	18	21
Total Current Liabilities	$ 238	$ 229	$ 254	$ 249	$ 228
Bank Loans (Noncurrent)	68	713	685	623	601
Shareholder Loans (Note 6).	299	259	269	259	229
Total Liabilities	$ 605	$1,201	$1,208	$1,131	$1,058
Common Stock	$ 2	$ 2	$ 2	$ 2	$ 2
Additional Paid-in Capital	436	436	436	436	436
Retained Earnings (deficit).	(632)	(564)	(446)	(244)	(153)
Total Shareholders' Equity	$(194)	$ (126)	$ (8)	$ 194	$ 285
Total Liabilities and Shareholders' Equity . . .	$ 411	$1,075	$1,200	$1,325	$1,343

Valuation Analyst: I imagine that regulations by the Environmental Protection Agency (EPA) have had a big impact on the industry.

Jane O'Neil: You might say "has had and is continuing to have" a big impact. Back in the mid-1980s, sales of wood stoves in the United States totaled approximately one million units annually. People used wood for heating because of both its lower cost and its greater dependability than oil. In 1988, just before the EPA began regulating the wood stove in-

EXHIBIT 2

Massachusetts Stove Company
Income Statements
(amounts in thousands)
(Case 11.2)

	Year Ended August 31			Six Months Ended
	1992	1993	1994	February 28, 1995
Sales	$1,165	$1,480	$1,637	$ 929
Cost of Goods Sold...............................	(550)	(727)	(759)	(417)
Depreciation (Notes 1 and 3)......................	(22)	(57)	(74)	(33)
Facilities Costs (Note 2)	(73)	(59)	(63)	(37)
Facilities Income (Note 2)	—	26	38	19
Gross Profit	$ 520	$ 663	$ 779	$ 461
Selling Expenses	(354)	(452)	(548)	(296)
Administrative Expenses	(21)	(37)	(39)	(19)
Operating Income	$ 145	$ 174	$ 192	$ 146
Interest Income	1	1	2	3
Interest Expense (Note 2).........................	(32)	(49)	(44)	(22)
Legal Expenses	(43)	—	—	—
Net Income before Taxes and Change in Accounting Principle......................	$ 71	$ 126	$ 150	$ 127
Income Tax Expense (Note 7)				
Current.......................................	(3)	(8)	(10)	(9)
Deferred.....................................	—	—	(32)	(27)
Net Income before Change in Accounting Principle ...	$ 68	$ 118	$ 108	$ 91
Cumulative Effect of Adopting FASB *Statement* No. 106..	—	—	94	—
Net Income	$ 68	$ 118	$ 202	$ 91

dustry, there were approximately 235 manufacturers. Today there are only about 35 firms left. The market demand has declined to around 180,000 units annually.

Valuation Analyst: Why didn't more firms try to obtain the EPA approval?

Jane O'Neil: There are two reasons. First, the market demand had already begun to contract. Second, the EPA approval process was expensive and full of uncertainties. Most firms in this industry were small like us. Given the assembly nature of the production process, the barriers to entry before the EPA regulations were low. The costs of redesigning existing stove models and going through the lengthy EPA approval process were prohibitive and highly uncertain. We felt we had an edge on the competition because we had added the catalytic combuster to our stoves in the mid-1980s. We did, however, have to redesign our stoves, make new molds for the castings, and engage in testing to obtain EPA approval.

Valuation Analyst: Doesn't your approval period last only five years? Will you have to go through this whole process again very soon?

Jane O'Neil: As long as the EPA standards and the design of our stoves don't change, we can obtain a five-year extension of the approval period. We now have EPA approval on

EXHIBIT 3

Massachusetts Stove Company
Statements of Cash Flows
(amounts in thousands)
(Case 11.2)

	Year Ended August 31			Six Months Ended February 28, 1995
	1992	1993	1994	
Operations				
Net Income	$ 68	$118	$202	$ 91
Cumulative Effect of Change in Accounting Principles	—	—	(94)	—
Depreciation	22	56	74	33
Deferred Income Taxes	—	—	32	27
(Increase) Decrease in Accounts Receivable	13	(44)	26	13
(Increase) Decrease in Inventories	(8)	(76)	(20)	48
Increase (Decrease) in Accounts Payable	(15)	(24)	(70)	3
Increase (Decrease) in Customer Advances	(24)	48	83	(28)
Increase (Decrease) in Other Current Liabilities	2	13	1	3
Cash Flow from Operations	$ 58	$ 91	$234	$190
Investing				
Capital Expenditures	$(69)	$ (93)	$ (16)	$ (7)
Financing				
Proceeds on Assumption of Long-Term Debt in Connection with Purchase of Building	$ 79	—	—	—
Repayment of Short-Term Loans—Bank	—	$ (13)	$ (12)	—
Repayment of Long-Term Loans—Bank	(14)	(27)	(69)	$ (21)
Increase in Shareholder Loans	—	10	—	—
Decrease in Shareholder Loans	(40)	—	(10)	(30)
Cash Flow from Financing	$ 25	$ (30)	$ (91)	$ (51)
Change in Cash	$ 14	$ (32)	$127	$132
Cash—Beginning of Year	37	51	19	146
Cash—End of Year	$ 51	$ 19	$146	$278

Tile Stove I through 1999 and on Tile Stove II through 1997. The major risk we run is that the EPA or a state environmental agency tightens the standards on pollutants. The states of Washington and Oregon, for example, just cut their emissions standards to one-half of the EPA prescribed levels. We expect to spend $60,000 to $90,000 over the next 12 to 14 months to redesign our Tile Stove I to meet these new standards. Our Tile Stove II model will require only minor modifications to meet the new regulations.

Valuation Analyst: Please tell me a bit about how you market your stoves.

Jane O'Neil: We use two channels: (1) wholesaling to retail hardware stores and (2) retail direct marketing. Our principal niche is retail direct marketing, which represented approximately 85 percent of our unit sales in fiscal 1994. We advertise in national construction and design magazines. Potential customers are encouraged either to call the company on our 800 number, send for additional information on our stoves, or visit our factory showroom. Here is a copy of the brochure we send them. You can see that it includes a picture of each stove model, a discussion of the benefits of wood burning and of ceramic tile, and a listing of the dimensions and other pertinent data on each stove. We also send a free video that shows the stoves in our factory showroom and the manufacturing process and includes presentations by me and by Mark Forest, who heads up our production operation.

Valuation Analyst: I would think that all customers would want to actually see the stove they are buying. The wholesaling of stoves to hardware stores and the selling of stoves from the factory showroom make sense to me. I would not think that customers would buy such an expensive item from a factory located in northern Massachusetts.

Jane O'Neil: That is just what we hope our competitors will continue to think because we have the direct retail marketing niche almost entirely to ourselves. Since 1991 we have compiled a list of approximately 100,000 people who have requested information about our stoves. We send these individuals three mailings each year for approximately four years, giving them additional information about our stoves and offering price reductions if they place an order by a particular date. I view this customer list as one of our most valuable assets, even though it doesn't appear on the balance sheet.

Valuation Analyst: What does it cost to develop and maintain this customer list?

Jane O'Neil: We spend approximately $6 in advertising to get a name on the mailing list and another $2 up front on promotional materials and postage. We spend approximately $1 annually for the additional mailings.

Valuation Analyst: How many of these people end up buying a stove?

Jane O'Neil: We received 41,500 new inquiries during the 1994 fiscal year. Of this total, we received and filled orders for approximately 500 stoves within six months of the initial inquiry. We also received and filled orders for another 350 stoves from the on-going customer list of 100,000 names. The remaining sales of 100 units came from our wholesale channel.

Valuation Analyst: I would think that repossessing a stove when a customer doesn't pay is a costly endeavor. How do you manage your credit risk?

Jane O'Neil: We have relatively little credit risk. We require full payment in cash or a third-party credit card before shipment. A local bank provides financing to credit-approved customers. We get our money up front before shipment and do not bear any risk if customers fail to repay their loans.

Valuation Analyst: Why did you exercise your option to purchase this building? I would think that renting would give you considerably more flexibility. You also wouldn't have to worry about leasing out the other 10,000 square feet and acting as a landlord.

Jane O'Neil: There are several reasons for this action. First, our relations with the former owner were deteriorating. We were continually hassled about our appropriate share of property taxes, the necessity for maintenance or repairs we requested, and so on. In addition, we felt that the purchase price of $608,400 ($24.34 per square foot) provided significant upside potential. We exercised our option when the commercial real estate market was at a low point. It appears that the market may have bottomed out at this point and will start to appreciate again. Other commercial buildings in the area have recently sold for around $27 per square foot. Third, the option permitted us to assume the unpaid balance on a loan from the New England Industrial Development Authority on the property. The loan carries an interest rate equal to 80 percent of the base rate of the Bank of Massachusetts and is reset each August. The potential difficulties of being a landlord have not been a problem so far. We have two tenants in the remaining 10,000 square feet of the building. We have priced the rentals essentially to break even. The tenants pay their share of property taxes, insurance, and maintenance.

Valuation Analyst: While we are talking about debt, tell me about the shareholder loans.

Jane O'Neil: Two of the loans, the one for $30,000 and the one for $90,000, are home equity loans. We used the proceeds in the business. You will note from the interim financial statements for the six months ended February 28, 1995, that we repaid the $30,000 loan. We hope to repay the $90,000 loan during the next two years if we generate sufficient funds. The noninterest-bearing loans for $138,750 are from several members of my family, my husband, and me. I have no plans to repay these loans during the next several years.

Valuation Analyst: I note that administrative expenses seem unusually low. Is there an explanation for this?

Jane O'Neil: Yes, there are a couple of people who draw no salary. In the mid-1980s we purchased a lawn products business. One of the key assets of that business was Roger Elliott, their design engineer. Roger has been "retired" for several years now but he continues to help us with the redesign of the stoves. Roger does not draw a salary. Also, my father, a retired business executive, serves as our chief financial officer but draws no salary. In addition, Mark Forest and I draw salaries that are considerably less than market levels would dictate, probably by about $50,000 a year for the two of us combined at the present time.

Valuation Analyst: I notice the relatively large net operating tax loss carryforward in the notes to the financial statements. How could this business manage to lose almost $250,000?

Jane O'Neil: You may not believe this, but the accumulated loss carryforward was almost $650,000 before we turned profitable in 1991! Almost all of the loss carryforward was incurred by the lawn products business before we purchased it in the mid-1980s. We discontinued the operations of this business in 1989 but can use their tax loss carryforward. We have used up approximately $400,000 of the loss carryforward since then. The deferred tax asset on the August 31, 1994, balance sheet reflects the tax savings from using the tax loss and tax credit carryforwards at a 23 percent tax rate, the tax rate applicable to the first $100,000 of taxable income.

Valuation Analyst: It appears that you will use up the remaining tax loss and tax credit carryforwards in the very near future and have to start paying taxes.

Jane O'Neil: That is correct. We have had to pay the 7 percent Massachusetts tax all along. At least the state tax is deductible in calculating the federal tax. We will likely pay federal taxes at the 35 percent statutory rate because the benefits of the lower 23 percent tax rate on the first $100,000 of taxable income is counterbalanced by a higher tax rate on taxable income exceeding $100,000 until such time as the overall tax rate is 35 percent. Depending on the levels of corporate and individual tax rates, we may choose to start paying salaries to my father and Roger Elliott and increase the compensation or benefits to Mark Forest and me.

Valuation Analyst: You have been quite helpful. I will go to work now on a valuation analysis.

REQUIRED

Perform a valuation of the shareholders' equity of Massachusetts Stove Company. Perform the valuation analysis using (1) the present value of future cash flows and (2) a valuation of individual assets and liabilities.

NOTES TO CONSOLIDATED FINANCIAL STATEMENTS FOR MASSACHUSETTS STOVE COMPANY

Note 1: Summary of Significant Accounting Policies.

Nature of Business. The company is engaged in the manufacture and sale of wood-burning stoves composed of cast iron and ceramic tile at a facility located in Greenfield, Massachusetts.

Consolidation. The consolidated financial statements include the accounts of Massachusetts Stove Company and its wholly owned subsidiary, Massachusetts Stove Realty Corp., after eliminating intercompany accounts and transactions (Note 2).

Inventories. Inventories are stated at lower of cost (first-in, first-out) or market (net realizable value). Inventories are composed of the following categories as of August 31:

	1992	1993	1994
Finished Goods	$ 70,144	$ 97,008	$ 90,299
Work in Process..........	115,883	177,229	208,994
Raw Materials	65,485	53,390	48,590
	$251,512	$327,627	$347,883

Depreciation. The company follows the policy of charging to expenses annual amounts of depreciation which allocate the cost of property and equipment over their estimated useful lives. The company uses the straight-line method for the building and building improvements and the straight-line and double-declining balance methods for equipment, furniture, and fixtures. Estimated useful lives are:

	Years
Building................................	31.5
Building Improvements	7.0
Equipment, Furniture, and Fixtures	5.0–7.0

Included in the equipment, furniture, and fixtures are the costs of developing prototypes for two new high-efficiency stoves. The new designs were required in order to obtain certification by the Environmental Protection Agency (EPA). Certifications for both stoves have been received and last for five years. The costs are being depreciated over the five-year life of the EPA certifications.

Income Taxes. The company provides for deferred income taxes using a balance sheet approach whereby deferred tax assets are recognized for operating loss and tax credit carryforwards. Deferred tax assets are adjusted for the effects of changes in tax laws and rates on the date of enactment. Reference should also be made to Note 7 regarding a change in the method of accounting for income taxes.

Note 2: Acquisition of Building and Facilities.   In June 1992, the company formed Massachusetts Stove Realty Corp., a wholly owned subsidiary, which in July 1992 purchased the land and building occupied by the company in Greenfield, Massachusetts, for $608,400. In connection with this acquisition, the company assumed the outstanding balance of a related mortgage loan (Note 4). Since the related mortgage exceeded the cost of the building, the company received $78,821 at closing.

The company occupies 60 percent of the building (15,000 square feet). The remaining 40 percent of the building (10,000 square feet) is rented to two commercial tenants under five-year leases expiring in January 1998. The tenants pay an annual base rent of $19,175 each plus their share of triple net costs (real estate taxes, insurance, and maintenance). The total base rent received by the company was $37,727 and $25,856 during the fiscal years ended August 31, 1994 and 1993, respectively. Triple net costs received from the tenants were recorded as a reduction of facilities costs.

Interest expense associated with the mortgage on the building was $32,573 and $32,795 for the years ended August 31, 1994 and 1993, respectively. These amounts are included with interest expense.

Note 3: Land, Building, and Equipment.   An analysis of changes in land, land improvements, stove development costs, equipment, furniture, and fixtures appears in Exhibit 4.

Note 4: Long-Term Notes Payable — Banks.   Long-term notes payable — banks consisted of the following at August 31:

	1992	1993	1994
New England Industrial Development Authority mortgage on land and building payable to bank in quarterly payments including principal and interest through August 2010, with variable interest adjusted annually in August to 80% of the Bank of Massachusetts base rate. The interest rate was 4.7 percent for the 1993 fiscal year, 4.8 percent for the 1994 fiscal year, and will be 5.8 percent for the 1995 fiscal year. A total of $150,000 of the notes payable to stockholders (Note 6) are subordinated to this mortgage. . .	$682,796	$664,241	$644,235
8% commercial loan payable to bank at $750 per month plus interest through February 1999, with variable interest at 2 points over the bank's base rate. Secured by machinery, equipment, and inventory.	58,500	49,500	—
	$741,296	$713,741	$644,235
Less — Current Portion.	(27,600)	(29,000)	(21,570)
	$713,696	$684,741	$622,665

Both Note 3 and Note 4 above are secured by the personal guarantees of four of the stockholders.

EXHIBIT 4

Analysis of Changes in Land, Building, and Equipment
(Case 11.2)

	Land	Building	Building Improvements	Development Costs — Tile Stove I	Development Costs — Tile Stove II	Equipment, Furniture, and Fixtures	Total
Cost							
Balance, August 31, 1991			—	$63,001	$ 27,859	$286,924	$ 377,784
Additions	$120,160	$492,903	—	—	53,617	11,693	678,373
Balance, August 31, 1992	$120,160	$492,903	$45,452	$63,001	$ 81,476	$298,617	$1,056,157
Additions	—	—	$45,452	—	30,238	16,959	92,649
Balance, August 31, 1993	$120,160	$492,903	$45,452	$63,001	$111,714	$315,576	$1,148,806
Additions	—	—	—	—	—	16,078	16,078
Balance, August 31, 1994	$120,160	$492,903	$45,452	$63,001	$111,714	$331,654	$1,164,884
Accumulated Depreciation							
Balance, August 31, 1991	—	—	—	$18,900	—	$255,447	$ 274,347
Additions	—	$ 3,263	—	12,600	—	6,473	22,336
Balance, August 31, 1992	—	$ 3,263	—	$31,500	—	$261,920	$ 296,683
Additions	—	15,648	$ 6,060	12,600	$ 11,171	11,078	56,557
Balance, August 31, 1993	—	$ 18,911	$ 6,060	$44,100	$ 11,171	$272,998	$ 353,240
Additions	—	15,648	6,493	12,600	22,343	16,332	73,416
Balance, August 31, 1994	—	$ 34,559	$12,553	$56,700	$ 33,514	$289,330	$ 426,656

Maturities on the long-term notes payable—banks require the following principal reductions for the years ended August 31.

1995	$ 21,570
1996	23,300
1997	25,100
1998	27,000
1999	29,200
Years Subsequent to 1998	518,065
	$644,235

Note 5: Short-Term Note Payable—Bank.

At August 31, 1994, the company had a bank line of credit available which expires in November 1994. The company can borrow up to $75,000 at two points above the Citibank prime rate. The note is secured by machinery, equipment, inventory and a personal guaranty of one of the stockholders. At August 31, 1994, there was no outstanding balance.

At August 31, 1993, note payable—bank consisted of a 270-day, 8 percent note payable January 18, 1994, to a bank. Secured by machinery, equipment and inventory.

At August 31, 1992, note payable—bank consisted of a variable rate demand note payable to a bank. The interest rate was two points over the bank's base rate. Secured by NYSE investments owned by two of the shareholders and by personal guarantees of three of the shareholders.

Note 6: Notes Payable—Stockholders.

Notes payable to stockholders consists of the following at August 31:

	1992	1993	1994
8.25 % stockholder loan. Loaned funds provided by bank demand note, variable interest payable quarterly at 1 point over the bank's base rate. Interest is being paid by the Company. Secured by NYSE collateral owned by a stockholder. Repayment of principal subordinated to 5.8% mortgage on land and building described above (Note 4)	$ 30,000	$ 30,000	$ 30,000
7.75% stockholder loan. Loan funds provided by residential mortgage note payable to bank, variable interest payable monthly at 2 points over the underlying mortgage rate. Interest is being paid by the Company. Repayment of principal subordinated to 5.8% mortgage on land and building described above (Note 4)	90,000	90,000	90,000
Noninterest-bearing notes payable to stockholders. Repayment of principal in the amount of $30,000 subordinated to 5.8% mortgage on land and building described above (Note 4)	138,750	148,750	138,750
Total	$258,750	$268,750	$258,750

Note 7: Accounting Change and Income Tax Matters. Effective September 1, 1993, the company adopted SFAS *Statement No. 109,* "Accounting for Income Taxes." The adoption of this statement changed the criteria for measuring the provision for income taxes and recognizing deferred tax assets on the balance sheet. Under the provisions of the accounting principles in effect prior to *Statement No. 109,* the tax benefit of unused net operating losses and tax credits were not recognized as assets unless the realization of those benefits was assured. Under the provisions of the new statement, these tax benefits are recognized unless it is more likely than not that some portion or all of the deferred tax assets will not be realized. The entire effect of the adoption of *Statement No. 109* results from the recognition of the tax benefits of net operating loss and tax credit carryforwards.

The effect of the adoption of *Statement No. 109* was to decrease income before cumulative effect of a change in accounting principle by $32,500. In addition, the cumulative effect of the change on prior years increased net income by $94,000 in the current year's income statement. The $94,000 reflects the tax savings from a net operating tax loss carryforward of $375,875 and tax credit carryforwards of $5,973 as of September 1, 1993. Prior years' financial statements have not been restated.

The provision for current income taxes consists of state taxes at 7 percent. State income taxes are deductible in computing federal taxable income. The company has utilized a portion of its net operating loss carryforward against its current federal taxable income.

As of August 31, 1994, the company had net operating loss carryforwards available to offset future federal taxable income as follows:

Years of Expiration	
1998	$ 79,124
1999	87,594
2000	48,598
2001	1,548
2003	29,361
	$246,225

As of August 31, 1994, the company had general business credits available to carryforward and offset future federal income taxes as follows:

Years of Expiration	
1997	$1,362
1999	615
2000	3,253
2001	743
	$5,973

INDEPENDENT ACCOUNTANTS' REPORT

To the Stockholders of
Massachusetts Stove Company

We have reviewed the accompanying consolidated balance sheets of Massachusetts Stove Company and Subsidiary as of August 31, 1992, 1993, and 1994, and the related consolidated statements of income and retained earnings (deficit), and cash flows for the years then ended, in accordance with standards established by the American Institute of Certified Public Accountants. All of the information included in these financial statements is the representation of the management of Massachusetts Stove Company and Subsidiary.

A review consists principally of inquiries of company personnel and analytical procedures applied to financial data. It is substantially less in scope than an audit conducted in accordance with generally accepted auditing standards, the objective of which is the expression of an opinion regarding the financial statements taken as a whole. Accordingly, we do not express such an opinion.

Based on our review, we are not aware of any material modifications that should be made to the accompanying consolidated financial statements in order for them to be in conformity with generally accepted accounting principles.

As discussed in Note 7 to the consolidated financial statements, during the year ended August 31, 1994, the company changed its method of accounting for income taxes.

Slybel and Slank

Greenfield, Massachusetts
September 29, 1994

CHAPTER 12

VALUATION: EARNINGS-BASED APPROACHES

Learning Objectives

1. Study the theoretical model that relates market prices to earnings (P-E ratio).
2. Study the theoretical model that relates market prices to the book value of common shareholders' equity (P-BV ratio).
3. Apply the theoretical models of the P-E ratio and the P-BV ratio to data of actual companies.
4. Understand the role of the following variables, or factors, in explaining why actual P-E and P-BV ratios may deviate from those suggested by the theoretical models: (a) cost of equity capital, (b) growth rates, (c) differences between current and expected future earnings, and (d) alternative accounting principles.

This chapter extends the discussion in the previous chapter by considering the relation between value (that is, market prices) and certain constructs of the accrual basis of accounting.[1] Specifically,

---

[1] Capital markets may be described as "efficient" if market participants react correctly and quickly to available information in the pricing of securities. The "correctly" portion of this definition implies that market participants identify the economic implications of available information so that market prices reflect economic values. For example, a change in accounting principles that increases reported earnings but has no cash-flow consequences should not cause market prices to change. The "quickly" portion of the definition suggests that market participants can earn abnormal returns using the information for only a very short period of time (hours or perhaps days). Market prices quickly capture any valuation-relevant signals in the information. This latter dimension of an efficient capital market

(continued)

1. What is the relation between the market price of a firm's common stock and its earnings for the current period (that is, the valuation significance of the *price-earnings ratio*)?
2. What is the relation between the market price of a firm's common stock and the book value of its common shareholders' equity (that is, the valuation significance of the *market value to book value ratio*)?

This chapter explores these relations at a theoretical level and summarizes recent research examining the relations at an empirical level. It also illustrates their use in the valuation of firms.

PRICE-EARNINGS (P-E) RATIOS

Analysts' reports and the financial press make frequent references to P-E ratios. Statements such as the following appear frequently:

- General Motors is selling for 12 times earnings.
- A P-E ratio of 18 for Digital Equipment is much too high. It should be selling for no more than 12 to 14 times earnings.
- Biotechnology firms are growing rapidly and should sell for 20 to 25 times earnings.

These statements suggest that there is a "correct" level for the P-E ratio of each firm, that there is a well-accepted underlying model that determines appropriate levels of P-E ratios. This section explores the theoretical relation between market prices and earnings. It also demonstrates the difficulties often encountered in reconciling actual P-E ratios with those indicated by the theoretical model.

---

implies little or no role for financial statement analysis. Analysts cannot study accounting information to find under- or overvalued securities. Analysts might, however, use market multiples of accounting variables (for example, price-earnings ratios) for publicly traded firms to value comparable firms that are not publicly traded. Research on the efficiency of capital markets has produced mixed results. Empirical tests of valuation models often observe unexplained variance between predicted market prices and actual market prices (that is, the R^2 is not 100 percent). The unexplained variance may result from (1) errors in measuring the independent or dependent variables (for example, net income may be a biased measure of economic earnings), (2) omission of important independent variables (for example, market prices may relate to both the level of earnings *and* the growth in earnings, or (3) misspecification of the relation between independent and dependent variables (for example, market price is a function of the level of earnings *times* the growth rate in earnings, not the level of earnings *plus* the growth rate). The presumption in an efficient capital market is that the unexplained variance is not due to systematic mispricing in the market (that is, market inefficiency). Unfortunately, the researcher cannot fully distinguish between modeling deficiencies and market inefficiencies when there is an unexplained variance. Note that market efficiency allows for random valuation errors at the level of the individual firm, but these random inefficiencies cancel out at an aggregated market level. For a discussion of these issues, see Ray Ball, "The Earnings-Price Anomaly," *Journal of Accounting and Economics* (1992), pp. 319–345.

DEVELOPMENT OF THEORETICAL MODEL

An understanding of the theoretical model requires a step-by-step development.

Cash Flows to the Investor. The theoretical relation between market prices and earnings draws on the classical dividend capitalization model.[2] The market price (P_t) of an equity security at time t equals the present value of the expected dividend stream discounted at a risk-adjusted discount rate (r).[3] Thus,

$$P_t = \sum_{t=1}^{n} \frac{\text{Expected Dividend}_t}{(1 + r)^t}$$

One of these dividends is the expected liquidating dividend upon dissolution of the firm. Thus,

$$P_t = \sum_{t=1}^{n-1} \frac{\text{Expected Dividend}_t}{(1 + r)^t} + \frac{\text{Expected Liquidating Dividend}_n}{(1 + r)^n}$$

A liquidating dividend occurs because a firm generates cash flows each period that it does not fully distribute to shareholders as a dividend. These retained cash flows plus returns generated on the retained cash flows compose the liquidating dividend. As long as a firm generates a return on the retained cash flows equal to the discount rate, or cost of equity capital, the firm's dividend policy has no effect on the market price of the common stock. This is the Miller and Modigliani dividend irrelevance proposition.[4]

Cash Flows to the Firm. The source of the cash flows for dividends is the cash flows generated by the firm. Cash flows received by the firm represent the generation of economic value; dividends merely represent the periodic distribution of this economic value to shareholders. Thus,

$$P_t = \sum_{t=1}^{n} \frac{\text{Expected Cash Flows}_t}{(1 + r)^t}$$

When a firm's expected leveraged free cash flows are projected to remain constant

---

[2]J. Williams, *The Theory of Investment and Value* (Cambridge, Massachusetts: Harvard University Press, 1938).

[3]Throughout this chapter, t refers to the accounting period that has just finished. The valuation is at the end of this period (for example, December 31). The period $t = 1$ refers to the first accounting period after the valuation.

[4]Merton H. Miller and Franco Modigliani, "Dividend Policy, Growth, and Valuation of Shares," *Journal of Business* (1961), pp. 411–432. Firms do, however, often generate returns that differ from the cost of equity capital, at least for a period of time. The excess or deficient returns may result from one-time (temporary) events or relate to longer-term earnings advantages or disadvantages. Later sections of this chapter discuss the valuation significance of these temporary and permanent dimensions of returns.

into perpetuity, a nongrowth scenario, then the preceding expression for market price simplifies to[5]

$$P_t = \frac{\text{Expected Cash Flows}_{t+1}}{r}$$

When leveraged free cash flows are projected to grow at a constant rate, g, then

$$P_t = \text{Expected Cash Flows}_{t+1} \times \frac{1}{r - g}$$

Expected Earnings. The next step in the theoretical formulation of the P-E ratio substitutes a firm's expected earnings for its expected leveraged free cash flows in the preceding formulation of market price. This substitution of earnings for cash flows rests on three foundations.

1. Over sufficiently long time periods, net income equals leveraged free cash flows. The effect of year-end accruals to convert cash flows to net income lessens as the measurement period increases.[6]
2. For a no-growth firm, net income equals leveraged-free cash flow. That is, net income before depreciation equals cash flow from operations (including debt service), depreciation expense equals investment expenditures, and debt issuances equal debt redemptions. For a firm experiencing a constant rate of growth, net income is a constant multiple of leveraged free cash flows.
3. Accrual-based earnings reflect changes in economic values more accurately than do free cash flows. One objective of generally accepted accounting principles (GAAP) is to reflect the economic consequences of transactions and events without regard to the timing of their related cash flows. Thus, firms recognize revenues when they have provided substantially all of the required goods or services and have received cash or a right to receive cash in the future. The delivery of the good or the rendering of services is viewed as the critical wealth-generating event, not the receipt of cash. Likewise, firms recognize expenses when they consume goods and services in operations, not when they expend cash. Another objective of GAAP is to measure the economic effects of transactions and events in as objective a manner as possible. Standard setters sometimes must trade off economic relevance and objectivity (for example, reporting most assets at acquisition cost instead of market values). Thus, accrual-based amounts might represent biased measures of economic values. The empirical issue is whether these biases are sufficiently similar across firms (for example, immediate expensing of research and development costs by technology-intensive firms or using acquisition

---

[5]Chapter 11 defined leveraged free cash flows as cash flows available to common shareholders. Operationally, leveraged free cash flows equal cash flow from operations plus or minus cash flow for investing plus or minus changes in borrowing.

[6]The cross-sectional correlations between earnings and stock prices increase as the earnings measurement interval increases. The values of R^2 for various intervals are 1 year, 5 percent; 2 years, 15 percent; 5 years, 33 percent, 10 years, 63 percent. See Peter D. Easton, Trevor S. Harris, and James A. Ohlson, "Aggregate Accounting Earnings Can Explain Most of Security Returns," *Journal of Accounting and Economics* (1992), pp. 119–142.

cost valuations for fixed assets by capital-intensive firms) that the capital market can incorporate them into valuations.

If one accepts the substitution of expected earnings for expected cash flows based on any, or all, of the above foundations, then market price equals

$$P_t = \sum_{t=1}^{n} \frac{\text{Expected Earnings}_t}{(1 + r)^t}$$

It is not intuitively obvious that one can "discount" earnings in the same sense that one discounts cash flows to a present value.[7] The discount rate must be reexpressed in terms of a capitalization rate (discussed below).

When a firm's earnings are expected to remain constant into perpetuity, then[8]

$$P_t = \frac{\text{Expected Earnings}_{t+1}}{r}$$

The constancy of earnings presumes an equilibrium state in which a firm generates a *permanent* level of earnings. When a firm's earnings are projected to grow at a constant rate, g, the expression for market price is

$$P_t = \text{Expected Earnings}_{t+1} \times \frac{1}{r - g}$$

Actual Earnings. The final link in the chain relating market prices to earnings substitutes actual earnings of the most recent period for expected permanent earnings. For the no-growth state,[9]

---

[7]If one accepts the argument above that accrual earnings reflect more accurately than cash flows the wealth-generating effects of operations and the firm could borrow off of that wealth creation, then discounting in the traditional sense is intuitively appealing.

[8]An alternative formulation of P_t expresses expected earnings in terms of certainty equivalents, using the probabilities of various outcomes, and then uses the risk-free rate to capitalize these earnings. The P-E ratio in this alternative setting reflects the real time value of delayed returns, not risk. We do not use this alternative formulation in this chapter.

[9]Theoretical precision requires the following specification of this model:

$$P_{t-1} = \frac{\text{Actual Earnings}_t}{r}$$

That is, market price at the beginning of period t equals the capitalized value of the current period's earnings. Assuming no dividends, market price at the end of period t should equal $P_{t-1} \times (1 + r)$. The market price at the end of period t declines, however, for the payment of dividends. Thus, the relation between price at the end of the period and earnings for the current period is

$$P_t + D_t = \frac{\text{Actual Earnings}_t}{r}$$

Most P-E ratios reported in the financial press ignore this dividend adjustment. Precision would dictate the restatement of dividends paid during the current period (most firms pay dividends quarterly) to their year-end equivalent amount assuming reinvestment of intraperiod dividends by shareholders. Another justification for ignoring the dividend adjustment is that the actual earnings of period t are a surrogate for expected earnings during period $t + 1$.

$$P_t = \frac{\text{Actual Earnings}_t}{r}$$

For the steady-growth rate case,

$$P_t = \text{Actual Earnings}_t \times \frac{1 + g}{r - g}$$

Two possible justifications for using actual earnings in period t as a surrogate for expected earnings in period $t + 1$ are (1) actual earnings represent the permanent earnings level for the firm or (2) earnings follow a random walk, so the actual earnings of the current period are the best predictor of future earnings.

The following summary depicts the chain relating market prices to dividends, cash flows and earnings discussed in this section:

Market Price = Present Value of Future Dividends to Shareholders

↓

= Present Value of Future Leveraged Free Cash Flows to the Firm

↓

= Capitalized Value of Future Earnings to the Firm

↓

= Capitalized Value of Current Earnings of the Firm

Synthesis of Theoretical Model. We can now express the above formulations for market price in terms of the price-earnings (P-E) ratio. For the no-growth firm:

$$\frac{P_t}{\text{Actual Earnings}_t} = \frac{1}{r}$$

where $1/r$ is the P-E ratio. For example, a discount rate of 12 percent translates into a P-E ratio of 8.3 (=1/.12). The P-E ratio is the multiple for capitalizing future earnings, a process analogous to discounting expected cash flows to their present value.[10] The P-E ratio in this formulation reflects the required rate of return by common equity investors. Given the relation between expected return and risk, the P-E ratio should serve as a measure of risk. Higher risk levels translate into lower P-E ratios and vice versa (that is, investors will not pay as much for a higher risk security as for a lower risk security with identical expected earnings).

The P-E ratio for the constant-growth setting is

$$\frac{P_t}{\text{Actual Earnings}_t} = \frac{1 + g}{r - g}$$

---

[10]The present value of an annuity of $1 approaches $1/r$ as the number of periods increases. For example, the present value after 40 periods is 8.24 and after 50 periods is 8.30.

In addition to risk, the P-E ratio reflects the value of earnings growth. The growth occurs because additional investments generate future earnings. The firm might finance these additional investments either through the retention of earnings or the raising of new capital (debt and/or equity).

Several empirical studies have examined the relation between P-E ratios, risk, and growth. Most studies used market beta as the measure of risk on the notion that the market prices only systematic risk. Growth was measured using realized growth rates of prior periods or analysts forecasts of future growth. These studies have found that approximately 50 percent[11] to 70 percent[12] of the variability in P-E ratios relate to risk and growth.

APPLICATION OF THEORETICAL P-E MODEL

Let us now apply the theoretical P-E model (growth version) to Coke and Pepsi. Consider the following data:

	Coke	Pepsi
Market Price per Share (December 31, Year 8)............	$44.63	$40.88
Earnings per Share (Year 8)	$ 1.68	$ 1.96
Market Beta.......................................	1.00	1.10
Cost of Equity Capital	14.00%[a]	15.10%[b]
Five-Year Compound Annual Growth Rate in Earnings	6.3%	15.2%

[a]14.0% = 3.0% + 1.0(14.0% − 3.0%)
[b]15.1% = 3.0% + 1.1(14.0% − 3.0%)

The P-E ratio for Coke according to the theoretical model is 13.8 $[(1 + .063) \div (.14 - .063)]$. Coke's actual P-E ratio is 26.6 ($44.63 ÷ $1.68). One possible reason for the divergence between the actual and the theoretical P-E ratios is that the computed cost of equity capital is too large. If we assume that the growth rate in earnings of 6.3 percent is sustainable, the theoretical model suggests a cost of equity capital of 10.3 percent [that is, $r = .103$ in the following formula: $26.6 = (1 + .063) \div (r - .063)$]. If we assume that 14 percent is an accurate measure of the cost of equity capital, then a P-E ratio of 26.6 implies an expected growth rate in earnings of 9.9 percent [that is, $g = .099$ in the following formula: $26.6 = (1 + g) \div (.14 - g)$].

We cannot apply the theoretical model to Pepsi because its historical growth rate in earnings exceeds the computed cost of equity capital. As is the case with Coke, we have either measured the cost of equity capital inaccurately, used a growth rate in earnings that is not sustainable, or used some combination. The actual P-E ratio of 20.6 ($40.88 ÷ $1.96) implies a cost of equity capital of 20.8 percent if the

[11]William Beaver and Dale Morse, "What Determines Price-Earnings Ratios?" *Financial Analysts Journal* (July–August 1978), pp. 65–76.

[12]Paul Zarowin, "What Determines Earnings-Price Ratios: Revisited," *Journal of Accounting, Auditing and Finance* (Summer 1990), pp. 439–454.

growth rate of 15.2 percent is sustainable or a growth rate in earnings of 9.8 percent if the cost of equity capital is 15.1 percent. Thus, actual P-E ratios may diverge from the values indicated by the model because of errors in measuring the cost of equity capital, the growth rate in earnings, or some combination of the two.

A third possible reason for the divergence of actual and theoretical P-E ratios is that actual earnings of the current period are an inaccurate surrogate for expected future (permanent) earnings. If the current period's earnings are less than the expected permanent level of earnings (for example, because the current period's earnings include an unusual or nonrecurring loss), then the P-E ratio will be greater than normal.[13] If the current period's earnings exceed their expected permanent level, then the P-E ratio will be less than normal. The task for the analyst is to assess whether the lower or higher level of earnings for the current period (and therefore higher or lower P-E ratio) represents a transitory phenomenon or a change to a new lower or higher level of permanent earnings.

Penman studied the relation between P-E ratios and changes in earnings per share for all firms on the Compustat data base for the years 1968 to 1985.[14] For each year, Penman grouped firms into twenty portfolios based on the level of their P-E ratios. He then computed the percentage change in earnings per share for the formation year and for each of the nine subsequent years. Penman then aggregated the results across years. Exhibit 12.1 presents a subset of the results.

The results for the formation year are consistent with transitory components in earnings. Firms with high P-E ratios experienced low percentage changes in earnings during the formation year relative to the preceding year. Firms with low P-E ratios experienced high percentage changes in earnings during the formation year.

The results for Year 1 after the formation year suggest a counterbalancing effect of the earnings change in the formation year (a low percentage earnings change followed by a high percentage earnings change and vice versa for portfolios 4 and 18, respectively).

EXHIBIT 12.1

Median Percentage Changes in Earnings Per Share for Portfolios Formed on Observed P-E Ratios for Formation Year and Subsequent Years

P/E Portfolio	Median Percentage Change in Earnings Per Share				
	Formation Year 0	Year 1	Year 2	Year 3	Year 4
4 (High)	.039	.522	.175	.178	.150
10 (Medium)	.140	.118	.116	.137	.158
18 (Low)	.184	.048	.102	.123	.131

[13]"Normal" means $1/r$ in the no-growth setting and $(1 + g)/(r - g)$ in the growth setting.

[14]Stephen H. Penman, "The Articulation of Price-Earnings Ratios and Market-to-Book Ratios and the Evaluation of Growth," University of California-Berkeley, 1993.

The results for subsequent years reflect the tendency toward mean reversion in percentage earnings changes to a level in the mid-teens. This result is consistent with the data presented for ROCE in Chapter 8, where Penman observed a mean reversion in ROCE toward the mid-teens. The mean reversion suggests systematic directional changes in earnings growth over time (that is, serial autocorrelation), but the reversion takes several years to occur. Thus, P-E ratios based on reported earnings incorporate the effects of both transitory earnings components and longer-term shifts in permanent earnings. The *ex post* observance of a market price change, or absence of such a change, will signal the transitory or permanent nature of the earnings change. The analyst, who must make buy, hold, or sell recommendations on particular equity securities, desires to anticipate this change in market prices before it occurs. The observation of a low or high P-E ratio for the current period by itself is not sufficient information to differentiate transitory and permanent earnings changes. The next section discusses the price to book value ratio, a measure that helps the analyst differentiate transitory and permanent earnings changes.

One additional factor that might explain the divergence between actual and theoretical P-E ratios, particularly in cross-sectional comparisons, is the effect of alternative accounting principles. Industries subject to particularly conservative accounting principles, such as technology-oriented industries that must expense research and development costs in the year incurred, will report lower earnings and higher P-E ratios than industries that can capitalize and amortize critical cost inputs, such as the cost of depreciable assets by capital-intensive firms. Firms that select conservative accounting principles (for example, LIFO for inventories during periods of rising prices and accelerated depreciation of fixed assets) will have lower earnings and higher P-E ratios than firms that select less conservative accounting principles.

Summarizing, P-E ratios appear related to

1. Risk.
2. Growth.
3. Differences between current and expected future (permanent) earnings.
4. Alternative accounting principles.

The analysts must assess each of these elements when evaluating reported P-E ratios and using P-E ratios to value nontraded firms. The theoretical model indicates the factors affecting the P-E ratios but does provide an unambiguous signal of the "correct" P-E ratio for a particular firm.

PRICE TO BOOK VALUE (P-BV) RATIOS

The P-E ratio relates a stock measure (market value at a point in time) to a flow measure (earnings for a period of time). The price to book value ratio relates a stock measure (market value) to a stock measure (book value) of common shareholders' equity. The book value of shareholders' equity reflects capital contributions plus accumulated earnings in excess of dividends. This section explores the theoretical and empirical relationship between market prices and book values.

DEVELOPMENT OF THEORETICAL MODEL

In the previous section, we developed the relation between market price and expected, or permanent, earnings as follows:

$$P_t = \sum_{t=1}^{n} \frac{\text{Expected Earnings}_t}{(1 + r)^t}$$

We might expand the numerator as follows:

$$P_t = \sum_{t=1}^{n} \frac{\text{Expected ROCE}_t \times BV_t}{(1 + r)^t}$$

where ROCE equals the rate of return on common shareholders' equity and BV equals the book value of common shareholders' equity at the beginning of the period. In equilibrium, a firm should earn a rate of return on capital (that is, ROCE) equal to the rate of return required by the market for its particular risk level. Thus, in equilibrium, ROCE $= r$ and $P_t = BV_t$. A P-BV ratio of 1.0 should therefore indicate a firm generating earnings at the required rate of return.

We can rewrite the above formulation for price as follows:

$$P_t = BV_t + \sum_{t=1}^{n} \left(\frac{\text{Expected ROCE}_t - r}{r} \right) (BV_t)$$

This formulation expresses price in terms of a firm's accumulated retained profitability (BV_t) and the present (capitalized) value of its expected excess or deficient earning power in the future. When the expected ROCE equals the discount rate (r), there is no excess earning power and the P-BV ratio equals 1.0. If the expected ROCE exceeds r (that is, the firm is expected to invest in positive net present value projects for some period of time in the future), then the P-BV ratio will exceed 1.0. The excess over 1.0 represents positive goodwill, the ability to generate higher returns than the market requires, given the firm's risk level. Because accounting does not record this goodwill on the balance sheet under GAAP (except for purchase method corporate acquisitions), assets and shareholders' equity are understated and the P-BV ratio will exceed 1.0. Likewise, a firm experiencing an ROCE less than r should have negative goodwill and a P-BV ratio less than 1.0. If GAAP recognized the positive and negative goodwill, the P-BV ratio in theory should equal 1.0. Over time, competition should eliminate the excess earning power of firms with positive goodwill and improved earnings performance or bankruptcy should eliminate the deficient earnings power of firms with negative goodwill. Thus, P-BV ratios should be mean reverting toward 1.0.

Price is also a function of the growth in book value. As the book value of shareholders' equity grows through the retention of earnings, the net assets available on which the firm generates the excess returns increase, thereby increasing market price. Note that expected future increases in the book value of shareholders' equity should not add to current market price if the firm earns an ROCE equal to the cost of equity capital (that is, expected growth *per se* should not add value).

We can reexpress the formula above for price in terms of the P-BV ratio as follows:

$$\frac{P_t}{BV_t} = 1.0 + \left(\frac{\text{Expected ROCE}_{t+1} - r}{r}\right)\left(\frac{BV_n}{BV_t}\right)$$

In this formulation, n is the point when expected ROCE converges on r (in the case of mean reversion of ROCE) or some distant terminal date (in the case of ROCE following a random walk).

Summarizing, the P-BV ratio is a function of (1) the expected level of profitability relative to the required rate of return and (2) growth in the book value of common shareholders' equity.

Several empirical studies have found that ROCE of the current period is a reliable predictor of expected future ROCE (implying either that ROCE follows a random walk or that it mean reverts slowly).[15] We might therefore rewrite the above formulation as follows:

$$\frac{P_t}{BV_t} = 1.0 + \left(\frac{\text{Actual ROCE}_t - r}{r}\right)\left(\frac{BV_n}{BV_t}\right)$$

This formulation permits the analyst to compute an expected current P-BV ratio, which might then serve as a basis for evaluating whether the current market price appears to be at a reasonable level.

APPLICATION OF THEORETICAL P-BV MODEL

Consider the following data for Coke and Pepsi:

	Coke	Pepsi
Market Price per Share (December 31, Year 8)	$44.63	$40.88
Book Value per Share (December 31, Year 8)	$ 3.53	$ 7.94
Cost of Equity Capital	14.0%	15.1%
ROCE for Year 8	56.7%	27.2%
Five-Year Compound Annual Growth Rate in Common Shareholders' Equity	6.5%	14.9%

The theoretical model for Coke and Pepsi suggests P-BV ratios as follows:

$$\frac{P_t}{BV_t} = 1.0 + \left(\frac{\text{Actual ROCE}_t - r}{r}\right)\left(\frac{BV_n}{BV_t}\right)$$

---

[15]Jane A. Ou and Stephen H. Penman, "Financial Statement Analysis and the Evaluation of Market-to-Book Ratios," University of California-Berkeley, 1993; Victor L. Bernard, "Accounting-Based Valuation Methods, Determinants of Market-to-Book Ratios and Implications for Financial Statement Analysis," University of Michigan, 1993.

Growth Rate Continues for 10 Years

$$\text{Coke: } 6.7 = 1.0 + \left(\frac{.567 - .140}{.140}\right)(1.065)^{10}$$

$$\text{Pepsi: } 4.2 = 1.0 + \left(\frac{.272 - .151}{.151}\right)(1.149)^{10}$$

Growth Rate Continues for 20 Years

$$\text{Coke: } 11.8 = 1.0 + \left(\frac{.567 - .140}{.140}\right)(1.065)^{20}$$

$$\text{Pepsi: } 13.9 = 1.0 + \left(\frac{.272 - .151}{.151}\right)(1.149)^{20}$$

The actual P-BV ratios are 12.6 for Coke (= \$44.63 ÷ 3.53) and 5.2 for Pepsi (=\$40.88 ÷ \$7.94).

As was the case with the P-E ratio, the differences between actual and theoretical levels of P-BV ratios may relate to (1) errors in measuring the cost of equity capital, (2) errors in measuring the growth rate in common shareholders' equity, (3) using an actual ROCE that includes transitory earnings (that is, it does not reflect the expected permanent level of ROCE), or (4) using an actual ROCE that incorporates biases caused by alternative accounting principles. The calculation of the P-BV ratios for Coke and Pepsi above suggests that several of these explanations might account for the divergence between their actual and theoretical ratios. The actual ROCE for Coke of 56.7 percent for Year 8 is higher than in previous years and probably not sustainable. Pepsi's historical growth rate in shareholders' equity derives from both the retention of earnings and the issuance of common stock in acquisitions. It is unlikely that Pepsi will continue to grow at this rate, particularly given the maturity of the consumer foods industry and the 6.3 percent growth rate for Coke. Also, the immediate expensing of advertising and product development costs each year biases the ROCE.

Empirical research on the P-BV ratio is of relatively recent origin. Penman, using the same database as in Exhibit 12.1, formed firms into 20 portfolios each year based on their P-BV ratios.[16] He then computed the median ROCE for each portfolio in the formation year and for each of the nine subsequent years. Exhibit 12.2 presents a portion of Penman's results.

The data in Exhibit 12.2 indicate that firms with the highest P-BV ratios have the highest ROCEs in the formation year and firms with the lowest P-BV ratios have the lowest ROCEs in the formation year. Firms in the median P-BV category display ROCEs similar to the long-term rate of return on common shares. These results are consistent with the P-BV ratio reflecting the presence or absence of positive or negative earning power relative to the cost of equity capital. Note also the slow but steady mean reversion in ROCEs over time, consistent with movement toward equilibrium.

---

[16]Penman, "The Articulation of Price-Earnings Ratios and Market-to-Book Ratios."

EXHIBIT 12.2

Median ROCEs for Portfolios Formed on Observed
P-BV Ratios for Formation Year and Subsequent Years

P-BV Portfolio	Median ROCE				
	Formation Year 0	Year 1	Year 2	Year 3	Year 4
4 (High)	.187	.186	.175	.164	.156
10 (Medium)	.135	.132	.129	.130	.133
18 (Low)	.077	.077	.090	.099	.107

RELATION OF P-E RATIOS AND P-BV RATIOS TO ROCE

We are now ready to relate the P-E ratio and the P-BV ratio to ROCE. Observe the following decomposition of the P-BV ratio:

$$\textbf{P-BV Ratio} = \textbf{P-E Ratio} \times \textbf{ROCE}$$

$$\frac{P_t}{BV_t} = \frac{P_t}{\text{Earnings}_t} \times \frac{\text{Earnings}_t}{BV_t}$$

The theoretical links between these three ratios appear below:

P-BV Ratio	=	P-E Ratio	×	ROCE
Function of • Relation between ROCE and r • Growth in book value • Alternative accounting principles		Function of • Risk(r) • Growth in earnings (transitory and permanent) • Alternative accounting principles		Function of • Profitability (transitory and permanent) • Alternative accounting principles

Figure 12.1 depicts the relation between these three ratios. The nine cells categorize various combination of P-BV ratios and P-E ratios. Each cell shows (for illustrative purposes) the discount rate (r), or cost of equity capital, at 15 percent, the realized ROCE of the current period (ROCE-C), and the expected permanent future ROCE (ROCE-F).[17]

---

[17]Figure 12.1 is patterned after a similar matrix in Penman, "The Articulation of Price-Earnings Ratios and Market-to-Book Ratios."

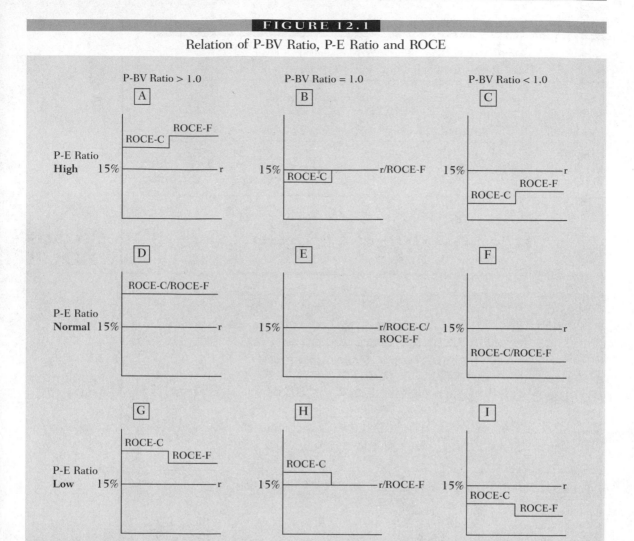

FIGURE 12.1

Relation of P-BV Ratio, P-E Ratio and ROCE

The columns in Figure 12.1 depict the P-BV ratio. When the P-BV ratio exceeds 1.0, ROCE-F exceeds r. When the P-BV ratio equals 1.0, ROCE-F = r. When the P-BV ratio is less than 1.0, ROCE-F is less than r.[18]

The rows in Exhibit 12.1 depict the P-E ratio. When the ratio is high, ROCE-C is less than ROCE-F. When the P-E ratio is normal, ROCE-C = ROCE-F. When the P-E ratio is low, ROCE-C exceeds ROCE-F.

We discuss these cells more fully below.

_____

[18]This discussion assumes that the P-BV ratio is not systematically biased by alternative accounting principles.

Equilibrium Case. Cell E depicts the equilibrium case. The firm expects to earn an ROCE of 15 percent in the future. Because this level of ROCE equals the market required rate of return of 15 percent, the firm has no excess earnings power, or goodwill. Thus, its P-BV ratio equals 1.0. In addition, the current period's ROCE of 15 percent equals the long-run expected ROCE (that is, the current period's ROCE includes no transitory earnings elements). Its P-E ratio will therefore equal 1/.15, reflecting only the market's required rate of return for the level of risk.

Current Earnings with Transitory Components. Consider now cells B and H. In these cases, the firm generates a lower ROCE (cell B) or higher ROCE (cell H) during the current period than its expected future level. The P-E ratio based on the current period's earnings is therefore higher or lower than normal. The task for the analysis is to assess whether or not the current period's ROCE represents a temporary phenomenon. A high or low P-E ratio coupled with a P-BV ratio of 1.0 suggests that the long-run expected ROCE equals the cost of equity capital. Thus, the current period's high P-E ratio (low ROCE-C) or low P-E ratio (high ROCE-C) is not expected to persist. The analyst should expect little market price change as a result of this transitory earnings aberration. Some market price change should occur, however, to the extent that the deviate earnings causes the firm to have more or less assets available on which to earn returns at the 15 percent expected rate in the future. Thus, cells B and H suggest that earnings include transitory elements.

Current Earnings Useful Predictor of Future Earnings. Consider now cells D and F. The P-E ratio is at a normal level (that is, the P-E ratio equals $1/r$).[19] Thus, the current period's profitability is expected to persist into the future. If the current period's ROCE is higher or lower than in the previous year, then the change in profitability during the current year is interpreted as a permanent earnings change. The market should price this new earnings level at the appropriate P-E ratio [6.7 = (1/.15) in this case]. Note that the market price will be higher for a higher level of earnings (cell D) and lower for a lower level of earnings (cell F) at that constant (normal) P-E ratio. The level of the P-BV ratio will indicate whether the new earnings level (ROCE-F) exceeds the cost of equity capital (cell D) or falls short (cell F).

Remaining Cells. The remaining four cells (A, C, G, and I) depict cases where the current earnings level is not expected to persist (indicated by high and low P-E ratios) and where the long-run expected ROCE exceeds or falls short of the cost of equity capital. The high P-E ratio based on the current period's earnings (cells A and C) indicate that the expected permanent level of earnings is higher than current earnings. This higher permanent level of ROCE will either exceed (cell A) or fall short (cell C) of the cost of equity capital. The low P-E ratios based on the current period's earnings (cells G and I) indicate that the expected permanent level of earnings is less than current earnings. This lower permanent level of earnings may exceed (cell G) or fall short (cell I) of the cost of equity capital.

---

[19]The analyst can assess normalcy in this regard by computing the cost of equity capital. See the discussion in Chapter 11.

USING P-E RATIOS AND P-BV RATIOS IN VALUING NONTRADED FIRMS

The analyst can value firms whose common shares are not publicly traded by using P-E ratios and P-BV rates of comparable firms that are publicly traded. The theoretical models assist in this valuation task by identifying the variables that the analyst should use in selecting comparable firms. The relevant variables for P-E and P-BV valuation models are

1. Expected (permanent) ROCE (profitability).
2. Cost of equity capital (risk).
3. Growth in earnings and shareholders' equity (growth).

Alford examined the accuracy of the P-E valuation models using industry, risk, ROCE, and earnings growth as the bases for selecting comparable firms.[20] The results indicate that industry membership, particularly at a three-digit SIC code level, provides the most effective comparisons. Firms in the same industry usually experience similar profitability, face similar risks, and grow at similar rates. Thus, industry membership serves as an effective proxy for the variables in the P-E valuation model. Alford observed some improvement in valuation accuracy by adding total assets (as a measure of risk) and ROCE to industry membership.[21] He found that adding growth to industry membership did not increase valuation accuracy.

SUMMARY

This chapter develops the theoretical rationale for relating market prices to earnings and to the book value of shareholders' equity. Relating market prices to earnings, using the P-E ratio, has been a frequently used technique by analysts for decades. There has been increasing recognition in recent years that transitory elements in the earnings of a particular period can cloud the interpretation of the P-E ratio as an indicator of value. Emphasis has shifted, particularly in academic research, to the P-BV ratio. This ratio is affected less by transitory earnings elements of a particular period.

Four variables, or factors, affect the P-E ratio and the P-BV ratio: (1) the cost of equity capital, (2) the growth rate in earnings or common shareholders' equity, (3) the presence of transitory components in the earnings or ROCEs of a particular year, and (4) biases in earnings or common shareholders' equity related to alternative accounting principles. Ongoing empirical research is endeavoring to identify the effects of each of these variables on reported P-E ratios and P-BV ratios. While this research is evolving, the analyst should view the theo-

---

[20]Andrew W. Alford, "The Effect of the Set of Comparable Firms on the Accuracy of the Price-Earnings Valuation Method," *Journal of Accounting Research* (Spring 1992), pp. 94–108.

[21]Recent research suggests that size (measured by total assets or market value of shareholders' equity) is a more accurate measure of risk than market beta in explaining market rates of return. See Eugene F. Fama and Kenneth R. French, "The Cross Section of Expected Stock Returns," *The Journal of Finance* (June 1992), pp. 427–465.

retical models as providing directional guidance in valuing firms rather than unambiguous indicators of value.

RODRIGUEZ HOME CENTER: EQUITY BUYOUT VALUATION*

Rodriguez Home Center, Inc. (RHC) operates a specialty retail store in Los Angeles, California, offering (fiscal 1995 sales mix in parentheses) furniture (27 percent), appliances (15 percent), audio and video electronics products (47 percent), selected jewelry (4 percent), and related products and services (7 percent). The company is known for low and competitive prices, a liberal return-of-merchandise policy, and a willingness to offer first-time credit to its customers. The company's bilingual sales staff and liberal credit terms have supported the development of a substantial customer base that is mostly Hispanic. RHC operates out of one department store and uses one warehouse, both of which it leases.

The company is wholly owned by Jose Rodriguez, who is 62 years old. His father founded RHC in 1956. The company's competitive advantage is the goodwill generated among the Hispanic community over the years. Although its product offerings are not unique, its competitively low prices for brand-name merchandise and credit extension policies have garnered an active customer list of 60,000 individuals. Two of its top three corporate officers as well as 14 of its 15 line managers are Hispanic. U.S. Census data indicate that the Hispanic community now composes 25 percent of the State of California's total population.

Jose Rodriguez is interested in selling his ownership in RHC and has approached his bank to assist in finding a buyer. The bank approached you as a partner in Southern California Investment Partners to see if your investment group might have an interest. The bank provided you with the attached financial statements (Exhibits 3, 4, and 5) and notes for the most recent five fiscal years. The bank indicated its willingness to maintain the working capital loan facility with the company on essentially the same terms as it currently does.

REQUIRED

You are asked to ascertain a reasonable purchase price for the equity ownership of Jose Rodriguez as of January 31, 1995. You should derive this valuation following three separate approaches:
   a. Present value of future cash flows of RHC.
   b. Multiples of earnings and book values, using both theoretical models and multiples of comparable companies.
   c. Market values of individual assets and liabilities (including goodwill).

The most comparable publicly traded companies in terms of product line are Second Family Group, Inc. (over-the-counter market) and Best Choice Company, Inc. (New York Stock Exchange). However, neither of these two companies offers in-store credit as Rodriguez does. Daytona Houston and C.J. Nickel offer in-store credit but a much broader product line than Rodriguez. Exhibit 1 presents selected data for these four companies. Exhibit 2 presents financial statement ratios for appliance, electronic, and furniture retailers.

---

*The author acknowledges the assistance of Gary M. Cypres in the preparation of this case.

EXHIBIT 1

Selected Data for Certain Retailers
For 1995 Fiscal Year
(Case 12.1)

	Second Family Group	Best Choice Company	Daytona Houston	C.J. Nickel
Sales (000s)	$78,222	$512,850	$14,739,000	$16,736,000
Assets (000s)	$32,779	$156,787	$ 8,524,000	$12,325,000
Net Income (000s)	$1,252	$5,683	$410,000	$ 577,000
Profit Margin for ROA	2.1%	1.6%	4.2%	4.6%
Assets Turnover................	2.5	3.5	1.9	1.3
Rate of Return on Assets	5.1%	5.5%	8.2%	6.2%
Common Earnings Leverage	68.4%	70.1%	65.7%	74.4%
Capital Structure Leverage.......	2.5	2.3	5.0	3.4
Rate of Return on Common Shareholders' Equity	8.7%	9.0%	26.7%	15.7%
Cost of Goods Sold/Sales........	72.5%	76.5%	72.3%	65.5%
Selling and Administrative Expense/Sales	24.7%	20.9%	18.6%	31.7%
Accounts Receivable Turnover....	107.2	74.3	11.6	4.9
Inventory Turnover	4.3	4.0	5.5	4.2
Accounts Payable Turnover	4.8	6.2	8.9	6.4
Current Ratio...................	1.2:1	1.6:1	1.5:1	2.6:1
Total Liabilities/Total Assets	58.6%	57.8%	75.7%	64.4%
Long-Term Debt/Total Assets	22.9%	22.4%	43.2%	25.4%
Interest Leverage Ratio..........	2.6	3.6	3.0	3.8
Five-Year Growth Rate Sales	10.4%	24.9%	12.3%	2.3%
Net Income	8.7%	15.7%	7.3%	4.8%
Market Value/Earnings..........	14.2	16.8	11.8	10.3
Market Value/Book Value of Equity...................	1.31	1.44	2.86	1.61
Market Beta..................	1.18	1.15	1.30	1.22

EXHIBIT 2

Financial Ratios for Selected Retailers for 1995 Fiscal Year
(Case 12.1)

	Appliances	Electronic Stores	Furniture Stores
Profit Margin for Return on Assets	2.7%	3.6%	3.3%
Asset Turnover........................	2.3	2.0	1.6
Return on Assets......................	6.3%	7.3%	5.4%
Return on Common Shareholders' Equity ..	13.4%	17.1%	10.2%
Cost of Goods Sold/Sales................	69.6%	65.5%	63.0%
Accounts Receivable Turnover............	24.3	33.2	12.8
Inventory Turnover	3.8	3.9	3.0
Current Ratio.........................	2.0:1	2.1:1	2.9:1
Total Liabilities/Total Assets	51.8%	50.0%	45.0%

EXHIBIT 3

Rodriguez Home Center, Inc.
Comparative Income Statements
(amounts in thousands)
(Case 12.1)

	For the Year Ended January 31				
	1991	1992	1993	1994	1995
Sales	$ 56,058	$ 69,670	$ 86,382	$ 98,534	$110,500
Cost of Goods Sold	(37,404)	(46,214)	(56,892)	(68,054)	(75,774)
Gross Margin	$ 18,654	$ 23,456	$ 29,490	$ 30,480	$ 34,726
Selling and Administrative Expenses	(20,149)	(23,566)	(29,262)	(34,161)	(36,184)
Finance Income	6,026	7,007	8,498	10,045	11,109
Credit Insurance Income	1,060	1,312	1,698	2,022	2,210
Interest Expense	(1,871)	(2,269)	(2,492)	(2,366)	(2,707)
Income before Income Taxes	$ 3,720	$ 5,940	$ 7,932	$ 6,020	$ 9,154
Income Tax Expense	(1,914)	(2,822)	(3,184)	(2,796)	(4,119)
Net Income	$ 1,806	$ 3,118	$ 4,748	$ 3,224	$ 5,035

EXHIBIT 4

Rodriguez Home Center, Inc.
Comparative Balance Sheets
(amounts in thousands)
(Case 12.1)

	January 31					
	1990	1991	1992	1993	1994	1995
Assets						
Cash	$ 243	$ 436	$ 786	$ 500	$ 802	$ 1,152
Accounts Receivable						
Gross	30,216	34,976	46,330	59,512	71,360	83,896
Deferred Interest	(2,288)	(2,648)	(4,904)	(5,520)	(7,174)	(9,224)
Allowance for Uncollectible						
Accounts	(578)	(670)	(1,116)	(1,600)	(2,000)	(2,400)
Net	$27,593	$32,094	$41,096	$52,892	$62,988	$73,424
Merchandise Inventories	7,562	10,250	11,294	16,612	16,392	15,646
Prepayments	36	56	106	2,362	3,618	3,004
Total Current Assets	$35,191	$42,400	$52,496	$71,866	$82,998	$92,074
Fixtures and Equipment (net)	3,038	2,906	2,454	2,338	3,116	2,870
Deposits	38	68	192	192	176	178
Total Assets	$38,267	$45,374	$55,142	$74,396	$86,290	$95,122

Exh. 4—Continued

			January 31			
	1990	**1991**	**1992**	**1993**	**1994**	**1995**
Liabilities and Shareholders' Equity						
Notes Payable to Bank	$16,410	$18,995	$24,186	$31,435	$37,312	$43,363
Current Portion of Long-Term Debt..	—	—	—	—	218	268
Accounts and Notes Payable—Trade .	9,869	11,646	11,154	13,514	16,764	14,305
Other Current Liabilities	2,486	3,425	5,376	10,273	8,794	9,165
Total Current Liabilities..........	$28,765	$34,066	$40,716	$55,222	$63,088	$67,101
Long-Term Debt	—	—	—	—	804	588
Total Liabilities	$28,765	$34,066	$40,716	$55,222	$63,892	$67,689
Common Stock	$ 36	$ 36	$ 36	$ 36	$ 36	$ 36
Retained Earnings................	9,466	11,272	14,390	19,138	22,362	27,397
Total Stockholders' Equity	$ 9,502	$11,308	$14,426	$19,174	$22,398	$27,433
Total Liabilities and Stockholders' Equity......................	$38,267	$45,374	$55,142	$74,396	$86,290	$95,122

EXHIBIT 5

Rodriguez Home Center, Inc.
Comparative Statement of Cash Flows
(amounts in thousands)
(Case 12.1)

	For the Year Ended January 31				
	1991	**1992**	**1993**	**1994**	**1995**
Operations					
Net Income	$ 1,806	$ 3,118	$ 4,748	$ 3,224	$ 5,035
Depreciation................................	512	558	608	730	714
(Increase) Decrease in Receivables	(4,308)	(8,652)	(12,082)	(9,794)	(10,086)
(Increase) Decrease in Inventories	(2,688)	(1,044)	(5,318)	220	746
(Increase) Decrease in Prepayments	(20)	(50)	(2,256)	(1,256)	614
Increase (Decrease) in Accounts Payable	1,777	(492)	2,360	3,250	(2,459)
Increase (Decrease) in Other Current Liabilities ..	939	1,951	4,897	(1,479)	371
Cash Flow from Operations..................	$(1,982)	$(4,611)	$(7,043)	$(5,105)	$ (5,065)
Investing					
Acquisition of Fixtures and Equipment	(380)	(106)	(492)	(1,508)	(468)
Other Investing Transactions	(30)	(124)	—	16	(2)
Cash Flow from Investing	$ (410)	$ (230)	$ (492)	$(1,492)	$ (470)
Financing					
Increase (Decrease) in Short-Term Debt	$ 2,585	$ 5,191	$ 7,249	$ 5,877	$ 6,051
Increase (Decrease) in Long-Term Debt	—	—	—	1,022	(166)
Cash Flow from Financing	$ 2,585	$ 5,191	$ 7,249	$ 6,899	$ 5,885
Net Change in Cash........................	$ 193	$ 350	$ (286)	$ 302	$ 350

Jose Rodriguez indicates that he recently received an appraisal report of the store fixtures and equipment conducted by Price Waterhouse. The company asked for this appraisal to assist in assessing the adequacy of its insurance coverage. The appraisal as of January 31, 1995, appears below (amounts in thousands):

Store Fixtures and Equipment	Fair Market Value
Automobiles and Trucks.............	$ 344.0
Furnitures and Equipment...........	1,621.0
Leasehold Improvements	1,461.6
Total	$3,426.6

The report indicates that the valuation of automobiles and trucks uses information from *Truck Blue Book, Truck Gazette,* and *Kelley Blue Book.* The valuation of furniture, equipment, and leasehold improvements uses various government price indices for the specific items to ascertain their reproduction cost in new condition. Price Waterhouse then adjusted this reproduction cost downward to reflect the current condition of these items.

NOTES TO FINANCIAL STATEMENTS

NOTE A: SUMMARY OF SIGNIFICANT ACCOUNTING POLICIES

Revenue Recognition. The company recognizes revenue from the sale of merchandise at the time of sale. It typically provides customers with financing for their purchases. The company adds interest at rates varying between 11 percent and 21 percent to the face (gross) amount of the receivable at the time of sale and recognizes this amount as revenue over the term of the installment contract using the interest method. The installment contracts provide for monthly payments and mature from 1 to 24 months from the time of the sale. The company's balance sheet uses 24 months as the operating cycle in accordance with the terms of the installment contracts.

Merchandise Inventories. The company states its inventories at lower of cost (first-in, first-out) or market.

Store Fixtures and Equipment. Store fixtures and equipment appear at acquisition cost. The company computes depreciation and amortization using the straight-line method over the estimated lives of assets as follows:

Automobiles and Trucks	3–5 years
Furniture and Equipment	5–7 years
Leasehold Improvements	Life of lease

Income Taxes. The company provides deferred taxes for timing differences between book and taxable income.

NOTE B: ACCOUNTS RECEIVABLE

An aging of the accounts receivable on January 31, 1995, reveals the following (dollar amounts in thousands):

Days Past Due	Number of Accounts	Gross Amount Outstanding
31–60 Days	2,996	$2,061
61–90 Days	1,594	1,025
91–120 Days	840	549
120–150 Days	414	304
More than 150 Days	638	393
	6,482	$4,332

The allowance for uncollectible accounts changed as follows (amounts in thousands):

	Fiscal Year Ending January 31				
	1991	1992	1993	1994	1995
Balance, Beginning of Fiscal Year.....	$ 578	$ 670	$ 1,116	$ 1,600	$ 2,000
Plus Bad Debt Expense	1,682	2,160	2,764	3,416	3,868
Minus Accounts Written Off........	(1,590)	(1,714)	(2,280)	(3,016)	(3,468)
Balance, End of Fiscal Year..........	$ 670	$ 1,116	$ 1,600	$ 2,000	$ 2,400

NOTE C: INVENTORIES

The book value of inventories exceeded their market value by $800,000 on January 31, 1995, and the company recorded a write-down to reflect a lower of cost or market valuation. The company took its first complete physical inventory on January 31, 1994, and discovered that the book inventory exceeded the physical inventory by $2,600,000. The company wrote down the book inventory to reflect this overstatement but did not restate inventory and cost of goods sold amounts for prior fiscal years.

NOTE D: STORE FIXTURES AND EQUIPMENT

Store fixtures and equipment consist of the following (amounts in thousands):

	January 31				
	1991	1992	1993	1994	1995
Automobiles and Trucks.............	$ 486	$ 544	$ 609	$ 683	$ 765
Furniture and Equipment...........	2,809	2,320	2,457	3,021	2,622
Leasehold Improvements	1,210	1,546	1,604	2,099	1,886
Software Development Costs........	210	360	440	507	698
Gross.........................	$ 4,715	$ 4,770	$ 5,110	$ 6,310	$ 5,971
Less Accumulated Depreciation......	(1,809)	(2,316)	(2,772)	(3,194)	(3,101)
Net	$ 2,906	$ 2,454	$ 2,338	$ 3,116	$ 2,870

Software development costs are capitalized and amortized in accordance with a reporting standard of the Financial Accounting Standards Board.

NOTE E: NOTES PAYABLE TO BANK

The company has a revolving line of credit agreement with a bank that provides for borrowings not to exceed the lower of $60,000,000 or 65 percent of eligible receivables. The amounts outstanding on this line bear interest at .5 percent over the bank's prime rate. Accounts receivable and inventories not otherwise secured by the company's trade notes (Note F) collateralize this line of credit. The bank may withdraw the line-of-credit facility at any time, with any unpaid notes then repayable over a maximum period of 12 months. The line-of-credit agreement contains restrictive covenants with regard to the maintenance of financial ratios.

At January 31, 1995, the company's borrowings under the line-of-credit facility total $43,363,000. These borrowings bear interest at rates ranging from 6.46 percent to 7.01 percent and have maturities from February 13, 1995, to July 22, 1995. The amount of unused credit under this line was $2,446,000 on January 31, 1995.

NOTE F: TRADE NOTES PAYABLE

Trade notes payable consist of inventory purchases made through a flooring arrangement with a finance company. The repayment terms typically require payment within 30 days. The flooring company possesses a first priority security interest in certain inventories. The supplier of the merchandise pays all finance charges.

NOTE G: LONG-TERM DEBT

Long-term debt consists of the following (amounts in thousands):

	January 31	
	1994	1995
Various Equipment Notes at Interest Rates Ranging from 8.75% to 9.25%, Secured by Assets, Maturing from 1995 to 1998.....	$ 808	$687
Obligations under Capital Leases	214	168
Total	$1,022	$855
Less Current Portion	218	267
	$ 804	$588

Maturities of the equipment notes and obligations under capital leases at January 31, 1995, are as follows (amounts in thousands):

Fiscal Year	Equipment Notes	Capital Leases
1996	$217	$ 67
1997	162	67
1998	176	66
1999	132	—
	$687	$200
Less Amount Represting Interest.........	—	31
	$687	$169

NOTE H: INCOME TAXES

The provision for income taxes consists of the following (amounts in thousands):

	For the Year Ended January 31				
	1991	1992	1993	1994	1995
Current Taxes					
Federal	$ 599	$1,144	$1,222	$2,286	$1,581
State	186	372	595	798	590
Deferred Taxes					
Federal	$ 868	$ 966	$1,010	$ (213)	$1,440
State	261	340	357	(75)	508
Total Provision.....	$1,914	$2,822	$3,184	$2,796	$4,119

Deferred taxes arise from timing differences related to revenue recognition and depreciation.

NOTE I: COMMITMENTS

The company leases its warehouse and certain computer equipment under five-year, noncancellable operating leases expiring in fiscal 1998. The warehouse lease provides for a minimum 4 percent rent escalation per year from fiscal 1995 onward and has two 5-year options to extend. The company also leases its retail showroom under a noncancellable lease expiring in fiscal 2000. The lease provides for cost-of-living rent escalation plus payment of certain executory costs, excluding property taxes, and has two 5-year options to extend.

Aggregate minimum lease payments are as follows (amounts in thousands):

Fiscal Year	Total
1996	$ 2,995
1997	3,037
1998	2,344
1999	1,526
2000	1,526
Thereafter	1,272
	$12,700

Rent expense for fiscal years 1994 and 1995 were $2,389,566 and $2,424,826, respectively.

CASE 12.2

REVCO D.S.: FRAUDULENT CONVEYANCE*

Investors in a firm's debt securities that were issued to finance a leveraged buyout (LBO) have increasingly used the legal concept of fraudulent conveyance in efforts to obtain financial restitution for losses they incurred when the issuing firm is unable to service its debt adequately after the LBO. The sponsoring equity participants in an LBO use the assets of a target firm as collateral for substantial debt borrowings. The proceeds of the debt issues plus a relatively small amount of funds contributed by the sponsoring equity participants finance the buyout of the shares of the pre-LBO shareholders. A presumption exists on the part of the new debt holders that the firm is solvent after the LBO. That is, the value of the firm's assets exceeds the claims of creditors. A subsequent finding that a firm is unable to service the LBO debt may suggest (1) that the value of liabilities exceeded the value of assets just after the LBO (either because lenders overstated the perceived value of the assets or because more corporate assets were used to buy out the pre-LBO shareholders than was appropriate) or (2) subsequent management decisions or operating conditions led to a deterioration of asset values or increase in liability values. Claimants use the fraudulent conveyance concept in the

*The author gratefully acknowledges the assistance of Dusty Philip in the preparation of this case.

first setting above, arguing that the sponsoring equity participants overpaid to buy out existing shareholders, leaving insufficient assets in the firm to service the debt.

Revco D.S., Inc., the largest retail drugstore chain in the United States, engaged in an LBO transaction totaling $1.45 billion on December 29, 1986. Revco subsequently filed for bankruptcy on July 28, 1988, causing substantial losses for debt and equity participants in the LBO. This case examines whether the value of Revco's net assets at the time of the LBO justified the buyout price.

ECONOMIC CHARACTERISTICS AND EXISTING CONDITIONS IN THE DRUGSTORE INDUSTRY

Between 1970 and 1985, the drugstore industry experienced a 15 percent annual growth rate in sales. Most of this growth occurred because of the increasingly dominating presence of large retail drugstore chains (Revco, Rite Aid, Eckerds, Walgreens). By 1985, these chains commanded a 60 percent market share, with independent drugstores, pharmacies, hospitals, variety stores, and supermarkets composing the remainder. Drugstores compete on the basis of price, convenience, quality, reliability, and delivery. The drugstore chains increased their market share at the expense of the smaller players for the following reasons:

1. Lower prices due to volume purchasing.
2. Greater convenience due to the larger number of locations.
3. Greater diversity of merchandise beyond pharmaceuticals.
4. Improving professional image.

By the mid-1980s, however, the drugstore industry began approaching maturity. The number of retail outlets nationwide reached a saturation point. In 1986, drugstores reported their smallest sales gains in a decade. Competition intensified among drugstores for a larger share of the now slower growing market. Among the more important industry trends were the following:

1. *Frequent Price Wars:* Firms began to trade off reduced profit margin for increased assets turnover.
2. *Increased Focus on Cost-Cutting:* Firms trimmed costs to offset the required price reductions. Many drugstores installed computer systems to improve productivity and service.
3. *Recentralization:* Firms began to reverse the trend over the preceding decade toward autonomous profit centers in an effort to eliminate overhead costs and increase coordination among drugstores.
4. *Consolidation:* Firms attempted to maintain their historical growth rates and increase their market share by acquiring existing drugstore chains. In addition, supermarket chains attempted to diversify into drugstores by participating in these acquisitions. Some of the major acquisitions included the following:

Acquiror/Acquiree

Pantry Pride/Adams Drugs
Kroger Co./Hook Drugs
K-Mart/Pay Less Drug Stores
Imasco/People's Drug Stores

5. *Diversification:* Drugstore chains diversified into higher growth, higher profit margin businesses, including auto parts, food distribution, children's toys, and books.
6. *Changed Product Mix:* Drugstores expanded their product line to include video cassette rentals and film processing.

Several positive signs appeared on the horizon for the drugstore industry in the mid-1980s.

1. *Aging of the Population:* Demographers expected the number of individuals over 65 years of age to increase 30 percent between 1986 and 1990 and those over 75 to increase by 74 percent. These age groups typically require substantially more prescription drugs than the general population.
2. *Increased Health Consciousness:* Individuals placed increasing emphasis on exercise, diet, and health monitoring beginning in the early 1980s, a trend expected to continue for the foreseeable future. Drugstores added products to satisfy consumer needs in these areas.
3. *Rising Hospital Costs:* Rising hospital costs were expected to lead to shorter hospital stays and increased emphasis on outpatient and at-home care, increasing the likelihood that patients would purchase drugs from drugstore chains rather than in-hospital pharmacies.
4. *New Tax Legislation:* Drugstores expected to benefit from the decrease in the statutory income tax rate from 46 percent to 34 percent.

HISTORICAL BACKGROUND OF REVCO

Exhibit 1 presents certain operating data for Revco for the fiscal years ending May 1982 to 1986. At the end of fiscal 1986, Revco operated more than 2,000 drugstores in the following geographical mix:

EXHIBIT 1

Revco—Operating Data
(Case 12.2)

	Fiscal year Ended May					Compound Annual Growth Rate
	1982	1983	1984	1985	1986	
Sales (in millions)	$ 1,555	$ 1,793	$ 2,227	$ 2,396	$ 2,743	15.2%
Number of Drugstores	1,593	1,661	1,778	1,898	2,031	6.3%
Drugstore Retail Square Footage (in thousands)	12,227	12,849	13,909	15,148	16,694	8.1%
Drugstore Sales as Percentage of Total Sales	94.5%	94.9%	95.3%	95.1%	95.4%	—
Drugstore Sales per Square Foot	$ 120	$ 132	$ 153	$ 150	$ 157	6.9%
Like-Drugstore Percentage Sales Growth	8.4%	12.3%	12.3%	5.8%	8.5%	—
Prescription Revenue as Percentage of Drugstore Sales	28.0%	29.6%	29.4%	30.5%	31.1%	—

Southeast......................	52.5%
Middle Atlantic................	8.5
Midwest......................	19.9
Southwest	19.1
Total.......................	100.0%

Revco's sales grew at a 15.2 percent compound annual rate during the five years preceding the LBO. Revco increased the number of drugstores at a 6.3 percent annual rate, using both internal growth and acquisitions. Prescription revenues remained a steady 30 percent of drugstore sales and drugstore revenues remained a steady 95 percent of total revenues. Revco employed an "everyday low price" strategy during this period rather than opting for periodic sales.

Exhibit 2 presents comparative income statements, Exhibit 3 presents comparative balance sheets, and Exhibit 4 presents comparative statements of cash flows for the 1982 to 1986 fiscal years. Additional information pertaining to these financial statements follows:

1. Revco leases drugstore and warehouse facilities using operating leases. The present value of its lease commitments when discounted at 10 percent follows:

May 31	Present Value of Operating Leases (in millions)
1981	$212
1982	$249
1983	$283
1984	$343
1985	$409
1986	$456

EXHIBIT 2

Revco D.S., Inc.
Income Statement
(amounts in millions)
(Case 12.2)

	1982	1983	1984	1985	1986
Sales Revenue	$ 1,555	$ 1,793	$ 2,227	$ 2,396	$ 2,743
Interest Revenue	2	2	3	2	3
Total Revenues.....................	$ 1,557	$ 1,795	$ 2,230	$ 2,398	$ 2,746
Cost of Goods Sold...................	(1,135)	(1,307)	(1,602)	(1,795)	(2,022)
Selling and Administrative Expenses	(321)	(360)	(448)	(520)	(596)
Interest Expense	(11)	(6)	(6)	(15)	(29)
Unusual Items	—	—	—	—	3
Income before Taxes.................	$ 90	$ 122	$ 174	$ 68	$ 102
Income Taxes.......................	(40)	(56)	(81)	(29)	(45)
Net Income	$ 50	$ 66	$ 93	$ 39	$ 57

EXHIBIT 3

Revco D.S., Inc.
Balance Sheet
(amounts in millions)
(Case 12.2)

	1981	1982	1983	1984	1985	1986
Assets						
Cash	$ 18	$ 27	$ 51	$ 18	$ 8	$ 45
Accounts Receivable	31	31	41	54	75	69
Inventories	258	276	317	472	492	502
Prepayments	11	11	16	19	26	24
Total Current Assets	$318	$345	$425	$563	$ 601	$ 640
Property, Plant, and Equipment						
Gross	$164	$199	$218	$271	$ 345	$ 428
Accumulated Depreciation	(46)	(58)	(69)	(84)	(102)	(127)
Net	$118	$141	$149	$187	$ 243	$ 301
Other Assets	11	15	24	27	31	46
Total Assets	$447	$501	$598	$777	$ 875	$ 987
Liabilities and Shareholders' Equity						
Accounts Payable	$ 78	$ 90	$100	$142	$ 145	$ 155
Notes Payable	—	—	—	51	121	—
Current Portion of Long-Term Debt	3	3	4	4	4	5
Other Current Liabilities	47	49	66	72	75	94
Total Current Liabilities	$128	$142	$170	$269	$ 345	$ 254
Long-Term Debt	66	66	43	39	45	305
Deferred Income Taxes	4	8	13	22	28	36
Total Liabilities	$198	$216	$226	$330	$ 418	$ 595
Common Stock	$ 14	$ 20	$ 32	$ 36	$ 36	$ 36
Additional Paid-in Capital	20	15	41	39	39	42
Retained Earnings	215	250	299	372	382	412
Treasury Stock	—	—	—	—	—	(98)
Total Shareholders' Equity	$249	$285	$372	$447	$ 457	$ 392
Total Liabilities and Shareholders' Equity	$447	$501	$598	$777	$ 875	$ 987

2. Revco uses a last-in, first-out (LIFO) cost-flow assumption for inventories and cost of goods sold. The excess of current cost over LIFO inventories at each year end follows:

May 31	Excess of Current Cost (in millions) over LIFO Inventories
1982	$ 82
1983	$ 94
1984	$103
1985	$118
1986	$128

EXHIBIT 4

Revco D.S., Inc.
Statement of Cash Flows
(amounts in millions)
(Case 12.2)

	1982	1983	1984	1985	1986
Operations					
Net Income	$ 50	$ 66	$ 93	$ 39	$ 57
Depreciation...................................	17	19	23	28	34
Other Addbacks...............................	4	6	10	6	2
Working Capital from Operations..............	$ 71	$ 91	$ 126	$ 73	$ 93
(Increase) Decrease in Accounts Receivable	1	(11)	(7)	(22)	9
(Increase) Decrease in Inventories	(18)	(41)	(142)	(20)	(10)
(Increase) Decrease in Prepayments..............	—	(4)	(2)	(7)	2
Increase (Decrease) in Accounts Payable..........	13	11	33	7	11
Increase (Decrease) in Other Current Liabilities ...	1	17	(2)	(1)	18
Cash Flow from Operations...................	$ 68	$ 63	$ 6	$ 30	$ 123
Investing					
Sale of Property, Plant, and Equipment...........	$ 2	$ 2	$ 1	$ 6	$ 2
Acquisition of Property, Plant, and Equipment.....	(42)	(29)	(58)	(90)	(82)
Other...	—	—	—	—	(16)
Cash Flow from Investing	$(40)	$(27)	$ (57)	$(84)	$ (96)
Financing					
Increase in Short-Term Borrowing...............	—	—	$ 49	$ 70	—
Increase in Long-Term Borrowing	$ 3	—	—	11	$ 261
Increase in Common Stock	1	$ 38	1	1	2
Decrease in Short-Term Borrowing	—	—	—	—	(121)
Decrease in Long-Term Borrowing..............	(3)	(24)	(7)	(5)	(5)
Decrease in Common Stock.....................	—	—	—	—	(99)
Dividends	(15)	(17)	(22)	(29)	(27)
Other...	(5)	(9)	(3)	(4)	(1)
Cash Flow from Financing	$(19)	$(12)	$ 18	$ 44	$ 10
Net Change in Cash...........................	$ 9	$ 24	$ (33)	$(10)	$ 37

3. Selected per share data follow:

	1982	1983	1984	1985	1986
Fiscal Year					
Earnings per Share	$1.39	$ 1.91	$ 2.54	$ 1.06	$ 1.72
Book Value Per Share	$8.12	$10.24	$12.22	$12.48	$12.11

4. On May 24, 1984, Revco acquired the outstanding common shares of Odd Lot Trading Company by issuing 4.4 million Revco common shares valued at $113 million. Revco treated the acquisition as a pooling of interests, recording the shares issued at the book value of Odd Lot's common shareholders' equity of $925 thousand. Odd Lot purchases closed-out merchandise and manufacturers' overruns from various vendors for resale at discount prices through their 153 stores located in nine states. Sales and earnings of Odd Lot generally compose less than 5 percent of Revco's total sales each year. Prior to the acquisition, Revco sold certain merchandise to Odd Lot. At the time of the acquisition, Revco was considered a target for an unfriendly takeover. The shares exchanged placed 4.4 million shares (12.0 percent) in what Revco considered friendly hands. Soon after the acquisition, the former owners and managers of Odd Lot made numerous suggestions to improve the operations and profitability of Revco's drugstore operations, suggestions that Sidney Dworkin, long-time chairman and CEO of Revco, did not appreciate. Revco fired these individuals in February 1985. On July 9, 1985, Revco repurchased the 4.4 million shares held by these individuals for $98.2 million in cash. Revco financed the stock repurchase using the proceeds from $95 million of long-term borrowing.

5. For the year ending May 1985, Revco recognized a pretax loss of $35 million from writing down inventories of Odd Lot. The latter company operated at a net loss of $9.5 million in fiscal 1985 and at a net loss of $8.6 million in fiscal 1986.

6. On July 1, 1985, Revco acquired the Carls Drug Store chain for $35 million in cash.

7. The income statement for the fiscal year ending May, 1986 includes the following unusual items (amounts shown are pretax in millions):

Gain from Sale of Computer Subsidiary	$ 6.6
Gain on Sale of Alarm Service Division	2.3
Premium for Short-Term Insurance Coverage Following Bankruptcy of Former Carrier	(5.0)
Expenses of Board of Directors to Examine Proposed LBO	(1.1)
Total Unusual Items	$ 2.8

The after-tax effect of the unusual items was $1.5 million.

8. Revco's market price per share was $27.50 in early 1986 just prior to rumors of an LBO hitting the market.

9. An independent appraisal of Revco's net assets as of September 1986 revealed assets (excluding any goodwill) of $1.433 billion and liabilities of .611 billion.

LBO TRANSACTION

The sponsoring equity participants in the LBO included the following:

Transcontinental Services Group	51.0%
Current Management	28.9
Salomon Brothers	13.1
Golenberg & Co.	1.4
Holders of Exchangeable Preferred Stock	5.6
Total	100.0%

These individuals obtained financing totaling $1.45 billion and used the proceeds to purchase the outstanding shares of Revco for $38.50 per share and to retire $117.5 million of existing debt. The new Revco entity also assumed $175.0 million of existing Revco debt. Exhibit 5 presents a cash-flow analysis relating to the LBO. Revco planned to sell seven nondrugstore subsidiaries soon after the LBO for their independently appraised value of $225 million and to use the proceeds to repay a portion of the term debt.

REQUIRED

Your task is to assess the reasonableness of the $38.50 buyout price for Revco's common shares. Your analysis should proceed as follows:

   a. Prepare a set of pro forma financial statements for Revco for the fiscal years 1987 to 1991, ignoring the financing for the LBO. That is, project (1) operating income after taxes but before interest expense and related tax effects, (2) assets and current liabilities excluding term debt and the current portion of long-term debt, and (3) cash flow from operations (excluding interest and related taxes) net of cash flow from investing activities. Discount the net cash flow from operating and investing activities, including any residual value at the end of fiscal 1991, using a weighted average cost of capital from the LBO. Assume a 40 percent income tax rate for fiscal 1987 and a 34 percent tax rate thereafter. The prime interest rate at the time of the transaction was 10 percent. The debentures were issued for their face value.

   b. A second approach to assessing the reasonableness of the buyout price is to examine the valuation of other drugstore chains. Exhibits 6 through 9 present historical ratio

---

EXHIBIT 5

Sources and Uses of Cash Relating to Revco LBO
(amounts in thousands)
(Case 12.2)

Sources

Term Bank Loan, priced at prime plus 1.75% or LIBOR + 2.75%, repayable over five years	$ 455,000
Senior Subordinated Debentures, 13.125%, due in December, 1993 and 1994	400,000
Subordinated Debentures, 13.30%, due in December, 1995 and 1996	210,000
Junior Subordinated Debentures, 13.30%, due in December 1997 to 2001	93,750
Convertible Preferred Stock, 850,000 shares with $12 per share dividend, convertible into 2.56 common shares each	85,000
Exchangeable Preferred Stock, 7,880,000 shares with $3.8125 per share dividend on liquidation preference ($25) exchangeable for $25 notes yielding 15.25%	130,020
Junior Preferred Stock, 1,203,875 shares with $4.40 per share dividend	30,098
Common Stock	34,381
Revco Cash	9,155
Total Sources	**$1,447,404**

Uses

Acquisition of Revco Common Stock, 32,433 shares at $38.50	$1,248,674
Repayment of Existing Debt	117,484
Cancellation of Revco Employee Stock Options	3,246
Fees and Commissions	78,000
Total Uses	**$1,447,404**

analyses (assuming the capitalization of all operating leases) for four drugstore chains as follows:

> *Fay's Drug Company:* This firm operated 150 drugstores throughout the Northeast in 1986. The average store size was approximately 15,000 square feet. Drugstore sales composed the vast majority of revenues. Fay's also operated several auto parts and paper supplies outlets.
> *Perry Drugstores:* This firm operated 139 drugstores, primarily in Michigan, in 1986. Perry focused its strategy on drugstores, auto parts, and health care, with drugstores the dominant segment by far.

EXHIBIT 6

Fay's Drug Company
Ratio Analysis
(Case 12.2)

	1982	1983	1984	1985	1986
Profitability Analysis					
Return on Assets:					
Profit Margin...........................	1.8%	2.4%	3.1%	2.7%	1.3%
× Asset Turnover	2.9	3.0	2.7	2.3	2.2
= Return on Assets	5.3%	7.3%	8.1%	6.2%	2.9%
Return on Common Equity					
Return on Assets.........................	5.3%	7.3%	8.1%	6.2%	2.9%
× Common Earnings Leverage.............	72.5%	84.3%	85.0%	86.1%	47.0%
× Capital Structure Leverage	4.1	3.8	3.0	2.9	3.4
= Return on Common Equity..............	15.5%	23.4%	20.7%	15.5%	4.6%
Operating Performance					
Gross Margin/Sales.......................	25.1%	24.9%	25.6%	25.5%	23.7%
Operating Profit before Tax/Revenues	3.2%	4.6%	5.6%	4.5%	1.9%
Net Income—Continued Operations/Revenues.	1.3%	2.0%	2.6%	2.4%	0.6%
Asset Turnover					
Sales/Average Accounts Receivable	61.8	63.1	76.1	68.3	58.0
COGS/Average Inventory	5.9	7.0	6.3	5.5	5.5
Sales/Average Fixed Assets...................	11.4	12.7	11.5	10.7	10.4
Risk Analysis					
Liquidity					
Current Ratio............................	1.78	1.98	1.74	1.81	2.56
Quick Ratio	0.52	0.76	0.49	0.52	0.68
Days Payables Held	38	30	33	38	32
Days Receivable Held	6	6	5	5	6
Days Inventory Held......................	62	52	58	67	66
Operating Cash Flow to Current Liabilities....	44.4%	40.5%	30.9%	16.6%	−20.5%
Solvency					
Total Liabilities/Total Assets	73.8%	73.8%	61.8%	67.9%	72.2%
Long-Term Debt/Total Assets	46.0%	46.8%	35.3%	41.5%	53.5%
Long-Term Debt/Owner's Equity	175.6%	178.5%	92.5%	129.2%	192.6%
Operating Cash Flow to Total Liabilities	17.2%	15.0%	12.2%	6.5%	−6.2%
Interest Coverage Ratio....................	3.51	6.52	6.62	6.32	1.47
Operating Cash Flow to Capital Expense	2.16	1.42	0.80	0.68	−0.40

EXHIBIT 7

Perry Drugstores
Ratio Analysis
(Case 12.2)

	1982	1983	1984	1985	1986
Profitability Analysis					
Return on Assets					
Profit Margin............................	1.8%	2.1%	2.4%	2.5%	1.7%
× Asset Turnover	2.2	2.0	1.8	1.8	1.7
= Return on Assets	4.0%	4.2%	4.4%	4.4%	2.9%
Return on Common Equity					
Return on Assets.........................	4.0%	4.2%	4.4%	4.4%	2.9%
× Common Earnings Leverage..............	65.1%	75.0%	87.2%	73.9%	51.9%
× Capital Structure Leverage	4.5	3.6	3.3	4.1	4.9
= Return on Common Equity..............	11.7%	11.5%	12.7%	13.3%	7.4%
Operating Performance					
Gross Margin/Sales......................	29.8%	29.9%	31.1%	30.4%	31.1%
Operating Profit before Tax/Revenues	3.0%	3.7%	3.9%	3.9%	2.9%
Net Income—Continued Operations/Revenues.	1.2%	1.6%	2.1%	1.8%	0.9%
Asset Turnover					
Sales/Average Accounts Receivables...........	65.3	72.2	59.5	38.4	33.2
COGS/Average Inventory	3.9	3.8	3.5	3.3	3.2
Sales/Average Fixed Assets..................	11.8	12.2	11.3	9.6	8.4
Risk Analysis					
Liquidity					
Current Ratio.............................	1.93	2.24	1.46	1.99	2.24
Quick Ratio	0.18	0.40	0.19	0.32	0.33
Days Payables Held	54	48	51	55	54
Days Receivable Held	6	5	6	10	11
Days Inventory Held	93	96	104	109	113
Operating Cash Flow to Current Liabilities....	−12.8%	4.0%	31.4%	−36.9%	−5.3%
Solvency					
Total Liabilities/Total Assets	77.8%	68.4%	71.2%	78.8%	80.6%
Long-Term Debt/Total Assets	51.1%	47.2%	38.7%	54.2%	58.7%
Long-Term Debt/Owner's Equity	229.7%	149.5%	134.2%	255.8%	302.4%
Operating Cash Flow to Total Liabilities	−4.6%	1.2%	11.7%	−12.6%	−1.4%
Interest Coverage Ratio.....................	2.55	3.73	6.90	3.23	1.86
Operating Cash Flow to Capital Expense	−0.83	0.21	0.69	−0.54	−0.15

Rite Aid Corporation: Rite Aid operated 1,403 drugstores throughout 20 states in 1986 (third largest in the industry behind Revco and Eckerd). The firm's average drugstore totaled 6,500 square feet. Rite Aid also operated auto parts, toy store, and book chains.

Walgreen Company: Walgreen operated 1,273 drugstores in 1986. Although Walgreen ranked fourth in number of stores, it ranked first in sales. The firm also operated a chain of restaurants.

EXHIBIT 8

Rite Aid Corporation
Ratio Analysis
(Case 12.2)

	1982	1983	1984	1985	1986
Profitability Analysis					
Return on Assets					
Profit Margin	4.5%	4.7%	5.0%	5.2%	4.8%
× Asset Turnover	2.1	2.1	2.0	1.9	1.8
= Return on Assets	9.5%	9.6%	10.1%	9.9%	8.4%
Return on Common Equity					
Return on Assets	9.5%	9.6%	10.1%	9.9%	8.4%
× Common Earnings Leverage	100.5%	101.6%	102.4%	98.0%	90.9%
× Capital Structure Leverage	2.0	2.1	2.1	2.2	2.5
= Return on Common Equity	19.6%	20.8%	21.3%	21.6%	19.1%
Operating Performance					
Gross Margin/Sales	26.2%	27.1%	28.2%	28.9%	28.7%
Operating Profit before Tax/Revenues	8.8%	9.1%	9.7%	10.1%	9.2%
Net Income—Continued Operations/Revenues	4.6%	5.2%	6.1%	5.1%	4.3%
Asset Turnover					
Sales/Average Accounts Receivable	31.4	34.8	38.9	35.5	25.2
COGS/Average Inventory	3.9	4.0	4.0	3.9	3.7
Sales/Average Fixed Assets	9.2	8.8	8.5	7.7	7.0
Risk Analysis					
Liquidity					
Current Ratio	1.90	1.77	2.26	1.74	2.09
Quick Ratio	0.31	0.36	0.34	0.30	0.45
Days Payables Held	32	29	30	30	27
Days Receivable Held	12	10	9	10	14
Days Inventory Held	94	90	91	93	98
Operating Cash Flow to Current Liabilities	25.5%	40.6%	65.0%	32.6%	0.8%
Solvency					
Total Liabilities/Total Assets	51.7%	54.1%	49.2%	60.1%	59.9%
Long-Term Debt/Total Assets	26.5%	26.3%	26.8%	32.7%	34.9%
Long-Term Debt/Owner's Equity	54.8%	57.4%	52.7%	82.0%	87.0%
Operating Cash Flow to Total Liabilities	12.5%	19.6%	28.5%	12.8%	0.3%
Interest Coverage Ratio	11.58	13.61	18.95	12.08	7.23
Operating Cash Flow to Capital Expense	0.70	1.10	1.59	0.35	0.28

The following market price information as of the end of fiscal 1986 for each firm may assist in your valuation:

	Fay's	Perry	Rite Aid	Walgreen
Price Earnings Ratio	17	19	19	22
Price to Book Value per Share	2.44	3.81	4.52	4.60

EXHIBIT 9

Walgreen Company
Ratio Analysis
(Case 12.2)

	1982	1983	1984	1985	1986
Profitability Analysis					
Return on Assets					
Profit Margin..........................	2.5%	2.9%	3.1%	3.1%	3.0%
× Asset Turnover	2.4	2.3	2.3	2.2	2.1
= Return on Assets	6.1%	6.8%	7.0%	6.8%	6.3%
Return on Common Equity					
Return on Assets......................	6.1%	6.8%	7.0%	6.8%	6.3%
× Common Earnings Leverage..............	108.2%	99.7%	97.7%	96.7%	94.6%
× Capital Structure Leverage	3.1	3.1	3.1	3.2	3.3
= Return on Common Equity..............	20.4%	21.1%	21.4%	21.0%	19.9%
Operating Performance					
Gross Margin/Sales.....................	30.5%	30.6%	30.7%	30.7%	30.3%
Operating Profit before Tax/Revenues	4.5%	5.3%	5.7%	5.7%	5.4%
Net Income—Continued Operations/Revenues.	2.7%	3.0%	3.1%	3.0%	2.8%
Asset Turnover					
Sales/Average Accounts Receivable	139.7	148.0	83.2	79.3	100.8
COGS/Average Inventory	5.3	5.3	5.2	5.1	5.0
Sales/Average Fixed Assets.................	9.3	9.3	9.5	9.4	8.7
Risk Analysis					
Liquidity					
Current Ratio..........................	1.52	1.55	1.66	1.76	1.85
Quick Ratio	0.25	0.30	0.33	0.33	0.36
Days Payables Held	27	29	28	27	27
Days Receivable Held	3	2	4	5	4
Days Inventory Held	69	69	70	72	72
Operating Cash Flow to Current Liabilities....	37.4%	38.9%	28.9%	29.6%	29.8%
Solvency					
Total Liabilities/Total Assets	67.4%	68.5%	67.9%	69.2%	70.5%
Long-Term Debt/Total Assets	38.7%	40.6%	39.0%	43.0%	44.9%
Long-Term Debt/Owner's Equity	118.5%	129.1%	121.4%	139.7%	152.3%
Operating Cash Flow to Total Liabilities	13.7%	14.3%	10.5%	9.9%	9.0%
Interest Coverage Ratio....................	14.92	20.45	26.73	30.33	18.33
Operating Cash Flow to Capital Expense	1.11	1.39	1.26	1.00	0.69

c. A third approach to assessing the reasonableness of the buyout price is to examine acquisitions of other drugstore chains around the time of the Revco LBO. Exhibit 10 presents data relating to five such acquisitions. The transaction involving Jack Eckerd Corporation was a management-led LBO, whereas the Pay Less Drug, Hook Drug, and Thrifty Corporation transactions involved acquisitions by other operating corporations.

EXHIBIT 10

Valuation Data on Six Drugstore Acquisitions
(Case 12.2)

Date	Company Acquired		Sales	EBIT[a]	EBIDT[b]
		Purchase Price of Common Stock as a Multiple of			
January 1985	Payless Drug Stores (144 store chain)	One-Year Prior	.58	8.3	6.9
		Five-Year Average	.69	11.0	9.0
February 1985	Hook Drug Inc. (300 store chain)	One-Year Prior	.46	9.5	7.7
		Five-Year Average	.56	10.6	8.7
October 1985	Jack Eckerd Corp. (drugstores, optical centers, clothing stores)	One-Year Prior	.47	9.0	6.9
		Five-Year Average	.53	8.2	6.8
May 1986	Thrifty Corp. (555 drugstores plus book, auto, and sporting goods stores)	One-Year Prior	.57	10.9	8.7
		Five-Year Average	.62	13.8	10.9
December 1986	Revco (2,000 drugstores)	One-Year Prior	.44	9.2	7.4
		Five-Year Average	.57	9.8	8.2

[a]EBIT is earnings before interest and taxes.

[b]EBIDT is earnings before interest, depreciation, and taxes.

SOURCE: Amounts adapted from Karen H. Wruck, "What Really Went Wrong with Revco?" *Journal of Applied Corporate Finance* (Summer, 1991), pp. 79–92.

CASE 12.3

KLEEN CLEANING SERVICES: PRICING AN INITIAL PUBLIC OFFERING

Larry Starr, founder and Chief Executive Officer of Kleen Cleaning Services, describes how his young and rapidly growing firm got its start.

I worked in my parents' residential and commercial cleaning business during high school. Our most challenging task was cleaning drapes. Most drapes require dry cleaning. Drapes, however, are heavy and bulky. Taking drapes down and transporting them to another location for dry cleaning were costly. What we needed was a machine that would perform the dry cleaning while the drapes remained hanging. The drawback of equipment available at the time was that it left too much dry cleaning fluid in the drapes, weighing them down and causing the hanging apparatus to pull loose from the wall or ceiling. While an engineering student at New York Technical Institute, I created a cleaning machine that adjusted the amount of cleaning fluids applied in relation to the humidity in the room on the day of application. The machine also contains a powerful blower for drying. These two functions reduce the weight problem of existing equipment. After graduation in 1990 I started Kleen Cleaning Services, specializing in the cleaning of drapes for residential and commercial [office buildings, movie theaters] customers.

Kleen Cleaning Services maintained a single office from 1990 to 1993 in New York City. It used telemarketing to obtain customers. Telemarketers would call potential customers at random, offering various low-priced packages of drapery cleaning services. The average price per job booked was $90. While performing the work, however, technicians were usually able to get customers to add additional drapes to the job so that the average job completed was $150.

Larry Starr was a key asset of the company during these early years. His energy and enthusiasm were contagious. He had an ability to relate quickly to all types of people (employees, customers). He was sold on Kleen and quickly brought others on board as well. As one employee stated: "Larry could charm the socks off of an Eskimo."

The success of the New York City office led Kleen to expand beginning in 1994. It opened three new offices in fiscal 1994 and another three offices in fiscal 1995, all located in the New York City area. Kleen also added restoration services beginning in fiscal 1995. Insurers of commercial buildings damaged by fire hire contractors to repair electrical, plumbing, and drywall damage and to clean carpets, drapes, and furniture. Kleen subcontracts the repair work and performs the cleaning services itself.

Kleen obtains restoration jobs from a single insurance consultant located in New York City. These jobs require up front capital since Kleen must purchase repair materials and cleaning supplies before receiving progress payments from insurance companies. Kleen engaged in short- and long-term borrowing and issued common stock to selected individuals during fiscal 1995 to finance restoration work. It also formed joint ventures with others in order to obtain the needed capital but must share the profits of this work with the joint venture partners. During fiscal 1995, Kleen obtained 55 percent of its revenues from restoration services and 45 percent from residential and commercial drapery cleaning. It has 291 employees, including 86 trained technicians, 86 technician trainees, 88 telemarketers, and 31 administrative personnel.

EXHIBIT 1

Kleen Cleaning Services—Income Statement
(amounts in thousands)
(Case 12.3)

	For the Year Ending January 31			Three Months Ended April 30 (unaudited)	
	1993	1994	1995	1994	1995
Sales	$ 575	$1,241	$ 4,845	$ 638	$ 5,497
Other Revenue	—	—	187	—	—
Cost of Goods Sold	(284)	(577)	(2,051)	(320)	(2,976)
Selling and Administrative	(139)	(306)	(1,125)	(91)	(623)
Interest	—	—	(43)	—	(64)
Income Taxes	—	(36)	(867)	(96)	(938)
Net Income	$ 152	$ 322	$ 946	$ 131	$ 896
Earnings per Share	$.03	$.06	$.12	$.02	$.11
Common Shares Outstanding	5,500	5,500	7,700	7,700	7,700

Exhibits 1, 2, and 3 present the financial statements of Kleen for fiscal years 1993 to 1995. Exhibit 4 presents selected financial statement ratios. Kleen was taxed as a sole proprietorship prior to January 31, 1994.

Kleen intends to make an initial public offering of its common stock on July 1, 1995. The stock ownership before and after the offering is as follows:

| | Before | | After | |
	Shares	Percentage	Shares	Percentage
Larry Starr..........	5,500,000	71%	5,500,000	55%
Other Individuals	2,200,000	29	2,150,000	22
Public Owners.......	—	—	2,350,000	23
	7,700,000	100%	10,000,000	100%

EXHIBIT 2

Kleen Cleaning Services—Balance Sheet
(amounts in thousands)
(Case 12.3)

| | January 31 | | | | (unaudited) April 30 |
	1992	1993	1994	1995	1995
Cash	$ 14	$ 4	$ 30	$ 87	$ 10
Accounts Receivable	—	30	—	694	2,461
Inventories	—	—	—	429	336
Prepayments......................	22	36	77	518	1,436
Total Current Assets.............	$ 36	$ 70	$107	$1,728	$4,243
Property, Plant, and Equipment					
Cost......................	$ 92	$126	$126	$3,223	$3,967
Accumulated Depreciation	(8)	(30)	(68)	(163)	(269)
Net	$ 84	$ 96	$ 58	$3,060	$3,698
Other Assets.....................	13	13	13	258	259
Total Assets	$133	$179	$178	$5,046	$8,200
Accounts Payable..................	—	$ 2	$ 3	$ 237	$ 363
Notes Payable.....................	—	—	—	1,356	1,972
Current Portion of Long-term Debt ...	—	—	—	147	198
Other Current Liabilities	—	—	—	28	1,572
Total Current Liabilities..........	—	$ 2	$ 3	$1,768	$4,105
Long-Term Debt	—	—	—	429	933
Deferred Income Taxes.............	—	—	—	819	236
Total Liabilities	—	$ 2	$ 3	$3,016	$5,274
Common Stock ($.01 par value)	$ 55	$ 55	$ 55	$ 77	$ 77
Additional Paid-in Capital	55	55	55	942	942
Retained Earnings..................	23	67	65	1,011	1,907
Total Shareholders' Equity........	$133	$177	$175	$2,030	$2,926
Total Equities....................	$133	$179	$178	$5,046	$8,200

EXHIBIT 3

Kleen Cleaning Services
Statement of Cash Flows
(amounts in thousands)
(Case 12.3)

	For the Year Ended January 31			Three Months Ended April 30 (unaudited)	
	1993	1994	1995	1994	1995
Operations					
Net Income	$ 152	$ 322	$ 946	$131	$ 896
Depreciation	22	38	97	6	106
Deferred Taxes	—	—	819	90	(583)
(Increase) Decrease in Accounts Receivable	(30)	30	(694)	(49)	(1,767)
(Increase) Decrease in Inventories	—	—	(429)	(31)	(220)
(Increase) Decrease in Prepayments	(14)	(41)	(441)	(67)	(605)
Increase (Decrease) in Accounts Payable	2	1	234	2	126
Increase (Decrease) in Other Current Liabilities	—	—	28	6	1,544
Cash Flow from Operations	$ 132	$ 350	$ 560	$ 88	$ (503)
Investing					
Acquisition of Fixed Assets	$ (34)	—	$(3,097)	—	$ (744)
Other Investing Transactions	—	—	(247)	—	(1)
Cash Flow for Investing	$ (34)	—	$(3,344)	—	$ (745)
Financing					
Increase in Short-Term Borrowing	—	—	$ 1,356	$ (2)	$ 616
Increase in Long-Term Borrowing	—	—	576	—	555
Issue of Common Stock	—	—	909	—	—
Dividends	$(108)	$(324)	—	—	—
Cash Flow for Financing	$(108)	$(324)	$ 2,841	$ (2)	$1,171
Change in Cash	$ (10)	$ 26	$ 57	$ 86	$ (77)
Cash at Beginning of Year	14	4	30	30	87
Cash at End of Year	$ 4	$ 30	$ 87	$116	$ 10

Kleen plans to use its share of the proceeds from the offering to open new offices (4 new offices scheduled for opening in fiscal 1996 and 10 for fiscal 1997) and to finance its growing restoration business without having to enter joint ventures. Kleen estimates that 80 percent of fiscal 1996 revenues will come from restoration work.

REQUIRED

At what price should the 2,350,000 Kleen common shares be issued on the market? Summarize the valuation process you employed.

EXHIBIT 4

Financial Statement Ratios for Kleen Cleaning Services, Business Services Industry, and Personal Services Industry (Case 12.3)

	Kleen Cleaners			Average, 1983 to 1992	
	1993	1994	1995	Business Services	Personal Services
Profit Margin for ROA.........................	26.4%	25.9%	20.1%	6.8%	5.7%
Total Assets Turnover.......................	3.7	7.0	1.9	1.2	1.4
Rate of Return on Assets........................	97.4%	180.4%	37.3%	8.4%	8.8%
Common Earnings Leverage.....................	1.00	1.00	.97	.89	.88
Capital Structure Leverage.....................	1.0	1.0	2.4	1.9	1.8
Rate of Return on Common Shareholders' Equity ...	98.1%	183.0%	85.8%	15.3%	15.0%
Cost of Goods Sold/Sales......................	49.4%	46.5%	42.3%	—	—
Selling & Administrative Expense/Sales...........	24.2%	24.7%	23.2%	—	—
Income Tax Expense on Operating Income/Sales....		2.9%	18.2%		
Fixed Asset Turnover	6.4	16.1	3.1	—	—
Price-Earnings Ratio..........................	—	—	—	19.3	15.1
Market Value to Book Value Ratio	—	—	—	2.4	2.1

REPORTS OF INDEPENDENT ACCOUNTANTS

Board of Directors
Kleen Cleaning Services
New York, NY

We have examined the consolidated balance sheet of Kleen Cleaning Services as of January 31, 1993, 1994, and 1995 and the respective related statements of income and cash flows for the years ended January 31, 1993, 1994, and 1995. Our examination was made in accordance with generally accepted accounting standards and accordingly, included such tests of the accounting records and such other auditing procedures as we considered necessary in the circumstances.

In our opinion, the accompanying statements together with the related notes present fairly the consolidated financial position of Kleen Cleaning Services at January 31, 1993, 1994, and 1995 and the results of operations and changes in cash flows for the year then ended in conformity with generally accepted accounting principles applied on a consistent basis.

Whitespan & Company
(local CPA firm)

Brunswick, New Jersey
June 1, 1995

Board of Directors
Kleen Cleaning Services
New York, NY

We have made a review of the consolidated balance sheet of Kleen Cleaning Services, Inc. and subsidiaries as of April 30, 1995, and the related consolidated statements of income, shareholders' equity and changes in financial position for the three-month period ended April 30, 1995, in accordance with standards established by the American Institute of Certified Public Accountants. A review of the consolidated financial statements for the comparative period of the prior year was not made.

A review of interim financial information consists principally of obtaining an understanding of the system for the preparation of interim financial information, applying analytical review procedures to financial data, and making inquiries of persons responsible for financial and accounting matters.

It is substantially less in scope than an examination in accordance with generally accepted auditing standards, which will be performed for the full year with the objective of expressing an opinion regarding the financial statements taken as a whole. Accordingly, we do not express such an opinion.

Based on our review, we are not aware of any material modifications that should be made to the consolidated interim financial statements referred to above for them to be in conformity with generally accepted accounting principles.

Andersenhouse & Mitchell
(Big-6 CPA firm)

New York, NY
June 1, 1995

The Coca-Cola Company and Subsidiaries
Consolidated Balance Sheets
(Dollars in millions except per share data)

December 31,	Year 8	Year 7
Assets		
Current		
Cash and cash equivalents.................................	$ 998	$ 956
Marketable securities, at cost.............................	80	107
	1,078	1,063
Trade accounts receivable, less allowances of $39 in Year 8 and $33 in Year 7....................................	1,210	1,055
Finance subsidiary receivables...........................	33	31
Inventories	1,049	1,019
Prepaid expenses and other assets	1,064	1,080
Total Current Assets....................................	$ 4,434	$ 4,248
Investments and Other Assets		
Investments		
Coca-Cola Enterprises Inc.	498	518
Coca-Cola Amatil Limited............................	592	548
Other, principally bottling companies	1,125	1,097
Finance subsidiary—receivables	226	95
Long-term receivables and other assets	868	637
	$ 3,309	$ 2,895

655

December 31,	Year 8	Year 7
Property, Plant, and Equipment		
Land	197	203
Buildings and improvements	1,616	1,529
Machinery and equipment	3,380	3,137
Containers	403	374
	$ 5,596	$ 5,243
Less allowances for depreciation	1,867	1,717
	$ 3,729	$ 3,526
Goodwill and Other Intangible Assets	549	383
	$12,021	$11,052
Liabilities and Share-Owners' Equity		
Current		
Accounts payable and accrued expenses	$ 2,217	$ 2,253
Loans and notes payable	1,409	1,967
Finance subsidiary notes payable.	244	105
Current maturities of long-term debt	19	15
Accrued taxes.	1,282	963
Total Current Liabilities.	$ 5,171	$ 5,303
Long-Term Debt	$ 1,428	$ 1,120
Other Liabilities	725	659
Deferred Income Taxes.	$ 113	$ 82
Share-Owners' Equity		
Common stock, $.25 par value—		
Authorized: 2,800,000,000 shares;		
Issued: 1,703,526,299 shares in Year 8; 1,696,202,840 shares		
in Year 7	$ 426	$ 424
Capital surplus.	1,086	871
Reinvested earnings	9,458	8,165
Unearned compensation related to outstanding restricted		
stock	(85)	(100)
Foreign currency translation adjustment	$ (420)	$ (271)
	$10,465	$ 9,089
Less treasury stock, at cost (406,072,817 common shares in		
Year 8; 389,431,622 common shares in Year 7).	$ 5,881	$ 5,201
	$ 4,584	$ 3,888
	$12,021	$11,052

See Notes to Consolidated Financial Statements.

The Coca-Cola Company and Subsidiaries
Consolidated Statements of Income
(Dollars in millions except per share data)

Year Ended December 31,	Year 8	Year 7	Year 6
Net Operating Revenues	$13,957	$13,074	$11,572
Cost of goods sold	5,160	5,055	4,649
Gross Profit	8,797	8,019	6,923
Selling, administrative and general expenses	5,695	5,249	4,604
Operating Income	3,102	2,770	2,319
Interest income	144	164	175
Interest expense	(168)	(171)	(192)
Equity income	91	65	40
Other income (deductions)—net	4	(82)	41
Gain on issuance of stock by Coca-Cola Amatil	12	—	—
Income before Income Taxes and Changes in Accounting Principles	3,185	2,746	2,383
Income taxes	997	863	765
Income before Changes in Accounting Principles	2,188	1,883	1,618
Transition effects of changes in accounting principles			
Postemployment benefits	(12)	—	—
Postretirement benefits other than pensions			
Consolidated operations	—	(146)	—
Equity investments	—	(73)	—
Net Income	2,176	1,664	1,618
Preferred stock dividends	—	—	1
Net Income Available to Common Share Owners	$ 2,176	$ 1,664	$ 1,617
Income per Common Share			
Before changes in accounting principles	$ 1.68	$ 1.43	$ 1.21
Transition effect of changes in accounting principles			
Postemployment benefits	(.01)	—	—
Postretirement benefits other than pensions			
Consolidated operations	—	(.11)	—
Equity investments	—	(.06)	—
Net Income per Common Share	$ 1.67	$ 1.26	$ 1.21
Average Common Shares Outstanding	1,302	1,317	1,333

See Notes to Consolidated Financial Statements.

Consolidated Statements of Cash Flows

Year Ended December 31, (in millions)	Year 8	Year 7	Year 6
Operating Activities			
Net income...	$ 2,176	$ 1,664	$ 1,618
Transition effects of changes in accounting principles.................	12	219	—
Depreciation and amortization......................................	360	322	261
Deferred income taxes	(62)	(27)	(94)
Equity income, net of dividends	(35)	(30)	(16)
Foreign currency adjustments	9	24	66
Gains on sales of assets	(84)	—	(35)
Other noncash items..	78	103	33
Net change in operating assets and liabilities	54	(43)	251
Net cash provided by operating activities............................	2,508	2,232	2,084
Investing Activities			
Decrease (increase) in current marketable securities	29	(52)	3
Additions to finance subsidiary receivables	(177)	(54)	(210)
Collections of finance subsidiary receivables.........................	44	254	52
Acquisitions and purchases of investments	(816)	(717)	(399)
Proceeds from disposals of investments and other assets	621	247	180
Purchases of property, plant and equipment	(800)	(1,083)	(792)
Proceeds from disposals of property, plant, and equipment	312	47	44
All other investing activities..	(98)	(1)	(2)
Net cash used in investing activities.................................	(885)	(1,359)	(1,124)
Net cash provided by operations after reinvestment	1,623	873	960
Financing Activities			
Issuances of debt..	445	1,381	990
Payments of debt..	(567)	(432)	(1,246)
Preferred stock redeemed...	—	—	(75)
Common stock issued...	145	131	39
Purchases of common stock for treasury..............................	(680)	(1,259)	(399)
Dividends (common and preferred)..................................	(883)	(738)	(640)
Net cash used in financing activities	(1,540)	(917)	(1,331)
Effect of Exchange Rate Changes on Cash and Cash Equivalents	(41)	(58)	—
Cash and Cash Equivalents			
Net increase (decrease) during the year..............................	42	(102)	(371)
Balance at beginning of year..	956	1,058	1,429
Balance at end of year	$ 998	$ 956	$ 1,058

See Notes to Consolidated Financial Statements.

The Coca-Cola Company and Subsidiaries
Consolidated Statements of Share-owners' Equity
(In millions except per share data)

Three Years Ended December 31, Year 8	Preferred Stock	Common Stock	Capital Surplus	Reinvested Earnings	Outstanding Restricted Stock	Foreign Currency Translation	Treasury Stock
Balance December 31, Year 5	$75	$420	$ 513	$6,261	$ (68)	$ 4	$(3,543)
Sales of stock to employees exercising stock options	—	1	38	—	—	—	(2)
Tax benefit from employees' stock option and restricted stock plans	—	—	20	—	—	—	—
Translation adjustments	—	—	—	—	—	(9)	—
Stock issued under restricted stock plans, less amortization of $22	—	1	69	—	(47)	—	—
Purchases of common stock for treasury	—	—	—	—	—	—	(397)
Redemption of preferred stock	(75)	—	—	—	—	—	—
Net Income	—	—	—	1,618	—	—	—
Dividends							
Preferred	—	—	—	(1)	—	—	—
Common (per share—$.48)	—	—	—	(639)	—	—	—
Balance December 31, Year 6	—	422	640	7,239	(115)	(5)	(3,942)
Sales of stock to employees exercising stock options	—	2	129	—	—	—	(34)
Tax benefit from employees' stock option and restricted stock plans	—	—	93	—	—	—	—
Translation adjustments	—	—	—	—	—	(266)	—
Stock issued under restricted stock plans, less amortization of $25	—	—	9	—	15	—	—
Purchases of common stock for treasury	—	—	—	—	—	—	(1,225)
Net income	—	—	—	1,664	—	—	—
Common dividends (per share—$.56)	—	—	—	(738)	—	—	—

continued

The Coca-Cola Company and Subsidiaries
Consolidated Statements of Share-owners' Equity
(In millions except per share data)—Continued

Three Years Ended December 31, Year 8	Preferred Stock	Common Stock	Capital Surplus	Reinvested Earnings	Outstanding Restricted Stock	Foreign Currency Translation	Treasury Stock
Balance December 31, Year 7	—	424	871	8,165	(100)	(271)	(5,201)
Sales of stock to employees exercising stock options	—	2	143	—	—	—	(94)
Tax benefit from employees' stock option and restricted stock plans	—	—	66	—	—	—	—
Translation adjustments	—	—	—	—	—	(149)	—
Stock issued under restricted stock plans, less amortization of $19	—	—	6	—	15	—	—
Purchases of common stock for treasury	—	—	—	—	—	—	(586)
Net income	—	—	—	2,176	—	—	—
Common dividends (per share—$.68)	—	—	—	(883)	—	—	—
Balance December 31, Year 8	$—	$426	$1,086	$9,458	$ (85)	$(420)	$(5,881)

See Notes to Consolidated Financial Statements.

NOTES TO CONSOLIDATED FINANCIAL STATEMENTS

1. ACCOUNTING POLICIES

The significant accounting policies and practices followed by The Coca-Cola Company and subsidiaries (the Company) are as follows:

Consolidation. The consolidated financial statements include the accounts of the company and all subsidiaries except where control is temporary or does not rest with the company. The company's investments in companies in which it has the ability to exercise significant influence over operating and financial policies, including certain investments where there is a temporary majority interest, are accounted for by the equity method. Accordingly, the company's share of the net earnings of these companies is included in consolidated net income. The company's investments in other companies are carried at cost. All significant intercompany accounts and transactions are eliminated.

Certain amounts in the prior years' financial statements have been reclassified to conform to the current-year presentation.

Net Income per Common Share. Net income per common share is computed by dividing net income less dividends on preferred stock by the weighted average number of common shares outstanding.

Cash Equivalents. Marketable securities that are highly liquid and have maturities of three months or less at the date of purchase are classified as cash equivalents.

Inventories. Inventories are valued at the lower of cost or market. In general, cost is determined on the basis of average cost or first-in, first-out methods. However, for certain inventories, cost is determined on the last-in, first-out (LIFO) method. The excess of current costs over LIFO stated values amounted to approximately $9 million and $24 million at December 31, Year 8 and Year 7, respectively.

Property, Plant, and Equipment. Property, plant, and equipment are stated at cost, less allowances for depreciation. Property, plant and equipment are depreciated principally by the straight-line method over the estimated useful lives of the assets. Depreciation expense was $333 million for Year 8 and $310 million for Year 7.

Goodwill and Other Intangible Assets. Goodwill and other intangible assets are stated on the basis of cost and are being amortized, principally on a straight-line basis, over the estimated future periods to be benefited (not exceeding 40 years). Amortization expense was $27 million in Year 8 and $12 million in Year 7. Accumulated amortization was approximately $50 million and $26 million at December 31, Year 8 and 7, respectively.

Changes in Accounting Principles.   Statement of Financial Accounting Standards No. 112, Employers' Accounting for Postemployment Benefits (SFAS 112) was adopted as of January 1, Year 8. SFAS 112 requires employers to accrue the costs of benefits to former or inactive employees after employment, but before retirement. The Company recorded an accumulated obligation of $12 million, which is net of deferred taxes of $8 million. The increase in annual pretax postemployment benefits expense in Year 8 was immaterial to Company operations.

In Year 8, the Financial Accounting Standards Board (FASB) issued Statement of Financial Accounting Standards No. 115, Accounting for Certain Investments in Debt and Equity Securities (SFAS 115). SFAS 115 requires that the carrying value of certain investments be adjusted to their fair value. The Company's required adoption date is January 1, Year 9. The Company expects to record an increase to share-owners' equity of approximately $65 million in Year 9 from the adoption of SFAS 115.

2. INVENTORIES

Inventories consist of the following (in millions):

December 31	Year 8	Year 7
Finished goods	$ 689	$ 620
Work in process	4	23
Raw materials and supplies	356	376
	$1,049	$1,019

3. BOTTLING INVESTMENTS

The Company invests in bottling companies to ensure the strongest and most efficient production, distribution and marketing systems possible.

Coca-Cola Enterprises (CCE) is the largest bottler of Company products in the world. The Company owns approximately 44 percent of the outstanding common stock of CCE, and, accordingly, accounts for its investment by the equity method of accounting. A summary of financial information for CCE is as follows (in millions):

	December 28, Year 8	December 29, Year 7
Current assets	$ 746	$ 701
Noncurrent assets	7,936	7,384
Total assets.......................	$8,682	$8,085
Current liabilities	$1,007	$1,304
Noncurrent liabilities	6,415	5,527
Total liabilities	$7,422	$6,831
Share-owners' equity	$1,260	$1,254
Company equity investment...........	$ 498	$ 518

Year ended December 31,	Year 8	Year 7	Year 6
Net operating revenues........................	$5,465	$5,127	$3,915
Cost of goods sold...........................	3,372	3,219	2,420
Gross profit	$2,093	$1,908	$1,495
Operating income	$ 385	$ 306	$ 120
Operating cash flow[1]	$ 804	$ 695	$ 538
Loss before changes in accounting principles	$ (15)	$ (15)	$ (83)
Net loss available to common share owners	$ (15)	$ (186)	$ (92)
Company equity loss........................	$ (6)	$ (6)	$ (40)

[1]Excludes nonrecurring charges.

The Year 7 net loss of CCE includes $171 million of noncash, after-tax charges resulting from the adoption of Statement of Financial Accounting Standards No. 106, Employers' Accounting for Post-retirement Benefits Other Than Pensions (SFAS 106) and Statement of Financial Accounting Standards No. 109, Accounting for Income Taxes (SFAS 109) as of January 1, Year 7. The Company's financial statements reflect the adoption of SFAS 109 by CCE as if it occurred on January 1, Year 4.

The Year 6 results of CCE include pretax restructuring charges of $152 million and a pretax charge of $15 million to increase insurance reserves.

In a Year 6 merger, CCE acquired Johnston Coca-Cola Bottling Group, Inc. (Johnston) for approximately $196 million in cash and 13 million shares of CCE common stock. The Company exchanged its 22 percent ownership interest in Johnston for approximately $81 million in cash and approximately 50,000 shares of CCE common stock, resulting in a pretax gain of $27 million to the Company. The Company's ownership interest in CCE was reduced from 49 percent to approximately 44 percent as a result of this transaction.

If the Johnston acquisition had been completed on January 1, Year 6, CCE's Year 6 pro forma net loss available to common share owners would have been approximately $137 million. Summarized financial information and net concentrate/syrup sales related to Johnston prior to its acquisition by CCE have been combined with other equity investments below.

Net concentrate/syrup sales to CCE were $961 million in Year 8, $889 million in Year 7 and $626 million in Year 6. CCE purchases sweeteners through the Company under a pass-through arrangement, and, accordingly, related collections from CCE and payments to suppliers are not included in the Company's consolidated statements of income. These transactions amounted to $211 million in Year 8, $225 million in Year 7 and $185 million in Year 6. The Company also provides certain administrative and other services to CCE under negotiated fee arrangements.

The Company engages in a wide range of marketing programs, media advertising and other similar arrangements to promote the sale of Company products in territories in which CCE operates. The Company's direct support for certain CCE marketing activities and participation with CCE in cooperative advertising and other marketing programs amounted to approximately $256 million, $253 million and $199 million in Year 8, Year 7 and Year 6, respectively.

In April Year 8, the Company purchased majority ownership interests in two bottling companies in Tennessee along with the rights to purchase the remaining minority interests. Such ownership interests and a bottling operation in the Netherlands were sold to CCE in June Year 8. The Company received approximately $260 million in cash plus the assumption of indebtedness and carrying costs resulting in an after-tax gain of $11 million or approximately $.01 per share.

In Year 7, The Company sold 100 percent of the common stock of the Erie, Pennsylvania, Coca-Cola bottler to CCE for approximately $11 million, which approximated the Company's original investment plus carrying costs. In January Year 9, the Company sold common stock representing a 9 percent voting interest in The Coca-Cola Bottling Company of New York, Inc. (CCNY) to CCE for approximately $6 million, which approximated the Company's investment.

If valued at the December 31, Year 8, quoted closing price of the publicly traded CCE shares, the calculated value of the Company's investment in CCE would have exceeded its carrying value by approximately $361 million.

Other Equity Investments. The Company owns approximately 51 percent of Coca-Cola Amatil Limited (CCA), an Australian-based bottler of Company products. In the fourth quarter of Year 8, CCA issued approximately 8 million shares of stock to acquire the Company's franchise bottler in Jakarta, Indonesia. This transaction resulted in a pretax gain of approximately $12 million and diluted the Company's ownership interest to the present level. The Company intends to reduce its ownership interest in CCA to below 50 percent. Accordingly, the investment has been accounted for by the equity method of accounting.

At December 31, Year 8, the excess of the Company's investment over its equity in the underlying net assets of CCA was approximately $191 million, which is being amortized over 40 years. The Company recorded equity income from CCA of $40 million, $28 million and $15 million in Year 8, Year 7 and Year 6, respectively. These amounts are net of the amortization charges discussed above.

In January Year 8, CCA sold its snack-food segment for approximately $299 million, and recognized a gain of $169 million. The Company's ownership interest in the sale proceeds received by CCA approximated the carrying value of the Company's investment in the snack-food segment.

In Year 8, the Company acquired a 30 percent equity interest in Coca-Cola FEMSA, S.A. de C.V., which operates bottling facilities in the Valley of Mexico and Mexico's southeastern region, for $195 million. At December 31, Year 8, the excess of the Company's investment over its equity in the underlying net assets of Coca-Cola FEMSA was approximately $130 million, which is being amortized over 40 years.

Also in Year 8, the Company entered into a joint venture with Coca-Cola Bottling Co. Consolidated (Consolidated), establishing the Piedmont Coca-Cola Bottling Partnership (Piedmont), which will operate certain bottling territories in the United States acquired from each company. The Company has made a cash contribution of $70 million to the partnership for a 50 percent ownership interest. Consolidated has contributed bottling assets valued at approximately $48 million and approximately $22 million in cash for the remaining 50 percent interest. Piedmont has purchased assets and stock of certain bottling companies from the Company for approximately $163 million, which approximated the Company's carrying cost, and certain bottling assets from Consolidated for approximately $130 million. The Company beneficially owns a 30 percent economic interest and a 23 percent voting interest in Consolidated.

Operating results include the Company's proportionate share of income from equity investments since the respective dates of investment. A summary of financial information for the Company's equity investments, other than CCE, is as follows (in millions):

December 31,	Year 8	Year 7
Current assets	$2,294	$1,945
Noncurrent assets	4,780	4,172
Total assets.....................	$7,074	$6,117
Current liabilities	$1,926	$2,219
Noncurrent liabilities	2,366	1,720
Total liabilities..................	$4,292	$3,939
Share-owners' equity	$2,782	$2,178
Company equity investment.........	$1,629	$1,387

Year ended December 31,	Year 8	Year 7	Year 6
Net operating revenues........................	$8,168	$7,027	$7,877
Cost of goods sold............................	5,385	4,740	5,244
Gross profit	$2,783	$2,287	$2,633
Operating income	$ 673	$ 364	$ 560
Operating cash flow	$ 984	$ 923	$ 979
Income before changes in accounting principles....	$ 258	$ 199	$ 214
Net income...................................	$ 258	$ 74	$ 214
Company equity income........................	$ 97	$ 71	$ 80

Net income for the Company's equity investments in Year 8 reflects an $86 million after-tax charge recorded by Coca-Cola Beverages Ltd., related to restructuring its operations in Canada.

Net sales to equity investees, other than CCE, were $1.2 billion in Year 8 and $1.3 billion in Year 7 and Year 6. The Company participates in various marketing, promotional and other activities with these investees, the majority of which are located outside the United States.

If valued at the December 31, Year 8, quoted closing price of shares actively traded on stock markets, the net calculated value of the Company's equity investments in publicly traded bottlers, other than CCE, would have exceeded the Company's carrying value by approximately $966 million.

The consolidated balance sheet caption "Other, principally bottling companies," also includes various investments that are accounted for by the cost method.

4. FINANCE SUBSIDIARY

Coca-Cola Financial Corporation (CCFC) provides loans and other forms of financing to Coca-Cola bottlers and customers for the acquisition of sales-related equipment and for other business purposes. The approximate contractual maturities of finance receivables for the five years succeeding December 31, Year 8, are as follows (in millions):

Year 9	Year 10	Year 11	Year 12	Year 13
$33	$32	$31	$16	$118

These amounts do not reflect possible prepayments or renewals.

In Year 8, CCFC provided a $100 million subordinated loan to CCNY and issued a $50 million letter of credit on CCNY's behalf, of which $18 million was outstanding at December 31, Year 8.

In connection with the Year 6 acquisition of Sunbelt Coca-Cola Bottling Company, Inc. by Consolidated, CCFC purchased 25,000 shares of Consolidated preferred stock for $50 million, provided to Consolidated a $153 million bridge loan and issued a $77 million letter of credit on Consolidated's behalf. Consolidated redeemed the 25,000 shares of preferred stock for $50 million plus accrued dividends in Year 7. Consolidated also repaid all amounts due under the bridge loan in Year 7. In Year 8, the letter of credit was withdrawn.

5. ACCOUNTS PAYABLE AND ACCRUED EXPENSES

Accounts payable and accrued expenses consist of the following (in millions):

December 31,	Year 8	Year 7
Accrued marketing	$ 371	$ 374
Container deposits..................................	122	117
Accrued compensation	119	99
Accounts payable and other accrued expenses	1,605	1,663
	$2,217	$2,253

6. SHORT-TERM BORROWINGS AND CREDIT ARRANGEMENTS

Loans and notes payable consist primarily of commercial paper issued in the United States. At December 31, Year 8, the Company had $1.4 billion in lines of credit and other short-term credit facilities contractually available, under which $150 million was outstanding. Included were $1.0 billion in lines designated to support commercial paper and other borrowings, under which no amounts were outstanding at December 31, Year 8. These facilities are subject to normal banking terms and conditions. Some of the financial arrangements require compensating balances, none of which are presently significant to the Company.

7. ACCRUED TAXES

Accrued taxes consist of the following (in millions):

December 31,	Year 8	Year 7
Income taxes	$1,106	$820
Sales, payroll and other taxes	176	143
	$1,282	$963

8. LONG-TERM DEBT

Long-term debt consists of the following (in millions):

December 31,	Year 8	Year 7
7 3/4% U.S. dollar notes due Year 11	$ 250	$ 250
5 3/4% Japanese yen notes due Year 11	270	241
5 3/4% German mark notes due Year 13[1]	147	156
7 7/8% U.S. dollar notes due Year 13	249	249
6 5/8% U.S. dollar notes due Year 17	149	149
6% U.S. dollar notes due Year 18	150	—
7 3/8% U.S. dollar notes due Year 18	148	—
Other due Year 9 to Year 28[2]	84	90
	1,447	1,135
Less current portion	19	15
	$1,428	$1,120

[1] Portions of these notes have been swapped for liabilities denominated in other currencies.
[2] The weighted average interest rate is approximately 7.8 percent.

Maturities of long-term debt for the five years succeeding December 31, Year 8, are as follows (in millions):

Year 9	Year 10	Year 11	Year 12	Year 13
$19	$43	$527	$5	$400

The above notes include various restrictions, none of which are presently significant to the Company.

Interest paid was approximately $158 million, $174 million and $160 million in Year 8, Year 7 and Year 6, respectively.

9. FINANCIAL INSTRUMENTS

The carrying amounts reflected in the consolidated balance sheets for cash, cash equivalents, loans and notes payable approximate the respective fair values due to the short maturities of these instruments. The fair values for marketable debt and equity securities, investments, receivables, long-term debt and hedging instruments are based primarily on quoted market prices for those or similar instruments. A comparison of the carrying value and fair value of these financial instruments is as follows (in millions):

December 31,	Carrying Value	Fair Value
Year 8		
Current marketable securities	$ 80	$ 82
Investments[1]	88	88
Finance subsidiary receivables	259	265
Long-term receivables and other assets	868	865
Long-term debt	(1,447)	(1,531)
Hedging instruments	31	(142)
Year 7		
Current marketable securities	$ 107	$ 108
Investments[1]	258	258
Finance subsidiary receivables	126	135
Long-term receivables and other assets	637	636
Long-term debt	(1,135)	(1,156)
Hedging instruments	102	99

[1]The consolidated balance sheet caption, Other, principally bottling companies, also includes equity investments of $1.0 billion and $839 million at December 31, Year 8 and Year 7, respectively.

Hedging Transactions. The Company has entered into hedging transactions to reduce its exposure to adverse fluctuations in interest and foreign exchange rates. While the hedging instruments are subject to the risk of loss from changes in exchange rates, these losses would generally be offset by gains on the exposures being hedged. Realized and unrealized gains and losses on hedging instruments that are designated and effective as hedges of firmly committed foreign currency transactions are recognized in income in the same period as the hedged transaction. Approximately $9 million of losses realized on settled contracts entered into as hedges of firmly committed transactions in Year 9, 10 and 11, were deferred at December 31, Year 8.

From time to time, the Company purchases foreign currency option contracts to hedge anticipated transactions over the succeeding three years. Net unrealized gains/losses from hedging anticipated transactions were not material at December 31, Year 8 or Year 7.

At December 31, Year 8 and Year 7, the Company had forward exchange contracts, swaps, options and other financial market instruments, principally to exchange foreign currencies for U.S. dollars, of $4.6 billion and $4.9 billion, respectively. These amounts are representative of amounts maintained through Year 8. Maturities of financial market instruments held at December 31, Year 8, are as follows (in millions):

Year 9	Year 10	Year 11	Year 12 through Year 18
$2,266	$753	$666	$961

Although pretax losses recognized on hedging transactions in Year 8 amounted to $29 million, such losses were fully offset by income recognized on the exposures being hedged.

Guarantees. At December 31, Year 8, the Company was contingently liable for guarantees of indebtedness owed by third parties of $140 million, of which $39 million is related to independent bottling licensees. In the opinion of management, it is not probable that the Company will be required to satisfy these guarantees. The fair value of these contingent liabilities is immaterial to the Company's consolidated financial statements.

10. PREFERRED STOCK

The Company canceled the 3,000 issued shares of its $1 par value Cumulative Money Market Preferred Stock (MMP) in Year 8 and returned the shares to the status of authorized but unissued shares. None of the MMP had been outstanding since Year 6, when the final 750 shares of the 3,000 shares originally issued were redeemed.

11. COMMON STOCK

Common shares outstanding and related changes for the three years ended December 31, Year 8, are as follows (in millions):

	Year 8	Year 7	Year 6
Outstanding at January 1.....................	1,307	1,329	1,336
Issued to employees exercising stock options.....	7	9	4
Issued under restricted stock plans.............	—	—	3
Purchased for treasury			
Share repurchase programs.................	(14)	(30)	(14)
Stock option plan activity...................	(3)	(1)	—
Stock outstanding at December 31	1,297	1,307	1,329

12. RESTRICTED STOCK, STOCK OPTIONS AND OTHER STOCK PLANS

The Company sponsors restricted stock award plans, stock option plans, Incentive Unit Agreements and Performance Unit Agreements.

Under the amended Year 4 Restricted Stock Award Plan and the amended Year 1 Restricted Stock Award Plan (the Restricted Stock Plans), 20 million and 12 million shares of restricted common stock, respectively, may be granted to certain officers and key employees of the Company.

At December 31, Year 8, 17 million shares were available for grant under the Restricted Stock Plans. The participant is entitled to vote and receive dividends on the shares, and, under the Year 1 Restricted Stock Award Plan, the participant is reimbursed by the Company for income taxes imposed on the award, but not for taxes generated by the reimbursement payment. The shares are subject to certain transfer restrictions and may be forfeited if the participant leaves the Company for reasons other than retirement, disability or death, absent a change in control of the Company. On July 18, Year 6, the Restricted Stock Plans were amended to specify age 62 as the minimum retirement age. The Year 1 Restricted Stock Award Plan was further amended to conform to the terms of the Year 4 Restricted Stock Award Plan by requiring a minimum of five years of service between the date of the award and retirement. The amendments affect shares granted after July 18, Year 6.

Under the Company's Year 6 Stock Option Plan (the Option Plan) a maximum of 60 million shares of the Company's common stock may be issued or transferred to certain officers and employees pursuant to stock options and stock appreciation rights granted under the Option Plan. The stock appreciation rights permit the holder, upon surrendering all or part of the related stock option, to receive cash, common stock or a combination thereof, in an amount up to 100 percent of the difference between the market price and the option price. No stock appreciation rights have been granted since Year 5, and the Company presently does not intend to grant additional stock appreciation rights in the future. Options outstanding at December 31, Year 8, also include various options granted under previous plans. Further information relating to options is as follows (in millions, except per share amounts):

	Year 8	Year 7	Year 6
Outstanding at January 1,	31	36	33
Granted	6	4	8
Exercised	(7)	(9)	(4)
Canceled	—	—	(1)
Outstanding at December 31,	30	31	36
Exercisable at December 31,	22	23	24
Shares available at December 31, for options that may be granted	45	51	55

	Year 8	Year 7	Year 6
Prices per share			
Exercised	$4–$41	$4–$28	$3–$28
Unexercised at December 31	$5–$44	$4–$41	$4–$30

In Year 3, the Company entered into Incentive Unit Agreements, whereby, subject to certain conditions, certain officers were granted the right to receive cash awards based on the market value of 1.2 million shares of the Company's common stock at the measurement dates. Under the Incentive Unit Agreements, the employee is reimbursed by the Company for income taxes imposed when the value of the units is paid, but not for taxes generated by the reimbursement payment. As of December 31, Year 8, 400,000 units have been paid and 800,000 units were outstanding.

In Year 1, the Company entered into Performance Unit Agreements, whereby certain officers were granted the right to receive cash awards based on the difference in the market value of approximately 2.2 million shares of the Company's common stock at the measurement dates and the base price of $5.16, the market value as of January 2, Year 1. As of December 31, Year 8, 780,000 units have been paid and approximately 1.4 million units were outstanding.

13. PENSION BENEFITS

The Company sponsors and/or contributes to pension plans covering substantially all U.S. employees and certain employees in international locations. The benefits are primarily based on years of service and the employees' compensation for certain periods during the last years of employment. Pension costs are generally funded currently, subject to regulatory funding limitations. The Company also sponsors nonqualified, unfunded defined benefit plans for certain officers and other employees. In addition, the Company and its subsidiaries have various pension plans and other forms of postretirement arrangements outside the United States. Total pension expense for all benefit plans, including defined benefit plans, amounted to approximately $57 million in Year 8, $49 million Year 7 and $42 million in Year 6. Net periodic pension cost for the Company's defined benefit plans consists of the following (in millions):

Year Ended December 31,	U.S. Plans			International Plans		
	Year 8	Year 7	Year 6	Year 8	Year 7	Year 6
Service cost—benefits earned during the period .	$ 17	$ 15	$ 13	$ 17	$ 18	$ 16
Interest cost on projected benefit obligation......	53	50	46	22	20	18
Actual return on plan assets	(77)	(36)	(113)	(27)	(19)	(18)
Net amortization and deferral	31	(9)	71	13	3	1
Net periodic pension cost.....................	$ 24	$ 20	$ 17	$ 25	$ 22	$ 17

The funded status for the Company's defined benefit plans is as follows (in millions):

December 31,	U.S. Plans				International Plans			
	Year 8	Year 7	Year 8	Year 7	Year 8	Year 7	Year 8	Year 7
	Assets Exceed Accumulated Benefits		Accumulated Benefits Exceed Assets		Assets Exceed Accumulated Benefits		Accumulated Benefits Exceed Assets	
Actuarial present value of benefit obligations Vested benefit obligation....	$481	$401	$ 109	$ 82	$139	$119	$110	$ 90
Accumulated benefit obligation	$523	$431	$ 111	$ 89	$151	$127	$126	$100
Projected benefit obligation .	$598	$520	$ 133	$ 101	$196	$167	$177	$148
Plan assets at fair value[1] ...	631	587	2	1	200	188	94	73
Plan assets in excess of (less than) projected benefit obligation	33	67	(131)[2]	(100)[2]	4	21	(83)	(75)
Unrecognized net (asset) liability at transition	(34)	(37)	17	19	(16)	(6)	34	33
Unrecognized prior service cost	8	23	15	3	—	—	9	8
Unrecognized net (gain) loss ..	(24)	(61)	36	24	28	2	(3)	(3)
Adjustment required to recognize minimum liability.	—	—	(46)	(33)	—	—	(7)	(3)
Accrued pension asset (liability) included in the consolidated balance sheet..	$ (17)	$ (8)	$(109)	$ (87)	$ 16	$ 17	$ (50)	$ (40)

[1]Primarily listed stocks, bonds and government securities.
[2]Substantially all of this amount relates to nonqualified, unfunded defined benefit plans.

The assumptions used in computing the preceding information are as follows:

	U.S. Plans			International Plans (weighted average rates)		
	Year 8	Year 7	Year 6	Year 8	Year 7	Year 6
Discount rates	7 1/4%	8 1/2%	9%	6 1/2%	7%	7 1/2%
Rates of increase in compensation levels....	4 3/4%	6%	6%	5%	5 1/2%	6%
Expected long-term rates of return on assets	9 1/2%	9 1/2%	9 1/2%	7%	7%	7 1/2%

14. OTHER POSTRETIREMENT BENEFITS

Company has plans providing postretirement health care and life insurance benefits to substantially all U.S. employees and certain international employees in international locations who retire with a minimum of five years of service. The Company adopted SFAS 106 for all U.S. and international plans as of January 1, Year 7. In Year 7, the Company recorded an accumulated obligation for consolidated operations of $146 million, which is net of $92 million in deferred tax benefits. The Company also recorded an additional charge of $73 million, net of $13 million of deferred tax benefits, representing the Company's proportionate share of accumulated postretirement benefit obligations recognized by bottling investees accounted for by the equity method.

Net periodic cost for the Company's postretirement health care and life insurance benefits consists of the following (in millions):

Year Ended December 31,	Year 8	Year 7
Service cost	$10	$ 9
Interest cost	21	20
Other.	(1)	—
	$30	$29

The Company contributes to a Voluntary Employees' Beneficiary Association trust that will be used to partially fund health care benefits for future retirees. The Company is funding benefits to the extent contributions are tax-deductible, which under current legislation is limited. In general, retiree health benefits are paid as covered expenses are incurred. The funded status for the Company's postretirement health care and life insurance plans is as follows (in millions):

December 31,	Year 8	Year 7
Accumulated postretirement benefit obligations		
Retirees.	$ 132	$ 111
Fully eligible active plan participants	35	34
Other active plan participants	131	113
Total benefit obligation.	298	258
Plan assets at fair value[1]	42	24
Plan assets less than benefit obligation	(256)	(234)
Unrecognized net loss.	23	—
Accrued postretirement benefit liability included in the consolidated balance sheet.	$(233)	$(234)

[1]Consists of corporate bonds, government securities and short-term investments.

The assumptions used in computing the preceding information are as follows:

Year Ended December 31,	Year 8	Year 7
Discount rate	7 1/4%	8 1/2%
Rate of increase in compensation levels	4 3/4%	6%

The rate of increase in the per capita costs of covered health care benefits is assumed to be 11 percent in Year 9, decreasing gradually to 5 1/2 percent by Year 20. Increasing the assumed health care cost trend rate by 1 percentage point would increase the accumulated postretirement benefit obligation as of December 31, Year 8, by approximately $35 million and increase net periodic post-retirement benefit cost by approximately $4 million in Year 8.

15. INCOME TAXES

Income before income taxes and changes in accounting principles consists of the following (in millions):

Year Ended December 31,	Year 8	Year 7	Year 6
United States	$1,035	$ 762	$ 648
International.......................	2,150	1,984	1,735
	$3,185	$2,746	$2,383

Income tax expense (benefit) consists of the following (in millions):

Year Ended December 31,	United States	State & Local	International	Total
Year 8				
Current..........	$356	$34	$669	$1,059
Deferred[1]	(64)	5	(3)	(62)
Year 7				
Current..........	$278	$36	$576	$ 890
Deferred[1]	(60)	(1)	34	(27)
Year 6				
Current..........	$233	$31	$595	$ 859
Deferred	(89)	(5)	—	(94)

[1]Additional deferred tax benefits of $8 million in Year 8 and $105 million in Year 7 have been included in the SFAS 112 and SFAS 106 transition effect charges, respectively.

The Company made income tax payments of approximately $650 million, $856 million and $672 million in Year 8, Year 7 and Year 6, respectively.

A reconciliation of the statutory U.S. federal rate and effective rates is as follows:

Year Ended December 31,	Year 8	Year 7	Year 6
Statutory U.S. federal rate	35.0%	34.0%	34.0%
State income taxes—net of federal benefit	1.0	1.0	1.0
Earnings in jurisdictions taxed at rates different from the U.S. federal rate	(5.1)	(3.8)	(3.1)
Equity income	(1.7)	(1.0)	(.6)
Other—net...	2.1	1.2	.8
	31.3%	31.4%	32.1%

The tax effects of temporary differences and carryforwards that give rise to significant portions of deferred tax assets and liabilities consist of the following (in millions):

December 31,	Year 8	Year 7
Deferred tax assets:		
Benefit plans	$298	$297
Liabilities and reserves	177	119
Net operating loss carryforwards........	141	101
Other...............................	120	84
Gross deferred tax assets	736	601
Valuation allowance...................	(75)	(63)
Total	$661	$538
Deferred tax liabilities:		
Property, plant, and equipment	$342	$312
Equity investments....................	180	197
Intangible assets......................	52	68
Other...............................	61	43
Total	$635	$620
Net deferred tax asset (liability)[1]	$ 26	$ (82)

[1]Deferred tax assets of $139 million have been included in the consolidated balance sheet caption marketable securities and other assets at December 31, Year 8.

At December 31, Year 8, the Company had $403 million of operating loss carryforwards available to reduce future taxable income of certain international subsidiaries. Loss carryforwards of $293 million must be utilized within the next five years, and $110 million can be utilized over an indefinite period. A valuation allowance has been provided for a portion of the deferred tax assets related to these loss carryforwards.

As the result of changes in U.S. tax law, the Company was required to record charges for additional taxes and tax-related expenses that reduced net income by approximately $51 million in Year 8. The Company's effective tax rate reflects the favorable U.S. tax treatment from manufacturing facilities in Puerto Rico that operate under a negotiated exemption grant that expires December 31, Year 24, as well as the tax benefit derived from significant operations outside the United States, which are taxed at rates lower than the U.S. statutory rate of 35 percent. Changes to U.S. tax law enacted in Year 8 will limit the utilization of the favorable tax treatment from operations in Puerto Rico beginning in Year 9, and will exert upward pressure on the Company's effective tax rate.

Appropriate U.S. and international taxes have been provided for earnings of subsidiary companies that are expected to be remitted to the parent company. The cumulative amount of unremitted earnings of international subsidiaries that are expected to be indefinitely reinvested, exclusive of amounts that, if remitted, would result in little or no tax, is approximately $426 million at December 31, Year 8. The taxes that would be paid upon remittance of these earnings are approximately $149 million.

16. Net Change in Operating Assets and Liabilities

The changes in operating assets and liabilities, net of effects of acquisitions and divestitures of businesses and unrealized exchange gains/losses, are as follows (in millions):

Year Ended December 31,	Year 8	Year 7	Year 6
Increase in trade accounts receivable	$(151)	$(147)	$ (32)
Increase in inventories	(41)	(138)	(3)
Increase in prepaid expenses and other assets.........	(76)	(112)	(326)
Increase (decrease) in accounts payable and accrued expenses......................................	(44)	405	267
Increase in accrued taxes........................	355	57	244
Increase (decrease) in other liabilities...............	11	(108)	101
	$ 54	$ (43)	$ 251

17. Acquisitions and Investments

During Year 8, the Company's acquisition and investment activity, which includes investments in bottling operations in Mexico, Belgium and the United States, totaled $816 million. During Year 7 and Year 6, the Company's acquisition and investment activity totaled $717 million and $399 million, respectively. None of the acquisitions in Year 7 or Year 6 were individually significant.

As discussed in Note 3, the Company purchased bottling operations in Tennessee that were subsequently sold to Coca-Cola Enterprises along with a bottling operation in the Netherlands. Note 3 also includes a discussion of the Company's Year 8 investments in bottling operations in Mexico and in the United States.

The acquisitions have been accounted for by the purchase method of accounting, and, accordingly, their results have been included in the consolidated financial statements from their respective dates of acquisition. Had the results of these businesses been included in operations commencing with Year 6, the reported results would not have been materially affected.

18. Nonrecurring Items

Upon a favorable court decision in Year 8, the Company reversed the previously recorded reserves for bottler litigation, resulting in a $13 million reduction to selling, administrative and general expenses and a $10 million reduction to interest expense. Selling, administrative and general expenses for Year 8 also include provisions of $63 million to increase efficiencies in European, domestic and corporate operations. Also in Year 8, equity income has been reduced by $42 million related to restructuring charges recorded by Coca-Cola Beverages Ltd. Other income (deductions)—net includes a $50 million pretax gain recorded by the foods business sector upon the sale of citrus groves in the United States, and a $34 million pretax gain recognized on the sale of property no longer required as a result of a consolidation of manufacturing operations in Japan.

Other income (deductions)-net in Year 6 includes a $69 million pretax gain on the sale of property no longer required as a result of consolidating manufacturing operations in Japan and a $27 million pretax gain on the sale of the Company's 22 percent ownership interest in Johnston to Coca-Cola Enterprises. Selling, administrative and general expenses and interest expense in Year 6 include the original charges of $13 million and $8 million, respectively, for bottler litigation reversed in Year 8. In addition, Year 6 equity income has been reduced by $44 million related to restructuring charges recorded by Coca-Cola Enterprises.

19. LINES OF BUSINESS

The Company operates in two major lines of business: soft drinks and foods (principally juice and juice drink products). Information concerning operations in these businesses is as follows (in millions):

| | Soft Drinks | | | | |
	United States	International	Foods	Corporate	Consolidated
Year 8					
Net operating revenues	$2,966	$9,205	$1,766	$ 20	$13,957
Operating income	618[1]	2,753[1]	127	(396)[1]	3,102
Identifiable operating assets	1,956	5,809	761	1,280[3]	9,806
Equity income				91[1]	91
Investments (principally bottling companies)				2,215	2,215
Capital expenditures	136	557	30	77	800
Depreciation and amortization.	91	172	38	59	360
Year 7					
Net operating revenues	$2,813	$8,551	$1,675	$ 35	$13,074
Operating income	510	2,521	112	(373)	2,770
Identifiable operating assets	1,812	5,251	791	1,035[3]	8,889
Equity income				65	65
Investments (principally bottling companies)				2,163	2,163
Capital expenditures	169	736	38	140	1,083
Depreciation and amortization.	87	157	35	43	322
Year 6					
Net operating revenues	$2,645	$7,245	$1,636	$ 46	$11,572
Operating income	469	2,141	104	(395)	2,319
Identifiable operating assets	1,447	4,742	755	1,124[3]	8,068
Equity income				40[2]	40
Investments (principally bottling companies)				2,121	2,121
Capital expenditures	131	547	57	57	792
Depreciation and amortization.	82	112	30	37	261

Intercompany transfers between sectors are not material.

[1]Operating income for soft drink operations in the United States, International operations and Corporate were reduced by $13 million, $33 million and $17 million, respectively, for provisions to increase efficiencies. Equity income was reduced by $42 million related to restructuring charges recorded by Coca-Cola Beverages Ltd.

[2]Reduced by $44 million related to restructuring charges recorded by Coca-Cola Enterprises.

[3]Corporate identifiable operating assets are composed principally of marketable securities and fixed assets.

Continued

Compound Growth Rates Ending Year 8	Soft Drinks		Foods	Consolidated
	United States	International		
Net operating revenues				
5 years	8%	15%	3%	12%
10 years	7%	14%	5%	11%
Operating income				
5 years	12%	16%	7%	14%
10 years	10%	17%	1%	14%

20. OPERATIONS IN GEOGRAPHIC AREAS

Information about the Company's operations in different geographic areas is as follows (in millions):

	United States	Africa	European Community	Latin America	Northeast Europe/ Middle East	Pacific & Canada	Corporate	Consolidated
Year 8								
Net operating revenues	$4,586	$255	$3,834	$1,683	$677	$2,902	$ 20	$13,957
Operating income	730[1]	152	872[1]	582	152	1,010	(396)[1]	3,102
Identifiable operating assets.............	2,682	153	2,777	1,220	604	1,090	1,280[3]	9,806
Equity income							91[1]	91
Investments (principally bottling companies)........							2,215	2,215
Capital expenditures..	165	6	239	141	129	43	77	800
Depreciation and amortization.......	127	3	99	33	22	17	59	360
Year 7[4]								
Net operating revenues	$4,339	$242	$3,984	$1,383	$546	$2,545	$ 35	$13,074
Operating income	608	129	889	502	108	907	(373)	2,770
Identifiable operating assets.............	2,563	139	2,587	1,185	435	945	1,035[3]	8,889
Equity income							65	65
Investments (principally bottling companies)........							2,163	2,163
Capital expenditures..	204	12	386	188	120	33	140	1,083
Depreciation and amortization.......	121	3	99	27	14	15	43	322

Continued

Continued

	United States	Africa	European Community	Latin America	Northeast Europe/ Middle East	Pacific & Canada	Corporate	Consolidated
Year 6[4]								
Net operating revenues	$4,125	$206	$3,338	$1,103	$408	$2,346	$ 46	$11,572
Operating income	560	105	768	405	99	777	(395)	2,319
Identifiable operating assets.............	2,161	126	2,558	815	297	987	1,124[3]	8,068
Equity income							40[2]	40
Investments (principally bottling companies)........							2,121	2,121
Capital expenditures..	185	6	331	106	55	52	57	792
Depreciation and amortization.......	111	2	66	23	7	15	37	261

Intercompany transfers between geographic areas are not material.

Identifiable liabilities of operations outside the United States amounted to approximately $1.9 billion at December 31, Year 8, and Year 7, and $1.8 billion at December 31, Year 6.

[1]Operating income for the United States, European Community and Corporate were reduced by $13 million, $33 million and $17 million, respectively, for provisions to increase efficiencies. Equity income was reduced by $42 million related to restructuring charges recorded by Coca-Cola Beverages Ltd.

[2]Reduced by $44 million related to restructuring charges recorded by Coca-Cola Enterprises.

[3]Corporate identifiable operating assets are composed principally of marketable securities and fixed assets.

[4]In Year 8, the Company divided its Northeast Europe/Africa group into the Northeast Europe/Middle East and Africa groups. Accordingly, previous years' results have been reclassified to reflect this change.

Compound Growth Rates	United States	Africa	European Community	Latin America	Northeast Europe/ Middle East	Pacific & Canada	Consolidated
Year 8							
Net operating revenues							
5 years	6%	11%	19%	24%	24%	7%	12%
10 years	6%	(4)%	18%	15%	21%	13%	11%
Operating income							
5 years	11%	20%	13%	27%	17%	12%	14%
10 years	8%	2%	19%	24%	22%	18%	14%

APPENDIX B

FINANCIAL STATEMENTS FOR PEPSICO, INC. AND SUBSIDIARIES

PepsiCo, Inc. and Subsidiaries
Consolidated Statement of Income
(in millions except per share amounts)
Fifty-two weeks ended December 25, Year 8 and December 26, Year 7
and December 28, Year 6

	Year 8	Year 7	Year 6
Net Sales	**$25,020.7**	$21,970.0	$19,292.2
Costs and Expenses, net			
Cost of sales	**11,946.1**	10,611.7	9,366.2
Selling, general and administrative expenses	**9,864.4**	8,721.2	7,605.9
Amortization of intangible assets	**303.7**	265.9	208.3
Operating Profit	**2,906.5**	2,371.2	2,111.8
Interest expense	**(572.7)**	(586.1)	(613.7)
Interest income	**88.7**	113.7	161.6
Income before Income Taxes and Cumulative Effect of Accounting Changes	**2,422.5**	1,898.8	1,659.7
Provision for Income Taxes	**834.6**	597.1	579.5
Income before Cumulative Effect of Accounting Changes	**1,587.9**	1,301.7	1,080.2
Cumulative Effect of Change in Accounting for Postretirement Benefits Other Than Pensions (net of income tax benefit of $218.6)	**—**	(356.7)	—
Cumulative Effect of Change in Accounting for Income Taxes	**—**	(570.7)	—
Net Income	**$ 1,587.9**	$ 374.3	$ 1,080.2
Income (Charge) Per Share			
Before cumulative effect of accounting changes	$ **1.96**	$ 1.61	$ 1.35
Cumulative effect of change in accounting for postretirement benefits other than pensions	**—**	(0.44)	—
Cumulative effect of change in accounting for income taxes	**—**	(0.71)	—
Net Income per Share	$ **1.96**	$ 0.46	$ 1.35
Average shares outstanding used to calculate income (charge) per share	**810.1**	806.7	802.5

See accompanying Notes to Consolidated Financial Statements.

PepsiCo, Inc. and Subsidiaries
Consolidated Balance Sheet
(in millions except per share amounts)
December 25, Year 8 and December 26, Year 7

	Year 8	Year 7
Assets		
Current Assets		
Cash and cash equivalents	$ 226.9	$ 169.9
Short-term investments, at cost which approximates market	1,629.3	1,888.5
	1,856.2	2,058.4
Accounts and notes receivable, less allowance:		
$128.3 in Year 8 and $112.0 in Year 7	1,883.4	1,588.5
Inventories	924.7	768.8
Prepaid expenses, taxes and other current assets	499.8	426.6
Total Current Assets	5,164.1	4,842.3
Investments in Affiliates and Other Assets	1,756.6	1,707.9
Property, Plant and Equipment, net	8,855.6	7,442.0
Intangible Assets, net	7,929.5	6,959.0
Total Assets	$23,705.8	$20,951.2
Liabilities and Shareholders' Equity		
Current Liabilities		
Short-term borrowings	$ 2,191.2	$ 706.8
Accounts payable	1,390.0	1,164.8
Income taxes payable	823.7	621.1
Accrued compensation and benefits	726.0	638.9
Accrued marketing	400.9	327.0
Other current liabilities	1,043.1	1,099.0
Total Current Liabilities	6,574.9	4,557.6
Long-term Debt	7,442.6	7,964.8
Other Liabilities	1,342.0	1,390.8
Deferred Income Taxes	2,007.6	1,682.3
Shareholders' Equity		
Capital stock, par value 1-2/3¢ per share: authorized 1,800.0 shares, issued		
863.1 shares	14.4	14.4
Capital in excess of par value	879.5	667.6
Retained earnings	6,541.9	5,439.7
Currency translation adjustment and other	(183.9)	(99.0)
	7,251.9	6,022.7
Less: Treasury stock, at cost:		
64.3 shares in Year 8 and Year 7	(913.2)	(667.0)
Total Shareholders' Equity	6,338.7	5,355.7
Total Liabilities and Shareholders' Equity	$23,705.8	$20,951.2

See accompanying Notes to Consolidated Financial Statements

PepsiCo, Inc. and Subsidiaries
Consolidated Statement of Cash Flows
Fifty-two weeks ended December 25, Year 8 and December 26, Year 7 and December 28,
Year 6
(in millions)

	Year 8	Year 7	Year 6
Cash Flows—Operating Activities			
Income before cumulative effect of accounting changes	$ 1,587.9	$ 1,301.7	$ 1,080.2
Adjustments to reconcile income before cumulative effect of of accounting changes to net cash provided by operating activities			
Depreciation and amortization.	1,444.2	1,214.9	1,034.5
Deferred income taxes	83.3	(52.0)	98.0
Other noncash charges and credits, net	344.8	315.6	227.2
Changes in operating working capital, excluding effect of acquisitions:			
Accounts and notes receivable.	(161.0)	(45.7)	(55.9)
Inventories	(89.5)	(11.8)	(54.8)
Prepaid expenses, taxes and other current assets	3.3	(27.4)	(75.6)
Accounts payable.	143.2	(102.0)	57.8
Income taxes payable	(125.1)	(16.9)	(3.4)
Other current liabilities	(96.7)	135.2	122.3
Net change in operating working capital	(325.8)	(68.6)	(9.6)
Net Cash Provided by Operating Activities.	3,134.4	2,711.6	2,430.3
Cash Flows—Investing Activities			
Acquisitions and investments in affiliates	(1,011.2)	(1,209.7)	(640.9)
Purchases of property, plant and equipment (Capital spending). . . .	(1,981.6)	(1,549.6)	(1,457.8)
Proceeds from sales of property, plant and equipment	72.5	89.0	69.6
Short-term investments, by original maturity:			
More than three months—purchases	(578.7)	(1,174.8)	(1,849.2)
More than three months—maturities	846.0	1,371.8	1,873.2
Three months or less, net	(8.3)	(249.4)	(164.9)
Other, net.	(109.4)	(30.8)	(105.8)
Net Cash Used for Investing Activities.	(2,770.7)	(2,753.5)	(2,275.8)

continued

continued	Year 8	Year 7	Year 6
Cash Flows—Financing Activities			
Proceeds from issuances of long-term debt	710.8	1,092.7	2,799.6
Payments of long-term debt	(1,201.9)	(616.3)	(1,348.5)
Short-term borrowings, by original maturity:			
More than three months—proceeds	3,033.6	911.2	2,551.9
More than three months—payments	(2,791.6)	(2,062.6)	(3,097.4)
Three months or less, net	839.0	1,075.3	(467.1)
Cash dividends paid	(461.6)	(395.5)	(343.2)
Purchases of treasury stock	(463.5)	(32.0)	(195.2)
Proceeds from exercises of stock options	68.6	82.8	15.8
Other, net	(36.7)	(30.9)	(47.0)
Net Cash Provided by (Used for) Financing Activities	(303.3)	24.7	(131.1)
Effect of Exchange Rate Changes on Cash and Cash Equivalents.	(3.4)	0.4	(7.5)
Net Increase (Decrease) in Cash and Cash Equivalents.	57.0	(16.8)	15.9
Cash and Cash Equivalents—Beginning of Year	169.9	186.7	170.8
Cash and Cash Equivalents—End of Year.	$ 226.9	$ 169.9	$ 186.7

Supplemental Cash Flow Information

Cash Flow Data

	Year 8	Year 7	Year 6
Interest paid	$ 549.5	$ 574.7	$ 490.1
Income taxes paid	$ 675.6	$ 519.7	$ 385.9

Schedule of Noncash Investing and Financing Activities

	Year 8	Year 7	Year 6
Liabilities assumed in connection with acquisitions	$ 897.0	$ 383.8	$ 70.9
Issuance of treasury stock and debt for acquisitions.	$ 364.5	$ 189.5	$ 162.7
Book value of net assets exchanged for investment in affiliates	$ 60.8	$ 86.7	$ —

See accompanying Notes to Consolidated Financial Statements

PepsiCo, Inc. and Subsidiaries
Consolidated Statement of Shareholders' Equity
(shares in thousands, dollars in millions except per share amounts)
Fifty-two weeks ended December 25, Year 8 and December 26, Year 7 and December 28, Year 6

| | Capital Stock | | | | Capital in Excess of Par Value | Retained Earnings | Currency Translation Adjustment and Other | Total |
| | Issued | | Treasury | | | | | |
	Shares	Amount	Shares	Amount				
Shareholders' Equity, December 29, Year 5	863,083	$14.4	(74,694)	$(611.4)	$365.0	$4,753.0	$383.2	$4,904.2
Year 6 net income						1,080.2		1,080.2
Cash dividends declared (per share-$0.46)						(363.2)		(363.2)
Currency translation adjustment							(52.9)	(52.9)
Purchase of treasury stock			(6,392)	(195.2)				(195.2)
Shares issued in connection with acquisitions			5,613	46.7	95.0			141.7
Stock option exercises, including tax benefits, and compensation awards			1,446	13.6	16.4			30.0
Other, principally conversion of debentures			45	0.4	0.2			0.6
Shareholders' Equity, December 28, Year 6	863,083	$14.4	(73,982)	$(745.9)	$476.6	$5,470.0	$ 330.3	$5,545.4
Year 7 net income						374.3		374.3
Cash dividends declared (per share-$0.51)						(404.6)		(404.6)
Currency translation adjustment							(429.3)	(429.3)
Shares issued in connection with acquisitions			4,265	44.2	115.3			159.5
Stock option exercises, including tax benefits, and compensation awards			6,333	65.5	75.5			141.0
Purchases of treasury stock			(1,000)	(32.0)				(32.0)
Other, principally conversion of debentures			107	1.2	0.2			1.4

continued

continued

	Capital Stock				Capital in Excess of Par Value	Retained Earnings	Currency Translation Adjustment and Other	Total
	Issued		Treasury					
	Shares	Amount	Shares	Amount				
Shareholders' Equity, December 26, Year 7	863,083	$14.4	(64,277)	$(667.0)	$667.6	$5,439.7	$(99.0)	$5,355.7
Year 8 net income						1,587.9		1,587.9
Cash dividends declared (per share-$0.61)						(485.7)		(485.7)
Currency translation adjustment							(77.0)	(77.0)
Purchases of treasury stock			(12,371)	(463.5)				(463.5)
Shares issued in connection with acquisitions			8,896	170.2	164.6			334.8
Stock option exercises, including tax benefits, and compensation awards			3,415	46.6	47.1			93.7
Pension liability adjustment, net of deferred taxes							(7.9)	(7.9)
Other, principally converstion of debentures			35	0.5	0.2			0.7
Shareholders' Equity, December 25, Year 8	863,083	$14.4	(64,302)	$(913.2)	$879.5	$6,541.9	$(183.9)	$6,338.7

See accompanying Notes to Consolidated Financial Statements

NOTES TO CONSOLIDATED FINANCIAL STATEMENTS

(tabular dollars in millions except per share amounts)

1. SUMMARY OF SIGNIFICANT ACCOUNTING POLICIES

Significant accounting policies are discussed below, and where applicable, in the Notes that follow.

Principles of Consolidation.   The financial statements reflect the consolidated accounts of PepsiCo, Inc. and its controlled affiliates. Intercompany accounts and transactions have been eliminated. Investments in affiliates in which PepsiCo exercises significant influence but not control are accounted for by the equity method, and the equity in net income is included in the Selling, general and administrative expenses in the Consolidated Statement of Income. Certain other reclassifications were made to prior year amounts to conform with the Year 8 presentation.

Marketing Costs.   Marketing costs are reported in Selling, general and administrative expenses and include costs of advertising, marketing and promotional programs. Promotional discounts are expensed as incurred, and other marketing costs not deferred are charged to expense ratably in relation to sales over the year in which incurred. Marketing costs deferred consist of media and personal service advertising prepayments, materials in inventory and production costs of future media advertising; these assets are expensed in the year used.

Cash Equivalents.   Cash equivalents represent funds temporarily invested (with original maturities not exceeding three months) as part of PepsiCo's management of day-to-day operating cash receipts and disbursements. All other investment portfolios, primarily held outside the U.S., are classified as short-term investments.

Net Income Per Share.   Net income per share is computed by dividing net income by the weighted average number of shares outstanding during each year.

Research and Development Expenses.   Research and development expenses, which are expensed as incurred, were $113 million, $102 million and $99 million in Year 8, Year 7 and Year 6, respectively.

2. BUSINESS SEGMENTS

Information regarding industry segments and geographic areas of operations is provided following the Notes to Consolidated Financial Statements.

3. UNUSUAL ITEMS

In Year 8, PepsiCo recorded a charge of $29.9 million ($0.04 per share) to increase its net deferred tax liabilities, as required by Statement of Financial Accounting Standards (SFAS) No. 109, "Accounting for Income Taxes," for the 1% statutory rate increase under U.S. tax legislation enacted in Year 8. (See Note 13.)

Unusual charges, principally for restructurings, totaled $193.5 million in Year 7 ($128.5 million after-tax or $0.16 per share) and $170.0 million in Year 6 ($119.8 million after-tax or $0.15 per share). In Year 7, PepsiCo adopted the Statement of Financial Accounting Standards No. 106, "Employers' Accounting for Postretirement Benefits Other Than Pensions" and SFAS No. 109 effective December 29, Year 6. (See Notes 10 and 13.) As compared to the previous accounting methods, the adoption of SFAS No. 106 and SFAS No. 109 reduced Year 7 operating profit by $72.8 million ($19.3 million after-tax or $0.02 per share).

4. Acquisitions and Investments in Affiliates

During Year 8 PepsiCo completed a number of acquisitions and affiliate investments in all three industry segments aggregating $1.4 billion, principally comprised of $1.0 billion in cash and $335 million in PepsiCo Capital Stock. Approximately $307 million of debt, including capital lease obligations, was assumed in these transactions, more than half of which was subsequently retired. This activity included acquisitions of domestic and international franchised restaurant operations, the buyout of PepsiCo's joint venture partners in a franchised bottling operation in Spain and the related acquisition of their fruit-flavored beverage operation, the acquisition of the remaining 85% interest in a large franchised bottling operation in the Northwestern U.S., the acquisition of a regional Mexican-style casual dining restaurant chain in the U.S. and equity investments in certain franchised bottling operations in Argentina and Mexico.

During Year 7, acquisitions and affiliate investment activity aggregated $1.4 billion, principally for cash. This activity included acquisitions of international (primarily Canada) and domestic franchised bottling operations and a number of domestic and international franchised restaurant operations, the buyout of PepsiCo's joint venture partner in a Canadian snack food business and an equity investment in a domestic casual dining restaurant chain featuring gourmet pizza. In addition, PepsiCo exchanged certain previously consolidated snack food operations in Europe with a net book value of $87 million for a 60% equity interest in an international snack food joint venture with General Mills, Inc. PepsiCo secured a controlling interest in its Mexican cookie affiliate, Gamesa, through an exchange of certain non-cookie operations of Gamesa for its joint venture partner's interest.

During Year 6, acquisition and affiliate investment activity aggregated $804 million, principally for cash, led by acquisitions of domestic franchised restaurant operations.

The acquisitions have been accounted for by the purchase method; accordingly, their results are included in the consolidated Financial Statements from their respective dates of acquisition. The aggregate impact of acquisitions was not material to PepsiCo's net sales, net income or net income per share; accordingly, no related pro forma information is provided.

5. Inventories

Inventories are valued at the lower of cost (computed on the average, first-in, first-out or last-in, first-out methods) or net realizable value. The cost of 41% of Year 8 inventories and 44% of Year 7 inventories was computed using the last-in, first-out

(LIFO) method. Use of the LIFO method increased the Year 8 total year-end inventory amount below by $8.9 million, but reduced the Year 7 amount by $3.4 million.

	Year 8	Year 7
Raw materials, supplies and in-process......	$463.9	$388.1
Finished goods.........................	460.8	380.7
	$924.7	$768.8

PepsiCo hedges certain raw material purchases through commodity futures contracts to reduce its exposure to market price fluctuations. Gains and losses on these contracts are included in the cost of the raw materials.

6. PROPERTY, PLANT, AND EQUIPMENT

Property, plant, and equipment are stated at cost. Depreciation is calculated principally on a straight-line basis over the estimated useful lives of the assets. Depreciation expense in Year 8, 7, and 6 was $1.1 billion, $923 million and $800 million, respectively.

	Year 8	Year 7
Land	$ 1,186.4	$ 1,010.0
Buildings and improvements	5,017.6	4,269.5
Capital leases, primarily buildings......	402.6	330.5
Machinery and equipment	7,643.4	6,485.2
	14,250.0	12,095.2
Accumulated depreciation.............	(5,394.4)	(4,653.2)
	$ 8,855.6	$ 7,442.0

7. INTANGIBLE ASSETS

Identifiable intangible assets arose from the allocation of purchase prices of business acquired, and consist principally of reacquired franchise rights and trademarks. Reacquired franchise rights relate to acquisitions of franchised bottling and restaurant operations, and the trademarks principally relate to acquisitions of international snack food operations and KFC. Values assigned to such identifiable intangibles were based on independent appraisals or internal estimates. Goodwill represents any residual purchase price after allocation to all identifiable net assets.

	Year 8	Year 7
Reacquired franchise rights.........	$3,959.7	$3,476.9
Trademarks......................	898.5	734.2
Other identifiable intangibles........	154.7	159.6
Goodwill.......................	2,916.6	2,588.3
	$7,929.5	$6,959.0

Intangible assets are amortized on a straight-line basis over appropriate periods generally ranging from 20 to 40 years. Accumulated amortization was $1.3 billion and $1.0 billion at year-end Year 8 and 7, respectively.

The recoverability of carrying values of intangible assets is evaluated on a recurring basis. The primary indicators of recoverability are current or forecasted profitability of the related acquired business, measured as profit before interest, but after amortization of the intangible assets. Consideration is also given to the estimated disposal values of certain identifiable intangible assets compared to their carrying values. For the three-year period ended December 25, Year 8, there were no adjustments to the carrying values of intangible assets resulting from these evaluations.

8. SHORT-TERM BORROWINGS AND LONG-TERM DEBT

	Year 8	Year 7
Short-Term Borrowings		
Commercial paper (3.3% and 3.5% weighted average interest rate at year-end 8 and 7, respectively)	$ 3,535.0	$ 2,113.6
Current maturities of long-term debt issuances	1,183.1	1,052.6
Notes (A)	394.0	600.0
Other borrowings	529.1	440.6
Amount reclassified to long-term debt (B)	$(3,450.0)	$(3,500.0)
	$ 2,191.2	$ 706.8
Long-Term Debt		
Short-term borrowings, reclassified (B)	$ 3,450.0	$ 3,500.0
Notes due Year 9 through Year 16 (6.5% and 6.6% weighted average interest rate at year-end 8 and 7, respectively) (A)	3,873.8	4,209.1
Zero coupon notes, $935 million due Year 9–Year 30 (14.4% semi-annual weighted average yield to maturity at year-end 8 and 7)	327.2	300.4
Swiss franc perpetual Foreign Interest Payment bonds (C)	212.2	211.4
Pound sterling 9 1/8% notes (D)	—	91.0
Swiss franc 5 1/4% bearer bonds due Year 10 (D)	90.1	89.1
Swiss franc 7 1/8% notes due Year 9 (D)	69.8	69.1
Capital lease obligations (See Note 9)	291.4	242.0
Other, due Year 9–Year 38 (6.6% and 6.8% weighted average interest rate at year-end 8 and 7, respectively)	311.2	305.3
	8,625.7	9,017.4
Less current maturities of long-term debt issuances	(1,183.1)	(1,052.6)
Total long-term debt	$ 7,442.6	$ 7,964.8

Long-term debt is carried net of any related discount or premium and unamortized debt issuance costs. The debt agreements include various restrictions, none of which is presently significant to PepsiCo.

The annual maturities of long-term debt through Year 13, excluding capital lease obligations and the reclassified short-term borrowings, are: Year 9-$1.2 billion; Year 10-$692 million; Year 11-$1.1 billion; Year 12-$278 million and Year 13-$1.1 billion.

(A) PepsiCo has entered into interest rate swap agreements to effectively convert $193 million and $725 million of fixed rate debt issuances to variable rate debt with a weighted average interest rate of 3.3% and 3.4% at year-end 8 and 7, respectively, as well as effectively convert $214 million of variable rate debt to fixed rate debt with an interest rate of 7.0% at year-end 8 and 7. The differential to be paid or received on interest rate swaps is accrued as interest rates change and is charged or credited to interest expense over the life of the agreements.

(B) At year-end 8 and 7, $3.5 billion of short-term borrowings were classified as long-term, reflecting PepsiCo's intent and ability to refinance these borrowings on a long-term basis, through either long-term debt issuances or rollover of existing short-term borrowings. At year-end 8 and 7, PepsiCo had revolving credit agreements covering potential borrowings aggregating $3.5 billion, with the current agreements expiring in Year 10 through 14. These unused credit facilities provide the ability to refinance short-term borrowings.

(C) The coupon rate of the Swiss franc 400 million perpetual Foreign Interest Payment bonds issued in Year 4 is 7 1/2% through Year 11. The interest payments are made in U.S. dollars at a fixed contractual exchange rate. The bonds have no stated maturity date. At the end of each 10-year period after the issuance of the bonds, PepsiCo and the bondholders each have the right to cause redemption of the bonds. If not redeemed, the coupon rate will be adjusted based on the prevailing yield of 10-year U.S. Treasury Securities. The principal of the bonds is denominated in Swiss francs. PepsiCo can, and intends to, limit the ultimate redemption amount to the U.S. dollar proceeds at issuance, which is the basis of the carrying value.

(D) PepsiCo has entered into currency exchange agreements to hedge its foreign currency exposure on these issues of non-U.S. dollar denominated debt. At year-end 8, the carrying value of this debt aggregated $160 million and the net receivable under related currency exchange agreements aggregated $41 million, resulting in a net effective U.S. dollar liability of $119 million with a weighted average fixed interest rate of 6.5%. At year-end 7, the aggregate carrying values of the debt and the net receivable under related currency exchange agreements were $249 million and $20 million, respectively, resulting in a net effective U.S. dollar liability of $229 million with a weighted average fixed interest rate of 7.2%. The carrying values of the currency exchange agreements are reflected in the Consolidated Balance Sheet as gross receivables and payables under the appropriate current and noncurrent asset and liability captions. Changes in the carrying value of a currency exchange agreement resulting from exchange rate movements are offset by changes in the carrying value of the related non-U.S. dollar denominated debt, as both values are based on current exchange rates.

The maturity dates of interest rate swaps and currency exchange agreements correspond with those of the related debt instruments. The counterparties to PepsiCo's interest rate swaps and currency exchange agreements consist of a diversified group of financial institutions. PepsiCo is exposed to credit risk to the extent of nonperformance by these counterparties; however, PepsiCo regularly monitors its positions and the credit ratings of these counterparties and considers the risk of default to be minimal. Additionally, due to the frequency of interest payments and receipts, PepsiCo's credit risk related to interest rate swaps is not significant.

9. LEASES

PepsiCo has noncancelable commitments under both capital and long-term operating leases, primarily for restaurant units. Certain of these units have been subleased to restaurant franchisees. Commitments on capital and operating leases expire at various dates and, in many cases, provide for rent escalations and renewal options. Most leases require payment of related occupancy costs which include property taxes, maintenance and insurance.

Future minimum commitments and sublease receivables under noncancelable leases are as follows:

| | Commitments | | Sublease Receivables | |
	Capital	Operating	Direct Financing	Operating
Year 9	$ 56.8	$ 247.2	$ 3.5	$ 9.7
Year 10	52.4	219.7	3.3	9.1
Year 11	46.5	197.7	3.1	8.2
Year 12	39.9	171.6	2.8	7.3
Year 13	59.8	155.5	2.4	6.1
Later years	229.0	894.9	9.0	25.5
	$484.4	$1,886.6	$24.1	$65.9

At year-end Year 8, the present value of minimum payments under capital leases was $291 million, after deducting $1 million for estimated executory costs (taxes, maintenance and insurance) and $192 million representing imputed interest. The present value of minimum receivables under direct financing subleases was $15 million after deducting $9 million of unearned interest income.

Total rental expense and income and the contingent portions of these totals were as follows:

	Year 8	Year 7	Year 6
Total rental expense	$419.8	$379.0	$323.2
Contingent portion of expense	$ 27.5	$ 27.5	$ 22.3
Total rental income	$ 16.6	$ 14.7	$ 13.0
Contingent portion of income	$ 4.4	$ 4.5	$ 4.8

Contingent rentals are based on sales by restaurants in excess of levels stipulated in the lease agreements.

10. POSTRETIREMENT BENEFITS OTHER THAN PENSIONS

PepsiCo provides postretirement health care benefits to eligible retired employees and their dependents, principally in the U.S. Retirees who have 10 years of service and attain age 55 while in service with PepsiCo are eligible to participate in the postretirement benefit plans. The plans in effect through Year 8 were largely non-contributory and not funded.

Effective December 29, Year 6, PepsiCo adopted Statement of Financial Accounting Standards No. 106 (SFAS 106), "Employers' Accounting for Postretirement Benefits Other Than Pensions." SFAS 106 requires PepsiCo to accrue the cost of postretirement benefits over the years employees provide services to the date of their full eligibility for such benefits. Previously, such costs were expensed as actual claims were incurred. PepsiCo elected to immediately recognize the transition obligation for future benefits to be paid related to past employee services, resulting in a noncash charge of $575.3 million pretax ($356.7 million after-tax or $0.44 per share) that represents the cumulative effect of the change in accounting for years prior to Year 7. The expense recognized in Year 7 exceeded the amount under the previous accounting method by $52.1 million pretax ($32.3 million after-tax or $0.04 per share). PepsiCo's cash flows have been unaffected by this accounting change as PepsiCo continues to largely fund postretirement benefit costs as the claims are incurred.

Effective in Year 8 and Year 7, PepsiCo introduced retiree cost-sharing and implemented programs intended to stem rising costs. Also, PepsiCo has adopted a provision which limits its future obligation to absorb health care cost inflation. These amendments resulted in an unrecognized prior service gain of $191 million, which is being amortized on a straight-line basis over the average remaining employee service period of 10 years as a reduction in postretirement benefit expense beginning in Year 8.

The Year 8 information presented below includes amounts for a small postretirement benefit plan in Puerto Rico. Although not yet measured, obligations related to other international postretirement benefit plans are not expected to be significant, since these benefits are generally provided through government-sponsored plans.

The postretirement benefit expense for Year 8 and Year 7 included the following components:

	Year 8	Year 7
Service cost of benefits earned	$ 14.7	$25.5
Interest cost on accumulated postretirement benefit obligation...	40.6	50.8
Amortization of prior service (gain) cost	(19.6)	0.1
Amortization of net loss	0.5	—
Postretirement benefit expense	$ 36.2	$ 76.4

The decline in the Year 8 expense was primarily due to the plan amendments, reflecting reductions in service and interest costs as well as the amortization of the unrecognized prior service gain. Expense recognized in Year 6 under the previous accounting method was $23.9 million.

The Year 8 and Year 7 postretirement benefit liability recorded in the Consolidated Balance Sheet included the following components:

	Year 8	Year 7
Actuarial present value of benefit obligations		
Retirees..	$(313.8)	$(251.2)
Fully eligible active plan participants...............	(107.3)	(132.5)
Other active plan participants.....................	(206.9)	(312.1)
Accumulated postretirement benefit obligation	(628.0)	(695.8)
Unrecognized prior service (gain) cost..............	(171.5)	.5
Unrecognized net loss............................	148.6	58.0
Postretirement benefit liability at year-end...........	$(650.9)	$(637.3)

The assumed discount rate used to determine the accumulated postretirement benefit obligation at year-end 8 and related expense for Year 9 is 6.8% compared to 8.2% used to determine the obligation at year-end 7 and related expense for Year 8. The decrease reflects the decline in interest rates. The discount rate represents the expected yield on a diversified portfolio of high-grade (AA rated or equivalent) fixed-income investments with cash flow streams approximating payments under the plans. The lower discount rate increased the accumulated postretirement benefit obligation by $99.6 million and is expected to increase expense in 1994 by $7.6 million.

As a result of plan amendments discussed above, separate assumed health care cost trend rates are used for current retirees and employees retiring after Year 8. The assumed health care cost trend rate for current retirees was 12.5% for Year 7, 11.5% for Year 8 and is 10.5% for Year 9, declining gradually to 5.5% in Year 19 and thereafter. A one-percentage-point increase in the assumed health care cost trend rate would have increased the Year 8 postretirement benefit expense by $6.4 million and would have increased the Year 8 accumulated postretirement benefit obligation by $82.7 million.

II. PENSION PLANS

PepsiCo sponsors noncontributory defined benefit pension plans covering substantially all full-time domestic employees as well as contributory and noncontributory defined benefit pension plans covering certain international employees. Benefits generally are based on years of service and compensation or stated amounts for each year of service. PepsiCo funds the domestic plans in amounts not less than minimum statutory funding requirements nor more than the maximum amount that can be deducted for federal income tax purposes. International plans are funded in amounts sufficient to comply with local statutory requirements. The plans' assets consist principally of equity securities, government and corporate debt securities and other fixed-income obligations. PepsiCo Capital Stock accounted for approximately 22% and 24% of the total market value of the domestic plans' assets for Year 8 and Year 7, respectively.

Full-time domestic employees not covered by these plans generally are covered by multiemployer defined benefit plans as part of collective-bargaining agreements. Pension expense for these multiemployer plans was not significant in the aggregate.

The international plans presented below are primarily comprised of those in the U.K. for all three years, those in Canada for Year 7 and Year 8, as well as those in Mexico and Japan for Year 8. Information for Year 7 and Year 6 has not been re-stated, since complete information for plans in Mexico and Japan, and for those in Canada in Year 6, was not available. Information for Year 7 and Year 6, which had previously been reported on a combined basis for all plans, has been disaggregated to enhance comparability with the Year 8 presentation.

The net pension expense for company-sponsored plans included the following components:

	Domestic Plans			International Plans		
	Year 8	Year 7	Year 6	Year 8	Year 7	Year 6
Service cost of benefits earned	$ 57.1	$ 52.3	$ 40.5	$ 12.4	$ 8.6	$ 6.2
Interest cost on projected benefit obligation. .	75.6	72.0	62.6	15.0	10.9	6.7
Return on plan assets						
Actual	(161.5)	(61.3)	(205.2)	(40.8)	(36.0)	(18.9)
Deferred gain (loss)	70.9	(26.2)	122.9	20.4	18.6	5.8
	(90.6)	(87.5)	(82.3)	(20.4)	(17.4)	(13.1)
Amortization of net transition (gain) loss	(19.0)	(19.0)	(19.0)	0.3	—	—
Net other amortization	8.8	8.2	5.1	1.7	(6.5)	0.4
Pension expense (income).	$ 31.9	$ 26.0	$ 6.9	$ 9.0	$ (4.4)	$ 0.2

Inclusion of the plans in Mexico and Japan increased the Year 8 pension expense by $5.5 million. Inclusion of the plans in Canada increased the Year 8 and Year 7 pension expense by $3.4 million and $0.9 million, respectively.

Reconciliations of the funded status of the plans to the pension liability included in the Consolidated Balance Sheet are as follows:

| | Domestic Plans | | | | International Plans | | | |
| | Assets Exceed Accumulated Benefits | | Accumulated Benefits Exceed Assets | | Assets Exceed Accumulated Benefits | | Accumulated Benefits Exceed Assets | |
	Year 8	Year 7	Year 8	Year 7	Year 8	Year 7	Year 8	Year 7
Actuarial present value of benefit obligations								
Vested benefits	$ (726.0)	$ (721.0)	$(192.8)	$(15.9)	$(138.8)	$ (98.5)	$(28.0)	$(18.0)
Nonvested benefits	(99.0)	(76.3)	(28.3)	(1.4)	(3.4)	(1.8)	(5.4)	(1.2)
Accumulated benefit obligation	(825.0)	(797.3)	(221.1)	(17.3)	(142.2)	(100.3)	(33.4)	(19.2)
Effect of projected compensation increases	(131.6)	(124.9)	(41.7)	(19.9)	(22.9)	(17.6)	(18.4)	(3.9)
Projected benefit obligation	(956.6)	(922.2)	(262.8)	(37.2)	(165.1)	(117.9)	(51.8)	(23.1)
Plan assets at fair value	1,018.7	1,096.2	185.2	2.4	221.7	186.1	17.3	14.5
Plan assets in excess of (less than) projected benefit obligation	62.1	174.0	(77.6)	(34.8)	56.6	68.2	(34.5)	(8.6)
Unrecognized prior service cost	11.7	44.0	49.9	4.9	3.2	3.0	0.5	0.3
Unrecognized net loss (gain)	16.0	(77.7)	26.1	14.2	11.9	3.7	7.7	6.0
Unrecognized net transition (gain) loss	(89.0)	(111.2)	(2.8)	0.4	(2.6)	(2.6)	8.1	(0.8)
Adjustment required to recognize minimum liability	—	—	(33.0)	—	—	—	(4.3)	—
Prepaid (accrued) pension liability	$ 0.8	$ 29.1	$ (37.4)	$(15.3)	$ 69.1	$ 72.3	$(22.5)	$ (3.1)

The assumptions used in computing the information above were as follows:

	Domestic Plans			International Plans		
	Year 8	Year 7	Year 6	Year 8	Year 7	Year 6
Discount rate—pension expense....	8.2%	8.4	9.5	9.0%	9.5	10.4
Expected long-term rate of return on plan assets.................	10.0%	10.0	10.0	10.8%	10.8	11.9
Discount rate—projected benefit obligation	7.0%	8.2	8.4	7.4%	9.0	10.2
Future compensation growth rate ...	3.3%–7.0%	3.3–7.0	3.3–7.4	3.5%–8.5%	5.0–7.0	6.8–7.0

The discount rates and rates of return for the international plans represent weighted averages.

The lower discount rates used in determining the Year 8 projected benefit obligation reflect the decline in interest rates. The discount rates represent the expected yields on a diversified portfolio of high-grade (AA rated or equivalent) fixed-income investments with cash flow streams approximating payments under the plans. The lower discount rates increased the projected benefit obligation for all plans and changed the funded status of certain plans from overfunded to underfunded. The lower discount rates are expected to result in an estimated $43.2 million noncash increase in pension expense related to Year 9.

In Year 9, PepsiCo will change the method for calculating the market-related value of plan assets used in determining the return-on-asset component of annual pension expense and the cumulative net unrecognized gain or loss subject to amortization. Under the current accounting method, the calculation of the market-related value of assets reflects amortization of the actual capital return on assets on a straight-line basis over a five-year period. Under the new method, the calculation of the market-related value of assets reflects the long-term rate of return expected by PepsiCo and amortization of the difference between the actual return (including capital, dividends and interest) and the expected return over a five-year period. PepsiCo believes the new method is widely used in practice and preferable because it results in calculated plan asset values that more closely approximate fair value, while still mitigating the effect of annual market-value fluctuations. Under both methods, only the cumulative net unrecognized gain or loss which exceeds 10% of the greater of the projected benefit obligation or the market-related value of plan assets is subject to amortization. The noncash benefit in Year 9 of adopting this change is expected to include a cumulative effect credit of approximately $37.5 million ($22.9 million after-tax) related to years prior to Year 9, and an estimated $35.0 million in lower pension expense related to Year 9 as compared to the current accounting method.

12. POSTEMPLOYMENT BENEFITS OTHER THAN TO RETIREES

In November Year 7, the Financial Accounting Standards Board issued Statement of Financial Accounting Standards No. 112 (SFAS 112), "Employers' Accounting for Postemployment Benefits." SFAS 112, which must be adopted in the first quarter of

Year 9, requires employers to accrue the cost of postemployment benefits (including continuation of salary and health care coverage, severance and disability-related benefits) to terminated or inactive employees (and their dependents) other than retirees. SFAS 112 requires immediate recognition of any unrecorded obligation upon adoption. PepsiCo accrues some, but not all postemployment benefits.

PepsiCo has not yet determined the severance amounts that will be accrued based on the occurrence of an event or over expected service lives, and therefore has not yet estimated the cumulative effect charge upon adoption of SFAS 112 or the incremental expense in Year 9 aside from the cumulative effect. The adoption of SFAS 112 will have no impact on cash flows as PepsiCo will continue to largely fund these benefit costs as incurred.

13. INCOME TAXES

Effective December 29, Year 6, PepsiCo adopted Statement of Financial Accounting Standards No. 109 (SFAS 109), "Accounting for Income Taxes." PepsiCo elected to adopt SFAS 109 on a prospective basis as a change in accounting principle, resulting in a noncash tax charge in Year 7 of $570.7 million ($0.71 per share) for the cumulative effect of the change related to years prior to Year 7. The cumulative effect primarily represents the recording of additional deferred tax liabilities related to identifiable intangible assets, principally acquired trademarks and reacquired franchise rights, that have no tax bases. These deferred tax liabilities would be paid only in the unlikely event the related intangible assets were sold in taxable transactions.

Detail of the provision for income taxes on income from continuing operations before cumulative effect of accounting changes:

	Year 8	Year 7	Year 6
Current—Federal	$466.8	$413.0	$315.5
Foreign	195.5	170.4	114.3
State	89.0	65.7	51.5
	751.3	649.1	481.3
Deferred—Federal	78.2	(18.8)	63.5
Foreign	(12.5)	(33.5)	25.3
State	17.6	0.3	9.4
	83.3	(52.0)	98.2
	$834.6	$597.1	$579.5

In Year 8, a charge of $29.9 million ($0.04 per share) was recorded to increase net deferred tax liabilities as of the beginning of Year 8 for the 1% statutory rate increase under the new U.S. tax legislation. The effect of the higher rate on the Year 8 increase in net deferred tax liabilities through the enactment date of the legislation was immaterial. Of the charge, $25.2 million is included in the deferred federal provision and $4.7 million related to Safe Harbor Leases (discussed below) is included in Selling, general and administrative expenses.

As compared to the previous accounting method, the adoption of SFAS 109 reduced Year 7 pretax income by $20.7 million, but also reduced the deferred provision for income taxes by $33.7 million, resulting in an increase of $13.0 million ($0.02 per share) in income before the cumulative effect.

The Year 6 amounts above were calculated under the previous accounting method. The Year 6 deferred provision arose principally from accelerated expense recognition for tax purposes as compared to financial reporting and included amounts related to depreciation of property, plant and equipment of $56.2 million, amortization of intangibles of $49.0 million and increased prefunding of employee benefits of $23.3 million, partially offset by $41.7 million related to restructuring charges.

Tax benefits associated with exercises of stock options totaled $23.4 million in Year 8, $57.5 million in Year 7 and $8.5 million in Year 6. These amounts were credited to shareholders' equity. A change in the functional currency of operations in Mexico from the U.S. dollar to local currency in Year 8 resulted in a $19.3 million decrease in the net deferred foreign tax liability that was credited to shareholders' equity.

U.S. and foreign income before income taxes and cumulative effect of accounting changes:

	Year 8	Year 7	Year 6
U.S.	$1,633.0	$1,196.8	$1,054.3
Foreign	789.5	702.0	605.4
	$2,422.5	$1,898.8	$1,659.7

PepsiCo operates centralized concentrate manufacturing facilities in Puerto Rico and Ireland under long-term tax incentives. The foreign amount in the above table includes approximately 50% (consistent with the allocation for tax purposes) of the income from U.S. sales of concentrate manufactured in Puerto Rico.

Reconciliation of the U.S. federal statutory tax rate to PepsiCo's effective tax rate on pretax income, based on the dollar impact of these major components on the provision for income taxes:

	Year 8	Year 7	Year 6
U.S. federal statutory tax rate	35.0%	34.0%	34.0%
State income tax, net of federal tax benefit	2.9	2.3	2.4
Effect of lower taxes on foreign income (including Puerto Rico and Ireland)	(3.3)	(5.0)	(2.7)
Reduction of prior year foreign accruals	(2.0)	—	—
Effect of Year 8 tax legislation on deferred income taxes	1.1	—	—
Nondeductible amortization of domestic goodwill (all years) and other intangible assets (Year 6 only)	0.8	0.9	1.8
Other, net	—	(0.8)	(0.6)
Effective tax rate	34.5%	31.4%	34.9%

Detail of the Year 8 and Year 7 deferred tax liabilities (assets):

	Year 8	Year 7
Intangible assets other than nondeductible goodwill	$ 1,551.0	$1,292.2
Property, plant and equipment	552.3	526.8
Safe Harbor Leases.	177.5	185.6
Zero coupon notes.	103.5	96.0
Other.	549.0	233.2
Gross deferred tax liabilities	2,933.3	2,333.8
Postretirement benefits.	(268.0)	(238.4)
Net operating loss carryforwards	(241.5)	(138.6)
Restructuring accruals	(42.0)	(73.2)
Deferred state income taxes.	(39.9)	(63.3)
Various accrued liabilities and other.	(697.6)	(383.0)
Gross deferred tax assets	(1,289.0)	(896.5)
Deferred tax assets valuation allowance.	249.0	181.3
Net deferred tax liability.	$ 1,893.3	$1,618.6
Included in:		
"Prepaid expenses, taxes and other current assets".	$ (138.2)	$ (107.9)
"Other current liabilities".	23.9	44.2
"Deferred Income Taxes"	2,007.6	1,682.3
	$ 1,893.3	$1,618.6

The valuation allowance related to deferred tax assets rose by $67.7 million in Year 8 and $38.5 million in Year 7, which offset higher deferred tax assets arising primarily from increased net operating loss carryforwards. The net operating loss carryforwards largely relate to a number of foreign and state jurisdictions and expire over a range of dates.

The deferred tax liability for Safe Harbor Leases (the Leases) is related to transactions, which PepsiCo entered into over a decade ago, that decreased income taxes paid by PepsiCo over the initial years of the Leases and are now increasing taxes payable. Additional taxes paid in Year 8 related to the Leases totaled $6.4 million, and taxes payable are estimated to be $40.5 million over the next five years. The provision for income taxes is not impacted by the Leases.

Deferred tax liabilities have not been recognized for bases differences related to investments in foreign subsidiaries and joint ventures. These differences, which consist primarily of unremitted earnings intended to be indefinitely reinvested, aggregated approximately $3.2 billion at year-end 8 and $2.4 billion at year-end 7, exclusive of amounts that if remitted in the future would result in little or no tax under current tax laws and the Puerto Rico tax incentive grant. Determination of the amount of unrecognized deferred tax liabilities is not practicable.

14. FRANCHISE ARRANGEMENTS

Franchise arrangements with restaurant franchisees generally provide for initial fees and continuing royalty payments to PepsiCo based upon a percentage of sales. The arrangements are intended to assist franchisees through, among other things, product development and marketing programs initiated by PepsiCo for both its company-owned and franchised operations. On a limited basis, franchisees have also entered into leases of restaurant properties leased or owned by PepsiCo. (See Note 9.) Royalty revenues, initial fees and rental payments from franchisees, which are included in Net Sales, aggregated $357 million, $344 million and $326 million in Year 8, Year 7 and Year 6, respectively. Franchise royalty revenues, which represent the majority of these amounts, are recognized when earned. PepsiCo also has franchise arrangements with beverage bottlers, which do not provide for royalty payments.

15. EMPLOYEE INCENTIVE PLANS

PepsiCo has established certain employee incentive plans under which stock options are granted. A stock option allows an employee to purchase a share of PepsiCo Capital Stock (Stock) in the future at the fair market value on the date of the grant.

Under the PepsiCo SharePower Stock Option Plan (SharePower), approved by the Board of Directors and effective in Year 4, essentially all employees other than executive officers, part-time and short-service employees may be granted stock options annually. The number of options granted is based on each employee's annual earnings. The options generally become exercisable ratably over five years from the grant date and must be exercised within 10 years of the grant date. SharePower options were granted to approximately 118,000 employees in Year 8 and 114,000 employees in Year 7.

The shareholder-Year 2 Long-Term Incentive Plan (the Plan), which has provisions similar to plans in place in prior years, provides incentives to eligible senior and middle management employees. In addition to grants of stock options, which are generally exercisable between 1 and 15 years from the grant date, the Plan allows for grants of performance share units (PSUs) to eligible senior management employees. A PSU is equivalent in value to a share of Stock at the grant date and vests for payment four years from the grant date, contingent upon attainment of prescribed performance goals. PSUs are not directly granted, as certain stock options granted may be surrendered by employees for a specified number of PSUs within 60 days of the option grant date. During Year 8, 96,165 stock options were surrendered for 32,055 PSUs. At year-end 8 and 7, there were 491,200 and 484,698 outstanding PSUs, respectively.

The Plan also provides for incentive stock units (ISUs), which were granted to eligible middle management employees. Since Year 4 these employees have been granted stock options rather than ISUs. ISUs vest for payment at specified dates over a six-year period, and each ISU is equivalent in value to a share of Stock at those respective dates. At year-end 8 and 7, there were 5,700 and 127,565 outstanding ISUs, respectively.

Grants under the Plan are approved by the Compensation Committee of the Board of Directors (the Committee), which is composed of outside directors. Payment of awards other than stock options is made in cash and/or Stock as approved by the Committee, and amounts expensed for such awards were $5 million, $11 million and $15 million in Year 8, Year 7 and Year 6, respectively. Under the Plan, a maximum of 54 million shares of Stock can be purchased or paid pursuant to grants. There were 20 million and 22 million shares available for future grants at year-end 8 and 7, respectively.

Year 8 and Year 7 activity for the stock option plans included:

(options in thousands)	SharePower	Long-Term Incentive
Outstanding at December 28, Year 6	23,801	27,834
Granted..............................	8,477	12,653
Exercised	(1,155)	(5,155)
Surrendered for PSUs...................	—	(503)
Canceled.............................	(2,327)	(1,839)
Outstanding at December 26, Year 7	28,796	32,990
Granted..............................	**9,121**	**2,834**
Exercised	(1,958)	(1,412)
Surrendered for PSUs...................	—	(96)
Canceled.............................	(2,524)	(966)
Outstanding at December 25, Year 8	33,435	33,350
Exercisable at December 25, Year 8	11,733	10,665
Option prices per share		
Exercised during Year 8	$17.58 to $36.75	$4.11 to $36.31
Exercised during Year 7	$17.58 to $35.25	$4.11 to $29.88
Outstanding at year-end 8	$17.58 to $36.75	$4.11 to $42.81

16. Fair Value of Financial Instruments

PepsiCo's financial instruments include cash, cash equivalents, short-term investments, debt, interest rate swap agreements, currency exchange agreements and guarantees. Because of the short maturity of cash equivalents and investments which mature in less than one year, the carrying value approximates fair value. The fair value of investments which mature in more than one year is based upon market quotes. The fair value of debt issuances, interest rate swap agreements and currency exchange agreements is estimated using market quotes, valuation models and calculations based on market rates. At year-end 8 and 7, the carrying value of all financial instruments was not materially different from fair value.

17. Contingencies

PepsiCo is subject to various claims and contingencies related to lawsuits, taxes, environmental and other matters arising out of the normal course of business. Management believes that the ultimate liability, if any, in excess of amounts already provided arising from such claims or contingencies is not likely to have a material adverse effect on PepsiCo's annual results of operations or financial condition. At year-end Year 8 and 7, PepsiCo was contingently liable under guarantees aggregating $276 million and $200 million, respectively. The guarantees are primarily issued to support financial arrangements of certain bottling and restaurant franchisees and PepsiCo joint ventures. PepsiCo manages the risk associated with these guarantees by performing appropriate credit reviews in addition to retaining certain rights as a franchisor or joint venture partner.

18. Segment Data

	Net Sales					Operating Profits				
	Year 8	Year 7	Year 6	Year 5	Year 4	Year 8	Year 7	Year 6	Year 5	Year 4
Industry Segments										
Beverages: Domestic	$ 5,918.1	$ 5,485.2	$ 5,171.5	$ 5,034.5	$ 4,623.3	$ 936.9	$ 686.3	$ 746.2	$ 673.8	$ 577.6
International	2,720.1	2,120.4	1,743.7	1,488.5	1,153.4	172.1	112.3	117.1	93.8	98.6
	8,638.2	7,605.6	6,915.2	6,523.0	5,776.7	1,109.0	798.6	863.3	767.6	676.2
Snack Foods: Domestic	4,365.3	3,950.4	3,737.9	3,471.5	3,211.3	900.7	775.5	616.6	732.3	667.8
International	2,661.5	2,181.7	1,512.2	1,295.3	810.5	288.9	209.2	140.1	160.3	105.9
	7,026.8	6,132.1	5,250.1	4,766.8	4,021.8	1,189.6	984.7	756.7	892.6	773.7
Restaurants: Domestic	8,025.7	7,115.4	6,258.4	5,540.9	4,684.8	685.1	597.8	479.4	447.2	356.5
International	1,330.0	1,116.9	868.5	684.8	565.9	92.9	120.7	96.2	75.2	57.8
	9,355.7	8,232.3	7,126.9	6,225.7	5,250.7	778.0	718.5	575.6	522.4	414.3
Combined Segments										
Domestic	18,309.1	16,551.0	15,167.8	14,046.9	12,519.4	2,522.7	2,059.6	1,842.2	1,853.3	1,601.9
International	6,711.6	5,419.0	4,124.4	3,468.6	2,529.8	553.9	442.2	353.4	329.3	262.3
	$25,020.7	$21,970.0	$19,292.2	$17,515.5	$15,049.2	$3,076.6	$2,501.8	$2,195.6	$2,182.6	$1,864.2
Unallocated Expenses, net						(170.1)	(130.6)	(83.8)	(140.5)	(91.6)
Operating Profit						$2,906.5	$2,371.2	$2,111.8	$2,042.1	$1,772.6
Results by Restaurant Chain										
Pizza Hut	$ 4,128.7	$ 3,603.5	$ 3,258.3	$ 2,949.9	$ 2,453.5	$ 372.1	$ 335.4	$ 314.5	$ 245.9	$ 205.5
Taco Bell	2,901.3	2,460.0	2,038.1	1,745.5	1,465.9	253.1	214.3	180.6	149.6	109.4
KFC	2,325.7	2,168.8	1,830.5	1,530.3	1,331.3	152.8	168.8	80.5	126.9	99.4
	$ 9,355.7	$ 8,232.3	$ 7,126.9	$ 6,225.7	$ 5,250.7	$ 778.0	$ 718.5	$ 575.6	$ 522.4	$ 414.3

	Net Sales			Segment Operating Profits			Identifiable Assets[b]		
	Year 8	Year 7	Year 6	Year 8	Year 7	Year 6	Year 8	Year 7	Year 6
Geographic Areas[a]									
United States	$18,309.1	$16,551.0	$15,167.8	$2,522.7	$2,059.6	$1,842.2	$13,589.5	$11,957.0	$10,777.8
Canada and Mexico	2,819.5	2,214.2	1,434.7	324.8	251.0	198.7	2,581.1	2,395.2	917.3
Europe	1,819.0	1,349.0	1,170.3	47.4	52.6	30.9	2,666.1	1,948.4	2,367.3
Other	2,073.1	1,855.8	1,519.4	181.7	138.6	123.8	1,675.1	1,282.0	1,138.7
Total	$25,020.7	$21,970.0	$19,292.2	$3,076.6	$2,501.8	$2,195.6	$20,511.8	$17,582.6	$15,201.1

Identifiable Assets

Industry Segments	Year 8	Year 7	Year 6
Beverages	$ 9,105.2	$ 7,857.5	$ 6,832.6
Snack Foods	4,994.5	4,628.0	4,114.3
Restaurants	6,412.1	5,097.1	4,254.2
Corporate	3,194.0	3,368.6	3,574.0
Total	$23,705.8	$20,951.2	$18,775.1

By Restaurant Chain:	Year 8	Year 7	Year 6
Pizza Hut	$2,232.9	$1,676.8	$1,454.3
Taco Bell	2,075.9	1,523.7	1,157.1
KFC	2,103.3	1,896.6	1,642.8
Total	$6,412.1	$5,097.1	$4,254.2

Capital Spending[b]

Industry Segments	Year 8	Year 7	Year 6
Beverages	$ 491.3	$ 343.7	$ 425.8
Snack Foods	491.4	446.2	406.0
Restaurants	1,004.4	757.2	648.4
Corporate	20.8	18.0	4.1
Total	$2,007.9	$1,565.1	$1,484.3
Domestic	$1,388.0	$1,069.0	$1,036.9
International	619.9	496.1	447.4
Total	$2,007.9	$1,565.1	$1,484.3

By Restaurant Chain:	Year 8	Year 7	Year 6
Pizza Hut	$ 295.0	$212.8	$214.7
Taco Bell	459.4	339.0	230.5
KFC	250.0	205.4	203.2
Total	$1,004.4	$757.2	$648.4

Acquisitions and Investments in Affiliates[c]

Industry Segments	Year 8	Year 7	Year 6
Beverages	$ 711.5	$ 717.5	$285.2
Snack Foods	75.5	201.3	47.7
Restaurants	588.7	480.4	470.7
Total	$1,375.7	$1,399.2	$803.6
Domestic	$ 757.3	$ 549.5	$608.3
International	618.4	849.7	195.3
Total	$1,375.7	$1,399.2	$803.6

By Restaurant Chain:	Year 8	Year 7	Year 6
Pizza Hut	$312.9	$247.7	$103.1
Taco Bell	186.8	72.4	52.3
KFC	89.0	160.3	315.3
Total	$588.7	$480.4	$470.7

Amortization of Intangible Assets

	Year 8	Year 7	Year 6
Beverages	$157.4	$137.6	$118.3
Snack Foods	40.9	40.5	35.9
Restaurants	105.4	87.8	54.1
Total	$303.7	$265.9	$208.3
By Restaurant Chain:			
Pizza Hut	$ 44.7	$33.3	$25.6
Taco Bell	23.0	16.4	11.4
KFC	37.7	38.1	17.1
Total	$105.4	$87.8	$54.1

Depreciation Expense

	Year 8	Year 7	Year 6
Beverages	$ 358.5	$290.6	$251.7
Snack Foods	279.2	251.2	215.8
Restaurants	457.2	374.3	324.4
Corporate	6.6	6.9	8.1
Total	$1,101.5	$923.0	$800.0
By Restaurant Chain:			
Pizza Hut	$193.4	$150.5	$136.6
Taco Bell	124.6	101.5	82.5
KFC	139.2	122.3	105.3
Total	$457.2	$374.3	$324.4

(a) The results of centralized concentrate manufacturing operations in Puerto Rico and Ireland have been allocated based upon sales to the respective areas.

(b) Includes noncash amounts related to capital leases, largely in the restaurant segment, of $26.3 in Year 8, $15.5 in Year 7 and $26.5 in Year 6.

(c) Includes noncash amounts related to treasury stock and debt issued in domestic transactions of $364.5 in Year 8, $189.5 in Year 7 and $162.7 in Year 6. Of these noncash amounts, 65%, 58% and 8%, respectively, related to the beverage segment and the balance related to the restaurant segment.

APPENDIX C

1A_FSAP OUTPUT FOR COKE AND PEPSICO.

1.1 CFA—CHANGES IN CASH FLOW

	Year 4	Year 5	Year 6	Year 7	Year 8
OPERATING:					
Income from Continued Operations	1,724	1,382	1,618	1,664	2,176
Depreciation and Amortization	184	244	261	322	360
Other Addbacks	37	98	99	346	99
Other Subtractions	-1,114	-261	-117	-56	-181
Decrease(Increase) in Receivables	-100	-88	-32	-147	-151
Decrease(Increase) in Inventory	-35	-169	-3	-138	-41
Decrease(Increase) in Other CA	-204	-66	-326	-112	-76
Increase(Decrease) A&N Payable—Trade	89	199	267	405	-44
Increase(Decrease) in Other CL	529	-55	317	-52	366
CASH FROM CONTINUED OPERATIONS	1,110	1,284	2,084	2,232	2,508
+ Cash from Discontinued Operations & Extraordinary Items	0	0	0	0	0
TOTAL CASH FROM OPERATIONS	1,110	1,284	2,084	2,232	2,508
INVESTING:					
Fixed Assets Acquired (Sold)	402	574	748	1,036	488
Investments Acquired (Sold)	956	108	-218	-523	-166
Other Investing Transactions	0	27	-158	199	-231
CASH BEFORE DIVIDENDS AND EXTERNAL FINANCING	1,664	845	960	872	1,623
Less Dividends:	490	552	640	738	883
CASH BEFORE EXTERNAL FINANCING	1,174	293	320	134	740
FINANCING:					
Increase(Decrease) ST Borrowing	165	472	-711	880	-419
Increase(Decrease) LT Borrowing	-240	38	454	69	297
Increase(Decrease) Capital Stock	-1,126	-502	-435	-1,128	-535
Other Financing Transactions	-22	33	1	-58	-41
CHANGE IN CASH	-49	334	-371	-103	42

1.2 CASH FLOW ANALYSIS—INTERPERIOD PERCENT CHANGES

	COMPOUND GROWTH RATE	INTERPERIOD PERCENT CHANGE			
		Year 5	Year 6	Year 7	Year 8
OPERATING:					
Income from Continued Operations	6.0%	-19.8%	17.1%	2.8%	30.8%
Depreciation and Amortization	18.3%	32.6%	7.0%	23.4%	11.8%
Other Addbacks	27.9%	164.9%	1.0%	249.5%	-71.4%
Other Subtractions	-36.5%	-76.6%	-55.2%	-52.1%	223.2%
Decrease(Increase) in Receivables	10.9%	-12.0%	-63.6%	359.4%	2.7%
Decrease(Increase) in Inventory	4.0%	382.9%	-98.2%	4500.0%	-70.3%
Decrease(Increase) in Other CA	-21.9%	-67.6%	393.9%	-65.6%	-32.1%
Increase(Decrease) A&N Payable-Trade	ERR	123.6%	34.2%	51.7%	-110.9%
Increase(Decrease) in Other CL	-8.8%	-110.4%	-676.4%	-116.4%	-803.8%
CASH FROM CONTINUED OPERATIONS	22.6%	15.7%	62.3%	7.1%	12.4%
+ Cash from Discontinued Operations & Extraordinary Items	0.0%	0.0%	0.0%	0.0%	0.0%
TOTAL CASH FROM OPERATIONS	22.6%	15.7%	62.3%	7.1%	12.4%
INVESTING:					
PP&E Acquired/Sold	5.0%	42.8%	30.3%	38.5%	-52.9%
Increase(Decrease) in Investments	344	-88.7%	-301.9%	139.9%	-68.3%
Other NC Operating Assets Acquired	0.0%	0.0%	-685.2%	-225.9%	-216.1%
CASH BEFORE DIVIDENDS AND EXTERNAL FINANCING	-0.6%	-49.2%	13.6%	-9.2%	86.1%
Less Dividends:	15.9%	12.7%	15.9%	15.3%	19.6%
CASH BEFORE EXTERNAL FINANCING	-10.9%	-75.0%	9.2%	-58.1%	452.2%
FINANCING:					
Increase(Decrease) ST Borrowing	ERR	186.1%	-250.6%	-223.8%	-147.6%
Increase(Decrease) LT borrowing	ERR	-115.8%	1094.7%	-84.8%	330.4%
Increase(Decrease) Capital Stock	-17.0%	-55.4%	-13.3%	159.3%	-52.6%
CHANGE IN CASH	ERR	-781.6%	-211.1%	-72.2%	-140.8%

2.1 PROFITABILITY FACTORS

	Year 4	Year 5	Year 6	Year 7	Year 8
RETURN ON ASSETS:					
Profit Margin	21.5%	15.0%	15.1%	13.6%	16.4%
x Asset Turnover	1.1	1.2	1.2	1.2	1.2
= Return On Assets	24.5%	17.5%	17.9%	16.7%	19.8%
RETURN ON COMMON EQUITY:					
Return On Assets	24.5%	17.5%	17.9%	16.7%	19.8%
x Common Earnings Leverage	88.3%	88.9%	92.6%	93.6%	95.2%
x Capital Structure Leverage	2.5	2.5	2.4	2.6	2.7
= Return On Common Equity	54.6%	39.2%	39.4%	40.0%	51.4%
OPERATING PERFORMANCE:					
Gross Margin/Sales	56.6%	58.9%	59.8%	61.3%	63.0%
Operating Profit Before Tax/Revenues	22.3%	21.3%	21.8%	22.1%	23.6%
Net Income-Continued Operations/Revenues	18.5%	13.1%	13.7%	12.6%	15.3%
ASSET TURNOVER					
Sales/Average Accounts Receivable	11.2	11.5	12.0	12.7	12.0
COGS/Average Inventory	5.0	4.8	4.7	5.0	5.0
Sales/Average Fixed Assets	4.7	4.6	4.4	4.1	3.8

2.2 RISK FACTORS

	Year 4	Year 5	Year 6	Year 7	Year 8
LIQUIDITY:					
Current	0.99	0.96	1.01	0.80	0.86
Quick Ratio	0.55	0.57	0.51	0.41	0.45
Days Payables Held	115	123	137	150	157
Days Receivable Held	33	32	30	29	30
Days Inventory Held	74	77	77	72	73
Operating Cash Flow To					
Current Liabilities	34.0%	32.3%	49.5%	47.4%	47.9%
SOLVENCY:					
Total Liabilities/Total Assets	57.9%	58.5%	56.7%	64.8%	61.9%
LT Debt/Total Assets	6.6%	5.8%	9.6%	10.1%	11.9%
LT Debt/Owner's Equity	15.7%	13.9%	22.3%	28.8%	31.2%
Operating Cash Flow to					
Total Liabilities	24.9%	25.1%	37.1%	34.4%	34.4%
Interest Coverage Ratio	6.73	9.76	13.35	17.06	19.96
Operating Cash Flow to Capital					
Expense	2.40	2.17	2.63	2.06	3.14

3.1 INCOME STATEMENT ITEMS AS PERCENT OF SALES

	Year 4	Year 5	Year 6	Year 7	Year 8
Sales	100.0%	100.0%	100.0%	100.0%	100.0%
Cost of Goods Sold	-43.4%	-41.1%	-40.2%	-38.7%	-37.0%
GROSS MARGIN	56.6%	58.9%	59.8%	61.3%	63.0%
Other Revenue	3.9%	2.9%	2.2%	1.1%	1.8%
Selling, General, &					
Administrative Expenses	-37.3%	-39.8%	-39.8%	-40.2%	-40.8%
Other Expenses & Losses	0.0%	0.0%	0.0%	0.0%	0.0%
Income Tax Expense on Operations	-7.5%	-6.9%	-7.2%	-7.0%	-7.6%
OPERATING MARGIN	15.6%	15.0%	15.1%	15.3%	16.5%
Interest Expense	-3.4%	-2.2%	-1.7%	-1.3%	-1.2%
Income Tax Savings on Interest	1.2%	0.8%	0.6%	0.4%	0.4%
Minority Interest in Earnings	0.0%	0.0%	0.0%	0.0%	0.0%
INCOME—CONTINUED OPERATIONS	13.3%	13.5%	14.0%	14.4%	15.7%
Income From Discontinued					
Operations	5.9%	0.0%	0.0%	0.0%	0.0%
Extraordinary Gains & Losses	0.0%	0.0%	0.0%	0.0%	0.0%
Changes in Accounting Principles	0.0%	0.0%	0.0%	-1.7%	-0.1%
NET INCOME	19.2%	13.5%	14.0%	12.7%	15.6%
Preferred Stock Dividend	0.2%	0.2%	0.0%	0.0%	0.0%
NET INCOME AVAILABLE TO					
COMMON SHAREHOLDERS	19.0%	13.3%	14.0%	12.7%	15.6%

3.2 INCOME STATEMENT ITEMS—INTERPERIOD PERCENT CHANGES

	COMPOUND GROWTH RATE	INTERPERIOD PERCENT CHANGES			
		Year 5	Year 6	Year 7	Year 8
Sales	11.7%	14.2%	13.1%	13.0%	6.8%
Cost of Goods Sold	7.3%	8.1%	10.4%	8.7%	2.1%
GROSS MARGIN	14.7%	18.8%	14.9%	15.8%	9.7%
Selling & Administrative					
Expense	14.2%	21.7%	13.0%	14.0%	8.5%
Income Tax Expense on					
Operations	11.8%	5.1%	16.8%	10.8%	14.7%
OPERATING MARGIN	13.3%	9.8%	13.8%	14.4%	15.0%

3.1 INCOME STATEMENT ITEMS AS PERCENT OF SALES—Continued

	Year 4	Year 5	Year 6	Year 7	Year 8
Interest Expense	-14.1%	-25.3%	-16.1%	-11.4%	-1.8%
Inc Tax Savings on Int	12.6%	-25.3%	-16.1%	-11.4%	1.1%
Minority Interest in Earnings	ERR	ERR	ERR	ERR	ERR
INCOME—CONTINUED OPERATIONS	16.4%	15.8%	17.1%	16.4%	16.1%
Income From Discontinued Operations	0.0%	-100.0%	0.0%	0.0%	0.0%
Extraordinary Gains & Losses	0.0%	0.0%	0.0%	0.0%	0.0%
Changes in Accounting Principles	0.0%	0.0%	0.0%	0.0%	-94.5%
NET INCOME	6.0%	-19.8%	17.1%	2.8%	30.8%
Preferred Stock Dividend	ERR	-18.2%	-94.4%	-100.0%	0.0%
NET INCOME AVAILABLE TO COMMON SHAREHOLDERS	6.3%	-19.9%	18.5%	2.9%	30.8%

4.1 BALANCE SHEET COMMON SIZE STATEMENT

	Year 4	Year 5	Year 6	Year 7	Year 8
ASSETS:					
Cash and Market Securities	14.3%	16.1%	10.9%	9.6%	9.0%
Accounts/Notes Receivable	9.9%	10.3%	9.5%	9.8%	10.3%
Inventories	9.5%	10.6%	9.7%	9.2%	8.7%
Other Current Assets	9.8%	7.7%	10.5%	9.8%	8.9%
CURRENT ASSETS	43.5%	44.7%	40.5%	38.4%	36.9%
Investments	29.3%	26.7%	28.2%	26.2%	27.5%
Property, Plant, & Equipment	39.8%	40.8%	43.5%	47.4%	46.6%
Less Accumulated Depreciation	15.4%	15.1%	15.2%	15.5%	15.5%
Other Assets	2.8%	3.0%	3.0%	3.5%	4.6%
TOTAL ASSETS	100.0%	100.0%	100.0%	100.0%	100.0%
LIABILITIES:					
Accounts Payable-Trade	16.7%	17.0%	18.7%	20.4%	18.4%
Notes Payable—Non-Trade	17.3%	20.5%	11.7%	18.7%	13.8%
Current Part LT Debt	0.0%	1.0%	1.1%	0.1%	0.2%
Other Current Liabilities	10.1%	7.7%	8.8%	8.7%	10.7%
CURRENT LIABILITIES	44.2%	46.3%	40.3%	48.0%	43.0%
Long-Term Debt	6.6%	5.8%	9.6%	10.1%	11.9%
Deferred Tax (NCL)	3.6%	2.9%	2.0%	0.7%	0.9%
Other NCL	3.5%	3.6%	4.8%	6.0%	6.0%
Minority Interest in Subsidiaries	0.0%	0.0%	0.0%	0.0%	0.0%
NONCURRENT LIABILITIES	13.8%	12.2%	16.4%	16.8%	18.9%
TOTAL LIABILITIES	57.9%	58.5%	56.7%	64.8%	61.9%
STOCKHOLDERS' EQUITY:					
Preferred Stock	3.6%	0.8%	0.0%	0.0%	0.0%
Common Stock	5.1%	4.5%	4.1%	3.8%	3.5%
Additional Paid-in Capital	4.7%	4.8%	5.1%	7.0%	8.3%
Retained Earnings	67.8%	69.5%	72.6%	73.9%	78.7%
Treasury Stock	39.1%	38.2%	38.6%	47.1%	48.9%
Cumulative Translation Adjustments	-0.1%	0.0%	0.0%	-2.5%	-3.5%
STOCKHOLDERS' EQUITY	42.1%	41.5%	43.3%	35.2%	38.1%
TOTAL EQUITY & LIABILITIES	100.0%	100.0%	100.0%	100.0%	100.0%

4.2 BALANCE SHEET—INTERPERIOD PERCENT CHANGES

	COMPOUND GROWTH RATE	INTERPERIOD PERCENT CHANGES				
		Year 4	Year 5	Year 6	Year 7	Year 8
ASSETS:						
Cash and Market Securities	-2.6%	-4.0%	26.3%	-25.2%	-4.8%	1.4%
Accounts/Notes Receivable	9.7%	4.7%	16.0%	1.9%	12.0%	14.5%
Inventories	6.1%	1.3%	24.5%	0.6%	3.1%	2.9%
Other Current Assets	18.7%	80.0%	-11.8%	49.3%	1.0%	-1.5%
CURRENT ASSETS	6.4%	11.1%	15.0%	0.0%	2.5%	4.4%
Investments	6.7%	1.5%	2.0%	16.6%	0.3%	14.3%
Property, Plant, & Equipment	14.0%	13.3%	14.9%	17.4%	10.0%	6.7%
Less Accumulated Depreciation	10.2%	10.8%	9.9%	11.1%	10.4%	8.7%
Other Assets	57.3%	307.0%	18.5%	10.5%	26.0%	43.3
TOTAL ASSETS	10.0%	11.2%	12.0%	10.2%	8.1%	8.8%
LIABILITIES:						
Accounts/Notes Payable-Trade	15.4%	28.3%	13.6%	21.4%	17.7%	-1.6%
Notes Payable: Nontrade	3.9%	5.1%	33.0%	-37.3%	73.7%	-20.2%
Current Part LT Debt	0.0%	0.0%	0.0%	13.4%	-86.4%	26.7%
Other Current Liabilities	24.7%	97.4%	-14.3%	25.3%	6.9%	33.1%
CURRENT LIABILITIES	12.5%	27.5%	17.4%	-4.1%	28.8%	-2.5%
Long-Term Debt	13.4%	-27.9%	-2.4%	83.8%	13.7%	27.5%
Deferred Tax (NCL)	-16.0%	9.6%	-10.5%	-24.5%	-59.0%	37.8%
Other NCL	28.6%	42.7%	12.9%	48.8%	33.4%	10.0%
Minority Interest in Subsidiaries	0.0%	0.0%	0.0%	0.0%	0.0%	0.0%
NONCURRENT LIABILITIES	12.9%	-7.9%	-0.5%	48.2%	10.8%	21.8%
TOTAL LIABILITIES	12.6%	16.8%	13.2%	6.8%	23.6%	3.8%
STOCKHOLDER'S EQUITY:						
Preferred Stock	ERR	0.0%	-75.0%	-100.0%	0.0%	0.0%
Common Stock	0.4%	0.5%	0.2%	0.5%	0.5%	0.5%
Additional Paid-in Capital	24.9%	19.1%	13.5%	18.0%	46.9%	29.8%
Retained Earnings	16.6%	28.1%	14.8%	15.2%	10.0%	15.8%
Treasury Stock	23.2%	56.4%	9.5%	11.3%	31.9%	13.1%
Cumulative Translation Adjustment	89.9%	-58.8%	-157.1%	-225.0%	5320.0%	55.0%
STOCKHOLDERS' EQUITY	6.5%	4.2%	10.4%	15.0%	-12.2%	17.9%
TOTAL EQUITY & LIABILITIES	10.0%	11.2%	12.0%	10.2%	8.1%	8.8%

5.1 PROFITABILITY ANALYSIS

						Return on Assets			
Level 1						Year 6	Year 7	Year 8	
						17.9%	16.7%	19.8%	

	Profit Margin						Asset Turnover		
Level 2	Year 6	Year 7	Year 8				Year 6	Year 7	Year 8
	15.1%	13.6%	16.4%				1.2	1.2	1.2
Level 3	Year 6	Year 7	Year 8				Year 6	Year 7	Year 8
Sales	100.0%	100.0%	100.0%	Receivable					
COG Sold	-40.2	-38.7	-37.0	Turnover			12.0	12.7	12.0
Sell & Ad	-39.8	-40.2	-40.8	Inventory					
Other(net)	2.2	1.1	1.8	Turnover			4.7	5.0	5.0
Increase Taxes	-7.2	-7.0	-7.6	Fixed Asset					
Operating Increase	15.1%	15.3%	16.5%	Turnover			4.4	4.1	3.8

1A_FSAP Output for PepsiCo

1.1 CFA—CHANGES IN CASH FLOW

	Year 4	Year 5	Year 6	Year 7	Year 8
OPERATING:					
Income from Continued Operations	901	1,091	1.080	374	1,588
Depreciation and Amortization	772	884	1,034	1,215	1,444
Other Addbacks	200	226	350	1,244	428
Other Subtractions	0	-118	0	-52	0
Decrease(Increase) in Receivables	-150	-125	-56	-46	-161
Decrease(Increase) in Inventory	-50	-21	-55	-12	-89
Decrease(Increase) in Other CA	7	-62	-100	-27	3
Increase(Decrease) A&N Payable-Trade	135	26	58	-102	143
Increase(Decrease) in Other CL	71	209	119	118	-222
CASH FROM CONTINUED OPERATIONS	1,886	2,110	2,430	2,712	3,134
+ Cash from Discontinued					
& Extraordinary Items	0	0	0	0	0
TOTAL CASH FROM OPERATIONS	1,886	2,110	2,430	2,712	3,134
INVESTING:					
Fixed Assets Acquired (Sold)	874	1,135	1,388	1,461	1,910
Investments Acquired (Sold)	-3,284	-682	-782	-1,262	-752
Other Investing Transactions	-98	-120	-106	-31	-109
CASH BEFORE DIVIDENDS AND					
EXTERNAL FINANCING	-2,370	173	154	-42	363
Less Dividends:	242	294	343	396	462
CASH BEFORE EXTERNAL FINANCING	-2,612	-121	-189	-438	-99
FINANCING:					
Increase(Decrease) ST Borrowing	2,925	-86	-1,013	-76	1,081
Increase(Decrease) LT Borrowing	-334	479	1,452	477	-491
Increase(Decrease) Capital Stock	0	-139	-179	51	-394
Other Financing Transactions	-46	-38	-55	-31	-40
CHANGE IN CASH	-67	95	16	-17	57

1.2 CASH FLOW ANALYSIS - INTERPERIOD PERCENT CHANGES

	COMPOUND GROWTH RATE	INTERPERIOD PERCENT CHANGES			
		Year 5	Year 6	Year 7	Year 8
OPERATING:					
Income from Continued Operations	15.2%	21.1%	-1.0%	-65.4%	324.6%
Depreciation and Amortization	16.9%	14.5%	17.0%	17.5%	18.8%
Other Addbacks	20.9%	13.0%	54.9%	255.4%	-65.6%
Other Subtractions	0.0%	0.0%	-100.0%	0.0%	-100.0%
Decrease(Increase) in Receivables	1.8%	-16.7%	-55.2%	-17.9%	250.0%
Decrease(Increase) in Inventory	15.5%	-58.0%	161.9%	-78.2%	641.7%
Decrease(Increase) in Other CA	-19.1%	-985.7%	61.3%	-73.0%	-111.1%
Increase(Decrease) A&N Payable-Trade	1.4%	-80.7%	123.1%	-275.9%	-240.2%
Increase(Decrease) in Other CL	ERR	194.4%	-43.1%	-0.8%	-288.1%
CASH FROM CONTINUED OPERATIONS	13.5%	11.9%	15.2%	11.6%	15.6%
+ Cash from Discontinued					
& Extraordinary Items	0.0%	0.0%	0.0%	0.0%	0.0%
TOTAL CASH FROM OPERATIONS	13.5%	11.9%	15.2%	11.6%	15.6%
INVESTING:					
PP&E Acquired/Sold	21.6%	29.9%	22.3%	5.3%	30.7%
Increase(Decrease) in Investments	-30.8%	-79.2%	14.7%	61.4%	-40.4%
Other NC Operating Assets Acquired	2.7%	22.4%	-11.7%	-70.8%	251.6%

1.2 CASH FLOW ANALYSIS - INTERPERIOD PERCENT CHANGES Continued

	COMPOUND GROWTH RATE	INTERPERIOD PERCENT CHANGES			
		Year 5	Year 6	Year 7	Year 8
CASH BEFORE DIVIDENDS AND EXTERNAL FINANCING	ERR	-107.3%	-11.0%	-127.3%	-964.3%
Less Dividends:	17.5%	21.5%	16.7%	15.5%	16.7%
CASH BEFORE EXTERNAL FINANCING	-55.9%	-95.4%	56.2%	131.7%	-77.4%
FINANCING:					
Increase(Decrease) ST Borrowing	-22.0%	-102.9%	1077.9%	-92.5%	-1522.4%
Increase(Decrease) LT Borrowing	10.1%	-243.4%	203.1%	-67.1%	-202.9%
Increase(Decrease) Capital Stock	0.0%	0.0%	28.8%	-128.5%	-872.5%
CHANGE IN CASH	ERR	-241.8%	-83.2%	-206.3%	-435.3%

2.1 PROFITABILITY FACTORS

	Year 4	Year 5	Year 6	Year 7	Year 8
RETURN ON ASSETS:					
Profit Margin	8.6%	8.6%	7.7%	3.5%	7.8%
x Asset Turnover	1.2	1.1	1.1	1.1	1.1
= Return On Assets	9.9%	9.5%	8.3%	3.8%	8.8%
RETURN ON COMMON EQUITY:					
Return On Assets	9.9%	9.5%	8.3%	3.8%	8.8%
x Common Earnings Leverage	69.1%	70.3%	72.7%	49.2%	81.0%
x Capital Structure Leverage	3.7	3.7	3.4	3.6	3.8
= Return On Common Equity	25.6%	24.5%	20.7%	6.9%	27.2%
OPERATING PERFORMANCE:					
Gross Margin/Sales	51.3%	52.0%	51.5%	52.2%	52.3%
Operating Profit Before Tax/Revenues	12.7%	13.1%	11.7%	11.3%	11.9%
Net Income-Continued Operations/Revenues	5.8%	6.1%	5.6%	1.7%	6.3%
ASSET TURNOVER					
Sales/Average Accounts Receivables	13.7	13.4	13.3	14.3	14.4
COGS/Average Inventory	15.0	15.1	15.0	14.7	14.1
Sales/Average Fixed Assets	3.2	3.3	3.1	3.1	3.1

2.2 RISK FACTORS

	Year 4	Year 5	Year 6	Year 7	Year 7
LIQUIDITY:					
Current	0.96	0.86	1.23	1.06	0.79
Quick Ratio	0.75	0.68	0.95	0.80	0.57
Days Payables Held	47	46	45	41	39
Days Receivable Held	27	27	27	26	25
Days Inventory Held	24	24	24	25	26
Operating Cash Flow To Current Liabilities	49.9%	49.9%	57.2%	65.5%	56.3%
SOLVENCY:					
Total Liabilities/Total Assets	74.3%	71.4%	70.5%	74.4%	73.3%
LT Debt/Total Assets	40.2%	32.7%	41.6%	38.0%	31.4%
LT Debt/Owner's Equity	156.2%	114.2%	140.8%	148.7%	117.4%
Operating Cash Flow to Total Liabilities	19.6%	18.0%	19.1%	18.8%	19.0%
Interest Coverage Ratio	3.21	3.42	3.70	4.24	5.23
Operating Cash Flow to Capital Expense	2.00	1.79	1.67	1.75	1.58

3.1 INCOME STATEMENT ITEMS AS PERCENT OF SALES

	Year 4	Year 5	Year 6	Year 7	Year 8
Sales	100.0%	100.0%	100.0%	100.0%	100.0%
Cost of Goods Sold	-48.7%	-48.0%	-48.5%	-47.8%	-47.7%
GROSS MARGIN	51.3%	52.0%	51.5%	52.2%	52.3%
Other Revenue	1.2%	1.0%	0.8%	0.5%	0.4%
Selling, General,					
& Administrative Expense	-39.6%	-40.4%	-40.5%	-41.4%	-40.6%
Other Expenses & Losses	0.0%	0.7%	0.0%	0.0%	0.0%
Income Tax Expense on Operations	-4.3%	-4.6%	-4.1%	-3.6%	-4.1%
OPERATING MARGIN	8.6%	8.7%	7.7%	7.7%	7.8%
Interest Expense	-4.0%	-3.9%	-3.2%	-2.7%	-2.3%
Income Tax Savings on Interest	1.4%	1.3%	1.1%	0.9%	0.8%
Minority Interest in Earnings	0.0%	0.0%	0.0%	0.0%	0.0%
INCOME—CONTINUED OPERATIONS	5.9%	6.1%	5.6%	5.9%	6.3%
Income From Discontinued					
Operations	0.0%	-0.1%	0.0%	0.0%	0.0%
Extraordinary Gains & Losses	0.0%	0.0%	0.0%	0.0%	0.0%
Changes in Accounting Principles	0.0%	0.0%	0.0%	-4.2%	0.0%
NET INCOME	5.9%	6.0%	5.6%	1.7%	6.3%
Preferred Stock Dividend	0.0%	0.0%	0.0%	0.0%	0.0%
NET INCOME AVAILABLE TO					
COMMON SHAREHOLDERS	5.9%	6.0%	5.6%	1.7%	6.3%

3.2 INCOME STATEMENT ITEMS—INTERPERIOD PERCENT CHANGES

	COMPOUND GROWTH RATE	INTERPERIOD PERCENT CHANGES			
		Year 5	Year 6	Year 7	Year 8
Sales	13.2%	16.8%	8.4%	13.9%	13.9%
Cost of Goods Sold	12.6%	15.2%	9.6%	12.0%	13.8%
GROSS MARGIN	13.7%	18.3%	7.3%	15.6%	13.9%
Selling & Administrative Expense	13.9%	19.2%	8.6%	16.5%	11.7%
Income Tax Expense on Operations	12.1%	23.5%	-2.7%	0.9%	30.1%
OPERATING MARGIN	10.7%	18.5%	-3.9%	13.7%	16.1%
Interest Expense	-1.6%	12.8%	-10.8%	-4.6%	-2.2%
Income Tax Savings on Interest	28.9%	12.8%	-10.8%	-4.6%	0.7%
Minority Interest in Earnings	ERR	ERR	ERR	ERR	ERR
INCOME—CONTINUED OPERATIONS	15.2%	21.1%	-1.0%	20.6%	22.0%
Income From Discontinued Operations	0.0%	0.0%	-100.0%	0.0%	0.0%
Extraordinary Gains & Losses	0.0%	0.0%	0.0%	0.0%	0.0%
Changes in Accounting Principles	0.0%	0.0%	0.0%	0.0%	-100.0%
NET INCOME	15.2%	19.5%	0.3%	-65.4%	324.6%
Preferred Stock Dividend	0.0%	0.0%	0.0%	0.0%	0.0%
NET INCOME AVAILABLE TO					
COMMON SHAREHOLDERS	15.2%	19.5%	0.3%	-65.4%	324.6%

4.1 BALANCE SHEET COMMON SIZE STATEMENT

	Year 4	Year 5	Year 6	Year 7	Year 8
ASSETS:					
Cash and Market Securities	10.1%	10.6%	10.8%	9.8%	7.8%
Accts/Notes Receivable	8.2%	8.3%	7.9%	7.6%	7.9%
Inventories	3.6%	3.4%	3.5%	3.7%	3.9%
Other Current Assets	1.5%	1.5%	2.1%	2.0%	2.1%
CURRENT ASSETS	23.5%	23.8%	24.3%	23.1%	21.8%

4.1 BALANCE SHEET COMMON SIZE STATEMENT—Continued

	Year 4	Year 5	Year 6	Year 7	Year 8
Investments	6.4%	8.8%	9.0%	8.2%	7.4%
Property, Plant, & Equipment	51.7%	52.4%	55.9%	57.7%	60.1%
Less Accumulated Depreciation	17.8%	19.1%	20.8%	22.2%	22.8%
Other Assets	36.2%	34.1%	31.6%	33.2%	33.4%
TOTAL ASSETS	100.0%	100.0%	100.0%	100.0%	100.0%
LIABILITIES:					
Accounts Payable-Trade	7.0%	6.5%	6.4%	5.6%	5.9%
Notes Payable—Non-Trade	5.7%	9.5%	1.2%	3.4%	9.2%
Current Part LT Debt	0.0%	0.0%	0.0%	0.0%	0.0%
Other Current Liabilities	11.7%	11.8%	12.2%	12.8%	12.6%
CURRENT LIABILITIES	24.4%	27.8%	19.0%	21.8%	27.7%
Long-Term Debt	40.2%	32.7%	41.6%	38.0%	31.4%
Deferred Tax (NCL)	5.7%	5.5%	5.7%	8.0%	8.5%
Other NCL	4.0%	3.7%	3.4%	6.6%	5.7%
Minority Interest in Subsidiaries	0.0%	1.7%	0.0%	0.0%	0.0%
NON-CURRENT LIABILITIES	49.9%	43.6%	50.6%	52.7%	45.5%
TOTAL LIABILITIES	74.3%	71.4%	70.5%	74.4%	73.3%
STOCKHOLDERS' EQUITY:					
Preferred Stock	0.0%	0.0%	0.0%	0.0%	0.0%
Common Stock	0.0%	0.1%	0.1%	0.1%	0.1%
Additional Paid-in Capital	2.2%	2.1%	2.5%	3.2%	3.7%
Retained Earnings	26.3%	27.7%	29.1%	26.0%	27.6%
Treasury Stock	3.3%	3.6%	4.0%	3.2%	3.9%
Cumulative Translation Adjustments	0.4%	2.2%	1.8%	-0.5%	-0.8%
STOCKHOLDERS' EQUITY	25.7%	28.6%	29.5%	25.6%	26.7%
TOTAL EQUITY & LIABILITIES	100.0%	100.0%	100.0%	100.0%	100.0%

4.2 BALANCE SHEET—INTERPERIOD PERCENT CHANGES

	COMPOUND GROWTH RATE	INTERPERIOD PERCENT CHANGES				
		Year 4	Year 5	Year 6	Year 7	Year 8
ASSETS:						
Cash and Market Securities	02.8%	-5.2%	18.4%	12.1%	1.1%	-9.9%
Accounts/Notes Receivable	14.0%	26.7%	14.1%	4.7%	7.2%	18.6%
Inventories	15.9%	23.3%	7.3%	12.8%	16.3%	20.3%
Other Current Assets	17.3%	2.7%	14.7%	46.0%	10.1%	17.4%
CURRENT ASSETS	9.6%	8.8%	15.0%	11.9%	6.0%	6.7%
Investments	16.3%	17.6%	55.1%	11.7%	1.5%	2.9%
Property, Plant, & Equipment	16.4%	17.4%	14.8%	17.0%	15.2%	17.8%
Less Accumulated Depreciation	19.7%	22.4%	21.5%	19.6%	19.1%	15.9%
Other Assets	25.2%	112.0%	6.8%	1.5%	17.3%	13.9%
TOTAL ASSETS	16.3%	35.9%	13.3%	9.5%	11.6%	13.1%
LIABILITIES:						
Accounts/Notes Payable-Trade	9.5%	19.8%	5.8%	7.3%	-2.7%	19.3%
Notes Payable:Nontrade	8.6%	-40.3%	87.9%	-86.0%	210.1%	209.9%
Current Part LT Debt	0.0%	0.0%	0.0%	0.0%	0.0%	0.0%
Other Current Liabilities	14.2%	14.9%	14.5%	13.3%	16.9%	11.5%
CURRENT LIABILITIES	11.2%	-4.7%	29.2%	-22.0%	22.4%	44.3%
Long-Term Debt	22.9%	128.8%	-7.8%	39.4%	2.0%	-6.6%
Deferred Tax (NCL)	20.2%	7.0%	10.0%	13.5%	57.2%	19.4%
Other NCL	15.8%	-5.3%	2.6%	0.8%	120.4%	-3.5%
Minority Interest in Subsidiaries	0.0%	0.0%	0.0%	-100.0%	0.0%	0.0%
NON-CURRENT LIABILITIES	21.4%	84.0%	-1.0%	27.3%	16.1%	-2.2%
TOTAL LIABILITIES	16.8%	40.9%	8.9%	8.1%	17.9%	11.4%

4.2 BALANCE SHEET—INTERPERIOD PERCENT CHANGES—Continued

	COMPOUND GROWTH RATE	INTERPERIOD PERCENT CHANGES				
		Year 4	Year 5	Year 6	Year 7	Year 8
STOCKHOLDER'S EQUITY:						
Preferred Stock	0.0%	0.0%	0.0%	0.0%	0.0%	0.0%
Common Stock	22.9%	0.0%	180.0%	0.0%	0.0%	0.0%
Additional Paid-in Capital	23.0%	7.1%	9.3%	30.7%	40.0%	31.6%
Retained Earnings	14.5%	19.5%	19.5%	15.1%	-0.5%	20.3%
Treasury Stock	12.4%	-3.5%	24.2%	22.1%	-10.6%	36.9%
Cumulative Translation Adjustments	ERR	175.0%	480.3%	-13.6%	-129.9%	85.9%
STOCKHOLDERS' EQUITY	14.9%	23.1%	26.0%	13.1%	-3.4%	18.3%
TOTAL EQUITY & LIABILITIES	16.3%	35.9%	13.3%	9.5%	11.6%	13.1%

5.1 PROFITABILITY ANALYSIS

Return on Assets

Level 1

	Year 6	Year 7	Year 8
	8.3%	3.8%	8.8%

Profit Margin   **Asset Turnover**

Level 2

	Year 6	Year 7	Year 8		Year 6	Year 7	Year 8
	7.7%	3.5%	7.8%		1.1	1.1	1.1

Level 3

	Year 6	Year 7	Year 8		Year 6	Year 7	Year 8
Sales	100.0%	100.0%	100.0%	Receivable Turnover	13.3	14.3	14.4
COG Sold	-48.5	-47.8	-47.7				
Sell & Ad	-40.5	-41.4	-40.6	Inventory Turnover	15.0	14.7	14.1
Other (net)	0.8	0.5	0.4				
Increase Taxes	-4.1	-3.6	-4.1	Fixed Asset Turnover	3.1	3.1	3.1
Operating Increase	7.7%	7.7%	7.8%				

INDEX